NATURE CONSERVATION LAW
(SECOND EDITION)

AUSTRALIA
LBC Information Services—Sydney

CANADA and USA
Carswell—Toronto

NEW ZEALAND
Brooker's—Auckland

SINGAPORE and MALAYSIA
Sweet & Maxwell Asia
Singapore and Kuala Lumpur

NATURE CONSERVATION LAW

Second edition

Colin T. Reid

Professor of Environmental Law
University of Dundee

EDINBURGH
W. GREEN/Sweet & Maxwell
2002

Published in 2002 by
W. Green & Son Ltd
21 ALVA STREET
Edinburgh EH2 4PS

www.wgreen.co.uk

Typeset by Wyvern 21 Ltd.
Printed and bound in Great Britain by
Creative Print and Design (Wales), Ebbw Vale

No natural forests were destroyed to make this product;
only farmed timber was used and replanted

A CIP catalogue record for this book is available from
the British Library.

ISBN 0414 01355 7

PREFACE

The aim, scope and structure of this book remain the same as in the first edition, where they are explained more fully. Since the first edition was completed in 1993, a lot has happened in terms of the law on conservation, including implementation of the Habitats and Species Directive, major reforms in England and Wales under the Countryside and Rights of Way Act 2000 and the imminent arrival of National Parks in Scotland. During this period the general legal background has been transformed by devolution. Even before devolution, the law north and south of the border was diverging on some issues and writing now at a time when reforms in the south have been implemented but in Scotland are still merely promised (see Addendum, below) has made parts of this book rather more fragmented than is ideal. At one stage it looked as if the Countryside and Rights of Way Act might be delayed and the book could have beaten it to the shelves, at others it has looked as if no matter how slowly either Parliament worked they would manage to overtake the book. As it is, the book captures what may be a temporary, lopsided phase, reflecting old and new approaches to conservation law.

Two key points made in the Preface to the first edition must be re-emphasised. Firstly, although the book is entitled *Nature Conservation Law*, no such sharply defined area of law exists. There is an increasing volume of law specifically dedicated to nature conservation, and this forms the core of the book, but many other areas of law will affect the survival of species and habitats and these too must be given some consideration.

Secondly, this is a book about *Nature Conservation Law*, not conservation policy or practice. It deals with the legal rules penalising certain conduct and establishing public authorities and their powers to intervene in the ways in which individuals treat wildlife and the land and waters that support it. Within the legal framework, it is the ways in which policies are shaped, powers are exercised and money spent that will decide how far-reaching and effective any conservation measures are in practice. Studying the law alone will give an incomplete, and indeed sometimes misleading, view of how nature conservation in Great Britain operates, especially since the law often gives wide discretion to authorities and individuals. Yet it is the law that sets the boundaries on what authorities are permitted or required to do and on what individuals can be forced to do or abstain from doing, so that an awareness of these limits is an essential part of any study and understanding of nature conservation in practice. This book tries to explain

v

that legal framework, not to offer a complete guide to conservation theory, administration, policy or practice.

The first edition of this book was geographically confined to the law in Great Britain, *i.e.* Scotland, England and Wales, and this remains the case in this edition. Northern Ireland has distinct legislation and administrative structures on most issues, whereas enough of the law in Scotland, England and Wales is the same or similar for these jurisdictions to be discussed together, despite the fact that they are now out of step in introducing changes to what were the common rules in the Wildlife and Countryside Act 1981. Apologies to my friends in Northern Ireland.

The bulk of the law described here is statutory. Although I hope that major amendments have been noted, I have not mentioned every minor adjustment to the legislation, *e.g.* when public authorities have been renamed or restructured, and all references should be read as referring to the legislation as amended. For the sake of brevity, the following abbreviations have been used for legislation that is frequently mentioned.

CA 1968	Countryside Act 1968
CNHR 1994	Conservation (Natural Habitats, etc.) Regulations 1994 (S.I. 1994 No. 2716)
CSA 1967	Countryside (Scotland) Act 1967
EA 1995	Environment Act 1995
EPA 1990	Environmental Protection Act 1990
NHSA 1991	Natural Heritage (Scotland) Act 1991
NPACA 1949	National Parks and Access to the Countryside Act 1949
NPSA 2000	National Parks (Scotland) Act 2000
TCPA 1990	Town and Country Planning Act 1990
TCPSA 1997	Town and Country Planning (Scotland) Act 1997
WCA 1981	Wildlife and Countryside Act 1981

For recent English cases I have not included the new "format-neutral" citations, but instead have relied on the official reports or other versions that should be fairly readily available—watch out for the fact that with the advent of electronic publishing, some series of reports have switched (without any visible indication) from citations based on year and page number to ones based on year and their own case number. I have added references (in Chapter 2) to the main web-pages of the statutory conservation bodies and relevant government departments, invaluable; these provide if at times overwhelming, sources of information.

I have endeavoured to state the law as at the end of December, 2001, but it has been possible to take account of some later developments.

Acknowledgements

So many people have been of assistance in preparing this book, that it is impossible to mention all of them by name, or even by category. Among the groups who have given me great assistance are: colleagues in the Department of Law at Dundee University who on the academic side have read and commented on snippets of my work and answered daft questions as I strayed beyond my competence and on the secretarial and technical side have enabled me to work with some efficiency; academic colleagues elsewhere, whose works and comments have been so useful; undergraduate and postgraduate students whose understanding, or lack of it, has helped to clarify my ideas or expression; library staff at Dundee University and elsewhere who have helped to track down materials of assorted kinds; and the staff of many government departments and public bodies who have been unfailingly helpful, even when faced with the most obscure and technical questions. Deborah Inglis and Mark MacGuire do however earn a separate mention for their work for me as student research assistants. To the publishers, I am grateful for their forbearance as the schedule for producing a text had to be extended and for their work in preparing the Tables and Index and producing the book. In advance, can I thank anyone who points out things that I may have missed or misunderstood in preparing this text; such comments will be received with gratitude, not resentment. Finally my thanks go to my family for their assorted help and forbearance and especially to my wife Anne for her assistance on scientific matters and in so many other ways.

Colin T. Reid,
Dundee
January 2002

ADDENDUM

The following paragraphs note some of the significant developments during the first few months of 2002 while this book was in production. Several of these seemed too important to let pass without mention and I am grateful to the publishers for the opportunity to add these notes at proof stage.

The fact that major changes to the Wildlife and Countryside Act 1981 have taken place in England and Wales but are only promised in Scotland is a feature that runs through this book (see para.1.1.24 and *passim*). The timetable for change in Scotland is now clearer since in announcing its legislative programme to the Scottish Parliament on May 30, 2002, the Scottish Executive stated that a draft Bill on nature conservation will be produced in the spring of 2003 but that provisions on wildlife crime, including custodial sentences and increased police powers, would be included in the Criminal Justice (Scotland) Bill currently before the Scottish Parliament. The wildlife crime changes are likely to be very similar to those south of the border and to be in force later in 2002, but the final form of the habitat and other reforms remains to be seen.

The most significant development in the courts is that the designation procedure for SSSIs has now survived a challenge arguing that it was incompatible with the European Convention on Human Rights (see paras 1.5.5–1.5.7, 5.5.7). In *R. on the application of Aggregate Industries U.K. Ltd v. English Nature* (High Court, April 24, 2002) the court followed the same approach as the House of Lords in the *Alconbury* case, holding that that the designation of an SSSI did amount to a determination of the landowner's civil rights, that in confirming the designation English Nature did not by itself provide an independent and impartial tribunal as required by article 6 of the Convention, but that the process as a whole, including the right to challenge designation in the courts, did meet the standards required by the Convention. The court also rejected challenges that the designation defeated the owner's legitimate expectations and had no justifiable basis.

In *R. v. London Borough of Hammersmith & Fulham, ex p. Burkett* (House of Lords, May 23, 2002) the House of Lords has held that the time-limit for seeking judicial review starts with the formal issue of the decision and made other significant comments on the issue of delay (see para.1.4.16).

The first National Park in Scotland will be established in July 2002 under the Loch Lomond and The Trossachs National Park Designation,

Transitional and Consequential Provisions (Scotland) Order 2002 (S.S.I. 2002 No. 201) (see para.5.11.34).

The structure of the water industry has been changed by the creation of Scottish Water as a single water and sewerage authority for Scotland by the Water Industry (Scotland) Act 2002. The Act imposes on Scottish Water duties to exercise its functions in the way best calculated to contribute to the achievement of sustainable development (s.51) and in order to further the conservation of flora, fauna and natural beauty (s.53), whilst there is an obligation to consult Scottish Natural Heritage before carrying out certain operations in several protected areas and likewise the National Park Authority in National Parks (s.54) (see paras 2.2.5, 2.2.10, 2.7.23, 5.5.39, 8.6.4). The Land Reform (Scotland) Bill currently before the Scottish Parliament also includes a significant role for sustainable development in relation to the community right to buy, while giving Scottish Natural Heritage limited powers to take action to protect the natural heritage on land open to the public under the new access rights.

Other legislative developments in Scotland include the passage of the Fur Farming (Prohibition) Scotland Act 2002 (see para. 7.2.6) and the Protection of Wild Mammals (Scotland) Act 2002, prohibiting hunting with dogs (see paras 3.4.10, 4.2.12)—this is due to come into force at the start of August 2002 but is subject to a legal challenge to its validity.

The Marine Wildlife Conservation Bill, allowing for the creation of marine areas of special interest in England and Wales is making good progress through Parliament (see section 5.4), whilst in April the U.K. and devolved governments published an important policy statement on marine conservation: *Safeguarding Our Seas: A Strategy for the Conservation and Sustainable Development of our Marine Environment.*

In relation to administrative structures, the Department for Transport, Local Government and the Regions has been dismantled and its remit is now covered by the Department for Transport (further details at http://www.dft.gov.uk) and the Office of the Deputy Prime Minister (further details at http://www.odpm.gov.uk) (see para.2.4.7). The Ministry of Agriculture, Fisheries and Food (Dissolution) Order 2002 (S.I. 2002 No. 794) makes a number of statutory amendments to deal with the dissolution of this long-standing Ministry which was often specifically referred to in legislation. In Scotland complaints against Scottish Natural Heritage are now handled by the Scottish Public Service Ombudsman under the Scottish Public Services Ombudsman Act 2002 (see paras 2.6.6, 2.6.20).

CTR
June 11, 2002

CONTENTS

TABLE OF CASES

TABLE OF EUROPEAN CASES

TABLE OF STATUTES

TABLE OF STATUTORY INSTRUMENTS

TABLE OF EUROPEAN AND OTHER MATERIALS

1. INTRODUCTION

Although the law has concerned itself with the natural world from the earliest times, nature conservation law in its present form is a modern development. Inspired first by Victorian reactions against cruelty and blatantly destructive over-exploitation, the law has developed in keeping with changing perceptions of environmental issues and of the value of wild plants and creatures. The conservation of wild plants and animals is now widely recognised as a desirable policy objective, and the protection and enhancement of biodiversity feature in many policy statements. To some this conclusion is justified by moral or religious arguments, to others by aesthetic considerations. Justifications also exist from a utilitarian viewpoint, accepting the desirability of preserving resources for future generations and of maintaining genetic diversity in order to provide the basis for future developments of benefit to mankind. Whatever the justification,[1] nature conservation is now accepted as a legitimate concern of the state and the law reflects this. **1.1.1**

However, nature conservation is not the only concern of the state, nor is it necessarily high in the list of priorities. The claims of nature conservation will often have to compete against those of many other interests, such as economic development, agricultural production and the protection of individual rights. Much of the law in this area has accordingly been shaped by the need to balance a concern for nature conservation with the other demands on the state, an exercise which is frequently left to the wide discretion of public bodies to be exercised in individual cases. In many situations, therefore, nature conservation may be forced to take a back seat, but at least it now has official and increasing recognition, and measures exist to ensure that those who are taking decisions do have to include the protection of habitats, plants and animals as one of the factors to be taken into account. **1.1.2**

The policy in the early law was quite different. There were laws which addressed humankind's dealings with the natural world, but the sole aim was to serve immediate human interests. The law provided for the exploitation of plants and animals as valuable natural resources and for protection against the damage which uncontrolled nature could cause to human interests. In both Scotland and England many laws were made and the legislation of the Scottish Parliament can serve to illustrate the sort of measures which were adopted. Although the fre- **1.1.3**

---

[1] House of Commons Environment, Transport and Regional Affairs Committee, *U.K. Biodiversity*, 20th Report of 1999–2000 (1999–2000 H.C. 441), para. 8.

quent repetition of many provisions suggests that the law was not always rigidly observed or enforced—a situation not unknown today in many areas of environmental law—this legislation does reveal the attitudes and legal responses to issues involving wildlife. Several broad categories of laws can be identified.

1.1.4 One major category is provided by the laws aimed at the destruction of pests. Legislation was directed against rooks, crows, and other birds which destroyed corn,[2] and against birds of prey,[3] wolves[4] and foxes.[5] Landowners were instructed to destroy the nests of rooks on pain of forfeiting any tree wherein they were nesting,[6] to destroy the nests and eggs of "foulys of reif,"[7] and to destroy birds of prey by all means possible.[8] Organised wolf hunts were to be held[9] and there was a bounty on the head of foxes.[10] In relation to wolves at least, these measures proved successful. Local rules also existed to further these aims, *e.g.* for some years in Shetland all tenants, ministers, gentlemen and bailies had to produce at the annual head court the heads of weasels, crows, ravens or eagles, or their eggs, of else pay a fine, the number of items required (and the fine) increasing with status of the person (one for a tenant, six for a bailie),[11] while the slayers of eagles were entitled to a reward.[12] Measures also existed against farmers who allowed their crops to be infested with "guld," the corn marigold.[13]

1.1.5 A second group of laws sought to protect animals that were a valuable resource to the community. Wild fowl were not to be slain at moulting time when they could not fly, and their eggs and nests were protected.[14] Hares were not to be killed "in time of snow,"[15] and for a period herons were given special protection, those who kept their nests and prevented others from killing them being entitled to the King's thanks.[16] Salmon, which were a major economic resource, were the subject of much legislation, regulating the size of cruives,[17] setting the

---

[2] *e.g.* A.P.S. II 51 c.32 (1457).
[3] *ibid.*
[4] See note 9, below.
[5] A.P.S. II 51 c.35 (1457).
[6] *ibid.*, II 6 c.20 (1424).
[7] *ibid.*, II 51 c.31 (1457).
[8] *ibid.*, II 51 c.32 (1457).
[9] *ibid.*, II 15 c.5 (1427), II 51 c.35 (1457).
[10] *ibid.*, II 51 c.35 (1457).
[11] G. Donaldson (ed.), *Court Book of Shetland 1615–1629* (1992), pp. 160, 167.
[12] *ibid.*, p. 165.
[13] Frag. Coll. 11–12 (A.P.S. I 750).
[14] A.P.S. II 51 c.31 (1457).
[15] *ibid.*, I 576 (1400), II 52 c.36 (1457).
[16] *ibid.*, II 235 c.19 (1493).
[17] *e.g. ibid.*, I 469 c.11 (1318), II 5 c.12 (1424), II 119 c.6 (1478).

close times and seasons,[18] prohibiting the taking of fish at mills,[19] and requiring the removal of obstructions and traps.[20] The law also protected[21] and encouraged[22] rabbit warrens and dovecotes, whose inhabitants were not treated as wild animals, and which were a valuable source of fresh meat to their owners, although presumably less welcome to those who were farming the surrounding land.

Such measures existed, of course, not for the benefit of the species **1.1.6** concerned, but to ensure that there were adequate numbers for continuing exploitation, and particularly for hunting. Hunting played a very important part in the lives of the monarch, the nobility and their followers,[23] and produced a wealth of legislation. The special laws for the forests,[24] in essence hunting reserves, served to protect them and their game for their noble owners, and incidentally from being converted to agricultural use or denuded for timber. More general provisions prohibited hunting on other lands,[25] restricted the killing of particular game to particular classes of society,[26] while the shooting of deer, other beasts and wild fowl was prohibited.[27]

A final category of legislation can be identified, often overlapping **1.1.7** with the above, namely laws which recognise and try to limit the harm which man was doing to the bounty of the natural world. Several of the acts relating to hunting comment on the dearth of game compared to its past abundance and for this reason impose temporary restrictions,[28] while the harvesting of solan geese (gannets) on the Bass Rock was regulated because of over-exploitation, especially as those who were interested only in the feathers were destroying the value of the birds as meat.[29] Other laws were a response to the fact that "the wood of Scotland is utterly destroyed,"[30] requiring that woods, trees and broom be planted[31] and that all fencing be done by living hedges, not

---

[18] *e.g. ibid.*, II 7 c.12 (1424), VII 655 c.114 (1669).

[19] *e.g. ibid.*, II 96 c.13 (1469), II 221 c.15 (1489).

[20] *e.g. ibid.*, II 119 c.6 (1478).

[21] *e.g. ibid.*, II 7 c.10 (1424).

[22] *e.g. ibid.*, II 243 c.21 (1503).

[23] ". . . in time of peace in all time bygone the said pastimes of hunting and hawking were the only means and instruments to keep the whole lieges bodies from not becoming altogether effeminate" (A.P.S. IV 236 c.34 (1600)).

[24] For a detailed study of this topic and an edited version of the forest laws see J.M. Gilbert, *Hunting and Hunting Reserves in Medieval Scotland* (1979).

[25] A.P.S. II 107 c.15 (1474).

[26] *e.g. ibid.*, II 486 c.15 (1551), permitting only gentlemen and nobles using hawks to kill certain wild fowl.

[27] *e.g. ibid.*, III 26 c.17 (1567).

[28] *e.g. ibid.*, II 486 c.15 (1551), II 96 c.13 (1469) (salmon).

[29] *ibid.*, III 614 c.140 (1592).

[30] *ibid.*, II 242 c.15 (1503).

[31] *e.g. ibid.*, II 51 c.27 (1457), II 243 c.21 (1503).

dry sticks.[32] In order to prevent erosion, especially in the wake of the disaster at Culbin where moving sandhills covered a village, the pulling of shrubs and vegetation on sand dunes was prohibited.[33]

1.1.8　　This considerable legal heritage in both jurisdictions has had a significant influence on the law relating to game and fishing, and its spirit lives on in some pest control measures. However, as far as the modern law of nature conservation is concerned, a new start was made in relation to birds in Victorian times, and it is only within recent decades that legal protection has been extended to animals, especially reptiles, insects, other invertebrates, and non-commercial fish, and that broad protection has been given to wild plants.[34]

1.1.9　　The modern legislation has its origin in two facets of nineteenth-century society. In the first place, there was the movement against cruelty to animals. The Society for the Prevention of Cruelty to Animals was founded in the 1820s (becoming the RSPCA in 1840) and in the following decades the concerns of its members and of those who shared their views expanded. The protection of wildlife, especially birds, was added to the struggles against the ill-treatment of horses and other domesticated animals and against bear-baiting, cock-fighting, etc. In addition to the more general provisions, specific measures were promoted to prevent particular manifestations of cruelty to wildlife, *e.g.* the banning of the use of pole-traps[35] and hooks[36] to catch birds.

1.1.10　　The second factor which prompted legislation was an awareness of the gross over-exploitation of wildlife which was taking place.[37] The huge numbers of birds killed by shooting parties, the use of birds essentially as moving targets without any part of the carcase being collected or used, and the widespread use of feathers in the fashion trade[38] were

---

[32] *ibid.*, II 51 c.30 (1457).

[33] *ibid.*, IX 452 c.54 (1695).

[34] On the development of the modern law see generally, D. Stamp, *Nature Conservation in Britain* (1969); J. Sheail, *Nature in Trust* (1976); D.E. Allen, *The Naturalist in Britain—A Social History* (1976); D. Evans, *A History of Nature Conservation in Britain* (2nd ed. (revised) 1997); J. Sheail, *Nature Conservation in Britain—The Formative Years* (1998).

[35] Wild Birds Protection Act 1904.

[36] Wild Birds Protection Act 1908.

[37] The ambivalent attitudes in the nineteenth century can be detected in many sources. In Jules Verne's *Twenty Thousand Leagues under the Sea* (1870) the author fears that "barbarous and inconsiderate greed" will lead to the disappearance of the last whale from the ocean (Part II, Chap. 12) but at the same time comments on an enormous heap of oysters, saying that "this mine was inexhaustible, for Nature's creative power is far beyond man's instinct of destruction" (Part II, Chap. 2).

[38] This prompted particular attention, and the "Fur, Fin and Feather" movement was effective in persuading many women to refrain from wearing the feathers of birds not killed for food; generally the animal welfare and nature conservation movement was one where women became deeply involved in political activities.

all aspects of this mistreatment of a natural resource, aside from the cruelty involved in many cases.

More ironically, particular damage was done by the growing public **1.1.11** interest in the natural world, as those with leisure to indulge their interest devoted their energies not simply to observing nature, but to amassing large collections of eggs and other specimens. Inevitably, the collectors were most interested in the rarest specimens and were prepared to pay for them, so that the damaging consequences of this hobby were concentrated on the species least able to bear the pressure.[39] The greater accessibility of the countryside through the spread of railways and later the motor car allowed more people to become involved in collecting, and the efforts of collectors had a very damaging effect on some species of birds, insects and plants, many of which were already suffering as a result of changes in land use and agriculture.

A number of societies with concern for nature conservation were **1.1.12** formed, *e.g.* the Selborne Society for the Protection of Birds, Plants and Pleasant Places, founded in 1885, and these, and those who shared their views, attempted to educate the public and to secure a measure of legal protection for birds, animals and plants. Slowly they made progress, and it is probably true to say that now it is only in a few cases (*e.g.* orchids and some birds of prey) that animals and plants in Britain are severely threatened by deliberate collecting or hunting as opposed to the incidental results of man's other activities.

It is birds which were the first recipients of protection under the **1.1.13** modern law, and which have been the subject of most legislation. Prompted particularly by the mass slaughter of sea-birds at Flamborough Head, as sport and to provide plumage for the fashion trade, the Sea Birds Preservation Act 1869 was passed, imposing a close season during the breeding months for over 30 kinds[40] of sea bird. A further 79 kinds of bird were similarly protected by the Wild Birds Protection Act 1872, the close season being extended by the Wild Fowl Preservation Act 1876. These early measures were replaced by the more general Wild Birds Protection Act 1880. It is interesting to note that at this stage the legislation already displayed many of the features of the current law: a schedule to list species given additional protection, offences

---

[39] "If a vulture is foolish enough to perch on rocks in Cork Harbour, as one did in 1843, it must expect to be shot and placed in a museum. It is far better, in the cause of science, that the three rustic buntings which landed on our shores should be captured and identified than that their lives should be spared." (H. Russell, "The Protection of Wild Birds", *The Nineteenth Century*, vol. 42 (1897) 614 at p. 616 (thanks to Dr. K. Last for this reference)).

[40] The birds were identified by common names, which meant that there was some uncertainty as to exactly which species were protected, with considerable overlap in the list as names might apply to more than one species (*e.g.* gull), and more than one name for a species was included (*e.g.* puffin and sea parrot).

based on the possession of dead birds with the onus on the accused to show their lawful origin, ministerial powers to vary the close seasons, powers to grant exemptions for all or some birds in particular areas, and provisions to assist in the enforcement of the law.

1.1.14   During the decades following the 1880 Act many amendments, extensions and refinements of the law were made before the law was again consolidated and reformed by the Protection of Birds Act 1954. In the intervening period there had been 14 statutes concerned with protecting birds, some general, some relating to particular species: the Wild Birds Protection Acts 1881, 1894, 1896, 1902, 1904 and 1908, the Sand Grouse Protection Act 1888, the Wild Birds Protection (St. Kilda) Act 1904, the Captive Birds Shooting (Prohibition) Act 1921, the Protection of Birds Acts 1925 and 1933, the Protection of Lapwings Act 1928, the Quail Protection Act 1937, and the Wild Birds (Ducks and Geese) Protection Act 1939. All of these were repealed by the 1954 Act, following which two further statutes were enacted, the Protection of Birds Act 1954 (Amendment) Act 1964 and the Protection of Birds Act 1967.

1.1.15   The main statutory provisions are now to be found in the Wildlife and Countryside Act 1981, which replaced the earlier legislation on the protection of wild birds, as well as that dealing with most other animals and plants and aspects of habitat conservation. Prompted by the need to implement the European Community's Directive on the conservation of wild birds[41] and by the United Kingdom's acceptance of the Bern Convention on the Conservation of European Wildlife and Natural Habitats,[42] as well as by more general pressure to do more for conservation, the 1981 Act recast the law on nature conservation in Britain. Its passage proved to be a battleground between conservationists and those with competing interests, with well over 2,000 amendments being proposed, and conservation and the environment firmly becoming issues of political importance. The 1981 Act has now itself been considerably revised for England and Wales by the Countryside and Rights of Way Act 2000.

1.1.16   While the protection of birds was dealt with by fairly far-reaching legislation as early as the 1880s, the protection of other animals has been more fragmented, and generally more recent. There had long been rules on game and fishing, which in regulating the exploitation of many species did contain an element of conservation, but the first statute primarily motivated by such concern was probably the Grey Seals (Protection) Act 1914.[43] This imposed a close season for the taking of

---

[41] Directive 79/409 see paras 7.4.3–7.4.13, below.

[42] See paras 7.5.15–7.5.21, below.

[43] This was also the earliest to use the scientific name to assist in identifying the species concerned.

such seals to coincide with the breeding period during which mothers and pups were on shore and particularly vulnerable to hunting parties. The 1914 Act was replaced by the Grey Seals (Protection) Act 1932, which in turn was replaced by the Conservation of Seals Act 1970, which extended protection to the common seal.[44]

As far as the conservation of other animals was concerned, it was **1.1.17** only badgers that attracted specific protective legislation, through the Badgers Act 1973,[45] while deer were made the subject of comprehensive provisions dealing with both their conservation and exploitation, in the Deer (Scotland) Act 1959 and the Deer Act 1963.[46] It was with the Conservation of Wild Creatures and Wild Plants Act 1975 that protection was extended to other species, species less likely to have a place in the public's affections (two bats, a lizard, a snake, a toad and a butterfly). As in so many areas, the law here was transformed and greatly extended by the Wildlife and Countryside Act 1981, with subsequent amendments to its Schedules conferring protection on an increasing number of cold-blooded creatures and invertebrates.

The fate of birds and other animals overseas was also not wholly **1.1.18** neglected. The Importation of Plumage (Prohibition) Act 1921 restricted the import of all feathers except those of the eider and ostrich. The Animals (Restriction of Importation) Act 1964 made similar provisions regarding some animals, alive or dead, but the law was wholly reshaped and greatly extended (covering plants as well as animals) by the Endangered Species (Import and Export) Act 1976, enacted largely to implement the Convention of International Trade in Endangered Species.[47]

Although the threat to wild plants from over-collecting[48] as well as **1.1.19** changes in land use was well known from the middle of the nineteenth century, no general provisions were enacted until the 1970s. A major concern was the conflict between any conservation measures and the rights of landowners to do as they wish on their own land, and to their own property since unlike wild animals, plants, being an accretion to the ground, are owned by the owner of the land.[49] Although byelaws prohibiting the picking or uprooting of plants were adopted by many counties, the Conservation of Wild Creatures and Wild Plants Act 1975 was the first national measure to prohibit (subject to a number of excep-

---

[44] See paras 3.4.21–3.4.26, below.

[45] Replaced by the Protection of Badgers Act 1992; see paras 3.4.12–3.4.20, below.

[46] See now the Deer (Scotland) Act 1996 and Deer Act 1991; see paras 4.2.16–4.2.29, below.

[47] See paras 7.3.6–7.3.22, below.

[48] Most notably, perhaps, the widespread devastation of ferns during the "fern fever" which raged from the 1840s to the 1870s; see D.E. Allen, *The Victorian Fern Craze— A History of Pteridomania* (1969), esp. pp. 54–55.

[49] See paras 6.1.2–6.1.5, below.

tions, particularly for landowners) the uprooting of plants, with 21 species being given further protection against being picked. Again, this is an area where the Wildlife and Countryside Act 1981 greatly changed the legal position, with protection being extended to many more species. As with the provisions on animals, the amendments since 1981 have granted protection to many more species which are not so widely appreciated by the public, *e.g.* mosses and liverworts.

1.1.20　　While these measures designed to protect particular species from direct harm were being introduced, measures were also being taken to protect habitat. Individuals and local and national societies had been active for years in protecting nature at locations throughout the country, and in persuading public bodies and other landowners to manage their land with at least some regard for the wild animals and plants which it supported. After many years of work by interested groups and a number of influential reports,[50] legislation in 1949 finally created a number of official designations.

1.1.21　　The National Parks and Access to the Countryside Act 1949 provided for the creation (in England and Wales only) of National Parks, where landscape and nature conservation were to be combined with the provision of access and facilities to allow public enjoyment of the countryside,[51] and of Areas of Outstanding Natural Beauty, areas where the planning system should have particular regard to natural beauty.[52] Nature reserves were given statutory recognition, at national and local level,[53] and the Act also created the system of Sites of Special Scientific Interest (SSSIs),[54] although in this first incarnation the designation served merely as a source of information for public bodies, without the owner or occupier of the site being even notified. Subsequent legislation provided for other designations, *e.g.* sanctuary orders under the Protection of Birds Act 1954. Again it was the Wildlife and Countryside Act 1981 that reformed this area of the law, with major changes to the system for SSSIs[55] and the creation of Nature Conservation Orders,[56] marine nature reserves[57] and protection for limestone pavement.[58]

1.1.22　　Since the 1981 Act there has been much more widespread official

---

[50] See generally J. Sheail, *op. cit.* (1976), Chaps 5–6, (1998) Chap.1; D. Evans, *op. cit.*, Chap. 4.

[51] See section 5.11, below.

[52] See paras 5.12.1–5.12.8, below; legislation in Scotland was passed for National Scenic Areas in 1986 (see paras.5.12.9–5.12.10, below) and for National Parks in 2000 (see paras 5.11.20–5.11.34, below).

[53] See section 5.3, below.

[54] See section 5.5, below.

[55] See *ibid*.

[56] Now limited to Scotland; see section 5.6, below.

[57] See section 5.4, below.

[58] See section 5.7, below.

recognition of nature conservation and of the value of biodiversity. The ways in which biodiversity is treated are more fully considered in the next section, and it is only gradually that the response is moving from the policy level to produce legal changes. But there have been major legal developments affecting both species and habitat conservation. The most important of these has been the adoption by the E.C. of the Habitats and Species Directive in 1992[59] and its implementation in Great Britain by the Habitats (Nature Conservation, etc.) Regulations 1994.[60] This measure not only required stricter protection for certain listed species, but imposed a requirement on Member States to ensure that habitat was adequately protected. This required the introduction of significantly stricter legal controls over the European sites qualifying for such protection, such that damaging operations can be not simply delayed but actually prohibited indefinitely.[61]

A second major development has been the reaction to concerns that Wildlife and Countryside Act 1981 Act was not adequate to ensure protection for habitat and wildlife. Despite the fact that it was largely doing its job in relation to the specific threats which it was designed to prevent,[62] it had not stopped the continuing loss of habitat through gradual deterioration or other causes outwith its scope and had not proved as effective as it might in enforcing the law (*e.g.* the absence of a power to impose custodial sentences meant that there was little deterrent against impecunious egg-thieves).[63] At the same time, the rush to re-designate sites during the 1980s in order to invoke the greater protection under the 1981 Act led in places to resentment over the role and approach of what were perceived as "outsiders" who arrived suddenly in an area and on the basis of supposed scientific data but no local knowledge started telling established land managers what they could and could not do on land that local people had managed for years in a way that had actually preserved its value for biodiversity.

1.1.23

In 1998 separate consultation papers proposed different approaches to reform of the SSSI system in Scotland and in England and Wales.[64] In England and Wales this has already led to legislation in the Countryside and Rights of Way Act 2000, strengthening aspects of the SSSI system[65] and amending the 1981 Act in other significant ways.[66] In

1.1.24

---

[59] Directive 92/43/E.C.; see paras 7.4.14–7.4.37, below.

[60] S.I. 1994 No. 2716.

[61] See section 5.2, below.

[62] K. Last, "Habitat Protection: Has the Wildlife and Countryside Act 1981 Made a Difference?" (1999) 11 J.E.L. 15.

[63] *Forsyth v. Cardle*, 1994 S.C.C.R. 769.

[64] *People and Nature: A New Approach to SSSI Designations in Scotland* (Scottish Office, 1998); *Sites of Special Scientific Interest: Better Protection and Management* (DETR, 1998).

[65] See paras 5.5.17–5.5.36, below.

[66] In contrast to the battles at the time of the 1981 Act, the wildlife provisions of the Countryside and Wildlife Bill produced very little debate or opposition, although the

Scotland, progress so far has been limited to the production of a refined policy statement and a promise of early action,[67] whilst legislative activity has been centred on bringing to fruition a separate initiative to establish the first National Parks in Scotland.[68] At the same time as these formal changes have been taking shape, the operation of the legal structures has been assisted by a much more sympathetic policy background. With a variety of pressures moving agricultural and forestry policy away from the simple objective of maximising production[69] and with financial difficulties facing many farmers, it has been possible for grant-aided conservation measures to be seen as worthwhile option for land managers seeking a reliable economic return, as opposed to something that inevitably obstructs the profitable use of the land.

1.1.25   In relation to the institutional arrangements for nature conservation, again the story is one of prolonged activity, with varying degrees of official involvement, by societies and interested individuals leading to several reports and committee investigations before formal action was taken.[70] The Nature Conservancy was established by royal charter in 1949. It derived its powers from the National Parks and Access to the Countryside Act 1949 and had as its main tasks the provision of scientific advice to the government, the establishment and maintenance of nature reserves, and the organisation of scientific research. Its links with the Natural Environment Research Council[71] were redrawn by the Science and Technology Act 1965, before it was given a full statutory basis and a new name, the Nature Conservancy Council, by the Nature Conservancy Council Act 1973. During the 1960s all public bodies were placed under a general duty to have regard to the desirability of conserving the natural beauty of the countryside, which includes its flora and fauna.[72]

1.1.26   The Environmental Protection Act 1990 and the Natural Heritage (Scotland) Act 1991 radically changed the institutional structure, dividing the Nature Conservancy Council on a geographical basis and creating new bodies: Scottish Natural Heritage (SNH), English Nature and the Countryside Council for Wales (CCW). In Scotland and Wales a

---

access provisions gave rise to much controversy and debate, threatening the passage of the Bill.

[67] *The Nature of Scotland: A Policy Statement* (Scottish Executive, 2001). In a written answer on 1 November, 2001 the First Minister said that: "The Executive now intends to come forward with legislative proposals at an early opportunity and a draft Bill will be published as soon as possible." (S.P. W.A. November 1, 2001, p. 383); see Addendum, above.

[68] National Parks (Scotland) Act 2000; see paras 5.11.20–5.11.34, below.

[69] See sections 6.4 and 8.4, below.

[70] See J. Sheail, *op. cit.* (1976) Chap. 8, (1998) Chap. 2.

[71] See para. 2.7.24, below and J. Sheail, *op.cit.* (1998) Chap. 7.

[72] Countryside (Scotland) Act, 1967, s.66; Countryside Act 1968, s.11; see para. 2.2.6, below.

further feature of the reform was the merging of the tasks acquired from the Nature Conservancy Council with those of the Countryside Commissions.[73] The Countryside Commission for Scotland had been created by the Countryside (Scotland) Act 1967, with broadly defined functions (but little direct power) with regard to the provision, development and improvement of facilities for enjoying the countryside and to the conservation and enhancement of its natural beauty and amenity. For England and Wales, the starting point was the National Parks Commission established under the 1949 Act, and it was by the Countryside Act 1968 that this body's functions were extended, with broad functions similar to those of the Scottish Commission being added to its more specific role in the National Parks. The Countryside Commission was restricted to functions in England and has now become the Countryside Agency, following the addition of further functions related to rural development.[74]

This geographical divide at agency level has now been followed by **1.1.27** the more fundamental constitutional transformation brought about by devolution, which transfers most responsibility for nature conservation issues to the Scottish Parliament and Executive, and some functions to the National Assembly for Wales.[75] Even before these measures took effect, there were some signs of divergence between Scotland on the one hand and England and Wales on the other. The legislation creating SNH had also created for Scotland only an Advisory Committee on SSSIs, the policy proposals on reforms to the SSSI system took significantly different approaches, and the proposals for National Parks in Scotland developed a model different from that in England and Wales.[76] The passage of the Countryside and Rights of Way Act 2000 for England and Wales and the National Parks (Scotland) Act 2000 for Scotland have confirmed the need to look at parts of law separately in each jurisdiction, although the need to comply with the E.C. Birds and Habitats and Species Directives will be a constraint on how far the various systems can diverge.[77]

This brief account has recorded merely the stages in the development **1.1.28** of the law, and is in no way a history of nature conservation in Britain. Any such history would emphasise the massive contribution made by committed individuals and societies of various kinds, a commitment to practical conservation work, to the promotion of the ideas of nature

---

[73] See section 2.6, below.

[74] See paras 2.7.1–2.7.5, below.

[75] See section 2.3, below.

[76] Although the National Parks (Scotland) Act 2000 was passed by the Scottish Parliament, the proposals on which it is based pre-date the implementation of the devolution arrangements.

[77] See paras 2.3.4–2.3.5, 2.3.7, below.

conservation and to the development of appropriate structures and policies for public bodies. It is to these unofficial efforts, rather than to the law, that the main credit must go for the conservation of as much of our natural heritage as has survived to this day.[78]

BIODIVERSITY

1.2.1   The history described so far has largely omitted the key term which has dominated policy discussion of nature conservation over the last decade: "biodiversity". This dominance is largely attributable to the Convention on Biological Diversity[79] signed at the "Earth Summit" in Rio in 1992, where the concept was introduced to a global audience, alongside that of sustainable development. Both of these terms have been eagerly seized by governments and others, partly as elements of a new and fashionable rhetoric as states try to show that they are environmentally aware, partly because the reporting and strategy-forming requirements of the Rio Conventions lead to the use of the terms in structuring responses to the international agreements, but also because of the convenience of the terms in encapsulating important ideas.

1.2.2   Whereas part of the attraction of the term "sustainable development" may lie in its lack of precise definition,[80] "biodiversity" does have a clearer, if broad, meaning. The definition given in the Convention on Biological Diversity is that:

> "'*Biological diversity*' means the variability among living organisms from all sources including, *inter alia*, terrestrial, marine and other aquatic ecosystems and the ecological complexes of which they are part; this includes diversity within species, between species and of ecosystems."[81]

The power of the definition is that it covers several different but interconnected forms of diversity, all of which must be considered if the natural heritage of the earth is to be passed down to future generations. Diversity between species, the presence of a number of distinct sorts of plant or animal, is perhaps the simplest aspect of this and is what drives the concern to prevent the extinction of endangered plants and animals. Diversity within species reflects the extent of genetic variation within species, and the fact that local populations may have traits different from those in other areas, traits that may prove essential to the

---

[78] See the works cited at note 34, above.
[79] See paras 7.5.22–7.5.24, below.
[80] See paras 2.2.2–2.2.5, below.
[81] Convention on Biological Diversity (1992), art. 2.

long-term survival or value of the species (*e.g.* disease resistance, adaptation to climate variations) and in some cases may eventually lead to differentiation as a separate species. Diversity of ecosystems is the basis for the conservation of different habitat types, whilst diversity within ecosystems is often a measure of the health and undisturbed nature of a habitat. Nature conservation must take account of all of these aspects of our biological heritage.[82]

Each of these can be measured and therefore provide useful ways of **1.2.3** assessing and monitoring the varied natural environment, but there are dangers in allowing what may appear to be clear statistical measures to dominate policy to the exclusion of a more rounded picture. There is often no simple answer on whether or not a group of similar organisms represent one "species" or several, and taxonomic debates (and fashions)[83] ebb and flow, quite apart from the issue of hybrids. Views on such issues, and that of diversity within species, are of course being fundamentally changed by developments in DNA techniques, which are revealing that we know a lot less about biological diversity than we thought we did. In relation to habitats, the number of species recorded for a site may often be a guide to the health of the ecosystem, but this clearly does not apply in extreme environments and may not capture the significance of a site in view of the dynamic nature of populations, land use patterns and climate, quite apart from being dependent on the quality of the original recording process.[84] Biological diversity is, though, a very useful concept that deserves its place at the heart of policy and practice.

One requirement of the Convention on Biological Diversity is the **1.2.4** development of "national strategies, plans or programme for the conservation and sustainable use of biological diversity".[85] The United Kingdom's response was to produce in 1994 *Biodiversity: the UK*

---

[82] "Too much of biodiversity policy is based on ignorance or prejudice or single-minded enthusiasm for a single species, and has often little understanding of the naturally evolving world." House of Commons Environment, Transport and Regional Affairs Committee, *U.K. Biodiversity*, 20th Report of 1999–2000 (1999–2000 H.C. 41), para 12.

[83] Arguments between "lumpers" (who are reluctant to acknowledge some minor differences as justifying separate recognition at species level) and "splitters" (who are more willing to assert the existence of separate species) can run on for decades, with a consequent to-ing and fro-ing of classification of species, sub-species, varieties and geographical races.

[84] Particularly for invertebrates and lower plants, the number of recorded species is often an indication more of the level of recording effort than of the number of species actually present. A detailed study over 15 years has recorded 1,782 species of animal and 42 species of plant in one suburban garden in Leicester (J. Owen, *The Ecology of a Garden: The First Fifteen Years* (1991)), whilst much shorter and less intensive study of a garden in Dundee has led to the recording of 52 species of hoverflies, seven bumblebees and 127 moths (data from Dr. Anne Reid).

[85] Convention on Biological Diversity (1992), art. 6.

Action Plan[86] which sets a framework within which more specific plans have been developed, in the form of Species and Habitat Action Plans and Local Biodiversity Action Plans.[87] The U.K. Biodiversity Steering Group published its report in 1995[88] which contained the first set of species and habitat plans. Since then the U.K. Biodiversity Group, which has members from government departments, the statutory conservation bodies, business, academic and research bodies and major conservation non-governmental organisations, has continued its work[89] and by the middle of 2001 there were 391 species action plans and 45 habitat action plans. These plans set out costed proposals for improving the conservation status of the species or habitat concerned, identifying the key bodies who can take the lead in implementing the plans and seeking "champions" to assist in providing the resources for such implementation. About 160 Local Biodiversity Action Plans are being produced by local partnerships involving the conservation bodies, local authorities, non-governmental organisations and other interests, with the intention of these plans guiding decision-making and land use and management decisions by the public and private sector.[90] None of these species, habitat or local plans, however, has any direct statutory status and there is no specific obligation on authorities to have regard to their terms, although clearly they will be relevant where there are general obligations in relation to conservation.[91]

1.2.5   All of this activity at policy level has had only a limited effect on the law itself, with the existing wildlife and planning provisions forming the background against which the more specific plans are to be put into effect. References to protecting or enhancing biodiversity appear frequently in the preambles to E.C. legislation,[92] but initially the term made only rare and insignificant appearances in domestic law. Certain management activities "for the purposes of enhancing biodiversity" are among those attracting support in an Environmentally Sens-

---

[86] Cm. 2428. There is also a European Community Biodiversity Strategy (COM (1998) 42 final).

[87] Full details are available at the U.K. Biodiversity website at www.ukbap.org.uk.

[88] *Biodiversity: The U.K. Steering Group Report* (1995) and see Government Response (Cm. 3260, 1996).

[89] *Sustaining the Variety of Life: 5 Years of the U.K. Biodiversity Action Plan* (Report of the U.K. Biodiversity Group to the U.K. Government, the Scottish Executive, the National Assembly for Wales and the Northern Ireland Executive) (2001).

[90] See generally House of Commons Committee on the Environment, Transport and Regional Affairs, *U.K. Biodiversity*, 20th Report of 1999–2000 (1999–2000 H.C. 441); V. Abernethy and M. Scott (eds), *A Flying Start: Local Biodiversity Action in Scotland* (Scottish Biodiversity Group, 2001).

[91] See paras 1.2.6–1.2.7, below.

[92] "Nature and Biodiversity" is identified as one of the four priority areas in the European Community's forthcoming Sixth Environmental Action Programme (COM (2001) 31 final).

itive Area,[93] whilst the "effect on biodiversity" is one of the adverse environmental effects of road traffic to be taken into account in setting targets for traffic reduction.[94] More recently, though, two enactments have given a more prominent role for biodiversity.

The major provision is in the Countryside and Rights of Way Act **1.2.6** 2000, which imposes general duties on the government in England and Wales. Government ministers, government departments and the National Assembly for Wales are to have regard to the purpose of conserving biological diversity in accordance with the UN Convention on Biological Diversity.[95] In particular, the Minister[96] has to publish a list of organisms and habitats of principal importance for this purpose, and to take and encourage others to take steps to further the conservation of the listed species and habitats. The list is to be prepared in consultation with the statutory conservation bodies and to be published. The impact of such a "balancing duty" is discussed more fully in Chapter 2 below.[97]

A more focused provision appears in the Greater London Authority **1.2.7** Act 1999, where the duties of the Mayor include the preparation of a "state of the environment report" for London, to include information on biodiversity,[98] and the preparation of the London Biodiversity Action Plan.[99] This plan must contain information on the ecology, wildlife and habitat of Greater London, proposals for conserving and promoting biodiversity and commitments to this end made by other bodies. The plan must take into account any biodiversity plans made by London borough councils. Outside London, though, the Local Biodiversity Action Plans have no statutory status. It has been strongly argued that such status should be conferred,[1] but this idea was not accepted by the government, although it was noted that these plans would be among the elements taken into account when local authorities prepare their community strategies as required under section 4 of the Local Govern-

---

[93] *e.g.* Environmentally Sensitive Areas (Stage III) Designation Order 2000 (S.I. 2000, No. 3051), Sched. 2, Pt. 3; see section 5.9, below.

[94] Road Traffic Reduction (National Targets) Act 1998, s.2.

[95] CRWA 2000, s.74; a similar duty on the Scottish Ministers is proposed in *The Nature of Scotland* (Scottish Executive, 2001), p. 10.

[96] For the sake of simplicity, the term "the Minister" is used throughout this book to cover not only Ministers of the U.K. government, but also the Scottish Ministers and the National Assembly of Wales as appropriate, depending on the extent of any devolution of the power or function in question; see section 2.3 below.

[97] See para. 2.2.6, below.

[98] Greater London Authority Act 1999, s.351.

[99] *ibid.*, s.352.

[1] See, *e.g.* House of Commons Committee on the Environment, Transport and Regional Affairs, *U.K. Biodiversity*, 20th Report of 1999–2000 (1999–2000 H.C. 441), paras 26–32.

ment Act 2000.[2] Legal (and financial) provisions to strengthen the efforts to improve our grossly inadequate knowledge of biological diversity (often dependent on volunteers) have also been called for but with very limited results.[3]

1.2.8   As well as being a key concept in policy debate, biodiversity is therefore beginning to make its mark in the legal framework for conservation. With its emphasis on diversity within species and within habitats, it may help to shift attention away from an undue concentration on a few endangered species and outstanding sites towards the wider needs of flora and fauna,[4] but so far the legal tools for securing biodiversity remain largely unchanged.

NATURE CONSERVATION AND THE GENERAL LAW

1.3.1   The law on nature conservation is a statutory creation, operating against the background provided by the general civil and criminal law. An outline of this legal background is necessary so that the need for and form of the statutory intervention can be appreciated. In particular the law relating to the ownership of wild animals, of plants and of land must be considered, as a significant factor in shaping the law on nature conservation has been the potential conflict between the private property rights of individuals and the public interest in securing conservation.

Ownership

1.3.2   As far as plants are concerned, the law is simple; all plants growing in the ground belong to the owner of the land. This is the case regardless of whether the plant occurs naturally or has been deliberately planted. Subject to the rights of anyone else with an interest in the land, landowners have the right to nurture or destroy the plant as they think fit, and statutory intervention has been necessary to restrict this freedom for a number of purposes, *e.g.* weed control, nature conservation and forestry. The legal position and its consequences are discussed more fully in Chapter 6.[5]

---

[2] See para. 2.2.3, below.

[3] See, *e.g.* House of Commons Committee on the Environment, Transport and Regional Affairs, *U.K. Biodiversity*, 20th Report of 1999–2000 (1999–2000 H.C. 441), paras 33–38.

[4] "Designated conservation sites have an important role in protecting biodiversity. . . . However, the main reservoir for biodiversity is the 'wider countryside', outwith these protected sites, and it is here that biodiversity action is likely to produce the greatest gains." *Action for Scotland's Biodiversity* (Scottish Biodiversity Group, 2000), p. 9.

[5] See paras 6.1.2–6.1.5, below.

The law relating to animals is more complicated. Apart from a hand-   **1.3.3**
ful of special rules relating to specific animals (such as the Crown's
rights in swans,[6] sturgeon and whales[7]), the starting point of the law,
which essentially follows Roman Law on this topic, is a distinction
between wild animals (animals *ferae naturae*) and domestic ones
(animals *mansuetae* or *domitae naturae*). The latter, such as dogs,
horses, sheep and cattle are treated in the same way as all other moveable property, being fully owned throughout their lives and subject to
the standard rules for lost or abandoned property. Wild animals are
treated differently. While in the wild, they are deemed to be ownerless,
res nullius, and become the subject of property only when seized and
actually taken into possession.[8] The categorisation of an animal is a
matter of law, and although generally straightforward may be uncertain
in some cases, *e.g.* where domesticated animals become feral[9] or in
relation to fish.[10]

In order for an animal *ferae naturae* to become the property of some-   **1.3.4**
one, it must be taken. This can be achieved by killing it or by taking it
into captivity, *e.g.* putting it in a cage or restricting it within a park or
enclosure.[11] A hunter who wounds an animal will be recognised as
having rights over it so long as he continues to give chase, but once
the chase is abandoned the animal is once again *res nullius* and free to
become the property of the first person to seize it. In relation to some
species, ownership is also recognised where the animal may be free to
roam, but consistently returns to the owner's premises, displaying what
is known as an *animus revertendi*. This applies, for example, to pigeons
returning to a dovecote[12] and bees returning to a hive,[13] but is thought
unlikely to extend to the habit of salmon returning to their spawning
grounds.[14]

The principle that property is acquired by the person who takes such   **1.3.5**
animals is subject to a qualification in England and Wales. It is accepted

---

[6] In England and Wales only; *Case of Swans* (1592) 7 Co.Rep. 15b.

[7] Stair, II. i. 5; Blackstone, *Commentaries* (1783) i, 223.

[8] Stair, II. i. 33; Erskine, II. i. 10; Blackstone, *Commentaries* (1783) ii, 389–395.

[9] *Falkland Islands Co. v. R.* (1863) 2 Moo. P.C. N.S. 266 (status of sheep and cattle found wild in the Falkland Islands after being introduced by earlier settlers).

[10] In *Valentine v. Kennedy*, 1985 S.C.C.R. 89 at p. 91 it was doubted that any fish, even non-indigenous ones specially reared, could be properly regarded as "tamed" and therefore other than *ferae naturae*; see also, on the status of snails, A.P. Herbert's *Cowfat v. Wheedle*, reprinted in many collections including *Uncommon Law* (1982).

[11] Stair, II. i. 33; Blackstone, *Commentaries* (1783) ii, 389–392.

[12] *Hamps v. Darby* [1948] 2 K.B. 311.

[13] *Kearry v. Pattinson* [1939] 1 K.B. 471.

[14] This is an obstacle to the potential development of a "salmon ranching" industry, whereby salmon are reared to be released into the open sea then harvested by their "owner" on their return to fresh water to spawn; see W. Howarth, *The Law of Aqua-culture* (1990), Chap. 17.

that once killed and taken wild animals cease to be *res nullius* and become the subject of property, but as the courts have not been willing to recognise that a poacher could gain ownership by his unlawful acts, property has been held to vest in the owner of the land.[15] In Scotland, however, the courts have been willing to follow the logic of the basic principle, so that property is acquired even by a poacher taking animals unlawfully, contrary to the game rights of the owner of the land concerned.[16] In such circumstances the landowner may be entitled to claim compensation from the poacher, but has no right to restitution of the animals taken.

1.3.6   The English approach has perhaps been influenced by the tendency there to describe the owner of game rights over land as having a qualified property right in the game there, a right perfected on the taking of the game.[17] This is arguably a misleading way of expressing the position as although a landowner may have the power to control any hunting on his land, and have the exclusive right to take the game, he does not have any true property rights in the animals unless and until he physically takes them. Those who take game without any right to it may commit a wrong against the person who is entitled to take the game,[18] but it is not truly an interference with his property in the game. Similarly misleading are references to a form of property in young animals and fledglings not yet able to fly.[19]

1.3.7   Ownership generally is lost once a wild animal ceases to be held in captivity (or to have an *animus revertendi*), but is retained so long as the owner is in pursuit.[20] In *Kearry v. Pattinson*,[21] a case involving bees swarming away from a hive, the English court considered the old statements that the owner retained his rights in animals escaping from captivity provided that he had the animals in sight and the power to pursue them. It was emphasised that the owner's rights lasted only as long as he had the lawful power to pursue the creatures, so that once the animals entered the land of another where their owner could not enter except as a trespasser, then they were no longer his property. In England and Wales, once an animal *ferae naturae* has ceased to be the property of someone, it reverts to its former status as *res nullius*, cap-

---

[15] *Blades v. Higgs* (1865) H.L.C. 621.

[16] Erskine, II, i, 10; *Leith v. Leith* (1862) 24 D. 1059 (Lord Curriehill at pp. 1077–1078); *Scott v. Everitt* (1853) 15 D. 288 (in the absence of a statutory entitlement police have no right to seize unlawfully taken game).

[17] See, *e.g. Case of Swans* (1592) 7 Co. Rep. 15b at 17b.

[18] The right to take game may be separated from the ownership or occupation of the land; see paras. 4.2.6–4.2.8, below.

[19] On the difficulties of applying the language and concepts of property to wild animals, see the Australian case *Yanner v. Eaton* [1999] H.C.A. 53.

[20] Stair, II. i. 33; Blackstone, *Commentaries* (1783) ii, 393.

[21] [1939] 1 K.B. 471.

able of being acquired by the first person to capture it again.[22] In Scotland the same rule, taken from Roman Law, applies and is a departure from the more general rule of feudal origin that property which has once been owned does not become *res nullius* once abandoned by its owner but reverts to the Crown, a rule which applies to animals not *ferae naturae*.[23]

The legal position on the ownership of wild animals has several **1.3.8** consequences for the criminal and civil law. As far as the criminal law is concerned, the basic position that wild animals (unless in captivity) are not the property of anyone, means that they cannot be stolen at common law. In Scotland, therefore, it has been held that if a charge of theft is based on the taking of an *animal ferae naturae*, the charge must set out how the animal ceased to be *res nullius* and came to be somebody's property.[24] The same would apply to a charge of malicious mischief or vandalism.[25] It is also specifically provided by the Theft Act 1607[26] that a person who takes fish from a proper stank or bees is guilty of theft, and the taking of oysters and mussels from marked beds is also theft.[27] In *Valentine v. Kennedy*[28] four men were held guilty of stealing trout which had escaped from a reservoir into surrounding burns, but the fish in question were rainbow trout which are not indigenous and which the men knew must have come from the reservoir. The sheriff commented that if the fish in question had been native brown trout a charge of theft would have been unlikely to succeed as it was unlikely that it could have been proved that the trout came from the reservoir and were not simply wild.

In England and Wales the position is governed by statute. Section **1.3.9** 4(4) of the Theft Act 1968 states that wild animals, tamed or untamed, are to be regarded as property for the purposes of the Act. However, it continues to provide that although wild animals which are tamed or ordinarily kept in captivity may be stolen, a charge of theft of a wild animal or its carcase will otherwise be possible only where the animal has been reduced into possession by or on behalf of another person and the possession has not since been lost or abandoned, or where another person is in the course of reducing the animal into possession. A similar

---

[22] *Hamps v. Darby* [1948] 2 K.B. 311.
[23] Erskine, II. i. 10; D.L. Carey Miller, *Corporeal Moveables in Scots Law* (1991), para. 2.02; *cf. Valentine v. Kennedy*, 1985 S.C.C.R. 89 at p. 91.
[24] *Wilson v. Dykes* (1872) 10 M. 444.
[25] Criminal Justice (Scotland) Act 1980, s.78.
[26] As amended by Statute Law Revision (Scotland) Act 1964, Scheds 1–2; see Lord Rodger of Earlsferry, "Stealing Fish" in R.F. Hunter (ed.) *Justice and Crime—Essays in Honour of the Rt. Hon. Lord Emslie* (1993).
[27] Oyster Fisheries (Scotland) Act 1840, s.1; Mussel Fisheries (Scotland) Act 1847, s.1.
[28] 1985 S.C.C.R. 89.

provision governs the position for criminal damage.[29] These provisions
in essence repeat the common law rules on ownership, including recognition of the traditional rules of the chase. A specific offence penalises
the taking or destruction of fish from a private fishery, the offence
being treated as less serious if committed by means of angling during
daylight.[30]

1.3.10   The civil law is also affected. As wild animals do not form the property of anyone, and do not in themselves have any other recognition in
the law, they fall outwith the law's protection. In the absence of statutory provisions, killing or destroying wild animals is not in itself a
wrong against anyone, as no legally recognised personal or property
rights are affected. The destructive conduct may involve a trespass or
breach of other rights which the law will acknowledge, but any action
must be based on the breach of those rights, and no legal value can be
attached to the wild animals. This may affect the likelihood of obtaining
a remedy, as the effect on wild animals of the unwanted conduct should
be disregarded and wild animals, not being the property of anyone,
have no legally recognised value.[31]

1.3.11   It follows that the standard civil law is of little use in securing the
direct protection of wild animals. It can be invoked only when some
legally recognised rights are also affected, *e.g.* a landowner may be
able to take action if a trespass or nuisance is involved, or the holder of
game or fishing rights may be able to intervene. However, conservation
groups and individuals who have an interest in preserving wildlife, but
no legal rights at stake, lack the standing to do anything.[32]

1.3.12   The law's failure to accord any value to wildlife may also have indirect consequences. Policies of land management and investment which
protect and encourage wild plants and animals at the expense of
maximising financial returns will be regarded as producing no legally
recognised return. For someone dealing with his own property this is
of no consequence, but much property is held by trustees who are under
a duty to do their best for the beneficiaries. The duty of the trustees
is to obtain the best return, regardless of moral, social and political
considerations,[33] especially where property is expressly held for invest-

---

[29] Criminal Damage Act 1971, s.10(1); a news report in the *The Times* of August 19, 1993
notes that a man was convicted under this Act after injuring some swans, which, exceptionally, are the property of the Queen at all times (see note 6, above); this enabled a
custodial sentence to be imposed, at a time when this was not available for the offences
under WCA 1981 that might otherwise have been the basis for prosecution.

[30] Larceny Act 1861, s.24, preserved by Theft Act 1968, s.32 and Sched. 1, para. 1;
Environment Agency v. Russell (unreported) (1997) 9 E.L.M. 19.

[31] A landowner might be able to create a value entitled to legal protection, *e.g.* by charging visitors to observe wild animals on his land.

[32] See section 1.3, below.

[33] *Martin v. Edinburgh District Council*, 1988 S.L.T. 329; *Cowan v. Scargill* [1985] Ch.
270; *Harries v. Church Commissioners for England* [1992] 1 W.L.R. 1241.

ment purposes, as is the case with considerable areas of land. Environmentally friendly management of land and recourse to "green investments" may well produce a satisfactory return. However, unless the power to be influenced by such matters is expressly included in the trust, trustees may be acting in breach of their duties if they allow a concern for nature conservation to stand in the way of obtaining any appropriate financial returns from the property which they hold, regardless of the value which they or others see in the conservation of nature.[34] On the other hand, the creation of a trust whose express purposes include the protection of wildlife on particular land will put the trustees in a stronger position to take action against anything which threatens this objective.

Land ownership

Under the general law it is the owners of a piece of land who enjoy the power to determine what happens on that land and therefore the extent to which plants and animals are conserved there. The owners of the land own the plants growing on it, they control who can enter the land, they decide the way in which the land is to be used. As far as nature conservation is concerned, this is a mixed blessing. If the owners are keen to protect wild plants and animals, they are in the position to ensure that this takes place by managing the land to preserve and enhance habitats, prohibiting activities which are likely to cause damage or disturbance, eliminating threats to the natural flora and fauna and excluding unwelcome visitors. On the other hand, if landowners do not wish to conserve nature, any measures requiring them to do so will amount to an infringement of their right to do as they wish with their own property,[35] and any enduring restrictions may affect the value of property considerably.

1.3.13

It follows that if an individual or conservation body wishes to conserve nature in a particular area, the best approach is to acquire the land, or a sufficient interest in the land in order to ensure that appropriate steps are taken.[36] If an interest in the land cannot be acquired, it may be sufficient to enter an agreement with the landowner which obliges him to act, or refrain from acting, in particular ways. Difficulties arise, however, in trying to ensure the long-term protection of sites and in ensuring that the successors of the parties to the initial deal

1.3.14

---

[34] The same issue may arise in other circumstances, *e.g.* in *Williams v. Schellenberg*, 1988 G.W.D. 29–1254 one *pro indiviso* proprietor of land argued that her interest had been damaged by the proprietor in occupation encouraging the designation of the land as an SSSI, thereby restricting its management and reducing its value.

[35] See paras 1.5.9–1.5.11, below.

[36] Many National Nature Reserves are not owned by the conservation bodies but leased or simply subject to management agreements.

continue the conservation measures. The law on land-ownership and related matters in Scotland is very different from that in England and Wales, and in both jurisdictions is a subject of some complexity. What follows is merely a brief indication of some of the issues and possibilities which arise.

1.3.15   As far as ownership of the land is concerned, if one wishes to secure the land for more than the lifetime of one individual, or to protect against an individual owner's change of mind, the solution lies in the complexities of the law on trusts, charities and associations. Land may be acquired by a conservation group in its own right if it is an incorporated association and therefore enjoys its own legal personality. Otherwise, the land must be vested in trustees, either for an association, or subject to a trust the objectives of which include the conservation of nature. Such a trust can avoid the legal restrictions on private trusts, in Scotland by being a public trust and in England and Wales by seeking charitable status. In the 1920s a trust to create a specific form of sanctuary for wild animals was held not to constitute a valid charitable trust as it had no benefit to the community,[37] but the protection of the environment, including its flora and fauna, is now recognised as a charitable purpose.[38] In the event of any doubt, the obstacle can readily be circumvented, *e.g.* by ensuring that the terms of the trust are drawn so as to include an educational element.

1.3.16   If outright ownership is not possible or desired, land may be taken on a lease, the terms of which allow the land to be managed in a way compatible with nature conservation. This is a common device as landowners may be reluctant to part with their land permanently, but be prepared to allow the land to be used for conservation purposes for a fixed term, at the end of which the owners will be free to reconsider how they wish the land to be used.

1.3.17   A simple agreement between the owner of the land and some other party to the effect that the owner will do or not do certain things in order to conserve or enhance the nature conservation value of the land is also possible, and can be framed so as to be legally enforceable. However, such an agreement suffers from the severe drawback that it will be a personal agreement, which binds only the original parties. Therefore if the owner dies or sells the land to another, the agreement is at an end. In relation to such "management agreements" entered by many official bodies, this problem is solved by statutory provisions which ensure that such agreements, once registered, do run with the land, binding successors to the original contracting owner.[39]

---

[37] *Re Grove-Grady* [1929] 1 Ch. 557; *cf. Re Verrall* [1916] 1 Ch 100, confirming as charitable the purposes of the National Trust.

[38] H. Picarda, *The Law and Practice Relating to Charities* (3rd ed., 1999), pp. 158–159, 164–166.

[39] *e.g.* NPACA 1949, s.16.

Without statutory intervention, it is unlikely that similar management **1.3.18** agreements between private parties can practically be prolonged and protected in such a way. In England and Wales agreements limiting the use of land, restrictive covenants, can run with the land, binding successors to the owner who initially agreed to the limitations, but this is possible only where the covenant is for the benefit of some land held by the other party to the agreement or his successors, and where the covenant has been registered. Moreover, it is only the holder of the benefited land who can enforce the covenant.

An agreement not to use or develop a site in certain ways may in **1.3.19** some circumstances be regarded as benefiting other land, but for this to be a useful conservation device, the conservation body or whoever made the initial agreement with the landowner must have done so in a capacity as owner of that benefited land, and only if it continues to be the owner of the benefited land (or the succeeding owner shares its views on this point) will the covenant be enforced. In practice, this requires a fairly unlikely combination of circumstances. Similar requirements that there be land which benefits from an obligation before it can be recognised as running with the burdened land prevent the development of "conservation easements," a concept which has developed in many states of the USA.[40]

In Scotland the position at present is fundamentally different because **1.3.20** of the continuing effects of the feudal system, but is about to be transformed. The feudal superior retains the right to insert restrictions and conditions in a feudal grant, so that a sale of land may be subject to a number of restrictions on the use of that land. Once recorded, these obligations can be enforced against the proprietor of the land and his successors by the superior or in some cases by others who hold neighbouring land granted by the same superior with the power to enforce such (usually mutually beneficial) restrictions. For sales where no feudal superior is involved, conditions can be imposed but face the same limitations as in England and Wales in that they will run with the land only if imposed for the benefit of some adjoining land and be enforceable only by those with an interest in such land.

The rights of the feudal superior will, however, be wholly removed **1.3.21** when the Abolition of Feudal Tenure (Scotland) Act 2000 comes into force. This Act forms part of the wholesale reform of Scottish land law which is still under way, and not all of the details of the new system are clear as yet. In particular, the full details of the future law on the existence and enforceability of title conditions, remain to be agreed, but in essence the ability to enforce such conditions will, as in England

---

[40] See, *e.g.* J.A. Blackie, "Conservation Easements and the Doctrine of Changed Conditions" (1989) 40 Hast. L. J. 1187.

and Wales, generally depend on the ownership of land that directly benefits from the condition that has been imposed.

1.3.22   However, special provision is made for "conservation burdens". The terms of the 2000 Act will enable prescribed conservation bodies and the Scottish Ministers to preserve any rights, currently resting on their role as feudal superiors, to enforce conditions designed to preserve or protect the special characteristics of the land, including its flora and fauna.[41] The scheme requires action in advance of the appointed day when the reshaping of land law will take effect, in the form of the execution and registration of a notice preserving the right to enforce, but once this has been done the conservation body or Ministers will still be able to enforce the conditions even though they have no interest in related land. The right to enforce conditions can subsequently be assigned between conservation bodies and the Ministers. The proposals on title conditions recommend provision for new burdens of this sort to be created.[42]

1.3.23   Even if it does prove possible for an agreement to run with the land as described above, in both jurisdictions a party can apply to the relevant Lands Tribunal to be discharged from his obligations under the agreement. The Tribunals have the power to modify or discharge the obligations if in Scotland they are found to be unreasonable or inappropriate, unduly burdensome or impeding some reasonable use of the land,[43] or in England and Wales if they are found to be obsolete or to be impeding a reasonable use of land, or if the proposed modification or discharge causes no injury to the beneficiary of the covenant.[44] It is clear therefore that resort must be had to statutory provisions if effective steps are to be taken to control the way in which land is managed so as to further nature conservation.

Other rights

1.3.24   Certain rights relating to wild animals may be held by someone other than the owner of the land concerned. The rights to take fish and game are incidents of the ownership of land, but can be separated from the land and granted to others.[45] In Scotland the right to take salmon is exceptionally a separate tenement, belonging to the Crown as part of the *regalia minora* unless granted to others, but generally the extent of

---

[41] Abolition of Feudal Tenure (Scotland) Act 2000, ss.26–32; the prescribed bodies will be listed by regulations made under s.26(1).

[42] See Scottish Law Commission, *Report on Real Burdens* (Scot. Law Com. No. 181, 2000) pp. 191–196 and draft Title Conditions (Scotland) Bill, Part III.

[43] Conveyancing and Feudal Reform (Scotland) Act 1970, s.1.

[44] Law of Property Act 1925, s.84 (as amended by Law of Property Act 1969, s.28).

[45] See generally W.M. Gordon, *Scottish Land Law* (2nd ed.,1999), Chaps 8 and 9; C. Parkes and J. Thornley, *Fair Game: The Law of Country Sports and the Protection of Wildlife* (new revised edition) (1997), Chaps 3 and 12.

any separation will depend on the terms of the particular grant by the owner of the land. The issue is complicated as the nature of the grant will depend on its terms—it may be viewed as a form of lease or merely as a personal licence granted by the landowner—and is to some extent affected by statute, especially in relation to agricultural land.[46] The provisions relating to game or fishing may also form part of a broader agreement and be affected by its character, *e.g.* it is common for landowners to reserve game and fishing rights when leasing land.

From a nature conservation point of view the separation of game and **1.3.25** fishing rights has significance in two ways. In the first place, if the wildlife of a site is to be protected, it may be necessary not only to ensure that suitable arrangements are made with the parties who own and occupy the land, but also to ascertain who holds the game and fishing rights and to make arrangements with them. Otherwise the measures undertaken to conserve nature may be undermined by the exercise of these separate rights over the land.

Secondly, game and fishing rights may be used as a means of fur- **1.3.26** thering conservation. In order to protect the species concerned, such rights may be acquired by those with an interest in conservation and then not exercised, thereby producing a *de facto* ban on shooting and fishing on the land, subject to statutory rights and pest control measures.[47] Short of such a policy, the existence of separate rights ensures that there is some party other than the owner of the land with an interest in its management. As measures to encourage a large and sustainable harvest of game and fish may also be of benefit to other wildlife,[48] particularly in preserving land in a comparatively natural state, free from intensive agriculture, the protection and enhancement of game rights may in itself be beneficial for nature conservation. It must be recognised though, that the protection of game can also lead to measures highly detrimental to some wild species, *e.g.* the unlawful destruction of birds of prey.

LEGAL STANDING

The general position on the ownership of wild plants and animals has **1.4.1** a further consequence of major significance for the law on nature conservation. This relates to the legal standing of those wishing to protect

---

[46] *e.g.*, the rights of a tenant to kill ground game (Ground Game Act 1880, s.3); see paras 4.2.6–4.2.8.

[47] A similar policy has been adopted in relation to salmon in Scotland by the Atlantic Salmon Conservation Trust, with the acquisition and dismantling of coastal netting stations in order to increase the stocks entering the rivers to breed.

[48] But not always, *e.g.* the large numbers of deer in parts of Scotland, allegedly encouraged by shooting interests, can do a lot of damage by overgrazing and preventing natural regeneration of woodland.

the interests of wild plants and animals, or rather to their general lack of standing. The courts will only entertain actions from parties with a legally recognised interest in the subject of the litigation, therefore the issue of standing is of crucial importance to the extent to which those concerned for nature conservation can invoke the courts' assistance to further their aims and prevent damaging activities taking place.

1.4.2   What qualifies a person as having legal standing depends on the nature of the action being raised, but generally the courts insist on some direct connection with the matter in dispute. It is not enough that a person is interested in an issue, in the way that a person may be interested in sport or the arts as their leisure pursuit; the law requires the person to have some legal interest in the subject matter. In relation to judicial review a slightly more relaxed standard may be imposed, but the courts will still look for some real connection with the issue and will firmly shut their doors to anyone who appears to be interfering in something which is not properly his or her business.

1.4.3   Many of the provisions designed to protect wildlife do so by creating criminal offences. The extent to which nature conservation groups or concerned individuals can ensure that alleged offenders are brought to justice varies. In Scotland the position is that proceedings are instigated by the public prosecutors in all but the most exceptional circumstances. As any private prosecutors will have to show that they have been personally wronged by the alleged crime,[49] there appears no likelihood of private prosecution in the case of offences created to protect wild plants and animals or habitat.

1.4.4   In England and Wales the position is different, and although most prosecutions are handled by the public authorities, especially now the Crown Prosecution Service, prosecutions may be brought by private individuals, even where they have not themselves been the victim of the alleged crime. This means that action can be taken to invoke the criminal law, and prosecutions have been successfully brought by individuals, usually with the support of some organisation, *e.g.* cases relating to birds raised by officers of the Royal Society for the Protection of Birds. However, as it is only the police who enjoy the various statutory powers of search, etc., which may well be necessary in order to obtain the requisite evidence, co-operation with the public authorities is useful. Throughout Great Britain many police forces now have designated "wildlife" or "nature conservation" officers in an effort to make the work of the police in this field more effective.

1.4.5   In the civil law, the position in both jurisdictions is essentially the same. If there is an agreement of some sort with terms designed to promote nature conservation, in all but a handful of cases it is only the

---

[49] *McBain v. Crichton*, 1961 J.C. 25.

parties to that agreement who have the standing to enforce it.[50] Therefore, unless they are parties to the original agreement, there is no scope
for conservation groups or the like to take action to ensure that a landowner keeps to the terms of a management agreement, or that the parties to a lease abide by terms designed to protect natural features.[51]

For actions in delict or tort, the pursuers must be able to show that **1.4.6**
they have suffered some legal wrong. As animals in the wild are not
owned by anyone, nobody suffers a wrong if they are harmed, so that
no recourse can be had to the courts. Plants are the property of the
owners of the land, so that they alone are in a position to respond to
damage done to them. Actions may be possible if the damaging conduct
can be shown to cause harm to the pursuers' domestic animals and in
Mull Shellfish Ltd v. Golden Sea Produce Ltd[52] the pursuers were
allowed to seek damages for harm caused to free floating mussel larvae
that would have settled on the equipment maintained for the commercial rearing and cultivation of mussels. Damage to an interest in the
land concerned, or in other land affected, will also create title to sue.[53]
Nevertheless, the class of potential pursuers is small and firmly
excludes conservation groups which may have a deep concern for, and
interest in, the well-being of the species being affected, but no patrimo-
nial interest which is being harmed.[54]

There is potential for European Community law to be argued as a **1.4.7**
source of rights providing a basis for action. The crucial question is
whether the relevant legislation is regarded as creating individual rights
which can be enforced through the courts. In some cases this is clear,
especially in relation to procedural rights, such as the opportunities for
public participation under the Environmental Assessment Directive.[55]
In relation to substantive rights the position is less certain, as shown in
Bowden v. Southwest-Services Ltd[56] where it was held that the Bathing
Water and Urban Waste Water Directives[57] did not have such a direct

---

[50] It may be possible to give effect to a clear intention to give a third party some rights
under an agreement if the contract is drafted so as to invoke the general rules on third
party rights provided in Scots law by the *jus quaesitum tertio* and in England and
Wales under the Contracts (Rights of Third Parties) Act 1999.

[51] Agreements which run with the land, binding successors to the original parties, are
discussed above (paras 1.3.17–1.3.23).

[52] 1992 S.L.T. 703.

[53] This would include game or fishing rights, which might form the basis for an action
where harm is caused to the natural environment.

[54] Potential liability for "biodiversity damage" and a role for public interest groups to
enforce this are among the proposals in the E.C.'s proposal for a Directive on Environmental Liability (COM (2002) 17 final).

[55] *e.g. R. v. Durham County Council, ex p. Huddleston* [2000] 2 C.M.L.R. 313 [2000]
Env. L.R. 488.

[56] [1999] 3 C.M.L.R. 180, [1999] Env.L.R. 438.

[57] Directives 76/160 and 91/271.

impact on the interests of fisherman to support a case, whereas it was at least arguable that the Shellfish Directive[58] did create individual rights for mollusc fishermen which could form the basis of a claim for damages where harm resulted from a failure to implement its terms properly. Since any E.C. measures directly protecting wildlife are unlikely to be regarded as creating individual rights, it is in such procedural or indirect contexts that access to the courts may be provided. Actions based on the European Convention on Human Rights are available only to those who qualify as "victims", as interpreted by the European Court of Human Rights, but this may be possible for those who are the victims of unfair decision-making procedures or whose property is affected. [59]

1.4.8   Most nature conservation law at some stage involves public authorities, either the statutory conservation bodies or central or local government in the exercise of their planning and other powers. As statutory bodies they must keep within the limits of their statutory powers and properly fulfil their responsibilities and follow the prescribed procedures for their action. In most cases considerable discretion is conferred on the authorities, but their conduct will usually be subject to judicial scrutiny,[60] and the courts will be prepared to intervene if they are found to be acting *ultra vires*, *i.e.* illegally, irrationally or in breach of procedural propriety.[61] In both Scotland and England special procedures exist for parties challenging the conduct of public authorities by means of judicial review,[62] and a fundamental element of both is that the court will only consider a case at the instance of someone with sufficient standing.[63] A similar point arises under many statutory schemes where rights of appeal or challenge are restricted to "persons aggrieved".

1.4.9   The general approach is that only a person with some direct connection with the issue will be recognised as having sufficient standing to invoke the court's powers of judicial review. Regrettably, though, it is not possible to provide a simple, reliable statement of when a party will have standing. Apart from difficulties in assessing the extent to

---

[58] Directive 79/923.

[59] Human Rights Act 1998, s.7; see para. 1.5.4, below.

[60] Either under statutory procedures allowing reference to the court, *e.g.* in relation to Nature Conservation Orders (WCA 1981, Sched. 11 para. 5), or by means of judicial review.

[61] *Council of Civil Service Unions v. Minister for the Civil Service* [1985] A.C. 374.

[62] In Scotland, Rule of Court 260B (introduced by Act of Sederunt (Rules of Court Amendment No.2) (Judicial Review) 1985 (S.I. 1985 No. 500)); in England and Wales, Supreme Court Act 1981, s.31, Part 54 of the Civil Procedure Rules 1998, as added by the Civil Procedure (Amendment No.4) Rules 2000 (S.I. 2000 No. 2092).

[63] Similarly, decisions of E.C. institutions can be challenged under art. 230 of the E.C. Treaty only by Member States or those with a "direct and individual concern" in the matter; see *Stichtung Greenpeace Council (Greenpeace International) v. Commission* (C-321/95P) [1998] E.C.R. I-1651.

which recent decisions mark a significant shift in the law and in taking account of differences between jurisdictions, the issue is clouded by the fact that even where there may be room for argument, the legal standing of a party is often not challenged. Moreover, parties may be connected with a case in more than one way, so that it is difficult to identify precisely what features of their connection establish their title and interest to sue. The differing fates of local residents challenging quarry developments in *R. v. North Somerset Council, ex p. Garnett* and *R. v. Somerset County Council, ex p. Dixon*[64] reveal that the extent of connection with a case required before the courts will recognise standing can vary.

In Scotland the courts view the issue of title and interest to sue as a preliminary matter, to be determined before the substance of the case is considered,[65] and the two elements of the test may be treated separately, so that a party who is viewed as having title to sue, may fail on the basis that in the particular circumstances he has no sufficient interest.[66] No comprehensive definitions exist, but as far as title is concerned reference is frequently made to Lord Dunedin's comment in *D. & J. Nicol v. Dundee Harbour Trustees*[67] that to have title a person "must be a party (using the word in its widest sense) to some legal relation which gives him some right which the person against whom he raises the action either infringes or denies". This idea has been given a broad interpretation and in *Wilson v. Independent Broadcasting Authority*[68] it has been held that where a public body owes a duty to the public, individual members of the public may have title to sue. **1.4.10**

However, even if person qualifies as having title to raise an issue, the court must also be satisfied that he has an interest to do so. This requires that the particular issue is of some real concern to the party, and not an academic issue or merely something which he is raising as a matter of general public spirited concern.[69] Such interest, though, need not be a formal legal or property interest, *e.g.* in *Kincardine and Deeside District Council v. Forestry Commissioners*[70] it was held that a local authority had interest on the basis of its "reasonable concern with a major project in their area which may affect the economy or amenity of the area generally". **1.4.11**

In England and Wales, procedural reforms to the process of judicial **1.4.12**

---

[64] Both reported in full at (1998) 10 J.E.L. 161, with commentary by J. Alder.
[65] *Scottish Old People's Welfare Council, Petrs*, 1987 S.L.T. 179; in some cases, though, it is accepted that the issue of standing may not be separable from a consideration of the merits, *Gordon v. Kirkcaldy District Council*, 1989 S.L.T. 507.
[66] As in *Scottish Old People's Welfare Council, Petitioners*, above.
[67] 1915 S.C.(H.L.) 7 at pp. 12–13.
[68] 1979 S.L.T. 279.
[69] *Scottish Old People's Welfare Council, Petitioners*, above.
[70] 1992 S.L.T. 1180 at p. 1184.

review in 1977 swept away a number of restrictive rules on *locus standi* and replaced them with the general test that the applicant must demonstrate "a sufficient interest in the matter to which the application relates".[71] This test has generally been given a fairly liberal interpretation, and been viewed as an issue which has to be considered as part of the broader consideration of the factual and legal circumstances of the case, not as a preliminary issue.[72] Some interest over and above that of the ordinary citizen has to be shown. If this is not possible, a party who does not have *locus standi* can attempt to persuade the Attorney General to instigate proceedings by way of a relator action, although the likelihood of success is small.[73]

1.4.13   The most significant development in recent years has been the courts' increasing willingness to grant standing to campaigning groups. Decisions allowing Greenpeace to challenge the commissioning of a nuclear reprocessing unit at Sellafield and the World Development Movement to challenge financial support for a dam in Malaysia appear to establish that standing can be granted to such bodies.[74] Important features in these decisions were the advantages of a single action from an organised group, as opposed to many individual cases, and the importance of maintaining the rule of law where there may be no individual with a stronger right to sue. These cases represent a marked change of attitude from that shown in the *Rose Theatre* case[75] at the start of the 1990s, but do seem to represent the current generally accepted view, so much so that in one recent case raised by Greenpeace the judge stated that its legal standing to bring proceedings was "well established".[76] It is not yet clear how far this shift in the law will be reflected in Scotland, where there is no authoritative decision in a directly relevant field. In significant recent cases involving conservation issues, the standing of the Worldwide Fund for Nature and the Royal Society for the Protection of Birds has not been challenged,[77] and the cases in other areas where organisations have been refused standing can be distinguished, either because of the potential presence of indi-

---

[71] Supreme Court Act 1981, s.31(3).

[72] *R. v. Inland Revenue Commissioners, ex p. National Federation of Self-employed and Small Businesses Ltd* [1982] A.C. 617.

[73] H.W.R. Wade, *Administrative Law* (8th ed.) (2000) pp. 570–576.

[74] *R. v. Inspectorate of Pollution, ex p. Greenpeace Ltd (No.2)* [1994] 4 All E.R. 329; *R. v. Secretary of State for Foreign and Commonwealth Affairs, ex p. World Development Movement Ltd* [1995] 1 W.L.R. 386.

[75] *R. v. Secretary of State for the Environment, ex p. Rose Theatre Trust Co.* [1990] 1 Q.B. 504.

[76] *R. v. Secretary of State for Trade and Industry, ex p. Greenpeace (No.2)* [2000] Env. L.R. 221 at p. 224, [2000] 2 C.M.L.R. 94 at p. 97 (Maurice Kay J.).

[77] *WWF U.K. v. Secretary of State for Scotland* [1999] 1 C.M.L.R. 1021, [1999] Env. L.R. 632; *RSPB v. Secretary of State for Scotland*, 2000 S.L.T. 1272.

viduals with a stronger interest[78] or because of the very different context of the dispute.[79]

In relation to more narrowly focused groups, *e.g.* residents' groups, the courts look at the substance of the party's interest in the matter, and the particular legal form of the party is not of crucial importance. Therefore if individuals would have title to sue in the particular circumstances, the fact that they have banded together to form an incorporated association which is in law a different person, is of no significance, and the association will enjoy standing to the extent that the individuals would personally.[80] However the capacity of unincorporated associations in England and Wales to become parties to legal action remains uncertain.[81]

1.4.14

Organisations or individuals can seek to strengthen their standing by ensuring that they take the opportunity to build a connection with any site in dispute and to participate in any formal procedures leading up to the decision they may wish to contest. In relation to planning decisions, the simplest way to become involved is through making representations in response to the initial application or at a public inquiry or other appeal proceedings, as it is well established that objectors have a clear right to ensure that proceedings have been conducted lawfully. Such involvement can transform someone from a concerned bystander, but a bystander nonetheless, into a legally interested party.[82] For example, in *Patmor Ltd v. City of Edinburgh District Licensing Board*[83] it was held that the holders of a gaming licence had no title in that capacity to challenge the grant of a licence to another company for similar premises in the area, despite their obvious concern as rival traders to limit competition, but did have title in their capacity as objectors to the new application, having formally taken advantage of

1.4.15

---

[78] *Scottish Old People's Welfare Council, Petitioners*, above.

[79] *The Rape Crisis Centre v. Secretary of State for the Home Department*, 2001 S.L.T. 389.

[80] *Scottish Old People's Welfare Council, Petitioners*, above at p. 185; *R. v. Hammersmith and Fulham London Borough Council, ex p. People Before Profit Ltd* (1982) 80 L.G.R. 322, at p. 333, *R. v. Secretary of State for the Environment , ex p. Rose Theatre Trust Co.* above, at p. 521.

[81] Discussed in Law Commission, *Administrative Law: Judicial Review and Statutory Appeals* (Law Comm. No.226, 1993–94 H.C. 669) at pp. 51–52; *R. v. Traffic Commissioners, ex p. "Brake"* [1996] COD 248.

[82] Despite the recent changes noted above, a court faced with the same circumstances as in *R. v. Poole Borough Council, ex p. Beebee* (1991) 3 J.E.L. 293, might still view the failure of the Worldwide Fund for Nature to make representations in response to the initial planning application to be fatal to its standing, in contrast to the long history of involvement with the site by the British Herpetological Society (survey work, financial input to the site, planning authority's express provision for an opportunity to relocate lizards).

[83] 1987 S.L.T. 492 (affirmed 1988 S.L.T. 850).

the opportunity to submit representations when the application was advertised. A failure to take an earlier opportunity to raise arguments may also lead to the court refusing to entertain them on the basis of acquiescence or estoppel.[84]

1.4.16   A further requirement to be noted in relation to judicial review is the need to act promptly.[85] In England and Wales the ability to refuse cases on the basis of "undue delay" takes statutory form,[86] and the maximum period allowed is three months from the contested decision.[87] This period is, however, the maximum, and action may be required well before it expires.[88] In Scotland the law is based on the doctrine of *mora* and acquiescence, with no fixed time periods but rather an assessment of whether the delay indicates acquiescence or would result in prejudice to others if the action were allowed to go ahead.[89] Especially where the decision to be challenged comes at the end of a protracted process, or the factual situation entails the interaction between different statutory procedures, there can be great difficulty in ascertaining exactly when "the clock starts running" for the purposes of determining whether action has been taken promptly.[90]

HUMAN RIGHTS

1.5.1   The transformation of the legal background in the United Kingdom as a result of legislation in 1998 also merits brief discussion. The impact of the Acts of Parliament giving effect to devolution is discussed in the following chapter,[91] but at this stage something has to be said about the new status of human rights. The Human Rights Act 1998, which came fully into force in October 2000, provides that it is unlawful for any

---

[84] *WWF U.K. v. Secretary of State for Scotland* [1999] 1 C.M.L.R. 1021, [1999] Env. L.R. 632.

[85] C. Reid, "Environmental Citizenship and the Courts" (2000) 3 Env. L. Rev. 177 at pp. 183–186.

[86] Supreme Court Act 1981, s.31(6).

[87] Civil Procedure Rules 1998, rule 54.5 (as added by Civil Procedure (Amendment No. 4) Rules 2000, (S.I. 2000 No. 2092)).

[88] *e.g. R. v. Secretary of State for Trade and Industry, ex p. Greenpeace (No. 1)* [1998] Env. L.R. 415; *R. v. Ceridigion County Council, ex p. McKeown* [1998] 2 P.L.R. 1; G. Roots and R. Walton, "Promptness and Delay in Judicial Review—an update on the continuing saga" [2001] J.P.L. 1360. See Addendum, above.

[89] *Swan v. Secretary of State for Scotland*, 1998 S.C. 479, noted at (1999) 11 J.E.L. 184.

[90] See, for example, *R. v. Secretary of State for Trade and Industry, ex p. Greenpeace (No. 1)* [1998] Env. L.R. 415 and *R. v. Secretary of State for Trade and Industry, ex p. Greenpeace (No. 2)* [2000] Env. L.R. 221, [2000] 2 C.M.L.R. 94; the initial licensing process took over 16 months, and then the need to await the outcome of the first case added a further dimension to the problem of determining when the basis for action had crystallised. See Addendum, above.

[91] See section 2.3, below.

"public authority" to act in a way that is incompatible with an individual's Convention rights; these are set out in Schedule 1 to the Act which in effect reproduces most of the content of the European Convention on Human Rights. Some key points of the legal framework will be mentioned and then the potential for specific rights to affect nature conservation law. Under the devolution arrangements any action incompatible with Convention rights is also outwith the powers of the Scottish Parliament and Executive and the National Assembly for Wales and can be declared invalid by the procedures in the devolution legislation.[92]

The "public authorities" which must not act in a way incompatible   **1.5.2**
with Convention Rights are defined to include courts and tribunals and other persons or bodies with at least some functions "of a public nature".[93] It is clear that Ministers are public authorities, as are local authorities, National Park authorities, the statutory conservation bodies, arguably the National Trusts and potentially bodies such as the RSPB to the extent that certain of their activities, such as managing an officially declared National Nature Reserve,[94] can be classed as "public". Action that is incompatible with Convention rights is unlawful and may in some circumstances give rise to a claim for damages where such an award is necessary to ensure "just satisfaction" for the recipient, taking all the circumstances into account; in many cases judicial review resulting in the quashing of the offending decision is likely to be the appropriate remedy.[95] If recourse to the British courts does not provide a satisfactory solution, it remains possible to raise a case before the European Court of Human Rights in Strasbourg, arguing that the United Kingdom has acted in breach of the Convention, although this is a lengthy process.

Where it is argued that the effect of legislation is incompatible with   **1.5.3**
Convention rights, the first duty of the courts is to "read and give effect to" legislation in a way that is compatible with Convention rights,[96] giving the courts more than the usual room for manoeuvre in finding a meaning that meets the requirements of the Convention. If legislation cannot be read in a way that is compatible, then subordinate legislation, including any legislation from the Scottish Parliament and the National Assembly for Wales, can be declared to be invalid. However there is no power to override an Act of the Westminster Parliament or Order

---

[92] Scotland Act 1998, ss.29(2), 57(2); Government of Wales Act 1998, s.107; these provisions took effect before the Human Rights Act 1998 came into force and in Scotland generated a large volume of litigation, mainly in relation to criminal procedure.

[93] Human Rights Act 1998, s.6; acts "of a private nature" of those bodies which have some public functions fall outwith the scope of the requirement.

[94] WCA 1981, s.35 ; see para. 5.3.9, below.

[95] Human Rights Act 1998, s.8.

[96] *ibid.*, s.3.

in Council made under the Royal Prerogative, and in these cases the most that the courts can do is issue a declaration of incompatibility, drawing the attention of Parliament and the government to the situation.[97] Remedial action to bring matters into line with Convention rights is expected but not legally required, thereby conserving the idea of parliamentary sovereignty and the powers of Parliament to have the final say. The position of Convention rights is thus very different from that of rights under E.C. law, which must be protected by the courts even though this involves overriding the terms of an Act of Parliament.[98]

1.5.4 Recourse to the courts is available only to those who claim to be "victims" of an infringement of their rights.[99] Although the Convention refers in its title to "human rights", and some of the rights protected are clearly limited to human beings,[1] it has long been accepted that many of the rights are also enjoyed by "legal" as well as "natural" persons, so that companies and some associations can also seek recourse if their rights or freedoms are unduly restricted. The test for being a victim is essentially that one has been directly affected by the breach of rights, but although there is some generosity for family members or where a class of people are affected,[2] the test does impose a stricter standard than that adopted in some judicial review cases permitting public interest groups access to the courts.[3]

1.5.5 In relation to nature conservation law the two articles most likely to give rise to argument are article 6, the right to a fair trial, and art.1 of Protocol 1, protection of property. Article 6 provides that "in the determination of his civil rights and obligations . . . everyone is entitled to a fair and public hearing within a reasonable time by an independent and impartial tribunal", and the application of this provision to statutory decision-making and appeal mechanisms has generated much argument, including cases from the United Kingdom before the European Court of Human Rights, long before the 1998 Act was enacted. The fundamental issue in this area so far as nature conservation is concerned arises from the fact that under the town and country planning system, and many other regimes on environmental matters, the right of appeal

---

[97] *ibid.*, s.4; measures of the Church Assembly, and the General Synod of the Church of England are similarly protected.

[98] *e.g. R. v. Secretary of State for Transport, ex p. Factortame Ltd (No. 2)* [1991] 1 A.C. 603.

[99] Human Rights Act 1998, s.7.

[1] *e.g.* the right to marry (art. 12).

[2] *e.g. Open Door Counselling and Dublin Well Women v. Ireland* (1992) 15 E.H.R.R. 244.

[3] In *R. (on the application of Vetterlein) v. Hampshire County Council* [2002] Env. L.R. 8 it was held that "generalised environmental concerns" are not enough to entitle an individual to invoke Convention rights as the basis of a claim.

against regulatory decisions lies not to the courts but to the Minister. It has been conceded by the government that in view of the Ministers' role in setting policy and the potential for government departments to be directly involved in proceedings, this procedure does not by itself offer appeal to a "fair and impartial" tribunal.[4] The question therefore becomes one of whether the potential for subsequent recourse to the courts (either under statutory procedures or by judicial review) is sufficient to ensure that the process as a whole meets the standards set in the Convention.

This issue has arisen in several cases. Before the 1998 Act, the European Court of Human Rights held in *Bryan v. United Kingdom*[5] that the recourse to the courts did mean that the planning process as a whole was sufficiently impartial, but at first instance the Court of Session in *County Properties Ltd v. Scottish Ministers*[6] and the English High Court in *R. v. Secretary of State for Environment, Transport & the Regions, ex p. Holding & Barnes plc*[7] held that the planning procedures did involve an infringement of rights under article 6. The English case was then referred to the House of Lords[8] where it was decided that the appeal procedures did in fact live up to the standards demanded by the Convention, a decision followed by the Inner House in Scotland.[9] The system of appeals to ministers and their delegates, with recourse to the courts for those aggrieved, can therefore be maintained. **1.5.6**

Nevertheless, the importance of providing legal protection for those whose rights are being affected by decisions taken within the legal structures for nature conservation has been reflected in legislative changes. The new structures for SSSIs in England and Wales incorporate appeal mechanisms so that certain decisions that are taken by the statutory conservation bodies and that affect the rights of owners and occupiers of land can be contested before an appeal body independent of the statutory conservation bodies making the initial decisions.[10] **1.5.7**

A slightly different issue arose in *Lafarge Redland Aggregates v. Scottish Ministers*,[11] where it was held that there was insufficient appearance of impartiality when the Ministers in determining a plan- **1.5.8**

---

[4] The potential for Ministers to call in decisions for their personal attention means that this criticism applies even where in practice appeals are delegated to inspectors or reporters.

[5] (1996) 21 E.H.R.R. 342; followed by the European Court in *Chapman v. United Kingdom* (2001) 33 E.H.R.R. 18.

[6] 2000 S.C. 430.

[7] [2001] 2 W.L.R. 1389 (known as the *Alconbury* case, after one of other cases in this joined action).

[8] [2001] 2 W.L.R. 1389.

[9] 2002 S.C. 79.

[10] WCA 1981, ss.28F, 28L (added by CRWA 2000, Sched. 9); see paras 5.5.7, 5.5.24, 5.5.28, below. See Addendum, above.

[11] 2000 S.L.T. 1361.

ning application referred the question of whether the area concerned should be proposed as a Special Area of Conservation[12] to Scottish Natural Heritage, which had been among the main objectors to the application. Taken at its extreme, this decision seems to render it impossible for the statutory conservation bodies to fulfil their function of providing advice to ministers and at the same time to play any active part in any procedures where ministers may have to make decisions affecting legal rights. Such a conclusion would call for a wide reassessment of the many roles of these bodies.[13] The exact scope of this decision, taken in the context of truly exceptional planning case, remains to be further explored, both under domestic rules of natural justice and the terms of article 6. A less controversial ground for finding that article 6 had been breached in this case was the inordinate delay in determining the planning application,[14] which had denied the applicants their right to a decision within a reasonable time.

1.5.9   In contrast to the procedural nature of the concerns under article 6, the second main issue raises substantive matters. Article 1 of Protocol 1 follows the pattern of most of the substantive articles of the Convention, with a broad statement of the right "to the peaceful enjoyment of ... possessions" followed by a qualification which permits a person to be deprived of his property "in the public interest and subject to conditions provided for by law." Issues under this article can arise in relation to nature conservation measures authorising compulsory purchase of land or restricting the owners' rights to do as they wish with their property.

1.5.10   These matters were discussed by the European Court of Human Rights in *Matos e Silva Lda v. Portugal*,[15] where the occupiers of land that had been identified for a nature reserve claimed that their rights had been infringed. The case is again somewhat exceptional in that the relevant legal proceedings affecting the site had been going on for many years, in itself conceded by the Portuguese government to amount to a breach of the applicants' rights under article 6 to have their rights determined within a reasonable time, but a few useful pointers are given. It was held that the restrictions on the occupiers' use of their land, in particular a prohibition on key forms of development, combined with steps paving the way for compulsory acquisition which blighted the chances of selling the land, did amount to an interference with the occupiers' right to enjoy their property. On the other hand, measures to protect the environment and for the purposes of town and country

---

[12] See section 5.2, below.
[13] See para. 2.6.7, below.
[14] Over five years after the end of the public inquiry (that itself came after lengthy proceedings), no decision had been made.
[15] (1997) 24 E.H.R.R. 573.

planning are in the public interest. The question was therefore one of determining whether a fair balance had been struck between the competing interests, and in the particular circumstances it was held that the occupiers were subject to an excessive burden in having to endure serious effects hindering their ordinary enjoyment of rights over the land for 13 years during which virtually no progress had been made towards the final acquisition of the land and establishment of the nature reserve.

This decision confirms that property rights can legitimately be restricted in pursuit of environmental objectives, and that whether there has been a breach of the Convention will depend on the individual circumstances, with the decision resting on ideas such as a fair balance of interests and whether the interference with the individual's rights can be justified as a proportionate measure to achieve one of the permissible public goals.[16] Many of the conservation measures discussed below do have the effect of restricting property rights, but if decisions are taken with due regard for the competing public and private interests, if appropriate appeal mechanisms operate promptly and if proper compensation is available in the event of compulsory acquisition, these should meet the standards of the Convention.

1.5.11

Other cases affecting property have given rise to arguments under article 8 of the Convention, the right to respect for one's home and private life, where again the legitimacy of action on environmental grounds has been recognised, provided that there is an appropriate balance between the public interest being promoted and the private rights of individuals.[17] The right to life (article 2) has been raised where health is at risk from pollution,[18] but this is unlikely to be an issue in relation to nature conservation, and the invocation of other rights will require a significant degree of legal ingenuity.

1.5.12

Overall, the Human Rights Act 1998 may not have much effect on the final results of the law in relation with respect to nature conservation, other than in relation to decision-making procedures, but it does provide a new discipline requiring decision-makers to ensure that in taking decisions for conservation purposes due regard is paid to the personal and property rights of individuals and companies who are affected by those decisions.

1.5.13

---

[16] *e.g. Hatton v. United Kingdom* (2002) 34 E.H.R.R. 1, where it was held that there was a breach of the Convention since the decision to approve a scheme for night-time flights at Heathrow airport had been taken without an adequate assessment of the extent of either the interference with the rights of nearby residents or the economic benefits that might justify such interference.

[17] *e.g. Powell and Rayner v. United Kingdom* (1990) 12 E.H.R.R. 355; *Buckley v. United Kingdom* (1996) 23 E.H.R.R. 101; *Chapman v. United Kingdom* (2001) 33 E.H.R.R. 18, *Hatton v. United Kingdom*, above.

[18] *e.g. Lopez Ostra v. Spain* (1995) 20 E.H.R.R. 277.

1.6.1   Over the last 50 years, there has been significant evolution in the legal approaches to providing protection for wild plants and animals. Since the general legal background offers few opportunities for furthering conservation beyond the initiatives of private individuals on their own land, the development of nature conservation has depended on action by Parliament and government. The legislation enacted and the legal, economic and other tools used to give effect to policies aiming at conservation have changed considerably. Although the criminal law has always been used to control actions directly harmful to particular species, until the 1990s habitat protection rested almost entirely on the voluntary principle, with the emphasis on persuasion rather than direct regulation. Now significant direct controls are in place, but accompanied by an emphasis on conservation as a process that requires not just the prevention of harmful acts but also the positive management of land and other resources, in a partnership between private owners and the conservation authorities.

1.6.2   A detailed analysis (legal, historical, social, economic, political) of the approaches and techniques adopted, and those which have been rejected, would be a fascinating and lengthy study, especially when comparisons are drawn over time, with other areas of policy, *e.g.* agriculture and planning, and with the situation in other countries. In the context of this book, however, it must suffice to look briefly at the voluntary principle that for so long dominated this area and to identify five elements in the mechanisms discussed in the following chapters to confer some protection on wild creatures and plants. These are the use of the criminal law, the acquisition of property rights, the imposition of notification requirements of various sorts, the use of agreements to provide long-term conservation, and the growing importance of management plans and schemes. Underlying all of this is a shift from a wholly voluntary approach to one that still favours voluntary measures but promotes these against a background where meaningful sanctions are available not only against those who clearly damage but also against those who fail to maintain the conservation interest of their land.

From Voluntary Principle to Partnership

1.6.3   The structure of the law on nature conservation was until recently completely dominated by reliance on the voluntary principle. The legal structures were based on persuasion, not compulsion. This was in marked contrast to other areas of law, so that whereas the controls imposed under the modern town and country planning system have always clearly prohibited activities that were considered undesirable, the nature conservation measures essentially offered protection only if the landowner agreed to accept restrictions, usually in exchange for compensation. A range of social, political and technical arguments can explain this disparity, but two key points can be identified. Firstly, nature conservation was not viewed as important enough to justify direct interference with private rights.[19] Secondly, there was a view that the land was best cared for through the stewardship of its existing owners, not through rules and regulations.

Reliance on the voluntary principle has had its strong supporters and critics. Supporters argue that the best guardians of the countryside and its valuable habitat are those who own it and live and work there. Successful conservation requires the continuing commitment of those on the ground, and this is best achieved by obtaining the willing co-operation of those involved. Any attempt to order them to manage their land in a particular way would in many cases be met with at best resentful compliance with the mere letter of the law, whereas proper conservation measures depend on a thorough acceptance of the objectives being pursued, so that the whole management of the land and of the activities on it takes account of the natural heritage. Even if it were possible to specify everything necessary to ensure appropriate management, the problems of monitoring and enforcement on a long-term basis mean that laws imposed on unwilling landowners would not prove a success. The need for continuing management of the land in appropriate ways provides a valid distinction with the planning system. For this reason, nature conservation is better served by offering assistance and encouragement so that landowners become willing partners in the conservation enterprise, not reluctant servants. **1.6.4**

The voluntary approach also emphasises the importance of education. The law cannot hope to deal with all of the matters of significance for nature conservation, nor to regulate all the sites that contribute to the overall health and richness of the environment, therefore a general raising of awareness of the value and requirements of conservation is what is called for. Through the operation of the statutory designations and consultation requirements, and through the provision of advice and information, people can be made aware of how they can protect and promote biodiversity, and in many cases do so without prejudicing any of their other interests. In the long-term this gentle encouragement to a change in attitudes will provide a more secure basis for nature conservation than will any specific legal measures which are subject to repeal or amendment to suit the political exigencies of the day. **1.6.5**

On the other hand, a negative assessment of the voluntary approach is to say that it gives far too much weight to private interests at the **1.6.7**

---

[19] A view held particularly by some of those with political influence: see, *e.g.* the debates in the House of Lords during the passage of the Natural Heritage (Scotland) Bill, especially on January 23, 1991; Hansard, H.L. Vol. 525, cols 173–185.

expense of the public interest in nature conservation. The rights of landowners to do as they please with their property are given undue protection,[20] and landowners (often already of considerable wealth) can receive large payments in order to do nothing. Conservation is seen as a public objective, yet the state uses bribery at the taxpayers' expense, not the power of the law, to promote it. Moreover the voluntary system that was adopted was open to abuse, as payments for maintaining the land in its desired condition could be triggered by proposals which were at best speculative and which the landowner never really intended to carry through. The overall approach left unsympathetic landowners free to ruin even the most valuable of sites, and put all habitat protection at the mercy of the willingness of landowners to co-operate and of the resources available to the conservation bodies for compensation payments. The relentless history of habitat destruction over past decades by itself condemns the voluntary approach as an inadequate way of achieving meaningful conservation.

1.6.8 Whatever one's assessment, it should be recognised that in the past the voluntary principle had to operate against a generally unsympathetic background, in which environmental concerns were a low priority for government and for individuals. With changes in official and public attitudes[21] and an official commitment to sustainability, that background has changed markedly since the early 1980s, and there is the potential for the voluntary principle really to come into its own, supported at last by adequate funding and by complementary policies in agriculture, forestry and other areas which have a major effect on the countryside. The past failures can to some extent be attributed to the fact that the principle was never given the opportunity to work properly.

1.6.9 The voluntary approach has, however, been abandoned as the sole basis for conservation measures. The need to guarantee the protection of sites in order to meet the requirements of the Habitats and Species Directive[22] meant that total reliance on voluntary measures was no longer tenable and growing public concern for conservation and awareness of the failings of the previous law have led further to the stronger measures introduced for England and Wales and promised for Scotland.[23] These do include prohibitions and a degree of compulsion

---

[20] *cf.* the restrictive approach to interpreting statutory provisions which interfere with property rights suggested in *North Uist Fisheries Ltd v. Secretary of State for Scotland,* 1992 S.L.T. 333; see para. 5.6.6, below.

[21] It is interesting to speculate whether the educational and persuasive impact of the voluntary approach itself contributed to this change, or whether the change was slowed by the fact that the voluntary approach appeared to give conservation a low priority in competition with other public goals.

[22] See para. 1.1.22, above.

[23] See para. 1.1.24, above.

at odds with a wholly voluntary approach,[24] but to a considerable extent they remain in the background. The foreground emphasis is still on co-operation and on a partnership between public bodies and private interests. Thus the mechanisms for European Sites and the reformed system of SSSIs in England and Wales still give prominence to management agreements as the key means of securing the protection of sites, and management schemes for SSSIs[25] do not by themselves impose direct obligations.

Establishing an effective partnership is undoubtedly made easier by the presence of the stronger measures "in the shadows", and also by the more sympathetic background created by the gradual changes in agricultural policy.[26] Both of these encourage landowners to co-operate with the conservation bodies and to see conservation-related measures as a sensible and indeed desirable part of their management of the land. It is thus possible to gain many of the advantages of the voluntary approach, whilst ensuring that its one great flaw is cured by the presence of compulsion as a measure of last resort.   **1.6.10**

A further element in securing partnership is the increased emphasis on the positive management of sites. Attention has shifted from merely trying to prevent specific activities that damage sites to endeavouring to protect them from gradual deterioration and to enhance their conservation value. The increased attention paid to management statements and schemes[27] is part of a wider move towards looking at the enhancement of areas and the financial mechanisms are reflecting this. A criticism of the older management agreements was that too often they rewarded those who had proposed damaging changes to their sites but did nothing for those who willingly cared for the wildlife on their land. Money was spent on stopping things happening rather than actually furthering conservation. Over the last 15 years there has been a significant change away from compensatory payments to positive payments for the active management and enhancement of the land.[28] The new attitude is boldly stated in the *Guidelines on Management Agreement Payments and Other Related Matters* issued in February 2001:[29] "Min-   **1.6.11**

---

[24] The extent of the increase in the legal powers of the conservation bodies is shown by the fact that appeal mechanisms have had to be introduced to review their actions, where none were needed before; see para. 5.5.24, below.

[25] See paras 5.5.26, below.

[26] See paras 8.4.3–8.4.8, below.

[27] See para. 1.6.28, below.

[28] Compensatory agreements now account for only four per cent of the land covered by management agreements in England (English Nature, *Annual Report for 2000–2001*, p. 9).

[29] DETR, 2001, para. 1.2; technically this applies to England only but the same approach is taken throughout Great Britain: "The continuing and future use of Management Agreements as a positive tool forms the backbone of [our strategy]" (*Natural Care Strategy*, SNH, 2001).

isters expect that management agreements on SSSIs will be used to facilitate their positive management. . . . Ministers are not prepared for public money to be paid out simply to prevent new operations which could destroy or damage these national assets."

1.6.12   We are currently in a state of transition, from a "toothless" system[30] that was totally dependent on the voluntary principle with almost nothing to support it if agreement could not be reached, to one where significant legal powers do exist to take the steps necessary to preserve and enhance the natural heritage, but voluntary partnership is the preferred means of achieving significant gains. The transition has still to take place fully in Scotland and has not had long enough to settle down in England and Wales, but the implementation of the Habitats and Species Directive "broke the mould" by introducing compulsion in place of a wholly voluntary approach. Already it must seem remarkable to those studying this area for the first time that the old, voluntary system was seen as the appropriate way to deal with the manifold threats to biodiversity in this country.

1.6.13   Whatever the overall approach, the law employs a combination of mechanisms to achieve its end. The rest of this section comments briefly on some of the key devices used in the protection of both species and habitats.

Criminal Law

1.6.14   The criminal law is used to mark out forms of conduct which are considered to be unacceptable in society. As well as the direct penalties and deterrent, the use of the criminal courts and the stigma of conviction should bring home to offenders, and the public generally, the fact that such actions are regarded as unacceptable. The law has been used to create a number of offences prohibiting the killing, injuring or other harm to wild animals and plants.[31]

1.6.15   There are good reasons for utilising laws which render harm to wild animals and plants criminal. In the first place the most obvious thing which man can do to protect wildlife is to refrain from killing, injuring or disturbing it, and making such conduct a crime is the most direct legal way of trying to prevent it. Secondly, from the legal point of view, such laws are comparatively simple. The undesirable conduct is defined, any necessary exceptions are stated, and then the operation of the law is left to the general system of law enforcement, with no need for special administrative arrangements. Thirdly, such laws are useful in terms of publicity and education, as they should be readily compre-

---

[30] Lord Mustill in *Southern Water Authority v Nature Conservancy Council* [1992] 1 W.L.R. 775 at p. 778.

[31] *e.g.* the intentional killing of most wild birds; see Chapter 3, below.

hensible, although public awareness of the law is not necessarily high, and there may be problems in relation to provisions designed to protect particular species which may not be widely recognised in the field.

However, there are factors which may reduce the effectiveness of **1.6.16** this approach to conservation legislation. By requiring the express prohibition of the undesirable conduct, there is a risk that some forms of harm, or some species in need of protection, will be omitted. The presence of gaps and possible loopholes may undermine the law, and it may be difficult to persuade the legislators to make the effort to enact the necessary amendments promptly. In the second place, criminal offences are likely to be directed against obvious and direct harm, so that the gradual deterioration of habitats and the harmful consequences incidental to other legitimate activities are likely to escape sanction.

A third problem which affects the use of any criminal law in this **1.6.17** area relates to enforcement. The central measures prohibiting direct harm against wildlife are supported by ones on possession and sale to catch more than just the instant when harm is done,[32] but even with the use of strict liability[33] and the onus being put on the accused to establish that they fall within any exceptions to an offence, it may be hard to secure the evidence necessary for a conviction. There may be problems in identifying the species which are given special protection, and by their very nature many of the offences are going to be committed in remote places away from the eyes of witnesses. In Scotland some recognition is given to these difficulties by the relaxation in some instances of the rules on corroboration, allowing the evidence of one witness to suffice for conviction.[34] It may also prove difficult to persuade a busy police force and prosecutor's office that nature conservation cases should be given any priority over the mass of more standard crimes with which they have to cope.

Likewise the effectiveness of the law can be undermined by the **1.6.18** courts imposing only low penalties on offenders, penalties which are trivial in proportion to the economic gain which has been achieved by ignoring the law and the irreparable nature of the harm done. Crimes against wildlife have attracted a number of substantial fines, remarkably so in view of the derisory fines that are too often imposed for offences in other areas of environmental law, and occasionally judges have stated that in fact prison sentences, if available, would have been an

---

[32] See para. 3.2.4, below.
[33] Strict liability describes the position where criminal liability rests on the simple fact that the accused carried out the prohibited act, without any need to show that it was done intentionally, recklessly, negligently or knowingly; *e.g.* see para. 3.3.13, below.
[34] *e.g.* Deer (Scotland) Act 1996, s.23(5); WCA 1981, s.19A (added by Prisoners and Criminal Proceedings (Scotland) Act 1993, s.36).

appropriate sentence.[35] The Countryside and Rights of Way Act 2000 now does provide for heavier sentences in England and Wales, and similar changes are promised for Scotland, but it remains to be seen whether there is a willingness to make use of these new powers.

1.6.19 The criminal law is also used in another way, as the final sanction to secure compliance with a number of essentially administrative schemes, *e.g.* in relation to the planning system.[36] In this context the use of the criminal law shares the features of its use in many other regulatory schemes, especially the general perception that the offences involved are not "real crimes." This means that the offences are given a low priority at all stages in the administration of justice, and that the consequences of conviction, in terms of penalty and stigma, are often minimal.[37]

Property Rights

1.6.20 In seeking to protect habitat, an obvious mechanism is to make use of the rights that the general law confers on owners of land. The landowner's rights to control what happens on the land and who has access to it provide a strong and simple way of ensuring that the land is managed in a particular way, and there is the advantage of making use of the normal rules of property law so that there is no need for any special rules or procedures. The large-scale acquisition of land and its transfer to stewards who can be guaranteed to secure its management for long-term conservation would therefore be an option for securing the future of the country's natural heritage.

1.6.21 This approach is used on some occasions,[38] but most designated habitat has not been taken under the direct control of the state in any form. The potential for greater use of ownership is available, with assorted powers of compulsory purchase where this is considered necessary,[39] but both the cost of compensating owners and a reluctance to use compulsory powers in this area have limited its deployment. There may, though, be more pressure to make greater use of these powers if

---

[35] See para. 3.2.6, below.

[36] See section 8.2., below.

[37] J. Rowan-Robinson, P. Watchman, C. Barker, *Crime and Regulation: A Study of the Enforcement of Regulatory Codes* (1990).

[38] Essentially this has been the case only for National Nature Reserves. In England, just over a fifth of the area included in National Nature Reserves is owned by English Nature, with almost a further two-fifths occupied under leases; English Nature, *Annual Report for 2000–2001*, p. 15; for Scotland, where some reserves are controlled through a patchwork of ownership, leases and agreements, see Scottish Natural Heritage, *Facts and Figures 2000–2001*, p. 19.

[39] *e.g.* in relation to European Sites, National Nature Reserves, or where management arrangements for an SSSI cannot be achieved or are broken (see paras 5.2.18, 5.3.4, 5.5.29, 5.6.6.7, below).

arrangements to encourage the positive management of sites in private ownership do not in fact secure them from deterioration[40] or do not succeed in achieving the enhancement of degraded habitats that is desired.

Notification

Notification procedures have played a central part in conservation **1.6.22** measures, and have worked in two directions. Firstly the conservation authorities have notified those dealing with land of the fact that it is of special value, so that those taking decisions about its management and use are aware of its conservation value and the harm that might be done. Secondly those dealing with the land have been required to notify the conservation authorities when they are planning to carry out activities that might affect it, so that there is an opportunity for conservation measures to be agreed or imposed.

The first form of notification occurs throughout the habitat protection **1.6.23** structures. The starting point of all these measures is the designation of particular sites so that the areas of special value are identified and people alerted to the need to have special consideration.[41] Under the original version of Sites of Special Scientific Interest only the planning authorities were notified of the designation, so that only a narrow range of decisions in relation to the land were affected, but under the more recent legislation notification is made not only to the owners and occupiers responsible for day-to-day management but also to a range of statutory undertakers who may be carrying out operations affecting the land.[42] Letting people know of the value of the land does not by itself guarantee any protection, but does avoid damage occurring through ignorance alone and should ensure that conservation issues are at least included in the list of factors influencing management decisions, even if they are given little or no weight. Awareness of the potential for harm may by itself be enough to lead sympathetic occupiers to change their plans, or at least to adapt them to accommodate conservation concerns. In a wider context this approach is manifested in the whole system of environmental impact assessment,[43] which does not by itself prevent any environmentally harmful developments taking place, but does try to ensure that decision-makers do at least take account of the environmental costs of a proposal as they consider whether or not to give consent.

A further dimension to this aspect of notification is the growing inter- **1.6.24**

---

[40] Especially in relation to European Sites; see para. 5.2.18, below.
[41] Although there are also more direct legal consequences, the listing of species as qualifying for enhanced protection also fulfils this notification role; see para. 3.2.3, below.
[42] See section 5.5, below.
[43] See section 8.3, below.

est in designations as accolades, "which have the potential to generate local pride in the quality of the natural heritage" and which might be "encouraged and publicised with view to promoting tourism and other local economic development".[44] The designation by itself can thus provide a focus for interest, education and enthusiasm, as well as adding an official "quality mark" which can be useful to anyone using the quality of the natural heritage of an area as a resource in attracting visitors or business of various sorts. Long-term conservation will only be achieved in a culture where nature is valued, and simply telling people of the value of what is around them has an important part to play in generating such a culture.

1.6.25   The second form of notification, from the occupier to the conservation authorities, has lain at the heart of the arrangements for SSSIs, and is still the basis for the system in Scotland.[45] The occupiers are not prohibited from carrying out activities, but must inform the statutory conservation body before doing so. This notification serves two purposes. The first is to make the occupiers realise that they are doing something potentially harmful to the site, reinforcing the impact of the designation, and the second, more important, is to give the body the opportunity to consider invoking any further conservation measures. Again, therefore, the notification requirements by themselves do not secure the protection of the site, but they provide the trigger for dialogue between occupiers and the conservation bodies and for invoking the range of conservation options available. This puts the onus on the effectiveness of those further options, and in the past these were limited to the negotiation of a management agreement. Only with the introduction of European Sites[46] and the new regime for SSSIs[47] in England and Wales has it been possible for the notification to be generally followed by a prohibition. Notification requirements alone, therefore cannot provide protection, but do have a part to play in informing, educating and encouraging the desired behaviour.

Agreements

1.6.26   The dominant mechanism for habitat protection over the last two decades has been the management agreement.[48] Any meaningful and long-term controls on the use of land have been the product of agreement

---

[44] *Natural Heritage Designations Review* (Scottish Office, 1996), p. 46.

[45] See section 5.5, below.

[46] See Section 5.2, below.

[47] See paras 5.5.21–5.5.22, below; in Scotland prohibitions are only available if a Nature Conservation Order is made (see section 5.6, below).

[48] See generally C. Rodgers and J. Bishop, *Management Agreements for Promoting Nature Conservation* (1998); A. Ross and J. Rowan-Robinson, "Behind Closed Doors: The Use of Agreements in the U.K. to Protect the Environment" (1999) 1 Env. L. Rev. 82.

rather than imposition.[49] This manifestation of the voluntary principle has allowed the requirements of each site to be individually addressed, although the transaction costs involved in negotiating individual agreements is increasingly leading to the use of standard schemes operating over shorter periods.[50] Over the years a very large number of agreements have been made[51] and they have taken different forms over the years, from the long-term nature reserve agreements made when reserves were established, through the compensatory agreements offered to prevent damaging operations being carried out on an SSSI to the positive agreements that are now being made to provide for the positive management and enhancement of sites.

The use of agreements encapsulates the voluntary principle and has been the focus of the arguments for and against that approach. Their current role is changing in two ways. Firstly, the powers that now enable the conservation authorities to take stronger action to secure conservation aims mean that the agreements are free to place more emphasis on positive action. Secondly, the changes in agricultural policy mean that conservation agreements can increasingly combine with, as opposed to competing against, at least some of the support schemes for agriculture. When they had to serve not only as an incentive but also as almost the only way of offering protection to threatened sites, agreements could be seen as a very weak mechanism, doomed to fail in the face of an unwilling landowner. Now they are not the only means of preventing harm occurring and are thus free to fulfil the role that they are best equipped for—a positive role in enabling measures to be taken beyond the bare minimum, and benefiting parties affected and showing a positive return for the public money spent.

1.6.27

Management Plans

As noted above, the emphasis on taking positive steps to conserve and enhance habitat, as opposed to seeking merely to prevent specific damage being done, has led to greater attention being paid to management plans and schemes. This manifests itself in several ways. The most notable recent development has come in relation to SSSIs in England and Wales (where the designation of a site must be accompanied by a management statement setting out views on the management of the land, similar statements must be produced for existing sites, and management schemes can be introduced,)[52] but this is just part of a

1.6.28

---

[49] See paras 5.1.7–5.1.8 below.

[50] *Natural Care Strategy* (SNH, 2001), p. 8.

[51] There were 1,259 agreements in force in Scotland in 2001 and it takes over 40 pages of fairly small print to list all their details; SNH, *Facts and Figures 2000–2001*, pp. 97–143.

[52] See paras 5.5.18 and 5.5.26, below.

wider feature. European Sites, National Parks and Areas of Outstanding Natural Beauty all require plans to guide their management and to co-ordinate the activities of the different public authorities and private interests concerned.[53] To these specific plans must be added the biodiversity plans being developed for particular species, habitats and local areas,[54] and the plans that underlie the management schemes being increasingly used as the basis for management agreements.[55]

1.6.29   Such plans are not an innovation, but increasingly they are enjoying statutory status or some means of ensuring their implementation. Their enhanced role, and the opportunities for consultation and participation as they are develop, are part of the wider move towards a more positive approach, based on a partnership for management, not prohibition. The details of what is done in practice may come to depend more and more on such plans and less on any formal legal provision.

1.6.30   The law frequently allows wide discretion to official bodies, and even where overt discretion is not created, the availability, or lack, of resources will inevitably affect considerably the way in which the law is administered. The legal framework may thus operate in different ways according to the different priorities of different bodies at any given time. Moreover, the increasing use of plans and grant schemes enables significant shifts in policy direction to take place without any need to change the law itself.[56] The crucial factor is whether there is the real political will to give priority to nature conservation, a priority which inevitably means that other interests must in some cases suffer. The law is currently in the process of changing to offer greater assist-ance to the protection of biodiversity. If the rhetoric of sustainability is carried through into practice, and environmental considerations are truly integrated with other policies, then even without further changes to the law, the impact of nature conservation measures may be consid-erably increased.

1.6.31   In deciding on the future of nature conservation law, attention will inevitably turn back to the big question of why we are conserving nature. The law at present to some extent contains both ecocentric and anthropocentric ideas, the former through the duty to designate sites when they meet certain scientific criteria,[57] the latter by permitting des-ignated sites to the destroyed where social and economic interests jus-

---

[53] See paras 5.2.27, 5.5.18, 5.11.10, 5.11.28, 5.12.7, below.

[54] See para. 1.2.4, above.

[55] *Natural Care Strategy* (SNH, 2001), p. 8.

[56] See, *e.g.* the many changes in forestry achieved even before the legislative steps to introduce environmental impact assessments and consent procedures for planting: C. Reid, ''Forestry, the Law and the Environment'' in C. Rodgers (ed.), *Nature Conserva-tion and Countryside Law* (1996).

[57] This applies the European designations and SSSIs; see sections 5.2 and 5.5, below.

tify this.[58] These differing approaches can coexist to some extent, but inevitably conflicts will arise. Even within each approach, there are difficulties. If an ecocentric approach is taken, what is the ultimate goal, given that many habitats are to a great extent artificial, the creation not of natural processes but of human intervention?[59] From a purely anthropocentric point of view, how does one balance, say, arguments of amenity against the demand for houses in the countryside, or the interests of farmers against those of other groups? The scope for differing views of what the law should be trying to do will ensure that debate will continue over its application and development.

---

[58] Through the structured decision-making in relation to projects affecting European Sites and the powers of the conservation bodies and planning authorities to consent to damaging activities on SSSIs; *ibid.*

[59] The reintroduction of extinct species raises questions about what environment we are trying to create, or recreate, since if one goes back far enough all of Great Britain should just be covered in ice.

2. THE AUTHORITIES RESPONSIBLE FOR NATURE CONSERVATION

2.1.1 Responsibility for matters affecting nature conservation is spread among a range of official bodies. Various departments of central government and the devolved administrations are involved, as are local government and the European Community. The most direct responsibility is borne by a group of public bodies which enjoy a degree of independence from government while in practical terms a major role is played by charitable organisations. The fragmentation of responsibility is exacerbated by the different structures which exist in the different jurisdictions in Great Britain, and by the effects of devolution.

2.1.2 In view of the many activities which can have an impact on the environment some division of responsibilities is inevitable. However, although it is sensible for there to be bodies dealing with all aspects of agriculture, of river quality, etc., such division can mean that the interests of nature conservation are pushed into the background. Because it is not the central concern of such bodies, conservation can be seen as a marginal issue, primarily the responsibility of others, and consequently not as something to be given any priority when policies are formulated or powers exercised. In this way, the approach to the countryside and the environment becomes fragmented and unnecessary conflicts and disputes can arise. What is required is an integrated approach, with co-operation between the various bodies so that complementary decisions are taken and conservation concerns are taken into consideration (whether or not they are fully accepted) from the earliest stage of formulating policy. Without such integration one can have the absurd situation of one official body offering grants to people to do things in the interests of agriculture or forestry while another official body offers payments in order to stop them in the interests of nature conservation.

2.1.3 Mechanisms for co-operation between the various authorities exist at different levels. The activities of the conservation bodies can to some extent be kept in line with other aspects of official policy by the power to issue ministerial directions and by requirements for ministerial consent before certain powers are exercised. The conservation authorities are also placed under a duty to have regard to more than just the interests of nature conservation in carrying out their functions. On the other hand, authorities whose main responsibilities lie elsewhere are bound to pay heed to the concerns of conservation both by similar "balancing obligations" and by more particular duties, especially by requirements that the statutory conservation bodies be consulted either before particular powers are exercised or on the general management of certain issues. However the advice which is proffered need not be followed and in view of an authority's prime responsibilities it may be quite proper for it to place other interests before those of nature conservation.

Moves have been made toward greater integration in recent years. **2.1.4**
Most noticeably the institutional divide between the bodies responsible
for landscape and natural beauty and those concerned with nature conservation was ended in Scotland and Wales with the creation of Scottish
Natural Heritage and the Countryside Council for Wales, although the
divide continues in England.[1] Such mergers allow for a broader
approach to be taken to issues affecting particular areas, but it must
also be recognised that real conflicts remain to be resolved before an
integrated policy can emerge, *e.g.* between the interests of public access
and recreation and those of nature conservation. The slow but now
perceptible increase in the weight of environmental considerations
within agricultural policy is a further manifestation of some progress
towards increased integration.[2]

More generally, the government's commitments on environmental **2.1.5**
matters have frequently referred to the need to integrate environmental
and other policies "to ensure . . . that we are not undoing in one area
what we are trying to do in another."[3] The current sustainable development strategy expressly refers to the "building of concern for wildlife
into other policies",[4] but although the rhetoric of such an integrated
approach is now common, the practical results are not always as obvious. The recent inquiry into United Kingdom Biodiversity by the House
of Commons Environment Committee found a lack of integration and
a limited commitment to biodiversity in some departments, and called
for more efforts to promote biodiversity, and monitor progress, across
all aspects of government.[5] There is certainly a long way to go before
a properly integrated approach is delivered in practice.

Whatever the formal policy and institutional structure, much will **2.1.6**
always depend on the attitudes and approaches of the people involved.
A simple awareness of environmental concerns on the part of those
responsible for branches of government and other activities will do
much to prevent needless damage and conflict being caused. Construct-
ive informal dialogue can achieve more in practice than the most carefully designed structure operating without goodwill or mutual understanding.[6]

---

[1] See section 2.6, below.
[2] See section 8.4, below.
[3] *This Common Inheritance: Britain's Environmental Strategy*, Cm. 1200 (1990), para.
1.6.
[4] *A Better Quality of Life: A Strategy for Sustainable Development for the U.K.*, Cm.
4345 (1999), para. 8.57.
[5] House of Commons Environment, Transport and Regional Affairs Committee, *U.K.
Biodiversity*, 20th Report of 1999–2000 (1999–2000 H.C. 441), paras 104–107.
[6] *cf.* Alexander Pope, *An Essay on Man* (1734) Epistle iii. 1.303:
   "For Forms of Government let fools contest;
     Whate'er is best administer'd is best."

SUSTAINABLE DEVELOPMENT AND BALANCING OBLIGATIONS

2.2.1   Before considering the authorities which have specific responsibilities for nature conservation, something should be said about two more general features of many public bodies. The first is the increasing imposition of duties in relation to sustainable development, requiring at least some attention to be paid to biodiversity and conservation. The second is the presence of more precise balancing obligations which require public authorities to have some regard to the environment in the exercise of their functions. Virtually all public authorities are the creatures of statute, and their powers and functions are defined by the legislation which creates them. It is only if legislation requires or permits them to do so that they are able to shape their policy and conduct with regard to the concerns of nature conservation. Without some such provision, authorities acting in the interests of conservation might well be found to be acting *ultra vires* and unlawfully by allowing an irrelevant consideration to influence the exercise of their statutory functions.[7] The presence of such provisions is therefore important if nature conservation is not to be ignored and is to be integrated into the policies and actions of bodies across the public sector.

Sustainable Development

2.2.2   Since the early 1990s, sustainable development has been accepted as a national policy goal,[8] and whatever the arguments over exactly what the term means,[9] it is clear that regard for biodiversity and nature conservation falls within its scope. The presence of obligations to have regard to or to further sustainable development therefore means that authorities must at least consider the impact of their activities on the natural environment. There are two main forms in which sustainable development makes an appearance in legislation, either as the focus of a specific strategy or as a factor to be considered in the exercise of functions.

2.2.3   The most specific obligation is placed on the National Assembly for

---

[7] *Associated Provincial Picture Houses Ltd v. Wednesbury Corporation* [1948] 1 K.B. 223. See for example the controversy over whether the gas industry regulator was legally entitled to provide funds for the Energy Saving Trust (1994) 231 ENDS Report 31.

[8] *Sustainable Development—The U.K. Strategy*, Cm. 2426 (1994); *A Better Quality of Life: A Strategy for Sustainable Development for the U.K.*, Cm. 4345 (1999).

[9] "It is a pity that the issue which everyone on the planet will have to tackle at some point has acquired this impenetrable title. It is even more problematic that no definition exists which can be understood by everyone and built into their lives." *Down to Earth—A Scottish Perspective on Sustainable Development* (Scottish Office, 1999), p. 4. See also para. 2.6.11, below.

Wales, which is required to produce a scheme setting out how it proposes to promote sustainable development in the exercise of its functions. It is further required to report annually on how the proposals were carried out and every four years (in the year following the elections) on how effective its proposals have been in promoting sustainable development.[10] Local authorities in England and Wales similarly have to prepare community strategies for promoting the economic, social and environmental well-being of their area and contributing to the achievement of sustainable development in the United Kingdom.[11] This obligation is supported by a general background power to do things likely to achieve the promotion or improvement of the environmental well-being of their area.[12]

In London, the Greater London Authority has a similar general power to promote the improvement of the environment in Greater London.[13] The state of the environment report to be produced every four years by the Mayor must expressly address biodiversity issues[14] and the Mayor must produce a biodiversity action plan—the only biodiversity plan required by statute in the country.[15] However, unlike the waste management and air quality strategies that also have to be produced, there is no explicit obligation on local authorities within London to have regard to this plan in their own actions.[16]

2.2.4

The Environment Agency has making a contribution to achieving sustainable development as part of its principal aim[17] and ministerial guidance on this goal must be given to the Environment Agency and to the Scottish Environment Protection Agency, and must be followed by them.[18] At a more general level, contributing to the achievement of sustainable development is among the functions of the regional development agencies in England and Wales,[19] whilst the Strategic Rail Authority,[20] the Rail Regulator and the Minister[21] all have to exercise their powers in relation to the railways so as to contribute to the same end. These requirements mirror the first legislative appearance of the concept of sustainability when the Natural Heritage (Scotland) Act

2.2.5

---

[10] Government of Wales Act 1998, s.121; the first scheme, *Learning to Live Differently* was approved in November 2000.

[11] Local Government Act 2000, s.4.

[12] *ibid.*, s.2.

[13] Greater London Authority Act 1999, s.30.

[14] *ibid.*, s.351.

[15] *ibid.*, s.352; see para. 1.2.4, above.

[16] *cf. ibid.*, ss.355, 364.

[17] Environmental Protection Act 1995, s.4.

[18] *ibid.*, ss.4, 31.

[19] Regional Development Agencies Act 1998, s.4.

[20] Transport Act 2000, s.207.

[21] Railways Act 1993, s.4, as amended by Transport Act 2000, s.224.

1991 required Scottish Natural Heritage to have regard to the desirability of securing that anything done in relation to the natural heritage of Scotland is undertaken in a manner which is sustainable.[22]

Balancing Obligations

2.2.6   The requirement on SNH to have regard to sustainability is typical of many balancing obligations that have been imposed on a range of public authorities. One of the most general requires that in the exercise of their statutory functions relating to land, every minister, government department and public body is obliged to have regard to the desirability of conserving the natural heritage (in Scotland)[23] or the natural beauty and amenity of the countryside (in England and Wales).[24] South of the border this has now been strengthened by an obligation on Ministers of the Crown, the National Assembly for Wales and government departments to have regard to the conservation of biological diversity in accordance with the Rio Convention on Biological Diversity.[25] As there is no obligation to act in the interests of conservation, merely to have regard to such matters, such provisions may not offer much by way of support for conservation. However, they do achieve something by ensuring that conservation is always a relevant consideration which cannot be wholly ignored when decisions are being taken and they do open the remote possibility of a legal challenge to the validity of any action which is clearly damaging to the natural heritage and cannot be supported by any other considerations. Moreover, the fact that natural beauty and heritage must be borne in mind adds weight to the voices of conservation groups and others in pressing their arguments on the authorities in question, albeit that no legal standing is conferred. Other considerations may in practice override those of the countryside in individual instances, but authorities cannot completely shut their eyes to the impact of their activities on wildlife and natural habitats.

2.2.7   In addition to the very general terms of these provisions, some obligation with respect to the countryside or conservation can be imposed on specific bodies or in relation to specific tasks. Particular obligations to have regard to the purposes for which land has become subject to various conservation designations are features of many regulatory schemes and are discussed in the context of each designation in

---

[22] NHSA 1991, s.1(1); see para. 2.6.11, below. See Addendum, above.

[23] CSA 1967, s.66 (amended by NHSA 1991, Sched. 10, para. 4(7)); for the meaning of "natural heritage" see para. 2.6.10, below.

[24] CA 1968, s.11; conserving natural beauty includes conserving flora, fauna and geological and physiographical features (*ibid.*, s.49(4)).

[25] CRWA 2000, s.74; see paras 1.2.6 above and 7.5.22–7.5.24, below.

Chapter 5 below.[26] Almost invariably, though, such duties are expressed
to be subject to the proper exercise of the primary statutory functions
of the bodies involved and provided that an authority can produce some
justification for its conduct based on these functions and some evidence
that the environmental impact was not wholly ignored, it is unlikely
that a court would be willing to hold that an authority was in breach of
such a broadly phrased duty.

One general formulation which is used is to require the authority in   **2.2.8**
question to seek a balance between various interests, including those
of conservation. The interests listed may be irreconcilable in many situations, but such an obligation does at least ensure that some thought is
given to the matters specified. Thus, "so far as may be consistent with
the proper discharge of [their] functions" under the Forestry Acts
1967–1979, the Forestry Commissioners must "endeavour to achieve a
reasonable balance between" the development and maintenance of forestry and timber production and the conservation and enhancement of
natural beauty and the conservation of flora, fauna and geological or
physiographical features of special interest.[27] The agriculture ministers
must seek a balance between the promotion and maintenance of a stable
and efficient agricultural industry, the economic and social interests of
rural areas, the conservation and enhancement of the natural beauty and
amenity of the countryside[28] and its features of archaeological interest,
and the promotion of the enjoyment of the countryside by the public.[29]
Similarly, in discharging their functions under the Sea Fisheries Acts,
ministers and local fisheries committees are obliged, so far as consistent
with the proper and efficient exercise of those functions, to have regard
to the conservation of marine flora and fauna and to endeavour to
achieve a reasonable balance between conservation and their other concerns.[30]

In some cases there is a fuller statement of the environmental   **2.2.9**
responsibilities of new public bodies, although the effect of such provisions is often merely to emphasise their existence rather than to confer
any greater legal weight. The formulations vary, even within the same
statute. Without prejudice to their general function of furthering the

---

[26] *e.g.*, National Parks in England and Wales (NPACA 1949, s.11A (added by EA 1995,
s.62)); Areas of Outstanding Natural Beauty (CRWA 2000, s.85); National Parks in
Scotland (NPSA 2000, s.14); SSSIs in England and Wales (WCA 1981, s.28G (added
by CRWA 2000, Sched. 9)).

[27] Forestry Act 1967, s.1(3A) (added by Wildlife and Countryside (Amendment) Act
1985, s.4).

[28] Expressly stated to include the conservation of flora and fauna and geological and
physiographical features.

[29] Agriculture Act 1986, s.17; there is also a provision enabling them to provide services
for the benefit of such conservation and enhancement (*ibid.*, s.1).

[30] Sea Fisheries (Wildlife Conservation) Act 1992, s.1.

improvement of the environment,[31] Scottish Enterprise is obliged merely to "have regard to . . . the desirability of safeguarding the environment",[32] whereas for Highlands and Islands Enterprise the duty is more fully expressed as being to:

"have regard to the desirability of safeguarding—

   (a) the natural beauty of the countryside in;
   (b) the flora and fauna of; and
   (c) the geological and geomorphological[33] features of special interest of, the Highlands and Islands."[34]

The fuller terms of the latter provision may result in environmental considerations appearing more significant, but it is unlikely that there is any difference in legal terms to the place of such issues in the authorities' deliberations.

2.2.10   More positive obligations are imposed on the authorities concerned with water resources and drainage in England and Wales.[35] One function of the Environment Agency in England and Wales is "to such extent as it considers desirable, generally to promote the conservation of . . . flora and fauna which are dependent on an aquatic environment" and the conservation of the natural beauty and amenity of waters and associated land.[36] Ministers, the Agency, internal drainage boards, and water and sewerage undertakers are all obliged not merely to have regard to the desirability of conservation, but (so far as is consistent with the relevant statutory functions) to exercise their powers so as to further the conservation and enhancement of natural beauty and the conservation of flora, fauna and geological or physiographical features of special interest, and to take into account the effect of their conduct on the beauty, wildlife and features of any affected area.[37] Such a formulation may somewhat increase the weight of environmental considerations, but as always the prime statutory functions of the authorities take priority.

2.2.11   As well as being attached to the general functions of particular

---

[31] Enterprise and New Towns (Scotland) Act 1990, s.1.

[32] *ibid.*, s.4(4).

[33] There is probably no practical significance in the use of "geomorphological" in place of the more usual "physiographical."

[34] Enterprise and New Towns (Scotland) Act 1990, s.5(3).

[35] See para. 2.7.22, below and Addendum, above.

[36] EA 1995, s.6.

[37] Water Industry Act 1991, s.3(2); Water Resources Act 1991, s.16(1); Land Drainage Act 1991, s.61A (added by Land Drainage Act 1994, s.1); the same applies to the British Waterways Board under s.22 of the British Waterways Act 1995 (a private Act of Parliament).

authorities, balancing obligations appear in relation to a range of specific tasks. The general obligations on the regulatory bodies for gas and electricity to have regard to the effect on the environment of gas transmission through pipelines[38] and of the generation, transmission and supply of electricity[39] are supplemented by more specific duties. The desirability of preserving natural beauty and conserving flora, fauna and geological and physiographical features must be taken into account at all stages in the preparation and approval of proposals for new pipelines,[40] and for the underground storage of gas,[41] while for electricity generating stations and transmission lines,[42] there is the further requirement that the proposals include measures to mitigate any adverse effects on the environment. Housing authorities must bear in mind the effect of their proposals on the beauty of the landscape or countryside.[43] The Cardiff Bay Development Corporation must have regard to the desirability of developing and conserving flora and fauna,[44] and in the interests of conservation additional conditions can be imposed on works otherwise automatically authorised under the Telecommunications Code[45] or approved for the Channel Tunnel.[46] The Coal Authority in dealing with its property must take into account the effect of proposals on the natural beauty, flora and fauna of the area and have regard to the desirability of preserving and conserving these.[47]

In many instances the presence of such balancing obligations is perhaps more symbolic than significant in view of the priority always granted to the main statutory functions of the bodies concerned, functions which may call for works and activities with serious adverse effects on the natural environment. However, the authorities cannot claim that they are not allowed to respond to the interests of nature conservation and cannot shut their eyes to the environmental impact of their activities nor their ears to the arguments of those pressing for conservation to be taken into account. There may be little likelihood of an authority ever being found to be in breach of such obligations, but their presence does give some legal weight to conservation interests.

2.2.12

---

[38] Gas Act 1986, s.4AA(5) (added by Utilities Act 2000, s.9).
[39] Electricity Act 1989, s.3A(5) (added by Utilities Act 2000, s.13).
[40] Pipelines Act 1962, s.43.
[41] Gas Act 1965, s.4(4).
[42] Electricity Act 1989, Sched. 9, paras1, 3.
[43] Housing Act 1985, s.607; Housing (Scotland) Act 1987, s.6(1).
[44] Cardiff Bay Barrage Act 1993, s.14; it is not clear exactly what "developing" flora and fauna means.
[45] Telecommunications Act 1984, s.10(4).
[46] Channel Tunnel Act 1987, Sched. 3, para. 2.
[47] Coal Industry Act 1994, s.3(7); see also *ibid.*, s.53.

DEVOLUTION

2.3.1   The implementation in 1999 of the devolution arrangements for Scotland and Wales has had a major impact on the way in which powers
relating to nature conservation are distributed throughout Great Britain.
The position is now much more complicated than before, and care must
be taken in ascertaining where governmental power now rests. One
obvious consequence is that the many statutory provisions conferring
powers or functions on "the Secretary of State" can no longer be taken
at face value, since the devolution arrangements may well have transferred the tasks to the Scottish Ministers or to the National Assembly
for Wales. There is a marked difference between Scotland and Wales
both in the mechanisms by which powers have been transferred and the
scope of the powers actually divided. The transfer of power to the
Scottish Parliament and Ministers extends to all matters not expressly
reserved for Westminster and Whitehall, and the Parliament has the
power to make primary legislation. In contrast, powers have been transferred to Wales only in relation to the matters expressly specified and
the legislative powers are restricted to the making of subordinate legislation.

Scotland

2.3.2   The Scotland Act 1998 created both the Scottish Parliament and the
Scottish Executive with wide powers. Full legislative and ministerial[48]
powers are transferred to these new authorities except in the area of
reserved matters,[49] but it is expressly provided that the United Kingdom
Parliament retains the power to legislate on any subject.[50] Nature conservation and most of the other matters covered in this book, *e.g.* agriculture, planning and the environment generally, clearly fall within the
scope of devolved matters, so that responsibility for these now lies
with the Scottish authorities.[51] Thus the changes to the Wildlife and
Countryside Act 1981 made by the Countryside and Rights of Way Act
2000 did not extend to Scotland, leaving the Scottish Parliament to
legislate on this topic as it thinks fit. Nevertheless, some of the reserva-
tions may be significant either by preventing the use of certain mechan-

---

[48]   Where previously power lay with the Secretary of State, it now lies with "the Scottish
Ministers".
[49]   The reserved matters are set out in Schedule 5 to the 1998 Act, with further restrictions
stated in Schedule 4.
[50]   Scotland Act 1998, s.28(7).
[51]   See generally G. Little, "Scottish Devolution and Environmental Law", (2000) 12
J.E.L. 155; C. Reid, "Devolution and the Environment" in A. Ross (ed.), *Environment
and Regulation* (Hume Papers on Public Policy); vol. 8, no. 2 (2000).

isms to achieve policy objectives,[52] or by retaining at Westminster control of policy areas with an indirect impact on conservation.[53] The scope of the Scottish Ministers' powers is actually wider than that of the Scottish Parliament since by the process of executive devolution it is possible for powers reserved to the United Kingdom government to be delegated to the Scottish Ministers in relation to their exercise in Scotland.[54]

Special provision is made for a number of public authorities whose functions straddle the border and whose activities include both reserved and devolved matters.[55] The "cross-border public authorities" designated under the Act must report to both the United Kingdom and Scottish Parliaments, and although ministerial powers are not devolved, the relevant United Kingdom minister can act in some matters only in consultation with the Scottish Ministers. More detailed provision can be made for individual bodies. The list of cross-border public authorities includes the Joint Nature Conservation Committee,[56] the Forestry Commission[57] and the Royal Commission on Environmental Pollution.[58] Special provision is also made for the border rivers.[59]

2.3.3

Important restrictions on the powers of the Scottish Parliament and Executive relate to E.C. law and international obligations. Within the range of devolved maters, the primary responsibility to ensure compliance with E.C. law rests on the Scottish authorities, and it is beyond the competence of the Parliament to legislate, or the Ministers to act, in a way which is incompatible with E.C. law.[60] However, it is expressly stated that the United Kingdom government can still exercise powers to implement E.C. law in Scotland.[61] This reflects the position

2.3.4

---

[52] *e.g.* the reservation of tax matters prevents the creation of new taxes or tax reliefs to further policy goals; Scotland Act 1998, Sched. 5, Head A.

[53] *e.g.* most energy matters and many transport ones are reserved; Scotland Act 1998, Sched. 5, Heads D and E.

[54] Scotland Act 1998, s.63; see *e.g.* the Scotland Act 1998 (Transfer of Functions to Scottish Ministers) Order 1999 (S.I. 1999 No.1750). To assist this process there is provision for the division of functions not previously exercised separately in Scotland; Scotland Act 1998, s.106; see *e.g.* the Scotland Act 1998 (Modification of Functions) Order 1999 (S.I. 1999 No.1756).

[55] Scotland Act 1998, ss.88–90.

[56] See paras 2.6.19–2.6.22, below.

[57] See paras 2.7.10–2.7.14, below.

[58] Scotland Act 1998 (Cross-border Public Authorities) (Specification) Order 1999 (S.I. 1999 No.1319).

[59] Under the Scotland Act 1998 (Border Rivers) Order 1999 (S.I. 1999 No.1746), the Scottish Ministers can exercise some powers over the Tweed in England and the Environment Agency over the border Esk in Scotland; although not a cross-border body, the Environment Agency is required to submit its annual report to the Scottish Ministers for laying before the Parliament.

[60] Scotland Act 1998, ss.29(2), 57(2).

[61] *ibid.*, s.57(1).

that it is the United Kingdom that is the Member State of the E.C. and therefore the United Kingdom government that is entitled to a seat in the Council when decisions are made but also responsible before the European Court of Justice for contraventions of E.C. law.[62] Thus in relation to such matters as compliance with E.C. Directives, it is expected that the Scottish authorities will ensure that all of the necessary measures are in place but any measures incompatible with the E.C. obligations can be challenged in the courts and held to be invalid, and Whitehall can intervene directly if it is thought that E.C. law is being breached. The Concordats between the London and devolved governments endeavour to establish arrangements for co-operation and consultation between the different administrations,[63] but the Scottish authorities have no formal involvement in British dealings with the E.C., which remain wholly in the hands of the United Kingdom government.

2.3.5   In relation to international obligations, the restrictions on the Scottish Parliament and Executive are enforced through political rather than judicial intervention. The Secretary of State, a member of the United Kingdom government, can intervene to prevent a Bill being presented for Royal Assent if he or she has reasonable grounds to believe that it would be incompatible with international obligations,[64] and on the same grounds can intervene to require the Scottish Ministers to take, or to desist from taking, any action, including making any delegated legislation or proposing any Bill.[65] The new Scottish authorities are therefore constrained to ensure that the United Kingdom's international obligations are properly respected in Scotland.[66] Again, since foreign affairs are a reserved matter, there is no formal role for the Scottish Parliament or Ministers in the negotiation of these obligations.

Wales

2.3.6   For Wales, the transfer of power under the Government of Wales Act 1998 has been much more limited. The National Assembly for Wales has no power to make primary legislation, but can make some subordinate legislation. The transfer of ministerial functions is formally to the

---

[62] It is no defence for the national government of a Member State to say that the matter is a responsibility of another tier of government; *e.g. Commission v. Belgium* (227–230/85) [1988] E.C.R. 1; *Commission v. Italy* (C-33/90) [1991] E.C.R. I-5987.

[63] *Memorandum of Understanding and Supplementary Agreements between the United Kingdom Government, Scottish Ministers and the Cabinet of the National Assembly for Wales*, Cm. 4444 (1999), pp. 18–23; the main Memorandum is supported by an Agreement on the Joint Ministerial Committee and Concordats on among other topics Co-ordination of European Union Policy Issues.

[64] Scotland Act 1998, s.35.

[65] *ibid.*, s.58.

[66] Where international or E.C. law sets targets or quotas, there is express power for these to be divided between the parts of the United Kingdom; Scotland Act 1998, s.106.

Assembly, although in practice many functions are delegated to committees or to the Assembly First Secretary and his or her fellow Assembly Secretaries.[67] There is no direct equivalent of the cross-border authorities in Scotland, but a number of public authorities can be required to provide witnesses and documents for the Assembly. These include the Joint Nature Conservation Committee and the Environment Agency.[68–73]

The areas of competence of the Assembly are specified by listing the enactments under which the Assembly can exercise ministerial powers.[74] These include many statutes falling within the scope of this book. In many cases it is only certain powers under an Act that are transferred, either by specifying the individual sections or sub-sections where power is passed, or by making exceptions when powers under an Act are transferred as a whole.[75] The position is further complicated by the fact that in some instances the powers are transferred only to the extent that they had previously been passed to the Secretary of State for Wales from other Ministers under earlier arrangements for administrative devolution;[76] this is especially prevalent in the area of agriculture and fisheries. In a number of further cases powers can be exercised concurrently by the Assembly and United Kingdom Ministers or remain in the hands of the United Kingdom government but can be exercised only after consulting or with the agreement of the Assembly.[77] There are similar provisions to those described above for Scotland to restrain the Assembly from acting in breach of E.C. or international obligations.[78]

2.3.7

---

[67] As authorised by Government of Wales Act 1998, s.62.

[68–73] Government of Wales Act 1998, s.74 and Sched. 5.

[74] Specified in the National Assembly for Wales (Transfer of Functions) Orders: Order 1999 (S.I. 1999 No.672); (No.2) Order 1999 (S.I. 1999 No.2787); Order 2000, (S.I. 2000 No.253); (Variation) Order 2000, (S.I. 2000 No.1829); and (No.2) Order 2000, (S.I. 2000 No.1830).

[75] As examples, ministerial powers under the whole of the Conservation of Seals Act 1970 is transferred, except for the power under s.1(2) (specification of permitted firearms and ammunition; see para. 3.4.22, below), whereas for long and complex pieces of legislation such as the Water Resources Act 1991, there is a detailed list of specific provisions where power is transferred; National Assembly for Wales (Transfer of Functions) Order 1999 (S.I. 1999 No.672), Sched. 1.

[76] *e.g.* Transfer of Functions (Wales) Order 1969 (S.I. 1969 No.388); Transfer of Functions (Wales) (No. 1) Order 1978 (S.I. 1978 No.272).

[77] *e.g.* both the Assembly and the Secretary of State have concurrent powers to grant licences under Part I of the Wildlife and Countryside Act 1981 (s.16), the agreement of the Assembly is required for the classification of the quality of waters (Water Resources Act 1991, s.82) and the Assembly must be consulted on the charging schemes for various environmental licences (Environment Act 1995, ss.41, 42); National Assembly for Wales (Transfer of Functions) Order 1999 (S.I. 1999 No.672), Sched. 2.

[78] Government of Wales Act 1998, ss.106, 108.

2.3.8   Given the very detailed nature of these transfer arrangements, any gen-
eralisation as to the scope of devolution to Wales is difficult. Many significant powers in relation to nature conservation are transferred to the
National Assembly,[79] *e.g.* most powers under the Conservation (Natural
Habitats, etc.) Regulations 1994[80] and under the legislation for specific
animals,[81] while others may be exercised concurrently by the Assembly
and the United Kingdom minister, *e.g.* the granting of licences under s.16
of the Wildlife and Countryside Act 1981. The position in relation to agriculture and fisheries, water, and town and country planning requires section by section analysis of the particular legislation and the Transfer of
Functions Orders before the full picture emerges.

Treatment in this Book

2.3.9   The complex distribution of power that results from these devolution
arrangements creates problems for authors writing about the exercise
of ministerial powers in more than one jurisdiction (and England and
Wales can no longer be treated as a single, undifferentiated
jurisdiction). Technically the correct approach is to specify in each case
which of the range of options applies, from Secretary of State throughout Great Britain, to Secretary of State in England, Scottish Ministers
in Scotland and National Assembly for Wales in Wales, noting the big
difference in the scope of the competences devolved to Scotland and
to Wales and the variations such as concurrent powers, consultative
arrangements and Scottish Ministers acting under executive devolution.
But that approach rapidly produces an almost unreadable text and tends
to obscure rather than assist any account of the substantive provisions.
Throughout this book, therefore, the term "the Minister" is used as a
short-hand phrase for the holder of powers that before 1999 lay in the
hands of one of the Secretaries of State. In practice for England this
will be the Secretary of State, for Scotland it will be in almost all cases
the Scottish Ministers (but with the possibility of intervention from
London especially in relation to implementing E.C. law), and for Wales
either the Secretary of State or the National Assembly.

CENTRAL GOVERNMENT

2.4.1   Although most of the detailed administration of nature conservation
lies in the hands of specialist bodies, especially the statutory conserva-

---

[79] See note 74, above.
[80] S.I. 1994 No.2716; there is no transfer of the powers under regs.71–78 (electricity and
pipelines).
[81] *e.g.* all of the powers under the Protection of Badgers Act 1992, most of those under
the Conservation of Seals Act 1970 and some under the Deer Act 1991 have been
transferred.

tion bodies, central government is deeply involved in the making of overall policy and retains many significant powers to control or influence the way in which the law operates in practice. This applies as much to the Scottish Executive within its area of competence as to the Westminster government. The strength of the government's commitment to nature conservation will determine its place (usually fairly low) in relation to conflicting concerns, such as promoting economic development or expanding the motorway system, and to competing claims for public funds. The policy lead given by central government will be crucial in determining where the balance between various interests is to be struck, especially as so much of the law relies on discretionary powers. More fundamentally, central government is responsible for providing the funds for the various conservation bodies and for promoting the legislation under which they operate.

In addition to functions within the domestic system, the central **2.4.2** authorities are responsible for handling conservation issues at European and international levels. It is the Westminster government, in the name of the Crown, which signs and ratifies international treaties. It is the Westminster government whose representatives on the Council of Ministers of the European Community negotiate and agree to European legislation, and it is the Westminster government which is ultimately responsible for ensuring that Community law is properly implemented and observed in this country.[82] The fact that the government may ultimately have to answer before the European Court of Justice for the state of our law gives central government an added incentive to keep a close eye on what is happening, even where the prime responsibility lies with the devolved administrations, and even more when it may initially rest with local authorities or other public bodies.

Within government, responsibility is divided between a number of **2.4.3** departments, and now between Westminster and the devolved administrations as discussed above. Whatever the practical arrangements, the formal approach has been for statutes to confer powers simply on "the Secretary of State," which means that any of Her Majesty's Principal Secretaries of State can lawfully exercise the power.[83] In relation to any legislation the pre-dates the devolution arrangements, any such reference to the Secretary of State must now be read in the light of the transfer of powers to the Scottish Parliament and National Assembly for Wales. The statutory language used after devolution became effective tends to reflect the new arrangements expressly.

The role of government ministers is often hidden behind the more **2.4.4** obvious and direct official powers lying in the hands of the conservation and other public bodies. However, although lying in the background,

---

[82] See para. 2.3.4, above.
[83] Interpretation Act 1978, Sched. 1; *Agee v. Lord Advocate*, 1977 S.L.T. (Notes) 54.

the power of central government should not be underestimated, especially in relation to the conservation bodies. This power comes in various forms. In the first place, it is the government which appoints the members of the boards of these bodies,[84] and in so doing can obviously influence the general approach which is likely to be taken by them. Secondly, as the finances which are to be available to these bodies are also determined by the government,[85] some control can be exercised over how much the agencies are actually able to achieve in carrying out their functions, *e.g.* the extent to which funds are available will obviously have a direct effect on the number, scale and nature of management agreements which can be offered to landowners.[86] There is also the possibility of direct involvement through the power of government to issue to the agencies directions which must be obeyed.[87]

2.4.5   In addition to these general powers over the statutory conservation bodies and other agencies, the government exercises controls over their activities in other ways. The making of grants and loans by such bodies is usually subject to government approval,[88] as is the exercise of any power of compulsory purchase.[89] Byelaws have to be confirmed by the Minister,[90] and some of the significant designations of land for conservation purposes have to be made or confirmed by the Minister.[91]

2.4.6   In other areas, such as agriculture and town and country planning, the role of government ministers is more direct. Regulations made by the Ministers govern most aspects of agriculture, and the grant schemes which play such an important role in shaping the industry[92] and in the management of the countryside[93] are created and administered by central government (within European Community guidelines). In the planning system, the Ministers make the detailed rules which exempt certain forms of development from the need for permission,[94] approve planning authorities' structure plans[95] and supervise other development plans,[96] decide appeals,[97] and can call in individual applications for

---

[84] *e.g.* NHSA 1991, Sched. 1, para. 3.
[85] *e.g. ibid.*, s.8.
[86] An issue highlighted after the decision in *Cameron v. Nature Conservancy Council,* 1991 S.L.T. (Lands Tr.) 85; see para. 5.5.16, below.
[87] *e.g.* NHSA 1991, s.11.
[88] *e.g. ibid.*, s.9.
[89] *e.g.* NPACA 1949, s.103(1) (substituted by Nature Conservancy Council Act 1973, Sched. 1, para. 2 and amended by EPA 1990, Sched. 9, para. 1).
[90] *e.g. ibid.*, s.106.
[91] *e.g.* Nature Conservation Orders, Environmentally Sensitive Areas; see sections 5.6, 5.9, below.
[92] *e.g.* capital grant schemes under Agriculture Act 1970, s.29.
[93] *e.g.* grants for conservation purposes under EA 1995, s.98.
[94] TCPSA 1997, s.30; TCPA 1990, s.59.
[95] *ibid.*, s.10; *ibid.*, ss.35, 35A.
[96] *ibid.*, s.19; *ibid.*, ss.18, 44.
[97] *ibid.*, s.47; *ibid.*, s.79.

their own determination.[98] The number of references throughout this book to "the Minister" is itself testament to the extent of direct power enjoyed by ministers in matters relevant for conservation.[99]

Central government, including the Scottish Executive, is thus deeply involved in the handling of nature conservation.[1] From the framing of the fundamental pieces of legislation to the determination of individual applications for grants or planning permission, the government can affect the whole form and direction of the law and policy throughout the country, a position strengthened by its control over the membership and finances of the public bodies established outside government to play the leading part in conservation matters. In practice governments have not generally exercised their powers so as to interfere with the detailed workings of the conservation bodies, but the extent of power and influence which lies in the hands of central government must always be remembered. **2.4.7**

LOCAL AUTHORITIES

The range of powers and responsibilities exercised by local authorities means that they are heavily involved in matters affecting nature conservation. The variety of structural arrangements throughout Great Britain renders it increasingly difficult to describe the formal distribution of powers and functions briefly but accurately. What follows favours brevity over comprehensive detail. The basic structure is that in Scotland and Wales there is a single tier of local government,[2] whereas in England there are both unitary and two-tier arrangements,[3] with a separate structure in London involving the London boroughs and the new institutions created by the Greater London Authority Act 1999. In all cases the creation of joint boards to carry out particular tasks (*e.g.* police and fire services in Scotland) and other co-operative arrangements of various sorts further complicate the position in practice. **2.5.1**

The wide discretion and broad powers enjoyed by local authorities **2.5.2**

---

[98] *ibid.*, s.46; *ibid.*, s.77.

[99] As discussed at para. 2.3.9 above, for the purposes of this book the term "the Minister" includes the National Assembly for Wales where powers have been devolved to it.

[1] Further information is available from the Scottish Executive at www.scotland.gov.uk, the National Assembly for Wales at www.wales.gov.uk, the Department for Environment, Food and Rural Affairs at www.defra.gov.uk and the Department for Transport, Local Government and the Regions at www.dtlr.gov.uk. See Addendum above.

[2] Local Government etc. (Scotland) Act 1994, Local Government (Wales) Act 1994.

[3] Metropolitan District Councils are single-tier authorities, whereas in other areas there is either a unitary authority or a divide between County and District Councils; Local Government Acts 1972, 1985 and 1992. For a number of purposes relevant to this book, the Isles of Scilly are treated as if they formed a separate county.

mean that there is much that an authority can do to further the interests of nature conservation if it is so minded. Within authorities, though, the demands of nature conservation must compete with the many other demands placed on local government and it is not surprising if authorities at times view economic development as more important than nature conservation when it comes to determining land use, and education, housing and social services as more deserving when it comes to the allocation of resources. The balance may, however, be affected in England and Wales by the imposition of the duty to prepare a community strategy promoting or improving the environmental, as well as social and economic, well-being of the area and contributing to sustainable development,[4] supported by the introduction of a new background power for authorities to do things considered likely to promote the environmental well-being of their area.[5] The express requirement to consider environmental issues as a whole, as opposed to a fragmented approach with particular planning, public health, pollution control and nuisance responsibilities considered separately, may promote a greater awareness of the potential for measures promoting biodiversity to play a part in enhancing overall amenity and the quality of life.

2.5.3   Perhaps the most obvious part played by local authorities is in the operation of the system of town and country planning. As this subject is well covered in more specialised works, it is not the intention to deal with it in any detail in this book.[6] At present it is enough to note that as planning authorities,[7] local authorities are responsible for the making of development plans for their areas[8] and for the approval of the individual applications for permission to carry out building, engineering or mining operations or to change the use of any land.[9] Within the scope of these powers, which exclude most agricultural and forestry matters,[10] the authorities have considerable control over changes in the use of land and thus on the sort of habitat which will be available within their areas, a control emphasised by the fact that a grant of planning permission can authorise activities in an SSSI, however damaging to its value as natural habitat.[11]

2.5.4   Direct powers over the countryside are also enjoyed by local author-

---

[4] Local Government Act 2000, s.4.

[5] *ibid.*, s.2.

[6] See section 8.2, below.

[7] Planning functions are generally divided between the two tiers of local government where these exist; TCPA 1990, s.1.

[8] TCPSA 1997, Pt II; TCPA 1990, Pt II.

[9] *ibid.*, Pt III; *ibid.*, Pt III.

[10] *ibid.*, s.26(2)(e); *ibid.*, s.55(2)(e).

[11] In Scotland WCA 1981, s.28(8); in England and Wales WCA 1981, s.28P(4) (added by CRWA 2000, Sched.9); see section 5.5, below.

ities. Local nature reserves can be created,[12] public access can be arranged through agreements or orders,[13] and management agreements can be made for the preservation and enhancement of the natural beauty of the countryside and the promotion of its enjoyment by the public.[14] Country parks (and in Scotland, regional parks) can be created[15] and there is a variety of powers to make byelaws[16] and appoint rangers or wardens[17] for areas where an authority has intervened in some way. The law also allows authorities more general powers which may be of relevance, *e.g.* in Scotland local authorities may undertake works for the preservation and enhancement of natural beauty,[18] and in England and Wales there is the new general power to act for the benefit of environmental well-being.[19]

An authority's other functions will also have an effect on habitat and   **2.5.5**
nature conservation. Local authorities act as coast protection authorit-ies,[20] and as roads and highways authorities,[21] in all of which capacities works with significant environmental impact can be undertaken or authorised. Involvement in aspects of public health[22] and pollution con-trol[23] gives authorities a role in environmental issues. The responsibility for providing recreational facilities[24] could also be invoked to justify

---

[12] NPACA 1949, s.21; see para. 5.3.10, below.

[13] CSA 1967, Pt II (this power is now shared with SNH; NHSA 1991, s.13); NPACA 1949, Pt V.

[14] *ibid.*, s.49A(2) (added by Countryside (Scotland) Act 1981, s.9, amended by NHSA 1991, Sched. 10, para. 4); WCA 1981, s.39.

[15] *ibid.*, ss.48, 48A (added *ibid.*, s.8); CA 1968, s.7.

[16] *e.g.*, for country parks and areas covered by access agreements: NPACA 1949, s.90; CSA 1967; s.54; CA 1968, s.41. New powers to make byelaws are conferred in Eng-land and Wales by the access provisions under the Countryside and Rights of Way Act 2000 (s.17).

[17] NPACA 1949, s.92; CSA 1967; s.65 (amended by Countryside (Scotland) Act 1981, Sched. 1, para. 4). Again further powers are conferred under the new access legislation (CRWA 2000, s.18) and in Scotland provisions for byelaws and rangers are included in the Land Reform (Scotland) Bill being considered during 2002.

[18] Local Government (Development and Finance) (Scotland) Act 1964, s.2 (amended by CSA 1967, s.52).

[19] Local Government Act 2000, s.2.

[20] Coast Protection Act 1949, s.1 (amended by Local Government Act 1972, Sched. 30, Local Government etc. (Scotland) Act 1994, Sched. 13, para. 32); in Scotland local authorities are also responsible for flood prevention (Flood Prevention (Scotland) Act 1961, s.1 (amended and applied by Local Government etc. (Scotland) Act 1994, Sched. 13, para. 56)).

[21] Roads (Scotland) Act 1984, s.151; Highways Act 1980 s.1.

[22] Public Health (Scotland) Act 1897, s.12 (as amended by Local Government etc. (Scotland) Act 1994, Sched. 13, para. 9); Public Health Act 1936, s.1 (amended by Local Government Act 1972, Sched. 14, para. 1; Local Government (Wales) Act 1994, Sched. 9, para. 3).

[23] EPA 1990, s.4.

[24] Local Government and Planning (Scotland) Act 1982, ss.14–18; Local Government (Miscellaneous Provisions) Act 1976, s.19.

support for facilities for bird-watching, etc., whilst the way in which an authority treats the land under its direct control (schools, offices, cemeteries) will also be of importance in terms of habitat on a local level. On occasions this may in itself become a controversial issue, as in *R. v. Somerset County Council, ex p. Fewings*[25] where it was held that the council had acted unlawfully in exercising its management powers over land in order to give effect to the councillors' ethical view that hunting was wrong, as opposed to acting after a broader consideration of what was to the benefit of its area.[26] As with central government, throughout this book the multitude of references to local authorities in their many capacities illustrates the range of powers which they enjoy and which are of importance for nature conservation.

STATUTORY CONSERVATION BODIES

2.6.1   Until 1991 responsibility for nature conservation and other countryside matters was divided along functional lines. There was a single body, the Nature Conservancy Council (NCC),[27] responsible for nature conservation throughout Great Britain, whilst separate bodies, the Countryside Commissions,[28] were responsible for the natural beauty of the countryside and promoting its enjoyment by the public. As the task of preserving the natural beauty of the countryside was expressly declared to include the conservation of its flora and fauna and its geological or physiographical features of special interest,[29] this division was somewhat artificial, but the NCC and the Commissions developed their own clear areas of activity.

2.6.2   This structure was transformed at the beginning of the 1990s and the main division now is on a geographical basis. In Scotland and in Wales new bodies were created, Scottish Natural Heritage[30] and the Countryside Council for Wales,[31] which exercise the functions of both the NCC and the Countryside Commissions. Only in England does a functional division remain, but here too there have been changes. The functions

---

[25] [1995] 1 W.L.R. 1035; see also *R. v. Sefton Metropolitan District Council, ex p. British Association of Shooting and Conservation Ltd* (2000) 2 L.G.L.R. 979.

[26] Local Government Act 1972, s.120.

[27] Established in its final form by the Nature Conservancy Council Act 1973.

[28] The Countryside Commission for Scotland, established under CSA 1967, and the Countryside Commission, which operated in England and Wales and was created by CA 1968 as successor to the National Parks Commission created by NPACA 1949.

[29] CSA 1967, s.78(2); CA 1968, s.49(4).

[30] NHSA 1991, Pt I; for one year a separate Nature Conservancy Council for Scotland was in existence (EPA 1990, s.128) before the 1991 Act created SNH as the integrated body.

[31] EPA 1990, ss.128, 130.

derived from the NCC are exercised by English Nature, originally established as the Nature Conservancy Council for England[32] but now with legal recognition of the shorter title, which had been in common usage since the body was created.[33] The functions of the Countryside Commission, no longer extending to Wales,[34] remained with it, but this body has now been revised and renamed as the Countryside Agency, following the acquisition of functions from the Development Commission when it was abolished as part of the wider reform of the development agencies in England.[35] Scottish Natural Heritage (SNH), the Countryside Council for Wales (CCW) and English Nature (EN) do not have a formal collective title, and are generally referred to here as the statutory conservation bodies.[36]

The aim of creating single bodies in Scotland and Wales was to provide the opportunity for an integrated approach to be taken to all conservation and countryside matters, and to recognise the fact that the issues and pressures affecting conservation in those countries are different from those in much of England.[37] In Scotland further elements were the desire to transfer the conservation body to the ambit of the Scottish Office[38] and the hope that a new body could establish better relations with local communities than had been the case with the NCC which had become involved in a number of very public controversies over

2.6.3

---

[32] *ibid.*, s.128.

[33] CRWA 2000, s.73.

[34] EPA 1990, s.130, Sched. 8.

[35] Regional Development Agencies Act 1998, ss.34–35; Development Commission (Transfer of Functions and Miscellaneous Provisions) Order 1999 (S.I. 1999 No.416). The Development Commission, often referred to as the Rural Development Commission, was created by the Miscellaneous Financial Provisions Act 1983. See paras 2.7.1–2.7.5, below.

[36] This term "conservation bodies" has been used in legislation (*e.g.* CRWA 2000, s.74), as has the term "nature conservation bodies" (*e.g.* CNHR 1994, reg. 4) but neither is ideal, since they could easily be seen as including the charitable and unofficial bodies which play an important part in practical conservation and in policy debates. "Statutory conservation bodies" is rather clumsy (and might be read as including the National Trusts in view of their unusual statutory position (see para. 2.8.4) or the bodies concerned with the conservation of cultural, as opposed to natural, heritage), but reduces the risk of confusion with "conservation boards" created in relation to Areas of Outstanding Natural Beauty (see paras 2.7.6–2.7.9, below) while the alternative of "conservation agencies" risks giving the false impression that the bodies are "Next Steps agencies" operating within the departmental structure of government rather than separate, non-departmental statutory corporations (T. Daintith and A. Page, *The Executive in the Constitution* (1999), pp. 37–50).

[37] On the background to the changes see S. Tromans, *The Environment Acts 1990–1995* (1996), pp. 343–345; F. Reynolds and W.R. Sheate, "Reorganization of the Conservation Authorities" in W. Howarth and C.P. Rodgers (eds). *Agriculture, Conservation and Land Use* (1992).

[38] All aspects of the NCC's work were under the supervision of the Department of the Environment.

land use during the 1980s.[39] The arguments for integration, however, were not seen as convincing enough for a similar merger to be carried out in England. The splitting of the NCC attracted much criticism as being likely to weaken the scientific base of the conservation authorities and as being an unhelpful fragmentation of responsibility when many issues require study and action at a British level,[40] to say nothing of the practical difficulties caused by dividing responsibility for such areas as the Solway Firth and Bristol Channel. The legislation was hotly debated, and the establishment of the Joint Nature Conservation Committee[41] did little to quieten the concern being expressed that the splitting of the NCC could only weaken the voice of nature conservation on important matters. In view of the vast range of conflicting factors that have influenced the weight given to conservation arguments during the past decade, it is difficult to judge how much impact the structural change has had by itself, while the subsequent moves towards devolution would in any event have demanded a geographical division of the main conservation responsibilities.

2.6.4 The structural changes in the administration of nature conservation did not affect the substantive rules to be applied. The conservation bodies operate by means of the same provisions as governed the powers and functions of the NCC, and the law largely remains the same throughout Great Britain. The one major exception relates to the provisions on Sites of Special Scientific Interest (SSSIs), where some changes to the law in Scotland were made at the time of the structural division,[42] and more significant divergence has occurred since devolution took effect.[43] At an administrative level, the conservation bodies can largely be discussed together since they share many features, indeed CCW and EN share the same constitutional provisions. The following paragraphs describe the common features of the bodies, before examining the special aspects of each in turn and the role of the Joint Committee.

Common features

2.6.5 Each body has about a dozen members,[44] all of whom are appointed by

---

[39] *e.g.* over the Flow Country and the management of geese on Islay.
[40] As ever, Northern Ireland is treated separately and is regarded as a special case, although in this instance its geographical separation might in fact justify a different approach in any event.
[41] EPA 1990, s.128(4); see paras 2.6.19–2.6.22, below.
[42] The establishment of the Advisory Committee; see para. 5.5.8, below.
[43] The law in England and Wales has been considerably changed under CRWA 2000; see section 5.5, below.
[44] Between eight and 12 members for SNH and CCW, between ten and 14 for EN (EPA 1990, s.128(2), NHSA 1991, Sched. 1, para. 3); the number of members can be varied by ministerial order (EPA 1990, s.128(3), NHSA 1991, Sched. 1, para. 8).

the relevant Minister[45] and on terms determined by him;[46] members may be removed in the event of bankruptcy, prolonged absence from the body's business (unless permission has been granted) or other causes rendering them unfit or unable to continue.[47] For SNH the Minister is bound to have regard to the desirability of ensuring so far as practicable that there are among the members persons of knowledge or experience of SNH's principal areas of activity,[48] and to satisfy himself that the members have no financial or other interest likely to be prejudicial to their performance in office.[49] In all cases a chairman and deputy chairman are appointed by the Minister[50] while the chief officer is appointed by the body with the Minister's approval.[51] Each body has control of its own procedure[52] and can appoint committees including outside members;[53] for example, this latter power has been used by SNH to establish three Area Boards in an attempt to maintain closer contacts with local communities.

Although independent of government departments, the conservation **2.6.6** bodies remain under a degree of central supervision. Annual reports and accounts must be prepared and are subject to scrutiny by the relevant Parliament and auditing body.[54] As well as being able to influence the bodies through the appointment of their members, the Minister has the power to give the bodies directions of a general or specific character with regard to the discharge of their functions, but not in relation to the detailed exercise of their nature conservation powers.[55] More significantly, the funds made available to the bodies are determined by the

---

[45] EPA 1990, s.128(2), NHSA 1991, Sched. 1, para. 3; membership of one of the bodies is a disqualification from being an M.P. (for SNH, House of Commons Disqualification Act 1975, Sched. 1 Pt II (amended by NHSA 1991 Sched. 10 para. 8); for CCW and EN, *ibid.*, Sched. 1 Pt III (amended by EPA 1990, Sched. 6, para. 24) (members in receipt of remuneration only)).

[46] *ibid.*, Sched. 6 para. 4, *ibid.*, Sched. 1, para. 7.

[47] *ibid.*, Sched. 6, para. 6, *ibid.*, Sched. 1, para. 9; the English and Welsh provisions refer to six consecutive months' absence, the Scottish ones to three months' as well as including a power to dismiss members who are "unsuitable" as well as unable or unfit to continue in office.

[48] NHSA 1991, Sched. 1, para. 4.

[49] *ibid.*, Sched. 1, para. 5; for this purpose the Minister can request information from members and potential members (*ibid.*, para. 6).

[50] EPA 1990, Sched. 6, para. 4; NHSA 1991, Sched. 1, para. 10.

[51] *ibid.*, Sched. 6, para. 8; *ibid.*, Sched. 1, para. 12.

[52] *ibid.*, Sched. 6, para. 12; *ibid.*, Sched. 1, para. 15.

[53] *ibid.*, Sched. 6, para. 14; *ibid.*, Sched. 1, para. 16.

[54] *ibid.*, Sched. 6, paras 19–21; *ibid.*, s.10. For EN financial scrutiny remains in the hands of the Comptroller and Auditor General, but for CCW it has been transferred to Auditor General for Wales by virtue of the National Assembly for Wales (Transfer of Functions) Order 1999 (S.I. 1999 No.672), Sched. 1, and for SNH to the Auditor General for Scotland by virtue of the Public Finance and Accountability (Scotland) Act 2000, Sched, 4, para. 10.

[55] *ibid.*, s.131(4); *ibid.*, s.11.

Minister[56] and the grants and loans made by the bodies are also subject to ministerial authorisation (specifically or by means of a general authorisation);[57] in England and Wales the Minister must act with Treasury approval. The conservation bodies also fall within the jurisdiction of the Ombudsman.[58] Although these powers have not in fact been used to interfere with the workings of the conservation bodies, or the NCC before them, it must be noted that the independence of the bodies could be undermined by the existence of such provisions.[59]

2.6.7   The conservation bodies are given a range of general functions and powers to enable them to carry out their responsibilities for nature conservation.[60] The bodies must take appropriate account of actual or possible ecological changes[61] and all of their functions must be exercised so as to secure compliance with the requirements of the Habitats Directive.[62] These functions include the provision of advice to government ministers on the development and implementation of policies for nature conservation, the provision of advice to any persons about nature conservation, the dissemination of relevant knowledge, and the commissioning and support (financial or other) of research.[63] The general powers enable the conservation bodies to initiate and carry out research themselves, to accept and apply gifts and contributions for the achievement of their purposes, to hold land, to make charges for their services and to do all other things incidental or conducive to their functions.[64] These provisions are wide enough to allow the bodies to operate freely without continually checking the limits of their legal powers and are in addition to the specific measures contained in the detailed provisions on nature conservation.

---

[56] *ibid.*, s.129; *ibid.*, s.8.

[57] *ibid.*, s.134; *ibid.*, s.9.

[58] Parliamentary Commissioner Act 1967, Sched. 2 (amended by EPA 1990, Sched. 6, para. 23; NHSA 1991, Sched. 10, para. 3); in Scotland matters now fall under the scrutiny of the Scottish Parliamentary Commissioner for Administration (Scotland Act 1998 (Transitory and Transitional Provisions) (Complaints of Maladministration) Order 1999 (S.I. 1999 No.1351)) [See Addendum, above] and in Wales of the Welsh Administration Ombudsman (Government of Wales Act 1998, s.111, Sched. 9 para. 14).

[59] The extent to which such powers entitle ministers to intervene in the affairs of non-departmental bodies was the focus of heated political debate in the aftermath of the failure of the Scottish Qualifications Authority to deliver accurate and timeous exam results in the summer of 2000; see *Scottish Parliament Official Report*, vol. 8 cols 142–144 (September 7, 2000).

[60] Defined for this purpose as "the conservation of flora, fauna or geological or physiographical features" (EPA 1990, s.131(6)).

[61] EPA 1990, s.131(6).

[62] CNHR 1994, reg. 3(2).

[63] EPA 1990, s.132(1); NHSA 1991, s.2(1).

[64] *ibid.*, s.132(2); *ibid.*, s.2(1), (2): the Scottish legislation expressly includes reference to the power to form partnerships and companies.

The substantive provisions are discussed in detail below, but in summary, the conservation bodies are responsible for the designation of nature reserves and the making of byelaws and management agreements for them, for the designation of SSSIs, the approval of activities within them and the making of management agreements for them, and for the licensing of activities relating to protected species. The bodies are also involved as consultees in many official procedures and are charged with the provision of advice to government at all levels on matters relating to nature conservation, from the formulation of policy to the desirability of particular acts and the protection of individual species. For all of these tasks a major research effort is necessary.   **2.6.8**

Scottish Natural Heritage

Scottish Natural Heritage (SNH)[65] was created by the Natural Heritage (Scotland) Act 1991, as the successor to both the Nature Conservancy Council for Scotland and the Countryside Commission for Scotland. Its general aims reflect those of its two predecessors, being: **2.6.9**

> "(a) to secure the conservation and enhancement of; and
> (b) to foster understanding and facilitate the enjoyment of, the natural heritage of Scotland."[66]

SNH is thus charged with the responsibility both for conservation and for recreation and amenity, a combination which offers the opportunity for an integrated approach to be taken on many countryside and environmental issues. However, much closer co-ordination with the authorities responsible for agriculture, forestry and other rural land uses is necessary before a truly integrated approach is possible, while the present dual objectives of SNH may lead to internal conflicts in areas where recreational pressure may damage fragile environments.[67]

The legislation creating SNH contains two novelties. First, the concept of the "natural heritage" of Scotland is introduced. This is defined as including the flora and fauna of Scotland, its geological and physiographical features, and its natural beauty and amenity,[68] thereby combining and replacing the somewhat ungainly terms which have been used in previous conservation and countryside legislation.   **2.6.10**

The second novelty is the reference to the concept of sustainability,   **2.6.11**

---

[65] Information about SNH can be found on its website at www.snh.org.uk.
[66] NHSA 1991, s.1(1).
[67] Issues such as the development of the Cairngorm funicular railway bring out this clear potential for conflict; see *WWF U.K. Ltd v. Secretary of State for Scotland* [1999] 1 C.M.L.R. 1021, [1999] Env. L.R. 632.
[68] NHSA 1991, s.1(3).

noted above.[69] As part of its general aims, SNH is required to have regard to the desirability of ensuring that anything done in relation to the natural heritage of Scotland "is undertaken in a manner which is sustainable."[70] The exact meaning and impact of this provision are far from clear, especially as no definition is provided of "sustainable". The most that was offered in the parliamentary debates was the quotation of very broad principles taken from a document prepared by the International Union for the Conservation of Nature.[71] The introduction of this concept can be viewed as either a strengthening or a weakening of the commitment to conservation. A strengthening may result from the test of sustainability being applied to all activities which in any way affect the natural heritage, assessing their acceptability in terms of their long-term impact on the natural environment. On the other hand the commitment to conservation could be weakened either if the social and economic aspects of the concept are given prominence over biodiversity issues, or if questions as to the sustainability of any new development divert attention from the more fundamental issue of whether any development at all should be allowed to interfere with the status quo. Whatever one's approach, sustainability remains more of a political, economic and ethical principle than a legal standard by which conduct can be judged. In view of the lack of definition and the fact that SNH is merely required "to have regard to" the desirability of securing sustainability, arguments over the meaning and effect of this provision are likely to take place at the policy rather than the legal level, and this provision has not been the focus of legal argument.

2.6.12　　In addition to having regard to the desirability of ensuring sustainability, SNH is required to pay heed to a number of other considerations, balancing the concerns of conservation with a range of other interests.[72] As with all such balancing obligations, the precise weight to be given to any consideration is left to the discretion of SNH in each instance, but the various factors must at least be borne in mind and will obviously exert some influence on the making of policy and determination of particular cases. In keeping with SNH's main responsibilities actual or possible ecological and other environmental changes to the natural heritage of Scotland must be considered,[73] and it is also to have regard to aspects of what is sometimes called the "cultural heritage," namely the need to conserve sites and landscapes of archaeological and

---

[69] See para. 2.2.5, above.

[70] NHSA 1991, s.1(1).

[71] A draft of *Caring for Our World—A Strategy for Sustainability*; H.C. 1990–91 First Scottish Standing Committee C, col. 55.

[72] NHSA 1991, s.3(1).

[73] This is the only consideration to be taken into account in the exercise of functions relating to the Joint Nature Conservation Committee (*ibid.*, s.3(2)).

historical interest. Such conservationist concerns are balanced by the duty to consider the needs of agriculture, fisheries and forestry and the need for social and economic development. There is also a duty to consider the interests of owners and occupiers of land and of local communities. These latter needs and interests will obviously conflict at times with those of nature conservation (and of promoting recreation), but any successful conservation policy must pay heed to the concerns of the people who often feel themselves as being the most endangered species in the remote areas valued for their natural features. The emphasis given to working closely with local communities is reflected in the arrangements for National Parks in Scotland,[74] and is a strong feature of the consultation paper in 1998 on changes to the system of SSSIs[75] and of the final policy statement *The Nature of Scotland*.[76]

2.6.13 From the Nature Conservancy Council for Scotland, SNH has inherited the detailed nature conservation functions described later in this book as well as a role as official consultee on many planning and related matters.[77] From the Countryside Commission for Scotland, it has inherited a range of advisory functions and concern for the promotion of public recreation in the countryside. SNH's latter role has been enhanced by the power for SNH itself to enter access agreements and to make access orders to provide public access to areas of the countryside for recreational purposes;[78] previously the Countryside Commission for Scotland had been restricted to an advisory role, with the relevant legal powers being exclusively in the hands of planning authorities.

2.6.14 The powers which the Countryside Commission for Scotland enjoyed have been retained and broadened in scope, both geographically, as they are no longer restricted to "the countryside,"[79] and in terms of their use, as they can now be exercised in connection with the full range of SNH's functions, not merely those inherited from the Commission. There is a general power to enter management agreements[80] and a power to undertake and promote development schemes designed to enhance or conserve or to foster understanding or enjoy-

---

[74] See paras 5.11.24–5.11.25, below.

[75] *People and Nature: A New Approach to SSSI Designation in Scotland* (Scottish Office, 1998) (see K. Last, "Mechanisms for Environmental Regulation" in A. Ross, (ed.), *Environment and Regulation* (Hume Papers on Public Policy; vol. 8 no. 2) (2000) 38 at p.58).

[76] Scottish Executive (2001).

[77] Detailed amendments to the relevant legislation to take account of this transfer of functions to SNH are made by EPA 1990, Sched. 9 and NHSA 1991, Sched. 2.

[78] NHSA 1991, s.13 and Sched. 3, amending Pt II of CSA 1967.

[79] The Commission was restricted to operating in "the countryside" as defined by CSA 1967, s.2.

[80] CSA 1967, s.49A (added by Countryside (Scotland) Act 1981, s.9 and amended by NHSA 1991, Sched. 10, para. 4).

ment of the natural heritage.[81] Such schemes must involve the application of new techniques and methods or serve to illustrate the appropriateness of such schemes to particular areas,[82] and wide powers, including that of compulsory purchase of land, are provided to allow such schemes to be carried out.[83] From both predecessors SNH acquired the power to make or propose byelaws for areas where it is exercising various powers[84] and the ability to offer grants, loans and other forms of assistance to those furthering its objectives.[85]

Countryside Council for Wales

2.6.15   The Countryside Council for Wales (CCW)[86] was created by the Environmental Protection Act 1990,[87] and like SNH is charged with the tasks previously carried out by separate conservation and countryside bodies. Responsibility for nature conservation in Wales and the relevant statutory powers and functions were transferred to CCW from the Nature Conservancy Council,[88] while it is provided that in Wales CCW is to exercise the functions of the Countryside Commission, which had previously operated in both England and Wales.[89] Thus, as in Scotland, there is in Wales a single body which should be able to offer a more integrated approach to countryside and conservation issues than was previously the case.

2.6.16   The conservation functions and powers of CCW are the same as those of the other conservation bodies, and the countryside ones as those enjoyed by the Countryside Commission.[90] The latter powers are to be exercised for dual purposes.[91] Firstly, CCW is to act for the conservation and enhancement of natural beauty in Wales[92] and of the

---

[81] NHSA 1991, s.5(1).

[82] *ibid.*, s.5(2).

[83] *ibid.*, s.5(3)–(11); any compulsory purchase of land must be approved by the Minister and is subject to special parliamentary procedure.

[84] *e.g.* for nature reserves (NPACA 1949, s.2) and for areas covered by access arrangements (CSA 1967, s.54(4) (amended by NHSA 1991, Sched. 10, para. 4)).

[85] Now governed by NHSA 1991, s.9.

[86] The name Cyngor Cefn Gwlad Cymru can also be used, by virtue of the Alternative Names in Welsh Order 1994 (S.I. 1994 No. 2889). Information about CCW can be found on its website at www.ccw.gov.uk.

[87] EPA 1990, ss.128, 130.

[88] The detailed amendments necessary to achieve this are contained in *ibid.*, Sched. 9.

[89] *ibid.*, s.130; the detailed amendments necessary are contained in *ibid.*, Sched. 8, in particular substituting a new s.1 and adding ss.4A, 50A and 86A to NPACA 1949.

[90] See paras 2.7.1–2.7.3, below; the additional powers in England transferred from the Development Commission to what is now the Countryside Agency do not extend to Wales.

[91] EPA 1990, s.130(2).

[92] The conservation of natural beauty includes the conservation of flora and fauna and geological and physiographical features; *ibid.*, s.130(3).

natural beauty and amenity of the countryside in Wales, both in areas designated as National Parks and Areas of Outstanding Natural Beauty and elsewhere.[93] Secondly, CCW is to encourage the provision and improvement of facilities for the enjoyment of the Welsh countryside and of opportunities for open-air recreation and the study of nature. At the same time CCW is required to have regard to the social and economic interests of rural areas in Wales,[94] but there are no more detailed balancing obligations to mirror those imposed on SNH.[95] As described below, the powers acquired from the Countryside Commission are largely advisory and supportive, rather than offering scope for the implementation of major independent initiatives. The National Assembly of Wales has the power to adjust the functions of CCW, but only so as to give it additional functions.[96]

English Nature

The integration of conservation and countryside responsibilities which took place in Scotland and Wales did not take place in England, so that after the division of the NCC and the transfer to CCW of countryside functions in Wales, England was left with two bodies, defined by both functional and geographical limits. In England, one body exercises responsibility for nature conservation, as successor to the NCC; this body's statutory name was originally the Nature Conservancy Council for England but it operated under the name English Nature (EN), and this change of name has now been given statutory recognition.[97] Meanwhile, the Countryside Commission continued as before to perform its functions in relation to the countryside and recreation, but now limited to activities in England,[98] but this body too has had a change of name, to the Countryside Agency, following an expansion of its functions.[99]   2.6.17

The Environmental Protection Act 1990 lays down the constitution and general functions of EN, as described above.[1] The functions of EN are the same as those conservation functions exercised by the other   2.6.18

---

[93] Earlier legislation had suggested that efforts should be concentrated on the designated areas by stating that the conservation and enhancement of natural beauty were to be sought "particularly" in the designated areas; NPACA 1949, s.1 as originally enacted.

[94] EPA 1990, s.130(2).

[95] See para. 2.6.12, above.

[96] Government of Wales Act 1998, s.28, Sched. 4, Pt III.

[97] CRWA 2000, s.73 and Sched. 8 (which substitutes the new name for the old in over 40 statutory references). Information about EN can be found on its website at www.english-nature.org.uk.

[98] EPA 1990, s.130.

[99] Development Commission (Transfer of Functions and Miscellaneous Provisions) Order 1999 (S.I. 1999 No. 416), art. 3; see paras 2.7.1–2.7.5, below.

[1] EPA 1990, ss.128–134, Sched. 6.

conservation bodies. These functions have been described in general terms above and are discussed in more detail throughout the following chapters.

Joint Nature Conservation Committee

2.6.19   In order to counter some of the disadvantages of splitting the NCC, the Environmental Protection Act 1990 requires the statutory conservation bodies to establish a Joint Nature Conservation Committee (JNCC).[2] The Committee is comprised of eleven voting members, being a chairman and three members appointed by the Secretary of State,[3] the chairman and one other member from each of the conservation bodies (chosen by the body itself), and the chairman of the Countryside Agency, with two non-voting members appointed by the Department of the Environment in Northern Ireland.[4] The chairman and Secretary of State's appointees are not to be members of any of the conservation bodies, and the ministerial appointees[5] are required to be people appearing to have experience in or scientific knowledge of nature conservation, chosen with regard to the recommendation of the chairman of the Committee and after such consultations as the Secretary of State considers appropriate.

2.6.20   Following devolution, the JNCC has been designated as a cross-border public authority under the Scotland Act 1998.[6] This means that the Scottish Ministers must be consulted before the Secretary of State makes any appointments, or exercises any other powers which are not restricted to reserved matters, and that the JNCC must report to the Scottish Parliament as well as to the Westminster Parliament.[7] There is also a wide power for the powers and functions of such cross-border public authorities to be adapted as is considered necessary or expedient following devolution, and for the transfer of property if functions are transferred to other bodies.[8] In Wales, the JNCC is one of the bodies which is made subject to the Assembly's powers to summon witnesses to give evidence and to produce documents in relation to the bodies' affairs in Wales.[9]

---

[2] *ibid.*, s.128(4); this provision and others relating to the JNCC have been amended by NHSA 1991, s.4 to take account of the subsequent creation of SNH. Information about the JNCC can be found on its website at www.jncc.gov.uk.

[3] See para. 2.6.20, below on how devolution has affected these arrangements.

[4] *ibid.*, Sched. 7, paras 2–4.

[5] But not the chairman.

[6] Scotland Act 1998 (Cross-border Public Authorities) (Specification) Order 1999 (S.I. 1999 No.1319).

[7] Scotland Act 1998, s.88; it also falls within the jurisdiction of the Scottish Parliamentary Commissioner for Administration (Scotland) Act 1998 (Transitory and Transitional Provisions) (Complaints of Maladministration) Order 1999 (S.I. 1999 No.1351).

[8] Scotland Act 1998, ss.88–89.

[9] Government of Wales Act 1998, s.74, Sched. 5.

The Committee shares the broad functions in relation to nature con- **2.6.21**
servation which the conservation bodies have inherited from the NCC.[10]
More specifically the bodies are entrusted with a range of "special
functions" which can be discharged only through the Committee,
although the Minister can issue directions that the conservation bodies
themselves should act.[11] The Committee has control of its own procedure[12] and is obliged to produce an annual report to the Minister, who
shall lay it before Parliament (subject now to the post-devolution
arrangements noted above) and to each of the statutory conservation
bodies.[13] The Minister in the exercise of the power to make grants to
the conservation bodies can specify that sums are to be used for the
purposes of the Committee.[14]

The "special functions to be discharged through the Committee **2.6.22**
relate to matters at an international level or which affect Great Britain
as whole, thereby seeking to ensure that after the splitting of the NCC
there continued to be consistency and coherence on matters of more
than local interest. In particular it is useful for there to be a single
body providing advice and information on dealings outside the United
Kingdom, a matter of growing importance as the government becomes
involved in more European Community and international measures,
which increasingly contain obligations for regular monitoring and
reporting. These special functions[15] are, firstly, the provision of advice
to the government on policies for or affecting nature conservation in
Great Britain as a whole[16] or outside Great Britain,[17] and, secondly, the
provision of advice and dissemination of knowledge to anyone about
the same matters. A matter concerns Great Britain as a whole if it is of
national[18] or international importance or otherwise affects the interests
of Great Britain as a whole (tests which can be satisfied by matters
arising in only one of the constituent parts of Great Britain) or if it is
a matter arising throughout Great Britain and raising issues common
to all three parts.[19] A third special function for the Committee is the
establishment of common standards throughout Great Britain for the
monitoring of and research into nature conservation and the analysis of

---

[10] EPA 1990, s.131(5); it is not subject to the express requirement imposed on the conservation bodies to exercise these functions so as to secure compliance with the Habitats
Directive (see para 2.6.7, above).
[11] *ibid.*, s.133.
[12] *ibid.*, Sched. 7, para. 8.
[13] *ibid.*, Sched. 7, para. 10.
[14] *ibid.*, s.129(2).
[15] *ibid.*, s.133.
[16] *i.e.* Scotland, England and Wales.
[17] The JNCC is involved in conservation matters for British territories overseas.
[18] Presumably the United Kingdom is the "nation" in mind.
[19] The JNCC acts as the scientific authority in relation to trade in endangered species;
see para. 7.3.20, below.

the resulting information. Fourthly, and most particularly, the Committee is charged with the periodic review of and making of recommendations for change to the lists of wild plants and animals given protection by virtue of Schedules 5 and 8 of the Wildlife and Countryside Act 1981.[20] The Committee can also commission or support research which in its opinion relates to any of the above matters. Advice and information can further be given to any of the conservation bodies on matters which in the opinion of the Committee concern nature conservation for Great Britain as a whole or outside Great Britain.

2.6.23   As these functions are very broadly defined, and the Committee shares the other functions of the conservation bodies, the legislative framework would allow the relationship between the Committee and the separate bodies to take several forms. The precise division of tasks and responsibilities is thus largely a matter of practice rather than legal regulation.

OTHER PUBLIC BODIES

Countryside Agency

2.7.1   The Countryside Agency[21] took its present name and form in 1999. Its origins lie with the National Parks Commission established in 1949,[22] which was transformed when the Countryside Act 1968 gave it responsibility for the countryside in general and the new name of Countryside Commission.[23] The Commission's constitution was restructured by the Wildlife and Countryside Act 1981,[24] which remains its primary legal basis. On the creation of CCW under the Environmental Protection Act 1990, the functions of the Commission in Wales were passed to this new body, so that the Commission itself was restricted to England only.[25] In 1999, when Regional Development Agencies were created for England, the functions of the Development Commission were transferred to the Countryside Commission which acquired its current name as the Countryside Agency.[26] The Agency's status and administration

---

[20] WCA 1981, ss.22(3), 24(1) (amended by EPA 1990, Sched. 9, para. 11); see paras 3.4.2, 6.2.4, below.
[21] Information about the Countryside Agency can be found on its website at www. countryside.gov.uk.
[22] NPACA 1949, s.1 (as originally enacted).
[23] CA 1968, ss.1–2.
[24] *ibid.*, Sched. 13.
[25] EPA 1990, s.130, Sched. 8.
[26] Development Commission (Transfer of Functions and Miscellaneous Provisions) Order 1999 (S.I. 1999 No.416). Despite the name, the Agency remains a separate statutory corporation, not a "Next Steps agency" within a government department; see note 36 on p. 70, above.

are essentially the same as for the conservation bodies, with members appointed by the Secretary of State, and the Agency is subject to similar provisions on ministerial directions, annual reports and accounts.[27] Its funds come from the government[28] and the Secretary of State and Treasury must approve arrangements for the grants and loans which it makes to others.[29]

The Agency's functions acquired from the Countryside Commission are the preservation and enhancement of natural beauty[30] and amenity in the countryside and the encouragement of the provision of facilities for the enjoyment of the countryside and open-air enjoyment therein.[31] Included in this is a concern for the need to secure public access to the countryside for recreational purposes and the study of nature.[32] This task is given greater prominence by the Agency's role in relation to the public rights of access to the countryside introduced by the Countryside and Rights of Way Act 2000. It is the Agency that is responsible for drawing up the definitive maps of open country over which access rights may be exercised[33] and it has a major role in dealing with exclusion or restriction of access.[34]

2.7.2

In the exercise of its functions, the Agency must have due regard to the needs of agriculture and forestry and to the economic and social interests of rural areas.[35] The Agency is the body primarily responsible for the designation of National Parks and Areas of Outstanding Natural Beauty, and within the former plays a major consultative and advisory role in relation to the park authorities.[36] Other than in the provision of information and publicity about the countryside and for the benefit of visitors to it,[37] it is only really in relation to experimental schemes demonstrating the application of new techniques or approaches that the Agency can take an executive role.[38] In other areas, particularly the promotion of public access by means of access and public path agreements and orders,[39] the Agency can make initiatives and offer advice, but ultimately depends on planning authorities and others to implement

2.7.3

---

[27] WCA 1981, Sched. 13.
[28] *ibid.*, s.47(2).
[29] Local Government Act 1974, s.9.
[30] This includes conservation of flora and fauna and geological and physiographical features; NPACA 1949, s.114(2) (amended by CA 1968, s.21(7)).
[31] CA 1968, s.1(2) (substituted by EPA 1990, Sched. 8, para. 1).
[32] *ibid.*, s.2(2) (amended by *ibid.*, Sched. 8, para. 2).
[33] CRWA 2000, ss.4–11.
[34] *ibid.*, ss.21–33.
[35] CA 1968, s.37.
[36] NPACA 1949, ss.5–6, 87; see sections 5.1, 5.12, below.
[37] CA 1968, s.2(8).
[38] *ibid.*, s.4, (partly substituted by WCA 1981, s.40).
[39] NPACA 1949, Pt V.

its ideas.[40] The tasks recently conferred on the Agency in relation to public rights of access to the countryside, will of course, greatly enhance its direct role on access issues. The Agency is further charged with the task of advising government at all levels on countryside matters, acting on its own initiative as well as in response to formal requests,[41] and is a consultee in many official procedures.

2.7.4 From the Development Commission[42] the Agency has acquired the function of keeping under review and advising the Secretary of State on all matters relating to the economic and social development of rural areas in England. The Agency can carry out measures likely to further such development, or can assist others with such measures.[43] Putting the functions from both sources together, the Agency itself describes its tasks as being:

> "—to conserve and enhance the countryside,
> —to promote social equity and economic opportunity for the people who live there and
> —to help everyone, wherever they live, to enjoy this national asset."[44]

2.7.5 As far as nature conservation is concerned, the Agency's major influence is likely to be in its encouragement of the preservation of habitat, particularly in National Parks, but more generally through its promotion of the countryside as a place to enjoy for its natural beauty. However, the growth of recreational use of areas of the countryside, and the extended rights of public access, in turn produce new threats of disturbance and damage to habitats, and the Agency will have to balance its twin aims of conserving natural beauty and encouraging recreation. The resolution of such conflicts and debate on them may be more open and subject to greater public scrutiny in England, where there are separate bodies to put forward the arguments for recreation and for nature conservation, than in Scotland and Wales where in the first instance such arguments must take place internally within a single organisation. On

---

[40] As well as advice it can provide practical help in the form of specially skilled staff; CA 1968, s.2(5).

[41] *ibid.*, s.2(4).

[42] The Development Commission was widely known as the Rural Development Commission and was created by the Miscellaneous Financial Provisions Act 1983 as a successor to the Development Commissioners under the Development and Road Improvement Funds Act 1909. It was formally dissolved by the Development Commission (Dissolution) Order 2000 (S.I. 2000 No.1505).

[43] Miscellaneous Financial Provisions Act 1983, s.1; Development Commission (Transfer of Functions and Miscellaneous Provisions) Order 1999 (S.I. 1999 No.416), art. 4.

[44] Taken from http://www.countryside.gov.uk/reception/more—01.htm (Dec. 2001).

the other hand, the ability of SNH and CCW to take a more integrated approach to the countryside, offers advantages over the English position.

National Park Authorities and Conservation Boards

In the National Parks that exist in England and Wales and are proposed for Scotland, a range of powers are exercised by the National Park Authorities.[45] These bodies enjoy many of the powers of local authorities and their general task is to further the purposes for which the National Parks are created. In England and Wales these are to conserve and enhance the natural beauty, wildlife and cultural heritage of the area and to promote opportunities for the understanding and enjoyment of its special qualities.[46] In Scotland these are to conserve and enhance the natural and cultural heritage of the area, promote sustainable use of its natural resources, promote the understanding and enjoyment of the area and to promote sustainable economic and social development of the area's communities.[47] In both cases the conservation and enhancement duty is to take priority in the event of a conflict between these purposes.[48]

2.7.6

The park authorities are comprised of members nominated by the local authorities for the area affected and those appointed by the Minister, but in Scotland a number of members are also directly elected.[49] The powers enjoyed by the authorities in England and Wales are different from those proposed for Scotland, where the order designating each park can specify the precise range of powers conferred on the authority. Central to their functions is the preparation of a park plan, which in Scotland enjoys statutory status.[50] The National Parks are discussed in more detail in section 5.11, below.

2.7.7

Despite their rather general title, conservation boards are in fact very limited in extent and in their geographical application. These are new bodies created under the Countryside and Rights of Way Act 2000 and able to acquire some powers from local authorities in order to conserve and enhance the natural beauty of an Area of Outstanding Natural Beauty (AONB) and to increase the public's understanding and enjoyment of the area's special qualities.[51] Each board is constituted individually by a ministerial order, with members who are local authority and parish council nominees and ministerial appointees.[52]

2.7.8

---

[45] See section 5.11, below.
[46] NPACA 1949, s.5(1), as amended by EA 1995, s.61; see para. 5.11.4, below.
[47] NPSA 2000, s.1; see para. 5.11.21, below.
[48] NPACA 1949, s.11A (added by EA 1995, s.62); NPSA 2000, s.9(6).
[49] See paras 5.11.7, 5.11.24–5.11.26, below.
[50] See paras 5.11.10, 5.11.28–5.11.29, below.
[51] CRWA 2000, s.87(1); in case of conflict, the former purpose is to take priority.
[52] *ibid.*, Sched. 13; see paras 5.12.5 below.

2.7.9   The order creating a conservation board can transfer to it any of the
functions of local authorities relating to the AONB, or arrange for these
to be exercisable concurrently by the board and authorities. Significantly, though, the key planning functions of the local authority cannot
be transferred or shared in this way.[53] One specific task for the boards
is to prepare and publish a management plan for their area.[54] The role
of conservation boards and the impact of Areas of Outstanding Natural
Beauty are discussed more fully in section 5.12, below.

Forestry

2.7.10   In view of the large areas affected and the dramatic impact on wildlife
habitat caused by the planting or felling of trees on a large scale, the
actions of the Forestry Commission can be of considerable significance
for nature conservation. The Commission fulfils a dual role, being
responsible for the management of the large areas of productive woodland still in public ownership, and for encouraging and regulating the
development of private forestry.[55] To cope with these potentially conflicting functions, the management of woodland and plantations is
entrusted to Forest Enterprise, an agency operating within the Commission, whilst the Commission now exercises its policy and regulatory
functions on a devolved basis.[56] In the past the Commission itself was
active in the establishment of new plantations, but the last Conservative
governments moved the main responsibility for extending afforestation
to the private sector, guided by the Commission's supervisory powers.

2.7.11   The Commission comprises a Chairman and up to ten Commissioners, appointed by the Crown, and including at least three with
knowledge and experience of forestry, one with relevant scientific
attainments and one with experience of the timber trade.[57] The Commission is subject to fairly standard provisions on preparing annual
reports and accounts, and is subject to ministerial direction.[58] The
formal structures for its operation have been significantly affected by
devolution, and it now has separate National Offices for Scotland, England and Wales. In relation to Scotland, forestry is a devolved matter,
and the Commission has been designated as a cross-border public

---

[53] *ibid.*, s.86.
[54] *ibid.*, s.89; see paras 5.12.1–5.12.8, below.
[55] Information about the Forestry Commission can be found on its website at www.
forestry.gov.uk.
[56] There is a further agency within the Commission, Forest Research, whose role is to
provide research, surveys and related services to the forest industry and advice to
support forestry policy.
[57] Forestry Act 1967, s.2 (amended by Forestry Act 1981, s.5).
[58] See especially *ibid.*, ss.1(4), 44, 45 and Sched. 1 (as amended—see note 61, below).

authority under the Scotland Act 1998,[59] which means that it reports to the Scottish Parliament as well as to Westminster.[60] The Forestry Act 1967 has been subjected to many amendments to reflect the division of functions and responsibilities arising from devolution.[61] In relation to Wales, the funding of the Commission's functions in Wales is now a responsibility of the Assembly,[62] and more detailed arrangements have been made to transfer ministerial powers to the Assembly[63] and for the separate exercise of the Commission's functions in Wales.[64]

The Commission's duty is to promote the interests of forestry, the **2.7.12** development of afforestation and the production and supply of timber and other forest products,[65] but this is now tempered by an obligation to endeavour to achieve a reasonable balance between these aims and the conservation and enhancement of natural beauty and the conservation of flora and fauna and geological and physiographical features of special interest.[66] This obligation reflected a growing appreciation within the Commission of environmental matters, and there has been a very significant shift in policies during the last two decades, although as trees grow only slowly, the effects of this will not be apparent for some time.[67] Forestry policy today is aimed at achieving a range of benefits, including maintenance and enhancement of biodiversity.[68]

The Forestry Commission's control over private forestry is achieved **2.7.13** in two ways, discussed more fully in Chapter 6.[69] As far as felling is concerned, there is a full statutory scheme which imposes a requirement for a felling licence to be obtained before any significant felling is carried out. For planting, formal approval is necessary only in those situations where an environmental impact assessment is required,[70] but

---

[59] Scotland Act 1998 (Cross-border Public Authorities) (Specification) Order 1999 (S.I. 1999 No. 1319).

[60] Scotland Act 1998, ss.88–90; see para. 2.3.3, above.

[61] Scotland Act 1998 (Cross-Border Public Authorities) (Adaptation of Functions etc.) Order 1999 (S.I. 1999 No. 1747), Sched. 12; Scotland Act 1998 (Cross-Border Public Authorities) (Forestry Commissioners) Order 2000 (S.I. 2000 No.746); property issues arising from devolution are dealt with by the Transfer of Property etc. (Scottish Ministers) Order 1999 (S.I. 1999 No.1104), art. 4.

[62] Government of Wales Act 1998, s.105.

[63] National Assembly for Wales (Transfer of Functions) Order 1999 (S.I. 1999 No.672), Sched. 1.

[64] Government of Wales Act 1998, Sched. 7.

[65] Forestry Act 1967, s.1(2).

[66] *ibid.*, s.1(3A) (added by Wildlife and Countryside (Amendment) Act 1985, s.4).

[67] See C. Reid, "The Changing Pattern of Environmental Regulation: British Forestry and the Environmental Agenda" (1997) 9 J.E.L. 23.

[68] See, *e.g. Sustainable Forestry: the U.K. Programme* (1994, Cm. 2429); *Forests for Scotland: The Scottish Forestry Strategy* (2000, SE/2000/199).

[69] See section 6.4, below.

[70] Environmental Impact Assessment (Forestry) (Scotland) Regulations 1999 (S.S.I. 1999 No. 43); Environmental Impact Assessment (Forestry) (England and Wales) Regulations 1999 (S.I. 1999 No.2228); see paras 6.4.25–6.4.29, below.

control is exercised through grant schemes operating in an economic context which means that no major planting will be economically viable without grant support.[71] These grant schemes now take into account considerations of habitat diversity, environmental protection and amenity as well as commercial timber production. These arrangements mean that the Commission will be involved in considering the desirability of any major forestry activities and is in a position to ensure that conservation matters are at least taken into account.

2.7.14 The Commission encourages visitors to parts of its land and has the power to provide facilities for them,[72] including in Scotland the express power to appoint rangers.[73] There is also a power to make byelaws to regulate the conduct of those on land managed by the Commission,[74] and byelaws have been made prohibiting the lighting of fires, any form of damage to trees and plants, the wilful disturbance of animals and their lairs of all sorts and the catching of butterflies, moths and dragonflies (one of the few legislative measures to make special mention of insects of any sort).[75] In other words, visitors must ensure that the natural environment in the woodland is disturbed as little as possible by their presence, so that on Forestry Commission land the general laws protecting plants and animals are considerably strengthened.

Crown Estate Commission

2.7.15 The Crown Estate Commissioners are responsible for administering the rights of the Crown in areas of land where the Crown retains a major interest,[76] most notably the foreshore and seabed.[77] Any activity, *e.g.* fish farming, which involves the positioning of structures on or over the seabed will require their permission. The Commissioners are appointed by the Crown,[78] are subject to ministerial direction[79] and report annually to Her Majesty and the U.K. Parliament.[80] Regulations can be made to control the conduct of the public granted access to Crown land.[81] The general duty of the Commissioners is, while main-

---

[71] See paras 6.4.12–6.4.16, below.

[72] CSA 1967, s.58; CA 1968, s.23.

[73] *ibid.*, s.65 (amended by Countryside (Scotland) Act 1981, Sched. 1, para. 4).

[74] Forestry Act 1967, s.46.

[75] Forestry Commission Byelaws 1982 (S.I. 1982 No. 648).

[76] Crown Estates Act 1961, s.1; information about the Crown Estate can be found on its website at www.crownestate.co.uk.

[77] See generally M.E. Deans, "The Crown Estate Commissioners—Their Role and Responsibilities in respect of the Foreshore and Sea-bed around Scotland" (1986) 4 Journal of Energy and Natural Resources Law 166.

[78] Crown Estates Act 1961, Sched. 1, para. 1.

[79] *ibid.*, s.1(4).

[80] *ibid.*, s.2.

[81] *ibid.*, s.6.

taining the Crown Estate as an estate in land, to maintain and enhance its value and the return obtained from it, but with due regard to the requirements of good management.[82] No specific environmental duty is placed on the Commissioners, but they are bound by the general balancing duties applicable to all public bodies.[83] Other than the requirement for environmental impact assessment of certain marine fish farming developments,[84] there are no other legal restrictions specifically imposed on the Commissioners for environmental or conservation grounds, and they enjoy a wide immunity from legal challenge to the exercise of their powers.[85] It is anomalous at least for significant regulatory powers to remain in the hands of a body so far removed from the normal structures of political, public and legal accountability.

Deer Commission for Scotland

In Scotland, the Deer Commission for Scotland has general responsibility for the conservation, control and sustainable management of deer, including their welfare.[86] The Commission is the successor to the Red Deer Commission, which was initially limited to concern for red deer but subsequently extended to other species.[87] The Commission is appointed by the Scottish Ministers and comprises a chairman and between nine and twelve members selected as being appropriate to represent the interests of persons or organisations concerned with deer management, agriculture, forestry, and the natural heritage. Nominations can be made by representative organisations and at least one third of the members must have knowledge and experience of deer management.[88] Local panels can be established to carry out the Commission's tasks in particular localities.[89] An annual report must be presented to the Ministers.[90]   **2.7.16**

The Commission advises both the Ministers[91] and landowners, collaborates with scientific investigations and supports or carries out its   **2.7.17**

---

[82] *ibid.*, s.1(3).

[83] CSA 1967, s.66; CA 1968, s.11; see para. 2.2.6, above.

[84] Environmental Impact Assessment (Fish Farming in Marine Waters) Regulations 1999 (S.I. 1999 No. 367); see para. 8.3.7, below.

[85] Crown Estates Act 1961, s.1(5); see *Walford v. Crown Estates Commissioners*, 1988 S.L.T. 377.

[86] Deer (Scotland) Act 1996, s.1; information about the Commission can be found on its website at www.dcs.gov.uk.

[87] Deer (Scotland) Act 1959, almost every section of which was amended by the Deer (Amendment) (Scotland) Act 1982.

[88] Deer (Scotland) Act 1996, s.1; if nominations are made by relevant bodies, the members reflecting the interests of deer managers must be selected from these (s.1(6)(c)).

[89] *ibid.*, s.4.

[90] *ibid.*, s.2(3).

[91] *ibid.*, s.2(1).

own research into matters affecting deer in Scotland.[92] It has power to deal with marauding deer and to introduce wider deer control schemes,[93] and can provide services and equipment to those involved in the control of deer.[94] Authority from the Commission acts as an exemption from the normal requirements for game licences to kill deer.[95] The details of the Commission's powers are discussed in relation to the law on deer generally.[96]

Scottish Environment Protection Agency and Environment Agency

2.7.18 The Scottish Environment Protection Agency (SEPA) and the Environment Agency were established by the Environment Act 1995 in order to create single bodies which would exercise a wide range of pollution control and related functions in Scotland and in England and Wales. SEPA took over the functions of Her Majesty's Industrial Pollution Inspectorate, river purification boards, many functions of local authorities, *e.g.* in relation to waste, and some powers of the Secretary of State. The Environment Agency similarly took over the functions of Her Majesty's Inspectorate of Pollution, the National Rivers Authority (much broader than those of the river purification boards) and some functions of local authorities (a narrower range than in Scotland) and the Secretary of State.[97] Both bodies are statutory corporations similar in form and status to the statutory conservation bodies.

2.7.19 The provisions establishing the Environment Agency state that its principal aim is to protect and enhance the environment, taken as a whole, so as to make a contribution towards the objective of achieving sustainable development; guidance towards this end can be given by the Minister.[98] SEPA does not have such an express general aim, but it too is subject to ministerial guidance as to the contribution it can make towards achieving sustainable development.[99] Both bodies are subject to broad duties to have regard to the desirability of conserving or enhancing the natural heritage (SEPA) or natural beauty, flora, fauna and geological and physiographical features (Environment Agency).[1] In particular, both agencies are under a duty, to the extent that they

---

[92] *ibid.*, s.3.
[93] *ibid.*, ss.6–10.
[94] *ibid.*, s.12.
[95] *ibid.*, s.38.
[96] See paras 4.2.17–4.2.23, below.
[97] EA 1995, ss.2, 21. Information about SEPA and the Environment Agency can be found on their websites at www.sepa.org.uk and www.environment-agency.gov.uk.
[98] EA 1995, s.4.
[99] *ibid.*, s.31.
[1] *ibid.*, ss.7, 32.

consider desirable, to promote the conservation of flora and fauna dependent on an aquatic environment and the conservation and enhancement of natural beauty.[2] Further duties apply where the activities or operations carried out or authorised by the agencies, might affect certain areas designated for their conservation value.[3]

Through their pollution control functions, especially with regard to water, and with the wider aquatic powers of the Environment Agency, both of these bodies may have a significant influence on nature conservation issues. The impact on biodiversity is a relevant factor in deciding on pollution permits of various kinds and measures to achieve improvements to water and atmospheric quality and precautions to prevent spillages and discharges benefit flora and fauna as much as humans.   **2.7.20**

Water

As noted above, authorities with responsibility for rivers and other aspects of the aquatic environment can also play a significant part in nature conservation. This is not the place for a detailed examination of water law in all its complexity;[4] all that the following paragraphs aim to do is to identify which authorities have responsibility for the major activities in this field.[5]   **2.7.21**

In England and Wales the water industry was restructured in 1989,[6] but the National Rivers Authority created at that time to safeguard and manage water resources[7] has since been subsumed within the Environment Agency. The Agency can impose restrictions on the abstraction or impounding of water,[8] setting a minimum acceptable flow for specific waters,[9] and imposing further restrictions in the event of drought.[10] It is responsible for issuing consents where activities are likely to lead to the entry (direct or indirect) of polluting matter into waters and for other pollution control measures,[11] and for the general supervision of   **2.7.22**

---

[2] *ibid.*, ss.6, 34.

[3] *ibid.*, ss.8, 35; see para. 5.5.39, below.

[4] See *Stair Memorial Encyclopaedia of the Laws of Scotland* (1989), Vol. 25, "Water and Water Rights," "Water Supply"; W. Howarth and D. McGillivray, *Water Pollution and Water Quality Law* (2001); W. Howarth, *Wisdom's Law of Watercourses* (5th ed., 1992); J.H. Bates, *Water and Drainage Law* (looseleaf).

[5] See further section 8.6, below.

[6] The restructuring was carried out by the Water Act 1989, but the relevant legislation was consolidated in the Water Industry Act 1991, the Water Resources Act 1991, the Statutory Water Companies Act 1991, the Land Drainage Act 1991 and the Water Consolidation (Consequential Provisions) Act 1991.

[7] Water Resources Act 1991, s.1.

[8] *ibid.*, Pt II, Chap. II.

[9] *ibid.*, Pt II, Chap. I.

[10] *ibid.*, Pt II, Chap. III.

[11] *ibid.*, Pt III.

flood defence.[12] The Agency has some responsibilities for fisheries[13] and may have navigation functions transferred to it from existing navigation and harbour authorities.[14] Land drainage is also under the supervision of the Agency,[15] although in most circumstances immediate responsibility lies with the internal drainage boards comprised of elected and appointed members under the Land Drainage Act 1991;[16] subsequent legislation has added duties to further the conservation of natural beauty, flora, fauna and geological and physiographical features in the exercise of drainage powers, with more precise obligations on designated sites.[17] All of these responsibilities can obviously have a major impact on the survival and quality of the habitat necessary for communities of aquatic plants and animals.

2.7.23   In Scotland similar powers exist, but they are distributed more widely within a structure that has been much altered during the last decade. SEPA has inherited all of the functions of the river purification authorities with respect to pollution control and flood warning systems,[18] whilst three new water authorities were created to take over water supply and sewerage functions as part of the wider restructuring of local government in the mid-1990s.[19] SEPA's general duty with regard to water is noted above, while the Scottish Ministers and the water authorities are subject to general duties to promote the conservation and effective use of water resources[20] and to further the conservation and enhancement of natural beauty and the conservation of flora, fauna, and geological and physiographical features of special interest.[21] The water authorities have further duties with regard to certain designated sites.[22] The water authorities are responsible the maintenance of water supplies, *e.g.* it is they who can initiate the procedure for drought

---

[12] *ibid.*, Pt IV.

[13] *ibid.*, Pt V.

[14] *ibid.*, s.2 and Sched. 2.

[15] Land Drainage Act 1991, s.7.

[16] *ibid.*, s.1 and Scheds. 1, 2.

[17] Land Drainage Act 1991, ss.61A, 61C, added by Land Drainage Act 1994, s.1; the duties are essentially the same as those that apply generally to the Environment Agency.

[18] EA 1995, s.21.

[19] Local Government etc. (Scotland) Act 1994, Part II. Under the Water Industry (Scotland) Act 2002, a single authority, Scottish Water, has taken over the functions of the three authorities created in 1994; see Addendum, above.

[20] Water (Scotland) Act 1980, s.1 (as substituted by Local Government etc. (Scotland) Act 1994, s.65(1)).

[21] Local Government etc. (Scotland) Act 1994, s.65(2); it seems surprising that after the creation of the phrase "natural heritage" as a more convenient replacement for this standard but rather awkward list of features to be conserved (NHSA 1991, s.1), the new phrase has not been more widely adopted in legislation.

[22] Local Government etc. (Scotland) Act 1994, s.73.

orders.[23] SEPA and the Ministers are responsible for controls on the abstraction of water for irrigation.[24] Flood prevention is a matter primarily for local authorities,[25] but SEPA has a role in flood warning and risk assessment.[26] Statutory control of land drainage is primarily in ministerial hands,[27] while matters affecting fisheries are dealt with by the Ministers, proprietors and district salmon fishery boards.[28] Responsibility for the aquatic environment is thus much more fragmented in Scotland, and the activities of a range of authorities can affect the habitat for aquatic life.

Natural Environment Research Council

The Natural Environment Research Council plays a major role in research relevant to nature conservation.[29] Established under royal charter and the Science and Technology Act 1965, its statutory functions are to carry out research in earth sciences and ecology, to facilitate, encourage and support such research by other institutions and people, and to disseminate knowledge and provide advice on these subjects.[30] It has no legal powers to intervene directly for the benefit of nature conservation, although it is represented on some other bodies which do have direct powers and must be consulted in some circumstances. However the research which it carries out in its own institutes and supports elsewhere is of major significance, and it is the parent body for, among others, the British Antarctic Survey, the British Geological Survey, the Institute of Terrestrial Ecology and the Institute of Freshwater Ecology.[31]

2.7.24

NON-GOVERNMENTAL BODIES

Non-governmental bodies have played a major part in the development of concern for nature conservation and in the achievement of practical measures to this end. A large number of charitable bodies have been

2.8.1

---

[23] NHSA 1991, Pt III (as amended by Local Government etc. (Scotland) Act 1994, Sched.13, para.170).

[24] *ibid.*, Pt II (as amended by EA 1995, Sched. 22, para. 96).

[25] Flood Prevention (Scotland) Act 1961, (as amended by Local Government etc.(Scotland) Act 1994, Sched. 13, para. 56 and Flood Prevention and Land Drainage (Scotland) Act 1997).

[26] Agriculture Act 1970, s.92 (as amended by EA 1995, Sched.22, para.14), EA 1995, s.25.

[27] Land Drainage (Scotland) Acts 1930 and 1958.

[28] Constituted under the Salmon Act 1986.

[29] Information about NERC can be found on its website at www.nerc.ac.uk.

[30] Science and Technology Act 1965, s.1(3).

[31] See J. Sheail, *Natural Environment Research Council: A History* (1992).

active in this field, providing a voice for those concerned for nature and actively seeking ways of conserving threatened habitat and species. Much can be achieved by small groups and even individuals in relation to particular sites, and apparently insignificant tasks such as the recording of the distribution and preferred habitat of species in an area provide essential information on biodiversity, creating the scientific base on which major decisions can be founded. The contribution made by such voluntary efforts to nature conservation in Britain is immense.

2.8.2   There is a large number of ways in which such activities can be organised, and few raise any legal issues specific to this area. The general law of trusts, charities and unincorporated associations must however be borne in mind, especially if an organisation wishes to acquire an interest in land or to enter other formal legal relationships in order to secure its aims. Careful attention to the legal formalities is essential if any effective long-term arrangements are to be made. Recent disputes over the acceptability of hunting over National Trust land have served to emphasise the significance of the land management decisions of such bodies and the extent and means by which they are or are not accountable to members and others.[32]

2.8.3   A number of charities, most notably the Royal Society for the Protection of Birds, do own and manage significant areas of land as nature reserves and this is one place where the law does come into contact with the activities of such voluntary bodies. Land which is being managed as a nature reserve by any body approved by a statutory conservation body and which the body considers to be of national importance can be declared by it to be a National Nature Reserve[33]; this means that the statutory body can make byelaws for the protection of the reserve in the same way as it can for those which it manages itself.[34] This power provides a means by which the voluntary efforts in this field can be integrated with the official ones and offers official recognition of the efforts made by the voluntary bodies to support those of the public conservation bodies.

National Trusts

2.8.4   The National Trusts occupy a position halfway between official and private organisations, in that although in no way governmental bodies, they do enjoy some statutory recognition. The National Trust was

---

[32] *ex p. Scott* [1998] 1 W.L.R. 226, deciding that the National Trust was not directly subject to judicial review and that the Charity Commissioners would have to authorise any legal proceedings; see below for the special status of the National Trusts. The legal position of charities in Scotland is very different.

[33] WCA 1981, s.35.

[34] NPACA 1949, s.20; see section 5.3, below.

incorporated under a private Act of Parliament in 1907,[35] and the National Trust for Scotland likewise in 1935,[36] and their constitutions are embodied in statute. Both have among their purposes

> "the permanent preservation for the benefit of the nation of lands ... of beauty or historic interest and .. . the preservation (so far as practicable) of their natural aspect and features and animal and plant life"[37]

so that nature conservation does fall within the purposes for which the Trusts can act.

Certain land which is held by the Trusts is declared to be inalienable,[38] so that there is a guarantee that it will continue to be used in accordance with the Trusts' purposes. Such land is accorded special treatment in other legislation, *e.g.* special procedures are required for its compulsory purchase.[39] On land in which they have an interest, the Trusts have the power to make byelaws, including ones to prevent any damage or disturbance to plants or animals,[40] and in England and Wales the power[41] to make and enforce restrictive covenants even though no adjacent land is held may allow something akin to a management agreement.[42] As the Trusts are significant landowners, particularly in areas of scenic beauty, considerable benefits for nature conservation can arise from these provisions.

2.8.5

EUROPEAN COMMUNITY

Although the European Community had been active on environmental issues for many years previously, it was only in 1987 that it was given express competence to act in this field. The impact of the Community is felt through its legislation on environmental topics and also through

2.9.1

---

[35] National Trust Act 1907; see also National Trust Charity Scheme Confirmation Act 1919 and National Trust Acts 1937, 1939, 1953, 1971, and Charities (National Trust for Places of Historic Interest or Natural Beauty) Order 1994 (S.I. 1994 No.2181).

[36] National Trust for Scotland Order Confirmation Act 1935; see also National Trust for Scotland Order Confirmation Acts 1938, 1947, 1952, 1961, 1973.

[37] National Trust Act 1907, s.4(1); National Trust for Scotland Order Confirmation Act 1935, Sched., s.4.

[38] *ibid.*, s.21; *ibid.*, s.22.

[39] Acquisition of Land (Authorisation Procedure) (Scotland) Act 1947, s.1(2); Acquisition of Land Act 1981, s.18.

[40] National Trust Act 1971, s.24; National Trust for Scotland Order Confirmation Act 1935, Sched., s.33.

[41] National Trust Act 1937, s.8.

[42] See paras 1.3.17–1.3.19, above and 5.1.7, below.

the influence of its policies in other areas, particularly agriculture, which play a major part in shaping the way in which individuals and businesses act within the United Kingdom.[43] The European dimension is now an integral part of the law on nature conservation; while the substantive rules are described where relevant in other chapters below, this section offers a brief outline of the basic framework of Community involvement in conservation matters.[44]

2.9.2 The powers and competence of the Community[45] depend upon the treaties which create it, and at first there was no reference in these to environmental matters. However, this did not prevent the Community from taking an interest in such issues and in addition to environmental considerations affecting its activities in other areas, a range of specifically environmental measures[46] were produced under the authority of two general provisions of the EEC Treaty as it stood at that time: article 100 which provided for the approximation (or harmonisation) of laws affecting the establishment or functioning of the common market, and article 235 which allowed measures to be taken where necessary for the attainment of the Community's objectives and where the Treaty had not specifically provided the necessary powers. These were not an altogether satisfactory basis for Community activity in this field and when the treaties were amended by the Single European Act which took effect in 1987, a new title was added conferring on the Community powers relating to the environment.[47] Subsequent amendments to the Treaty have strengthened the position of environmental law.

2.9.3 The Treaty, in its current form as agreed at Amsterdam in 1997,[48]

---

[43] C. Reid, "Nature Conservation Law" in J. Holder (ed.), *The Impact of EC Environmental Law in the United Kingdom* (1997).

[44] There is a growing literature on E.C. environmental law, including: D. Gillies, *A Guide to E.C. Environmental Law* (1999); J. Kiss and D. Shelton, *Manual of Environmental Law* (2nd ed., 1997); L. Kramer, *E.C. Environmental Law* (2000); J. Scott, *E.C. Environmental Law* (1998).

[45] Although often the terms are used as if interchangeable, there is a significant legal difference between the European Union and the European Community. The former term covers the full range of co-operation arrangements between the 15 Member States, including areas such as foreign affairs, whereas the latter refers to the formal structure of institutions, legislation and decision-making processes which have legal force in the Member States within the areas of competence specified in the E.C. Treaty.

[46] *e.g.* the Directive on the Conservation of Wild Birds (79/409) made in 1979; see section 7.4, below.

[47] Title VII of the EEC Treaty (arts 130r–130t), added by art. 25 of the single European Act; for a detailed account of these provisions see L. Kramer, *EEC Treaty and Environmental Protection* (1990).

[48] The article numbers given here refer to the consolidated version of the Treaty approved at Amsterdam in 1997 (in force 1999). The further amendments agreed by the Treaty of Nice (2000) will not alter the relevant parts of the Treaty apart from substituting a new art. 175(2), altering the decision-making procedure on some topics.

makes it clear that environmental matters are important to the Community and contains specific environmental provisions. Promoting "a high level of protection and improvement of the quality of the environment" is one of the Community's express tasks[49] and "environmental protection requirements must be integrated into the definition and implementation" of the Community's other policies and activities.[50] This last point is particularly important given the environmental impact of policies in other areas, such as agriculture and fisheries, and even the extent to which free trade requirements can stand in the way of national environmental policies.

The specific environmental provisions in Title XIX call on the Community to take action to contribute to the objectives of preserving, protecting and improving the environment, protecting human health, the prudent and rational utilisation of natural resources, and promoting measures at international level.[51] Community action should aim at a high level of protection, taking into account the diversity within the Community, and be based on the precautionary principle and the principles that preventive action should be taken, that environmental damage should be rectified at source and that the polluter should pay.[52] Regard must be had to scientific and technical data, environmental conditions in the different regions of the Community, potential costs and benefits of any action or lack of action, and the economic and social development of the Community, including the balanced development of its regions.[53] A variety of decision-making procedures are prescribed for different topics, including the involvement of the European Parliament and consulation with the Economic and Social Committee and the Committee of the Regions, and on some matters there is scope of majority voting in the Council of Ministers.[54] Member States remain free to adopt more stringent protective measures for themselves, provided that these are compatible with the Treaty, *e.g.* that they do not impose an undue restriction on free trade.[55] Environmental policy has been laid down in broad terms in a series of Environmental Action

2.9.4

---

[49] E.C. Treaty, art. 2.

[50] art. 6; this must be done "in particular with a view to promoting sustainable development".

[51] art. 174(1).

[52] art. 174(2).

[53] art. 174(3).

[54] art. 175; art. 175(2) will be replaced when the Treaty of Nice comes into force.

[55] *ibid.*, art.176; see, for example, *Ditlev Bluhme* (C-67/97) [1998] E.C.R. I-8033, where it was argued (unsuccessfully) that measures banning the keeping of other kinds of bees in order to protect a local subspecies on a remote Danish island did not fall within the permitted grounds for infringing the principle of the free movement of goods. See further paras 7.3.25–7.3.28.

Programmes, and nature and biodiversity form one of the priority areas in the Sixth Programme, scheduled for adoption in 2002.[56]

2.9.5   Legislation from the Community comes in the form of Regulations and Directives. Regulations automatically become part of the domestic law of the Member States and must be followed by individuals and enforced by the authorities in the same way as other laws within the national legal system. Directives are addressed to the Member States which are required to take whatever measures are necessaary to ensure that the objectives set out in Directive are achieved within their own national legal systems within the period specified in the Directive. Therefore where the national law does not already provide for the requirements of the Directive, new national legislation should be introduced, and in the United Kingdom this can be achieved by delegated legislation under the European Communities Act 1972.[57] Any implementing measures are to be interpreted so far as possible to ensure that the terms of the Directive are in fact completely satisifed.[58]

2.9.6   If a Directive has not been fully or properly implemented, the European Commission (frequently acting on the basis of a complaint from an individual) can take steps to ensure that the defaulting state does fulfil its obligation to give effect to the Directive. This process can lead ultimately to an action before the European Court of Justice, with fines being imposed on a Member State that fails to respond to a judgment against it.[59] Such actions have been necessary on many occasions to enforce the implementation of Directives on environmental topics.[60] A Directive which has not been implemented by the due date may also have direct effect.[61] This means that individuals in their dealings with a branch of defaulting state[62] (but not against other individuals)[63] can

---

[56] COM (2001) 31 final.

[57] European Communities Act 1972 s.2(2); to give one example, it was under this authority that the Conservation (Natural Habitats, etc.) Regulations 1994 were made to implement the Habitats and Species Directive; see para. 1.1.22, above.

[58] *Litster v. Forth Dry Dock and Engineering Co. Ltd*, 1989 S.L.T. 540, [1990] 1 A.C. 546.

[59] E.C. Treaty, art. 228; *Commission v. Greece* (C-387/97) [2000] E.C.R. I-5047.

[60] *e.g.* in relation to the United Kingdom's failure to implement the Nitrates Directive; *Commission v. United Kingdom* (C-69/99) [2000] E.C.R. I-10979; (see para. 8.4.20, below).

[61] *Van Duyn v. Home Office* (41/74) [1974] E.C.R. 1337, *Pubblico Ministero v. Ratti* (148/78) [1979] E.C.R. 1629.

[62] This covers all public authorities and other bodies given powers or responsibilities over and above those of private individuals and companies; *Foster v. British Gas plc* (C-188/89) [1990] E.C.R. I-3313, [1991] 1 Q.B. 405.

[63] *Marshall v. Southampton and South West Hampshire Area Health Authority (Teaching)* (152/84) [1986] E.C.R. 723, [1986] Q.B. 401; *Faccini Dori v. Recreb srl* (C-91/92) [1994] E.C.R. I-3325; this does not exclude all indirect consequences for individuals as in *R. v. Durham City Council, ex p. Huddleston* [2000] 1 W.L.R. 1484.

rely on its terms as if they had been implemented in national law, provided that the relevant provisions are sufficiently precise and unconditional for it to be clear exactly what the legal position would have been had the Directive been properly implemented.[64] An individual who has suffered harm as a direct result of a Member State failing to implement a Directive may also be entitled to claim compensation from that state.[65]

It is thus important to know what is provided in Community Law, both as a guide to the proper interpretation of domestic law implementing its terms and as a source of law which may supplement or override[66] domestic provisions. Although some of the measures on the protection of particular species are precise enough to be given direct effect, much of the legislation on nature conservation contains too great an element of discretion on the part of the Member State to be given direct effect,[67] and it is unlikely that any individual will be able to demonstrate a sufficiently direct loss to benefit from the potential for compensation. Nevertheless, the terms of the Directives must be followed by the Member States and the detailed discussion of E.C. measures in the following chapters show many cases where Member States have been found to be acting unlawfully through a failure to comply fully with Directives.[68]

2.9.7

Community law has had a major impact on all aspects of environmental law in Great Britain. As far as nature conservation is concerned, the need to comply with the Birds Directive was one of the factors which led to the Wildlife and Countryside Act 1981, whilst the implementation of the Habitats and Species Directive called for very significant changes to the law, greatly strengthening the protection given to designated sites.[69] This has in turn influenced the more recent changes to site protection in England and Wales, whilst the E.C. initiatives on environmental impact assessment, nitrate pollution of water and many other topics have also changed the legal rules and approach in this

2.9.8

---

[64] *Becker v. Finanzamt Munster-Innenstadt* (8/81) [1982] E.C.R. 53.

[65] *Francovich, Bonifaci and Others v. Italy* (C-6/90, C-9/90) [1991] E.C.R. I-5357; *Brasserie du Pêcheur SA v. Germany, R. v. Secretary of State for Transport, ex p. Factortame Ltd* (No.4) (C-46/93, 48/93) [1996] E.C.R. I-1029.

[66] *R. v. Secretary of State for Transport, ex p. Factortame Ltd (No. 2)* [1991] 1 A.C. 603.

[67] See, *e.g.* comments on the Birds Directive in *Kincardine and Deeside District Council v. Forestry Commissioners*, 1992 S.L.T. 1180 at p. 1187; more general discussions include L. Kramer, "The Implementation of Community Environmental Directives within Member States: Some Implications of the Direct Effect Doctrine" (1991) 3 J.E.L. 39; C. Hilson, "Community Rights in Environmental Law: Rhetoric or Reality?" in J. Holder (ed.), *The Impact of E.C. Environmental Law in the United Kingdom* (1997). See also para. 1.4.7, above.

[68] *e.g.*, in the designation of wildlife sites; see paras 7.4.9–7.4.10, 7.4.21.

[69] See para. 1.1.22, above.

country. It may be rare for Community law to be given direct effect so as to override the domestic legislation on a topic, but the threat of enforcement action before the European Court of Justice and the publicity which even the consideration of the issue by the Commission can attract, mean the Community law acts as a fundamental consideration in the development and operation of the law in Great Britain.

3. PROTECTION OF WILD ANIMALS

The most straightforward legal approach to protecting wildlife is to **3.1.1**
enact laws punishing people who cause it direct harm.[1] Most of the
early legislation designed to preserve game and other species considered to be of value took this form, and similar laws continue to play a
major role in nature conservation, although increasingly supported by
measures to protect the habitat necessary for the continued survival of
the protected species. The long-term decline of some species is the
direct result of man's deliberate conduct in exterminating them, for
food, fur and feathers, for sport or display, or to prevent harm to more
valued species. Putting an end to such direct assaults is an obvious and
essential first step in seeking to protect wildlife.

Such laws can be relatively simple. Certain actions directed towards **3.1.2**
certain specified animals are prohibited; the law affects everybody and
is of general application. The straightforward nature of such measures
means that they can be simple to understand, with real benefits in terms
of publicity and education. Although detracting from the simplicity of
the law, a further advantage of structuring the law on the basis of prohibiting direct harm to wildlife is that the particular threats to each
species can be specifically addressed. Some creatures are in need of
more protection than others; some are the special victims of particular
conduct. In other cases a degree of exploitation may be tolerated whilst
protection is also required in some situations. Enacting a separate law
for each species would achieve the maximum of individual attention,
but this would be quite unacceptable in terms of the legislative time and
effort required, to say nothing of producing an unworkably fragmented
system. To reduce this problem, species can be grouped into a handful
of categories, and different regimes designed for each category,
offering different levels of protection whilst leaving the law in a relatively manageable state.

Aside from the risk of excessive fragmentation, three factors may **3.1.3**
reduce the effectiveness of this very direct approach to conservation
legislation. By requiring the express prohibition of the undesired conduct, there is a risk that some forms of harm, or some species in need
of protection, will be omitted, or will come to be appreciated only after
the law is in place. In particular, conduct that causes very real, but
indirect, harm to the survival of a species may escape. The presence of
gaps and possible loopholes may undermine the law, and it may be
difficult to persuade the legislators to make the effort to enact the necessary amendments promptly. In the second place, such legislation is

---

[1] See generally K. Last, "The Protection of Species" in J. Rowan-Robinson and D.
McKenzie-Skene, *Countryside Law in Scotland* (2000).

likely to favour the large and "cuddly" animals. More tends to be
known about such animals, they are more in the public's eye, and
elected legislators are more likely to act on behalf of those creatures
which enjoy public sympathy than those whose importance or value is
not widely appreciated.[2] Thus there is in Britain special legislation for
badgers and seals, but no Woodlice Act is readily conceivable, however
endangered or ecologically vital some species of woodlice may be in
the wild.

3.1.4   The third feature which besets specific legislation is that of identifying the creatures and plants to which protection is given. A law which
makes it a criminal offence to disturb certain species will only work if
potential offenders can identify those species and moderate their conduct accordingly. How many people can tell the difference between the
reed warbler and the strictly protected marsh warbler,[3] between the
black-headed gull and the protected little and Mediterranean gulls? This
is a problem which is even more severe in relation to the law on plants
and invertebrates. The good intentions of such legislation may be
undermined by a lack of public knowledge which makes a nonsense of
the attempt to categorise species carefully. At a more detailed level the
problems of hybridisation and arguments over taxonomy and classification can undermine even the attempt to specify clearly individual
species.

3.1.5   The law relating to wildlife is, however, not concerned only with its
protection. It is also concerned to permit and regulate the exploitation
of wild creatures through various forms of hunting, and to secure the
destruction of those creatures viewed as pests. There are thus provisions
imposing requirements to destroy damaging species, regulating who
can hunt for animals and controlling the means which can be used to
kill or take animals and birds. Any attempt to present an overall picture
of the law regulating the harm which can be done to wildlife must
therefore bring together provisions from these somewhat different
areas. It may seem odd in a book on nature conservation to discuss
laws designed to allow, or even require, the destruction of wildlife, but
such measures play an essential part in the overall legal background
for conservation, and even the law on hunting plays a part in conservation by imposing a degree of regulation as opposed to allowing a
destructive or indiscriminate free-for-all. Moreover, such measures may
be used to achieve incidental benefits for wildlife generally, *e.g.* by

---

[2] See, for example, the leader in *The Times* (January 4, 1991) and subsequent letters
(January 12, 1991) after adders were given statutory protection.

[3] A leading field guide to birds describes the marsh warbler as "Very hard to tell from
Reed and Blyth's Reed [Warblers], except by song, though adults more olive-brown
with whiter throat and pinker legs"; H. Heinzel, *et al.*, *The Birds of Britain and Europe*
(5th ed., 1995), p. 282.

acquiring but not exercising the right to hunt game, interested parties can offer some protection to animals and birds in a particular area.

The law remains fragmented, and this chapter and the next endeavour to integrate the various threads of the law, presenting a picture based on the eventual legal results, rather than the structure of the legislation. The arrangement which follows draws a general distinction between measures which have as their primary objective the conservation of wildlife, those which seek primarily to regulate the exploitation of particular species, those which restrict the means by which creatures can be killed or caught, and those which require the destruction of species. This distinction is artificial, since the law in most cases contains elements of all four functions, but it does offer a rough framework on which to structure what would otherwise be a compilation of isolated pieces of legislation in either chronological or some arbitrary order. A degree of repetition has been inevitable in the attempt to present as coherent a guide as possible to this jumble of law.

3.1.6

OVERVIEW, LEGAL FRAMEWORK AND ENFORCEMENT

Unfortunately, the law on species protection within Great Britain has become fragmented. The Wildlife and Countryside Act 1981 provided a coherent and comparatively straightforward statement of the law in this area but in addition to minor amendments over the years it has since been overtaken by two significant measures. The first of these is the Conservation (Natural Habitats, etc.) Regulations 1994,[4] introduced to ensure protection for the species and habitats singled out in the E.C. Habitats and Species Directive.[5] In relation to species protection, this creates a separate set of rules which largely overlap those contained in the 1981 Act, but with marginal differences which ensure that great care has to be taken in studying the detail of the law. The second is the Countryside and Rights of Way Act 2000, which in addition to the more substantial changes to habitat protection, has changed several features of the law on species protection in England and Wales. Broadly similar amendments can be expected in Scotland in due course,[6] but for the time being the differences between the 1981 Act as it applies in Scotland and as it applies in England and Wales add a further layer of complexity. Before looking at the specific provisions protecting wild animals, it is worth making some general comments about each element of the legislative framework.

3.2.1

---

[4] S.I. 1994 No. 2716.
[5] Directive 92/43.
[6] *The Nature of Scotland* (Scottish Executive, 2001), Annex B; see para. 3.2.18, below.

Wildlife and Countryside Act 1981

3.2.2   The Wildlife and Countryside Act 1981 remains the single most important statute relating to the protection of wildlife and creates a large
number of offences relating to the killing and taking of birds, other
animals and plants. These provisions, contained in Part I of the Act,
will be considered in detail below,[7] and in relation to species protection,
the changes introduced by the Countryside and Rights of Way Act 2000
take the form of detailed amendments to the 1981 Act. Some points of
general application can usefully be considered at this stage.

Schedules

3.2.3   The Act relies heavily on the use of Schedules to identify categories of
species which are to enjoy differing levels of protection under the Act.
In this way the needs of many species can be catered for without the
Act becoming too fragmented or even more complex. This approach
also has the advantage that whilst the basic provisions are contained in
parliamentary legislation, their detailed application is determined by the
content of the schedules, which can be more easily amended. The Minister is given wide powers to alter the various schedules, and many of
the other details of the legislation, by means of statutory instruments,[8]
in most cases subject to only the negative resolution procedure at the
parliamentary stage.[9] This enables the law to retain some flexibility and
to respond to changing pressures or scientific appreciation of the status
of particular species. There is an obligation on the conservation bodies,
acting jointly through the JNCC, to review the schedules of protected
animals and plants every five years.[10] A common feature is that
offences in relation to the species given additional protection attract a
more severe "special penalty" than if other species are involved.

Possession and Sale

3.2.4   The central provisions in Part I of the Act outlawing the killing and
taking of animals, birds and their eggs are backed up by a number of
other provisions to overcome the difficulty of proving all of the elements of such offences. When a dead eagle, an osprey's egg or an
otter's pelt is discovered, it may be impossible for anyone but the persons involved to know exactly when and in what circumstances it was
killed or taken. The difficulties of providing legal proof of deliberate

---

[7] See section 6.2, below, in relation to plants.
[8] WCA 1981, s.22.
[9] *ibid.*, s.26; express parliamentary approval is required for amendments to the provisions on the methods of killing or taking birds or animals (s.26(3)).
[10] *ibid.*, s.24(l) (amended by EPA 1995, Sched. 9 para. 11).

killing, etc., are so great that most offenders would probably escape were it not for the supporting provisions which exist. It is therefore made an offence simply to possess wild birds and animals, and strict liability is employed. The strict liability is mitigated by a number of defences, but the onus is placed on the accused to show that his conduct has been innocent, a reflection both of the fact that he alone is likely to be in a position to provide evidence on such matters, and of the policy that those who wish to keep wild animals or birds (alive or dead) or birds' eggs should do so at their own risk.[11]

Enforcement

The enforcement of the law is assisted by a range of powers granted under s.19 of the Act.[12] A police officer who reasonably suspects that a person is committing or has committed an offence under Part I of the Act and reasonably suspects that evidence of the commission of the offence may be found, is authorised without warrant to stop and search the person, and to search or examine anything which the suspect is using or has in his possession. There is also a power to seize and detain anything which may be evidence of the commission of an offence; it has been held that this power is of general application, and is not restricted to circumstances where there has been a search under the previous provisions.[13] A suspect who fails to give his name and address to the police officer's satisfaction may be arrested without warrant,[14] but these are the only circumstances in which an arrest is authorised.[15] In order to exercise these powers, a power of entry to land other than a dwelling house is given where the suspicion is that an offence is currently being committed. Warrants are available from justices of the peace[16] to authorise entry and search in relation to certain of the offences under the Act.[17] In Scotland, the standard rules on corroboration are relaxed in relation to charges of taking or destroying birds' eggs, enabling convictions to be obtained on the evidence of a single witness.[18] Further enforcement powers have been added for England

3.2.5

---

[11] See *Kirkland v. Robinson* [1987] Crim. L.R. 643.
[12] As amended by the Police and Criminal Evidence Act 1984, Sched. 6 para. 25, Sched. 7.
[13] *Whitelaw v. Haining*, 1992 S.L.T. 956.
[14] WCA 1981, s.19(1)(c) for Scotland; for England and Wales this provision has been repealed by the Police and Criminal Evidence Act 1984, Sched. 7, but the general power of arrest under s.25 of that Act is available.
[15] *Morrison v. O'Donnell*, 2001 S.C.C.R. 272, where it was held to be unlawful to detain a suspect and search him at a police station, although the power of stop and search could have been used at the place where the suspect was found.
[16] Expressly including sheriffs in Scotland.
[17] WCA 1981, s.19(3).
[18] *ibid.*, s.19A, added by Prisoners and Criminal Proceedings (Scotland) Act 1993, s.36.

and Wales by virtue of the Countryside and Rights of Way Act 2000 (see below).

3.2.6 The 1981 Act did not allow for penalties other than fines in relation to the wildlife protection offences. This led to repeated criticism, and to difficulties in the courts when dealing with those who committed serious offences but had only limited resources.[19] The Countryside and Rights of Way Act 2000 now changes this, but in relation to England and Wales only. Nonetheless, under the 1981 Act itself the sanctions on conviction are strengthened by the fact that the court can order the forfeiture of any items taken in breach of the Act or of vehicles, animals (*e.g.* dogs) or other things used to commit the crime.[20] In keeping with much modern legislation, there is an express provision that where a crime is committed by a company or other body corporate, there can also be personal liability for any director, manager or the like through whose consent, connivance or neglect the crime is committed.[21] Attempts to commit crimes under the species protection provisions of the Act are expressly declared to be crimes in themselves, and possession for the purposes of committing an offence of items capable of being used to that end is also a crime in its own right.[22]

Licences

3.2.7 A further general feature of the 1981 Act is the possibility for exemptions to be granted from many of the Act's provisions, over and above the general defences which exist. Licences which authorise conduct which would otherwise be an offence may be obtained for a variety of reasons, from Ministers or the statutory conservation bodies.[23] These licences may be conditional, may be general or specific, may be personal or in favour of a class of people and will be of fixed duration.[24]

---

[19] *Seiga v. Walkingshaw*, 1994 S.C.C.R. 146; *Forsyth v. Cardle*, 1994 S.C.C.R. 769.

[20] WCA 1981, s.21(6).

[21] WCA 1981, s.69; in the 1994 Regulations, the equivalent provisions is expressly extended to apply to partnerships in Scotland with personal liability for any partner who is responsible in this way (CNHR 1994, reg. 106(2)).

[22] WCA 1981, s.18.

[23] WCA 1981, s.16. Such licences clearly provide a defence to a charge under the 1981 Act, but where more than one person has an interest in the land concerned, there is scope for argument over the precise nature of the rights conferred by them. In *Re Wildfowl Trust (Holdings) Ltd* (unreported, Outer House January 19, 1994) the landlord and tenant disputed whether a licence issued to the tenant to kill geese fell within the terms of the lease creating an exception for "conjunct rights conferred upon the tenant by statute" and therefore allowed the tenant to shoot the geese despite the landlords' reservation of exclusive hunting rights; the issue was never authoritatively resolved and the decision on whether to grant an interim interdict was resolved on the balance of convenience in favour of allowing the tenant to shoot.

[24] *ibid.*, s.16(5); licences authorising the killing of birds or animals must specify the area and method of killing and have a maximum validity of two years (s.16(6)).

A table of which authorities can grant a licence and for what purposes appears as Appendix C below.[25] The possibility of obtaining a licence must always be borne in mind when the prohibitions in the Act are being considered, and the scope and availability of licences can considerably alter the effect of the law in practice.[26] General licences are issued separately for England, Scotland and Wales, in most cases to the same effect, but there are many differences of detail which may be significant. Since the licences are of limited duration[27] and not published in any standard form, finding out exactly what one is permitted to do in any part of the country at any particular time is far from as straightforward as it should be.[28] The licences are subject to conditions and in some cases to recording and reporting requirements.

"Authorised persons"

One definition of general application can also be conveniently discussed here. In several places the Act declares that it is permissible for an "authorised person" to do acts which are otherwise criminal. For these purposes an authorised person is defined as: the owner or occupier of the land where the action takes place or someone authorised by him, a person authorised in writing by the local authority for the area,[29] or a person authorised in writing by the Environment Agency, a water undertaker or a sewerage undertaker. In relation to birds, authorisation in writing can also be provided by the conservation bodies, a district salmon fishery board in Scotland or a local fisheries committee in England and Wales.[30] Many of the general licences issued under the Act also permit "authorised persons" to do particular things, but the licences give their own, sometimes much narrower, definitions of who is an "authorised person" for the purposes of the particular licence.

3.2.8

Taking

A final point to mention in passing is that although in some contexts references to the taking of animals includes references to their taking by killing (especially in the context of the taking of game), in the legal

3.2.9

---

[25] The statutory conservation bodies in their "Facts and Figures" publications give details of the licences granted for the purposes within their jurisdiction (see Appendix C), *e.g.* in 2000–01, SNH issued a total of 667 and English Nature 1,736 licences under the 1981 Act, the Conservation (Natural Habitats, etc.) Regulations 1994 and the Protection of Badgers Act 1992.

[26] *e.g.*, in relation to pest species of birds; see paras 3.3.8–3.3.9, below.

[27] The licence references given below are to those in force in December 2001, but many expired and were due to be replaced early in 2002.

[28] Although the staff in the departments involved are very helpful, there is not even a system of collating and numbering all the different general licences.

[29] Where there are not unitary authorities, both authorities have this power.

[30] WCA 1981, s.27 (amended by the Water Act 1989, Sched. 25, para. 66, Sched. 27; Local Government Act 1985, Sched. 17; EPA 1990, Sched. 9, para. 11.).

context "taking"appears to mean only their capture.[31] This contrasts
with the position in the U.S.A. where the legislation protecting endangered species prohibits their "taking" and gives this term the wide
definition of "harass, harm, pursue, hunt, shoot, wound, kill, trap, capture or collect,"[32] which has been interpreted as extending to cover
"significant habitat modification or degradation where it actually kills
or injures wildlife by significantly impairing essential behavioral patterns, including breeding, feeding or sheltering".[33] Capturing animals
(whether to kill them or to keep them) in theory poses different problems from direct killing in terms of legal control, but since in almost
all cases the taking of animals is regulated along with their killing, it
is possible to deal with both together.

Conservation (Natural Habitats, etc.) Regulations 1994

3.2.10   The simplicity of having virtually all of the key laws on species protection in one place was lost when the decision was taken to implement
the Habitats and Species Directive by means of separate legislation, as
opposed to integrating its provisions with those of the 1981 Act. This
was very much in keeping with the policy at the time of adopting the
"copy-out" approach to implementing E.C. Directives, simply trans-
posing their provisions more or less directly into United Kingdom law
as opposed to ensuring that the terms of the Directive were met by
amending or adding to existing provisions.[34] This approach has the
advantage of simplicity for the legislator, as well as guaranteeing that
there has been complete legal implementation of the measure in a way
that is transparent to the Brussels authorities, without argument over
whether the adjustments to existing law do in fact fully implement all
the provisions of the Directive. On the other hand, for the user of the
law, the result is complexity and confusion, as two largely overlapping
sets of law have to be examined, taking careful note of where there are
differences in the details of the law, and even worse, trying to work
out whether minor differences in wording actually signify a difference
in meaning.

3.2.11   The species protection measures in the Directive are very similar to
those already in the 1981 Act, prohibiting the deliberate killing or
taking of protected species, disturbance to breeding and resting sites,

---

[31] The legislation consistently uses separate words for killing and taking; *cf. Wells v.
Hardy* [1964] 2 Q.B. 447, catching and returning fish is not "taking" for the Larceny
Act 1861.

[32] Endangered Species Act 1973 (U.S.A.), s.3.

[33] Interior Department regulations approved by the Supreme Court in *Babbitt v. Sweet
Home Chapter of Communities for a Great Oregon*, 515 U.S. 687 (1995).

[34] L.Ramsey, "Copy Out Technique: More of a 'Cop Out' than a Solution?" (1996) 17
Stat. L.R. 218.

possession or sale of the creatures or derivatives and restrictions on the methods of killing or taking where such is permissible at all. The result is that for some species there are two overlapping layers of law to be considered: the provisions in the 1981 Act and the further provisions in the 1994 Regulations. It may, of course, also be possible to have direct recourse to the Directive itself if the Act and Regulations do not in fact ensure that its provisions are properly reflected in the law.[35]

The provisions in the Regulations, discussed more fully below, larg- **3.2.12** ely repeat those in the Act, but there are some differences in the scope of the protection, *e.g.* extending the offence of destroying breeding sites to cover non-intentional activity, some differences in the scope of permissible exceptions and some places where there are differences in phrasing which probably do not represent differences in substance, *e.g.* is "deliberately" killing an animal (the offence under the Regulations) any different from "intentionally" doing so (the offence under the Act)? The result is to add complexity to the law and to exaggerate the differences between the protection measures for different categories of species. It is therefore particularly important to check the status of a species on the various statutory lists so that the laws applying to it can be identified.

The Regulations also have their own provisions on attempts, pos- **3.2.13** sessing items with intent to commit crimes, corporate liability, forfeit- ure and powers of search and seizure.[36]

Countryside and Rights of Way Act 2000

After much criticism, from many sources, of weaknesses in the 1981 **3.2.14** Act, and of government for not doing anything to overcome these, the Countryside and Rights of Way Act 2000 brought about a number of changes to the provisions in the Wildlife and Countryside Act.[37] The most significant of these relate to the rules on Sites of Special Scientific Interest, but a number of important amendments have been made to the species protection provisions as well. The changes here apply only in England and Wales, but the Scottish Executive has proposed broadly parallel amendments for Scotland.[38]

The changes achieve three main things. First, they extend the crimes **3.2.15** of disturbing certain birds and animals to cover actions taken recklessly as well as intentionally.[39] Secondly, they increase the maximum penalty

---

[35] See para. 2.9.6, above, on the direct effect of E.C. Directives.
[36] CNHR 1994, regs 100–101, 103, 106.
[37] J. Lowther, "Wildlife Offences with Added Bite: Evaluating Recent Amendments to the Wildlife and Countryside Act 1981" (2001) 13 E.L.M. 249.
[38] *The Nature of Scotland: A Policy Statement* (Scottish Executive, 2001).
[39] WCA 1981, ss.1(5), 9(4), amended by CRWA 2000, Sched. 12, paras 1, 5; see paras 3.3.5, 3.4.2, below.

for offences under Part I of the 1981 Act to six months' imprisonment.[40] This change creates the possibility of a custodial sentence for the first time, and also does away with the distinction between offences in the 1981 Act, under which a "special penalty" in the form of a higher fine could be imposed for certain offences. The Act also enables custodial sentences to be imposed[41] under regulations made to implement the Habitats and Species Directive and E.C. measures on trade on endangered species.[42]

3.2.16   Thirdly, the 2000 Act enables the Secretary of State to designate individuals as "wildlife inspectors" by means of written authorisation and grants these inspectors a range of powers.[43] Inspectors are authorised to enter and inspect premises in relation to offences involving the selling of protected species, compliance with the provisions on keeping wild birds, offences in relation to the introduction of new species and to verify statements made in relation to any relevant registration or licence.[44] Inspectors must also be allowed to inspect any specimen, including live wild birds or other animals, plants and derivatives from plants, birds and animals. Obstructing or impersonating an inspector is a crime, as is failing to give assistance reasonably requested from the person in possession or control of a live bird or animal for the purpose of examining the creature. These provisions supersede the specific powers of entry, etc. conferred by individual provisions of the 1981.[45] The power for magistrates to issue warrants to search premises is extended to apply to all the wildlife crime offences under Part I of the 1981 Act.[46]

3.2.17   The powers of inspectors and police officers extend to requiring the taking of samples of blood or tissue in order to determine the identity or ancestry of a sample, an essential prerequisite of applying the expanding range of DNA and other techniques that enable the origins of live or dead animals or plants creatures to be traced.[47] Samples can

---

[40] WCA 1981, s.21 as amended by CRWA 2000, Sched. 12, para. 10. The time limit for summary prosecution is also altered (*ibid.*, s.20 as amended by *ibid.*, para. 9).

[41] CRWA 2000, s.81(2); regulations made under the European Communities Act 1972 are not normally permitted to provide for any penalty greater than fines of a certain level in relation to offences created by the regulations (European Communities Act 1972, Sched. 2, para. 1(1)(d)).

[42] Primarily Regulation (E.C.) 338/97; see section 7.4, below.

[43] WCA 1981, ss.19ZA and 19ZB, inserted by CRWA 2000, Sched. 12 para. 8.

[44] Respectively, offences under ss.6, 9(5) and 13(2), offences under s.7, offences under s.14 and registration under s.7(1) and certain licences under s.16, all of WCA 1981; WCA 1981, s.19ZA(3) and (9). The powers to enter dwellings is more restricted; *ibid.*, s.19ZA(4).

[45] CRWA 2000 Sched. 16 Part IV, repealing WCA 1981 ss.6(9) and (10), 7(6) and (7), 14 (5) and (6).

[46] WCA 1981, s.19(3) as amended by CRWA 2000, Sched. 9 para. 7.

[47] WCA 1981, s.19ZB.

be taken from live birds, animals or plants only where the person concerned is satisfied on reasonable grounds that no lasting harm will be done by taking the sample. Samples from live birds or animals may be taken only by a veterinary surgeon, and the person having control of a live creature must give such assistance as is reasonably required to enable a sample to be taken. The powers of entry granted to police officers and inspectors are extended to enable them to be accompanied by a vet for the purpose of taking a sample. Again, obstruction and refusing reasonable assistance are offences.

Although a Bill has been promised "at an early opportunity",[48] it **3.2.18** remains to be seen whether, when and in what form the Scottish Parliament enacts legislation introducing similar changes in Scotland. It is to be hoped that where exactly the same result is desired, the same wording is used in order to avoid yet further complexity for the users of the law.

Birds and Eggs

The main legislation concerning birds is to be found in Part I of the **3.3.1** Wildlife and Countryside Act 1981 which replaced the previous legislation protecting birds. The starting point for the law is the simple statement in section 1(1) that it is an offence for any person intentionally to kill, injure or take any wild bird. However, in order to meet the requirements of different species, birds are divided into various categories: some are covered simply by the general law, some given added protection, others are given protection during a close season only and pest species are in practice deprived of the general protection granted to others. In all cases it must be remembered that licences may be granted allowing exemptions from the various prohibitions in the 1981 Act, but the methods by which birds can be killed or taken are always controlled.[49] Legal protection for birds is also granted by the provisions of the European Community's Birds Directive, which requires Member States to establish a general system of protection for all species naturally occurring in the wild state, seeking to maintain their populations at (or restore them to) a level corresponding to ecological, scientific and cultural requirements, taking account of economic and recreational requirements.[50] The Birds Directive is discussed further in Chapter 7. Separate rules apply to game birds.[51]

---

[48] In a written answer by the First Minister to the Scottish Parliament; SP WA 1 November, 2001, p. 383.

[49] See paras 4.4.15–4.4.17, below.

[50] Directive 79/409, arts 1, 5; see section 7.4, below. See Addendum, above.

[51] See section 4.2, below.

The general position

3.3.2   It is an offence for any person intentionally to do any of the following:
to kill, injure or take any wild bird, to take, damage or destroy the nest
of a wild bird while it is in use or being built, or to take or destroy the
egg of any wild bird.[52] A wild bird is defined as being any bird ordinarily resident in, or a visitor to, Great Britain in a wild state, other than
poultry or game birds, and anything calculated to prevent the hatching
of an egg is included within the meaning of destroying eggs.[53] The
offence does not apply to birds shown to have been bred in captivity.[54]
It is not altogether clear whether the intention applies only to the killing, etc. or extends to require knowledge that the bird was "wild" for
the purposes of the Act. In relation to the taking or destruction of eggs,
the law of corroboration is relaxed in Scotland so that a person may be
convicted on the evidence of one witness.[55]

3.3.3   A number of defences are provided to limit the scope of this general
prohibition. A person's taking of disabled birds in order to tend and
release them is excluded, as is the mercy killing of seriously disabled
birds with no reasonable chance of recovery, provided in both cases
that the original injury was not the result of that person's unlawful
act.[56] A more general defence excludes acts which are the incidental
result of a lawful operation and could not reasonably have been
avoided, *e.g.* the destruction of nests when felling woodland.[57] In each
of these cases the onus is on the accused to show that they fall within
the terms of the defence. Further allowances are made for authorised
persons.[58] They are allowed a defence if they can show that their action
was necessary for the purpose of preserving public health, public safety
or air safety, for preventing the spread of disease, or for preventing
serious damage to livestock, crops, fruit, growing timber or fisheries.[59]
However, this defence is only available where the authorised person
can show that there is no other satisfactory solution, and provided that
the Minister is informed and that it was not apparent in advance that
the action was necessary, so as to allow for a licence to be sought.[60] A
more specific exemption allows the gathering for human consumption
of gannets on Sula Sgeir, gull's eggs, and (before April 15th each year)

---

[52] WCA 1981, s.1(1).
[53] *ibid.*, s.27.
[54] *ibid.*, s.1(6).
[55] *ibid.*, s.19A (added by Prisoners and Criminal Proceedings (Scotland) Act 1993, s.36).
[56] *ibid.*, s.4(2)(a), (b).
[57] *ibid.*, s.4(2)(c).
[58] See para. 3.2.8, above.
[59] WCA 1981, s.4(3).
[60] *ibid.*, s.4(4)–(6), added by Wildlife and Countryside Act 1981 (Amendment) Regulations 1995 (S.I. 1995 No. 2825), reg. 2.

lapwings' eggs, provided that this is done in accordance with a licence from the Minister.[61]

Further exceptions are created by the general licences issued by Ministers,[62] *e.g.* permission to remove abandoned eggs from nest boxes between 1st August and 31st January, provided that the eggs are not kept,[63] and to take mallard eggs before 31st March for incubation to assist birds unlikely to withstand adverse weather conditions,[64] while individual licences can be issued to deal with particular situations. No offence is committed[65] if the action in question is required by ministers in the exercise of their powers relating to agricultural pest control,[66] or is done under the Animal Health Act 1981 or an order made under it.[67] As noted above, the definition of "wild bird" means that poultry (domestic fowls, geese, ducks, guinea fowls, pigeons, quails and turkeys) and game birds (pheasant, partridge, grouse (moor game), black (heath) game and ptarmigan) fall outside the range of this protection,[68] as do birds shown to have been bred in captivity.[69]

3.3.4

Protected birds

A number of birds listed in Schedule 1 to the 1981 Act enjoy enhanced protection. Almost 100 species are listed.[70] The general position is modified in three ways in relation to such birds. Firstly, in addition to the offences mentioned above, it is an offence intentionally to disturb any wild bird included in Schedule 1 whilst it is building a nest or is at or near its nest containing eggs or young, or intentionally to disturb the dependent young of such a bird.[71] In England and Wales this provision now extends to reckless as well as intentional conduct.[72] Over-

3.3.5

---

[61] *ibid.*, s.16(2); licences were issued during 2001 to sell for human consumption the eggs of greater and lesser black-backed and herring gulls (WLF100082, SEGEN/11, WLF 015—the references are to the licences for England, Scotland and Wales respectively, in force at the end of 2001).

[62] See para. 3.2.7, above.

[63] Licences WLF100068, SEGEN15, and WLF 006.

[64] Licences WLF100069, SEGEN16 and WLF 014.

[65] WCA 1981, s.4(1).

[66] Agriculture Act 1947, s.98; Agriculture (Scotland) Act 1948, s.39; see para. 4.5.2, below.

[67] See para. 4.5.11, below.

[68] WCA 1981, s.27.

[69] *ibid.*, s.1(6).

[70] See Appendix A.

[71] WCA 1981, s.1(5).

[72] *ibid.*, as amended by CRWA 2000, Sched. 12, para. 1. In English criminal law there are two separate definitions of "reckless", a subjective one based on the accused being aware of the possible harmful consequences of their conduct but carrying on regardless, and an objective one, extending to situations where the accused press on in the face of a risk of harm obvious to a reasonable person, regardless of whether they have in fact appreciated that risk. The objective definition is arguably the more likely one

zealous photographers and birdwatchers may be in danger of falling foul of this provision. Secondly, some of the defences noted above do not apply in relation to Schedule 1 birds. The exemption for acts done under the Animal Health Act 1981 is restricted to acts done in pursuance of orders made under sections 21 and 22 of that Act (wildlife destruction orders),[73] and none of the further defences available to authorised persons apply.[74] In the case of three species of bird which are listed in Schedule 1 but may be hunted,[75] the special rules apply only during the close season.[76] The birds concerned are goldeneye, pintail, and (in parts of northwest Scotland only) greylag geese. Thirdly, in Scotland anyone convicted of offences in relation to these birds is liable to a significantly increased fine as a "special penalty".[77]

3.3.6 Birds listed in Annex I of the Birds Directive[78] are also entitled to "special conservation measures concerning their habitat", primarily the designation and care of Special Protection Areas, and these are discussed with other habitat protection measures in Chapter 5. The interaction of domestic and E.C. law may be significant, as in *RSPB v. Secretary of State for Scotland*,[79] where it was accepted that the fairly broad power under the Wildlife and Countryside Act 1981 to grant licences to kill wild geese was in law constrained by the narrower tests set in the Birds Directive.

Birds which may be hunted

3.3.7 Game birds are excluded from the scope of most of the 1981 Act and the general position described above is modified in order to allow the hunting of a number of other species of birds, listed in Part I of Schedule 2 to the Act.[80] The Birds Directive similarly permits the hunting of some species, listed in Annex II.[81] No offence is committed by killing or taking such birds outside the close season, or by injuring them in

---

to apply here. See generally J. Smith, *Smith and Hogan—Criminal Law* (10th ed., 2002) pp. 77–84.

[73] *ibid.*, s.4(1); see para. 4.5.11, below.

[74] *ibid.*, s.4(3).

[75] *ibid.*, Sched. 1, Pt II; see Appendix A.

[76] *ibid.*, s.1(7); the close season is February 21–August 31 for areas below high-water mark, February 1–August 31 for other areas (*ibid.*, s.2(4)); see Appendix B.

[77] *ibid.*, s.1(4); as noted above, these "special penalties" have been overtaken in England and Wales by the introduction of custodial sentences under CRWA 2000 (see para. 3.2.15, above).

[78] Directive 79/409.

[79] 2000 S.L.T. 22 (O.H.) and 1272; see para. 3.3.12, below.

[80] See Appendix A; the three species listed in Part II of Schedule 1 and thereby enjoying enhanced protection during the close season also appear in Part I of Schedule 2.

[81] Birds Directive, art. 7.

the attempt to kill them,[82] although certain methods are prohibited in relation to all birds,[83] and it remains an offence to injure such a bird deliberately, except in the course of trying to kill it. The various close seasons are defined in the Act[84] and hunting is not permitted in Scotland on Sundays or on Christmas Day, nor on Sundays in any area of England and Wales prescribed by the Minister.[85] The Minister has the power to make orders varying the close seasons.[86] After consulting a representative of shooting interests he may also make orders offering to any birds listed in Part II of Schedule 1 or Part I of Schedule 2 special protection for a period of up to 14 days at a time. These orders, intended for periods of exceptionally severe weather or other temporary crises for the birds, operate so as to apply the rules for the close season during the period of special protection, and may affect all or only part of the country.[87] In England and Wales, some of these birds enjoy further protection in that it is an offence for anyone to take or destroy their eggs unless authorised by the person with the right to kill game on the land in question.[88]

Pests and Licences

The statutory provisions originally contained a considerable relaxation of the general protection for wild birds to allow authorised persons to deal with birds widely regarded as pests. The birds were listed in Part II of Schedule 2 and no offence was committed by an authorised person who killed or took such a bird, destroyed, damaged or took its nest or destroyed or took its eggs.[89] However this legislative exception for pest species was considered to fall foul of the terms of the Birds Directive[90] which imposes a prohibition on the killing and taking of all wild birds[91] and permits derogations only where certain criteria are met.[92] Accordingly, all of the species have now been removed from Part II of Schedule 2 and in its place a number of licences have been issued by the Minister under s.16 of the 1981 Act.[93]

3.3.8

---

[82] WCA 1981, s.2(1); see Appendix B for a table of close seasons for the birds covered here and for game birds.
[83] See paras 4.4.15–4.4.17, below.
[84] WCA 1981, s.2(4).
[85] *ibid.*, s.2(3). The Wild Birds (Sundays) Orders made under s.2 of the Protection of Birds Act 1954 presumably continue in effect in prescribing such areas; S.I.s 1955 No. 1286, 1956 No. 1310, 1957 No. 429, 1963 No. 1700.
[86] *ibid.*, s.2(5).
[87] *ibid.*, s.2(6).
[88] Game Act 1831, s.24, applying to game and "any swan, wild duck, teal and widgeon."
[89] WCA 1981, s.2(2).
[90] See para. 7.4.7, below.
[91] Directive 79/409, art. 5.
[92] *ibid.*, art. 9.
[93] See para. 3.2.7, above.

3.3.9   The general licences permit authorised persons to kill or take the listed species[94] or their eggs for a variety of purposes. Even if this limitation does not appear on the face of the licence, the licences cover only action taken for one of the specified statutory purposes and do not permit the general killing of the pest species.[95] Separate licences cover firstly the prevention of the spread of disease, the prevention of serious damage to livestock, foodstuffs, crops, vegetables, fruit, growing timber, fisheries and inland water, secondly the conservation of wild birds,[96] secondly the preservation of public health, public safety or air safety and the protection of any collection of wild birds,[97] and thirdly action for the purpose of conserving wild birds.[98] The licences are annual but apply to all authorised persons as defined in the licences,[99] so that there is no need for individual applications to be made. The change of form, from statutory exception to general licences, does not have any real impact on the practical effect of the law, but makes it even harder for anyone to find out exactly what they are or are not permitted to do (and therefore whether or not they are committing a crime), and removes the details of the law from any direct parliamentary scrutiny.

3.3.10   Other licences cover more specific situations, *e.g.* authorising aerodrome managers to take action against black-headed and common gulls and lapwings, and in certain places against oystercatchers, greylag geese and curlews.[1] Individual licences may be granted in relation to more localised problems, *e.g.* in relation to geese damaging agricultural crops[2] or cormorants damaging fisheries.[3]

3.3.11   Under the Birds Directive these exceptions from the general protection for birds are permitted only for certain purposes and if certain criteria are met. The purposes are in the interests of public health and safety, including air safety, to prevent serious damage to crops, livestock, forests, and water, to protect flora and fauna, for research and repopulation and to permit the limited keeping and "other judicious use" of small numbers of birds.[4] The grounds for granting licences

---

[94] The species covered are; crow, great black-backed gull, lesser black-backed gull, herring gull, jackdaw, jay, magpie, feral pigeon, rook, collared dove, house sparrow, starling, woodpigeon. The last four species are not covered by the licences authorising action for the conservation of other species of bird.

[95] *RSPCA v. Cundey* (unreported, High Court (Admin.) October 22, 2001).

[96] The general licence in England and Wales has no specific reference number; in Scotland it is licence PS/2001.

[97] Licences WLF100088, SEGEN/10 and WLF 008.

[98] Licences WLF100087, SEGEN/09 and WLF 020.

[99] See para. 3.2.8, above.

[1] Licences WLF100085, SEGEN/13 and WLF 017.

[2] As in *RSPB v. Secretary of State for Scotland*, 2000 S.L.T. 1272; see below.

[3] According to press reports citing RSPB Scotland, during 1999 in Scotland 22 licences to kill robins were issued.

[4] Directive 79/409, art. 9(1).

under section 16 of the 1981 Act largely match these, but it can be argued that the general defence for actions which are the incidental results of lawful actions permits harm to birds in too wide a range of circumstances. It is also specified in the Directive that there should be no other satisfactory solution before a derogation is made. In *RSPB v. Secretary of State for Scotland*[5] it was argued that the provision of compensation to farmers for damage done to their crops by geese provided an alternative to allowing some geese to be shot, but it was held that the alternatives to be considered must be ones that actually prevent the harm arising.[6]

In relation to protected species within Special Protection Areas, the basis for derogation is even more restricted in that there is an obligation to prevent any disturbances affecting the birds, so far as these are significant having regard to the objectives of the relevant provision.[7] The shooting of geese under the licence granted in *RSPB v. Secretary of State for Scotland*[8] clearly would be a disturbance, and it was held that the "significance" had to determined looking at the impact both locally and on the wider position of the species, bearing in mind the objectives of the relevant article, as amended by the Habitats and Species Directive. **3.3.12**

Possession

In view of the difficulty of proving that someone has intentionally killed a wild bird, and in order to suppress the demand for birds and their eggs, the 1981 Act renders their possession unlawful. It is a criminal offence to possess any live or dead wild bird or anything derived from one, or to possess the egg of any wild bird or part of an egg.[9] Unlike the earlier legislation,[10] the offences are not limited to birds which have been recently killed or taken, and a stuffed and mounted bird continues to be a "dead wild bird" the possession of which may be a criminal offence.[11] Subject to the exceptions noted below, these are offences of strict liability, as decided in *Kirkland v. Robinson*.[12] In deciding that the law did impose strict liability the court was influenced by the contrast with the other offences created by the same section, *e.g.* killing **3.3.13**

---

[5] 2000 S.L.T. 22 (O.H.); this point was not argued in the Inner House (2000 S.L.T. 1272).
[6] See also *Ligue Royale Belge pour la Protection des Oiseaux ASBL v. Région Wallonne* (C–10/96) [1996] I–E.C.R. 6775.
[7] See para. 7.4.24, below.
[8] Above.
[9] WCA 1981, s.1(2).
[10] Protection of Birds Act 1954, s.1.
[11] *Robinson v. Everett* [1988] Crim. L.R. 699.
[12] [1987] Crim. L.R. 643.

birds, which expressly require intentional conduct, by the presence of statutory defences to mitigate the potential harshness of strict liability, and by the importance of environmental protection. It was right that those who chose to possess wild birds should do so at their own risk.

3.3.14   The offence of possession is widely drawn, rendering it unlawful for any persons to have in their possession or control any live or dead wild bird, any part of one, anything derived from such a bird or any egg (whole or part) of a wild bird.[13] Where the bird is protected under Schedule 1 to the Act, the penalties for offenders in Scotland are increased.[14] Those in possession of the bird or egg can establish a defence if they can show that the bird or egg had not been killed or taken (in other words had come under their control by natural means), or had been killed or taken otherwise than in contravention of the 1981 Act or its predecessors[15] (in other words was the product of lawful activity or had been taken before 1954). A defence is also available if it can be shown that the bird or egg had at some stage been sold otherwise than in contravention of the 1981 Act or its predecessors.[16] The offences do not apply in relation to any bird shown to have been bred in captivity.[17]

Keeping

3.3.15   The keeping of certain live wild birds is covered by the general possession offence described above, but a number of other provisions exist to regulate the keeping of birds, and the conditions in which they are kept. In practice the application of these rules is significantly affected by a number of general licences relating to the keeping of birds issued by the Minister under the powers in section 16 of the Act. In addition to the licences on the keeping of certain species, general licences authorise veterinary surgeons and certain others to keep wild birds for treatment and rehabilitation.[18] For many species a person with a bird in his possession or control must ensure that the bird is registered and ringed or marked in accordance with regulations made by the Minister.[19] The

---

[13] WCA 1981, s.1(2); the reference to derivatives has led to general licences being issued in England and Wales authorising the retention of blood and tissue samples obtained as part of forensic investigations into offences under the Act (WLF 100104 and WLF 024).

[14] *ibid.*, s.1(4); see note 47 on p. 112, above.

[15] Protection of Birds Acts 1954–1967.

[16] WCA 1981, s.1(3).

[17] *ibid.*, s.1(6).

[18] Licences WLF 100075, WLF 10099, SEGEN 19 and WLF 021 and WLF 025. Licences in England and Wales also permit the keeping of birds by some official bodies without registration, pending legal proceedings (WLF 100077 and WLF 003).

[19] WCA 1981, s.7(1); Wildlife and Countryside (Registration and Ringing of Certain Captive Birds) Regulations 1982 (S.I. 1982 No. 1221) (amended by Wildlife and Countryside (Registration and Ringing of Certain Captive Birds, (Amendment) Regu-

species to which this provision may apply are listed in Schedule 4 to
the 1981 Act.[20]

In order to ensure proper compliance with these rules, those **3.3.16**
authorised by the Minister enjoy powers of entry to inspect premises
where birds covered by Schedule 4 are being kept, and obstruction of
such inspectors is an offence.[21] The law here is severe on persistent
offenders. Regardless of whether the bird is registered and ringed, it is
an offence for a bird listed in Schedule 4 to be kept by any person who
has been convicted within the last five years of certain offences (*e.g.*
in relation to the birds given extra protection under Schedule 1),[22] or
within the last three years of an offence relating to the protection of
birds or other animals or their ill-treatment.[23] It is also an offence for
anybody knowingly to dispose or offer to dispose of a Schedule 4 bird
to anyone falling within these categories of past offenders.[24]

It is an offence to cause or permit certain birds to be shown for the **3.3.17**
purposes of competitions or at premises where a competition is taking
place.[25] This prohibition applies to any live wild bird, or bird which
has a wild bird as a parent, other than the species listed in Part I of
Schedule 3 and ringed or marked in accordance with regulations made
by the Minister.[26] Licences cover the showing of certain captive-bred
wild birds.[27]

In order to prevent unnecessary suffering, the general rule is laid **3.3.18**
down that if birds are kept it must be in a cage or other receptacle
which is large enough to allow the bird to stretch its wings freely.
Failure to comply with this rule is an offence attracting the special
penalty in Scotland.[28] This rule applies to all birds, not just wild birds,
with the exceptions of poultry, birds in the course of conveyance, birds

---

lations 1991 and 1994, S.I.s 1991 No. 478, 1994 No. 1151)). Provision for a fee to be
charged for registration was added by the Birds (Registration Charges) Act 1997.

[20] See Appendix A. Further information is available at www.defra.gov.uk/wildlife–
countryside/citesbird/birdreg/index.htm.

[21] WCA 1981, s.7(6), (7); in England and Wales now replaced by the wider powers of
wildlife inspectors (see para. 3.2. 16–3.2.17, above).

[22] These were originally, and in Scotland still are, defined as those attracting the "special
penalty"; in England and Wales there is now a list of the relevant offences, including
those affecting birds included in Sched.1 and those concerning the methods for taking
and conditions for keeping wild birds (WCA 1981, s.7(3A), as inserted by CRWA
2000, Sched. 12, para. 4).

[23] WCA 1981, s.7(3); spent convictions under the Rehabilitation of Offenders Act 1974
are to disregarded (*ibid.*, s.7(5)).

[24] *ibid.*, s.7(4).

[25] *ibid.*, s.6(3).

[26] *ibid.*, s.6(5); Wildlife and Countryside (Ringing of Certain Birds) Regulations 1982,
S.I. 1982 No. 1220. In Scotland the "special penalty" applies if the offence is committed in relation to a Schedule 1 bird (WCA 1981, s.64).

[27] *e.g.* WLF 100094, SEGEN 03 and WLF 001.

[28] WCA 1981, s.8(1).

undergoing examination or treatment by a veterinary practitioner, and birds being shown at a public exhibition or competition provided that the bird is not confined in the smaller cage for more than 72 hours.[29] It is also a crime (with the special penalty) for anyone to promote, take part in or organise an event in which captive birds are liberated for the purpose of being shot immediately after they have been freed.[30] The owners and occupiers of land used for this purpose are likewise liable.

Sale

3.3.19   The sale of birds and their eggs is also strictly controlled. The provisions on sale are expressed so as to cover not merely the sale of birds or eggs, a requirement which may be difficult to prove and prevent early intervention by the authorities, but also offering or exposing for sale, possessing or transporting for the purpose of sale, and publishing or causing to be published an advertisement likely to be understood as meaning that a person does or intends to buy or sell.[31] In this way all activities relating to a sale should be covered and there should be little if any room for defences based on technicalities or a failure to prove that a formal legal sale has taken place.

3.3.20   There is a complete prohibition on the sale of the eggs of wild birds or of live wild birds other than those listed in Part I of Schedule 3,[32] and only then provided that they have been bred in captivity and are ringed or marked in accordance with regulations made by the Minister.[33] For dead wild birds and things derived from them, the prohibition extends to all species apart from those listed in Parts II and III of Schedule 3. For dead birds listed in Part III of the Schedule sale is permitted only during the shooting season, from September 1–February 28.[34] The 1981 Act contained a scheme limiting sales to registered dealers,[35] but this remains in operation only in Scotland.[36] Registration for the purposes of selling dead birds is not available to anyone within five years of being convicted of an offence under Part I of the 1981

---

[29] *ibid.*, s.8(2).

[30] *ibid.*, s.8(3).

[31] *ibid.*, s.6(1), (2).

[32] *ibid.*, s.6(1); see Appendix A. Again the Birds Directive (art. 6) similarly allows the sale of some species, listed in Annex III.

[33] *ibid.*, s.6(5); Wildlife and Countryside (Ringing of Certain Birds) Regulations 1982 (S.I. 1982 No. 1220).

[34] *ibid.*, s.6(6).

[35] *ibid.*, s.6(2); Wildlife and Countryside (Registration to Sell, etc., Certain Dead Wild Birds) Regulations 1982, (S.I. 1982 No. 1219) (amended by Wildlife and Countryside (Registration to Sell, etc., Certain Dead Wild Birds) (Amendment) Regulations 1991 (S.I. 1991 No. 479)). A fee may be charged for registration under the Birds (Registration Charges) Act 1997.

[36] Relevant provisions repealed for England and Wales by CRWA 2000, Sched. 16.

Act attracting the special penalty, or within three years of a conviction for an offence concerning the protection or ill-treatment of birds or other animals.[37] The Minister may authorise people to enter and inspect premises where a registered person keeps wild birds, and obstruction of such inspectors is an offence.[38] Again, the application of these rules in practice is affected by a number of general licences issued under section 16 of the Act.[39] The sale of game birds is subject to separate licensing requirements.[40]

ANIMALS

The law relating to other animals is more fragmented than that concerned with birds. In addition to the provisions of the Wildlife and Countryside Act 1981, with its recent amendments for England and Wales, there are a number of European protected species qualifying for protection under the Conservation (Natural Habitats, etc.) Regulations 1994. Older legislation dealing with pests and game must also be considered, and there are a sizeable number of provisions which relate to individual species, *e.g.* the Protection of Badgers Act 1992. The law on animals generally is blighted by the proliferation of different legislative definitions of "animal", sometimes referring to domestic animals only and frequently defying any scientific classification. In every case where a statute refers to "animals" it is wise to check that the animal which one has in mind is in the particular circumstances an animal for the purposes of the provision in question.   **3.4.1**

Protected animals

Under the Wildlife and Countryside Act 1981, a number of animals are given protection similar to that given to those birds listed in Schedule 1 to the Act. The protected animals are listed in Schedule 5[41] and it is an offence for any person intentionally to kill, injure or take a wild animal of those species.[42] It is an offence to have in one's possession or control any such animal, whether alive or dead, or anything derived   **3.4.2**

---

[37] *ibid.*, s.6(8); spent convictions under the Rehabilitation of Offenders Act 1974 are to be disregarded.

[38] *ibid.*, s.6(9), (10); in England and Wales now replaced by the wider powers of wildlife inspectors (see para.3.2.16, above).

[39] *e.g.* authorising the sale of certain gulls' eggs for human consumption (WLF 100082, SEGEN 11 and WLF 015).

[40] See para. 4.2.9, below.

[41] See Appendix A.

[42] WCA 1981, s.9(1).

from one.[43] As is the case with birds, it is a defence to show that the animal was not killed or taken, or was not killed or taken in contravention of the 1981 Act or its predecessor (the Conservation of Wild Creatures and Wild Plants Act 1975) or had been sold without contravening those provisions.[44] It is a further offence for anyone intentionally to damage, destroy or obstruct access to any place a wild animal included in Schedule 5 uses for shelter or protection, or intentionally to disturb an animal while using such a place; in England and Wales, this has been extended to include those who act recklessly.[45] However this latter offence does not apply to anything done within a dwelling-house, where it is permissible to evict or disturb protected animals, with the exception of bats which enjoy the benefits of special protection in this regard.[46] The sale, offer for sale, etc., or advertising of protected animals is also prohibited.[47] In any proceedings a particular animal is generally presumed to be wild unless the contrary is shown.[48] A number of species are listed in Schedule 5 but only in relation to certain aspects of the protection described here, *e.g.* it is only the rules on sale that apply to several butterfly species.[49]

3.4.3   The above provisions do not apply in certain circumstances. It is not an offence for a person to take a disabled animal for the purpose of treating it and releasing it, nor to kill an animal so severely disabled as to have no reasonable chance of recovery, provided in both cases that it was not that person's unlawful act which caused the disability.[50] More generally, no offence is committed where the otherwise unlawful conduct towards the animal is the incidental result of a lawful operation and could not reasonably have been avoided, *e.g.* the disturbance entailed in lawful agricultural or forestry operations.[51] No offence is committed by actions done under a ministerial requirement relating to agricultural pest control[52] or under the Animal Health Act 1981.[53] A

---

[43] *ibid.,* s.9(1).

[44] *ibid.,* s.9(3).

[45] *ibid.,* s.9(4), amended for England and Wales by CRWA 2000 Sched. 12, para. 5.

[46] *ibid.,* s.10(2), (5); see para. 3.4.11, below.

[47] *ibid.,* s.9(5). In England and Wales general licences authorise the sale outside the breeding seasons of adult specimens of common frogs, common toads and smooth and palmate newts, provided that they were not taken from the wild during the breeding season and excluding newts taken from certain counties (WLF 100105 and WLF 026).

[48] *ibid.,* s.9(6); the presumption applies to offences under subss. (1), (2), (5(a)).

[49] See Appendix A for details.

[50] WCA 1981, s.10(3)(a), (b).

[51] *ibid.,* s.10(3)(c).

[52] Agriculture Act 1947, s.98; Agriculture (Scotland) Act 1948, s.39; see para. 4.5.2, below.

[53] WCA 1981, s.10(1); see para. 4.5.11, below.

further defence is available to "authorised persons,"[54] who are allowed
to kill or injure animals where it can shown that the action was necessary to prevent serious damage to livestock, food for livestock, crops,
fruit, growing timber or other forms of property or fisheries.[55] This
defence is not available if the need for the action became apparent
beforehand, unless an application has been made for a licence to
authorise the conduct and that application is still being considered.[56]
As with the rest of Part I of the 1981 Act, licences may be obtained
authorising actions which would otherwise constitute offences.[57]

A lesser degree of protection is granted to the animals listed in
Schedule 6 to the 1981 Act.[58] Their protection is limited to a prohibition
on the use of certain methods of killing or taking them.[59] These include
the use of the following devices in killing or taking the listed animals,[60]
or their setting (for whatever purpose) in circumstances calculated to
cause bodily injury to such animals:[61] traps or snares, electrical devices
for killing or stunning, poisonous, poisoned or stupefying substances,
or nets.[62] A limited defence is available in relation to the setting of the
prohibited devices in that no offence is committed if the accused can
show that the article was set for the purpose of the lawful killing of
animals in the interests of public health, agriculture, forestry, fisheries
or nature conservation, and all reasonable precautions were taken to
prevent injury to the animals protected under Schedule 6.[63] Also prohibited is the use of: automatic or semi-automatic weapons, devices for
illuminating a target, sighting devices for night shooting, artificial
lights, mirrors or dazzling devices, gas or smoke, sound recordings
employed as decoys, and mechanically propelled vehicles used in
immediate pursuit of animals, for the purpose of driving, killing or
taking them.[64] A person who knowingly causes or permits the acts
rendered unlawful by these provisions is also guilty of an offence,[65] so
that a landowner who deliberately does nothing to stop his gamekeeper
offending may himself be prosecuted.

3.4.4

---

[54] See para. 3.2.8, above.
[55] WCA 1981, s.10(4).
[56] *ibid.*, s.10(6); if the application is granted, the licence will authorise the action taken,
if refused, the action is unlawful.
[57] *ibid.*, s.16; see para. 3.2.7, above and Appendix C.
[58] See Appendix A.
[59] WCA 1981, s.11(2); see section 4.4, below for the general law on methods of killing
and taking animals.
[60] *ibid.*, s.11(2)(b).
[61] *ibid.*, s.11(2)(a).
[62] The setting of nets is not itself prohibited.
[63] WCA 1981, s.11(6), (7) (added by Wildlife and Countryside (Amendment) Act 1991,
s.2).
[64] *ibid.*, s.11(2)(c)–(e).
[65] *ibid.*, s.11(2)(d) (added by Wildlife and Countryside (Amendment) Act 1991, s.2).

European Protected Species

3.4.5   An additional layer of protection is given to those species that qualify
as European protected species by virtue of their inclusion in the Habitats and Species Directive, implemented by the Conservation (Natural
Habitats, etc.) Regulations 1994. The measures to protect these species,
that include fish as well as mammals, reptiles, amphibians and one
butterfly,[66] are broadly parallel to those contained in the 1981 Act as
described above, but with slight differences, in substance as well as
wording. For those species listed in Schedule 2 to the Regulations (*e.g.*
otters, wild cat, bats, dormice, turtles), deliberately killing, capturing,
or disturbing any individual or taking their eggs is an offence.[67] This list
offers more protection than the 1981 Act in that it extends to deliberate
disturbance of the animals in all circumstances, not just while using a
place of rest or shelter.[68] It is also an offence to keep, sell, offer for
sale or exchange any of the protected species, alive or dead, or anything
derived from them.

3.4.6   More significant differences apply in relation to resting and breeding
sites. Most notably, under the Regulations it is an offence simply to
damage or destroy a breeding site or resting place of such animals,[69]
whereas under the 1981 Act such conduct is criminal only if done
intentionally or (in England and Wales) recklessly.[70] There are also
differences in the scope of the conduct prohibited. The 1981 Act covers
the obstruction of sites as well as their damage or destruction and refers
to "any structure or place [used] for shelter or protection", whereas the
Regulations are limited to damage or destruction of "breeding sites or
resting places". Since the European protected species are also protected
species under the 1981 Act, these overlapping provisions do not make
the law simple to follow, quite apart from issues such trying to work
out how the "resting place" of marine species can be identified and at
what stage pollution can be said to have damaged such a site. The
potential for these provisions to have an effect beyond direct criminal
charges was shown in *R. v. Cornwall County Council, ex p. Hardy*,[71]
where planning permission for a landfill site was quashed because the
environmental information considered during the environmental impact
assessment of the proposal had not properly investigated the likelihood
of disturbance to the roosting sites of bats.

---

[66] See Appendix A.

[67] CNHR 1994, reg. 39.

[68] Disturbance presumably includes causing injury to the animals, which is expressly
covered by s.9 of the 1981 Act but not mentioned in the Regulations.

[69] CNHR 1994, reg. 39(1).

[70] WCA 1981, s.9(4), as amended for England and Wales by CRWA 2000, Sched. 12,
para. 5.

[71] [2001] Env. L.R. 25.

As usual, there are a number of defences and exceptions,[72] essen- **3.4.7**
tially the same as under then 1981 Act, as well as provision for
licences authorising acts otherwise prohibited.[73] In a dwelling house,
European protected species (other than bats)[74] can be disturbed and
their breeding and resting places destroyed, and as under the 1981
Act, there are defences for action taken under statutory pest control
and animal health measures and for the tending and mercy killing
of animals injured other than by the accused's unlawful act. Owners
and occupiers of land, and those authorised by them or by local
authorities, can take action where necessary to prevent serious
damage to property, fisheries, livestock, crops or growing timber,
but only if the need for such action was not apparent in advance so
as to allow a licence to be sought. Where the killing or disturbance is
the incidental result of a lawful operation and could not reasonably
have been avoided, again there is a defence, but as noted above in
relation to the Birds Directive, the breadth of this provision, especially given that there is strict liability for damaging breeding and
resting places, may be too wide to satisfy the restrictions on permitting harm laid down in the Directive itself.[75] Moreover, the European
Commission has threatened to take legal action against the United
Kingdom on the basis that licences seem to be granted simply as a
formality after the grant of planning permission, without careful
weighing of the arguments for and against allowing damage to the
breeding sites and resting places of protected species.[76]

There is also a further group of species, listed in Schedule 3 to the **3.4.8**
1994 Regulations, that enjoy limited protection by virtue of restrictions
on the ways in which they can be taken or killed.[77] The same restrictions apply when any of the species listed in Schedule 2 may be taken
or killed. For the mammals listed (mountain hare, pine marten, polecat,
several seals), the prohibited means are: live decoys that are blind or
mutilated, tape recorders, electrical devices capable of killing or stunning, mirrors, devices for dazzling or for illuminating targets, night
sights, explosives, non-selective nets or traps, crossbows, poison, gass-
ing or smoking out, and automatic and semi-automatic weapons. For
the fish (including Atlantic salmon whilst in fresh water), the prohibition is on poison and explosives. The use of aircraft and moving motor
vehicles is also prohibited.

---

[72] CNHR 1994, reg. 40.
[73] CNHR 1994, regs 44–46.
[74] See para. 3.4.11, below.
[75] Habitats and Species Directive, art. 16; see para. 7.4.33, below.
[76] Press release IP/01/189, February 12, 2001.
[77] CNHR 1994, reg. 41; see Appendix A.

Cruelty

3.4.9   Laws against cruelty to animals have been in existence for a long time[78] but mostly do not apply to wild animals.[79] The Protection of Animals Act 1911 and Protection of Animals (Scotland) Act 1912 make any cruel ill-treatment of animals a crime, but limit the definition of "animal" for this purpose to domestic and captive animals.[80] This left wild animals unprotected other than through the various prohibitions on cruel and indiscriminate means of hunting and killing, although inventive prosecutors could sometimes find a way to intervene, *e.g.* the use of criminal damage in the case of swans as a result of their peculiar status as property of the Queen,[81] and breach of the peace in Scotland where using a hedgehog as a football in a public place was held to meet the requirements of conduct likely to cause alarm, upset or annoyance or to provoke a disturbance of the peace.[82]

3.4.10   The position has now been changed in relation to mammals as a result of the Wild Mammals (Protection) Act 1996. This makes it an offence for any person to mutilate, kick, beat, impale, stab, burn, stone, crush, drown, drag or asphyxiate any wild mammal with intent to inflict unnecessary suffering.[83] "Wild mammals" are defined as any that are not domestic or captive within the meaning of the Protection of Animals Acts 1911 and 1912, so that there is no opportunity for cases to fall into a gap between the two sets of rules.[84] There are exceptions to the general prohibition to allow for mercy killing, the swift and humane killing of mammals injured in lawful hunting or pest control activities, acts that are authorised by any statute and the results of any

---

[78] Since the Cruel Treatment of Cattle Act 1822 in England and Wales and the Cruelty to Animals (Scotland) Act 1850 in Scotland.

[79] See generally M. Radford, *Animal Welfare Law in Britain: Regulation and Responsibility* (Oxford, 2000), esp. Chaps 8–10; A. Stevenson, "Animals and the Scope of Anti-Cruelty Legislation" 1997 J.R. 12; S. Harrop, "The Dynamics of Wild Animal Welfare Law" (1997) 9 J.E.L. 287.

[80] There is a full statutory definition in each Act of what counts as a "domestic" animal, and for an animal to be "captive" requires more than a temporary inability for it to get away from those harming it; *Rowley v. Murphy* [1964] 2 Q.B. 43, *Barrington v. Colbert* (1998) 162 J.P. 642.

[81] News report in *The Times*, August 19, 1993.

[82] News report *The Scotsman*, October 10, 1993; in England similar facts have been expressly held to fall outwith the scope of the 1911 Act because the hedgehog could not be held to be in captivity (*Hudnott v. Campbell*, *The Times*, June 27, 1986—thanks to M. Radford for this reference). In Scotland, see also *Dempster v. Ruxton*, 1999 G.W.D. 1–24, where breach of the peace was used in relation to beating a fox to death.

[83] Wild Mammals Act 1996, s.1; on a strict interpretation any other method of causing suffering will fall outwith the scope of this offence, and note that the intent to cause suffering must be shown.

[84] *ibid.*, s.3.

lawful hunting by trap, snare, bird or dog[85] or of the lawful use of poisons.[86] The law therefore does prohibit deliberate cruelty to mammals, but other forms of animal remain unprotected. For birds, reasonable protection is offered by the wide provisions of the Wildlife and Countryside Act 1981, which penalise any intentional injuring of birds,[87] but for other forms of animal, there is no direct legal protection against cruel treatment, unless they have been included in one of the statutory lists of protected species.

Bats

Bats are given full protection under Schedules 5 and 6 to the 1981 Act, **3.4.11** and are European protected species. The protection given under the 1981 Act and 1994 Regulations[88] is extended by a restriction of the exemptions normally permitting action against protected species. In general no offence is committed by the killing, injuring or taking of a protected animal or the disturbance of its shelter if the action in question is carried out in a dwelling-house, or is the incidental result of a lawful operation and could not reasonably be avoided.[89] In relation to bats however, these defences are limited to action taken within the living area of a dwelling-house (in other words the inhabited rooms, not a loft or outbuilding), or taken after the relevant conservation body has been notified of the intended action.[90] In the latter case, the body must be given a reasonable time to advise whether the action should be carried out and if so, how. This provision is intended particularly to protect bats from the harmful effects of wood treatments and preservatives applied in roof-spaces where they may be roosting, but note that the role of the conservation body is simply to offer advice, which need not be followed.

Badgers

The badger is protected against being killed or taken by certain means **3.4.12** under Schedule 6 to the Wildlife and Countryside Act 1981,[91] but receives more general protection under the Protection of Badgers Act

---

[85] The question of whether hunting with dogs should be prohibited on grounds of cruelty is, of course, the subject of heated political debate and Bills to outlaw such hunting have been discussed in both the Westminster and Holyrood Parliaments. See Addendum, above.

[86] Wild Mammals (Protection) Act 1996, s.2.

[87] See para. 3.3.2, above.

[88] See *R. v. Cornwall County Council, ex p. Hardy*: para. 3.4.6, above.

[89] WCA 1981, s.10(2), (3)(c), offering defences to s.9; CNHR 1994, reg. 40(2), (3)(c), offering defences to reg. 39.

[90] *ibid.*, s.10(5); *ibid.*, reg. 40(4).

[91] See para. 3.4.4, above.

1992.[92] The structure and provisions of the 1992 Act are broadly similar to those for protected species under the 1981 Act, with generally worded prohibitions on killing and taking being supported by provisions on possession and sale, and qualified by a number of defences, but the scope and, in particular, the wording of the two Acts differ so that where badgers are involved the precise wording of the 1992 Act must be carefully studied.

3.4.13   It is an offence wilfully to kill, injure or take a badger, or to attempt to do so, otherwise than as permitted under the Act.[93] Moreover, the onus of proof is reversed in relation to this offence, in that where someone is charged with attempting to kill, injure or take a badger, and there is evidence from which it can reasonably be concluded that he was involved in such an attempt, he is presumed to have been so involved unless the contrary is shown.[94] It is also an offence[95] cruelly to ill-treat a badger, to use any badger tongs in the course of killing or taking a badger or attempting to do so, to use against badgers any firearm other than one of the specified size and power,[96] or to dig for badgers. In relation to digging for badgers, the onus of proof is again reversed, with evidence from which it could reasonably be concluded that a person was digging for a badger giving rise to a presumption that he was so doing unless the contrary is shown.[97]

3.4.14   These prohibitions designed to protect badgers are subject to a number of exceptions. They do not apply to a person taking or attempting to take a badger in order to tend it when it has been disabled otherwise than by his own act, to the killing or attempted killing of a badger appearing to be so seriously injured or in such a condition that killing it would be an act of mercy, nor to the unavoidable killing or injuring of a badger as an incidental result of a lawful action.[98] Conduct authorised under the Animals (Scientific Procedures) Act 1986 is also exempt. Killing a badger, taking one or injuring one while attempting to kill or take it is not an offence if the accused can show that his conduct was necessary for the purpose of preventing serious damage to land, crops, poultry or other forms of property.[99] However, the benefit of this provision is not available if the need for such action became

---

[92] Consolidating the Badgers Act 1973, which had been amended on several occasions, the Badgers Act 1991 and the Badgers (Further Protection) Act 1991.

[93] Protection of Badgers Act 1992, s.1(1).

[94] *ibid.*, s.1(2).

[95] *ibid.*, s.2(1).

[96] A smooth bore weapon of not less than 20 bore or a rifle using ammunition having a muzzle energy of not less than 160 footpounds and a bullet weighing not less than 38 grains; *ibid.*, s.2(1)(d).

[97] *ibid.*, s.2(2).

[98] *ibid.*, s.6.

[99] *ibid.*, s.7(1).

apparent beforehand unless an application for a licence authorising the action has been made and is still under consideration.[1]

In order to back up these offences, it is further provided that it is an offence to have in one's possession or control a dead badger, or any part of one or anything derived from one.[2] This is an offence of strict liability, but specific defences are provided if it can be shown that the badger had not been killed or had been killed otherwise than in contravention of the Act or the Badgers Act 1973, or that the badger or other article had at some stage been sold in circumstances such that the purchaser had no reason to believe that the badger had been killed in contravention of the Acts.[3] A person commits a crime by selling or offering for sale a live badger, or by having one in his possession or under his control,[4] unless he has possession or control of it in the course of his business as a carrier, or unless it was disabled otherwise than by his own act and is being kept to be tended.[5] Ringing or otherwise marking a badger is also an offence unless a licence is obtained.[6]

3.4.15

Protection is extended to badger setts, defined for the purposes of the Act "any structure or place which displays signs indicating current use by a badger."[7] It is an offence intentionally or recklessly[8] to interfere with a badger sett by damaging or destroying it, by obstructing access to it, by causing a dog to enter it or by disturbing a badger in occupation. In *Green v. DPP*[9] it was held that the ground above a badger sett did not fall within the scope of this offence, so that digging above a sett but without destabilising or damaging the tunnels or chambers was not in itself an offence. A defence is provided for action necessary to prevent serious damage to land, crops, poultry or other forms of property,[10] provided that if the need for such action was known in advance a licence had been applied for and is still under consideration.[11] It is a defence that the conduct was the incidental result of a lawful operation and could not reasonably have been avoided,[12] but this does not apply to interference in the form of causing a dog to enter the sett or the destruction of the sett. It follows that a licence is required

3.4.16

---

[1] *ibid.*, s.7(2).
[2] *ibid.*, s.1(3).
[3] *ibid.*, s.1(4).
[4] *ibid.*, s.3.
[5] *ibid.*, s.9.
[6] *ibid.*, s.5.
[7] *ibid.*, s.14.
[8] In England and Wales this probably means recklessly in the more objective sense established in *R. v. Caldwell* [1982] A.C. 341; Scots law probably also interprets this in an objective sense, *Allen v. Patterson*, 1980 J.C. 57.
[9] [2001] Env. L.R. 15.
[10] Protection of Badgers Act 1992, s.8(1).
[11] *ibid.*, s.8(2) applying s.7(2).
[12] *ibid.*, s.8(3).

for the destruction of a sett, even if this is merely incidental to some lawful operation, *e.g.* development authorised by planning permission.[13] Subject to restrictions as to the methods and materials used,[14] obstruction of the entrance to a badger sett for the purpose of hunting foxes with hounds is no offence, provided that it is authorised by the owner or occupier of the land and a recognised Hunt.[15]

3.4.17   Licences authorising conduct prohibited under the Act are available from the statutory conservation bodies and the agriculture ministers. The bodies can grant licences in relation to any action taken for scientific or educational purposes, for the purpose of the conservation of badgers, for the purpose of zoological gardens, or for marking badgers. The bodies can also grant licences permitting interference with badger setts for the purposes of development authorised under the town and country planning legislation, for preserving scheduled ancient monuments[16] or carrying out archaeological investigations of them, and for investigations into any offence or for gathering evidence for any court proceedings.[17] Both the bodies and the Minister can grant licences to interfere with setts for the purpose of controlling foxes in order to protect livestock, game or wild life.[18]

3.4.18   The agriculture ministers can grant licences for the killing or taking of badgers in order to prevent the spread of disease[19] or to prevent serious damage to land, crops, poultry or other forms of property. Licences for interference with badger setts can be granted for the same purposes and for any agricultural or forestry operation or for drainage works.[20] The Minister must consult the appropriate conservation body on the exercise of his functions under this provision and must not grant a licence unless he has received the body's general advice of the circumstances in which such licences should be granted.[21] In Scotland this

---

[13] English Nature granted 245 licences in relation to setts interfering with development in 2000–2001; data from the "Facts and Figures" section of their web-pages at www.english–nature.gov.uk.

[14] "Loose soil" is one of the permitted materials and in *Lovett v. Bussey, The Times*, April 24, 1998, it was held that whether soil was loose was a question of fact, but that clay soils should be broken up sufficiently to ensure that they do not form a compacted structure.

[15] *ibid.*, s.8(4)–(9); a Hunt Master who has given clear instructions as to the lawful way of stopping up a sett is not liable if the hunt servants act illegally; *RSPCA v. Farquhar* (1995) 7 E.L.M. 67.

[16] Under the Ancient Monuments and Archaeological Areas Act 1979.

[17] Protection of Badgers Act 1992, s.10(1).

[18] *ibid.*, s.10(3).

[19] On the controversial issue of badgers and the spread of bovine tuberculosis, see the House of Commons Agriculture Committee, *Badgers and Bovine Tuberculosis*, 5th Report of 1998–99 (1998–99 H.C. 233), and *Badgers and Bovine Tuberculosis: Follow Up*, 1st Report of 2000–01 (2000–01 H.C. 92).

[20] Protection of Badgers Act 1992, s.10(2).

[21] *ibid.*, s.10(6).

provision is restricted to licences granted for the protection of land and property[22]; in England and Wales it extends to licences granted for any of the above purposes except for preventing the spread of disease.[23]

Licences can be revoked at any time by the authority which granted them,[24] but are not to be unreasonably withheld or revoked.[25] Action authorised under a licence can not constitute an offence under the general restrictions on the placing of poison,[26] but failure to adhere to the conditions in a licence is itself an offence, regardless of any other liability.[27]

3.4.19

A number of provisions exist to assist in the enforcement of the law protecting badgers. Anyone found on any land committing an offence of killing, injuring or taking a badger or in possession of a dead badger can be required to leave the land by the owner or occupier (or their servants), or by a constable and required to give his full name and address. Wilful refusal to comply with these requirements is an offence.[28] The police are also given powers to stop and search suspected offenders, to arrest them and to seize anything which may be evidence of the commission of an offence. The power of seizure extends to articles liable to forfeit under the further provisions which state that on conviction the court shall order the forfeiture of any badger or skin which was the subject of the offence and may order the forfeiture of any weapon or item used in the commission of the offence.[29] Further provisions authorise the destruction or disposal of any dog used in committing an offence and the disqualification of the offender from having custody of a dog.[30]

3.4.20

Seals

The Conservation of Seals Act 1970 offers legal protection to seals in a number of ways.[31] As usual, though, there are a number of exceptions and the possibility of licences being granted to authorise for certain purposes action which is normally prohibited.

3.4.21

In the first place, there is a prohibition on the use of poison of any sort for killing or taking seals, and it is an offence to use firearms

3.4.22

---

[22] *ibid.,* s.10(7).
[23] *ibid.,* s.10(6).
[24] *ibid.,* s.10(8).
[25] *ibid.,* s.10(9).
[26] *ibid.,* s. 10(10), referring to Protection of Animals Act 1911, s.8, and Protection of Animals (Scotland) Act 1912, s.7; see para. 4.4.3, below.
[27] *ibid.,* s.10(8).
[28] *ibid.,* s.1(5).
[29] *ibid.,* s.11.
[30] *ibid.,* s.13.
[31] See generally D. McGillivray, "Seal Conservation Legislation in the U.K.—Past, Present, Future" (1995) to Int. J. of Marine and Coastal Law 19.

other than those of prescribed power to kill, injure or take a seal.[32] The possession of poison or prohibited firearms or ammunition with intent to kill or take a seal is itself an offence.[33] The rules restricting the means of killing do not apply to a person's mercy killing of a seal so seriously disabled that it has no reasonable chance of recovery, provided that it was not his own act that disabled it in the first place.[34] Seals are further protected under Schedule 3 to the Conservation (Natural Habitats, etc.) Regulations 1994, which provide additional limits on the methods by which they can be killed or captured,[35] and under Annex V of the Habitats and Species Directive, which calls on their conservation status to be kept under review and entitles them to protection from any indiscriminate means of killing capable of causing serious disturbance to populations.[36]

3.4.23   A close season is laid down for both species of seal found in British waters and it is an offence wilfully to kill, injure or take a seal during the close seasons. For grey seals the close season is September 1–December 31, for common seals June 1–August 31.[37] The effect of these close seasons can be extended by orders made by the Minister where it appears necessary for the proper conservation of seals. Such orders can apply to specific areas and to either or both species,[38] and in practice greatly extend the protection offered to seals. In particular this protection was considerably extended following the epidemic in 1988 which killed many seals in the North Sea, and after several temporary measures, including a ban on killing common seals off Shetland,[39] there is now a prohibition on killing, injuring or taking either species of seal on the North Sea coast of England.[40]

3.4.24   A number of defences are available. No offence is committed by the taking of a disabled seal in order to tend it (provided that the tender did not cause the injury), by a mercy killing, by the unavoidable killing or injuring of a seal as an incidental result of a lawful action, or by the

---

[32] Conservation of Seals Act 1970, s.1; the permitted firearms are rifles using ammunition of muzzle energy of not less than 600 footpounds and bullets weighing not less than 45 grains; the Minister can amend this prescription by statutory instrument (*ibid.*, s.1(2)).

[33] *ibid.*, s.8(2).

[34] *ibid.*, s.9(2).

[35] CNHR 1994, reg. 41; see para. 3.4.8, above.

[36] See paras 7.4.32–7.4.35, below. The effect of the Directive is extended to oil and gas operations offshore (beyond territorial waters) by the Offshore Petroleum Activities (Conservation of Habitats) Regulations 2001 (S.I. 2001 No.1754).

[37] Conservation of Seals Act 1970, s.2.

[38] *ibid.*, s.3.

[39] Conservation of Seals (Common Seals) (Shetland Islands Area) Order 1991 (S.I. 1991 No. 2638), revoked by Conservation of Seals (Common Seals) (Shetland Islands Area) Order 1991 Revocation Order 1998 (S.I. 1998 No.923).

[40] Conservation of Seals (England) Order 1999 (S.I. 1999 No. 3052).

killing or injuring of a seal in order to prevent damage to a fishing net or tackle, or to fish which are in a net.[41] This last defence is available only when the seal is in the vicinity of fishing net or tackle, and only to the person in possession of the equipment or someone acting at his request. It does not allow those seeking to reduce competition for fish stocks to kill seals which are not immediately threatening fishery operations.[42]

Licences may be granted by the Minister for a number of purposes authorising the killing or taking of seals, but in no case can the use of strychnine be authorised.[43] The licences can be granted for scientific or educational purposes, for the purposes of a zoo or other collection, for the prevention of damage to fisheries, for the reduction of a population surplus of seals either for management purposes or to use them as a resource, or for the protection of flora or fauna in nature reserves, marine nature reserves, SSSIs and land protected by a Nature Conservation Order. Before granting licences, the Minister is to consult with the Natural Environment Research Council, and he must have the consent of the relevant statutory conservation body before granting a licence for a nature reserve or SSSI.[44] Contravening the conditions in a licence is itself an offence, regardless of other liabilities.[45]   **3.4.25**

In order to assist in the enforcement of the Act and to allow any authorised culling to take place, there are provisions for powers of entry,[46] for powers of arrest, search and seizure,[47] for the forfeiture of unlawfully taken seals or sealskin and of firearms, etc. used in committing offences,[48] and provisions regulating the jurisdiction of courts where offences are committed on the coast or at sea.[49] The Natural Environment Research Council is to provide the Minister with scientific advice on the management of seal populations.[50]   **3.4.26**

Whales

All species of whales, dolphins and porpoises are given protection under Schedule 5 to the Wildlife and Countryside Act 1981, and are   **3.4.27**

---

[41] Conservation of Seals Act 1970, s.9.
[42] For the position affecting fish farms see W. Howarth, *The Law of Aquaculture* (1990), pp. 149–152.
[43] Conservation of Seals Act 1970, s.10 (amended by WCA 1981, Sched. 7, para. 7).
[44] *ibid.*, s.10(3).
[45] *ibid.*, s.10(2).
[46] *ibid.*, s.11.
[47] *ibid.*, s.4 (amended for England and Wales by the Police and Criminal Evidence Act 1984, Sched. 7, Pt I).
[48] *ibid.*, s.6.
[49] *ibid.*, s.7.
[50] *ibid.*, s.13.

European protected species,[51] but a number of other provisions also exist. The catching of all species of cetacean, or their treatment once caught, is prohibited within the coastal waters of the United Kingdom.[52] Any British ship involved in the catching or treatment of whales or any factory treating whales or producing whale oil must have a licence from the Minister, and no such licences are currently in force.[53] However, the Minister may issue permits granting exemptions from these provisions for scientific or other exceptional purposes.[54] In England and Wales, it is an offence intentionally or recklessly to disturb any dolphin or whale,[55] while in Scotland it is an offence to drive ashore any of the smaller types of whale commonly known as bottlenose or pilot whales.[56]

Fish

3.4.28 Fish do not have the same place in the public's affection as seals and whales and the hunting of fish is still widely accepted as a legitimate pastime, as well as a commercial activity. The protection of fish has thus attracted considerably less attention than that devoted to marine mammals, but the law has not ignored fish. Fish can benefit directly from the more general legislation on nature conservation, and a few species of fish are protected under Schedule 5 to the Wildlife and Countryside Act 1981.[57] The sturgeon is a European protected species under the 1994 Regulations,[58] while several species are listed in Schedule 3 to those Regulations and therefore benefit from the express prohibition on the use of poison and explosives,[59] although these are already outlawed by more general fisheries measures. The basking shark is given additional protection by the introduction in England and Wales of a specific provision making it an offence intentionally or recklessly to disturb specimens.[60]

3.4.29 Nonetheless, the majority of legislation dealing with fish is designed to regulate the exploitation of fish stocks and is discussed in Chapter 4. The law on fishing, as well as trying to regulate the catching of

---

[51] See paras 3.4.2, 3.4.5–3.4.8, above. The restrictions under the Directive are applied to oil and gas operations offshore (beyond territorial waters) by the Offshore Petroleum Activities (Conservation of Habitats) Regulations 2001 (S.I. 2001 No.1754).

[52] Whaling Industry (Regulation) Act 1934, ss.1, 2 (amended by the Fisheries Act 1981, s.35).

[53] *ibid.*, s.4.

[54] *ibid.*, s.7.

[55] WCA 1981, s.9(4A), added by CRWA 2000, Sched. 12, para. 5.

[56] Fisheries Act 1981, s.36.

[57] See para. 3.4.2, above.

[58] See paras 3.4.5–3.4.7, above.

[59] See para. 3.4.8, above.

[60] WCA 1981, s.9(4A), added by CRWA 2000, Sched. 12, para. 5.

certain species so as protect future stocks, can have incidental benefits for the conservation of aquatic fauna. The restrictions on when and how fishing can take place serve to provide some protection for fish and aquatic animals in generally. In particular, the prohibitions on the use of indiscriminate and destructive methods of fishing, such as electric devices and poison, will obviously benefit all forms of aquatic life.[61] Moreover, the value of waters for fishing can provide a strong incentive for their retention in an unpolluted state, to the benefit of animal and plant life generally.[62]

---

[61] See paras 4.3.10–4.3.12, below.
[62] *e.g.* the effect of the Shellfish Waters Directive (79/923).

4. EXPLOITATION AND DESTRUCTION OF WILDLIFE

4.1.1   Animals and birds have been hunted for food since the beginning of human existence, and more recently for sport. It was in order to protect wildlife for such purposes that the first laws affecting them were made, and the law regulating hunting and fishing continues to play a major role in controlling what can be done to wildlife. It therefore deserves to be considered in a book on nature conservation. An account of the full complexities of the law in this field, especially in relation to the administration and detailed control of fishing, inland and marine, would take this book beyond reasonable size, and what follows is a brief guide, with an emphasis on those parts of the law which may have most impact on nature conservation. Fuller accounts exist of the law on game and inland fisheries, but unfortunately it is much harder to keep track of ever-changing mass of legislation, national and European, on offshore fishing.[1]

4.1.2   Although the law dealt with in this chapter is designed to allow the killing and taking of wildlife, it may be of considerable benefit to nature conservation. It was in order to preserve deer for royal hunting that areas of forest were shut off from agricultural or commercial forestry use, with lasting benefits to many forms of plant and animal life. The law stipulating close seasons, etc., seeks at least to ensure that the species concerned are not exterminated, albeit with a view only to their future exploitation, and other controls may serve to limit the likelihood of harm afflicting species other then the intended targets. On a more practical level, the economic potential of shooting rights, etc., may help to prevent areas of "natural" countryside being destroyed by other forms of exploitation. Moreover, the offences created to punish those hunting particular species by unauthorised means, in unauthorised places or at unauthorised times may also offer a means of taking action against those engaged in activities which are harmful to other species, *e.g.* the likelihood of game being caught might allow the game laws to be invoked against those using nets to catch wildlife, even though game was not their intended target. By acquiring, but then not exercising, game rights over land those interested in nature conservation may be able to achieve a degree of protection for some species in the area, otherwise possible only at the expense of acquiring the land itself.

4.1.3   The legal provisions requiring the destruction of animals are not so likely to produce such incidental benefits. Some pest control measures may be of benefit to other species, but generally the significance of the law lies not in any potential benefits for nature conservation, but in the

---

[1] See paras 4.3.14–4.3.16, below.

ways in which it can conflict with and even override other measures adopted to further conservation, *e.g.* requiring the destruction of wild animals even within nature reserves.

This chapter is organised in an attempt to bring some order to a very fragmented area of law. First the law on hunting, shooting and fishing is considered for its effect in regulating who is permitted to kill or take wildlife and in what circumstances. Then the various provisions affecting the methods which can be used for killing and catching animals are considered. Finally the law requiring or permitting the destruction of wildlife is examined.

4.1.4

HUNTING AND SHOOTING

Game laws

Although the broad objectives and basic structure of the law of game are the same in Scotland and in England and Wales, there are many differences of considerable importance.[2] The law is further complicated by the existence of a number of overlapping provisions. One initial problem common to both jurisdictions is the absence of clear and consistent definitions of what is meant by "game."

4.2.1

The meaning of game

There is no single definition of "game" in either Scotland or England and Wales. Different statutes provide their own definitions, definitions which themselves give rise to doubts since they usually state that game "includes" the species which are listed rather than offering a complete definition. In both jurisdictions it is clear that the term "ground game" refers to hares and rabbits only,[3] but the broader position is less clear. As a common core, though, it can be said that the following will be regarded as game in virtually all circumstances: hares, pheasants, partridges, grouse, heath or moor game and black game.[4]

4.2.2

The position in Scotland is particularly complex. The Game (Scotland) Act 1772 contains provisions affecting hares, partridges, pheasants, muir fowl, tarmagans (ptarmigan), heath fowl and snipe.[5]

4.2.3

---

[2] See generally, S. Scott Robinson,*The Law of Game, Salmon and Freshwater Fishing in Scotland* (1990); W. Gordon, *Scottish Land Law* (2nd ed.) (1999), Chap. 9; A. Nicol, "Hunting and Shooting" in J. Rowan-Robinson and D. McKenzie Skene, *Countryside Law in Scotland* (2000); C. Parkes and J. Thornley, *Fair Game: The Law of Country Sports and the Protection of Wildlife* (1997) (new revised ed.).

[3] Ground Game Act 1880, s.8.

[4] Heath, moor and black game are terms covering the red and black grouse and ptarmigan.

[5] Game (Scotland) Act 1772, ss.1, 3.

The Night Poaching Act 1828 defines game as including the species listed in the core definition given above, with the addition of bustards,[6] and also applies to rabbits.[7] The Game (Scotland) Act 1832 applies to game, woodcock, snipe, wild ducks and conies (rabbits); no definition of game is given, but that in the 1828 Act is generally accepted to apply here.[8] It has also been held that capercaillie are game for the purposes of the 1832 Act, but it is now a protected species.[9] The Game Licences Act 1860 requires a licence for hunting game (again the 1828 definition is accepted in the absence of a definition in the Act),[10] woodcock, snipe, rabbits and deer.[11] For the Poaching Prevention Act 1862, game includes the species in the core definition above, the eggs of the birds listed there, woodcock, snipe and rabbits.[12] Only deer, pheasants, partridges, grouse and black game qualify as game for the purpose of compensating agricultural tenants for damage caused by game;[13] the control of rabbits and hares lies within the hands of the tenants.[14]

4.2.4 In England and Wales, the core definition noted above is the one which appears in the Game Act 1831.[15] The Night Poaching Act 1828 includes bustards within the definition,[16] and the Poaching Prevention Act 1862 applies to the core species and to rabbits, woodcock, snipe and the eggs of the birds in the core definition.[17] The Game Licences Act 1860 requires a licence for the hunting of game (undefined, but probably the core definition with the inclusion of bustards as in the 1828 Act) and of deer, rabbits, woodcock and snipe.[18]

4.2.5 Game birds are excluded from the provisions of Part I of the Wildlife and Countryside Act 1981 which give protection to wild birds, and are

---

[6] Night Poaching Act 1828, s.13.

[7] *ibid.*, s.1.

[8] Scott-Robinson, *op. cit.*, p. 9; deer were originally included in the 1832 Act but removed by the Deer (Scotland) Act 1959, Sched. 3.

[9] *Colquhoun's Trs. v. Lee*, 1957 S.L.T. (Sh.Ct.) 50; the status of the capercaillie is complicated by the fact that it became extinct in Britain during the second half of the eighteenth century, but it was reintroduced to Scotland from Sweden in 1837. The legal status of the capercaillie changed when it was given protection under WCA 1981, Sched.1 by the Wildlife and Countryside Act 1981 (Amendment) (Scotland) Regulations 2001 (S.S.I. 2001 No. 337).

[10] Scott Robinson, *op. cit.*, p. 14.

[11] Game Licences Act 1860, ss.2, 4.

[12] Poaching Prevention Act 1862, s.1.

[13] Agricultural Holdings (Scotland) Act 1991, s.53; the equivalent English legislation no longer refers to "damage from game" but to "damage from wild animals or birds the right to kill and take which is vested in the landlord or anyone (other than the tenant himself) claiming under the landlord" (Agricultural Holdings Act 1986, s.20).

[14] Ground Game Act 1880; see para. 4.2.8, below.

[15] Game Act 1831, s.2.

[16] Night Poaching Act 1828, s.13.

[17] Poaching Prevention Act 1862, s.1.

[18] Game Licences Act 1860, ss.2, 4.

defined for that purpose as pheasant, partridge, grouse (or moor game), black (or heath) game, or ptarmigan.[19] The other species of wildfowl (ducks and geese) which are hunted do fall within the 1981 Act and their hunting is regulated by the provisions there.[20]

Killing and taking game

The right to take and kill game is one of the incidents of the owner-   **4.2.6**
ship of land. The animals and birds themselves are *res nullius*, capable of appropriation by anyone who can take them, but no one has the right to enter land to take game in the absence of permission from the owner. This position at common law is backed up by a large number of statut-ory provisions creating offences relating to trespass in pursuit of game. The right to take game may, however, be severed from other rights in the land and is frequently the subject of a separate lease or is reserved, for his own use or for separate leasing, when the proprietor allows a tenant to occupy the land. The particular extent of the rights granted or reserved, and other matters relating to the management of the land will depend on the terms of individual agreements.[21] Where land is held by a public authority, statutory controls may constrain the wide discretion the landowner normally has over the exercise of game rights.[22]

The holder of the right to take game is entitled to access to the land   **4.2.7**
to exercise his right, and can authorise other people to exercise the right with him or in his stead. Those involved in killing or taking game, deer, woodcock and snipe must have a game licence under the Game Licences Act 1860.[23] A number of exceptions exist including: the taking of woodcock by nets or springes, the hunting of hares with hounds, the taking of rabbits on enclosed land by or with the permission of the proprietor or tenant, the taking or killing of deer in enclosed lands by or with the permission of the owner or occupier.[24] No licence is required for the killing of hares by the owner or occupier of the land,[25] and the law also provides that members of the Royal Family and gamekeepers appointed by the Queen are exempt from the licensing

---

[19] WCA 1981, s.27.

[20] See para. 4.2.15, below.

[21] See, *e.g. Re Wildfowl Trust (Holdings) Ltd* (unreported; Outer House January 19, 1994) on the relationship between the game rights reserved in a lease, the tenant's statutory rights and licences granted under the Wildlife and Countryside Act 1981.

[22] *R. v. Somerset County Concil, ex p. Fewings* [1995] 1 W.L.R. 1037, *R. v. Sefton Metropolitan Borough Council, ex p. British Association of Shooting and Conservation Ltd* [2001] Env. L.R. 10.

[23] Game Licences Act 1860, s.4 (amended by Protection of Birds Act 1954, Sched. 6).

[24] *ibid.*, s.5; for deer see paras 4.2.16–4.2.29, below.

[25] *ibid.*; this exception applies to those authorised under the provisions (which are differ-ently worded) of the Hares Act 1848, s.1 (England and Wales), and the Hares (Scotland) Act 1848, s.1.

requirements.[26] When someone is discovered doing acts requiring a licence, the licence must be displayed on request from an Inland Revenue officer, gamekeeper, owner or occupier of the land or the holder of a game licence.[27] A licence is valid for the whole United Kingdom unless it has been taken out solely in a person's capacity as a gamekeeper.[28]

4.2.8   The occupier of land does however have the right to take and kill ground game (*i.e.* rabbits and hares) on his land.[29] This right is inseparable from the occupation of the land but may be exercised only by the occupier and those authorised by him in writing. Only the occupier and one other person (who must fall within certain categories) are allowed to use firearms. No game licence is required for the exercise of this right.[30]

4.2.9   There are also limits on who can sell game. A dealer in game must obtain both a licence from the district council (or equivalent local authority)[31] and an excise licence,[32] and there are specific hygiene rules to be followed.[33]

Close seasons and methods of taking

4.2.10   The taking and killing of game is prohibited during the close seasons. A table showing the open seasons for game appears below.[34] In England the taking or killing of game on Sundays and on Christmas Day is prohibited[35] but no such legal prohibition applies to game in Scotland.[36] There is no close season on the killing of rabbits and hares, although rights under the Ground Game Act 1880 may be exercised on open moorland and unenclosed land in England and Wales only between September 1 and March 31, with the use of firearms permitted only between December 11 and March 31 unless all interested parties agree to waive this further restriction.[37] In Scotland such rights may be exercised all year, but the use of firearms is not permitted in April, May or

---

[26] *ibid.*, s.5.
[27] *ibid.*, s.10.
[28] *ibid.*, s.18.
[29] Ground Game Act 1880, s.1.
[30] *ibid.*, s.4.
[31] Game Act 1831, s.18, extended to apply to Scotland by Game Licences Act 1860, s.13.
[32] Game Licences Act 1860, s.14.
[33] Wild Game Meat (Hygiene and Inspection) Regulations 1995 (S.I. 1995 No. 2148).
[34] Appendix B.
[35] Game Act 1831, s.3.
[36] See Parkes and Thornley, *op. cit.*, p. 58; *cf.* the position for wildfowl, para. 4.2.15, below.
[37] Ground Game Act 1880, s.1(2); Ground Game Act 1906, ss.1, 2.

June.[38] The close seasons do not apply in Scotland to the taking of pheasants and partridges for breeding purposes.[39] The means by which it is permissible to kill and take game are dealt with later.[40]

Close seasons also apply to the sale of game. Game birds cannot be bought or sold ten days after the start of their close seasons.[41] The sale of indigenous hares is prohibited in the months of March, April, May, June and July.[42] **4.2.11**

Poaching

It is a criminal offence unlawfully to take or kill game or rabbits at night,[43] to enter land with any gun, net or other instrument in pursuit of game at night,[44] or trespass in pursuit of game, woodcock, snipe or rabbits during the day.[45] Greater penalties are incurred if at night there are three or more offenders or they are armed,[46] and by day if there are five or more offenders or (in Scotland only) if the offender has a blackened or otherwise disguised face.[47] These provisions do not apply to those hunting with hounds for hares, foxes or (in England and Wales only) deer.[48] In England and Wales it is also an offence for a person without the right to take game, to remove or destroy the eggs of any game bird, swan, wild duck, teal or widgeon.[49] **4.2.12**

Enforcement

Any person found trespassing in pursuit of game can be required by the person holding the game rights, the occupier of the land or their servants to give his name and address and to leave the land. If he fails to comply with such a request he can be apprehended by the same people; at night he can be apprehended immediately, without preliminaries.[50] Any game found on such a suspected offender can be seized,[51] **4.2.13**

---

[38] Ground Game Act 1880, s.1(2) (amended by Agriculture (Scotland) Act 1948, s.48).
[39] Game (Scotland) Act 1772, s.2.
[40] See section 4.4, below.
[41] Game Act 1831, s.4 (amended by Game Act 1970, s.1).
[42] Hares Preservation Act 1892, s.2.
[43] Night Poaching Act 1828, s.1, extended to apply to roads and highways by Night Poaching Act 1844, s.1.
[44] Night Poaching Act 1828, s.1.
[45] Game Act 1831, s.30; Game (Scotland) Act 1832, s.1.
[46] Night Poaching Act 1828, s.9.
[47] Game Act 1831, s.30; Game (Scotland) Act 1832, s.1.
[48] *ibid.*, s.35; *ibid.*, s.4. See Addendum, above.
[49] Game Act 1831, s.24; see also para. 3.3.6, above.
[50] *ibid.*, s.31; Game (Scotland) Act 1832, s.2; Night Poaching Act 1828, s.2.
[51] Game Act 1831 s.36; Game (Scotland) Act 1832, s.5.

and any assault on those exercising such powers is an offence.[52] Where an accused argues that he is in fact authorised in his conduct, the onus of proving any licence, etc., lies on him.[53]

Wildfowl

4.2.14   Wild ducks and geese generally fall outwith the scope of the game legislation, although wild ducks are included in the scope of some provisions. In Scotland it is an offence to trespass during the day in pursuit of wild ducks,[54] and in England and Wales it is an offence for someone with no game rights on the land to remove or destroy their eggs.[55] Snipe and woodcock are similarly covered by some of the provisions on game discussed above. No game licence is required to shoot wildfowl. Landowners may restrict access to their land, and although it appears that in Scotland the foreshore can be used by the public for shooting wildfowl,[56] in England and Wales restrictions imposed from a number of sources limit any such use.[57]

4.2.15   Wild ducks, wild geese, snipe, woodcock and other birds which do not count as "game" do, however, fall within the provisions of Part I of the Wildlife and Countryside Act 1981. This imposes a general prohibition on any intentional killing or taking of wild birds, except for those species listed in Part I of Schedule 2 to the Act.[58] These species (including snipe, woodcock, and several ducks and geese) may be killed or taken except during the close seasons, on Sundays and Christmas Day in Scotland, and on Sundays in areas of England and Wales prescribed by the Secretary of State.[59] The means by which these and all other sorts of wild bird may be killed or taken are also regulated.[60]

Deer

4.2.16   The law concerning deer offers these animals protection at some times of the year and in some circumstances, regulates their hunting, controls the means by which they can be killed or taken and provides for their destruction as pests.[61] As the law is found in modern legislation provid-

---

[52] *ibid.*, s.32; *ibid.*, s.6.

[53] *ibid.*, s.42; *ibid.*, s.12.

[54] Game (Scotland) Act 1832, s.1.

[55] Game Act 1831, s.24.

[56] *Hope v. Bennewith* (1904) 6 F. 1004.

[57] See Parkes and Thornley, *op. cit.*, pp. 222–224.

[58] The Birds Directive also permits the hunting of some species of ducks and geese provided that this is in accordance with national laws; art.7 and Annex II.

[59] WCA 1981, ss.1, 2; see paras 3.3.1–3.3.7, above.

[60] See paras 4.4.15–4.4.17, below.

[61] See generally C. Parkes and J. Thornley, *op. cit.*, Chap.11 and *Deer: Law and Liabilities* (2000).

ing more or less comprehensive codes, it is sensible to examine all aspects of the law together. The law in Scotland is somewhat different from that in England and Wales. During the 1990s the legislation in each jurisdiction was consolidated, but although the overall effect of the two sets of legislation is broadly similar, the existence of the Deer Commission in Scotland and the many detailed differences mean that the two jurisdictions have to be treated separately. One point that does apply throughout Great Britain is that is it an offence to release to the wild any muntjac, or sika deer (or hybrids with sika ancestry), while in relation to many Scottish islands the prohibition extends to the release of any red or sika deer or hybrids.[62]

Scotland

The relevant legislation in Scotland is the Deer (Scotland) Act 1996.[63] **4.2.17** The control and conservation of deer is supervised by the Deer Commission for Scotland, which has a significantly wider remit than its predecessor, the Red Deer Commission. As the change of name suggests, the Commission is now responsible for more species of deer in Scotland, namely red, sika, roe and fallow and hybrids of these species,[64] while its concerns have been extended to include measures to protect the natural heritage.[65] The Commission may impose control schemes and grant authority for its own staff or others to kill deer in certain circumstances. Generally though, as with game, the right to take or kill deer is a right enjoyed by the owners of the land or those to whom they have transferred this right. A game licence is required to take or kill deer,[66] except where the deer are killed or taken on enclosed land by or with the permission of the owner or occupier,[67] or through the actions of those authorised or required to take action by the Deer Commission.[68] Licences are also required for dealing in venison.[69]

There are close seasons for four species of deer in Scotland, set out **4.2.18** in Appendix B, and during the close season it is an offence to take or

---

[62] WCA 1981 s.14 and Sched.9 (see paras 7.2.3–7.2.4, below) as applied by Wildlife and Countyside Act 1981 (Variation of Schedule 9) Order 1997 (S.I. 1997 No.226) (for muntjac) and Wildlife and Countyside Act 1981 (Variation of Schedule 9) Order 1999 (S.I. 1999 No.1002) (for sika and red deer).

[63] Replacing the Deer (Scotland) Act 1959, as amended, primarily by the Deer (Amendment) (Scotland) Acts 1967, 1982 and 1996.

[64] Deer (Scotland) Act 1996, ss.1, 45(1).

[65] See para. 2.6.10, above; "natural heritage" is widely defined to include flora and fauna, geological and physiographical features and the natural beauty and amenity of the countryside (*ibid.*, s.45).

[66] Game Licences Act 1860, s.4.

[67] *ibid.*, s.5.

[68] Deer (Scotland) Act 1996, s.38.

[69] *ibid.*, ss.33–36.

wilfully to kill or injure any deer.[70] This prohibition does not apply to farmed deer which are enclosed and properly marked,[71] nor to action required or authorised by the Deer Commission in relation to deer causing damage.[72] Also excluded is action taken by the occupier of agricultural land or enclosed woodland or others authorised by him[73] where deer are found on arable land or enclosed grassland or woodland, where the occupier has reasonable cause to believe that serious damage will be caused to crops, pasture, trees, animal or human foodstuffs unless the deer are killed.[74] Licences granted for scientific purposes by the Commission can also authorise conduct normally prohibited during the close season.[75] It is also lawful to do acts in order to prevent suffering by injured or diseased deer or by a calf or fawn deprived of its mother.[76]

4.2.19 The only lawful method of taking, killing or injuring a deer is by shooting with a firearm.[77] The permitted categories of firearms and ammunition are prescribed in Regulations made by the Minister, which also prohibit the use of certain forms of sights, and allow him to grant special exemptions.[78] The use of shotguns is permitted in the case of action against deer causing serious damage to crops etc., but only with the specified forms of ammunition. Taking, killing or injuring a deer at night is unlawful, unless the Deer Commission has authorised the occupier of agricultural land or woodland, or his nominee, where this is necessary to prevent serious damage to crops, pasture, foodstuffs or woodland and no other reasonable control measures would be adequate.[79] The discharge of any firearm or missile at a deer from any moving vehicle is prohibited,[80] as is the use of aircraft to transport live deer unless the animal is inside the aircraft[81] or the operation is approved by a veterinary practitioner.[82] Also prohibited is the use of

---

[70] *ibid.*, s.5.

[71] *ibid.*, s.43.

[72] *ibid.*, s.14.

[73] Only certain categories of person can be authorised without the approval of the Deer Commission.

[74] Deer (Scotland) Act 1996, s.26.

[75] *ibid.*, s.5(7).

[76] *ibid.*, s.25; unlike the "mercy killing" provisions in the Wildlife and Countryside Act 1981 and in relation to seals and badgers, this is not qualified to deny the benefit of the exception to a person who caused the suffering in the first place, although such an initial act may well itself be an offence unprotected by the exception.

[77] *ibid.*, s.17(3).

[78] *ibid.*, ss.17(4), 21; Deer (Firearms) (Scotland) Order 1985 (S.I. 1985 No.1168) (see Appendix B).

[79] *ibid.*, s.18.

[80] *ibid.*, s.20(1)(a); "vehicle" includes any aircraft, hovercraft or boat (s.45(1)).

[81] So that deer cannot be carried in a sling or net under a helicopter.

[82] *ibid.*, s.20(1)(b),(2).

vehicles to drive deer on unenclosed land with a view to killing or injuring the deer, or to taking them alive.[83] The wilful injury of any deer with a firearm is an offence.[84]

As noted above, the law is relaxed in relation to the close seasons in order to allow occupiers to take action to control deer which are causing serious damage to agriculture or forestry, and is similarly relaxed to allow for control measures authorised by the Deer Commission.[85] The Commission can authorise the killing of deer where it is satisfied that they are causing serious damage to woodland or agricultural production, causing injury to livestock (*e.g.* by serious overgrazing of pasture or competition for supplementary feeding) or constitute an actual or potential danger to public safety, and further that the killing of the deer is necessary to resolve the problem and that none of the Commission's others powers is adequate to deal with the situation.[86] Any competent person can be authorised to kill the deer, the authorisation lasting for 28 days, and where the power is exercised the landowner must be notified and people likely to be on the land warned. Where the deer are coming from particular land, the person with the right to kill deer there must first be requested to take the necessary action, and authorisation for others to act can only be given once he has proved unable or unwilling to satisfy the request. These powers can also be exercised where the Commission is satisfied that serious damage is being caused to the natural heritage either on enclosed land or on unenclosed land where the damage is the result of the presence of a significantly higher density of deer population than is usual in all the circumstances.[87]

4.2.20

More general control measures can be introduced by means of a control scheme for the reduction in numbers, or total exclusion, of deer in a locality where they are causing or are likely to cause, damage or have become an actual or potential danger to public safety.[88] The relevant forms of harm are damage to woodland, to agricultural production, to livestock, including by serious overgrazing, or to the natural heritage, covering both direct and indirect damage and harm to actual or proposed alterations or enhancements of the natural heritage.[89] The Deer Commission is to form a preliminary view on the necessary measures and consult with the owners and occupiers of the land affected. If all

4.2.21

---

[83] *ibid.*, s.19.

[84] *ibid.*, s.21(5).

[85] *ibid.*, s.10.

[86] Where action is required for public safety and killing the deer might by itself constitute such a danger, the authorisation can be for the taking and removal of the deer from the land in question; *ibid.*, s.10(5).

[87] *ibid.*, s.11.

[88] *ibid.*, s.7.

[89] Thus if large numbers of deer were likely to impede the proposed natural regeneration of an area of native woodland, action could be taken at an early stage.

parties agree on the steps to be taken, who is to take them, the time limit for action and any other matters necessary for the agreement to work, a control agreement is drawn up by the Commission and takes effect.

4.2.22   Where it is not possible to reach a control agreement or an agreement is not being carried out, the Commission can impose a control scheme, but only in a more restricted range of circumstances.[90] There must be actual and serious damage or the deer must be a danger to public safety, and a scheme cannot be imposed where the agreement was proposed for the purpose of altering or enhancing the natural heritage. The scheme sets out the area affected, the number and mix of deer to be killed or removed and the steps to be taken by different owners and occupiers, but cannot impose an obligation on owners or occupiers to construct any fence. Control schemes have to be confirmed by the Minister before taking effect. Wilful failure to comply with a requirement imposed by a scheme is a criminal offence, as is obstruction of those acting in execution of a scheme or agreement.[91] In the event of any failure to comply with a scheme, the Commission must itself carry out any requirements of the scheme which it is satisfied are still necessary, recovering the cost through the sale of the deer killed and any sum still outstanding from the owner or occupier.[92]

4.2.23   The enforcement of the law relating to deer is assisted by a number of provisions. It is an offence for anyone who has no right to do so to take, kill or injure deer or to remove a deer carcase,[93] and where more than one person are acting together the penalties for this and the other offences noted above relating to killing or taking deer at unlawful times or by unlawful means are increased.[94] Trespassing in pursuit of deer is not itself an offence, but it is likely that a firearms offence will be involved.[95] The possession of deer in circumstances where there are reasonable grounds for suspecting that it has been unlawfully taken is an offence, as is the possession of firearms unlawful for this purpose.[96] Powers of arrest, search and seizure are conferred,[97] and for some offences a single witness suffices for conviction.[98] Those authorised by

---

[90] Deer (Scotland) Act 1996, s.8.

[91] *ibid.*, s.13.

[92] *ibid.*, ss.8(8), 9.

[93] *ibid.*, s.17; the provision about removing carcasses is necessary because it has been held that the "taking" of deer entails their killing or capture, not just the acquisition of a carcass; *Miln v. Maher*, 1979 J.C. 58.

[94] *ibid.*, s.22.

[95] *Ferguson v Macphail*, 1987 SCCR 52.

[96] Deer (Scotland) Act 1996, s.23.

[97] *ibid.*, ss.27–28.

[98] *ibid.*, s.23(5).

the Deer Commission enjoy wide powers of entry to land to control deer causing damage, to take a census of deer and to determine whether a control agreement or scheme is required.[99]

England and Wales

The legislation for England and Wales was consolidated in the Deer Act 1991.[1] As in Scotland, the right to take deer lies primarily with the owner of the land, but this right can be transferred separately and occupiers are given some rights in relation to deer causing damage. A game licence is required except for the taking or killing of deer on enclosed land by or with the permission of the owner or occupier.[2] Only licensed game dealers can deal in venison.[3]

4.2.24

For the four main species of deer close seasons are specified, different from those in Scotland.[4] It is an offence to take or intentionally to kill any deer during the close season,[5] except for action taken to prevent the suffering of diseased or injured deer,[6] to meet the requirements of an order for agricultural pest control,[7] or where a person falling within certain limited categories acts to prevent damage by deer on cultivated land, pasture or enclosed woodland.[8] The close season does not apply to deer farms where the deer which are clearly marked and kept on enclosed land,[9] and the Countryside Council for Wales and English Nature can grant licences for removing live deer from one area to another or the taking of live deer for scientific or educational purposes.[10]

4.2.25

It is an offence to set any trap or snare or to lay any poison in positions likely to cause bodily injury to deer, or to use these methods or a net to take or kill deer.[11] Also prohibited is the use of any firearm other than those permitted by the Minister (different from those allowed in Scotland),[12] any arrow, spear or similar missile or any drugged or poisoned missile.[13] Motor vehicles cannot be used to drive deer or for

4.2.26

---

[99] *ibid.*, s.15.

[1] Replacing the Deer Act 1963, as amended by the Wildlife and Countryside Act 1981 and by the Deer Act 1987, and the Deer Act 1980.

[2] Game Licences Act 1860, ss.4, 5.

[3] Deer Act 1991, s.10.

[4] *ibid.* s.2 and Sched. 1; see Appendix B.

[5] *ibid.*, s.2(1).

[6] *ibid.*, s.6(2).

[7] *ibid.*, s.6(1), referring to action required under s.98 of the Agriculture Act 1948; see para. 4.5.2 below.

[8] *ibid.*, s.7; see para. 4.2.28 below.

[9] *ibid.*, s.2(3).

[10] *ibid.*, s.8.

[11] *ibid.*, s.4(1).

[12] Specified in *ibid.*, Sched. 2; see Appendix B.

[13] *ibid.*, s.4(2).

the discharge of any firearm or missile, unless in relation to enclosed land where deer are normally kept and with the occupier's written permission.[14] Hunting deer with hounds remains lawful, but has generated much controversy, resulting in some landowners banning the activity from their land. Where a public authority or charity has taken such a decision this has itself proved controversial and led to litigation. In *R. v. Somerset County Council, ex p. Fewings*[15] it was held that the decision on moral grounds to ban hunting from the council's land did not fall within the council's limited statutory power to manage the land for certain purposes, whilst in *ex p. Scott*[16] a challenge to a similar decision by the National Trust fell on procedural grounds.

4.2.27   It is also an offence to take or wilfully kill deer at night,[17] except in the case of deer taken in accordance with requirements for agricultural pest control.[18] Action taken to relieve the suffering of diseased or injured deer is exempt from the prohibitions on night shooting and the use of traps and nets, and a wider range of firearms can be used.[19] The use of nets, traps and devices to project these can be authorised by the conservation bodies in relation to live deer for scientific and educational purposes or for the purpose of removing deer from one area to another.[20]

4.2.28   The control of deer as pests can be undertaken under the more general rules on pest control under s.98 of the Agriculture Act 1948 by which the agriculture ministers can make pest control orders requiring measures to combat deer and other pests.[21] More generally and as noted above, the law on the close seasons and night shooting are relaxed to allow action to be taking against deer causing damage.[22] The relaxation is available only to the occupier of the land,[23] members of his household or staff authorised by him and the person who has the right to kill deer on the land (if different from the occupier),[24] and covers the shooting of deer with prescribed firearms[25] on cultivated land, pasture or enclosed woodland.[26] It applies where it can be shown that there is reasonable

---

[14] *ibid.*, s.4(4),(5).
[15] [1995] 1 W.L.R. 1037.
[16] [1998] 1 W.L.R. 226.
[17] Deer Act 1991, s.3.
[18] *ibid.*, s.6(1).
[19] *ibid.*, s.6(3),(4).
[20] *ibid.*, s.8.
[21] See para. 4.5.2, below.
[22] Deer Act 1991, s.7.
[23] *i.e.* the occupier of the land on which the shooting takes place, *Traill v. Buckingham* [1972] 1 W.L.R. 459.
[24] Deer Act 1991, s.7(4).
[25] For this purpose including shotguns using specified ammunition; *ibid.*, s.7(2); see Appendix B.
[26] *ibid.*, s.7(1).

cause to suspect deer of the same species of causing damage to crops, vegetables, fruit, growing timber or other forms of property, that it is likely that further serious damage will be caused, and that the killing is necessary to prevent such damage.[27] This provision may, however be restricted by the Minister in relation to particular species or particular areas.[28]

Trespass in search or pursuit of deer with the intention of killing or injuring is an offence, as is any intentional taking, killing or injuring of deer, pursuit of deer or removal of carcases without the consent of the owner, occupier or other lawful authority.[29] An authorised person may require a person suspected of committing these offences to give his name and address and to quit the land,[30] and more general powers of search and seizure are provided to assist in the enforcement of the Acts.[31] **4.2.29**

FISHING

Fish and fishing are the subject of considerable legal attention. Although a few fish are among the protected species under the Wildlife and Countryside Act 1981 and the Conservation (Natural Habitats, etc.) Regulations 1994, most of the law is not expressly conservationist in intention. Nevertheless, the measures designed to protect stocks from over-exploitation and to protect private fishing rights do operate to the benefit of aquatic species generally and are the main way (other than pollution controls[32]) in which the law intervenes with the aquatic environment. Moreover, as with game rights, the economic value of fishing rights can provide a strong incentive for their owners to take steps to protect the quality of waters to the benefit of wildlife more generally. The following paragraphs offer an outline of the law on issues which are most likely to have consequences for nature conservation. **4.3.1**

Inland fishing is burdened with considerable legal controls, with significant differences between Scotland and England and Wales.[33] On the **4.3.2**

---

[27] *ibid.*, s.7(3).

[28] *ibid.*, s.7(5).

[29] *ibid.*, s.1(1),(2); belief that one has consent or other lawful authority, or that consent would be given were the circumstances known is a defence (s.1(3)).

[30] *ibid.*, s.1(4).

[31] *ibid.*, s.12. .

[32] See sections 8.5 and 8.6, below.

[33] See generally, S. Scott Robinson, *The Law of Game, Salmon and Freshwater Fishing in Scotland* (1990); W.M. Gordon, *Scottish Land Law* (2nd ed., 1999), Chap. 8; C. Hardie, "Fishing" in J. Rowan-Robinson and D. Mackenzie-Skene, *Countryside Law in Scotland* (2000); W. Howarth, *Freshwater Fishery Law* (1987); R.I. Millichamp, *A Guide to Angling Law* (1990); C. Parkes and J. Thornley, *Fair Game* (new revised ed., 1997), Chap. 12; P. Carty and S. Payne, *Angling and the Law* (1998).

border, special regimes apply to the Tweed and to the Solway, Esk and Sark; in some cases the Tweed is dealt with as a Scottish river throughout its length and the Esk as an English one.[34] As with taking and killing game, the right to catch fish is largely an incident of the ownership of land, but can be sold and leased separately. In addition to any restrictions imposed by proprietors, the law lays down some general rules relating to closed times and means of fishing, but to some extent the details of the regulation of fisheries is left to the byelaws of the administrative bodies vested with powers in this area. In England and Wales a key role is played by the Environment Agency[35] which as well as gaining some powers from ministers,[36] inherited this function from the National Rivers Authority which had in turn inherited it from the water authorities abolished by the Water Act 1989.[37] Fish farms and other waters where fish are kept in captivity and artificially reared are exempt from many of the provisions noted below.[38]

4.3.3   In Scotland, the law concerning salmon fishing is different from that for other sorts of fish. The right to catch salmon originally lay with the Crown as part of the *regalia minora* (except in Orkney and Shetland where udal law provided differently), but in very many instances the right has been granted to others. Salmon fishings can constitute a separate heritable tenement which can be held independently of any proprietorial rights in the land affected. In relation to other fish, the general rule is that in rivers which are tidal and in tidal lochs the right to catch fish is enjoyed by the public at large.[39] In other waters fishing rights lie with the riparian proprietors, but may be expressly transferred to others, although not as a separate holding. In England and Wales, the right to fish for salmon is not treated separately. The general distinction between public and private fisheries exists, but the Environment Agency operates a licensing scheme to regulate fishing for salmon, trout, freshwater fish and eels.[40] In both jurisdictions the rights of the public may be considerably curtailed in practical terms by the absence of any means of access to the waters where fishing may be permissible.

4.3.4   In Scotland, the proprietors of salmon fisheries in a district may form a district salmon fishery board, now regulated by the Salmon Act 1986. Such boards may do such acts, execute such works and incur such expenditure as appears expedient for the protection and improvement

---

[34] *e.g.* EA 1995, s.6(7); Scotland Act 1998 (Border Rivers) Order 1999 (S.I. 1999 No.1746).

[35] EA 1995, s.6(6), Sched. 15.

[36] *ibid.*, Sched. 15, paras 7–16.

[37] Water Act 1989, s.141, Sched. 17; see now Water Resources Act 1991, Pt V.

[38] See generally W. Howarth, *The Law of Aquaculture* (1990).

[39] Scottish Law Commission, *Discussion Paper on Law of the Foreshore and Seabed* (No. 113) (2001), pp. 17–19.

[40] Salmon and Freshwater Fisheries Act 1975, s.25.

of fisheries in their district, for the increase of salmon and the stocking of waters with salmon.[41] Ministerial powers to make regulations to conserve salmon have recently been introduced.[42] For other sorts of fish,[43] the Minister can make Protection Orders regulating and imposing controls and charges on fishing in specified areas and authorising wardens to exercise enforcement powers.[44] In England and Wales, in addition to operating the licensing scheme, the Environment Agency is responsible for maintaining, improving and developing fisheries for salmon, trout and other species,[45] whilst the Minister may make general regulations.[46]

In Scotland, it is an offence to fish for or take any unseasonable or unclean salmon (*i.e.* one which has spawned or is on the eve of spawning)[47] unless it is taken by accident and returned to the water with the least possible injury.[48] It is also unlawful knowingly to take any smolt or fry (*i.e.* young salmon before their migration to the sea), or to obstruct the passage of smolt or fry or the passage of mature salmon to spawning grounds during the annual close time, or to injure any spawn or spawning bed or shallow where spawn might be.[49] These prohibitions do not extend to action taken for the propagation of salmon or other scientific purposes nor to the incidental results of the cleaning of any dam or lade or exercise of property rights over the bed of a watercourse.[50] It is also lawful for a district salmon fishery board to take measures to prevent salmon reaching beds where from the nature of the stream their spawn might be destroyed.[51] Fixed engines (*i.e.* fixed nets or traps of any sort) are prohibited in inland waters,[52] and the construction and use of dams, sluices and gratings is also controlled.[53]

4.3.5

In England and Wales the intentional killing or taking of any immature or unclean (*i.e.* about to spawn or not yet recovered from

4.3.6

---

[41] Salmon Act 1986, s.16. The boards can raise money by means of an assessment on the fisheries in the district (*ibid.*, s.15).

[42] *ibid.*, ss.10A–10E, added by Salmon Conservation (Scotland) Act 2001.

[43] On the meaning of "freshwater fish" see *McLeod v. Keith*, 1997 S.C.C.R. 475.

[44] Freshwater and Salmon Fisheries (Scotland) Act 1976, s.1.

[45] EA 1995, s.6(6).

[46] Freshwater and Salmon Fisheries Act 1976, s.115.

[47] *Brady v. Barbour (No. 2)*, 1995 S.L.T. 920.

[48] Salmon Fisheries (Scotland) Act 1868, s.20.

[49] *ibid.*, s.19; this provision has been used to prevent an attempt to raft down a salmon river which might have disturbed shallows used by spawning salmon.

[50] *ibid.*

[51] *ibid.*

[52] Salmon and Freshwater Fisheries (Protection) (Scotland) Act 1951, s.2(1); a handful of long-standing cruives may remain in legitimate use; see Scott Robinson, *op. cit.*, p. 102.

[53] Salmon (Fish Passes and Screens) (Scotland) Regulations 1994 (S.I. 1994 No.2524); *Heritage Fisheries Ltd v. Duke of Roxburghe*, 2000 S.L.T. 800.

spawning) fish is an offence.[54] It is also an offence wilfully to disturb
any spawn or spawning fish or any bed, bank or shallow where spawn
or spawning fish might be, except in the exercise of a legal right to
extract material (*e.g.* gravel) from the waters or in cases authorised
by the Environment Agency for the purposes of artificial propagation,
scientific activities or the development of private fisheries.[55] Fish passes
in English and Welsh waters containing salmon or migratory trout are
controlled by the Environment Agency, which can require their construction and maintenance when dams are being built or altered, or
itself build fish passes.[56] The wilful alteration or injury to a fish pass,
and any act obstructing the use of one or scaring, hindering or preventing fish from using it is an offence, as is a failure on the part of
the owner or occupier to comply with a notice from the Agency to
restore a fish pass which has fallen into disrepair.[57] The law also regulates the use of sluices and provides for gratings to be installed and
maintained to protect fish from being caught in mill races etc.[58] Fixed
engines (*i.e.* any form of fixed net or trap for catching fish) and fishing
weirs are also prohibited unless expressly authorised.[59]

4.3.7   In both jurisdictions, fishing is prohibited during the close times and
there are also requirements relating to the removal of nets and other
equipment during the close times to reduce the likelihood of their being
improperly used.[60] In Scotland there is in relation to salmon a weekly
close time, from 6.00 p.m. on Friday until 6.00 a.m. on Monday, during
which it is illegal to fish by nets whilst fishing by rod and line is
unlawful on a Sunday.[61] There is also an annual close time of at least
168 days during which fishing is prohibited, although for fishing by rod
and line a shorter period may be prescribed.[62] Each district or part of a
district may have a different period set and there are considerable variations throughout Scotland. For trout the close season runs from
October 7 to March 14,[63] with no weekly close time.

---

[54] Salmon and Freshwater Fisheries Act 1975, s.2(2), (3); see *Pyle v. Welsh Water Authority* (unreported, noted in Howarth, *Freshwater Fishery Law* (1987) p. 36).

[55] *ibid.*, s.2(4), (5); *National Rivers Authority v. Jones* (unreported, *The Times*, March 10, 1992).

[56] Salmon and Freshwater Fisheries Act 1975, ss.9, 10, amended by EA 1995, Sched. 15, paras 10, 11.

[57] *ibid.*, s.12.

[58] *ibid.*, ss.13, 14 (as substituted by EA 1995, Sched. 15 para. 13), 15.

[59] *ibid.*, ss.6–7.

[60] *e.g.*, Salmon Fisheries (Scotland) Act 1868, s.23.

[61] Salmon and Freshwater Fisheries (Protection) (Scotland) Act 1951, s.13 (as amended by Freshwater and Salmon Fisheries (Scotland) Act 1976, s.7 and Sched. 3) and Salmon (Weekly Close Time) (Scotland) Regulations 1988 (S.I. 1988 No. 390).

[62] Salmon Act 1986, s.6.

[63] Freshwater Fisheries (Scotland) Act 1902, s.1 (amended by Trout (Scotland) Act 1933, s.1).

In England and Wales the close time can be set by local byelaws **4.3.8** made by the Environment Agency, but in accordance with minimum times provided by statute, which also specifies the dates and times to be applied in the absence of local rules.[64] For salmon there must be an annual close time of at least 153 days for nets, etc.,[65] and 92 days for rod and line[66] and a weekly close time of 42 hours.[67] For trout the minimum close times are 181 and 153 days[68] with a 42 hour weekly close time as for salmon. For other freshwater fish and rainbow trout the close time can be dispensed with by byelaws, but otherwise extends for at least 93 days.[69] The close season for catching salmon and trout by putt and putcher (a form of fixed trap) is set at 242 days.[70]

The law also restricts the possession and sale of fish during the close **4.3.9** seasons and provides wide enforcement powers to allow for the search and seizure of unlawfully taken fish and equipment used. Provisions exist for the introduction of a scheme for licensing salmon dealers.[71]

Only a limited number of methods are permissible in the catching of **4.3.10** fish, with further limitations applying to protected species under the Wildlife and Countryside Act 1981 and the Conservation (Natural Habitats, etc.) Regulations 1994.[72] In addition to the prohibition of the use of poison discussed more fully below,[73] there are prohibitions in both jurisdictions on the use of explosive or electrical devices.[74] In relation to these and the other activities mentioned below, authorisation for their use can be given for scientific purposes or the development of fisheries by the district salmon fishery board (in some cases only) or the Minister in Scotland, or by the Environment Agency in England and Wales.[75] In relation to salmon in Scotland, authorisation may also be granted for the purpose of conserving any creature or other living thing.[76]

The only lawful methods of taking salmon in Scotland are by rod **4.3.11** and line or by net and coble in relation to inland waters, with bag nets, fly nets or other stake nets[77] being permissible in the other waters of a

---

[64] Salmon and Freshwater Fisheries Act 1975, s.19 and Sched, 1.
[65] Aug. 31–Feb. 1.
[66] Oct. 31–Feb. 1.
[67] 6.00 a.m. Saturday–6.00a.m. Monday.
[68] Aug. 31 and Sep. 30 until March 1.
[69] March 14–June 16.
[70] Aug. 31–May 1.
[71] Salmon Act 1986, ss. 20, 31.
[72] See paras 3.4.2–3.4.8 above.
[73] See paras 4.4.10–4.4.11, below.
[74] Salmon and Freshwater Fisheries (Protection) (Scotland) Act 1951, s.4; Salmon and Freshwater Fisheries Act 1975, s.5.
[75] *ibid.*, s.9; *ibid.*, ss.1, 2.
[76] Salmon Act 1986, s.28.
[77] On the status of haaf nets in the Solway, see *Salar Properties (U.K.) Ltd v. Annandale and Eskdale District Council, The Times*, March 19, 1992.

salmon fishery district.[78] Regulations made by the Secretary of State can define what is meant by the various means of netting[79] and specify for particular areas certain forms of bait and lure for the purposes of the definition of "rod and line."[80] For other fish in inland waters the only permitted method of catching fish is by rod and line, except that where all the proprietors agree nets may be used in a loch or pond and that the proprietor or occupier may catch fish other than trout or salmon with nets or traps.[81] These rules do not prevent the use of a gaff or landing net in conjunction with rod and line.[82] Contravening these provisions is an offence, and the penalties are increased if two or more offenders are involved.[83] The taking of salmon leaping at or trying to ascend falls or going through a fish pass is also an offence.[84]

4.3.12   In England and Wales, the approach of the legislation is to ban the unlawful methods of fishing rather than to specify the lawful ones. The prohibited methods include the use of firearms, wires, spears, lights, and the use of stones or missiles to facilitate the catching of fish.[85] Also prohibited is the use of fish roe[86] and in relation to salmon or migratory trout the use of nets which stretch across more than three-quarters of the width of a stream or have too small a mesh.[87] Fixed engines, fishing weirs, mills and dams are also prohibited unless containing the requisite gaps, etc., to allow the passage of fish and protect the flow of water and unless authorised expressly by the Environment Agency, by general authorisation from the Minister or through being lawfully in use in

---

[78] Salmon and Freshwater Fisheries (Protection) (Scotland) Act 1951, s.2(1), (1A) (added by Salmon Act 1986, s.21); the boards' waters extend seaward three miles from the mean low-water springs (Salmon Act 1986, s.1(1)).

[79] *ibid.*, s.2(2A) (added by Salmon Act 1986, s.21); Salmon (Definition of Methods of Net Fishing and Construction of Nets) (Scotland) Regulations 1992 (S.I. 1992 No. 1974); Salmon (Definition of Methods of Net Fishing and Construction of Nets) (Scotland) (Amendment) Regulations 1993 and 1994 (S.I. 1993 No. 257 and 1994 No. 111).

[80] Salmon Act 1986, s.8, relating to the definition in Salmon and Freshwater Fisheries (Protection) (Scotland) Act 1951, s.24.

[81] Salmon and Freshwater Fisheries (Protection) (Scotland) Act 1951, s.2(2).

[82] *ibid.*, s.2(3).

[83] *ibid.*, s.3.

[84] Salmon Fisheries (Scotland) Act 1868, s.15.

[85] Salmon and Freshwater Fisheries Act 1975, s.1; possession of such implements with the intention of using them to catch fish is itself an offence, but gaffs used as an auxiliary to rod and line are permitted. Contrary to the inventive argument for the defence in *Alton v. Parker* (1891) 30 L.R. I.R. 87, the prohibition on using an "otter" or "otter lath" applies to the use of certain floating devices, not to the use of trained live otters to catch fish.

[86] *ibid.*, s.2.

[87] *ibid.*, s.3; landing nets used as an auxiliary to rod and line are permitted.

1861 by ancient right.[88] Byelaws can add to the range of prohibited methods.

At sea, there is a general public right to fish in tidal waters, but many different rules apply, arising both from the salmon legislation and the rules on marine fishing. One species which has attracted special attention is the basking shark, which as well as being a protected species under Schedule 5 to the Wildlife and Countryside Act 1981[89] now benefits in England and Wales from a provision making any intentional or reckless disturbance an offence.[90] **4.3.13**

For marine fishing generally, the law is mostly of recent origin and is designed to protect stocks from the depredations of fishing fleets which have become extremely, perhaps excessively, efficient, whilst at the same time balancing the competing economic and social interests of a large number of states within and outwith the European Community.[91] Regulations emerge in shoals from Brussels and national governments to regulate the total allowable catches and the allocation and the use of national quotas, banning the fishing for particular species in particular places by boats from particular countries at particular times, as well as controlling the types of fishing gear, vessels and methods of fishing which are permitted, and the number of days during which fishermen can be at sea.[92] All use of explosives, poisonous or stupefying substances or electrical current for catching marine species (not just fish) is banned, and it is unlawful to sell specimens caught using any form of projectile.[93] **4.3.14**

At national level there are wide powers for ministers to make orders regulating the minimum sizes of fish which can be caught and landed, the types of fishing gear permissible, and the areas and seasons in which fishing can take place, while there are licensing arrangements for fishing boats. In the exercise of these powers ministers must have regard to the conservation of marine flora and fauna and seek a reasonable **4.3.15**

---

[88] *ibid.*, ss.6–8; see *Gray v. Blarney* [1991] 1 All E.R. 1; *Mott v. Environment Agency*, *The Times*, January 25, 1999; *R. v. National Rivers Authority, ex p. Haughey* [1997] Env. L.R. 14.

[89] Wildlife and Countryside Act 1981 (Variation of Schedules 5 and 8) Order 1998 (S.I. 1998 No.878).

[90] WCA 1981, s.9(4A), added by CRWA 2000, Sched. 12, para. 5.

[91] On E.C. policy see Fisheries Management and Nature Conservation in the Marine Environment (COM (1999) 363) and the European Commission's Green Paper, *The Future of the Common Fisheries Policy* (COM (2001) 135 final). General information can be obtained at http://europa.eu.int/comm/fisheries. (check)

[92] The Scottish Fisheries Protection Agency lists almost 70 pieces of U.K. legislation alone in its *Annual Report and Accounts 1999–2000*, Annex D.

[93] Regulation (E.C.) 850/98, art. 31; see also Salmon and Freshwater Fisheries (Protection) (Scotland) Act 1951, s.4 and Salmon and Freshwater Fisheries Act 1975, s.5.

balance between conservation and their other concerns under the fisheries legislation.[94]

4.3.16 All of these measures, by controlling the volume, nature and location of fishing activity, have considerable significance for the conservation of marine species, albeit with the traditional aim of ensuring continued exploitation rather than seeking to conserve the environment. The details of this very rapidly changing mass of legislation lie beyond the scope of this work, [95] but those concerned with nature conservation should be aware of the existence of this legal structure which offers potential for furthering conservationist aims and controlling the destructive side-effects for other species of certain forms of fishing gear or techniques. Indeed some measures have been expressly adopted in order to benefit wider conservation interests, *e.g.* restrictions on fishing for sand eels in the North Sea in order to conserve the food supply for the many seabirds that nest on the east coast of Britain.[96]

4.3.17 The taking of shellfish is also surrounded by legislation, supported by special measures to protect water quality in designated shellfish waters.[97] Private fisheries can be established for oysters, mussels, cockles, clams, scallops and queens and within these the holders of the right to take shellfish can regulate fishing.[98] Private fisheries for oysters and mussels are also protected in Scotland by older legislation prohibiting others from dredging or otherwise disturbing or taking shellfish from such beds.[99] In addition to making provision for the minimum permissible size of creatures to be caught,[1] general rules lay down close

---

[94] Sea Fisheries (Wildlife Conservation) Act 1992, s.1.

[95] For an account of the legal regime, see the entries on "Fisheries", *Stair Memorial Encyclopaedia of The Laws of Scotland* (1990), Vol. 11, and *Halsbury's Laws of England* (4th ed., 1977), Vol. 18; and especially the relevant Supplements.

[96] Regulation (E.C.) 850/98, art. 29a, as added by Regulation (E.C.) 1298/2000.

[97] The Shellfish Waters Directive 79/923/EEC, implemented mainly through the Surface Waters (Shellfish) Classification Regulations 1997 (S.I. 1997 No.1332) and the Surface Waters (Shellfish) Classification (Scotland) Regulations 1997 (S.I. 1997 No.2470); it has been held that a breach of this Directive may create a right to compensation for shellfish fishermen who are adversely affected (*Bowden v. Southwest-Services Ltd* [1999] 3 C.M.L.R. 180, [1999] Env. L.R. 438).

[98] Sea Fisheries (Shellfish) Act 1967, ss.1–3 (amended by Sea Fisheries Act 1968, s.15, extended by Shellfish (Specification of Molluscs) Regulations 1987 (S.I. 1987 No. 218), Shellfish (Specification of Crustaceans) Regulations 2001 (S.I. 2001 No.1381) and Shellfish (Specification of Molluscs and Crustaceans) (Scotland) Regulations 1999 (S.S.I. 1999 No. 139)).

[99] Oyster Fisheries (Scotland) Act 1840; Mussel Fisheries (Scotland) Act 1847.

[1] Sea Fish (Conservation) Act 1967, s.1; *e.g.* recent rules on lobsters, spider crabs and edible crabs: (Undersized Lobsters (Scotland) Order 2000 (S.S.I. 2000 No.197); Undersized Lobsters Order 1993 (S.I. 1993 No. 1178); Undersized Spider Crabs (Scotland) Order 2000 (S.S.I. 2000 No.198); Undersized Spider Crabs Order 2000 (S.I. 2000 No.1502); Undersized Edible Crabs (Scotland) Order 2000 (S.S.I. 2000 No.228); Undersized Edible Crabs Order 2000 (S.I. 2000 No.2029).

seasons for the sale of indigenous oysters[2] and ban the possession or sale of edible crabs which are carrying spawn or have just cast their shells.[3]

On a related issue, it has been held that in England and Wales there is a public right to dig for bait (usually worms) on the foreshore, as an ancillary to the public right of fishing there.[4] It was stressed however, that this right is just an ancillary one and that no taking of bait for commercial purposes would be legitimate.

4.3.18

METHODS OF KILLING AND TAKING

The means by which wild creatures can be caught and killed is the subject of considerable legislation which prohibits or controls the use of poison and traps as well as the use of certain aids to taking animals. For some protected species there are further limits on the means by which they can be killed or captured, whilst more detailed rules apply to specific species, *e.g.* badgers, seals and deer where there are strict controls on the sort of firearms and ammunition which can be used in hunting them.[5] Byelaws can add to the prohibitions in many situations.

4.4.1

Poison

The use of poisons is controlled in various ways. Pesticides and their use are controlled generally by Part III of the Food and Environment Protection Act 1985[6] and the regulations made under it, largely implementing E.C. measures on this topic.[7] The basic conditions for the supply, storage and use of pesticides require that all reasonable precautions are taken to protect the health of human beings, creatures and plants and to safeguard the environment,[8] while notification must be given to various authorities before any aerial applications, including

4.4.2

---

[2] Sea Fisheries (Shellfish) Act 1967, s.16.

[3] *ibid.*, s.17; this does not apply if it can be shown that the crabs are for use as bait.

[4] *Anderson v. Alnwick District Council* [1993] 1 W.L.R. 1156; the same has been decided for Northern Ireland (*Adair v. National Trust for Places of Historic Interest and Scenic Beauty* [1998] N.I. 33).

[5] See paras 3.4.13, 3.4.22, 4.2.19, 4.2.26, above.

[6] As amended by the Pesticides Act 1998.

[7] Control of Pesticides Regulations 1986 (S.I. 1986 No. 1510) (as amended); Pesticides (Maximum Residue Levels in Crops, Food and Feeding Stuffs) (England and Wales) Regulations 1999 (S.I. 1999 No.3483); Pesticides (Maximum Residue Levels in Crops, Food and Feeding Stuffs) (Scotland) Regulations 2000 (S.S.I. 2000 No.22) (as amended).

[8] Control of Pesticides Regulations 1986, Sched. 2, para. 2, Sched. 3, para. 2 (as substituted by Control of Pesticides (Amendment) Regulations 1997 (S.I. 1997 No. 188, Sched. 1)).

notice to the statutory conservation bodies of any spraying within 1,500m of a National, Local or Marine Nature Reserve or an SSSI.[9] Similarly, the release of many poisonous substances is controlled by the laws regulating pollution.[10] The discharge and deposit of waste in liquid, gas or solid form are all controlled, with licences or other forms of approval being required for a large range of activities. These provisions should offer a degree of protection against conduct which would cause harm to the environment.

Animals

4.4.3   For the more specific legislation, perhaps the most convenient starting point is offered by the general provisions in section 8 of the Protection of Animals Act 1911[11] and section 7 of the Protection of Animals (Scotland) Act 1912. These sections make it an offence knowingly to place, or cause to be placed, on any land or in any building any poison or any fluid or edible matter (other than sown seed or grain) which has been rendered poisonous. This general prohibition on the laying of poison is however qualified by the existence of a defence if the poison is placed in order to destroy vermin in the interests of public health, agriculture or the protection of other animals or for manuring the land, provided that all reasonable precautions are taken to protect dogs, cats, fowls and other domestic animals.[12] In *Walkingshaw v. McClymont*,[13] the sheriff doubted whether there could ever be adequate precautions to satisfy this legal test when the aim of the exercise was to leave poisoned meat in the open countryside where a fox could get access to it. These sections also prohibit the sale of any seed or grain which has been rendered poisonous, except for their bona fide use in agriculture.

4.4.4   The use of a particular poison can be prohibited or restricted by the Minister if he is satisfied that it cannot be used for destroying animals, or particular kinds of animals, without causing undue suffering and that there are suitable alternative methods for destroying them which are adequate.[14] Only mammals count as "animals" for the purposes of this

---

[9]   *ibid.*, Sched. 4 (as substituted by *ibid.*).
[10] See generally, C. Reid (ed.), *Environmental Law in Scotland* (2nd ed., 1997); S. Bell and D. McGillivray, *Environmental Law* (5th ed., 2000).
[11] As amended by the Protection of Animals (Amendment) Act 1927, s.1.
[12] The wording of the two provisions differs slightly: the Scottish provision refers simply to the destruction of "vermin" (in *Walkingshaw v. McClymont* (below) held to include foxes), whereas the English one refers to "insects and other invertebrates, rats, mice, or other small ground vermin"; the Scottish provision refers to precautions to "prevent access" to the poison by dogs, etc., whereas the English one refers to precautions to "prevent injury" by the poison and includes wild birds within the categories entitled to protection.
[13] 1996 S.L.T. (Sh.Ct) 107.
[14] Animals (Cruel Poisons) Act 1962, s.2.

provision.[15] The effect of the regulations is to take the use of such poisons outwith the scope of the defences provided in section 8 of the Protection of Animals Act 1911 and section 7 of the Protection of Animals (Scotland) Act 1912, so that their use is a criminal offence. This power has been exercised so as to prohibit the use of phosphorous and red squill in all cases and the use of strychnine for all mammals except moles.[16] The sale and storage of poisons generally is controlled under the Poisons Act 1972 and the Poisons Rules[17] made under it.

Just as the use of a poison can be expressly taken outwith the scope of the defences in the 1911 and 1912 Acts, the use of poisons can be expressly brought within their scope. This can be achieved by minister-ial approvals under the Food and Environment Protection Act 1985.[18] More specifically, the use of particular poisons against grey squirrels and coypus can be authorised by the agriculture ministers in particular circumstances;[19] regulations have been made in the exercise of this power to permit the use of warfarin in destroying grey squirrels throughout England and Wales.[20]   **4.4.5**

The use of poison against rabbits and hares used to be prohibited throughout Great Britain under section 6 of the Ground Game Act 1880. For Scotland this provision has been repealed,[21] but it would appear that the prohibition on using poison to kill hares, contained in the Hares (Scotland) Act 1848,[22] remains in force. In England and Wales, the relevant part of section 6 of the 1880 Act has also ceased to have effect,[23] but again there is older legislation relating to hares.[24] It is expressly stated that it is not an offence under the Protection of Animals Act 1911 to use poisonous gas in rabbit holes[25] or in other burrows, etc. for the purpose of killing rodents of all sorts, foxes and moles under the agricultural pest control provisions of section 98 of the Agricultural Act 1947.[26] A similar provision allows the use of poison-   **4.4.6**

---

[15] *ibid.*, s.3.
[16] Animals (Cruel Poisons) Regulations 1963 (S.I. 1963 No. 1278); phosphorous is ele-mentary yellow phosphorous and red squill is any powder or extract made from the plant *Urginea maritima* (L.) Baker (the sea squill).
[17] Primarily the Poisons Rules 1982 (S.I. 1982 No.218), as amended.
[18] Food and Environment Protection Act 1985, s.16(14).
[19] Agriculture (Miscellaneous Provisions) Act 1972, s.19.
[20] Grey Squirrels (Warfarin) Order 1973 (S.I. 1973 No. 744); the laying of warfarin inside buildings is authorised throughout England and Wales, and its use outdoors in specified areas.
[21] Agriculture (Scotland) Act 1948, Sched. 10.
[22] Hares (Scotland) Act 1848, s.4.
[23] Prevention of Damage by Rabbits Act 1939, s.5(2); this repeal did not however extend to Greater London.
[24] Hares Act 1848, s.5.
[25] Prevention of Damage by Rabbits Act 1939, s.4.
[26] See para. 4.5.2, below.

ous gas in agricultural pest control in Scotland.[27] It is an offence knowingly to use or to permit the use of a rabbit infected with myxomatosis to spread the disease to unaffected rabbits.[28]

4.4.7   In relation to other particular species, the use of poison will not be an offence under the 1911 and 1912 Acts if its use falls within the scope of a licence granted by the statutory conservation bodies under the Protection of Badgers Act 1992 for scientific or educational purposes, or for the conservation of badgers.[29] The use of poison to kill seals is an offence,[30] as is its use against deer.[31] The use of poison is prohibited in relation to those species given protection under Schedule 6 to the Wildlife and Countryside Act 1981,[32] and under the Habitats and Species Directives.[33]

Birds

4.4.8   In addition to benefiting from the general restrictions on the use of poisons described above, the use of poisonous, poisoned or stupefying substances to kill or take wild birds is expressly prohibited.[34] The offence lies in setting such substances in such a place that they are calculated to cause bodily injury to any wild bird, even though birds may not be the intended victims. For the purpose of this provision, game birds are included within the definition of "wild birds."[35] Those who knowingly cause or permit such action are also guilty, but there is a defence for the setting of substances to kill or take in the interests of public health, agriculture, forestry, fisheries or nature conservation any wild animals which can lawfully be killed or taken in that way. This defence applies, however, only where all reasonable precautions have been taken to prevent injury to wild birds.[36] It has been held that this provision creates three separate offences, of using poisonous, using poisoned and using stupefying substances, and a charge of using a

---

[27] Agriculture (Scotland) Act 1948, s.49.

[28] Pests Act 1954, s.12.

[29] Protection of Badgers Act 1992, s.10(10); see para. 3.4.19, above.

[30] Conservation of Seals Act 1970, s.1(1): licences may be granted to allow the use of poisons other than strychnine (s.10(1)); see para. 3.4.22, above.

[31] In England and Wales this is expressly provided in s.4 of the Deer Act 1991, whereas in Scotland it is included in the general prohibition on using any method other than shooting with a firearm to kill deer (Deer (Scotland) Act 1996, s.17(3)); see paras 4.2.19, 4.2.26, above.

[32] WCA 1981, s.11(2) (amended by Wildlife and Countryside (Amendment) Act 1991, s.2); see para. 3.4.4, above.

[33] Directive 92/43, Annex VI; CNHR 1994, Sched.3; see paras 3.4.8, above and 7.4.35, below.

[34] WCA 1981, s.5(1) (amended by Wildlife and Countryside (Amendment) Act 1991, s.1); see also the Birds Directive, art. 8 and Annex IV.

[35] *ibid.*, s.27(1).

[36] *ibid.*, s.5(4), (4A) (added Wildlife and Countryside (Amendment) Act 1991 s.1).

poisoned substance failed when it was held that the substance in question was properly described as a narcotic and hence stupefying, not poisoned, substance.[37]

A further measure intended to protect wild birds is that the supply, but not the use, of lead weights for fishing is prohibited, a measure intended to reduce the danger to birds which risk being poisoned when such weights are ingested and worn down in their craw.[38] In England, the use of lead shot is prohibited for all shooting below the high water mark, at certain listed SSSIs and for specified wildfowl.[39]   **4.4.9**

Fish

The use of poison against fish is strictly prohibited and using poison to catch any marine organism is prohibited by E.C. law.[40] In Scotland it is an offence to put poison or any noxious substance in or near water with the aim of taking fish,[41] and it is also unlawful to possess poison for this purpose.[42] Permission can be granted by the Minister for the use of poison for scientific purposes or to protect or develop stocks of fish, or (in relation to salmon only) to conserve any creature or other living thing.[43]   **4.4.10**

In England and Wales the same offence exists,[44] as does a broader offence of causing of knowingly permitting to be put into waters which contain fish any matter which causes the water to become poisonous or injurious to fish, their spawn, spawning grounds or food.[45] The very broad terms of that offence are qualified so as not to apply to actions authorised by law (*e.g.* licensed discharges of waste) provided that the best practicable means within reasonable costs are used to prevent the matter causing injury.[46] Prosecutions may be raised only by the Environment Agency or a person certified by the Minister as having a material interest in the waters affected, a provision which limits the scope for environmental groups to utilise this provision to act against any   **4.4.11**

---

[37] *Robinson v. Hughes* [1987] Crim. L.R. 644.
[38] Control of Pollution (Anglers' Lead Weights) Regulations 1986 (S.I. 1986 No. 1992) (amended by Control of Pollution (Anglers' Lead Weights) (Amendment) Regulations 1993 (S.I. 1993 No. 49)); very large (over 28.35gm.) and very small (under 0.06gm.) weights are excluded.
[39] Environmental Protection (Restriction on Use of Lead Shot) (England) Regulations 1999 (S.I. 1999 No.2170).
[40] Regulation (E.C.) 850/98, art. 31.
[41] Salmon and Freshwater Fisheries (Protection) (Scotland) Act 1951, s.4.
[42] *ibid.*, s.7.
[43] *ibid.*, s.9; Salmon Act 1986, s.28.
[44] Salmon and Freshwater Fisheries Act 1975, s.5.
[45] *ibid.*, s.4.
[46] *ibid.*, s.4(2).

pollution of waters.[47] The Agency, acting with ministerial approval, may authorise the use of noxious substances for scientific purposes or in order to improve stocks of fish.[48]

Traps and Other Methods

Animals

4.4.12 The law controls both the sort of traps which can be used in catching animals and how they can be used. It is an offence to use or knowingly to permit the use of any spring trap other than one approved under regulations made by the Minister and used in circumstances covered by its approval.[49] The approval for a trap may be general or subject to conditions as to the circumstances of its use or the animals against which it is used, and the Minister may also grant licences authorising the experimental use of traps. The prohibition of the use of spring traps does not extend to those specified in regulations as being adapted solely for the destruction of rats, mice or other small ground vermin.[50] It is also an offence to sell or expose for sale any spring trap with a view to its use other than in accordance with the formal approvals, or to possess any spring trap for a purpose which is unlawful.[51]

4.4.13 Where a spring trap is used against hares or rabbits, it must be placed in a rabbit hole, and it is an offence to use or knowingly permit its use elsewhere.[52] Somewhat surprisingly, the meaning of "in a rabbit hole" has been the subject of decisions of the appellate courts.[53] The use of traps in accordance with a licence from the agriculture minister is outside this prohibition, and a licence to this effect may be embodied in a rabbit clearance order[54] or a notice served for the purpose of agricultural pest control.[55] Where spring traps are used against hares and rabbits, the traps must be inspected at least once a day.[56]

4.4.14 A number of other means of taking animals is also prohibited. The

---

[47] *ibid.*, s.4(3).

[48] *ibid.*, s.5.

[49] Agriculture (Scotland) Act 1948, s.50 (substituted by Pests Act 1954, s.10); Pests Act 1954, s.8; Small Ground Vermin Traps Order 1958 (S.I. 1958 No. 24).

[50] The current regulations are the Spring Traps Approval Order 1995 (S.I. 1995 No.2427) and the Spring Traps Approval (Scotland) Order 1996 (S.I. 1996 No.2202).

[51] Agriculture (Scotland) Act 1948; Pests Act 1954, s.8.

[52] Agriculture (Scotland) Act 1948, s.50A (added by Pests Act 1954, s.10); Pests Act 1954, s.9.

[53] *Brown v. Thompson* (1882) 9 R. 1183, *Fraser v. Lawson* (1882) 10 R. 396, both considering the equivalent provision in the Ground Game Act 1880, s.6.

[54] Pests Act 1954, s.1; see para. 4.5.5, below.

[55] Agriculture Act 1947, s.98; Agriculture (Scotland) Act 1948, s.39; see para. 4.5.2, below.

[56] Protection of Animals Act 1911, s.10; Protection of Animals (Scotland) Act 1912, s.9.

use of leg-hold traps is prohibited throughout the European Community.[57] It is an offence to place any self-locking snare so as to cause injury to any wild animal coming into contact with it, or to use a self-locking snare in any way in order to kill or take a wild animal.[58] Also prohibited are the use of any live mammal or bird as a decoy, any bow or crossbow, or explosive other than ammunition for a firearm.[59] A person who knowingly causes or permits the use of such methods is also guilty of an offence. A wider range of devices are prohibited in relation to those animals given enhanced protection under Schedule 6 to the Wildlife and Countryside Act 1981, and similarly for certain species (both protected ones and those which may be hunted) under the Conservation (Natural Habitats, etc.) Regulations 1994.[60] There is further legislation relating to badgers, deer and seals.[61]

Birds

The use of a large number of methods of killing and taking wild birds, **4.4.15** which for this purpose include game birds, is prohibited under the Wildlife and Countryside Act 1981, the list of prohibitions being subject to alteration by an order of the Minister.[62] Such orders can only be made after a draft of the order has been approved by both Houses of Parliament,[63] and changes can be made to the rules affecting firearms only in order to comply with Britain's international obligations.[64]

It is an offence to use any of the following[65]: **4.4.16**

   (a) a springe, trap, gin, snare, hook and line;
   (b) an electrical device for killing, stupefying or frightening;
   (c) a poisonous, poisoned or stupefying substance[66];
   (d) a baited board or bird lime or any similar substance;
   (e) a bow or crossbow;
   (f) an explosive other than ammunition for a firearm;
   (g) an automatic or semi-automatic[67] weapon or shot-gun with a barrel or more than 1.75 inches at the muzzle;

---

[57] Reg. 251/91, art. 2.
[58] WCA 1981, s.11(1) (amended by Wildlife and Countryside (Amendment) Act 1991, s.2).
[59] *ibid.*
[60] CNHR 1994, reg. 41 and Sched. 3.
[61] See section 3.4, above.
[62] WCA 1981, s.5(2).
[63] *ibid.*, s.26(3).
[64] *ibid.*, s.5(3).
[65] *ibid.*, s.5(1) (amended by Wildlife and Countryside (Amendment) Act 1991, s.1); see also art. 8 and Annex IV of the Birds Directive.
[66] See para. 4.4.8, above.
[67] General licences permit the use of semi-automatic weapons against pest species in certain circumstances (WLF 100091, the Scottish licence has no code, WLF 019).

(h) a device for illuminating a target, any form of artificial lighting, any mirror or dazzling device or any sighting device for night shooting;[68]

(i) a gas or smoke;

(j) a chemical wetting agent;

(k) a decoy in the form of a sound recording or any live bird or animal which is in any way tethered, secured or maimed;[69]

(l) a mechanically propelled vehicle in immediate pursuit of a bird.

In relation to items (a)–(c), the offence depends on the offending article being of such a nature and being so placed that it is calculated to cause injury to any wild bird coming into contact with it; in relation to the others what is covered is the use of the banned method for killing or taking a wild bird.[70] The offences extend to those who knowingly cause or permit the prohibited actions. It is also an offence to be involved in any way with an event where captive birds are liberated for the purpose of being shot immediately after their release.[71]

4.4.17   The ban on the use of nets or traps does not extend to their use by an authorised person in order to catch pest species which may be listed in Part II of Schedule 2 to the Act, and their use is permitted in the licences which have in effect replaced Part II of Schedule 2.[72] Larsen traps (which make use of a live decoy) are authorised, subject to conditions, for catching crows, jackdaws, jays, magpies and rooks.[73] Nets and traps may also be used to capture game birds when it is shown that the taking of the bird is solely for breeding purposes, and also legitimate is the use of nets in a duck decoy which was in use in 1954, immediately before the passing of the Protection of Birds Act 1954. These exceptions however, do not permit the use of nets for taking birds in flight, nor the use of any net propelled otherwise than by hand.[74] In relation to the offences of setting articles such that they are likely to cause injury, a defence is available if it can be shown that they were positioned for the lawful killing of any wild animal in the interests of

---

[68] General licences permit the use of these devices against feral pigeons, house sparrows and starlings (WLF 100090, SEGEN 05, WLF 0009).

[69] In *Holden v. Lancaster Justices*, *The Times*, October 10, 1998, it was held that birds with clipped wing feathers were not "maimed" for the purposes of this provision. Larsen traps that use live decoys are permitted in some circumstances; see para. 4.4.17, below.

[70] WCA 1981, s.5(1).

[71] *ibid.*, s.8(3).

[72] See paras 3.3.8–3.3.9, above.

[73] Licences WLF 100089, SEGEN 01, WLF 002.

[74] WCA 1981, s.5(5).

public health, agriculture, forestry, fisheries or nature conservation, and that all reasonable precautions were taken to prevent injury to wild birds.[75]

Fish

Only a limited number of methods are permissible in the catching of **4.4.18** fish. These have been discussed above.[76]

DESTRUCTION OF WILDLIFE

The control of pests has been a concern of the law for centuries, and **4.5.1** until comparatively recently the total extermination of many species would have been regarded as a legitimate aim. Today, although the law does to a considerable extent provide protection to wildlife, regard must also be had to the law regulating its destruction, as such measures can have a significant effect on what can and cannot be done to kill or capture wild animals. The controls on the use of poison and many of the other matters already considered serve to regulate how many pest control operations can be carried out, and in several places exceptions to the law have been noted, whereby the occupiers of land and other limited classes of people are permitted, for the purposes of protecting human, animal and plant health and of protecting property, to take steps normally forbidden by measures enacted to further the interests of nature conservation. There also exists a fragmented mass of provisions specifically directed at the control of pests. Most of these are rarely, if ever, invoked, but they could require action directly contrary to the interests of nature conservation.

One major power is that of the agriculture ministers to serve notices **4.5.2** requiring steps to be taken to take or destroy pests.[77] This power can be exercised where it appears expedient for preventing damage to crops, pasture, animal or human foodstuffs, livestock, trees, hedges, banks or works on land and can require action against rabbits, hares, other rodents, foxes, moles, wild birds (other than those enjoying special

---

[75] *ibid.*, s.5(4A) (added by Wildlife and Countryside (Amendment) Act 1991, s.1).

[76] See section 4.3, above.

[77] Agriculture Act 1947, s.98 (amended by Pests Act 1954, s.2 and Sched.; Protection of Birds Act 1954, Sched. 3, para. 1; Agriculture Act 1958, Sched. 3); Agriculture (Scotland) Act 1948, s.39 (amended by Pests Act 1954, s.2 and Sched.; WCA 1981, s.72(4)).

protection)[78] and (in England and Wales) deer.[79] The notice is to be served on the person who is entitled to take the specified action, who will usually be the owner or the occupier of the land but may be some-one different if game and shooting rights are held separately. The specified measures may not include any killing which is otherwise prohibited by law, with the exception of the killing of game which may be required during the close season.[80] A notice under these provisions may also call for the destruction or reduction of breeding places or cover for rabbits, or for steps to limit their movement.[81]

4.5.3   There is no right of appeal against such a notice, and failure to comply with one within the specified time is an offence.[82] Moreover, in the event of a failure to comply, the Minister may arrange for the necessary steps to be taken and recover the expenses incurred.[83] Powers of entry and inspection are provided to assist the Minister in the exercise of the functions under these provisions.[84] The Minister may also provide (at a reasonable charge) services and equipment to assist in compliance with a notice,[85] and anyone who has incurred costs in complying can apply to have these shared on a just and equitable basis with others who have an interest in the land.[86]

4.5.4   The Forestry Commissioners also enjoy the power to take action to control pests.[87] The Commissioners may act where they are satisfied that trees are being or are likely to be damaged by rabbits, hares or vermin (including squirrels)[88] owing to the failure of an occupier of

---

[78] The Scottish Act has been amended to refer to WCA 1981, Sched. 1 whereas the English one appears still to refer to the Protection of Birds Act 1954, repealed by WCA 1981; however the provisions of WCA 1981, s.4, setting the limits on the defences available to those acting in accordance with notices as described here ensures that the law is in fact the same (see para. 3.3.5, above).

[79] Fallow, red, roe and sika deer (and hybrids) are removed from the scope of this provision in Scotland by s.42A of the Agriculture (Scotland) Act 1948, added by Deer (Amendment) (Scotland) Act 1996, Sched. 1 para. 2 and amended by Deer (Scotland) Act 1996, Sched. 4 para. 1. This means that if muntjac deer become a problem in Scotland, action against them could be taken under these provisions.

[80] As specified in the Game (Scotland) Act 1772 and the Game Act 1831, s.3; see para. 4.2.10, above.

[81] Agriculture Act 1947, s.98(7); Agriculture (Scotland) Act 1948, s.39(5) (both added by Pests Act 1954, s.2).

[82] *ibid.*, s.100(1); *ibid.*, s.41(1).

[83] *ibid.*, s.100(2); *ibid.*, s.41(2).

[84] *ibid.*, s.106; *ibid.*, s.82.

[85] *ibid.*, s.101; *ibid.*, s.42.

[86] Applications are to the county court in England and Wales (*ibid.*, s. 100(5)) and to the Land Court in Scotland (*ibid.*, s.41(4)).

[87] Forestry Act 1967, s.7.

[88] The red squirrel is protected under Sched. 5 to the Wildlife and Countryside Act 1981, and no exemption is allowed for action against protected animals under these forestry provisions, in contrast to the exceptions allowed for agricultural pest control (WCA 1981, s.10(1)); see para. 3.4.3, above.

land to take adequate steps to destroy the animals or prevent their causing damage. The owner and occupier of the land must be given an opportunity to take the requisite action before the Commissioners take steps themselves, but the costs of such steps can be recovered by the Commissioners from the occupier.

In addition to the measures requiring the clearance of land offering them cover,[89] further attention is given to rabbits. Rabbit clearance areas may be designated by the agriculture ministers after consultation with local representatives of farmers, landowners, other farm and forestry interests and after local publicity for the proposal.[90] Within these areas, the occupiers of land have an obligation to take the necessary steps to kill or take wild rabbits, or where destruction is not reasonably practicable, to prevent their causing damage.[91] The existence of a rabbit clearance order does not entitle the occupier of the land to any right to kill rabbits with firearms additional to that conferred by the Ground Game Act 1880,[92] but authorisation for the additional use of firearms can be given by the Minister where such measures are necessary and the person entitled to grant authorisation has unreasonably withheld it.[93] All of England and Wales is designated as a rabbit clearance area, except for the City of London, the Isles of Scilly and Skokholm Island,[94] and all of Scotland is similarly designated apart from the Outer Hebrides and Jura.[95]

Rats and mice come under the responsibility of local authorities by virtue of the Prevention of Damage by Pests Act 1949.[96] The authorities are under a duty to keep their areas free from rats and mice, and in particular should inspect their areas for such creatures, destroy them on their own land and enforce the duties placed on the occupiers of land by the 1949 Act.[97] Occupiers of land[98] must forthwith notify the authority when it comes to their knowledge that rats or mice are resorting to or living on their land in significant numbers.[99] If the authority con-

4.5.5

4.5.6

---

[89] See para. 4.5.2, above.
[90] Pests Act 1954, s.1.
[91] *ibid.*, s.1(2).
[92] See para. 4.2.10, above.
[93] Pests Act 1954, s.1(3)–(5).
[94] Rabbit Clearance Order No.148 (1972).
[95] Details available from the Plant and Environment Policy Division of the Scottish Executive Environment and Rural Affairs Department.
[96] In England, primarily district councils; Prevention of Damage by Pests Act 1949, s.1. The legislation has been much amended to cope with the changes in local government structure since 1949 and functions can be transferred to housing action trusts in England and Wales (Housing Act 1988, s.68(1)).
[97] Prevention of Damage by Pests Act 1949, s.2.
[98] Other than agricultural land, unless otherwise prescribed (no agricultural land has yet been prescribed).
[99] Prevention of Damage by Pests Act 1949, s.3.

siders it necessary, notices[1] may be served requiring the occupier to take reasonable steps as specified to destroy rats and mice on their land.[2] There is a right of appeal against notices and failure to comply is an offence. In the event of non-compliance the council can arrange for the steps to be taken and recover the costs involved.[3]

4.5.7   In order to ensure the destruction of rats and mice escaping from hay stacks (Scotland) or ricks (England and Wales), regulations may impose special requirements on those involved in the threshing or dismantling of ricks and stacks.[4] The regulations which had been made under this provision for England and Wales have been revoked,[5] but those for Scotland remain in force,[6] affecting all stacks of grain, beans, peas, tares or mashlum and requiring such measures as the placing of fences round the stack before it is dismantled and the taking of all practicable steps to destroy any rats or mice escaping.

4.5.8   The provisions on the control of deer which are causing damage have already been discussed.[7] The measures to control non-indigenous pests such as mink are discussed below.[8]

4.5.9   As far as birds are concerned, the general provisions on agricultural pest control apply to them as much as to earth-bound pests, and the protection given to wild birds is relaxed in order to allow action to be taken against the main pest species. Although the Wildlife and Country-side Act 1981 provides for authorised persons[9] to be permitted to kill or take species listed in Part II of Schedule 2 to the Act, and to destroy, damage or take their eggs or nests,[10] no species are now listed in that Part of the Schedule and the authority for such action now rests in licences granted under the Act.[11] Where action is required by ministers

---

[1] The notice must require sufficiently specific steps for the occupiers to know what is required of them (*Perry v. Garner* [1953] 1 Q.B. 335), but there is no specific statutory form required, provided that the content of the notice and the authority of its source are clear (*Albon v. Railtrack plc* [1998] C.L.Y. 2295, reported as *Basildon District Council v. Railtrack plc* at [1998] E.H.L.R. 83).

[2] Prevention of Damage by Pests Act 1949, ss.4–6.

[3] *ibid.*, s.5. In *Leeds City Council v. Spencer, The Times*, May 24, 1999, [1999] E.H.L.R. 394 a claim was successfully resisted when the problem had been caused by the council's failure to carry out its own obligations under the waste legislation.

[4] *ibid.*, s.8.

[5] Prevention of Damage by Pests (Threshing and Dismantling of Ricks) (Revocation) Regulations 1978 (S.I. 1978 No. 1614).

[6] Prevention of Damage by Pests (Threshing and Dismantling of Stacks) (Scotland) Regulations 1950 (S.I. 1950 No. 980) (rendered metric by the Prevention of Damage by Pests (Threshing and Dismantling of Stacks) (Scotland) Amendment Regulations 1976 (S.I. 1976 No. 1236)).

[7] See paras 4.2.20–4.2.22, 4.2.28, above.

[8] See para. 7.2.6, below.

[9] See para. 3.2.8, above.

[10] WCA 1981, s.2(2).

[11] See paras 3.3.8–3.3.12, above.

in the exercise of their powers of agricultural pest control,[12] the death or injury of birds or damage to their eggs is not an offence except in relation to those species given enhanced protection under Schedule 1 to the 1981 Act.[13] In England and Wales, there is a further power for local authorities to take steps for abating or mitigating nuisance, annoyance or damage caused by the congregation in built-up areas of house doves, pigeons, starlings or sparrows.[14] Reasonable precautions must be taken to ensure that the seizure and destruction of birds is carried out humanely, and the provision does not authorise action contrary to the terms of the 1981 Act.[15]

The Minister has the power to take steps to eliminate pests affecting shellfish from waters other than those covered by private fisheries.[16] **4.5.10**

The legislation on animal health also provides for the destruction of wildlife. The agriculture ministers have the power to declare infected areas within which wide powers may be exercised.[17] If an area has been declared as being infected with rabies, provision can be made for the destruction of foxes and other wild animals in the area by persons authorised by the Minister.[18] In relation to other diseases, the destruction of any species of wild mammal or bird may be authorised if the Minister are satisfied that a disease existing among the wild members of a species is being transmitted to other animals,[19] and that the destruction of such wild creatures is necessary to eliminate or substantially reduce the incidence of the disease.[20] Orders made under this provision may authorise the use of methods for destroying animals which are otherwise unlawful, but only if such methods are the most appropriate in the light of all relevant circumstances, including the need to avoid unnecessary suffering.[21] The statutory conservation bodies must be consulted before such orders can be made.[22] In nature reserves managed by these bodies seven days' notice must be given before any exercise of the powers of entry to enforce and carry out the required steps, and as far as possible action in such reserves is to be taken with regard to minimising the harm to the flora, fauna and other features of such **4.5.11**

---

[12] See para. 4.5.2, above.

[13] WCA 1981, s.4(1).

[14] Public Health Act 1961, s.74.

[15] The species in question are all covered by the licences granted under the 1981 Act.

[16] Sea Fisheries (Shellfish) Act 1967, s.15.

[17] Animal Health Act 1981, s.17 (amended by Animal Health and Welfare Act 1984, s.4).

[18] *ibid.*, ss.19, 20.

[19] The animals which are protected by the Act are cattle, sheep, goats, other ruminating animals and swine, but the Minister can extend this definition to cover all other mammals (except man) and four-footed creatures (*ibid.*, s.87).

[20] *ibid.*, s.21.

[21] *ibid.*, s.21(4).

[22] *ibid.*, s.21(3).

reserves.[23] The recent foot and mouth disease outbreak has emphasised the extent of the legal powers available under the animal health provisions, but the relevant orders have not required the destruction of wildlife other than rats and stray and feral animals.[24] There are no provisions in the legislation relating to fish[25] and bees[26] authorising the destruction of animals in the wild.

---

[23] *ibid.*, s.22(7).
[24] Foot and Mouth Disease Order 1983 (S.I. 1983 No.1950), art. 9(1), rule 2(d), and art. 25 (as amended by several orders during 2001).
[25] Diseases of Fish Acts 1937 and 1983.
[26] Bees Act 1980; Bee Diseases Control Order 1982 (S.I. 1982 No. 107).

5. CONSERVATION OF HABITAT

By itself, the law protecting individual creatures can never secure their survival. Without suitable habitat offering food and shelter, no animal can survive and it is the loss of habitat, rather than any form of direct attack, which poses the greatest threat to most species today. The protection of habitat is equally vital to any attempt to conserve wild plants. If the law is going to seek the conservation of wildlife, it must therefore take steps to ensure the continued existence of the range and expanse of habitat necessary for this. In some countries this can be achieved by setting aside large areas of land for the exclusive use of wildlife, but in heavily populated islands such as Great Britain this approach is not possible. Moreover abandoning the land to nature would in any event prove futile in many areas, since virtually all of Britain's "natural" countryside is in fact the product of centuries of man's involvement with the land and some degree of continuing management is required if it is to survive in its present diversity. The conservation of habitat has instead been addressed by the creation of a large number of different designations of land, each with its own objectives, procedures and legal consequences.[1]

5.1.1

The piecemeal development of the law has resulted in there being about a dozen different legal regimes governing areas of land which have been identified as requiring protection in some form on account of their environmental quality. These regimes reflect different objectives: Areas of Outstanding Natural Beauty and National Scenic Areas are identified solely for their landscape, National Parks in England were created to serve the twin purposes of protecting landscape and providing opportunities for recreation, National Nature Reserves aim solely at the conservation and study of nature, while Environmentally Sensitive Areas have their origins in moves to reduce agricultural overproduction.[2] The effects of each designation vary in the extent to which the owner or occupier of land is restricted, the emphasis placed on voluntary agreements, the circumstances in which compensation is available, and the restrictions placed on visitors to the land. The fragmented structure of the law, exacerbated by the number of different public authorities involved, inevitably leads to confusion and at times exaggerated fears on the part of residents and landowners as to the effects of designation.

5.1.2

Historically, the trend has been towards stricter controls. When

5.1.3

---

[1] See J. Rowan-Robinson, C. Philp and M. de la Torre, "The Protection of Habitats" in J. Rowan-Robinson and D. McKenzie-Skene, *Countryside Law in Scotland* (2000).
[2] Nitrate Vulnerable Zones, created to protect water quality, are discussed at paras 8.4.18–8.4.21, below.

SSSIs were first introduced in 1949,[3] the landowner was not even
informed and the designation served simply to inform the planning
authority of the value of the area. The Wildlife and Countryside Act
1981[4] strengthened the regime by requiring the owner or occupier to
give notice before carrying out certain potentially damaging operations,
but contained no direct power to prevent these. Subsequently, the
regime for European Sites[5] did introduce provisions allowing damaging
operations to be prohibited. Now a wider range of controls, requiring
the positive management of land as opposed to merely prohibiting
activities, has been introduced for SSSIs in England and Wales.[6] There
has thus been a great strengthening of the degree of control exercised
over the owners and occupiers of land, albeit accompanied by great
emphasis on a partnership approach and assistance for landowners
taking positive steps to maintain and enhance the conservation value of
their land. This trend has been the product of greater public and political willingness to accept environmental objectives, including nature
conservation, as a legitimate reason for restricting the freedom of landowners to do as they wish with their land, coupled with appreciation
of the failure of the previous regimes to cope adequately with the varied
threats to important habitats and to biodiversity.

5.1.4   Throughout, though, there is a danger that by concentrating attention
and effort on the designated sites, the health of the wider countryside
(and of urban habitats) is ignored. There is a risk that the efforts for
designated sites are seen as being a complete response to the need to
take action to conserve biodiversity, overlooking the harm being done
in other areas. Biodiversity cannot be secured by the conservation of a
range of designated sites, however extensive, if the surrounding landscape has been become a "no-go area" for wildlife. Ensuring that the
whole of the country offers supportive habitats for species of many
sorts is harder than looking after a few designated sites, but ultimately
more valuable.

5.1.5   The starting-point for all designations is that while some protection
is offered to all land through the operation of the general law—planning
controls, pollution controls, nuisance, etc.—particular areas can be
identified which are so valuable or so sensitive that further measures
are justified in order to protect them. The first task therefore is to establish the criteria for identifying those sites which are to benefit from

---

[3] NPACA 1949, s.23.
[4] WCA 1981, s.28 (as originally enacted).
[5] CNHR 1994, Part II.
[6] WCA 1981, ss.28–28R, as substituted by CRWA 2000, Sched. 9; similar strengthening
of the regime is proposed for Scotland in *The Nature of Scotland* (Scottish Executive,
2001).

enhanced protection and procedures for their designation. Then an appropriate legal regime must be adopted to offer the desired level of protection. The following are the most commonly used legal devices.[7]

Ownership

Taking the land into the ownership of a body dedicated to nature con-   **5.1.6**
servation is probably the strongest way of securing that it will be managed in the interests of conservation. The owner is in the best position
to ensure that damaging activities are avoided, to exclude visitors who
might cause disturbance and to undertake any positive action required
to maintain or enhance the value of the area as habitat for wildlife.
Although there is provision for land being acquired, compulsorily in
some circumstances, the acquisition of land by public authorities has
not been a major element in the approach to conservation. The cost of
large-scale acquisitions, respect for property rights and a confidence in
the ability of landowners to treat their land with respect have combined
to limit the area of land taken over by the state. Outside the statutory
schemes, several non-governmental bodies, such as the National Trusts,
the Royal Society for the Protection of Birds and the John Muir Trust
have become significant landowners in sensitive areas of the country,
extending beyond any formal designations the area of land managed in
the interests of conservation.

Management Agreements

In place of the state acquiring land directly, the preference has been to   **5.1.7**
allow existing owners and occupiers to retain their interest in the land,
but to encourage them to use their land in ways which respect the
needs of wildlife. In many situations reliance is placed on management
agreements, whereby those with an interest in land agree with public
authorities to deal with the land in a particular way in exchange for
compensation which covers any expense incurred or profits foregone.[8]
Such agreements can include both negative and positive obligations on
the part of the occupier, prohibiting certain forms of harmful activity
and requiring certain beneficial ones, and they can run with the land,
binding the successors to those who entered the agreements.

It is hoped that since such agreements are voluntarily entered and   **5.1.8**
offer compensation for the restrictions imposed on the land there should
be more willing, and hence more effective, compliance with the agreed

---

[7] See also paras 1.6.14–1.6.29; K. Last, "Mechanisms for Environmental Regulation—
A Study of Habitat Conservation" in A. Ross (ed.), *Environment and Regulation*
(Hume Papers on Public Policy, vol.8, No.2) (2000).
[8] C. Rodgers and J. Bishop, *Management Agreements for Promoting Nature Conservation* (1998).

measures than if they were imposed by law, while a system of individual agreements allows all the particular needs and problems of each site to be taken into account in a way impossible if general legislation were employed. Critics, however, point out that this system of "buying off" landowners is not only unduly expensive, but also enables unscrupulous landowners, by threatening to develop their land, to blackmail the authorities into paying out large sums, regardless of how speculative the proposed development might be. This has led to increasing emphasis on the positive aspects of these arrangements—paying for the active management of the land with conservation in mind rather than offering compensation to desist from causing harm.[9] The costs of negotiating individual agreements has also led to a greater reliance on focused schemes that offer standard payments in exchange for standard management requirements.[10]

Byelaws

5.1.9   Where legal restrictions are required, particularly to regulate the conduct of visitors to the land as opposed to that of those with a legal interest in it, recourse is frequently had to byelaws. Again this allows the particular needs of each site to be taken into account and the restrictions to be shaped accordingly. Moreover, the consultation and confirmation procedures associated with the making of byelaws allow there to be some check on what is being done in the name of nature conservation. However, there can be difficulties in ensuring that byelaws are brought to the notice of the public, and visitors to a site often will not know that they have crossed into a special area, far less that they are now bound by an additional set of legal controls.

Planning controls

5.1.10   Throughout Great Britain, the town and country planning system offers a degree of control over many forms of development which could damage the value of an area as far as wildlife is concerned. One way of providing enhanced protection to those areas identified as being of particular value is to ensure that this value is properly respected in the operation of the planning system, which can be strengthened by the

---

[9] "Ministers expect that management agreements on SSSIs will be used to facilitate their positive management . . . Ministers are not prepared for public money to be paid out simply to prevent new operations which could destroy or damage these national assets." *(Guidelines on Management Agreement Payments and Other Related Matters* (DETR, 2001) para. 1.2).

[10] *e.g.* SNH's Peatland Management Scheme.

addition of further controls for particular areas.[11] Thus, development plans will reflect the status and objectives of the various designated areas, environmental impact assessments (or at the very least consultation with the conservation bodies) may be required when particular proposals are being considered, and express permission may be required for certain minor forms of development which are normally permitted without the need for individual application or consideration. However, two drawbacks of reliance on the planning system must be noted. In the first place, planning controls are operated by local authorities and central government departments which have responsibilities beyond nature conservation, in particular a concern for the economic well-being of their areas, and where conflicts arise, the interests of conservation may often be sacrificed in favour of other policy objectives. Secondly, planning controls do not extend to most activities in agriculture and forestry, so that many things which can be done on or to the land and which damage its value as a habitat for wildlife fall outwith the scope of planning controls.[12]

Notifications

A further technique is used to avoid the imposition of too great a burden of legal restrictions. Where certain activities may be harmful, what the law provides is not that the activity is prohibited nor that it requires some form of official approval, but rather that the appropriate official body must simply be notified of the proposed activity before it takes place. Such notification enables the authority, where it considers it appropriate, to invoke any of the other control mechanisms which may be available in the circumstances. In this way it should be possible for steps to be taken where necessary to prevent damage occurring, whilst avoiding both the blanket imposition of restrictions which may often be inappropriate or unnecessary, and the formality, delay and bureaucracy of a system of licences, permissions or approvals. The efficacy of such an approach is, however, dependent on both adequate knowledge of and compliance with the notification requirement, and the availability of and willingness to use[13] suitable tools to ensure that damage can in fact be avoided in those cases where it is considered necessary to intervene.

5.1.11

---

[11] See section 8.2, below.

[12] Extending planning controls to agricultural, forestry, sporting and conservation-related developments was suggested for Scotland in the *Recommendations for Action* from the Land Reform Policy Group (1996, Scottish Office; p. 35), but no concrete proposals have materialised.

[13] In Scotland prior to 1998 only six cases of unlawful operations on SSSIs were reported by SNH and its predecessors to the procurator fiscal, and none was prosecuted (A. Osborne; LL.M. dissertation at Aberdeen University).

Management Plans

5.1.12 The management plans and statements created for designated areas are acquiring more significance as a result of the increasing emphasis on a positive approach to conservation issues based on partnership between a range of public bodies and landowners. In some cases, such as National Parks[14] and Areas of Outstanding Natural Beauty[15] in England and Wales, there is no specific obligation on others to take these plans into account, although obviously they are very relevant to any general obligation to have regard to the objectives of the designated area. In other cases, though, the plans are given significant status, *e.g.* for National Parks in Scotland there is a duty on public authorities to have regard to the Park Plans,[16] whilst for SSSIs in England and Wales, management statements must now be prepared for all sites. A management scheme can be introduced and action taken against occupiers if failing to comply with the scheme is damaging the conservation value of the site.[17] The Habitats and Species Directive also establishes a role for management plans.[18] The focus thus shifts from prohibiting a few specified activities to endeavouring to give effect to a wider management plan, which is given some direct legal standing, with potential for further measures to ensure implementation if necessary.

5.1.13 The techniques listed above appear in various forms throughout the legal regimes for the various designated areas, often in combination and with additional devices not mentioned here. More generally, the fact of designation should alert people to the value of a site and may influence their treatment of it, *e.g.* a public authority subject to a duty to have regard to the conservation of the countryside, biological diversity, etc.,[19] should consider the consequences of its action for nature conservation before doing anything which affects a designated site.[20] As with so much of the law affecting nature conservation, the fragmented form of the law means that any general comments are of limited practical value, and the detailed rules for each of the designations must now be considered. This fragmentation is exacerbated by differences within Great Britain, so that the rules for Sites of Special Scientific Interest are currently significantly different in Scotland from those in

---

[14] See para. 5.11.10, below.
[15] See paras 5.12.7, below.
[16] See paras 5.11.28–5.11.29, below; planning authorities are required to pay "special attention" to the desirability of exercising their powers consistently with the Plan.
[17] See paras 5.5.18, 5.5.26–28, below.
[18] Directive 92/43, art. 6(1).
[19] See section 2.2, above.
[20] Land which has been designated may also be eligible for the exemption from Inheritance Tax available in the event of certain transfers to non-commercial organisations; Inheritance Tax Act (née Capital Transfer Tax Act) 1984, s.26.

England and Wales,[21] whilst the National Parks north and south of the border are very different creatures.[22] The various designations are not exclusive, and it is common for the same piece of land to be covered by a number of different legal regimes, in particular as a Site of Special Scientific Interest and as part of a broader conservation or landscape area.

The rest of this chapter deals with all of the designations given statut- **5.1.14** ory recognition, but many others exist, with varying degrees of official recognition. In England and Wales stretches of Heritage Coast have been identified, and in Scotland there are Preferred Coastal Conserva- tion Zones. There is an inventory, originally compiled by the Nature Conservancy Council, of Ancient and Semi-natural Woodlands which are worthy of particular care, while the Forestry Commission designates some of its land as Forest Parks. At the international level there are a number of Biosphere Reserves, designated under UNESCO's Man and the Biosphere Programme, and Biogenetic Reserves under a Council of Europe programme. There are also many other local or more specialised designations. In all cases, however, if these designations are to have any legal impact on the way in which the land is treated, the sites must also be included in one of the statutory designations described below. The table below indicates the extent of the main designations.

EUROPEAN SITES

European Sites were created to give effect to the E.C. Birds and Habitat **5.2.1** and Species Directives. When first introduced, they marked a signific- ant strengthening of the protection available to any sites in Great Bri- tain, but have now to some extent been overtaken by the new arrange- ments for SSSIs in England and Wales under the Countryside and Rights of Way Act 2000.[23] The sites designated under the European measures together comprise the Natura 2000 network and E.C. law dictates the key elements of the regime affecting them.[24] Status as a European Site under British law can be acquired in four ways. The first comprises Special Protection Areas designated under the Birds Direct- ive, while the remaining three are sites at different stages of the process of designating Special Areas of Conservation under the Habitats and Species Directive.[25]

---

[21] Some of these differences, such as the existence of the advisory committee in Scotland (see para. 5.5.8, below), pre-date devolution and the changes introduced by the Coun- tryside and Rights of Way Act 2000.
[22] See section 5.11, below.
[23] See paras 5.5.17–5.5.36, below.
[24] See generally, C. Rodgers, "Managing Natura 2000: Priorities for Implementing Euro- pean Wildlife Law" [2001] J.P.L. 265.
[25] CNHR 1994, reg. 10.

Protected Areas in Great Britain
(by number and area in hectares)

	Scotland	England	Wales	Cross-border	Total
European Sites					
—Special Protection Areas	131	76	13	3	223
	489,932	600,580	68,968	81,414	1,240,894
—candidate Special Areas of Conservation	219	213	85	7	524
	797,241	796,050	580,308	115,888	2,289,486
National Nature Reserves	72	208	65	—	345
	116,361	83,703	18,791	—	218,855
Marine Nature Reserves	—	1	1	—	2
	—	—	—	—	
Sites of Special Scientific Interest	1,449	4,115	1,021	—	6,585
	957,710	1,097,766	226,872	—	2,282,348
Ramsar Sites	50	66	7	4	127
	283,137	294,284	11,367	82,973	671,761
National Scenic Areas	40	—	—	—	40
	1,001,800	—	—	—	1,001,800
Areas of Outstanding Natural Beauty	—	36	4	1	4
	—	2,018,400	72,700	32,600	2,123,700

Data from reports and web-pages of the statutory conservation bodies, as at April 2001 with some later data.

Special Protection Areas

Under the Directive on the Conservation of Wild Birds,[26] the Member   **5.2.2**
States of the European Communities are obliged to take measures for
the conservation of wild birds in their territories. In particular, states
must designate the most suitable territories in number and size as Special Protection Areas (SPAs) for the conservation of the many rarer
species listed in Annex I to the Directive,[27] and take "similar measures"
for migratory birds not so listed.[28] The obligation once such an area
has been established was originally that Member States were to take
"appropriate steps to avoid pollution or deterioration of habitats or any
disturbances affecting the birds,"[29] but this was amended by the Habitats and Species Directive so that the obligations are now the same as
for Special Areas of Conservation.[30]

Both the designation and treatment of Special Protection Areas have   **5.2.3**
given rise to considerable litigation. In relation to designation, there is
a clear obligation on states to carry out this process,[31] and to ensure
that a sufficient number and size of areas are designated.[32] A series of
cases have emphasised that designation is to be carried out on the basis
of ornithological criteria alone, without regard for competing economic
or social interests.[33] This does allow Member States an element of discretion in identifying the precise areas to be designated, but this is
strictly limited as to the criteria to be used.

The most significant British contribution to the case law has been *R.*   **5.2.4**
v. Secretary of State for the Environment, ex p. RSPB,[34] in which the
European Court of Justice confirmed that in determining whether a
particular area is to be designated, economic or other factors cannot be
taken into account. The case arose from the Secretary of State's exclusion of a substantial area of Lappel Bank from an SPA designated in
the Medway estuary, a decision admittedly taken with regard to the
economic factors arising from the potential for expanding the port of
Sheerness. The European Court of Justice held that such factors should

---

[26] Directive 79/409; see paras 7.4.3–7.4.13, below.

[27] *ibid.*, art. 4(1).

[28] *ibid.*, art. 4(2).

[29] *ibid.*, art. 4(4).

[30] Directive 92/43, art. 7, applying art. 6(2)–(4).

[31] *Commission v. Italy* (C-334/89) [1991] E.C.R. I-93.

[32] *Commission v. Netherlands* (C-3/96) [1998] E.C.R. I-3031; *Commission v. France* (C-96/98) [1999] E.C.R. I-8351 (Marais Poitevin).

[33] *Commission v. Germany* (C-57/89) [1991] E.C.R. I-883 (Leybucht Dykes); *Commission v. Spain* (C-355/90) [1993] E.C.R. I-4223 (Santoña Marshes); *R. v. Secretary of State for the Environment, ex p. RSPB* (C-44/95) [1996] E.C.R. I-3805, [1997] Q.B. 206 (Lappel Bank) *Commission v. Netherlands* (C-3/96) [1998] E.C.R. I-3031. See para. 5.2.7, below in relation to Special Areas of Conservation.

[34] (C-44/95) [1996] E.C.R. I-3805, [1997] Q.B. 206.

have had no place in the decision, but by the time the case was concluded, the area in question was already being developed.[35] At a more detailed level, the issue of the boundary to be drawn was raised in *WWF U.K. Ltd v. Secretary of State for Scotland*.[36] The Court of Session held that deciding on a precise boundary was an integral part of the task of identifying the most suitable territories to be designated and rejected the argument that the Secretary of State had unduly fettered his discretion by using the boundaries of existing SSSIs as the starting point for this process. The Directive inevitably left a degree of discretion to Member States in fixing the exact boundaries, but this discretion was to be exercised on ornithological criteria alone.

5.2.5   In terms of protecting an SPA once designated, the European Court of Justice's interpretation of the original provisions of the Birds Directive in the *Leybucht Dykes* case made it clear that was only in exceptional circumstances that any action which reduced the size (and by clear implication, the quality) of an SPA could be permitted, and held that the balancing of conservation interests with economic and recreational requirements had no place in the treatment of Special Protection Areas once they have been declared.[37] Member States were unhappy at this almost absolute priority given to conservation and the Directive was amended by the application of the provisions in the Habitats and Species Directive, which do permit conservation concerns to be sacrificed in limited circumstances where there are reasons of overriding public interest.[38] Nevertheless, there still remains a strong obligation to ensure adequate protection for designated SPAs, and even for areas that should have been included within SPAs.[39]

Special Areas of Conservation

5.2.6   The status of European Sites within Great Britain is also conferred on three categories of site (four in England) identified in relation to Special Areas of Conservation (SACs) under the Habitats and Species Directive.[40] The first of these is sites that have completed the full designation

---

[35] An injunction pending the final outcome of the case was refused because the RSPB could not provide the required undertaking in damages (to compensate the port for the delays if it was finally held that there was no flaw in the initial decision), and the courts did not see E.C. law as providing a way of circumventing this requirement; for discussion of this point in the Court of Appeal and commentary by J. Harte see (1995) 7 J.E.L. 245, especially at pp. 276–277. In *Commission v. Germany* ((C-57/89) [1991] E.C.R. I-883 at p. 889), which is perhaps analogous, interim measures were refused by the European Court of Justice.

[36] [1999] 1 C.M.L.R. 1021, [1999] Env. L.R. 632.

[37] *Commission v. Germany* (C-57/89, [1991] E.C.R. I-883.

[38] See paras 5.2.20–5.2.26, below.

[39] *Commission v. France* (C-96/98) [1999] E.C.R. I-8351 (Marais Poitevin).

[40] CNHR 1994, reg. 10.

process at national and Community level[41] and have been formally designated by the Minister as SACs.[42] The second comprises those sites which after nomination at national level have been selected by the Commission as sites of Community importance and therefore require only formal designation at national level to become full SACs. The third category covers sites which have not been nominated at national level as candidate SACs but which the Commission proposes on the basis that they host priority habitats or species. This third category are treated as European Sites only during the period that their status is being considered at E.C. level and are not covered by the provisions in relation to plans and projects which play a significant part in protecting the other categories of site.[43] The fourth category, which applies in England only, are sites which the government has submitted to the Commission as candidates for inclusion in the list of sites of Community importance.[44] At present the designation processes have not reached the stage where there are any sites formally designated as SACs,[45] but as a matter of policy[46] (and of law in England in view of the fourth category noted above), all candidate SACs (*i.e.* sites nominated as potential SACs by the British authorities) should be treated if they do have that status.

The criteria for nominating or selecting an SAC are set out in Annex III of the Directive and require Member States to identify areas which represent the habitats or host the species listed in the Directive as requiring protection; those requiring special care are listed as priority habitats and species.[47] As with SPAs, it has been held that nomination is to be based on the scientific criteria alone. In *R. v. Secretary of State for the Environment, Transport and the Regions, ex p. First Corporation Shipping Ltd*,[48] the proposal to nominate the Severn Estuary as a candidate SAC was challenged by the port authority for Bristol, the argument being based on the terms of article 2(3) of the Directive which states that measures taken pursuant to the Directive should take into account economic, social and cultural requirements. The European

5.2.7

---

[41] Designation is governed by arts 4 and 5 of the Directive; see paras 7.4.21–7.4.23, below.

[42] CNHR 1994, reg. 8; ministerial designation must be within six years of the site's acceptance at E.C. level.

[43] *ibid.*, reg. 10(2), disapplying regs 20(1),(2), 24 and 48; see below for details.

[44] *ibid.*, reg. 10(1)(e) added by the Conservation (Natural Habitats, etc.) (England) (Amendment) Regulations 2000 (S.I. 2000 No.192).

[45] The steps so far towards designation for the United Kingdom are given in the *First Report by the United Kingdom under Article 17 on implementation of the Directive from June 1994 to December 2000* (DEFRA, 2001) (hereafter "*First Implementation Report*"), p. 18.

[46] *e.g.* NPPG 14, *Natural Heritage* (Scottish Office, 1999), para. 39.

[47] See para. 7.4.19, below; details of the selection process in the U.K. are given in the *First Implementation Report*, pp.9–20.

[48] (C-371/98) [2000] E.C.R. I-9253.

Court of Justice rejected this argument, stating that the requirement to set up "a coherent European ecological network" of SACs under art. 3 of the Directive could only be satisfied if all eligible sites were nominated at the first stage, since without detailed knowledge of the economic, social and cultural requirements in other states Member States could not judge whether omitting a particular site would jeopardise that overall objective. Only if all sites that met the technical criteria were put forward would the Commission have an exhaustive list from which to ensure that the coherent network was established.

Protection

5.2.8 The protection of European Sites rests on a number of measures in domestic law. In order to fulfil their statutory duty to protect them from damage or deterioration, ministers and conservation authorities can make use of management agreements, notification procedures delaying or prohibiting damaging operations, byelaws and compulsory purchase, whilst any plan or project likely to have adverse consequences on the site is to be given approval only if strict conditions are met. Several of these mechanisms control not just activities within the boundaries of a site, but also those outwith the boundaries that may have an effect on the state of the site. The whole framework is now somewhat awkward since it was designed to build on the legal structures for SSSIs and increase that level of protection for the benefit of European Sites, whereas the new provisions for SSSIs in England and Wales establish a significantly different regime, in some respects offering greater, rather than lesser, protection than applies for European Sites.[49] Where a site is covered by both designations, there may be cases in England and Wales where the conservation authorities' reliance on the new SSSI provisions is preferable for utilising the measures for European Sites.

5.2.9 Within Great Britain, the Minister is under a duty to keep a register of European Sites[50] and to notify the appropriate statutory conservation body when an entry is made or amended.[51] It is then the duty of that body to notify the owners and occupiers of land within the site, the relevant local planning authority and anyone else that the Minister directs.[52] The entry on the register is a local land charge in England and Wales, while in Scotland the planning authority has to maintain a register of European Sites of which they have been notified.[53]

5.2.10 The starting point for conservation responsibilities is that the Minister and the nature conservation bodies are under a duty to exercise

---

[49] The potential for making management notices is one example.
[50] CNHR 1994, reg. 11.
[51] *ibid.*, reg. 12.
[52] *ibid.*, reg. 13.
[53] *ibid.*, regs 14, 15.

their functions under the main conservation legislation so as to secure compliance with the Habitats and Species Directive,[54] which requires for European Sites that appropriate steps are taken to avoid deterioration of the habitats or disturbance of the species for which they have been designated.[55] All other "competent authorities"[56] are under the lesser duty to have regard to the requirements of the Directive.[57] The stronger duty could have been fulfilled by a willingness to make full use of the powers of compulsory purchase under that legislation to take the land into ownership which would ensure that it was managed for conservation purposes, but the approach taken was to rely primarily on the existing mechanisms used for SSSIs, strengthening them where necessary to ease the task of securing compliance with the Directive. Since almost all European Sites will already have been designated as SSSIs, and possibly as nature reserves, provision is made for existing management agreements, orders, notifications and byelaws to continue to have effect as if made under the provisions for European Sites.[58]

Throughout the various mechanisms described below, and in relation to various other potential threats to a European Site, there is a general requirement that applies whenever a plan or project that might affect the site is being considered for approval, in essence permitting approval to be given only if there is to be no adverse effect on the site or there is an overriding reason for giving approval. This is more fully discussed below. **5.2.11**

In keeping with the preference that was so dominant for a voluntary approach to nature conservation,[59] the first mechanism provided for the protection of European Sites is the management agreement. The appropriate nature conservation body can make an agreement with the owner, lessee and occupier of land within a European Site for its management, **5.2.12**

---

[54] *ibid.*, reg. 3(2); the legislation covered is Part III of NPACA 1949 (nature reserves), s.49A of CSA 1967 (management agreements), s.15 of CA 1968 (management agreements), Part I and ss.28–38 of WCA 1981 (species protection, SSSIs, other habitat protection), ss.131–134 of EPA 1990 (nature conservation bodies and functions), ss. 2, 3, 5, 6, 7 and 11 of NHSA 1991 (duties and functions of SNH, Natural Heritage Areas) and the 1994 Regulations themselves. For the obligation in relation to marine sites see para. 5.2.30, below.

[55] Directive 92/43, art. 6(2); see *Managing Natura 2000 Sites: The Provisions of Article 6 of the 'Habitats' Directive 92/43/EEC* (European Commission, 2000).

[56] This term covers Ministers, government departments, public or statutory undertakers, public bodies and holders of public office; CNHR 1994 reg. 6(1).

[57] *ibid.*, reg. 3(4).

[58] *ibid.*, regs 17, 18, 21, 27, 31.

[59] The need for stronger powers to meet the obligations under E.C. law for European Sites itself played a major part in overcoming the political reluctance to move from a wholly voluntary approach to one where there are more direct regulatory powers in the background; see paras 1.6.3–1.6.12, above.

conservation, restoration or protection.[60] The power to make agreements is extended to apply to land adjacent to such a site as well; this
is one of several features where the legal regime for European Sites
can have an impact outwith the boundaries of the sites themselves.
These agreements may provide for the management of the land and the
carrying out of specific activities or tasks and can provide for payments
for the costs of work or as compensation for restrictions imposed by
the agreement.[61] The agreement can thus be to secure long-term management or simply to carry out particular works, and the scope to control activities outwith the boundaries of the site may be important, particularly where water flow or drainage are significant to the state of the
site. An agreement can run with the land, binding the successors to the
original parties, in England and Wales as if it were a restrictive covenant that the conservation body is entitled to enforce (but without the
Lands Tribunal having the power to discharge or modify it), and in
Scotland by direct provision enabling the conservation body to register
the agreement in the Land Register or Register of Sasines and then
enforce it against anyone with an interest in the land.[62]

5.2.13   The second mechanism makes use of the fact that most European
Sites will already be designated as SSSIs and modifies the restrictions
on the rights of owners and occupiers to carry out the potentially damaging operations notified when the SSSI was designated. The 1994
Regulations build on the system created by the Wildlife and Countryside Act 1981, and still applying in Scotland.[63] The process for designating an SSSI includes notification of a list of potentially damaging
operations (PDOs) that the conservation body considers likely to
damage the flora, fauna or geological or physiographical features for
which the land was designated. For European Sites the basic pattern
established for SSSIs is adjusted by permitting the conservation body
at any time to amend the original notification, with regard to both the
reason for designation and the list of PDOs.[64] This avoids the position
where the conservation body has "only one bite at the cherry", a situ-

---

[60] CNHR 1994, reg. 16. The power to enter management agreements is expressly con-
ferred on a number of limited owners of land, including tenants for life under the
Settled Land Act 1925, universities and colleges under the Universities and Colleges
Estates Act 1925, certain church lands, liferenters in posession and trustees (reg. 86).

[61] There are further rules on the payment of farm capital grants (CNHR 1994, regs 88–89).

[62] Third parties *bona fide* onerously acquiring their interest prior to recording of the
agreement are not bound.

[63] The modifications for England and Wales introduced by the Countryside and Rights
of Way Act 2000 have brought the systems for SSSIs and European Sites into much
closer alignment on some issues, *e.g.* in relation to prohibiting operations, modifying
the list of PDOs and making byelaws, but the automatic prohibition on PDOs unless
consent is given and the new provisions for management notices in SSSIs go beyond
what is available for European Sites as such; see section 5.5, below.

[64] CNHR 1994, reg. 18.

ation that risks either gaps in the notification or an excessively thorough listing of all imaginable features and operations with the consequent excessive regulatory burden on the owners.

The owner or occupier must give written notice before carrying out any **5.2.14** of these operations and can proceed only if one of a number of conditions is met.[65] These are that the conservation body has given its written consent,[66] that the operation is carried out in accordance with a management agreement or that four months have passed from the date of the notification.[67] In the absence of a reasonable excuse, carrying out the operation without notice or without these conditions being met is a crime, but it expressly stated that a reasonable excuse is provided by either an emergency, provided that details are notified to the conservation body as soon as possible, or by the grant of planning permission for the operation.[68] These provisions therefore do not prohibit operations that are potentially damaging, but merely impose a four month delay, during which time a management agreement can be reached or stronger measures imposed.

The stronger measures available include a special nature conserva- **5.2.15** tion order.[69] These orders are made by the Minister after consultation with the conservation body in relation to operations that appear likely to destroy or damage the valuable flora, fauna or features of the site. Orders take effect as soon as they are made, and can be amended, but lapse after nine months unless the Minister confirms that he has considered the order and does not propose to amend or revoke it. Notice of an order, and the means of making representations or objections (at least 28 days must be permitted for this) must be served on every owner and occupier of the land and on the local planning authority as well as advertised in the London or Edinburgh Gazette and at least one local newspaper; the requirement to notify owners and occupiers can be replaced by notices fixed to conspicuous objects on the land. In the absence of representations or objections, the Minister is to consider the

---

[65] *ibid.*, reg. 19.

[66] See paras 5.2.20–5.2.24, below on the requirements before consent can be given.

[67] The four month period can by agreement be extended indefinitely; if notice to terminate this agreement is given, then at least one further month must pass before the operation becomes lawful (CNHR 1994, reg. 87).

[68] By referring to an "operation authorised by a planning permission granted on an application under [the planning legislation]" (CNHR 1994, reg. 23(4)(b)), the scope of the defence is limited to operations with the benefit of an express grant of permission, not those with deemed permission under the General Permitted Development Orders (see para. 8.2.9, below). The grant of planning permission will only be lawful in circumstances where the tests for any approval for plans or projects affecting a site are met (see paras 5.2.20–5.2.24, below).

[69] CNHR 1994, reg. 22; during 2001 there were special nature conservation orders in force affecting nine sites in Scotland and 14 in England (SNH, *Facts and Figures 2000–2001*, pp. 53–54; "Facts and Figures" section of English Nature's web-pages at www.english-nature.gov.uk.

order and confirm, amend or revoke it. Where there are representations or objections within the specified period, then a local inquiry or hearing must be held before the Minister considers the order and its conformation, amendment or revocation. The confirmation order must be publicised in the same way and any legal challenge to its validity must be made within six weeks.[70] Orders are registered as local land charges or in the Land Register of Scotland or General Register of Sasines, and must be included in the annual reports of the conservation bodies.[71]

5.2.16   Where an order is in force, the owner or occupier is again required to give notice before carrying out any of the listed operations, and these may proceed only if the conservation body gives its written consent or if the operation is carried out in accordance with a management agreement.[72] Where a special nature conservation order has been made, therefore, the controls on owners and occupiers are considerably strengthened, in that operations can be prohibited indefinitely, as opposed to merely delayed for four months.[73] A breach of these provisions is a criminal offence, but again the presence of a reasonable excuse provides a defence, including emergencies and operations with planning permission. The offence attracts a higher penalty than under the more general provisions, and in addition to any other penalty, the offender may be ordered to carry out operations in order to restore the land to its former condition.[74] If the effect of a special nature conservation order is to lower the value of an agricultural unit, compensation is payable by the conservation body to any applicant with an interest in the land.[75]

5.2.17   The controls so far discussed apply only to the owners and occupiers of land, but sites can be damaged by the activities of others. In order to prevent this, the nature conservation body can make byelaws for the site under the provisions for making byelaws for nature reserves.[76] The byelaws can apply to land surrounding or adjoining the site as well as the site itself and may address a wide range of issues including entry or movement of people, animals or vehicles, killing or disturbing any creatures, taking or interference with vegetation or soil, depositing of

---

[70] *ibid.*, Sched. 1.

[71] *ibid.*, reg. 22 (4)(6).

[72] *ibid.*, reg. 23.

[73] This is now automatically the position for SSSIs in England and Wales, without the need for the Minister to make any further order; see para. 5.5.21, below.

[74] CNHR 1994, reg. 26.

[75] *ibid.*, reg. 25. The amount of compensation represents the difference between the value of the interest in the land as it is and as it would be if the order had not been made, and there are rules on assessment, payment of interest, disputes, etc. (*ibid.*, regs 91–93).

[76] *ibid.*, reg. 28, applying NPACA 1949, s.20 which in turn applies ss.236–238 of the Local Government Act 1972 and ss.201–204 of the Local Government Act (Scotland) 1973, with byelaws subject to ministerial approval (reg.94); see para. 5.3.5, below.

rubbish or the lighting of fires. The byelaws, however, cannot limit the exercise of rights of the owner, occupier or lessee of the land,[77] the exercise of public rights of way or the exercise of functions of certain statutory undertakers, drainage and fisheries bodies and telecommunication operators.[78] Compensation is payable where a person's rights are restricted by byelaws.[79]

The final tool available to secure that a site does not suffer deterioration or damage is compulsory purchase.[80] This is available where the conservation body is satisfied that it is impossible to reach a management agreement in relation to an interest in land within the site[81] on terms that appear to it to be reasonable, or where an agreement has been reached but broken in a way that prevents or impairs the satisfactory management of the site. If the breach is capable of remedy, compulsory purchase is only possible if there has been a failure to remedy it within a reasonable time of the conservation body serving a notice requiring the remedying of the breach. Disputes over whether there has been a breach are referred to arbitration in the hands of an appointee of the Lord Chancellor or Lord President. In England and Wales, reliance on the new powers for management notices for SSSIs may provide a less dramatic alternative where deterioration is to be prevented.[82] **5.2.18**

Other provisions in the 1994 Regulations provide a range of authorised officials with powers of entry to ascertain if an offence has been committed, if special nature conservation order should be made, to assess compensation and to survey land with a view to acquiring an interest in it.[83] **5.2.19**

Plans and Projects

A major feature of the regime for protecting European Sites is the restriction on the circumstances in which approval can be give for any plan or project affecting a site. The basic rules, taken directly from the Habitats and Species Directive,[84] are laid out in the 1994 Regulations, which also make specific provisions in order to incorporate these requirements into a number of specific approval mechanisms. The rules **5.2.20**

---

[77] Control over these parties is achieved by the restrictions on PDOs or by means of a management agreement.

[78] CNHR 1994, reg. 29.

[79] *ibid.*, regs 30, 96, 97.

[80] *ibid.*, reg. 32; the Acquisition of Land Act 1981, Compulsory Purchase Act 1965 and the Acquisition of Land (Authorisation Procedure) (Scotland) Act 1947 apply to such purchases (*ibid.*, reg. 98).

[81] Note that whereas the power to enter management agreements extends to land adjacent to a European Site, the power of compulsory purchase is restricted to the site itself.

[82] See paras 5.5.26–5.5.28, below.

[83] CNHR 1994 regs.90, 95, 99.

[84] Directive 92/43, art. 6.

apply to any plan or project which is likely to have a significant effect on a European site and is not directly connected with or necessary to the management of the site,[85] and not just to projects on the site itself, but to all those that may have a significant effect on it.[86] The body responsible for giving approval must make an assessment of the implications for the site, and it is provided that the proposer of the plan must provide any information that is reasonably required and that the authorising body must consult the relevant statutory conservation body, and may consult the public.

5.2.21 Approval can be given only if the authorising body is satisfied that there will be no adverse effect on the integrity of the site[87] or, if there will be an adverse effect, that a number of very strict conditions are met. The determination of whether there are adverse effects is to be taken in the light of the Directive's objectives of avoiding any "significant" disturbance,[88] and consideration is to be given to both the effects on the survival across its natural range of the species being protected and the effects on the species on the particular site.[89] In many circumstances the determination of effects will take place as part of a formal environmental impact assessment of the proposal required as part of the approval process,[90] but this need not be the case, *e.g.* the statutory conservation bodies in deciding whether to permit a PDO will be required to assess the proposal's impact on the conservation value of the site but not to carry out a full environmental impact assessment. The ability to use conditions in any permission to obviate any potential adverse effects is also relevant.[91]

5.2.22 The main requirement where there is an adverse effect is that the

---

[85] The meaning of "plan or project" was considered at first instance in *RSPB v. Secretary of State for Scotland*, 2000 S.L.T. 22 at pp. 27–28. A broad definition, including all decisions which would lead to some activity on the site was rejected, and the phrase was seen as referring to what is normally regarded as development or land use proposals, extraneous to the management of the site.

[86] These requirements do not apply to sites that are European Sites only by virtue of the Commission considering that they be added to those nominated by the British authorities (CNHR 1994, regs 10(2), 48(7)); see para. 5.2.6, above.

[87] In *WWF–U.K. Ltd v. Secretary of State for Scotland* [1999] 1 C.M.L.R. 1021, [1999] Env. L.R. 632, Lord Nimmo Smith accepted the definition given in para. 2 of Appendix A to Annex D to Scottish Office Circular 6/1995: "The integrity of a site is the coherence of its ecological structure and function, across its whole area, that enables it to sustain the habitat, complex of habitats and/or the levels of populations of the species for which it was classified."

[88] Habitats and Species Directive, art. 6(2); see para. 5.2.27, below.

[89] *RSPB v. Secretary of State for Scotland*, 2000 S.L.T. 1272.

[90] See section 8.3, below.

[91] In *WWF–U.K. v. Secretary of State for Scotland* (above), it was accepted that it may be impossible to guarantee the absence of adverse effects, but what was required was for the authority to identify potential risks so far as foreseeable and to put in place a legally enforceable framework to prevent them materialising.

plan or project can be approved only if it is to be carried out for "imperative reasons of overriding public interest".[92] These reasons may include social or economic ones,[93] but in relation to some sites only a restricted category of reasons will be acceptable. Where the site hosts a priority species or habitat, then only reasons relating to human health, public safety, beneficial consequences of primary importance to the environment or reasons expressly accepted by the European Commission can be accepted. The further condition to be met is that there are no alternative solutions, although it is not clear how radical the consideration of options must be.[94] It is therefore at this stage of considering particular damaging proposals, not at designation, that there is some scope for a balancing of the needs of conservation against other public interests. The hurdle to be overcome before damaging activities can be permitted is a high one, especially in relation to priority sites, but the scope for conservation to be overridden in some circumstances has made the whole scheme much more acceptable to Member States across Europe than the more absolutist approach initially adopted under the Birds Directive.

If a project is permitted to proceed despite its damaging effects, there is an obligation on the Minister to ensue that any necessary compensatory measures are taken to ensure that the overall coherence of Natura 2000 is protected.[95] Thus when the Cardiff Bay barrage scheme resulted in the loss of important feeding grounds for waders, a new wetlands reserve was created on the Gwent Levels east of Newport.[96] **5.2.23**

These requirements to scrutinise carefully new plans and projects extend to require a review of existing approvals when a site becomes a European Site, and their revocation or amendment if they cannot be justified according to the same criteria as for new plans.[97] Such review, however, does not affect the validity of any action already taken in pursuance of the approval before the site was designated. This means that a planning permission for development on a site, or consent from **5.2.24**

---

[92] CNHR 1994, reg. 49, following art. 6(4) of the Directive.

[93] In *R. v. Secretary of State for Transport, ex p. Berkshire, Buckinghamshire and Oxfordshire Naturalists Trust* [1997] Env. L.R. 80 it was held that this test would have been satisfied in relation to the Newbury bypass by virtue of the relief offered from the environmental problems caused by heavy traffic along the existing road, improved road safety and the relief of the economic burden of traffic delays; see also para. 7.4.25, below.

[94] If the proposal is for a power station, do the alternatives include simply different locations or extend to requiring greater energy efficiency so as to avoid the need for the new station? *cf.* para. 3.3.11, above.

[95] CNHR 1994, reg. 53.

[96] This has in turn given rise to legal disputes over the exercise of compulsory purchase powers to establish the new reserve: *Walters v. Welsh Development Agency* [2001] R.V.R. 93.

[97] CNHR 1994, regs 50–51.

the conservation body for a PDO granted when the site was simply an SSSI, would have to be reviewed if it was not yet implemented when the site was designated as a European Site, but that there are no consequences if the permission or consent has already been acted on. If revocation or modification of an approval is necessary, this should be done through the relevant statutory procedures, which may well involve the payment of compensation.[98]

5.2.25 These general requirements in relation to all forms of official approval, consent, permission or authorisation are supplemented by a number of more specific provisions which embed these requirements in the specific contexts of a number of particular approval regimes. Thus there are specific provisions in relation to roads and highways, electricity works, pipe-lines, orders under the Transport and Works Act 1992 and environmental consents in relation to integrated pollution prevention and control, waste management licensing and water pollution.[99] The most thorough express incorporation relates to the grant of planning permission, where there are special rules for special development orders, simplified planning zones and enterprise zones,[1] as well as detailed rules on the grant of permission and on when and how existing permissions are to be reviewed.[2] There are also rules that prevent permitted development rights extending to authorise activities that should not be permitted under the rules designed to protect European Sites.

5.2.26 Certain activities that qualify as "development" and therefore would require planning permission are given automatic permission by means of the General Permitted Development Orders, so that there is no need to apply for an express grant of planning permission before proceeding.[3] This automatic permission is now subject to a condition that if the development is likely to have a significant effect on a European Site and is not directly concerned with the management of the site, then it can proceed only if certain further stages have been completed.[4] The developers must obtain written approval from the planning authority before the development can proceed, and this can be granted only if the authority is satisfied that there will be no adverse effect on the integrity of the site. The relevant statutory conservation body can be asked for its opinion, which is conclusive, on whether such an effect is likely.[5] If the planning authority is not satisfied that there will be no adverse effect, then the development

---

[98] *e.g.* TCPA 1990, ss.97, 106; TCPSA 1997, ss.65, 232.

[99] CNHR 1994, regs 69–70, 71–74, 75–78, 79–82, and 83–85 respectively.

[1] *ibid.*, regs 64–67.

[2] *ibid.*, regs 54–59.

[3] See para. 8.2.8, below.

[4] CNHR 1994, regs 60–63.

[5] The developer may seek this opinion directly, in which case the conservation body must notify its response to both developer and planning authority, or may apply for approval from the planning authority, which must consult the conservation body.

does not enjoy permitted development rights and the developers must apply for planning permission in the standard way, and their application will be subject to scrutiny applying the same tests as for other plans affecting European Sites. It is asking a lot of landowners and developers, including those outwith the boundaries of a European Site, to be so vigilant when planning what is normally permitted development that they will notice when their operations may affect such a site and then to raise an issue which will at best delay their activities and at worst impose a requirement to seek express permission with the real risk of refusal.

Management

Underlying these detailed regulatory mechanisms are the fundamental management obligations required by the terms of the Habitats and Species Directive. For each SAC, Member States are required to establish the necessary conservation measures, involving management plans to meet the ecological requirements of the habitats types and species being protected.[6] For both SACs and SPAs states are further required to take appropriate steps to avoid the deterioration of natural habitats and the habitats of the species for which the site was designated, as well as any disturbance of those species that could be significant to the purposes of the Directive.[7] If the overall effect of the management arrangements do not protect a site adequately, then action could be taken by the European Commission before the European Court of Justice[8]

5.2.27

Taken together all of these measures offer a strong armoury for securing the conservation of European Sites, albeit that the underlying model on which they are based has been largely overtaken by the changes to SSSIs in England and Wales. Nevertheless, the effectiveness of this armoury depends on the willingness to make use of the powerful tools that are provided. A particular example, which has attracted the attention of the European Commission, is the absence of measures which protect sites from deterioration through neglect (*e.g.* failure to maintain the drainage system, failure to prevent scrub encroaching on grassland).[9] The power of compulsory purchase in the absence of a satisfactory management agreement does provide a means of taking over such sites and ensuring their long-term conservation, but there is no guarantee that this will happen and the Commission has started

5.2.28

---

[6] Directive 92/43, art. 6(1); the varied authorities and means by which this obligation is met in Great Britain are detailed in the *First Implementation Report*, pp. 25–28.

[7] *ibid.*, art. 6(2) see para. 3.3.12, above.

[8] *e.g. Commission v. France* (C-96/98) [1999] E.C.R. I-8351; *Commissions v. Greece* (C-103/00), Jan. 30, 2002 (E.C.J.).

[9] Although there are real problems in relation to many inherently dynamic habitats, *e.g.* coastal lagoons, especially when any measures to preserve them artificially will in turn have an adverse effect on other valuable habitats.

proceedings for non-compliance with the Directive on this account. Also criticised is the failure to ensure adequate surveillance to monitor the health of habitats and species, and the failure to include development plans within the scope of the strict rules for approving plans likely to affect sites.[10] European Sites thus have the potential to offer strong protection to valuable habitats, but that result is not wholly guaranteed.

Marine European Sites

5.2.29　　European Sites are not restricted to those on land, but can include areas offshore, and several marine habitats and marine species are among those given protection by the Habitats and Species Directive.[11] In an important case it has been held that the terms of the Directive are not limited to territorial waters but extend to all areas over which Member States exercise sovereign rights, requiring the application of the Directive's provisions to activities offshore.[12] In relation to offshore oil and gas operations, effect has been given to that decision through the Offshore Petroleum Activities (Conservation of Habitats) Regulations 2001,[13] while plans have been announced to designate the Darwin Mounds, near Rockall, 120 miles offshore, as the first SAC outside territorial waters.[14]

5.2.30　　The starting point for the protection of marine sites is that as well as the obligation on Ministers and conservation bodies to exercise their conservation-related powers so as to secure compliance with the Directive,[15] the same obligation to secure compliance is extended to a range of other bodies in relation to their functions relevant to marine conservation. This obligation is imposed on all "competent authorities"[16] in the exercise of their powers under a range of specific statutory provisions covering fisheries, pollution and harbours.[17] Compared to the

---

[10] Press release IP/01/1192 (August 2001).

[11] L. Warren, "Marine Protection under the E.C. Habitats and Species Directive" (1996) 17 ECOS 28; P. Jones, "Marine Nature Reserves in Britain: Past Lessons, Current Status and Future Issues" (1999) 23 Marine Policy 375 at pp. 388–395.

[12] *R. v. Secretary of State for Trade and Industry, ex p. Greenpeace Ltd* [2000] 2 C.M.L.R. 94, [2000] Env. L.R. 221. See also D. Owen, "The Application of the Wild Birds Directive beyond the Territorial Sea of European Community Member States" (2001) 13 J.E.L. 39.

[13] S.I. 2001 No.1754.

[14] *The Times*, October 24, 2001.

[15] See para. 5.2.10, above.

[16] See para. *ibid.*

[17] The list covers: the Sea Fisheries Acts (as defined in s.1 of the Sea Fisheries (Wildlife Conservation) Act 1992); the Dockyard Ports Regulation Act 1865; the Military Lands Act 1900, s.2(2); the Harbours Act 1964; the Control of Pollution Act 1974, Part II (water pollution); WCA 1981 ss.36–37 (marine nature reserves); the Civic Government (Scotland) Act 1982, ss.120–122 (control of the seashore and adjacent waters); the Water Resources Act 1991; the Land Drainage Act 1991; and the 1994 Regulations themselves (CNHR 1994, reg. 3).

position onshore, there is thus a much wider range of public authorities required to see to it that the Directive is implemented, as opposed to simply being required to have regard to its terms. Where applicable, the powers described above in relation to primarily land-based sites can be used to achieve protection (*e.g.* the wording of the law would appear to permit the use of management agreements to regulate activities on the shore adjacent to a marine European Site), but more specific powers are also conferred.

The relevant statutory conservation body is required to install markers indicating the existence and extent of the site and to notify other public authorities of the conservation objectives for the site and of operations that may damage or disturb the features or species for which it has been designated.[18] Any of the "relevant authorities"[19] may establish a management scheme under which their functions shall be exercised so as to secure compliance with the Directive, or the Minister may direct one or more authorities to establish such a scheme.[20] This direction can include specific measures that are to be taken, the appointment of one authority to co-ordinate the scheme and instructions on reporting back to the Minister. There is also a power for the conservation bodies to make byelaws for a European Marine Site, subject to the same limitations as apply for marine nature reserves.[21] The effect of such byelaws is even further restricted by the express provision that they cannot interfere with the exercise of any functions by a relevant authority nor with any statutory function nor with the right of any person.

5.2.31

To the extent that any plans or projects affecting a European Site are subject to official approval, the general rules described above apply, permitting approval to be given only where there is likely to be no adverse effect, or that there are no alternative solutions and the project is required for imperative reasons of overriding public interest. The government was held to have acted unlawfully by failing to apply these rules to the granting of oil and gas exploration licences in the Atlantic off the north-west of Scotland,[22] and in response the Offshore Petroleum Activities (Conservation of Habitats) Regulations 2001[23] have

5.2.32

---

[18] CNHR 1994, reg. 33.

[19] This term covers the statutory conservation bodies, local authorities, navigation and harbour authorities, the Environment Agency and the Scottish Environment Protection Agency, water and sewerage undertakers, internal drainage boards and local fisheries committees; CNHR 1994, reg. 5.

[20] CNHR 1994, reg.34–35.

[21] *ibid.*, reg. 36; see section 5.4, below.

[22] *R. v. Secretary of State for Trade and Industry, ex p. Greenpeace Ltd* [2000] 2 C.M.L.R. 94, [2000] Env. L.R. 221.

[23] S.I. 2001 No.1754.

been made, ensuring that licences, consents and approvals for offshore activities are granted only when the tests set in the Directive are met.

5.2.33   There are difficulties in applying the Habitats and Species Directive to marine sites, both in identifying the key areas of habitat to be protected[24] and the means of protecting habitat and species from disturbance, especially when inshore water quality may be affected by diffuse pollution from many sources.[25] Nevertheless, marine conservation continues to lag behind the conservation of terrestrial sites,[26] but the decision on the application of the Directive beyond territorial waters has already forced a greater concentration on exactly what the Directive requires and how it can be implemented.[27]

NATURE RESERVES

5.3.1   Nature reserves are defined in the National Parks and Access to the Countryside Act 1949 as:

> "land managed for the purpose—
>
> > (a)   of providing, under suitable conditions and control, special opportunities for the study of, and research into, matters relating to the fauna and flora of Great Britain and the physical conditions in which they live, and for the study of geological and physiographical features of special interest in the area, or
> >
> > (b)   of preserving flora, fauna or geological or physiographical features of special interest in the area,
>
> or for both those purposes."[28]

The study and conservation of nature are thus the prime objectives in the management of the land, in marked contrast to the other designations (apart from European Sites) where nature conservation is either

---

[24] See, *e.g.*, art. 3(4) of the Directive which states that for "aquatic species that range over wide areas" the areas to be proposed for protection must be "clearly identifiable [areas] representing the physical and biological factors essential to their life and reproduction".

[25] J. Baxter and A. Davidson, "Management of Scotland's Marine and Coastal Special Areas of Conservation" in J. Baxter *et al.* (eds), *Scotland's Living Coastline* (1999).

[26] House of Commons Environment, Transport and Regional Affairs Committee, *U.K. Biodiversity*, 20th Report of 1999–2000 (1999–2000 H.C. 441), paras 53–54.

[27] The various statutory conservation bodies and others operate a website devoted to this issue at www.ukmarinesac.org.uk.

[28] NPACA 1949, s.15.

accommodated within the landowner's own use of the land or is balanced with or subordinate to other aims such as the provision of recreation or the protection of landscape. The focus on nature conservation is perhaps most clearly shown by the fact that in order to protect a reserve byelaws can be made excluding all visitors from the area.[29]

The establishment, maintenance and management of nature reserves **5.3.2**
is one of the general functions of the statutory conservation bodies,[30] and is achieved by the use of management agreements or by the acquisition of land, supported by byelaws. Areas of the foreshore and of tidal waters can be included in a reserve.[31] The powers relating to nature reserves can be exercised where it appears to the conservation body expedient in the national interest that land should be managed as a nature reserve.[32] A declaration by the body that land is being managed as a nature reserve is conclusive; the conservation body is under a duty to make a similar declaration if the land ceases to be managed in this way and all declarations must be publicised in the way best suited to informing those concerned.[33]

A management agreement may be made with any owner, lessee or **5.3.3**
occupier of the land. For the purpose of securing that the land is managed as a nature reserve, the agreement may impose restrictions on the exercise of any rights over the land by the parties, provide for the land to be managed in a particular manner and provide for work to be carried out on the land. The agreement may further provide for any management or other works to be carried out and/or paid for by the owner of the land, the conservation body or other persons, and may contain terms relating to payments by the body, in particular sums in compensation for the restriction of the parties' rights.[34] Special provision is made to allow agreements to be made with those with less than full ownership of the land, *e.g.* liferenters, tenants for life and trustees.[35] In Scotland agreements are to be registered in the Register of Sasines[36] and once registered can be enforced by the conservation body against the parties and those deriving title from them.[37] In England and Wales the agree-

---

[29] See para. 5.3.5, below.
[30] EPA 1990, s.132(1); NHSA 1991, s.4(7).
[31] NPACA 1949, s.114(1); *Burnet v. Barclay*, 1955 S.L.T. 282, *Evans v. Godber* [1974] 1 W.L.R. 1317.
[32] *ibid.*, s.16.
[33] *ibid.*, s.19.
[34] *ibid.*, s.16(2), (3).
[35] *ibid.*, ss.16(4), (5), 26; this is achieved by applying to management agreements the provisions for forestry dedication agreements in ss.1–4 of the Forestry Act 1947, saved for this purpose when repealed by the Forestry Act 1967, Sched. 7, Pt II, para. 3.
[36] By virtue of the Land Registration (Scotland) Act 1979, s.29(2), all references to the Register of Sasines extend to the Land Register.
[37] NPACA 1949, s.16(5), applying Forestry Act 1947 s.3(2) (see note 35 above); the agreement does not bind a person who *bona fide* onerously acquired his interest in the

ment operates essentially as a restrictive covenant with the body in the position of an absolute owner of adjacent land capable of benefiting from the covenant and for whose benefit the convenant is expressed.[38] These provisions mean that the agreement runs with the land and remains in force despite any change of occupation or ownership.

5.3.4   The statutory conservation bodies may acquire any interest in the land forming a nature reserve by agreement,[39] or in some cases compulsorily. The power of compulsory purchase can be exercised, firstly, where the body considers it expedient in the national interest that land should be managed as a nature reserve and has been unable to obtain on what it considers to be reasonable terms an agreement relating to the interest in question securing that the land will be satisfactorily managed for this purpose.[40] The second situation in which compulsory purchase is possible is where a management agreement for a nature reserve has been breached.[41] This option is without prejudice to any of the conservation body's other legal remedies, but where the breach is one capable of remedy, it can only be invoked if the defaulting party has not put things right within a reasonable time after being served with a notice from the body requiring remedial action.[42] The approval of the Minister must be obtained before any compulsory acquisition, which proceeds under the provisions of the Acquisition of Land (Authorisation Procedure) (Scotland) Act 1947 and the Acquisition of Land Act 1981 or the Compulsory Purchase Act 1965.[43]

5.3.5   Byelaws for the protection of a nature reserve can be made by a statutory conservation body where land is being managed as a reserve, whether directly by the body or under a management agreement, and has been declared to be a nature reserve.[44] Such byelaws must be confirmed by the Minister and are made under the procedures for local authority byelaws, modified to refer to the conservation bodies and to require copies of proposed and confirmed byelaws to be available for inspection at local authority offices in the relevant areas as well as

---

land prior to the registration of the agreement, nor those deriving title from such a person.

[38]   NPACA 1949, s.16(4), applying Forestry Act 1947 s.1(2), (3) (see note 35 above).

[39]   There is no express provision on the agreed acquisition of land for nature reserves, but it is covered by the general powers of the conservation bodies; EPA 1990, s.132(3), NHSA 1991, s.2(1).

[40]   NPACA 1949, s.17.

[41]   Any dispute over whether an agreement has been breached is to be determined by an arbiter appointed by the Lord President of the Court of Session or an arbitrator appointed by the Lord Chancellor.

[42]   NPACA 1949, s.18.

[43]   *ibid.*, s.103 (amended by Nature Conservancy Council Act 1973, Sched. 1, para. 2; Acquisition of Land Act 1981, Sched. 4, para. 8).

[44]   *ibid.*, s.20.

at the body's own headquarters.[45] In particular, byelaws can be made prohibiting or restricting the depositing of any rubbish or litter, the lighting of any fires or other acts likely to cause a fire, and the movement of any persons, vehicles, boats or animals into or within the reserve. Any killing, taking or disturbing of animals or plants, interference with the soil or damage to any objects in the reserve may be prohibited or restricted, as may the shooting of birds within the area surrounding or adjoining the reserve to the extent that this is required to protect the reserve itself. The byelaws may also provide for permits to be granted permitting things otherwise prohibited.[46]

There are, however, limits to the scope of the byelaws. The exercise of any right vested in a person as owner, lessee or occupier of the land cannot be interfered with—any restriction on such rights must be achieved directly by means of a management agreement, not through byelaws.[47] Where the exercise of other vested rights (whether arising from an interest in the land, a licence or an agreement) is prevented or hindered by the byelaws, compensation is payable by the conservation body.[48] Also beyond the reach of byelaws is any interference with the exercise of a public right of way,[49] with the functions of statutory undertakers, drainage authorities or salmon fishery district boards, or with the running of telecommunications systems.[50] **5.3.6**

The special status of nature reserves is recognised in a number of other statutory schemes. Among other points, orders can be made restricting or prohibiting vehicles on roads in a reserve[51] and in England and Wales the statutory conservation bodies must be consulted before a road building or improvement scheme in or near a reserve is initiated.[52] Land in a nature reserve cannot be accepted into the Farm **5.3.7**

---

[45] *ibid.*, s.106; Nature Conservancy Council (Byelaws) Regulations 1975 (S.I. 1975 No. 1970), adapting Local Government Act 1972, ss.236–238; Nature Conservancy Council (Byelaws) (Scotland) Regulations 1984 (S.I. 1984 No. 918), adapting Local Government (Scotland) Act 1973, ss.202–204 (amended by Civic Government (Scotland) Act 1982, s.110).

[46] *ibid.*, s.20(2).

[47] *ibid.*, s.20(2).

[48] *ibid.*, s.20(3).

[49] A right of navigation is not a public right of way for this purpose (*Evans v. Godber* [1974] 1 W.L.R. 1317; *cf. Attorney General (ex rel. Yorkshire Derwent Trust Ltd) v. Brotherton* [1992] 1 A.C. 425); the exercise of rights on the foreshore may be restricted (*Burnet v. Barclay*, 1955 S.L.T. 282).

[50] Added by Telecommunications Act 1984, Sched. 4, para. 28.

[51] Road Traffic Regulation Act 1984, s.22.

[52] Highways Act 1980, s.105A (added by the Highways (Assessment of Environmental Effects) Regulations 1988, S.I. 1988 No. 1241, reg. 2); the equivalent Scottish provision does not include nature reserves among the designations invoking such consultation, but since the sites will usually be SSSIs in any event, they will in practice be covered by this requirement—Roads (Scotland) Act 1984, s.20A (substituted by the Environmental Impact Assessment (Scotland) Regulations 1999 (S.S.I. 1999 No. 1), reg. 49, and applying *ibid.*, reg. 2(1)).

Woodland Premium Scheme[53] and any exercise in a nature reserve of the powers under the Animal Health Act 1981 to destroy wildlife requires prior notice and efforts to minimise the harm done.[54]

National Nature Reserves

5.3.8   What has been described so far are nature reserves managed by or by agreement with the statutory conservation bodies. There is, however, a potential for confusion as to their title and status. This arises because it is possible for reserves to be formally declared "National Nature Reserves" under the Wildlife and Countryside Act 1981.[55] This title can be conferred by a declaration[56] by a statutory conservation body where it considers that a nature reserve is of national importance. The risk of confusion lies in the fact that the title "National Nature Reserve" was in widespread but unofficial use for reserves managed by the Nature Conservancy Council before being given statutory recognition in 1981. A problem may occur in relation to future legislation as it could be argued that any reference to National Nature Reserves applies only to reserves which have been formally declared as such under the 1981 Act, thereby excluding many older ones if they have not been subject to any such statutory declaration.[57]

5.3.9   National Nature Reserves under the 1981 Act can be on land governed by a management agreement with the statutory conservation body, held and managed as a reserve directly by the body, or managed by another body approved by the statutory conservation body.[58] This last provision is particularly significant since it means that reserves managed by organisations such as the RSPB can be brought within the statutory scheme for nature reserves. A major consequence of this is that at the request of the organisation managing the reserve, the conservation body can make byelaws for such a reserve as if it were one managed through the statutory body itself.[59] This allows further legal sanctions to supplement the restrictions imposed by the managing body by virtue of its interest in the land.

Local Nature Reserves

5.3.10   Nature reserves can also be established by local authorities. It is within the powers of planning authorities in Scotland and Wales and county, county boroughs and districts and National Park authorities in England

---

[53] Farm Woodland Premium Scheme 1997 (S.I. 1997 No. 829, para. 5(1)).
[54] Animal Health Act 1981, s.22(7); see para. 4.5.11, above.
[55] WCA 1981, s.35.
[56] Governed by NPACA 1949, s.19.
[57] See, *e.g.* the Farm Woodland Premium Scheme 1997 (S.I. 1997 No. 829), para. 2(1) which expressly covers both categories.
[58] WCA 1981, s.35(1).
[59] *ibid.*, s.35(3).

to establish nature reserves where they consider it expedient that the land should be so managed.[60] The local authorities enjoy the same powers in this regard as the statutory conservation bodies, including powers of compulsory purchase, with references to "the interests of the locality" being substituted for those to "the national interest."[61] The existence of the power to create local nature reserves allows the protection of small sites which are not of national significance, but which do offer valuable habitat, and enables authorities to provide opportunities for the study of nature as a recreational or educational facility. As always, though, there are competing demands on the resources of local authorities.[62]

MARINE NATURE RESERVES

Although nature reserves can extend to include areas covered by the sea,[63] the legal machinery of land ownership and management agreements is not apt to deal with the conservation of the marine environment. Special provision was made in 1981 for the creation of Marine Nature Reserves, but weaknesses in the legislation and an unwillingness to proceed in the absence of total consensus from all interested parties have meant that these reserves have had little impact in practice.[64]   **5.4.1**

Marine Nature Reserves can be created for areas of land covered by tidal waters, including the foreshore, or parts of the sea which lie within the baselines for measuring the territorial sea[65] or lie seaward of the baselines or coast to a distance of three nautical miles.[66] By Order in Council, other areas of the sea within British territorial waters   **5.4.2**

---

[60] NPACA 1949, s.21(1); Local Government Act 1972 Sched. 17, para. 34; EA 1995, Sched. 9, para.3; for National Parks in Scotland see para. 5.11.31, below.

[61] NPACA 1949, s.21(4).

[62] *e.g.*, in *Giddens v. Barlow District Auditor* (1972) 70 L.G.R. 485 expenditure on the purchase of a wood as a local nature reserve was challenged, unsuccessfully, by a ratepayer on the grounds that it was providing facilities which would benefit only a privileged minority.

[63] See para. 5.3.2, above.

[64] See generally, J. Gibson, "Marine Nature Reserves" [1984] J.P.L. 699; J. Gibson, "Marine Nature Reserves in the United Kingdom" (1988) 3 Int. J. of Estuarine and Coastal Law 328; P. Jones, "Marine Nature Reserves in Britain: Past Lessons, Current Status and Future Issues" (1999) 23 Marine Policy 375; D. Laffoley and T. Bines, *Protection and Management of Nationally Important Marine Habitats and Species* (English Nature, 2000).

[65] Such baselines are drawn in accordance with international law and include lines drawn across the mouths of bays and firths and a line enclosing the Minch and all of the Inner and Outer Hebrides.

[66] WCA 1981, s.36(1) (amended by Territorial Sea Act 1987, Sched. 1, para. 6); a nautical mile is defined in s.1(7) of the 1987 Act as an international nautical mile of 1852 metres.

(currently extending to 12 nautical miles from the shore-line or baselines) can become eligible for designation.[67] Reserves are designated by the Minister on the basis of an application made by a statutory conservation body where it appears expedient that the land and covering waters should be managed for the purposes of conserving or studying the marine flora and fauna or the geological and physiographical features of special interest in the area. Once a reserve has been designated, it is managed by the conservation body for either or both of these purposes.[68]

5.4.3   The procedure for designation requires the conservation body's application to be accompanied by a copy of the byelaws which are proposed for the protection of the reserve[69] and provides for the Minister to give wide publicity to the proposed designation and accompanying byelaws. As well as notices in the local press and at prominent positions at local authority offices within the locality, notices must be served on all those with a vested interest in or right over the land affected and on a wide range of public authorities.[70] In the event of there being objections or representations which are not withdrawn, the Minister must arrange for there to be a hearing or local inquiry before he decides whether to make an order giving effect to the designation.[71] Similar publicity is required for orders once they have been made[72] and there is a limited power to challenge the validity of an order within 42 days of its notification, after which the order is not to be questioned in any legal proceedings.[73]

5.4.4   The impact of an area being designated as a Marine Nature Reserve lies in the provisions of the byelaws which are made for it, since other than through the byelaws, the effect of designation is simply to empower the conservation body to manage a reserve and to install markers indicating its existence and extent.[74] Byelaws are made by the body for the protection of reserves[75] in accordance with the procedures for the making of local authority byelaws, as modified by regulations.[76]

---

[67] Territorial Sea Act 1987, s.3(2)(b).
[68] WCA 1981, s.36(1).
[69] *ibid.*, s.36(2).
[70] *ibid.*, Sched. 12, paras 2–3; the public authorities concerned are the "relevant authorities" (see para. 5.4.6, below) and such other bodies as the Minister considers appropriate.
[71] *ibid.*, Sched. 12, para. 4; if he decides to make the order with modifications a similar procedure must be followed if additional land is affected (*ibid.*, para. 5).
[72] *ibid.*, Sched. 12, para. 7.
[73] *ibid.*, Sched. 12, para. 8.
[74] *ibid.*, s.36(1), (5).
[75] *ibid.*, s.37(1).
[76] *ibid.*, s.37(5), applying the Local Government Act 1972, ss.236–238 (as modified by Wildlife and Countryside (Byelaws for Marine Nature Reserves) Regulations 1986 (S.I. 1986 No. 143)) and the Local Government (Scotland) Act 1973, ss.202–204 (amended by Civic Government (Scotland) Act 1982, s.110).

As well as being the confirming authority for byelaws,[77] the Minister, after consulting the conservation body, can direct it to revoke or amend any byelaws which it has made.[78]

The byelaws may protect the reserve by prohibiting or restricting the entry or movement of individuals or vessels, the killing, destruction or disturbance of animals or plants, interference with the sea bed, damage to any object in the reserve, or the deposit of rubbish in the reserve.[79] The byelaws can vary for different parts of the reserve and allow the granting of permits to do things otherwise prohibited. These apparently wide powers are, however, severely restricted in several ways. First, the byelaws cannot prohibit or restrict the exercise of any right of passage by a vessel other than a pleasure boat, nor exclude even pleasure boats from all parts of the reserve at all times of the year.[80] There is no definition of a pleasure boat and many doubtful cases can be imagined. Secondly, the byelaws cannot render unlawful the discharge of any substance from a vessel,[81] nor anything done more than 30 metres below the sea bed,[82] nor anything done for securing the safety of any vessel, preventing damage to a vessel or its cargo or saving life.[83]

5.4.5

The third restriction on the scope of the byelaws also extends to anything else which a conservation body might do in the exercise of its powers to manage a reserve. This is that nothing which is done can interfere with the exercise of any functions conferred by an Act of Parliament (before or after the creation of the reserve and the making of byelaws), with the exercise of any right of any person or with the exercise of any function of a "relevant authority."[84] The "relevant authorities" for this purpose include all tiers of local authority, the Environment Agency and the Scottish Environment Protection Agency, water and sewerage undertakers, navigation, harbour and pilotage authorities, lighthouse authorities, salmon district fishery boards and local fisheries committees.[85]

5.4.6

Marine conservation is always difficult because of the wide range of influences which can affect the different elements of the marine environment from the surface to the sea-bed, and because of difficulties in enforcing any restrictions. The current structure does not make it

5.4.7

---

[77] *ibid.*, s.37(6).
[78] *ibid.*, s.37(7).
[79] *ibid.*, s.37(2).
[80] *ibid.*, s.27(3).
[81] Such deposits are controlled by Part II of the Food and Environment Protection Act 1985 and other legislation on marine pollution.
[82] Detailed legal regimes exist to control the exploitation of minerals on the continental shelf.
[83] WCA 1981, s.37(4).
[84] *ibid.*, s.36(6).
[85] *ibid.*, s.36(7) (amended by Water Act 1989, Sched. 25, para. 66).

easy to develop an integrated approach to conservation at the coast, considering both onshore and offshore issues. Moreover, in marine reserves the exclusion from the regulatory powers of authorities whose activities can have a major impact on the seashore and inshore waters, together with the other exclusions, severely weaken the whole mechanism of Marine Nature Reserves. This has been further weakened by slow progress towards designating reserves, with the government reluctant to proceed without full consensus from all interested parties. Only two Marine Nature Reserves had been designated in Great Britain, with a third (much larger) one at Strangford Lough in Northern Ireland.

SITES OF SPECIAL SCIENTIFIC INTEREST

5.5.1 Whereas in nature reserves the land is primarily dedicated to the interests of nature conservation, much of the valuable habitat in Britain is provided by land which is used for other purposes, and can continue to be so used without damaging its value for wildlife. Those areas of particular value do, however, require some recognition and a degree of protection if they are not to be destroyed by their development for building, quarrying, etc., or damaged by other changes in their management. The objectives of the system of Sites of Special Scientific Interest (SSSIs) are to identify valuable sites, to notify those responsible for them of their value and to provide a mechanism whereby changes to the land which might harm that value are considered by the conservation authorities before they take place, offering the opportunity for a range of controls to be agreed or imposed at that stage.

5.5.2 SSSIs were first introduced in 1949,[86] but the original provisions were weak, merely requiring special consideration within the town and country planning system (the owners and occupiers of the land were not even informed of the designation) and a new system was introduced by the Wildlife and Countryside Act 1981.[87] This new regime applied only to SSSIs which had been notified in accordance with the procedures in the 1981 Act, and throughout the 1980s a major task for the Nature Conservancy Council was the renotification of those SSSIs created under the previous legislation so that they could benefit from the new provisions. This task was completed in the early 1990s.

5.5.3 Although the system of SSSIs could be judged a success in tackling

---

[86] NPACA 1949, s.23; the legislation has in the past always referred to "areas which are of special interest," but the term Sites of Special Scientific Interest has been the universal usage, and is now recognised for England and Wales in WCA 1981, s.52 (as amended by CRWA 2000, Sched. 9, para. 5(2)).

[87] See generally S. Ball, "Sites of Special Scientific Interest" [1985] J.P.L. 767.

the main threats that the 1981 Act was designed to counter,[88] there was growing dissatisfaction at the failure of the legal mechanisms to prevent damage to protected sites.[89] In part inspired by the stronger measures introduced to secure compliance with the Habitats and Species Directive, proposals for reforming and strengthening the system of SSSIs were produced in 1998. There were separate consultation papers for England and Wales[90] and for Scotland.[91] These papers reflected different approaches, apparent from their very titles, for England and Wales emphasising "Better Protection" whilst in Scotland dealing with "People and Nature". The Scottish proposals paid more attention to the role of conservation in wider land use policies and the interests and concerns of the local community, an approach perhaps influenced by the much greater areas of land in Scotland covered by the designation and by the economic and social problems faced in many of the remote rural areas affected.[92]

The arrival of devolution has made it even easier for the proposals **5.5.4** to follow separate legislative paths, and in England and Wales fundamental changes to the system of SSSIs were introduced in the Countryside and Rights of Way Act 2000. In Scotland, reform has been promised[93] but it will be 2003 at the earliest before legislation is forthcoming. This means that there are currently two quite different regimes for SSSIs in Great Britain. The Scottish position, resting on the 1981 Act as originally enacted, remains a delaying mechanism whereby operations on the land can be delayed for a few months, but unless other stricter controls are applied, it is not possible to prevent the occupiers carrying out their wishes, however damaging to the conservation value of the site. In England and Wales, under the 1981 Act as amended by the Countryside and Rights of Way Act 2000, the SSSI scheme imposes stricter controls, with the power to prohibit damaging operations and to adjust the scope of the controls as time passes. It also offers mechanisms for securing the positive management of the site as

---

[88] K. Last, "Habitat Protection: Has the Wildlife and Countryside Act 1981 made a Difference?" (1999) 11 J.E.L. 15.

[89] In 2000–01,15 per cent of SSSIs in England were said to be in decline or destroyed (H.C. Written Answers, col.493W (December 6, 2001)).

[90] *Sites of Special Scientific Interest: Better Protection and Management* (DETR, 1998).

[91] *People and Nature: A New Approach to SSSI Designation in Scotland* (Scottish Office, 1998).

[92] K. Last, "Mechanisms for Environmental Regulation—A Study of Habitat Conservation" in A. Ross (ed.), *Environment and Regulation* (Hume Papers on Public Policy vol.8, no.1) (2000), at pp. 57–58.

[93] *The Nature of Scotland* (Scottish Executive, 2001); see para. 1.1.24, above. Aside from difficulties in policy formulation, progress on this issue in Scotland has been slowed by the priority given to the creation of National Parks and the wider issue of land reform.

well as for regulating the activities of third parties, while imposing duties on a range of statutory bodies. In this section, the Scottish position is described first before the amended scheme south of the border.

Scotland

5.5.5   Scottish Natural Heritage (SNH) is under a duty to notify as SSSIs those areas of land which are, in its opinion, of special interest by reason of any of their flora, fauna, or geological or physiographical features.[94] All owners and occupiers of the land concerned, the relevant planning authority and the Minister must receive copies of the notification,[95] which must set out why the land is of special interest and specify those operations (known as "potentially damaging operations") which appear likely to damage the flora, fauna or other special features of the land and thus fall within the scope of the SSSI controls.[96] The notification takes effect at once,[97] but a period of at least three months must be allowed for representations or objections to be made.[98] SNH must consider any representations which are made and within nine months of the original notification must notify the same people that the notification is being withdrawn, confirmed or confirmed with modifications (which cannot extend the area of the SSSI).[99] SNH has to compile and maintain a register of notifications for each planning authority, copies of which must be available for inspection at the authorities' offices.[1]

5.5.6   The precise scope of the duty to designate was considered in the English case of *R. v. Nature Conservancy Council, ex p. London Brick Property Ltd*[2] where a disused clay-pit was being designated on the basis that it provided valuable habitat for over 60 species of water-

---

[94] WCA 1981, s.28(1).

[95] *ibid.*, s.28(1); the service of notices is governed by WCA 1981, s.70A (added by Wildlife and Countryside (Service of Notices) Act 1985, s.1, amended by Planning (Consequential Provisions) (Scotland) Act 1997, Sched. 2, para. 34) which applies the provisions of TCPSA 1997, s.271.

[96] *ibid.*, s.28(4); the word "operations" in the term "potentially damaging operations" does not bear the specialised meaning which it has been given in construing the planning legislation (*Sweet v. Secretary of State for the Environment* [1989] 2 P.L.R. 14, (1989) 1 J.E.L. 245).

[97] Prior to the Wildlife and Countryside (Amendment) Act 1985 the notice took effect only once confirmed by the Nature Conservancy Council (the predecessor to SNH), but it was found that in the period between initial notification and confirmation some unscrupulous occupiers were taking steps which destroyed the features of the land which were of value, thereby defeating the whole system.

[98] WCA 1981, s.28(2) (amended by Wildlife and Countryside (Amendment) Act 1985, s.2(2)).

[99] *ibid.*, s.28 (4A)–(4C) (added by *ibid.*, s.2(4)).

[1] WCA 1981, s.28(12–12B) (amended by *ibid.* s.2(8)).

[2] [1996] Env. L.R. 1, [1996] J.P.L. 227.

beetle. This habitat existed only because of the particular regime of drainage and pumping that had been actively carried out by the owners, and since the pumping had now stopped and the SSSI mechanisms operated to prevent damaging operations, rather than to require positive actions, it was argued that the site should not be designated. The court held that although there was a duty to notify sites that were found to have features of special interest, at the stage of confirmation there was a degree of discretion. The presence of features of special interest provided a strong reason for exercising that discretion so as to confirm the site. If those features were inevitably doomed, that would render designation unreasonable, but there was no need for the survival of the features to be guaranteed before designation could be confirmed. In cases such as this, although there was no power to require positive action from the owners, there was still scope for management agreements to bring about the steps necessary to maintain the site. Only in exceptional circumstances, therefore, should designation not be followed through once the presence of the special features is established.

During the consultation and confirmation process it is important that the grounds of the designation are made clear. In *R. v. Nature Conservancy Council, ex p. Bolton Metropolitan Borough Council*,[3] the confirmation of an SSSI was held to be invalid on the grounds of a breach of natural justice since the Nature Conservancy Council had failed to correct what was clearly a mistaken belief on the part of the objectors that there was only one issue on which they were asked to respond, namely the potential of the site for restoration as an actively growing raised mire, whereas the present state of the site was also an important consideration. The confirmation process, whereby the conservation body both makes the initial designation and acts as the confirming authority, has been challenged in England as failing to provide landowners with a fair and independent hearing, in breach of article 6 of the European Convention on Human Rights;[4] interim injunction was granted to prevent English Nature confirming a designation but no final decision reached on this point.[5]

5.5.7

One additional feature that applies in Scotland, but never did elsewhere in Great Britain, is that designations are also subject to consideration by the advisory committee on SSSIs established under the Natural Heritage (Scotland) Act 1991.[6] The task of this committee, whose members must be scientifically qualified and independent of SNH,[7] is

5.5.8

---

[3] [1995] Env. L.R. 237, [1996] J.P.L. 237.

[4] As given effect by the Human Rights Act 1998; see para. 1.5.5, above.

[5] *William Sinclair Holdings Ltd v. English Nature* [2002] Env. L.R. 4. See Addendum, above.

[6] NHSA 1991, s.12; N. Collar, "Sites of Special Scientific Interest: Resolving objections" (1995) 40 J.L.S.S. 139.

[7] *ibid.*, s.12(2).

to consider the grounds on which an area has been declared to be of special interest and to advise SNH on whether there is adequate scientific justification for designation—the committee cannot consider the range of activities notified as potentially damaging operations or any other aspect of the designation. Cases are referred to the committee if in response to the initial notification the owner or occupier makes representations to SNH about the grounds for designation.[8] The advice from the committee must be received and considered by SNH before the notification of an SSSI is confirmed, and a copy of its advice is sent to the owner or occupier concerned.[9] The committee has a purely advisory role, although if a designation is confirmed by SNH against the advice of the committee, a dissatisfied owner or occupier might be tempted to seek to challenge that decision in the courts by means of judicial review. Ultimately, though, the test for designating SSSIs is whether a conservation body is "*of the opinion* that any area of land is of special interest,"[10] and the courts are likely to be reluctant to embark on any assessment of conflicting opinions from two expert scientific bodies.

5.5.9   The committee's role is not limited to new designations. Cases are also to be referred to it when the owner or occupier makes representations that any of the grounds for designation, as specified in the original notification,[11] have ceased to be valid.[12] In most cases, if the representations are not withdrawn within six months (this allows SNH time to assess the position itself and discuss the matter with the owner or occupier concerned), the case must then be referred to the committee, whose views must be considered before SNH decides whether to revoke or vary the designation.[13] This applies to designations made more than ten years ago or to more recent ones where relevant representations were made by the owner or occupier at the time of designation.[14] In all other circumstances, the procedure can be invoked no earlier than ten years after designation or ten years after the designation was last considered by the committee.[15]

---

[8] *ibid.*, s.12(5).

[9] *ibid.*, s.12(7); there are no provisions on the time within which the committee must provide its advice, but the notification lapses unless confirmed within nine months (WCA 1981, s.28(4A) (added by Wildlife and Countryside (Amendment) Act 1985, s.2)).

[10] WCA 1981, s.28(1), emphasis added.

[11] *ibid.*, s.28(4)(a).

[12] NHSA 1991, s.12(6).

[13] *ibid.*, s.12(6), (7). These provisions suggests the potential to revoke the designation as an SSSI, but no express power to do so appears in the 1981 Act; a denotification procedure has been added in the new provisions for England and Wales; see para.5.5.20, below.

[14] *ibid.*, s.12(6).

[15] *ibid.*, s.12(8).

This advisory procedure is much weaker than the full reconsideration **5.5.10**
of all aspects of designation which was originally proposed by the
members of the House of Lords dissatisfied with the previous arrangements. A particular difficulty may arise in those instances where large
areas have been designated, since it may be argued that not all of the
land concerned is in fact of special interest. However in a case involving Nature Conservation Orders,[16] an English court was prepared to
hold that it was appropriate to consider a local environment as a whole,
without distinguishing the particular places of greater and lesser importance.[17] A further potential problem is the extent to which "buffer
zones" can be established around valuable sites; such zones may contain little of particular interest themselves, but without them important
sites may be left vulnerable to damage or disturbance.[18] Greater powers
to vary the original designation are among the changes south of the
border discussed below.

The notification of an SSSI will contain a list of potentially damaging **5.5.11**
operations (PDOs), operations which appear to SNH likely to damage
the flora, fauna or special features of the site.[19] These will obviously
vary from site to site, but commonly listed operations include the cultivation of the land (ploughing, reseeding, etc.), changes to the grazing
regime, the dumping of any materials, the application of fertilisers,
pesticides or herbicides, the burning of vegetation, drainage works and
the filling of ditches, pools or marshland, the planting or felling of
trees, building, extraction of minerals and the killing or removal of any
wild animal.[20] One of the weaknesses of the SSSI system is that in
order to cover all activities which if carried to excess might damage a
site, landowners are often presented with very daunting lists of PDOs,
which give the impression that almost anything they could contemplate
doing on their land, including things which they have been doing for
years and which may very well have contributed to the conservation
value of the site, are to come under some form of control. This impression of far-reaching control and interference with what a person can do
on his own land means that the relationship between SNH and landowners can often start off on the wrong footing.

---

[16] See section 5.6, below.
[17] *Sweet v. Secretary of State for the Environment* [1989] 2 P.L.R. 14, (1989) 1 J.E.L.
245, *cf. R. v. Canterbury City Council, ex p. Halford* (1992) 64 P. & C.R. 513, where
a similar approach was taken to conservation areas. The new provisions for England
and Wales make it clear that it is the value of the area as a whole that is to be
considered; see para. 5.5.20, below.
[18] See N. Collar, *op. cit.*
[19] WCA 1981, s.28(4); on the meaning of "likely to damage" see *North Uist Fisheries
Ltd v. Secretary of State for Scotland*, 1992 S.L.T. 333, discussed at para. 5.6.6, below.
[20] Examples are given in Appendix 2 of L. Livingstone, *et al., Management Agreements
for Nature Conservation in Scotland* (1990).

5.5.12 The PDOs are not prohibited. Indeed, the most that can happen without agreement is that they can be delayed for four months. The legal requirement is that the owners or occupiers give written notice to SNH of their intention to carry out any of the operations.[21] They are then not permitted to carry out or permit the operation until four months have passed, unless SNH has given its consent to the particular operation, or the operation is carried out in accordance with a management agreement governing the land.[22] It is a criminal offence for the owner or occupier to proceed within the four months "without reasonable excuse"[23]; it is expressly provided that a reasonable excuse exists in the event of the operation being authorised by an express grant of planning permission[24] or being an emergency operation which has been notified to SNH as soon as practicable.[25] For the purposes of these provisions an "occupier" is someone with a legal interest in the land in question, and does not include someone on the land merely to carry out particular works.[26]

5.5.13 The reason for imposing a four-month delay is to give SNH the opportunity to consider the effect of the proposed operations and to act accordingly. If the operation is acceptable, consent will be given; if not the time can be used to find an appropriate means of preventing the operation, either by negotiating a management agreement for the site or by applying for further legal controls to be imposed through a Nature Conservation Order.[27]

5.5.14 In accordance with the voluntary principle which provided the basis for the 1981 Act, the main tool for protecting SSSIs is intended to be the management agreement, made between the conservation body and the owner and occupier of the land. An agreement can provide for compensation to be paid to the owner or occupier of an SSSI in return for his acceptance of restrictions on the use of the land, and may also provide for payments to be made in return for positive steps taken by the owner or occupier to maintain or improve the nature conservation

---

[21] WCA 1981, s.28(5) (amended by Wildlife and Countryside (Amendment) Act 1985, s.2(5)).

[22] *ibid.*, s.28(6) (amended by *ibid.*, s.2(6)).

[23] *ibid.*, s.28(7); D. Withrington and W. Jones, "Enforcement of Conservation Legislation: Protecting Sites of Special Scientific Interest", in W. Howarth and C. Rodgers (eds), *Agriculture, Conservation and Land Use* (1992).

[24] What is required is: "Planning permission granted on an application under Part III of the Town and Country Planning (Scotland) Act 1999" (*ibid.*, s.28(8)(a), amended by Planning (Consequential Provisions) (Scotland) Act 1997, Sched, 2, para. 34). This formulation means that a reasonable excuse is not provided by the fact that the operation is "permitted development" under the terms of the General Permitted Development Orders or otherwise exempt from normal planning control.

[25] *ibid.*, s.28(8).

[26] *Southern Water Authority v. Nature Conservancy Council* [1992] 1 W.L.R. 775.

[27] See section 5.6, below.

value of the site.[28] Agreements can also be made for land adjacent to
an SSSI where expedient for conserving the features of the site itself.[29]
By giving consent to the management of the site within agreed practices, the agreement can also obviate the need for individual notification
and consent every time something falling within the broad terms of the
PDOs is proposed.[30] The aims of the agreement may often be to maintain the existing way in which the land is being used, *e.g.* grazing to
prevent the growth of scrub, so that in the end, and despite the apparently daunting list of PDOs and fears of external controls which accom-
pany designation as an SSSI, the landowner may be continuing exactly
as before. One of the anomalies of the SSSI system has been that management agreements, and hence compensation, tended to be offered
only when an owner or occupier proposed[31] to carry out damaging
operations, whereas those who voluntarily managed their land in a way
which conserves its natural interest may receive no recognition or
reward.[32] This is now being realised and to some extent corrected with
greater emphasis on encouraging good management of land.[33]

The period available for negotiating an agreement was extended in **5.5.15**
1985 to the present four months from the original three,[34] but in many
cases this is still not long enough for the terms of an agreement to be
settled and formalised.[35] However, it is possible for the period to be
extended by agreement, terminable at one month's notice, and during
the extended period the proposed PDO cannot be carried out without
the consent of SNH.[36] Once a management agreement has been made
it will bind successors in title to the original parties, and provision is
made for agreements to be made by those who have less than full
ownership of the land.[37] Agreements are registered in the Register of
Sasines.[38]

The level of compensation available under a management agreement **5.5.16**
is determined in accordance with ministerial guidance, but this is not

---

[28] Agreements can be made under NPACA 1949, s.16 or CA 1968, s.15, which contains
essentially the same provisions specifically for SSSIs.
[29] CA 1968, s.15 (amended by EPA 1990, Sched. 9, para. 4).
[30] WCA 1981, s.28(6)(b).
[31] Some might say "threatened."
[32] L. Livingstone *et al.*, *op. cit.*, sections 3.4–3.5.
[33] See, for example, the *Natural Care Strategy* produced by SNH in 2001.
[34] Wildlife and Countryside (Amendment) Act 1985, s.2(6), amending WCA 1981,
s.28(6).
[35] L. Livingstone *et al.*, *op. cit.*, section 3.6.
[36] WCA 1981, s.28(6A)–(6C) (added by Wildlife and Countryside (Amendment) Act
1985, s.2(7)).
[37] NPACA, 1949 s.16(4), (5); CA, s.15(4), (6), both applying Forestry Act 1947 ss.1–4,
saved for this purpose when repealed by Forestry Act 1967, Sched. 7, Pt. II, para. 3.
[38] NPACA 1949, s.16(4), (5); CA, s.15(4), (6).

subject to any direct parliamentary or other controls.[39] The guidelines lay down the basis on which annual and lump sum payments are to be made to owners and occupiers who have entered agreements. If the level of compensation cannot be agreed, there is provision for arbitration on this issue, after which SNH must either amend its offer in terms of the arbiter's determination or withdraw the offer.[40] In one case in Scotland where this procedure has been invoked, the parties agreed to refer the case to the Lands Tribunal for Scotland.[41] The decision of the Tribunal, applying the criteria in the guidelines, produced a figure much higher than had been offered,[42] and raised the issue of how widely management agreements could and should be offered in view of the many other calls on the conservation bodies' finances.

England and Wales

5.5.17　The Countryside and Rights of Way Act 2000 fundamentally changed the system of SSSIs in operation in England and Wales, replacing section 28 of the Wildlife and Countryside Act 1981 with new sections 28-28R.[43] The new regime introduces stronger but more flexible controls on owners and occupiers within SSSIs, including provision to require positive actions to maintain a site, but also extends controls to other people whose activities can affect the site, especially by means of new criminal offences, byelaws and clear obligations on public authorities and statutory undertakers to have regard to the special features of a site.

5.5.18　The initial designation procedure is the essentially the same as before,[44] except that the initial notification must also be advertised in a local newspaper.[45] The most significant difference is that the notification must include a statement about the management of the land, including views on the conservation and enhancement of the species or features prompting the designation. With its emphasis on explaining what

---

[39] WCA 1981, s.50(2).

[40] *ibid.*, s.50(3).

[41] *Cameron v. Nature Conservancy Council*, 1991 S.L.T. (Lands Tr.) 85; the Tribunal has jurisdiction to accept the reference under s.1(5) of the Lands Tribunal Act 1949. See also *Thomas v Countryside Council for Wales* [1994] 4 All E.R. 853 (in passing it can be noted that the description of the SSSI system by Rougier J. as one where "a statutory body is given arbitrary power to interfere with the manner in which an ordinary citizen is going about a perfectly lawful occupation on his own land" (at p.859) seems to overstate the impact of an SSSI under the original provisions of the 1981 Act).

[42] The final sum was £555,000 for SSSIs covering ca. 3160 hectares.

[43] S. Payne, "From Carrots to Sticks—Natural Habitat Protection after the Countryside and Rights of Way Act 2000" (2001) 13 E.L.M. 239.

[44] See paras 5.5.5–5.5.7, above.

[45] WCA 1981, s.28. Here and in the following notes the references are to the new provisions of WCA 1981 added by CRWA 2000, Sched. 9.

might be appropriate for the site and on enhancement, this provision reflects the current concern with partnership and positive management, as well as meeting the requirement for management plans under the Habitat and Species Directive.[46] Similar statements must be produced within five years for all existing SSSIs.[47]

Whereas under the old provisions designation was a one-off process, **5.5.19** the new law allows for amendments and makes express provision for the designation of additional land. Variation notices allow the details of the original designation to be changed, but not the area of land covered, and are made and confirmed by the same procedure as for designation.[48] The power to vary the designation means that it is possible to adjust the grounds for designation to match changing physical conditions or changing appreciation of the special features on a site, whilst the potential to amend the list of PDOs removes the disadvantage of the scope of protection being frozen for ever on the basis of the original list of PDOs. This will allow for action to be taken if a new danger emerges, but also should improve relationships with the landowners, since it should be possible for the initial notification to include a shorter list of PDOs, reducing the regulatory burden, safe in the knowledge it is possible to add more extensive controls if necessary. An additional feature to deal with changing circumstances is the new obligation on owners of land in an SSSI to notify the conservation body when they dispose of any interest in the land or become aware that it is occupied by an additional or different occupier.[49]

The area of land covered by an SSSI can also be extended. There **5.5.20** are two different bases for doing this. The first is by the "notification of additional land" which applies when the conservation body is of the opinion that if land adjacent to an existing SSSI were combined with the designated land, then the combined area would meet the criterion of being of special interest.[50] The special interest in the additional land by itself may be limited, but its value as a "buffer zone" in relation to the extended site as a whole justifies designation. The second is by "enlargement of an SSSI", where an area of land that includes, but extends beyond the boundaries of, an existing SSSI meets the criterion of being of special interest.[51] In both cases the procedure is the same as for initial designation, with special provisions to deal with matters arising from the status, management and control of the land originally

---

[46] See para.5.2.27, above.
[47] CRWA 2000, Sched.11, para.6; a similar process is under way in Scotland on a non-statutory basis.
[48] WCA 1981, s.28A.
[49] *ibid.*, s.28Q.
[50] *ibid.*, s.28B.
[51] *ibid.*, s.28C.

designated. There is also provision for the denotification of an SSSI where the land is no longer of special interest.[52] The procedure to be followed is again essentially the same as for initial notification, except that the Minister, the Environment Agency and relevant statutory undertakers must also be informed. The denotification takes effect when the notice that the land is to be denotified is confirmed by the conservation body.

5.5.21 Management agreements will still form a major element in the way in which SSSIs are protected, and the new financial guidelines for England emphasise the need to secure positive management and the fact that public money is not to be used simply to prevent new damaging operations.[53] The negotiation of such agreements, however, will take place against a very different background since the formal controls on land that is designated as an SSSI are much stricter under the new rules. The initial requirement is still for the owner or occupier to give notice before carrying out any of the PDOs that have been notified (at any stage), but these can lawfully be carried out only if the conservation body gives it express consent or the operation is carried out in accordance with a management agreement, management scheme or management notice (see below).[54] This transforms the effect of an SSSI from being simply a delaying device into a form of prohibition, overridden only when the conservation body gives its consent, directly or through management arrangements. Consent can be given subject to conditions or for a limited period, and a consent can subsequently be withdrawn or modified, in which case a payment must be made to any owner or occupier suffering loss as a result.[55]

5.5.22 In the absence of a reasonable excuse, the owner or occupier commits an offence by carrying out a PDO without giving the required notice or without the relevant authorisation being given.[56] It is stated that a reasonable excuse is provided by the granting of planning permission for the operation[57] or by the granting of an authorisation by a public authority or statutory undertaker which has complied with the obligations in relation to operations affecting SSSIs included in the reforms to the 1981 Act.[58] Emergency operations also constitute a reas-

---

[52] WCA 1981, s.28D; the absence of such a provision in the 1981 Act was noted in *R. v. Nature Conservancy Council, ex p. London Brick Property Ltd* [1996] Env. L.R. 1 [1996] J.P.L. 227.

[53] *Guidelines on Management Agreement Payments and Other Related Matters* (DETR, 2001), paras 1.1–1.2.

[54] WCA 1981, s.28E.

[55] *ibid.*, s.28M(1).

[56] *ibid.*, s.28E(1).

[57] As before, the provision is phrased so as to apply only where there has been an application and express grant of planning permission, not to operations which are permitted development.

[58] See paras 5.5.30–5.5.33, below.

onable excuse, provided that the conservation body is notified as soon as practicable.

The maximum penalty for this offence is now an unlimited fine, and **5.5.23** for all offences in relation to SSSIs the courts are directed to have regard to any financial benefit arising from the offence. This is an attempt to ensure that the penalties take into account not only the damage done by the offence (which can be hard to quantify and even harder to convert to financial terms) but also what the offender has gained by not taking the requisite care of the site, whether by increased income or reduced costs, thereby avoiding the situation where a calcu-lating offender can decide that on a strict cost-benefit analysis it is better to run the risk of prosecution and a fine than to incur the addi-tional expenditure, or forgo the additional profit, involved in protecting the site. Whether the courts will in fact be willing to impose high fines remains to be seen.[59] A further significant sanction is provided by the power of the courts to order the restoration of the land, a power previ-ously limited to the context of Nature Conservation Orders.[60] The con-sent of the Director of Public Prosecutions is required before anyone other than a statutory conservation body can start a prosecution for these offences[61] and in the past the number of offences actually leading to prosecutions has been low.

When the maximum effect of an SSSI was simply to delay operations **5.5.24** for at most four months, there was no need for there to be a formal appeal mechanism. Now that the impact extends to an indefinite pro-hibition, an appeal structure has been instituted,[62] not least to comply with the requirement of article 6 of the European Convention on Human Rights[63] that any decisions determining civil rights (in this case the extent to which landowners are free to carry out normally lawful opera-tions on their own land) should be made by means of a fair hearing before an independent and impartial tribunal. Owners or occupiers have the right to appeal to the Minister if consent is refused, if they are aggrieved by any conditions in the consent or by the withdrawal or modification of a consent, or if there is a deemed refusal in that the conservation body has not made its decision to grant or refuse consent within four months of being notified of the intended operation. The appeal must be made within two months of the conservation body's decision (or the expiry of the four-month period) and may involve a

---

[59] A similar provision in relation to breaches of enforcement notices in planning law does not always produce fines that match the gains of the offenders; TCPA 1990, s.179(9).

[60] WCA 1981, s.31; see para. 5.6.9, below.

[61] *ibid.*, s.28P; this applies to all the offences under the new provisions.

[62] *ibid.*, s.28F.

[63] Given effect through the Human Rights Act 1998; see paras 1.5.5–1.5.7, above.

private hearing or public inquiry. The Minister can delegate the hearing of appeals to others, *e.g.* planning inspectors,[64] and detailed appeal regulations can be made.[65]

5.5.25   A further significant extension of powers in relation to SSSIs is the ability to control the actions of third parties, not just the owners and occupiers, closing a further weakness identified in the original provisions of the 1981 Act, and again bringing the powers in relation to SSSIs into closer alignment with those for European sites. The conservation bodies are able to make byelaws for SSSIs, applying the same provisions as for nature reserves.[66] This gives the conservation body the power to regulate the activities not just of the owners and occupiers, but also of visitors to the land.[67] The extension of controls to third parties is also achieved through a new criminal offence whereby it is a crime for anyone (not just the owner or occupier) who knows that his or her actions are taking effect within an SSSI intentionally or recklessly to damage the flora, fauna or features which have led to the site being designated, or intentionally or recklessly to disturb any such fauna.[68] No offence is committed if there is a reasonable excuse for this conduct, and an express grant of planning permission or other formal authorisation[69] provides such an excuse, as does an emergency provided that details of it are notified to the conservation body as soon as reasonably practicable.

5.5.26   The reforms to the system of SSSIs are not just about imposing stricter controls stopping people from doing things. They are also designed to improve the management of sites through the production of a management statement[70] and through the provision of mechanisms for securing the positive management of SSSIs by means of management schemes and notices. For all or part of an SSSI, the conservation body can make a management scheme for conserving or restoring the special features of the site.[71] Owners and occupiers must be consulted about a proposed scheme and then formally notified of it, with at least three months allowed for the making of representations about the

---

[64] WCA 1981, s.28F(8)–(9) and Sched.10A.

[65] *ibid.*, s.28F (6)–(7). Consultations were held on such regulations in autumn 2001; see [2001] J.P.L. 1046.

[66] WCA 1981, s.28R; see paras 5.3.5–5.3.6, above.

[67] For controls on the activities of statutory undertakers, see paras 5.5.30–5.5.33, below; for the special position where there are rights over common land, see C. Rodgers, "Environmental Management of Common Land: Towards a New Legal Framework?" (1999) 11 J.E.L. 231.

[68] WCA 1981, s.28P(6)–(7); this does not apply to the authorities and undertakers covered by the new duties discussed below.

[69] Subject to the authorising body having fulfilled its obligations with respect to SSSIs; see paras 5.5.30–5.5.33, below.

[70] See para. 5.5.18, above.

[71] WCA 1981, s.28J.

scheme, representations which must be taken into account. The scheme is then to be confirmed (with or without modifications)[72] or withdrawn by the conservation body within nine months of its notification, and takes effect when it is notified to all owners and occupiers. The scheme can be cancelled or modified at any time through the same procedures. The scheme by itself does not directly regulate the way in which land is managed, although potentially damaging operations can proceed without express consent from the conservation body if in accordance with a scheme,[73] and management agreements can provide for any matter covered by the scheme. Payments can also be made to those covered by a management scheme.[74] The greater legal importance of a management scheme is in paving the way for a management notice if the site is suffering harm.

Management notices can be made by the conservation body where it **5.5.27** appears to it that an owner or occupier is not giving effect to the provisions of a management scheme and that as a result any of the flora, fauna or other special features of the site are being inadequately conserved or restored.[75] The conservation body thus has a means of ensuring that the terms of the scheme are being carried into effect in order to achieve the protection or restoration of features on the site, emphasising the need for positive management, not simply the prevention of damaging operations, if sites are to be conserved. This extends to situations where deterioration is occurring through neglect, as well as through bad management and therefore greatly extends the powers of the law to achieve the conservation of habitat. Management notices may only be served where the conservation body is satisfied that it cannot reach on reasonable terms an agreement for the management of the land in accordance with the scheme and copies of the notice must be served on all the owners and occupiers of the land affected.

The effect of a management notice is to require the owner or occu- **5.5.28** pier to carry out work on the land or to do other things with respect to the land by the date specified. The actions specified must be reasonable in order to ensure that the land is managed in accordance with the scheme, and the notice must explain the effect of the notice and the rights of appeal. If the work specified is not carried out by the due date, the conservation body may enter the land and carry out the work itself, and recover the expenses from the defaulting owner or occupier. There is a right of appeal to the Minister against the service of a management notice, and an appeal, which can proceed by written submissions, by hearing or by local inquiry, has the effect of suspending the operation

---

[72] Modifications cannot make the scheme more onerous.
[73] WCA 1981, s.28E(3); see para. 5.5.21, above.
[74] *ibid.*, s.28M(2).
[75] *ibid.*, s.28K.

of a notice.[76] The grounds of appeal may include that some other owner or occupier should take, or pay for, any or all of the matters specified in the notice, and in this case the appellant must serve a copy of the appeal on those others. The Minister's decision can be to vary the effect of notice so that it imposes requirements on others or requires them to make a payment to the appellant, bearing in mind their relative interests in the land, their relative responsibility for the state of the land that prompted the notice, and the relative degree of benefit they will each derive from carrying out the notice.

5.5.29   There is also now the possibility of compulsory purchase as a means of ensuring that a site is conserved.[77] This is possible only where a management agreement has not been achievable on reasonable terms, or it has been broken in such a way that the land is not being properly managed. Disputes over whether there has been a breach are to be resolved by an arbitrator appointed by the Lord Chancellor. Once the land has been acquired it can be managed by the conservation body or disposed of on terms designed to secure that it is satisfactorily managed.

5.5.30   A further feature of the reforms in England and Wales is the introduction of clearer obligations on a range of public authorities and statutory undertakers. A duty is imposed to take reasonable steps, consistent with the authority's function, to further the conservation and enhancement of the natural features for which an SSSI has been designated. This duty is imposed on Ministers, the National Assembly for Wales, local authorities, those holding any Crown or statutory office and statutory undertakers.[78] The special nature of SSSIs must therefore be recognised in the exercise of many functions and duties. There may still be circumstances where statutory responsibilities lead an authority to act in a way adverse to the conservation of an SSSI, but the scope for claiming that the impact on an SSSI is an irrelevant, and therefore unlawful, consideration when options are being examined is much reduced.

5.5.31   These public authorities and statutory undertakers are subject to more precise obligations in relation to operations that they carry out or authorise and which might damage the features of an SSSI, and these apply even if the operation will take place outside the boundaries of the SSSI itself, an important point especially when operations affecting

---

[76] *ibid.*, s.28L; appeal regulations may be made by the Minister.

[77] *ibid.*, s.28N, applying NPACA 1949, s.103.

[78] *ibid.*, s.28G. "Statutory undertakers" have the same meaning as in s.262 of TCPA 1990; the failure of the original provisions to control damaging operations by a statutory undertaker was one of the features that led to comments on the ineffectiveness of the whole SSSI regime in *Southern Water Authority v. Nature Conservancy Council* [1992] 1 W.L.R. 775. There are some exceptions for operations under the Channel Tunnel Acts 1987 and 1996 (see CRWA 2000, Sched. 10, paras 6 and 11).

drainage and water flow are concerned.[79] The authority or undertaker must notify the conservation body of such operations, and in relation to operations that it is to carry out itself, it may initially proceed only if the conservation body assents.[80] If assent is refused,[81] the operation can only take place if the authority or undertaker gives the conservation body further notice[82] of when it is to go ahead, if it informs the conservation body of how it has taken account of any advice from the body, if the operations are carried out in such a way as to give rise to[83] as little damage as possible to the features of the site and if, so far as is reasonably practicable, the site is restored to its former condition if any damage does occur. The operation is thus not prohibited, but its effects are mitigated and the conservation body does have a short period of time to prepare any protective measures or try further negotiations to halt the operation.

In relation to operations to be authorised by the authority or undertaker, it must allow at least 28 days from the notice, unless the conservation body says sooner that it can proceed, and must take into account any advice from the body as it decides whether to approve the operation and what conditions, if any to impose.[84] If the authority or undertaker decides not to follow the conservation body's advice on any issue, it must notify the body of the permission actually granted, and must ensure that there is a period of at last 21 days between that notice and the start of the operation. Again, this means that damaging operations cannot be prevented, but does ensure that the decision to grant permission is not taken in ignorance of the damaging consequences for an SSSI.[85] **5.5.32**

These obligations on public authorities and statutory undertakers are enforced through the criminal law.[86] It is an offence to proceed with an **5.5.33**

---

[79] Recognising and raising awareness of the potential for harm may be a major issue if this provision is to operate successfully. Incidents such as the harm to the special flora of the Avon Gorge from pollution by debris falling during the shot-blasting of the Clifton Suspension Bridge can only be avoided if those commissioning the work, contractors and conservation groups recognise the need for special care and communicate clearly with each other. Here the problem arose not so much from the operation itself but from the choice of materials (copper slag, with high zinc levels) and their precise composition and form (which allowed the metals to leach into the soil), neither of which may have seemed to have been particularly significant issues to some of those concerned. See F. Pearce, "Poison Rains Down on Rare Plants", *New Scientist*, February 24, 1996; *The Times*, March 30, 1996.

[80] WCA 1981, s.28H.

[81] There is a deemed refusal if the conservation body does not respond in 28 days.

[82] At least 28 days' notice must be given.

[83] This somewhat unusual statutory phrase appears designed to cover more indirect consequences than the more usual "cause".

[84] WCA 1981, s.28I.

[85] In this respect these arrangements play a role similar to that of environmental impact assessments; see section 8.3, below.

[86] WCA 1981, s.28P(2)–(3); prosecutions can be brought only by the statutory conservation bodies or with the consent of the Director of Public Prosecutions (*ibid.*, s.28P(10)).

operation that does cause damage without serving the initial notice that a potentially harmful operation is proposed, or notice that the operation is to go ahead, unless there is a reasonable excuse for this failure. Failing to carry out the work so as to give rise to as little damage as reasonably practicable or to restore the site is also an offence. The sanction can include an order to restore the site.[87]

5.5.34　　The new law took effect on January 30, 2001 and there are transitional measures so that designations, notices and notifications under the old provisions continue in force and in order to cover cases where procedures were under way at that date.[88] The transitional provisions include the power for the conservation body to issue a stop notice in relation to operations which the owner or occupier had notified to the conservation body before October 30, 2000[89] and which are authorised only by virtue of the passage of four months, in other words where there has been no express consent from the conservation body directly or by virtue of the terms of a management agreement.[90] The stop notice must specify the land affected, the operations to be stopped and the date when the notice takes effect.[91] The effect of the stop notice is to apply the new provisions in relation to the authorisation of operations, so that the operation is lawful only if there is express consent, either directly or through the terms of a management agreement, scheme or notice. Compensation is payable to any occupier suffering loss as a result of the notice. There is a right of appeal against stop notices, but these continue in effect pending the appeal.

5.5.35　　A further feature of the changes for England and Wales is that the provisions on Nature Conservation Orders no longer have effect.[92] The new provisions for all SSSIs now include, and indeed surpass, the additional powers which could be used to strengthen the protection granted by to SSSIs under the 1981 Act as originally enacted. Again there are transitional provisions to deal with orders in force when the new law came into effect.[93] The new provisions also give the statutory conservation bodies wide powers of entry to land where necessary in relation to any stage or aspect of the SSSI regime, from whether the site merits designation to determining what if any management arrangements should be made and whether these are being followed.[94]

5.5.36　　The overall effect of the new provisions in England and Wales has

---

[87] *ibid.*, s.31.

[88] CRWA 2000, Sched. 11.

[89] The time-scale is altered where there was an agreement to extend the standard four-month period of delay.

[90] CRWA 2000, Sched. 11, paras 9–12.

[91] At least three days after the date of the notice unless special reasons demand otherwise.

[92] CRWA 2000, Sched. 9, para. 2.

[93] *ibid.*, Sched. 11, paras 15–19.

[94] WCA 1981, s.51, as amended by CRWA 2000, s.80.

been to transform the SSSI from a means of delaying the owner or occupier in carrying out damaging operations while a voluntary solution was sought into a comprehensive set of controls which has the potential to secure lasting protection, affecting both the management of an SSSI and the actions of third parties. The gap between the law in Scotland and that south of the border are such that the two versions of SSSI are fundamentally different creatures.

General

The existence of an SSSI has effects in other legal regimes. As far as agricultural developments are concerned, special rules apply to the consideration of applications for farm capital grants for land designated as an SSSI.[95] The agriculture ministers must exercise their functions under the grant schemes so as to further the conservation of the special features of the site, so far as is consistent with the purposes of the grant provisions, and consideration must be given to any objection from the statutory conservation body that the activities in question are damaging to the flora, fauna or special geological or physiographical features of the site.[96] Where a grant has been refused as a result of objections from the conservation body, the body must within three months offer to enter a management agreement for the site.[97]   **5.5.37**

As regards forms of development falling within the scope of the town and country planning system, the express grant of planning permission authorises the carrying out of any PDO.[98] This enables the planning authority, for which nature conservation may not be a priority in the light of the economic and social needs of its area, to permit development on an SSSI which can totally destroy its conservation value. Under planning rules, the conservation body must be consulted on any application which may affect an SSSI, not only those for development on the site itself,[99] and its views will be taken into account, but other considerations material to the decision may outweigh its objections. In England and Wales, though, the planning authority is one of the public   **5.5.38**

---

[95] "Farm capital grants" are defined as those provided by schemes under s.29 of the Agriculture Act 1970 or regulations giving effect to European Community provisions; WCA 1981, s.32(3) (substituted by Agriculture Act 1986, s.20(3)).

[96] WCA 1981, s.32(1), (amended by Agriculture Act 1986, s.20); in England the legislation requires the Agriculture Minister to consult with the Secretary of State for the Environment, and the statutory words have not been altered to reflect the unification of ministerial roles following the creation of the Department for the Environment, Food and Rural Affairs. See Addendum, above.

[97] *ibid.*, s.32(2).

[98] *ibid.*, s.28(8) (Scotland); s.28P(4) (England and Wales).

[99] Town and Country Planning (General Development Procedure) Order 1995 (S.I. 1995 No. 419), art. 10(1); Town and Country Planning (General Development Procedure) (Scotland) Order 1992 (S.I. 1992 No. 224), art. 15(1).

bodies now subject to the more stringent notice requirements and
obligations to have regard to protecting the SSSI when considering
whether to grant permission for any actions that might damage an
SSSI.[1] The fact that the land in question is an SSSI may also trigger
the requirement for an environmental assessment to be carried out,[2] and
SSSIs cannot be included in a Simplified Planning Zone (an area where
planning controls are considerably relaxed in order to stimulate
development).[3]

5.5.39   The environmental obligations of both SEPA and the Environment
Agency are also likely to affect SSSIs. Where a conservation body
considers that land is of special interest because of its flora, fauna or
geological or physiographical features, may be affected by the schemes,
works, or other activities carried out or authorised by the agencies, then
the body must notify the agency of the special interest of the land.[4] The
basic test for identifying land of special interest is the same as for
SSSIs, but the provision is not restricted to land formally notified as an
SSSI, whilst SSSIs which are safe from disturbance by the activities of
the relevant bodies may be excluded. Before a relevant body carries
out or authorises any works, etc., which it considers likely to destroy
or damage the special features of a site which has been notified, it must
consult with the conservation body; in the case of emergency works,
no prior consultation is required, but notification must be given as soon
as practicable. In England and Wales these specific requirements are
overtaken to a considerable extent by the wider obligations on all public
authorities and statutory undertakers in relation to SSSIs. A further
provision in England and Wales is that the Minister may require that
an appropriate management agreement is entered before certain land of
special scientific interest held by water undertakers is sold.[5]

5.5.40   The system of SSSIs is the cornerstone of habitat protection in Britain, but on all sides there was some dissatisfaction with its operation.
From the point of view of conservation interests, the system did not do
enough to guarantee the protection of sites, since damaging operations
could be delayed for only a short time, the protection could be overridden by a planning authority granting permission for a development and
only the activities of owners and occupiers were restricted, leaving the
conduct of those with lesser rights over the land, *e.g.* commoners, of
statutory undertakers and of visitors uncontrolled. Moreover the whole
approach was based on preventing particular damage, not ensuring the
positive management of the land, so that the value of a site could be

---

[1] WCA 1981, s.28I; see para. 5.5.32, above.
[2] See section 8.3, below.
[3] TCPA 1990, s.87(1); TCPSA 1997, s.54.
[4] EA 1995, ss.8, 35.
[5] Water Industry Act 1991, s.156.

lost by neglect, *e.g.* by scrub invading grassland, without any PDO being involved and hence no trigger for the (limited) further measures to be taken. Landowners and occupiers were often unhappy at the designation of their land on purely scientific grounds with no right of appeal and limited consideration for their ability to make a return from the land, whilst the system of notifying all potentially damaging operations presented them with what seemed to be a frightening array of restrictions, apparently removing totally their right to treat their land as their own. Criticism came from both sides over the compensation scheme and the purely negative approach of the PDO system.

Some of the difficulties, from the landowners' side at least, were caused not by the actual impact of the designation but by the initial impression of a much stronger set of restrictions than existed in practice. In Scotland many of these problems were considerably exacerbated by the poor handling of matters by the NCC during the 1980s when it was under great pressure to complete quickly the renotification of sites so that they could benefit from the 1981 Act. The strength of feeling on the issue was amply illustrated by the views expressed by several members of the House of Lords during the passage of the Natural Heritage (Scotland) Act 1991, when attempts were made to introduce a total reassessment of all SSSI designations.   **5.5.41**

The unhappiness with the provisions of the 1981 Act meant that during the late 1990s there was clear consensus on the need for reform. In Scotland, this has not yet borne fruit and the fairly weak scheme created by the 1981 legislation continues, although changes are promised. In England and Wales, however, the Countryside and Rights of Way Act 2000 has transformed the position, dealing with many of the criticisms from both sides and producing a new regulatory framework that seeks to tackle in a more positive way a wider range of threats to the future of SSSIs. The facts that there is such a difference between the legal controls in the different jurisdictions and that the new SSSI regime is in some respects stronger than that for European Sites means that the current legal position for these key conservation sites is particularly fragmented and awkward. It is to be hoped that the promised legislation in Scotland does emerge soon and that (unless there are real differences of policy) the various authorities can together produce a coherent and broadly consistent structure so that the different designations can work together clearly in a way that is simple to understand.   **5.5.42**

Nature Conservation Orders

Nature Conservation Orders are now available only in Scotland and offer more protection for a site than can be provided by its designation as an SSSI. The protection offered by such Orders is an enhanced   **5.6.1** version of that offered by SSSIs under the original terms of the 1981 Act, the main differences being that damaging operations can be delayed for longer, it is not merely owners and occupiers who are affected and a wider range of sanctions and compensation is available to ensure the success of the law.[6] The extended powers that now apply to all SSSIs in England and Wales now exceed these additional controls and Nature Conservation Orders have been abolished for those jurisdictions.[7] Any Nature Conservation Order in force for a site that becomes a European Site is converted into a Special Nature Conservation Order.[8]

5.6.2   There are three grounds for making a Nature Conservation Order: to secure the survival in Great Britain of any kind of animal or plant; to comply with any international obligation; or to conserve the flora, fauna or geological or physiographical features of a site which is of national importance.[9] Orders are made by the Scottish Ministers, after consultation with SNH, and can be made for any land which is considered by the Ministers to be of special interest by reason of its flora, fauna and geological or physiographical features;[10] this is the same test as for SSSIs, and any relevant land should already have been designated as such. Orders are thus made to supplement the SSSI system, protecting the most valuable, or most threatened, sites where the test of national or international importance can be met. It has been held that in determining the boundaries of the land to be covered by an Order it is acceptable to treat a locality as a single environment and to designate it as such, without distinguishing between the different elements within it of greater and lesser importance.[11]

5.6.3   Orders take effect at once, but there is then a nine-month period during which the Order must be considered, at the end of which it expires unless a formal decision on its future has been notified.[12] Once an Order has been made, it must be advertised in the local press and notices stating its general effect, where copies are available and where and when objections can be made, must be sent to all owners and occupiers of the land in question and to the relevant planning authorities.[13] If any objections or representations are withdrawn, or none is made, the Ministers may consider the Order as soon as practicable; if

---

[6] In March 2001, there were 11 Nature Conservation Orders in force in Scotland; SNH, *Facts and Figures 2000–2001*, p. 53.
[7] CRWA 2000, Sched.10, para. 7; Sched. 16.
[8] See paras 5.2.15–5.2.16, above.
[9] WCA 1981, s.29(1).
[10] *ibid.*, s.29(2).
[11] *Sweet v. Secretary of State for the Environment* [1989] 2 P.L.R. 14, (1989) 1 J.E.L. 245; *cf. R. v. Canterbury City Council, ex p. Halford* (1992) 64 P. & C.R. 513, where a similar approach was taken to conservation areas.
[12] WCA 1981, Sched. 11, para. 1.
[13] *ibid.*, para. 2; at least 28 days must be allowed for objections.

there are objections or representations, they must hold a local inquiry or hearing before proceeding. Once they have considered the Order, and any response to it, the Ministers may decide to allow the Order to stand, or that it should be amended or revoked.[14] The Ministers' decision must be publicised and notified in the same way as the original Order,[15] and after six weeks, during which there is a limited right to challenge its validity,[16] the Order cannot then be questioned in any legal proceedings.[17] Orders are registered in the Land Register for Scotland or the General Register of Sasines.[18] An Order can be made even though there are potentially conflicting statutory duties on other authorities that might lead to damaging operations being carried out.[19]

Each Nature Conservation Order specifies a number of potentially damaging operations which appear likely to destroy or damage the features which led to the Order being made.[20] It is an offence for any person to carry out any of these operations without reasonable excuse; this contrasts with the position for SSSIs where only the owner and occupier are subject to the restrictions imposed.[21] For owners and occupiers the same mechanism applies as for SSSIs, in that any proposal to carry out a PDO must be notified to SNH and can proceed without risk of liability provided that SNH has given its consent, the operation is in accordance with a management agreement or a certain time, initially three months,[22] has passed. It is again provided expressly that a reasonable excuse for any action is provided by an express grant of planning permission or by emergency operations notified to SNH as soon as practicable.[23]

5.6.4

The effect of these provisions was considered in *North Uist Fisheries Ltd v. Secretary of State for Scotland*,[24] where occupiers whose fish-farming activities were covered by the potentially damaging operations listed in an Order successfully challenged the validity of its confirmation. The occupiers objected to the making of the Order, leading to a

5.6.5

---

[14] *ibid.*, paras 3–4; amendments cannot extend the area covered (*ibid.*, para. 5).

[15] *ibid.*, para. 6.

[16] *ibid.*, para. 7; the operation of this procedure is illustrated in *Sweet v. Secretary of State for the Environment* (above) and *North Uist Fisheries Ltd v. Secretary of State for Scotland* (below) where Orders were challenged in the courts.

[17] *R. v. Secretary of State for the Environment, ex p. Upton Brickworks Ltd* [1992] J.P.L. 1044.

[18] WCA 1981, s.29(10).

[19] *Ward v. Secretary of State for the Environment* [1996] J.P.L. 200, where the highway authority's obligations to maintain a bridleway did not prevent an Order being made in relation to the land affected.

[20] *ibid.*, s.29(3).

[21] *ibid.*, s.29(8).

[22] *ibid.*, s.29(4) (amended by EPA 1990, Sched. 9, para. 11), (5).

[23] *ibid.*, s.29(9).

[24] 1992 S.L.T. 333; reported with commentary at (1992) 4 J.E.L. 241.

public inquiry being arranged prior to its confirmation or expiry, but they also continued their activities and gave notice of their intention to carry out the operations. The court said that they had been acting unlawfully in carrying out a specified operation within three months of giving notice (no prosecution was in fact started), but that after the three-month period those activities were legitimate. Accordingly the decision to confirm the Order after the subsequent inquiry was invalid because it had failed to take into account the fact that the fish-farming activities, which were the main target of the Order, had acquired legitimacy and could no longer be restricted by the procedure for notification, etc., created by the Order. This case shows the unsuitability of the system for controlling existing operations as opposed to proposed ones, and demonstrates the need for the conservation body to be alert to the way in which the operation of the three-month deadline can pre-empt the fuller consideration of an issue at an inquiry to be held within the nine-month deadline for an Order to be confirmed.

5.6.6 A further point of note in the case, although not necessary for the decision, was the view expressed on the scope of the potentially damaging operations notified when an Order is made. The legislation refers to operations "likely to destroy or damage" the valuable features of the site,[25] and the court favoured the view that this should be read as referring to operations which would probably cause damage, not just those which might possibly have that result. This conclusion follows the traditional approach of giving a strict interpretation to any provision giving rise to a risk of criminal conviction or interfering with property rights, but certainly goes against the precautionary principle which is one of the foundations of European Community environmental law. The difficulty of demonstrating exactly how a complex ecosystem will be affected by any given operation means that if this view were accepted it may be impossible for the potentially damaging operations to cover many activities where experts confidently predict, but cannot prove, that the activities carry a real risk of damaging the site.

5.6.7 The basic period for which an owner or occupier must wait after notifying his intention to carry out a PDO is three months.[26] However, where SNH offers to enter either an agreement to purchase the interest in the land or a management agreement providing compensation, the period is extended to twelve months from the notification or three months from the rejection or withdrawal of the offer, whichever is the later.[27] Compulsory acquisition of the interest in the land is a further option open to SNH and where such an order is made, the period of delay expires when SNH enters the land or the Ministers decide not

---

[25] WCA 1981, s.29(3); similar wording is used in relation to SSSIs in *ibid.*, s.28(4).
[26] *ibid.*, s.29(5)(c).
[27] *ibid.*, s.29(6).

to confirm the order.[28] The period available for negotiating a suitable management agreement or the purchase of the land is thus extended by the law itself, as opposed to relying on agreement between the parties as is the case in SSSIs. As for SSSIs, if a farm capital grant is refused as a result of objections from SNH, a management agreement must be offered.[29]

Those whose land is affected by a Nature Conservation Order may be entitled to some compensation, regardless of whether a management agreement is entered. Where an Order is made for land comprised in an agricultural unit,[30] anyone with an interest in the land can claim compensation from SNH if he can show that the value of his interest is less than it would have been had no Order been made. The compensation is the difference between the two values.[31] Compensation is also available to a person with an interest in the land who has notified SNH of his intention to carry out a potentially damaging operation; the compensation is payable where the period during which he is prevented from carrying out the operation has been extended from the basic three months (as the result of an offer of a management agreement, etc.[32]) and it can be shown that as a result of this extended delay before he can proceed he has suffered loss or damage or has incurred expenditure which has been rendered abortive. No compensation is available under this heading for any reduction in the value of an interest in the land.[33] Disputes over compensation are referred to the Lands Tribunal for Scotland,[34] and a number of associated issues are governed by the application of the rules in the Land Compensation (Scotland) Act 1963.[35]

5.6.8

If a person has been convicted of carrying out operations which have damaged or destroyed the special features of land covered by a Nature Conservation Order, in addition to imposing a higher penalty than is possible for damage in an SSSI, the court may order him to carry out within a certain period work to restore the land to its former condition.[36]

5.6.9

---

[28] *ibid.*, s.29(7).

[29] *ibid.*, s.32.

[30] "Land which is occupied as a unit for agricultural purposes, including any dwelling-house or other building occupied by the same person for the purpose of farming the land"; *ibid.*, s.30(11).

[31] *ibid.*, s.30(2); a claim must be made in writing within six months of the notification of the Ministers' decision after considering the Order (Wildlife and Countryside (Claims for Compensation under section 30) Regulations 1982 (S.I. 1982 No. 1346), reg. 2).

[32] See para. 5.6.7, above.

[33] WCA 1981, s.30(3); claims must be made in writing within six months of the end of the extended period (Wildlife and Countryside (Claims for Compensation under section 30) Regulations 1982 (S.I. 1982 No. 1346), reg. 3).

[34] *ibid.*, s.30(8).

[35] *ibid.*, s.30(4)–(7), (9).

[36] *ibid.*, s.31(1); there are rules on how such an order is to be treated for appeals against conviction or sentence (*ibid.*, s.31(2), (3), (7)).

It is an offence to fail to comply with such an order within the pre-scribed period, with a daily fine for continuing default.[37] Where the restoration work has not been carried out, SNH itself may enter the land and carry out the work, recovering expenses from the person in default.[38] If circumstances change so that compliance with the order is impracticable or unnecessary, the order may be discharged or varied by the court on the application of the person against whom it was made.[39] In England and Wales this sanction is now available for offences invol-ving SSSIs.[40]

LIMESTONE PAVEMENT ORDERS

5.7.1 Special provision is made for the protection of areas of limestone pave-ment, *i.e.* areas of limestone wholly or partly exposed on the surface of the ground and fissured by natural erosion[41]—such areas are of con-siderable botanical and geological value and many are designated as SSSIs. The making of Limestone Pavement Orders is a two-stage pro-cess. In the first place, any area of limestone pavement of special inter-est by reason of its fauna, flora or geological or physiographical fea-tures is to be identified by the statutory conservation bodies, or additionally by the Countryside Agency in England, and notified to the local planning authority for that area.[42] The decision to make an Order then rests with the Minister or the planning authority;[43] this power is to be exercised where it appears that the character or appearance of the land is likely to be adversely affected by the removal or disturbance of the limestone.[44] The procedure for making Orders is the same as for Nature Conservation Orders, with the Order taking effect at once but being reviewed by the Minister after an opportunity for objections and representation to be made; the Minister considers all Orders, whether made by himself or a planning authority.[45]

5.7.2 The effect of an Order is to designate the land affected and to pro-

---

[37] *ibid.*, s.31(5).

[38] *ibid.*, s.31(6).

[39] *ibid.*, s.31(4).

[40] *ibid.*, s.31 as amended by CRWA 2000, Sched. 9, para. 3.

[41] WCA 1981, s.34(6). There are about 2,600 hectares of this habitat in Great Britain and further information can be found on the web-pages of the Limestone Pavement Action Group at www.limestone-pavements.org.uk.

[42] *ibid.*, s.34(1); county and district authority in England except where there is a National Park acting as planning authority, a metropolitan county or Greater London (*ibid.*, s.52(2)).

[43] The county planning authority in non-metropolitan counties of England (*ibid.*, s.34(6)).

[44] *ibid.*, s.34(2).

[45] *ibid.*, Sched. 11; see para. 5.6.3, above.

hibit the removal or disturbance of limestone on or in it.[46] It is an offence without reasonable excuse to remove or disturb limestone on or in any designated land.[47] A reasonable excuse is however provided if the action is authorised by a grant of planning permission in response to an application under the planning legislation; as with SSSIs, there must be an express grant of permission, thereby excluding operations having only deemed permission under the General Permitted Development Orders, *e.g.* some agricultural operations.[48] Since any significant extraction of limestone is likely to require planning permission in any case as a "mining operation,"[49] the legal protection offered against disturbance is primarily in relation to activities which fall outwith the scope of planning control, or are incidental to other operations. No compensation is available to those whose land is designated under a Limestone Pavement Order.

AREAS OF SPECIAL PROTECTION

Sites which are of particular importance for birds can be offered additional protection through the creation of Areas of Special Protection. This designation replaced the more clearly named Bird Sanctuaries,[50] and should not be confused with Special Protection Areas under the European Community's Birds Directive.[51] The effect of such areas is primarily on visitors, since there are wide exemptions preserving the rights of those with any interest in the land. Orders creating Areas of Special Protection are made by the Minister, and the legislation lays down no specific criteria for when an order can be made.[52] Any proposed order must be notified to all owners and occupiers of the land affected, individually in writing or through the local press where individual notification is impracticable,[53] and three months are allowed for objections or representations to be made.[54] The order can be made by the Minister only if all the owners and occupiers consent, or at least if there are no objections or any objections are withdrawn.[55] Orders are

5.8.1

---

[46] *ibid.*, s.34(2).

[47] *ibid.*, s.34(4).

[48] *ibid.*, s.34(5).

[49] TCPA 1990, s.55; TCPSA 1997, s.26.

[50] Bird Sanctuaries were governed by the Protection of Birds Act 1954, s.3 and, although there is no express provision, it is considered that the sanctuaries designated under that Act continue in effect as if created under the 1981 Act; *Halsbury's Statutory Instruments* (Vol. 2) (1993 reissue), p. 225.

[51] Directive 79/409; see paras 5.2.2–5.2.5, above and 7.4.3–7.4.13, below.

[52] WCA 1981, s.3(1).

[53] *ibid.*, s.3(4).

[54] *ibid.*, s.3(5)(6).

[55] *ibid.*, s.3(5).

made by statutory instrument subject to annulment by either House of Parliament.[56]

5.8.2　Orders can contain a variety of provisions, strengthening the general law protecting wild birds. Within the designated area it may become an offence intentionally to kill, injure or take any wild bird, to take, damage or destroy the nest of a wild bird while it is in use or being built, to take or destroy eggs, to disturb wild birds while they are building or tending a nest or to disturb the dependent young of a wild bird; these prohibitions can apply to all wild birds or to specified species.[57] The effect of the order may thus be to apply the enhanced protection normally offered only to those species listed in Schedule 1 to the 1981 Act to all birds in the Area of Special Protection.[58] It can also be made an offence for any person to enter the designated area, or any part of it, at any time or during certain periods, *e.g.* protecting ground-nesting birds during the nesting season.[59] The order can also apply more severe penalties to any offence against the general law protecting birds, animals and plants committed in the designated area.[60]

5.8.3　There are, however, many exceptions to the prohibitions which can apply within Areas of Special Protection. Those with rights over the land are protected from restrictions not only by the fact that designations cannot be made in the face of objections by owners or occupiers, but also by the rule that none of the prohibitions in an order can affect the exercise by any persons of rights vested in them, as owner or occupier of the land or under any licence or agreement.[61] Further exceptions apply to "authorised persons"[62] in relation to birds which may be listed in Part II of Schedule 2 to the 1981 Act;[63] it is not an offence for authorised persons to kill or take such birds, to take or destroy their eggs or to destroy or disturb their nests or young.[64] The defences which apply to the general law protecting wild birds under the 1981 Act also apply to offences under the provisions of an order creating an Area of Special Protection.[65] The effect of Areas of Special Protection is thus

---

[56] *ibid.*, s.26(2).

[57] *ibid.*, s.3(1)(a).

[58] See para. 3.3.5, above.

[59] WCA 1981, s.3(1)(b).

[60] *ibid.*, s.3(1)(c) (amended for England and Wales by CRWA 2000, Sched. 12 para.2); the offences in question are those under *ibid.*, Pt I.

[61] *ibid.*, s.3(3).

[62] "Authorised persons" include owners, occupiers and those authorised by local authorities, the statutory conservation bodies and a range of statutory bodies; *ibid.*, s.27(1) (see para. 3.2.8, above).

[63] The control of pest species is now authorised by licences rather than this provision; see paras 3.3.8–3.3.9, above.

[64] WCA 1981, s.3(2).

[65] *ibid.*, s.4; see paras 3.3.3.–3.3.4, above.

not to offer complete protection to all birds, but rather to provide a limited sanctuary for some birds without interfering with existing rights in the land.[66]

ENVIRONMENTALLY SENSITIVE AREAS

Much of the landscape and habitat in Great Britain has been shaped by agricultural practices, but has been threatened by the pressure on farmers to change to more intensive and more efficient, but environmentally more harmful, methods if they are to make a living in the agricultural markets. The aim of Environmentally Sensitive Areas (ESAs) is to support agricultural practices which are compatible with conserving natural habitats, whilst ensuring an adequate income for the farmers who do not resort to damaging intensification. The origin of the designation lay in an E.C. Regulation seeking to improve the efficiency of agricultural structures, which also allowed Member States to introduce special schemes to encourage the use of environmentally beneficial agricultural practices in areas of ecological or landscape importance.[67] It now forms part of the wider agri-environment and rural development programmes that have emerged in the last decade, under an E.C. Regulation on support for rural development from the European Agricultural Guidance and Guarantee Fund.[68] The scheme adopted in this country is contained in the Agriculture Act 1986,[69] as amended.[70] Although the law is still in force for Scotland, support is now offered through the Rural Stewardship Scheme[71] which applies throughout Scotland so that the designation of ESAs is no longer of so much relevance except for the continuing effect of agreements that commenced under the ESA provisions.

5.9.1

The designation of ESAs is in the hands of the Minister, acting with

5.9.2

---

[66] There are eight Areas of Special Protection in Scotland, mostly designated in the late 1950s and early 1960s; SNH, *Facts and Figures 2000–2001*, p. 56.

[67] Regulation (E.E.C.) 797/85, art. 19, and subsequently Regulation (E.E.C.) 2078/92. On the early development see: D. Baldock, *et al.*, "Environmentally Sensitive Areas: Incrementalism or Reform?" (1990) 6 J. Rural Studies 143; P. Wathern, "Less Favoured and Environmentally Sensitive Areas: A European Dimension to the Rural Environment" in W. Howarth and C.P. Rodgers (eds). Agriculture, Conservation and Land Use (1992), Chap. 9; M. Whitby (ed.), *Incentives for Countryside Management: The Case of Environmentally Sensitive Areas* (1994).

[68] Regulation (E.C.) 1257/99.

[69] Agriculture Act 1986, s.18 (amended by EPA, Sched. 9, para. 13; NHSA, Sched. 10, para. 12; Agricultural Holdings (Scotland) Act 1991, Sched. 11, para. 45).

[70] Amended by the Agriculture Act 1986 (Amendment) Regulations 1994 and 1997 (S.I.s 1994 No.249, 1997 No.457).

[71] Rural Stewardship Scheme (Scotland) Regulations 2001 (S.S.I. 2001 No.300); see para.8.4.10, below.

the consent of the Treasury and after consultations in Scotland with Scottish Natural Heritage, in Wales with the Countryside Council for Wales, and in England with the Countryside Agency and English Nature.[72] The areas to be designated are those where it appears particularly desirable to conserve or enhance the natural beauty of the area, to conserve the flora, fauna, geological or physiographical features of the area or to protect buildings or other objects of archaeological, architectural or historic interest, and where these aims are likely to be facilitated by the maintenance or adoption of particular agricultural methods.[73] Orders are made by statutory instrument subject to annulment in Parliament.[74]

5.9.3   Once an ESA has been designated, the Minister is empowered to enter agreements with those having an interest in agricultural land whereby in exchange for prescribed payments that person agrees to manage the land in accordance with the agreement.[75] Although each agreement may differ, the designation order may lay down certain terms for all the agreements in that area,[76] including ones as to public access,[77] and the withholding of payments or imposition of penalties if required by E.C. measures.[78] Special provision is made to allow agreements to be made by those with less than full ownership of the land,[79] and by grazings committees on crofting land.[80] In Scotland, agreements may be registered in the Land Register of Scotland or the General Register of Sasines, and once registered can be enforced by the Minister against those deriving title from the original party.[81] In England and Wales the agreement is binding on those deriving title from the original party unless the contrary is stated.[82] The effect of these provisions is that agreements may run with the land, but that this is an issue to be decided when each individual agreement is made.

5.9.4   The designation of the ESA does not have any automatic consequences; it merely enables the Minister to enter agreements with individual farmers in the area, and the initiative must come largely from the farmers themselves. It is hoped that farmers will be encouraged to continue with more traditional farming methods by the availability of

---

[72] Agriculture Act 1986. s.18(1), (2).

[73] *ibid.*, s.18(1).

[74] *ibid.*, s.18(12).

[75] *ibid.*, s.18(3).

[76] *ibid.*, s.18(4).

[77] *ibid.*, s.18(4)(aa) (added by Agriculture Act 1986 (Amendment) Regulations 1994 (S.I. 1994 No. 249)).

[78] *ibid.*, s.18(4A) (added by Agriculture Act 1986 (Amendment) Regulations 1997 (S.I. 1997 No. 457)).

[79] *ibid.*, s.18(9).

[80] *ibid.*, s.19(4)–(7).

[81] *ibid.*, s.19(1)–(3).

[82] *ibid.*, s.18(7).

payments under the scheme to take the place of the income they could otherwise earn by converting to more intensive methods. The Minister must keep under review the effects of the scheme on each area and publish information on this.[83] The level of take-up, administration and monitoring of the scheme were criticised by the Public Accounts Committee in 1998,[84] and since then there have been many changes. More significantly, though, the scheme now operates in greater harmony with many other aspects of agricultural policy and agri-environment support, as opposed to standing almost alone against a strong tide in favour of greater intensification.

The number of areas designated has increased over the years, and the terms of the designations have been amended as the details of the scheme and the context of other support mechanisms have evolved. In England there has been a major revision and consolidation of the orders leading to the Environmentally Sensitive Areas (Stage I) to (Stage IV) Orders 2000.[85] In Scotland the arrangements for ESAs have been overtaken by the Rural Stewardship Scheme that applies throughout the country.

5.9.5

NATURAL HERITAGE AREAS

One uniquely Scottish designation is that of Natural Heritage Areas (NHAs). The legislative provisions for these were contained in the Natural Heritage (Scotland) Act 1991, but no such Area has been designated and the development of National Parks in Scotland makes it extremely doubtful that any ever will be created. The aim is to provide a framework which is apt for larger areas than can be properly dealt with by SSSIs and which takes account of all aspects of the natural heritage, in contrast to the more limited objectives of National Scenic Areas.[86] After such consultations as it thinks fit, SNH may recommend to the Scottish Ministers those areas which are of outstanding value to the natural heritage of Scotland[87] and where special protection measures are appropriate.[88] Following a recommendation, the Ministers may make a direction designating the area, but they must advertise any proposed designation and consider any representations made within the

5.10.1

---

[83] *ibid.*, s.18(8).
[84] House of Commons Public Accounts Committee, *Protecting Environmentally Sensitive Areas*, 39th Report of 1997–98 (1997–98 H.C. 513).
[85] S.I.s 2000 Nos 3049–3052.
[86] See paras 5.12.9–5.12.10, below.
[87] The "natural heritage of Scotland" includes the flora and fauna of Scotland, its geological and physiographical features and its natural beauty and amenity; NHSA 1991, s.1(3).
[88] *ibid.*, s.6(1).

specified period of at least three months.[89] A direction creating an NHA must be advertised in the local press.[90] The same procedure is followed where SNH recommends that it is no longer appropriate for all or part of an NHA to be designated as such and that the designation should be varied or cancelled.[91]

5.10.2   The legal effect of the designation of an NHA is minimal. The planning authority is obliged to maintain a list available for public inspection of any NHA in its district and to ensure that where an NHA has been designated special attention is paid to the desirability of preserving or enhancing its character or appearance in the exercise, with respect to any land in that area, of any powers under the Town and Country Planning (Scotland) Act 1997.[92]

5.10.3   However, the consultation paper issued when the proposal to introduce NHAs was first produced suggested a much greater significance in practice.[93] The intention was that for such areas, an overall Management Statement should be prepared, to be submitted to and approved by the Ministers when the recommendation for designation is made. This Management Statement should be prepared by SNH in co-operation with relevant public and private interests, and set forth a basis for sustainable land use throughout the area that can be implemented through the "voluntary principle". SNH will then oversee the implementation of the Management Statement, possibly with the assistance of a management committee, co-ordinating the activities and strategies of the various interested parties.[94]

5.10.4   SNH's role in achieving the aims of the NHA would include involvement in the preparation of alterations to the planning authorities' development plans for the area and as a consultee in the consideration of applications for forestry grants, felling licences and agricultural grants. No new powers would be involved, but use would be made of the existing provisions for management agreements,[95] financial assistance, consultation and advice in order to assist the implementation of the Statement, with the powers to designate SSSIs and make access orders available as a last resort. The Ministers might also be asked to make

---

[89] *ibid.*, s.6(3), (4).

[90] *ibid.*, s.6(5).

[91] *ibid.*, s.6(6), (7).

[92] TCPSA 1997, s.264.

[93] *Consultation Paper on Natural Heritage Areas*, Scottish Office, March 6, 1991.

[94] See the discussion of possible NHA status for the Cairngorms in *Common Sense and Sustainability: A Partnership for the Cairngorms*, Report of the Cairngorms Working Party (1992), section 4.4.1.

[95] The power to make management agreements extends to anything "necessary to secure the conservation and enhancement or to foster the understanding and enjoyment of the natural heritage of Scotland"; CSA 1967, s.49A (added by Countryside (Scotland) Act 1981 s.9, amended by NHSA 1991, Sched. 10, para. 4).

directions removing permitted development status from certain forms of development in such areas, as is presently the case in National Scenic Areas (*e.g.* in relation to vehicle tracks).[96] The aim throughout, though, would be to integrate the strategies of the many public bodies and private individuals whose activities can affect the natural heritage of the area, and to lead them to co-operate in preserving and enhancing the value of the area.

Many of these features now appear in the scheme for National Parks **5.10.5** under the National Parks (Scotland) Act 2000[97] and it is now clear that to the extent that there is a role for a designation such as this it will be filled by the National Parks.[98] Nevertheless, the legislative provisions for NHAs remain on the statute book. There are already far too many different designations and repealing these provisions and formally burying NHAs would be a small, but welcome, step towards a neater and more coherent set of laws on conservation.

NATIONAL PARKS

National Parks have developed very differently in England and Wales **5.11.1** and in Scotland. South of the border, the National Parks were created under the National Parks and Access to the Countryside Act 1949, but at that time it was decided that there was no need for them in Scotland,[99] and it is only under the very different provisions of the National Parks (Scotland) Act 2000 that the first National Park in Scotland is due to be created in 2002.

In both jurisdictions, the Parks are very different from the interna- **5.11.2** tionally accepted concept of national parks. The International Union for the Conservation of Nature has recommended that the term "national park" be reserved for relatively large areas where ecosystems are not materially altered by human exploitation and occupation, where the highest competent authority of the country has taken steps to prevent or eliminate exploitation and occupation and where visitors are allowed to enter under special conditions for "inspirational, educative, cultural and recreative purposes." It is further recommended that the term should not be used for inhabited and exploited areas where land-

---

[96] See para. 5.12.10, below.

[97] See paras 5.11.20–5.11.33, below.

[98] The *Natural Heritage Designations Review: Discussion Paper* produced by the Scottish Office in December 1996 supported a role for NHAs (Chap.5), building on the work done by the Cairngorms Partnership, but NHAs were seen largely as an alternative to National Parks and once policy changed in favour of National Parks, official documents stated that it was unlikely that any NHAs would ever be created (*e.g.* NPPG 14 *Natural Heritage* (1999), para. 34).

[99] *National Parks and the Conservation of Nature in Scotland* (Cmd. 7235, 1947).

scape planning and measures for the development of tourism have led
to areas where industrialisation and urbanisation are controlled and
public outdoor recreation takes priority over the conservation of ecosystems.[1] The systems of National Parks in Great Britain contravene this
recommendation in many ways.[2]

5.11.3   The National Parks are not areas unaffected by man (indeed none of
this country is free from significant human interference), and they are
places where many people continue to live and to make a living off the
land or in industrial or tourist developments. The original emphasis was
firmly on recreation and the preservation of natural beauty rather than
nature conservation, and indeed the Parks were better regarded as part
of the town and country planning system, as areas where slightly
stricter controls apply, than as a major element of the law relating to
nature conservation. This is not to say that the Parks do not play a part
in this latter objective, but their impact tends to be indirect and to
depend on the way in which discretionary powers are exercised.[3] The
changes introduced by the Environment Act 1995 give a greater role to
the conservation of wildlife (and cultural heritage) while the Scottish
model gives priority to conserving and enhancing the natural (and
cultural) heritage of the area, but still requires regard for economic and
social development.

England and Wales

5.11.4   The National Park system in England and Wales was introduced by the
National Parks and Access to the Countryside Act 1949, but has been
amended many times, most notably by the Environment Act 1995
which rewrote the purposes of the Parks and established in all cases
Park Authorities to take over functions previously left in the hands
of local authorities. The scheme was initially designed to further two
objectives, the preservation and enhancement of natural beauty and the
promotion of the enjoyment of the countryside by the public.[4] These
objectives were revised by the 1995 Act and the purposes are now
stated to be "conserving and enhancing the natural beauty, wildlife and
cultural heritage" of the areas concerned and "promoting opportunities
for the understanding and enjoyment" of their special qualities by the
public.[5] This is a wider definition, expressly mentioning wildlife, as

[1] Resolution 1 of 10th General Assembly of IUCN, New Delhi, December 1, 1969.
[2] For many purposes the Norfolk and Suffolk Broads are treated as a National Park,
although subject to the individual legal regime established by the Norfolk and Suffolk
Broads Act 1988; see paras 5.11.17–5.11.19, below.
[3] See generally, A. McEwan and M. McEwan, *National Parks: Conservation or Cos-
metics?* (1982).
[4] NPACA 1949, s.5(1) (as originally enacted).
[5] NPACA 1949, s.5(1) (as amended by EA 1995, s.61).

opposed to this being included within the meaning of "natural beauty", whilst emphasising the appreciation of special qualities of the Parks, as opposed to their use as a resource for recreation. The designation, management and legal rules for National Parks all seek to accomplish these objectives, and it is for these purposes that the powers given to the authorities involved can be exercised. Furthermore, all ministers, public bodies and office-holders and statutory undertakers are under an obligation to have regard to the twin purposes of National Parks in the exercise of their functions affecting land in a National Park.[6]

Although the preservation of the natural beauty of an area has always **5.11.5** included the preservation of its flora, fauna and geological and physio-graphical features,[7] the emphasis in National Parks was on protecting wildlife and natural features as part of the beauty of the countryside to be enjoyed and made available to the public. One of the difficulties faced by the National Parks is that the twin objectives (in either form) which they are created to serve are not always compatible. Increasing recreational use can put too much pressure on a fragile environment, and even those seeking to appreciate the peace of the countryside can destroy habitats through disturbance and erosion, to say nothing of the effect of the facilities required to transport and cater for large numbers of visitors. The dual objectives of the Parks must always be borne in mind and the interests of conservation must always be tempered by those of recreation and enjoyment, although in the event of conflict greater weight must be given to the conservation and enhancement of the natural beauty, wildlife and cultural heritage[8] (although there can of course be conflicts between these as well).

The areas which can be chosen as National Parks are extensive tracts **5.11.6** of country where action to further the twin objectives is particularly desirable because of their natural beauty and the opportunities they afford for open-air recreation in view of their character and location in relation to centres of population action.[9] Designation is in the hands of the Countryside Agency (in England) and the Countryside Council for Wales (in Wales),[10] subject to confirmation by the Minister after the

---

[6] NPACA 1949, s.11A(2), (added by EA 1995, s.62).

[7] *ibid.*, s.114(2) (amended by CA 1968, s.21(7) and EA 1995, Sched. 10 para. 2(8)); note the older usage of "preservation" as opposed to the current "conservation," which is thought to be more apt for living ecosystems.

[8] NPACA 1949 s.11A(2), added by EA 1995, s.62. This is known as the "Sandford Principle", following the *Report of the National Park Policies Review Committee* (1974), chaired by Lord Sandford.

[9] *ibid.*, s.5(2).

[10] All of the powers with respect to National Parks previously exercised by the Country-side Commission for the whole of England and Wales were transferred in Wales to the Countryside Council for Wales whilst remaining in the hands of the Countryside Commission for land in England (*ibid.*, s.4A (added by EPA 1990, Sched. 8, para. 2)); the changes from Countryside Commission to Countryside Agency were effected by

proposal has been advertised and notified to all local authorities affected. If objections or representations are made, a local inquiry or a hearing must be held,[11] and further consultations are required if the Minister
decides to confirm the proposed designation with modifications.[12] The
order designating a Park can be subsequently varied by the Minister or
the Agency or Council, subject to the same procedural rules.[13]

5.11.7   The administrative arrangements for the National Parks were altered
by the Environment Act 1995 which provided for the creation of a Park
Authority for each Park,[14] effected by the National Park Authorities
(Wales) Order 1995 and the National Park Authorities (England) Order
1996.[15] These Authorities are constituted by the Minister and the Act
lays down a detailed framework for their constitution.[16] Some of the
members are appointed by the relevant local authorities, the remainder
by the Minister,[17] and in England some of these must come from parish
councils or meetings. Different numbers of members, between 15 and
38, have been appointed to the Authorities created. Their main task is
to pursue the twin purposes of the National Parks, but also to seek to
foster the economic and social well-being of local communities.[18]

5.11.8   The Park Authorities' most significant powers lie in relation to the
planning system, where they act as the local planning authority for the
area covered by the Park and therefore exercise development control.[19]
As well as it being likely that different policies will be applied, the
normal planning controls are made more strict by means of restrictions
to the range of works which qualify as "permitted development" and
are thus exempt from the requirement to obtain express planning per-

---

the Development Commission (Transfer of Functions and Miscellaneous Provisions)
Order 1999 (S.I. 1999 No. 416), Sched. 1; see para. 2.7.1, above.

[11]   An inquiry must be held if there are representations from a local authority; NPACA
1949, Sched. 1, para. 2.

[12]   *ibid.*, s.7, Sched. 1; National Parks and Access to the Countryside Regulations 1950,
S.I. 1950 No. 1066, Pt IV.

[13]   *ibid.*, s.7(4); WCA 1981, s.45.

[14]   EA 1995, s.63.

[15]   S.I.s 1995 No. 2803 and 1996 No.1243. There were transitional measures for the
existing boards and committees which had responsibility for the Parks (EA 1995 ss.63–
64).

[16]   EA 1995, Sched. 7.

[17]   The proportions of members of each class are set out in the Act: in Wales two-thirds
of the members are appointed by the local authorities, in England the direct ministerial
appointments are to be two less than the local authority ones and the parish members
one less than half the number of direct ministerial appointments (EA 1995, Sched. 7,
para. 1).

[18]   This is to be achieved through co-operation with other public bodies, and no significant
expenditure is to be incurred for this purpose (NPACA 1949, s.11(A)(1)); *cf.* the higher
status given to economic and social development by their inclusion in the National
Park aims for Scottish Parks (see para. 5.11.21, below).

[19]   TCPA 1990, s.4A, added by EA 1995, s.67.

mission.[20] The authorities also enjoy a variety of other functions which had been placed in the hands of the planning authority, ranging from providing caravan sites and declaring local nature reserves to making byelaws and responsibilities in relation to ancient monuments and listed buildings.[21] There is also a general power to do anything calculated to facilitate (or conducive or incidental to) the achievement of the Park purposes.[22] Funding for the Park Authorities comes from the Minister,[23] supplemented by the Authorities' power to issue levies to the local authorities within the Park areas.[24]

Whilst executive power rests with the Park Authorities, an important advisory role is played by the Countryside Agency and the Countryside Council for Wales.[25] These bodies must be consulted before many of the powers of the Authorities are exercised, and must keep the general position in the National Parks under review. In particular, the Agency and Council are to make recommendations to ministers, Park and local authorities on the accomplishment of the objectives for which National Parks were created, advise on arrangements for the administration of the parks, give advice when consulted by ministers or Park Authorities on the preparation of development plans or the handling of individual applications for planning permission, and make representations when developments incompatible with the aims of a Park are proposed and when their own advice is not being followed.[26] The Agency and Council can also make recommendations on the payment of grants to authorities to assist in the management of the parks.[27] Only in very limited circumstances, *e.g.* for experimental schemes,[28] can the Agency or Council take direct action themselves.[29] **5.11.9**

Each Park Authority must prepare a National Park Management Plan formulating its policy for the management of the Park and the exercise of its own functions, and must review and revise this plan at least every five years.[30] This plan must be drawn up in consultation with the Countryside Agency or Countryside Council for Wales and with the local authorities affected and forms the basis on which the Park will be **5.11.10**

---

[20] Town and Country Planning (General Permitted Development) Order 1995 (S.I. 1995), No. 418), Scheds 1 and 2.
[21] EA 1995, Sched. 9.
[22] See para. 5.11.13, below.
[23] EA 1995, s.72.
[24] EA 1995, s.71, applying Local Government Finance Act 1988, s.74 and associated regulations.
[25] As successors to the Countryside Commission that was originally created as the National Parks Commission; NPACA 1949, s.1; see para. 2.7.1, above.
[26] *ibid.*, s.6(3), (4).
[27] CA 1968, s.2(9).
[28] *ibid.*, s.4 (amended by WCA 1981, s.40).
[29] See paras 2.6.16, 2.7.3, above.
[30] EA 1995, s.66.

managed with an eye to achieving the objectives of conserving and enhancing the natural beauty, wildlife and cultural heritage of the Park and promoting the understanding and enjoyment of its special features. The plan covers a wider range of issues than the standard development plans under the planning system,[31] but does not enjoy the same statutory status.[32]

5.11.11   For each Park a map must be drawn up by the Park Authority showing those areas of the Park whose natural beauty it is especially important to conserve.[33] The areas in question are areas of mountain, moor, heath, woodland, down, cliff and foreshore,[34] and they are to be identified in accordance with guidelines issued by the Countryside Agency and Countryside Council for Wales.[35] Such maps, which must be revised at least every five years,[36] are to be for sale to the public, and serve as a guide identifying those areas where the Authorities are likely to seek to exercise their various powers to regulate land use, etc.

5.11.12   While the operation of the planning system can be used to protect National Parks from many forms of development, agricultural and forestry developments are largely outwith the scope of such controls. However special provisions have been introduced to protect areas of moor and heath within the Parks. Where such an area has been designated by the Minister,[37] it is an offence to plough the land, convert it into agricultural land or carry out on it other agricultural or forestry operations which have been specified as likely to affect its character or appearance.[38] These prohibitions do not apply if the land in question has been agricultural land within the last twenty years,[39] or if the owner or occupier has given written notice to the Park Authority and one of a number of other conditions is satisfied. The Authority must notify the Minister and the Agency or Council.[40] Once notice has been given, the operation can go ahead as soon as consent has been given by the Authority, after three months if no decision has been made by the Authority by that time, or after twelve months if consent has been

---

[31] The Agency or Council must be consulted in the preparation of the development plans for a National Park; NPACA 1949, s.9.

[32] See paras 8.2.4–8.2.6, above.

[33] WCA 1981, s.43(1) (amended by Wildlife and Countryside (Amendment) Act 1985, s.3).

[34] *ibid.*, s.43(3) (added by *ibid.*).

[35] *ibid.*, s.43(1A)–(1C) (added by *ibid.*).

[36] *ibid.*, s.43(1) (amended by *ibid.*).

[37] *ibid.*, s.42(1); designating orders are to be made by statutory instrument subject to annulment by either House of Parliament (WCA 1981, s.42(8)).

[38] *ibid.*, s.42(2).

[39] *ibid.*, s.42(2); "agricultural land" does not include land used only for rough grazing (*ibid.*, s.52(1)) and any conversion in breach of this section or of its predecessor (CA 1968, s.14) is to be disregarded (WCA 1981, s.42(7)).

[40] *ibid.*, s.42(6).

refused.[41] As with the original provisions for SSSIs, the period of delay is intended to allow time for negotiations for management agreements or other measures to be introduced to deal with the situation. Where there is an application for a farm capital grant for land in a National Park, the outcome should so far as possible be consistent with the twin objectives of the Parks, and if a grant is refused following an objection from the Park Authority, an offer must be made by it to enter a management agreement.[42]

The Park Authorities in National Parks enjoy a range of powers to **5.11.13** further the aims of the Parks. They can arrange for the provision of facilities for visitors, including accommodation, refreshments, litter bins, camping sites and parking places[43] as well as study centres and other facilities for learning about the history and natural history of the area.[44] Where there is a shortage of such facilities, arrangements can be made to facilitate the use of waterways for boating, bathing, fishing and other forms of recreation.[45] Traffic on roads in National Parks can be restricted to conserve and enhance their natural beauty and to afford better opportunities for recreation, enjoyment of the amenities of the area and the study of nature.[46] More generally Park Authorities are given a general competence to do anything calculated to facilitate or conducive or incidental to the accomplishment of the Park objectives, although this does not enable them to raise money outside their express powers to do so or to overcome any statutory restriction on the exercise of their express powers.[47] In particular grants and loans can be made to other bodies and individuals to further these aims.[48]

A further important power to assist in preserving the character of the **5.11.14** National Parks, is the power of the Planning Authority to make byelaws. These can be made for the preservation of order, to ensure that people do not behave so as to cause undue interference with the enjoyment of others, and to protect from damage the land or anything thereon or therein.[49] In particular byelaws can cover matters such as traffic controls, litter and the lighting of fires.[50] For lakes and other stretches of open water in the parks byelaws can be made prohibiting or restricting traffic of any description on the water for the purposes of ensuring the safety of those using the lake, regulating all forms of sport

---

[41] *ibid.*, s.42(3), (4).
[42] *ibid.*, s.41(3)–(5) (amended by Agriculture Act 1986 s.20(4)); *cf.* para. 5.5.37, above.
[43] NPACA 1949, s.12; CA 1968, s.12(2).
[44] CA 1968, s.12(1).
[45] NPACA 1949, s.13; CA 1968, s.12(3).
[46] Road Traffic Regulation Act 1984, s.22.
[47] EA 1995, s.65(5),(6).
[48] WCA 1981, s.44, as amended by EA 1995, s.69(4).
[49] NPACA 1949, s.90(1).
[50] *ibid.*, s.90(3).

or recreation which use vessels, conserving the natural beauty and amenity of the lake and surrounding area and preventing any nuisance or damage, particularly nuisance caused by excessive noise.[51] In all cases the Agency or Council must be consulted before the byelaws are made,[52] and the byelaws must be confirmed by the Minister in accordance with the standard procedures for local authority byelaws.[53] Wardens can be appointed, to secure compliance with the byelaws, advise and assist the public, and perform other functions as directed by the Authorities.[54]

5.11.15 Land in National Parks can be acquired by the Minister where he considers this expedient,[55] and is to be passed into the hands of others to be managed for the twin purposes of the Park.[56] The terms on which land is passed on may include a financial contribution from the government for the management of the land.[57] The way in which land is dealt with by other authorities is also affected, *e.g.* before disposing of land in a National Park, water and sewerage undertakers must consult the Agency or Council and may enter management agreements to impose other conditions before the land is transferred.[58] The water legislation also provides that, as with SSSIs, areas within the Parks can be identified by the authorities as being of special value so that any body concerned with authorising or carrying out works must notify the Agency or Council in advance.[59]

5.11.16 What all of this means is that the relevant authorities in National Parks enjoy wide powers which can be used for the benefit of nature conservation as part of the general aim of conserving and enhancing the natural beauty and wildlife of these areas. The potential is there for things to be done to assist conservation through stricter planning controls, the making of byelaws and the funding or carrying out of particular projects, and to assist in educating the public through the provision of study centres. However the mere fact that an area has been designated a National Park has very little immediate and direct significance for nature conservation—the controls on converting moor and heath

---

[51] CA 1968, s.13.

[52] NPACA 1949, s.90(4); CA 1968, s.13(4).

[53] *ibid.*, s.106; *ibid.*, s.13(8); the procedure is set out in the Local Government Act 1972, ss.236–238.

[54] *ibid.*, s.92; *ibid.*, ss.13(9), 42; WCA 1981, s.49.

[55] *ibid.*, s.14(1); acquisition is by agreement and with the consent of the Treasury.

[56] *ibid.*, s.14(2).

[57] *ibid.*, s.14(3).

[58] Water Industry Act 1991, s.156; the disposal of houses in National Parks may also be restricted in the effort to avoid the spread of holiday homes at the expense of accommodation for those living in the parks (Housing Act 1985, s.37 (amended by Housing Act 1988, s.125); Housing Associations Act 1985, s.11 and Sched. 2, para, 3).

[59] Water Industry Act 1991, s.4; Water Resources Act 1991, s.17; Land Drainage Act 1991, s.13; see para. 5.5.39, above.

apply only once introduced to an area by ministerial order—and even where action is taken to conserve nature the authority must balance this against the need to promote the enjoyment of the land.

Norfolk and Suffolk Broads

Special provisions have been made for the Norfolk and Suffolk Broads, **5.11.17** similar to those for the National Parks, but taking account of the special requirements arising from the fact that it is the waterways which are the main features of interest both for recreation and conservation.[60] A Broads Authority has been established with membership drawn from the relevant local authorities, water and navigation bodies, the Countryside Agency and English Nature, boating, farming and land-owning interests.[61] The general duty of this authority is to manage the Broads for the purposes of conserving and enhancing their natural beauty,[62] promoting the enjoyment of the Broads by the public and protecting the interests of navigation.[63] Thus, as with the National Parks, nature conservation must be balanced with and may be subordinated to the interests of recreation, and also in this case of the preservation and development of rights of navigation.

Many of the provisions for the National Parks are repeated for the **5.11.18** Broads. A map must be drawn up and regularly revised showing the areas whose natural beauty it is especially important to conserve,[64] and a Broads Plan must be prepared to set out the policy for managing the area.[65] Particular areas can be designated within which specified operations which might affect their character or appearance can go ahead only after the Broads Authority has been notified and has given its consent or a period of time has passed. The areas which can be designated are areas of grazing marsh, fen marsh, reed-bed or broad-leaved woodland and the time periods are three months if no response is given and twelve months if consent is refused.[66] Byelaws can be made for areas owned or occupied by the Authority or commonly used by the public.[67] The Broads Authority counts as a local authority and the Broads as a National Park for many other pieces of legislation.[68]

---

[60] Norfolk and Suffolk Broads Act 1988; see generally M. Shaw, "The Broads Act 1988: A Framework for Environmental Planning and Management" [1989] J.P.L. 241.

[61] *ibid.*, s.1 (amended by EPA 1990, Sched. 9, para. 15; Water (Local Statutory Provisions) (Consequential Amendments) Order 1989 (S.I. 1989 No. 1380), art. 4).

[62] This includes conserving the flora, fauna, geological and physiographical features of the area (*ibid.*, s.25(2)); it is worth remarking that the "natural beauty" of the Broads is largely man-made, being the result of the flooding of early peat workings.

[63] *ibid.*, s.2.

[64] *ibid.*, s.4.

[65] *ibid.*, s.3.

[66] *ibid.*, s.5.

[67] *ibid.*, s.6.

[68] See *ibid.*, Sched. 6.

5.11.19   The importance of the waterways is reflected by the creation of a separate Navigation Committee with membership drawn from the Broads Authority, the owners and hirers of pleasure craft and other users of the area.[69] This Committee is responsible for maintaining, improving and developing for the purposes of navigation the area specified as the "navigation area."[70] There is a power for the Committee to make byelaws for the good management of the area, the conservation of its natural beauty and amenities and the promotion of its use for recreational purposes.[71]

Scotland

5.11.20   The belated introduction of National Parks in Scotland followed considerable debate[72] and consultation that spanned the period of devolution and it was the Scottish Parliament that passed the National Parks (Scotland) Act 2000. The Act sets out the framework for the Parks and the procedure for their creation, but leaves many of the significant details to be determined on a case by case basis, as demonstrated by the differences between the first two proposals. As would be expected half a century after the initial legislation south of the border, the Scottish provisions reflect wider environmental concerns, but a further feature is a greater concern for ensuring a strong local voice in the running of the parks.

5.11.21   The Act begins by setting out the "National Park aims", namely:

> "(a) to conserve and enhance the natural and cultural heritage of the area,
> (b) to promote sustainable use of the natural resources of the area,
> (c) to promote understanding and enjoyment (including enjoyment in the form of recreation) of the special qualities of the area by the public, and
> (d) to promote sustainable economic and social development of the area's communities."[73]

It is stated that the general purpose of the Park Authorities is to ensure that these aims are collectively achieved in a co-ordinated way in rela-

---

[69] *ibid.*, s.9.

[70] *ibid.*, s.10(1); the "navigation area" is defined in s.8(1).

[71] *ibid.*, s.10(3).

[72] At times political sensitivity to the fact that Scotland was one of the few countries in the world without any areas labelled as National Parks seemed to play at least as significant a role as a clear idea of what the Parks would add to the existing catalogue of designations.

[73] NPSA 2000, s.1.

tion to each Park.[74] Crucially, in the event of any conflict between these aims, greater weight must be given to the first aim.[75]

Proposals to establish a National Park may be made by the Scottish **5.11.22** Ministers where it appears to them that an area is of outstanding national importance on account of its natural heritage, or a combination of natural and cultural heritage, and has a distinctive character and coherent identity. The third requirement is that designation as a National Park will meet the special needs of the area and be the best means of ensuring that the National Park aims are collectively achieved in a co-ordinated way.[76] The proposal is then followed by a report from SNH (or another public body appointed for this purpose[77]) considering the desirability of the designation, the area to be designated, the functions for the Park Authority, the costs involved and any other specified matters. Preparation of this report must involve consultation with local authorities, community councils, representatives of those who live, work or carry on business in the area, and must take into account the views expressed.[78] Alternatively, the Ministers themselves can prepare a statement addressing the same issues and after similar consultation.[79] In either case, a local inquiry can then be held in relation to any matter arising in the report or statement.[80]

At this stage the proposal can be halted, but if it is proceeding, the **5.11.23** final stage is for the Ministers to make a designation order, which must have regard to the report or statement. The order must be approved in draft by the Scottish Parliament, after consultation with every local authority and community council for the area concerned, local representatives and the public. The draft may be revised in the light of the responses, with the Parliament being informed of the views received during the consultation and any changes made at this stage.[81] The final designation order is then made by statutory instrument,[82] and copies must be sent to the local authorities affected and kept available for public inspection.[83]

The detailed administrative arrangements for and the precise powers **5.11.24** of each National Park authority are to be determined on a individual

---

[74] *ibid.*, s.9(1).
[75] *ibid.*, s.9(6).
[76] *ibid.*, s.2(2).
[77] In both cases so far SNH has been chosen.
[78] NPSA 2000, s.3.
[79] *ibid.*, s.4.
[80] *ibid.*, s.5; the inquiry is governed by s.210 of the Local Government (Scotland) Act 1973.
[81] *ibid.*, s.6.
[82] *ibid.*, s.34.
[83] *ibid.*, s.7.

basis for each Park, but a framework is laid down in the Act.[84] The maximum number of members of the Park Authority is 25, some to be nominated by the Scottish Ministers, some by the relevant local authorities and some (at least a fifth of the number) directly elected by those living in the Park. In the two cases so far, the full 25 have been proposed with five directly elected and ten nominated in each class.[85] A further requirement is that a proportion of the appointed members (at least a fifth) must be "local members", that is have their sole or main residence in the Park or are councillors for a local authority or ward or community council within the Park. The Ministers must consult local authorities and community councils, local representatives and others as they think fit before making their nominations, and the nominees must appear to the Ministers to have knowledge or experience relevant to the Park's functions, with the potential for the designation order to specify particular interests to be covered.

5.11.25   The late introduction of provisions for directly elected representatives and local members shows the general determination as the Bill went through the Parliament that there should be a very strong local voice in the running of the Parks. They should not be in the hands of outside "experts". This determination is also reflected in the roles for the local authorities and the thorough consultation procedures which are to take place at many stages and which make particular reference to the role of community councils.

5.11.26   The maximum period of appointment for members is five years, renewable, and there are detailed rules on removal from office in the event of bankruptcy, incapacity or prolonged absence, the filling of vacancies and members' interests.[86] A Convener is to be chosen from among the members and a chief executive appointed, with the approval of the Ministers, and the Authority must appoint at least one Advisory Group. The Authority can appoint non-members to committees and has wide power to delegate to committees and officers. It can also agree that any of its functions shall be exercised by a local authority, or exercise functions on behalf of a local authority[87] or the Scottish Ministers.[88]

5.11.27   The Ministers have the power to issue general or specific directions to a Park Authority and also guidance as to the exercise of functions by Park Authorities. The Authorities must comply with any directions

---

[84] *ibid.*, Sched. 1.

[85] *Report on the proposal for a Loch Lomond and The Trossachs National Park* and *Report on the proposal for a National Park in the Cairngorms* (SNH, 2001). See Addendum, above.

[86] NPSA 2000, Sched. 1.

[87] *ibid.*, s.17.

[88] *ibid.*, s.18; ministerial functions in relation to delegated legislation or under the 2000 Act itself cannot be delegated.

or guidance, but these can be made only after consultation with the Authorities affected and guidance must be published and is subject to a negative resolution procedure in the Scottish Parliament.[89] Ministers must also determine the financial duties and procedures for Park Authorities, and the Ministers enjoy powers to pay grants and loans, approve borrowing, offer guarantees and require the payment of any surplus to the Ministers.[90] The Park's accounts are subject to scrutiny by the Auditor General for Scotland and Park Authorities must prepare annual reports and accounts, to be laid before Parliament.[91]

The Park Authority's purpose is to ensure that the National Park **5.11.28** aims are collectively achieved in a co-ordinated way.[92] Central to the management of a National Park is the National Park Plan and there is a clear statutory duty on the Scottish Ministers, the Authority, local authorities and all other public bodies and office holders to have regard to the Plan in the exercise of their functions so far as they affect the Park.[93] The Plan is made by the Park Authority and sets out its policy for managing the Park and for co-ordinating the exercise of the Author-ity's functions and those of other public bodies in relation to the Park.[94] Production of the Plan requires consultation with the relevant local authorities, community councils, representative groups and the public, and the views received must be taken into account. The Plan is subject to approval by the Scottish Ministers, with or without modification, and copies must be available for public inspection.[95] In the event of a Plan being rejected, a revised one must be submitted within the deadline stated at the time. Plans are to be reviewed through a similar procedure at least every five years.[96]

The effectiveness of the Plan in securing real co-ordination and co- **5.11.29** operation between the many authorities whose activities can help or hinder the achievement of the Park's aims, and in providing a means of compromise when these aims conflict, will obviously be crucial to the smooth working and success of the Parks. In particular, there is a clear need for the Park plan and the development plans for the area to be consistent, which emphasises the importance of the structural arrangements for town and country planning. With respect to land within a National Park, planning authorities are under an obligation to

---

[89] *ibid.*, s.16; the draft guidance must be laid before the Parliament for 40 days and if a resolution is passed that the guidance should not be given, then the Ministers must comply with that.
[90] *ibid.*, ss.21–24.
[91] *ibid.*, ss.25–26.
[92] *ibid.*, s.9(1).
[93] *ibid.*, s.14.
[94] *ibid.*, s.11.
[95] *ibid.*, s.12.
[96] *ibid.*, s.13.

pay "special attention" to the desirability of exercising powers consistently with the Park Plan.[97]

5.11.30   In relation to its own efforts to fulfil the Park objectives, key mechanisms available to the Authority include planning powers and the making of byelaws, management rules and management agreements but the full range of powers is to be determined in the individual designation orders. The most important area left undetermined is the extent to which the Authority is to act as the planning authority for the Park. The Act specifies the two options of the Authority becoming the planning authority with full powers or taking over responsibility solely for development planning, but also allows for other combinations. The proposal for the Loch Lomond and the Trossachs National Park is for the Park Authority to be the planning authority, responsible for development control and the local plan, but sharing responsibility with local authorities for the structure plan, whereas for the Cairngorms development planning is likely to remain in the hands of local authorities, but with the Park Authority involved in joint arrangements for both levels of development plan.[98]

5.11.31   Other specific functions covered by the proposed designation orders include the power to create local nature reserves, the development of grant and management schemes in various contexts, responsibility for rights of way, powers to provide recreational facilities, power to request road traffic management orders and a role as statutory consultee on many issues.[99]

5.11.32   The Park Authority has the power to enter management agreements with those holding any interest in land in order to do, or secure the doing of, whatever the parties consider necessary to achieve the Park aims. This is a very broad power, and is not even formally restricted to land within the Park itself. These agreements are subject to the usual terms in relation to running with the land, registration etc. The Authority can also make byelaws to protect the natural and cultural heritage of the Park, to prevent damage to the land or anything in, on or under it, or to secure the public's enjoyment of and safety in the National Park.[1] In particular, fires, litter, nuisances, vehicles other than on roads and the exercise of recreational activities can be controlled. Proposed byelaws must be advertised and there must be consultation with local authorities, community councils and representative groups. The byelaws must be confirmed by the Scottish Ministers.[2] A further mechanism

---

[97] TCPSA 1997, s.264A, added by NPSA 2000, Sched. 5, para. 18.
[98] See note 85 on p. 242, above.
[99] *ibid.*
[1] NPSA 2000, Sched. 2, para. 8.
[2] *ibid.*, applying ss.202–204 of the Local Government (Scotland) Act 1973.

available is the making of management rules for land owned, occupied or managed by the authority.[3]

The Authority also has a range of general powers to do things calcu- **5.11.33** lated to facilitate or conducive or incidental to accomplishing the National Park functions or others conferred on it.[4] To enable it to carry out its tasks it can provide advice and assistance, carry out research, make charges and pay grants, promote or oppose private legislation, and has wide powers to enter contracts, form businesses of various sorts and invest its funds.[5] More specifically, the Authority has the power for any of its functions to acquire land by agreement or by compulsory purchase (with Ministerial approval).[6] In a number of respects, *e.g.* public access to meetings and documents,[7] and as a consultee under a range of statutory procedures, including designation of SSSIs,[8] the Authority is treated as a local authority.

The first National Park in Scotland, for Loch Lomond and the Tros- **5.11.34** sachs, is due to be formally established in the summer of 2002, with the Cairngorms scheduled to follow in early 2003.

LANDSCAPE AND PLANNING DESIGNATIONS

Areas of Outstanding Natural Beauty (England and Wales only)

Areas of Outstanding Natural Beauty (AONBs) are areas in England **5.12.1** and Wales which are not in a National Park,[9] but are of such outstanding natural beauty that it is desirable that special provisions, primarily changes to the planning system, should apply to them.[10] The provisions for these were overhauled and considerably strengthened by the Countryside and Rights of Way Act 2000, with a duty placed on public bodies to have regard to their purposes, a new emphasis on the preparation of management plans and the potential to establish a conservation board for any individual AONB to further the purposes of the designation. Conservation of the natural beauty of an area includes conservation of its flora, fauna, and geological and physiographical features.[11]

The areas are selected and designated by the Countryside Agency **5.12.2**

---

[3] *ibid.*, Sched. 2, para. 10, applying ss.112–118 of Civic Government (Scotland) Act 1982.

[4] *ibid.*, s.9.

[5] *ibid.*, Sched. 2.

[6] Governed by the Land (Authorisation Procedure) (Scotland) Act 1947; *ibid.* para. 5.

[7] NPSA 2000, Sched. 2, para. 12.

[8] WCA 1981, s.28(1)(aa), inserted for Scotland by NPSA 2000, Sched. 5, para. 8.

[9] Epping Forest and Burnham Beeches are also excluded; CRWA 2000 s.92(3).

[10] CRWA 2000, s.82.

[11] *ibid.*, s.92(2).

and the Countryside Council for Wales, who must consult all the local authorities in the area and advertise the proposal. The designation must be confirmed by the Minister, who must receive any representations or objections made in response to the proposal and consult the Agency or Council and local authorities if he intends to refuse to confirm the order or to confirm it with modifications.[12] Designation orders can be varied by the Minister and the Agency or Council, and must be kept available for inspection by these bodies and by the local authorities in the areas affected.

5.12.3 Once an AONB has been created, all ministers, public bodies (including local authorities), statutory undertakers and public office holders are under a duty to have regard to the purpose of conserving and enhancing the natural beauty of the AONB when they exercise any functions in relation to or so as to affect land in an AONB.[13] This duty is therefore limited to land-related functions, but does apply to land outwith the boundaries of the AONB if there will be an effect inside. The Countryside Agency and Countryside Council for Wales have roles in some ways similar to that in relation to National Parks, having the same duty to give advice and rights to be consulted on development plans and access arrangements.[14] Local authorities also enjoy a general power to take such action as appears expedient to conserve or enhance the natural beauty of the area.[15]

5.12.4 Some impacts of designation as an AONB apply automatically. Within an AONB, the Countryside Agency or Countryside Council for Wales must be consulted by the planning authority on the preparation of development plans and on the making of arrangements for public access to land for recreation.[16] Certain permitted development rights are withdrawn,[17] and as for National Parks there are special rules on the disposal of certain land by water and sewerage undertakers and housing bodies.[18] The planning authority is also empowered to make byelaws for its own land in an AONB[19] and to appoint wardens,[20] whilst orders can be made by the Minister restricting traffic on roads in the area.[21]

---

[12] CRWA 2000, s.83.

[13] *ibid.*, s.85.

[14] *ibid.*, s.84(1), applying CA ss.6(4)(e), 9, 64(5), 64(5),(5A).

[15] *ibid.*, s.84(4); this provision is not as sweeping as it seems, since it applies only to remove certain statutory limitations on the capacities of authorities, not to confer wholly new powers, and it does not overcome any limitations applying where express powers are given (*ibid.*, s.84(5)–(6)).

[16] *ibid.*, s.84, applying NPACA ss.6(4)(e), 9, 64(5), 65(5),(5A).

[17] Town and Country Planning (General Permitted Development) Order 1995 (S.I. 1995 No. 418), Scheds 1, 2.

[18] See para. 5.11.15, above.

[19] NPACA 1949, s.90.

[20] *ibid.*, s.92.

[21] Road Traffic Regulation Act 1984, s.22.

The details of further impacts depend partly on whether a conserva- **5.12.5**
tion board has been established. The initiative to establish a board
comes from the Minister who must consult the Countryside Agency or
Countryside Council for Wales and all the local authorities for the area
and can proceed only if a majority of the local authorities consent.[22]
The order creating a board is made by means of a statutory instrument
which must be approved in draft by both Houses of Parliament.[23]
Boards are created separately for each AONB and their composition
and powers may vary. At least 40 per cent of the total membership
must be local authority members and the parish members in England
must further comprise at least 20 per cent of the total.[24] The local
authority members come from the authorities in whose areas the AONB
lies, and the appointing local authorities are to have regard to the desirability of appointing members with wards or electoral divisions actually
within the boundaries of the AONB.[25] A parish member must be a
member of a parish council lying within the AONB or the chairman of
a parish meeting in such a parish that does not have a separate parish
council; in the latter case it is the parish meeting that appoints the
member.[26] The Minister's appointees are named after consultation with
the Countryside Agency or the Countryside Council for Wales.

In its activities, the board is bound to have regard to the purposes of **5.12.6**
conserving and enhancing the natural beauty of its area and also of
increasing the public's understanding and enjoyment of the special
qualities of the area, giving priority to the former in the event of any
conflict.[27] Its powers are to do things calculated to facilitate or conducive to the achievement of those purposes, but subject to limits, most
notably the absence of any power to raise money except as specifically
authorised.[28] Specific functions of local authorities can be transferred
to the board, or become exercisable concurrently by the authority and
board. Development control and development planning powers under
the town and country planning legislation must remain wholly with the
local authority, but some minor powers, *e.g.* in relation to tree preservation notices, can be transferred.[29] The board is also required to seek to

---

[22] CRWA 2000, s.86.
[23] *ibid.*, s.88.
[24] *ibid.*, Sched. 13, para. 3.
[25] *ibid.*, Sched. 13, para. 4.
[26] *ibid.*, Sched. 13, para. 5; for both local authority and parish members there are further provisions on the termination of membership if they lose the status that rendered them eligible.
[27] *ibid.*, s.87(1).
[28] *ibid.*, s.87(4)–(6), Sched. 14.
[29] *ibid.*, s.86(3)–(4); the transfer cannot include the local authorities' functions under Parts II (development plans), III (development control), VII (enforcement) and XIII (Crown land) of the TCPA 1990.

foster the economic and social well-being of local communities in the area, but to do so by co-operation with other bodies, not by incurring any significant expenditure.[30] Grants can be made to conservation boards by the Minister.[31]

5.12.7   Whether or not a conservation board has been created, a management plan for the AONB must be prepared, formulating the policy for managing the area and the exercise of powers in relation to it.[32] If there is a board for the area, the plan must be produced by it within two years of its establishment. If there no board, this task is for the local authority, to be accomplished within three years of the designation as an AONB or by May 1, 2004,[33] unless a board is established in the meantime. There are provisions for the adoption of existing plans prepared by local authorities and for the review of plans at least every five years. The Countryside Agency or Countryside Council for Wales must be notified of the proposal to make a plan, as must every local authority affected in the case of those prepared by a conservation board, and their views must be taken into consideration.[34] These plans, however, have no statutory force[35] and there is no obligation on other bodies to pay regard to them, although they will be relevant in the context of the general obligation on all public bodies to have regard to conserving and enhancing the natural beauty of the area.[36]

5.12.8   The effect of the provisions in the Countryside and Rights of Way Act 2000 is to make AONBs much more similar to National Parks. Conservation boards may provide a focus for the management of the area, but the significant powers remain in the hands of the local authorities. Measures to conserve the natural beauty of an area may help to preserve the quality of the general habitat. The designation of an AONB will, however, have no direct effect on many agricultural or forestry developments that may significantly alter the landscape and habitat quality.

National Scenic Areas (Scotland only)

5.12.9   The aim of National Scenic Areas (NSAs) is to strengthen aspects of the town and country planning system in order to preserve areas of high landscape value. NSAs are areas of outstanding scenic value and beauty in a national context where special protection measures are considered appropriate, and which were designated by the Secretary of

---

[30] *ibid.*, s.87(2).
[31] *ibid.*, s.91.
[32] *ibid.*, s.89.
[33] Three years from the relevant provisions coming into force.
[34] CRWA 2000, s.90.
[35] *cf.* National Park Plans in Scotland; para. 5.11.28, above.
[36] CRWA 2000, s.85; see paras 5.12.3, above.

State after consultation with the Countryside Commission for Scotland and other bodies as he thought fit.[37] In practice the areas designated were those proposed in the Commission's report "Scotland's Scenic Heritage" in 1978. No new NSAs can be created, and in theory their place was being taken, in part at least, by Natural Heritage Areas. It seems unlikely that any Natural Heritage Areas will in fact be designated,[38] whilst the framework for National Parks seems disproportionate to the limited task of landscape protection. The future of NSAs is thus uncertain, but there is support for a continuing and indeed expanded role for a designation based on scenic values, operating as an accolade rather than to provide strong regulatory powers.[39] Nevertheless, existing designations continue unless and until cancelled by the same procedure.[40] Planning authorities maintain a list of NSAs in their area.[41]

Once an area has been designated, special attention must be paid to the desirability of preserving or enhancing its character or appearance in the exercise of functions under the Town and Country Planning (Scotland) Act 1997.[42] In order to assist this, permitted development rights have been withdrawn from certain forms of development in NSAs, *e.g.* the construction of vehicle tracks.[43] For planning, SNH must be consulted on certain kinds of application and any decision contrary to its advice must be notified to the Minister.[44] Traffic on roads can be restricted for the sake of the natural beauty of the area or to offer better opportunities for recreation or the study of nature.[45] Within NSAs therefore there is a slight strengthening of planning controls and the beauty of the landscape is to be given special attention, but there is nothing to assist directly the interests of nature conservation.

5.12.10

---

[37] Town and Country Planning (Scotland) Act 1972, s.262C(1) (added by Housing and Planning Act 1986, Sched. 11, para. 38); see note 40, below.

[38] See para. 5.10.5, above.

[39] *National Scenic Areas: Scottish Natural Heritage's Advice to Government* (SNH, 1999).

[40] By virtue of NHSA 1991, s.6(8), (9) and Sched. 11, s.262C of the 1972 Act was partly repealed and the remainder amended so as to apply to Natural Heritage Areas, but its provisions continued to have effect unaltered in so far as they apply to areas which have already been designated as NSAs. When the planning legislation was consolidated, s.262C was in turn replaced by s.264 of TCPSA 1997, which refers exclusively to Natural Heritage Areas, but again the original provisions of s.262C were saved and continue to apply to existing NSAs (Planning (Consequential Provisions) (Scotland) Act 1997, Sched. 3, para. 11).

[41] Town and Country Planning (Scotland) Act 1972, s.262C(3) (as saved for existing NSAs; see above).

[42] *ibid.*, s.262C(4) (as saved for existing NSAs; see above).

[43] Town and Country Planning (Restriction of Permitted Development) (National Scenic Areas) (Scotland) Direction 1987; see SDD circular 9/1987.

[44] Town and Country Planning (Notification of Applications) (National Scenic Areas) (Scotland) Direction 1987; see SDD circular 9/1987.

[45] Road Traffic Regulation Act 1984, s.22.

Conservation Areas

5.12.11 Planning controls and policies are also made more strict in conservation areas.[46] Local planning authorities are under an obligation to designate as conservation areas those parts of their areas which are of special architectural or historic interest, the character or appearance of which it is desirable to preserve or enhance.[47] Once a conservation area has been designated, greater publicity has to be given to certain planning applications,[48] stricter controls on demolition apply,[49] whilst further restrictions can be imposed through directions made by the planning authority.[50] Certain permitted development rights are withdrawn, as is the case for National Parks, Areas of Outstanding Natural Beauty and National Scenic Areas.[51] In all cases, any plan to cut down, lop or prune trees in a conservation area must be notified to the planning authority six weeks in advance, so as to allow time to consider whether a tree preservation order should be made protecting the trees.[52] Generally, the authority should develop proposals to preserve and enhance its conservation areas, acting positively as well as simply preventing degradation.[53] These provisions may serve to protect areas from intensive development and to protect small areas of trees, village greens, ponds, large gardens and other habitats of value.

INTERNATIONAL DESIGNATIONS

5.13.1 In addition to the measures introduced by the European Community to give protection to particular sites,[54] international agreements may also call for the protection of sites of particular importance. Whilst designations under international treaties may have no direct impact on the law within this country, they may be significant in terms of policy-making and the management of particular sites.[55]

5.13.2 In relation to international designations, these generally have no

---

[46] Planning (Listed Buildings and Conservation Areas) Act 1990, Pt II; Planning (Listed Buildings and Conservation Areas) (Scotland) Act 1997, Pt II.

[47] *ibid.*, s.69; *ibid.*, s.61.

[48] *ibid.*, s.73; *ibid.*, s.65.

[49] *ibid.*, s.74; *ibid.*, s.66.

[50] Town and Country Planning (General Permitted Development Order) 1995 (S.I. 1995 No. 418), art. 4; Town and Country Planning (General Permitted Development) (Scotland) Order 1992, (S.I. 1992 No. 223), art. 4.

[51] *ibid.*, Sched. 1; *ibid.* Scheds 1, 2.

[52] TCPA 1990, s.211; TCPSA 1997, s.172; see section 6.5, below.

[53] Planning (Listed Buildings and Conservation Areas) Act 1990, s.71; Planning (Listed Buildings and Conservation Areas) (Scotland) Act 1997, s.63.

[54] See section 5.2, above.

[55] See section 7.5, below.

direct legal consequences within Great Britain, although the international obligations have helped to shape the law here[56] and do influence the selection of sites to benefit from the application of the domestic provisions discussed above. The additional designation emphasises the importance of, and commitment to, nature conservation measures for the sites and can be a major factor in ensuring that the policy affecting the management and protection of a site does in fact give adequate protection to the natural features in question, especially in relation to the exercise of discretionary powers. Even where there is little likelihood of meaningful action at the international level if such sites are damaged, the bad publicity generated by allowing damage to habitats which the government itself has stated to be of international importance can play a real part in securing continued protection. The two most important current designations are discussed here: Ramsar sites and World Heritage sites.

5.13.3   There are also many other designations under a host of international schemes, with varying degrees of official recognition and support but usually lacking any legal significance, *e.g.* Biogenetic Reserves under the Bern Convention.[57] Among these Biosphere Reserves deserve brief mention. These are areas recognised under the UNESCO Man and Biosphere programme established in 1971. During the 1970s 13 Biosphere Reserves were designated in Great Britain, but the programme has developed significantly during the United Kingdom's absence from UNESCO between 1985 and 1997 and work is under way on how the revised programme might be applied here.

Ramsar Sites

5.13.4   The Convention of Wetlands of International Importance, especially as Waterfowl Habitat, known as the Ramsar Convention,[58] makes various provisions for the protection of wetlands, which throughout the world are disappearing as a result of drainage, land reclamation and pollution.[59] Among the measures is the establishment of a List of Wetlands of International Importance, which states undertake to protect.[60] The selection of sites for the List is the responsibility of states themselves, taking account of each site's significance in terms of ecology, botany, zoology, limnology or hydrology. More precise criteria for have been adopted and revised by Conferences of the Parties, suggesting, for example, that sites regularly supporting 20,000 waterbirds or 1 per cent.

---

[56] *e.g.*, WCA 1981; see para. 1.1.15, above.
[57] See paras 7.5.15–7.5.21, below.
[58] After the town in northern Iran where it was signed in 1971.
[59] See paras 7.5.6–7.5.9, below. Further information can be obtained from the official Ramsar web-pages at www.ramsar.org.
[60] Ramsar Convention, art. 2.

of the population of a species should be designated.[61] The List is maintained by the IUCN,[62] which must also be informed of changes to the ecological character of the wetlands as a result of technological developments, pollution or human interference.[63]

5.13.5 Once a wetland has been added to the List, the state is obliged to formulate and implement its planning so as to promote the conservation of the site and the wise use of wetlands,[64] and for all wetlands states must promote the establishment of nature reserves with adequate supervision by wardens.[65] The concept of "wise use" has been the subject of further guidance developed at the Conferences of the Parties.[66] Sites which have been placed on the List can be reduced in size or deleted altogether if this is required by an "urgent national interest," but so far as possible the state concerned should compensate for such loss by the creation of additional nature reserves for birds and the protection, in the same area or elsewhere, of an adequate portion of the same habitat.[67] These obligations are far from precise and leave plenty of room for discretion on the part of each state, to say nothing of the difficulties of enforcing any such obligations in international law.

5.13.6 In Great Britain, the Convention had no recognition in the law until recently, and even now this is very restricted. Legal recognition exists only in England and Wales and is limited to an obligation on the Minister to notify the conservation bodies when a site has been designated for the List and on them in turn to notify the relevant planning authority, owner and occupier, water undertaker and internal drainage board and the Environment Agency.[68] This means that those responsible for the main activities that may affect a site will at least be aware of its significance.

5.13.7 The primary means of implementing the Convention's terms therefore remains the overlap between the sites selected for Ramsar designation and those enjoying protection under domestic provisions, as European Sites, nature reserves or SSSIs. As discussed above, this may not guarantee their protection, or even their protection in all but cases of "urgent national interest," but does provide mechanisms for taking

---

[61] The Criteria are published on the Ramsar web-pages at www.ramsar.org/key–criteria.htm.

[62] International Union for the Conservation of Nature; see P. Birnie and A. Boyle, *International Law and the Environment* (2nd ed.) (2002), pp.67–68.

[63] Ramsar Convention, arts 3, 8.

[64] *ibid.*, art. 3.

[65] *ibid.*, art. 4.1.

[66] Again available at the Ramsar web-pages at www.ramsar.org/key—wiseuse.htm; D. Farrier and L. Tucker, "Wise Use of Wetlands under the Ramsar Convention: A Challenge for Meaningful Implementation of International Law" (2000) 12 J.E.L. 21.

[67] Ramsar Convention, art. 4.2.

[68] WCA 1981, s.37A, inserted by CRWA 2000, s.77.

action to secure their conservation, reinforced now by the fact that in England and Wales the key parties are formally notified of a site's Ramsar status. Planning advice and other guidance has advised on the need to promote the conservation of such sites and avoid as far as possible the loss of wetland resources, and in November 2000 the Ramsar Policy Statement made by the Environment Minister noted the large overlap between Ramsar sites and European Sites, and in essence stated that Ramsar sites should be treated in the same way as those under the Natura 2000 programme.[69]

World Heritage Sites

The Convention Concerning the Protection of the World Cultural and Natural Heritage (World Heritage Convention) was signed in 1972 to provide international recognition and assistance for the protection of monuments, buildings and sites which are the natural and man-made treasures of the world.[70] As far as nature conservation is concerned, a state can nominate any site within its territory for inclusion in the World Heritage List. The basic criterion is that the area be of "outstanding universal value" from a scientific, aesthetic or nature conservation point of view,[71] but before being added to the List each site must be approved by the World Heritage Committee which is responsible for compiling the List.[72] This Committee uses strict operational guidelines in making its decisions. Only sites which are of the utmost value and are adequately protected, both by the scale and integrity of the area and by domestic law will be accepted.[73] **5.13.8**

Each state has a duty to ensure "the protection, conservation, preservation, presentation and transmission to future generations" of the natural heritage in its territory and "to do all it can to this end, to the utmost of its own resources" and where appropriate with international assistance.[74] Effective and active measures are required, including the adoption of relevant policies, the establishment of appropriately staffed and resourced services to protect and conserve the natural heritage, the development and promotion of scientific and technical research and the **5.13.9**

---

[69] Statement by Michael Meacher in relation to England; available at http://www.defra.gov.uk/wildlife-countryside/ewd/ewd10.htm; he notes that only 6 of the 75 Ramsar sites in England do not co-incide with or substantially overlap European Sites.

[70] See paras 7.5.10–7.5.14, below; further information is available from the web-pages at www.unesco.org/whc.

[71] World Heritage Convention, art. 2.

[72] *ibid.*, art. 11.

[73] S. Lyster, *International Wildlife Law* (1985), pp. 212–218.

[74] World Heritage Convention, art. 4; the commitment to international co-operation and the provision of resources for poorer countries is of particular importance for the protection of the natural heritage in many parts of the world.

adoption of the necessary legal, financial and scientific measures.[75] As with most international agreements, these provisions are broadly drafted, but the Australian High Court was prepared to hold that they did impose a duty on the state to act, although recognising that discretion was left as to precisely how this duty would be fulfilled.[76]

5.13.10   Again in Great Britain implementation of the Convention is carried out through the nomination of sites already subject to protective measures in domestic law, *e.g.* St Kilda which is a National Nature Reserve. The nature of sites eligible for inclusion and the more specific criteria for listing combine to mean that only sites enjoying the fullest protection will be accepted, chiefly Nature Reserves. Apart from St. Kilda (and the Giant's Causeway in Northern Ireland), the sites in the United Kingdom have been designated for their archaeological, architectural or historical interest, but in December 2001 parts of the Dorset and East Devon coastline were added to the List on account of their geological value as sources of fossils.[77] Where a site has been accepted for the List, it must be protected and conserved from all threats.

---

[75] *ibid.*, art. 5.

[76] *Commonwealth of Australia v. State of Tasmania* (1983) 46 A.L.R, 625, 68 I.L.R. 266.

[77] Meeting of the World Heritage Committee in Helsinki, December 11–14, 2001.

6. PLANTS

THE GENERAL LAW

The legal position of plants is very different from that of wild animals. **6.1.1**
Every growing plant is the legal property of someone, and thus is subject to the ordinary laws of property, as well as to the special laws
devised to deal with the conservation and regulation of plants. This
might suggest that plants enjoy a greater degree of protection than other
forms of wildlife, but in practice this tends not to be the case as people
do not think of wild plants as being privately owned, and the owners
themselves tend to value only those plants from which they gain some
appreciable benefit, commercial or aesthetic. In considering the law
affecting plants it is necessary to consider how plants are dealt with by
the general law, examining the issues of ownership and the ways in
which plants are treated by the ordinary criminal law, before turning to
the specific legislation which has been enacted to deal directly with
issues arising in relation to plants. The new provisions on hedgerows
are then considered before the fuller provisions affecting trees in relation to forestry and town and country planning.

Ownership

The rule that plants belong to the owner of the soil in which they grow **6.1.2**
is of long standing[1] and is common to both Scots and English law.[2]
Indeed the proposition that plants growing in the soil belong to the
owner of the soil appears to be such a basic idea that it is more or less
taken for granted, and any discussion and dispute has centred on its
application between those holding different interests in the land.

If the rule were strictly applied, problems would arise where interests **6.1.3**
in land are held by different people, *e.g.* in relation to agricultural tenants, as crops which they had planted would not be theirs to harvest
and sell, but would belong to the landlord. In both jurisdictions the
position of tenants was protected by the development of a rule that
annual crops were treated as the tenant's moveable or personal property
as opposed to the landlord's heritable or real property. In Scotland this
exception tends to be discussed as part of the law of property in general,[3] whereas in England and Wales discussion has tended to appear

---

[1] See, for example, in Roman Law D.41.1.7.13, 41.1.9.pr.
[2] See generally D.L. Carey Miller, *Corporeal Moveables in Scots Law* (1991), paras
3.04–3.08; W.M. Gordon, *Scottish Land Law* (2nd ed., 1999), paras 5.38–5.40; W.S.
Holdsworth, *A History of English Law* (2nd ed., 1937), Vol. 7, pp. 485–488.
[3] Stair, II, i, 34; Carey Miller, *op. cit.*; Gordon, *op. cit.*

in the more specialised context of succession and emblements,[4] with many other points affecting the right to take growing plants being dealt with in land law by the rules on waste and *profits à prendre*.[5] In practice such matters are nowadays dealt with by the specific terms of individual leases, etc., or by statutory rules.[6]

6.1.4   The legal consequence of plants being property which is owned by someone is that any unauthorised interference with a plant will amount to a civil wrong at common law. Consequently the owner could sue anyone who damages or takes his plants or obtain an interdict or injunction to prevent any harm which is threatened. Although this is an area lacking in reported authority, any damage to plants being usually only an incidental part of a wider claim,[7] it would appear that any deliberate or negligent harm caused to wild plants certainly could give rise to liability, with the possibility of wider liability if the claim can be framed in trespass, whether to land or (in England) to property. It would follow that anyone picking wild flowers or even causing damage by walking on vegetation could face a civil action at the instance of the owner of the plants affected.

6.1.5   However, although wild plants may be part of their owner's property, they are not generally recognised as having any monetary value, so that the pursuer may be unable to demonstrate that any loss has been suffered by the harm done. This will pose a major practical problem in assessing the value of damage done, and may even lead the courts to say that in fact no actionable wrong has occurred.[8] The aesthetic or spiritual value placed on the wild plants is unlikely to affect this position, although a trust established for the purposes of nature conservation may have a stronger case if the achievement of its aims are being affected by damage to its plants, especially if it is seeking an interdict rather than damages.

---

[4] Modern texts tend not to offer any detailed discussion of these "vegetable chattels", but they are discussed in older books on personal property, *e.g.* J. Williams, T.C. Williams and W.J. Byrne, *Principles of the Law of Personal Property* (18th ed., 1926), pp. 161–162.

[5] R.M. Megarry, H.W.R. Wade and C. Harpum, *The Law of Real Property* (6th ed., 2000), pp.80–86, 1162–1164.

[6] Agricultural Holdings Act 1986; Agricultural Holdings (Scotland) Act 1991.

[7] In the well-known nuisance case of *St. Helens Smelting Co. v. Tipping* (1865) 11 H.L.C. 642 the primary damage alleged related to "hedges, trees, shrubs, fruit and herbage", while an example of a reported action based solely on plants is *Mills v. Brooker* [1919] 1 K.B. 555, where a neighbour was successfully sued in conversion for taking apples from trees overhanging his boundary.

[8] *e.g.* in *Winans v. Macrae* (1885) 12 R. 1051 one of the grounds for refusing interdict to prevent a cottar's pet lamb straying onto a 200,000 acre shooting estate where it might indeed have taken "a blade of grass," was that no appreciable wrong had been suffered so as to justify the court's intervention (Lord Young at pp. 1063–64).

Criminal Law

Since plants are private property, they are protected by the general criminal law. This is very much the case in Scotland, although in England and Wales statutory exceptions have been created to limit considerably the application of the law to wild plants. In Scotland there is nothing to restrict the application to plants growing wild of the ordinary law of theft, malicious mischief, vandalism and fire-raising[9] so that anyone taking or damaging a plant without the permission of the owner or other lawful excuse is guilty of a crime. The few reported cases have dealt with plants that were being to some extent cultivated, *e.g.* in *Rigg v. Trotter*[10] the accused were convicted of malicious mischief after treading down plants in a nursery and destroying turf prepared for and partially laid for a bowling green, while *James Miln*[11] involved the shearing and taking of grass and the pulling up of growing pease, and *John Young*[12] the digging of potatoes. Likewise in *H.M. Advocate v. Alexander Robertson*[13] the plants concerned in a charge of theft were turnips, although here the court reserved its opinion on whether this was an appropriate charge where the alleged theft was achieved by pasturing sheep in a field.

6.1.6

Exactly the same should apply to wild plants, which are as much the landowner's property as the most carefully nurtured crops or garden plants, although in such circumstances it may be more difficult to establish the necessary *mens rea*. In *Ward v. Robertson*[14] the court was not prepared to say that a person was guilty of malicious mischief simply by reason of damage done by walking across a field of cultivated grass where the accused had not deliberately sought to do harm and indeed had thought that no harm was being done. It was suggested, though, that a conviction might have been possible had there been evidence of a deliberate trampling down of grass, or if the field had contained other crops in which case knowledge that harm was being done might have been inferred. In the case of picking wild flowers, it may be obvious that damage is being done, but belief that the owner would not object might again raise difficulties in establishing *mens rea*.

6.1.7

In England and Wales the position is different, as wild plants are expressly excluded from the law of theft and criminal damage. For theft, it is provided that a person who picks flowers, fruit or foliage from a plant growing wild, or who picks any fungus growing wild, does not steal them, unless he does so for reward or for sale or for

6.1.8

---

[9] For muirburn see para. 8.4.13, below.
[10] (1714) Hume, i, 123.
[11] (1758) Hume, i, 79.
[12] (1800) Hume, i, 79.
[13] (1867) 5 Irv. 480.
[14] 1938 J.C. 32.

some other commercial purpose.[15] A theft charge is therefore possible only if there is a commercial motive or if an entire plant is uprooted and taken, as opposed to merely parts of the plant being removed.[16] For criminal damage, no offence is committed if the only property affected is any fungus growing wild or the flowers, fruit or foliage of a plant growing wild. Again, therefore the uprooting of a plant or its total destruction may give rise to prosecution, but lesser damage cannot.[17]

STATUTORY PROVISIONS

6.2.1	Statutory measures relating to wild plants largely mirror those for wild animals, with the establishment of a general level of protection which is enhanced for certain species, while legislation also allows for pest control and measures against the spread of disease. Aside from the enforcement difficulties resulting from the fact that few people can identify the rare species entitled to special protection (especially as there are often similar cultivated or more common species) two particular problems afflict legislation relating to plants.

6.2.2	Firstly, the naming of plants in legislation can be problematic, as common names frequently apply to more than one species, or vary throughout the country, while plant taxonomists are continually reassessing the classification of plants, so that the scientific names,[18] and indeed the recognition of plants as distinct species, may be liable to change. Secondly, plants hybridise much more easily than animals, so that particularly in relation to weed species, one can be faced in the field with hybrids which do not fall exactly within the terms of the legislation but which may be as vigorous as the named species. Both of these issues affect the Japanese knotweed, an invasive alien which it is illegal to spread in the wild.[19] In the legislation it is referred to as *Polygonum cuspidatum*, but it is generally known to botanists today *Fallopia japonica*, whilst previously called other names, including *Reynoutria japonica*.[20] In the wild in Britain, hybrids have been found

---

[15] Theft Act 1968, s.4(3).

[16] Every year or so there are press reports of convictions based on the digging up of large numbers of snowdrop or bluebell bulbs.

[17] Criminal Damage Act 1971, s.10(1).

[18] In any event the legislation rarely gives the full scientific name, almost invariably omitting the reference to the author who described the plant, a reference which forms an integral part of the proper scientific name.

[19] See para. 6.2.11, below; for the history of this plant see J. Bailey and A. Connolly, "Prize-winners to Pariahs—A History of Japanese Knotweed *s.l.* (Polygonaceae) in the British Isles", Watsonia 23: 93 (2000).

[20] Full names, *Polygonum cuspidatum* Siebold and Zucc., *Fallopia japonica* (Houtt.) Ronse Decraene, *Reynoutria japonica* Houtt.; a closely related species is *Fallopia sachalinensis* (F. Schmidt ex Maxim.) Ronse Decraene.

between this plant and *Fallopia sachalinensis*,[21] and these show a wide diversity, calling into question the adequacy of the current taxonomy. The first problem is one of untidiness rather than substance, as the alternative names are well recorded and the relevant plant can be identified, but the second is potentially more serious, since on a strict interpretation (arguably appropriate where criminal liability can be imposed) the legal provisions will apply only to the named, pure-bred, species, not to hybrids.[22]

Protection

Wild plants are given general legal protection under the Wildlife and Countryside Act 1981, with additional protection for some species under both that Act and the Habitats and Species Directive. Under section 13 of the 1981 Act, it is an offence for anyone other than an authorised person[23] intentionally to uproot any wild plant, unless he or she can show that the uprooting was the incidental result of a lawful act and could not reasonably have been avoided. A "wild plant" is one which is growing wild and is of a kind which ordinarily grows in Great Britain in a wild state,[24] a definition which may leave uncertain the status of certain plants which have escaped from gardens and which are not part of the indigenous British flora but are now widespread in a wild state, *e.g.* giant hogweed.[25] Licences may be granted by the appropriate bodies to authorise conduct otherwise unlawful under the provisions discussed here in and in the next paragraphs.[26]

6.2.3

Further protection is offered to the many plants (including mosses and lichens) listed in Schedule 8 to the 1981 Act. It is an offence for anyone (even an authorised person) intentionally to pick, uproot or destroy any wild plant listed in that Schedule,[27] although again there is a defence where the harm is shown to be the incidental result of lawful operations which could not reasonably have been avoided.[28] It is also an offence to sell or offer for sale any live or dead plant listed in Schedule 8 (or any part or derivative of such a plant), or to possess or

6.2.4

---

[21] The hybrids are known as *Fallopia x bohemica*, and the genetic complexity of this species (or cluster of species) is discussed by M. Hollingsworth and J. Bailey, "Hybridisation and clonal diversity in some introduced *Fallopia* species (Polygonaceae)" Watsonia 23: 111 (2000).

[22] *cf.* the Scottish deer legislation where express reference is made to hybrids; Deer (Scotland) Act 1996, s.45(1).

[23] "Authorised persons" include the owner and occupier of the land and those authorised by the local authority (WCA 1981, s.26(1)); see para. 3.2.8, above.

[24] *ibid.*, s.27(1).

[25] See para. 6.2.11, below.

[26] WCA 1981, s.16; CNHR 1994, regs. 44–45; see Appendix C.

[27] WCA 1981, s.13(1)(a); see Appendix A.

[28] *ibid.*, s.13(2).

transport such items for the purpose of sale;[29] for the purpose of this provision any plant is presumed to be wild unless the contrary is shown.[30] An offence is also committed if a person publishes or causes to be published an advertisement indicating that he does or intends to buy or sell such plants or their derivatives.[31]

6.2.5   A small group of the plants included in Schedule 8 are also listed as European protected species[32] and thus fall under the terms of the Habitats and Species Directive as implemented by the Conservation (Natural Habitats, etc.) Regulations 1994. As is the case with animals,[33] the Regulations essentially duplicate the measures contained in the 1981 Act, but with slight changes of wording which might be significant. The main offence is based on "deliberate", as opposed to "intentional" conduct and extends to collecting and cutting the plant as well as picking, uprooting or destroying, and covers all stages of the plant's biological cycle. It is therefore clearer that collecting seed from the listed plants is an offence. Again there a defence for the incidental results of a lawful operation where these could not reasonably be avoided, although this is considerably wider than the scope of derogations permitted under article 16 of the Habitats and Species Directive.[34] The Regulations also repeat offences based on activities relating to the sale or exchange of the plants, and the presumption that plants are wild unless the contrary is shown.[35]

6.2.6   These provisions offer plants some protection from intentional direct harm, but obviously the conservation of plants will rely heavily on the various mechanisms to safeguard habitats as a whole.[36] It is only by ensuring broader protection under such measures that the conditions necessary for plants to survive and propagate can be ensured and that the non-listed plants can be safeguarded against the actions of the owner or occupier of the land. A further practical problem faced by those concerned with botanical conservation (as by those concerned with invertebrates) is that although there is widespread public support for protecting birds and other high-profile animals, the public generally shows little regard for the native flora, apart from, perhaps, a few dramatic orchids.

6.2.7   Very different forms of statutory protection are offered to certain plants through provisions on hedgerows and the system of tree preservation orders, discussed in sections 6.3 and 6.5, below.

---

[29] *ibid.*, s.13(2)(a).
[30] *ibid.*, s.13(4).
[31] *ibid.*, s.13(2)(b).
[32] CNHR 1994, Sched.4; see Annex A.
[33] See para.3.4.5, above.
[34] See paras 7.4.29, 7.4.33–7.4.34, below.
[35] CNHR 1994, reg. 43.
[36] See C. de Klemm, *Wild Plant Conservation and the Law* (1990).

Weeds

In the days before modern herbicides, the control of weeds was a major **6.2.8**
problem for agriculture. Nostalgic appreciation of the beauty of a
wheatfield sprinkled with the bright flowers of poppies and cornflowers
overlooks the fact that to farmers these weeds posed a serious threat to
the yield and value of their crop. The law did not ignore this threat,
and in mediaeval Scotland legislation stated that not only did the tenant
have to cleanse his land of *maneleta,* or guld (the corn marigold), but
he was liable to a fine of one sheep for each plant found.[37]

The current legislation is to be found in the Weeds Act 1959, under **6.2.9**
which the Minister can require the occupier of any land to take such
action as may be necessary to prevent the spread of certain "injurious
weeds."[38] The weeds affected are spear thistle, creeping or field thistle,
curled dock, broad-leaved dock, and ragwort[39]; further weeds can be
added to this list by the Minister. If occupiers unreasonably fail to
comply with a notice requiring them to take action against injurious
weeds, an offence is committed, and a failure to take the required action
within 14 days of conviction is a further offence.[40] If an occupier does
not take the necessary steps, action can be taken by the Minister himself,[41] the costs being recovered from the occupier.[42] The owner of the
land is involved only where the Minister has had to take direct action
and it is not practicable to trace the occupier; in these circumstances
the cost of the intervention can be recovered from the owner, but the
owner has the right to recover from the missing occupier.[43]

More generally, it would appear that as weeds are not being deliber- **6.2.10**
ately cultivated, they fall within the definition of "wild plants" for the
purpose of section 13 of the Wildlife and Countryside Act 1981, and
therefore it is an offence for anyone other than an "authorised person"
intentionally to uproot such a plant.[44] However, it may be expected that
permission from the owner or occupier of the land will readily be given

---

[37] Frag. Coll. 11, 12 (A.P.S. I 750).
[38] Weeds Act 1959, s.1.
[39] *Cirsium vulgare* (Savi) Ten., *Cirsium arvense* L. Scop., *Rumex crispus* L., *Rumex obtusifolius* L., *Senecio jacobaea* L.; for once the statute includes the authors' names, but omits the conventional capital letter for the generic name.
[40] Weeds Act 1959, s.2.
[41] The standard legal phrasing conjures a lovely image of a team of Her Majesty's Minis-ters, in their best pinstripe suits of course, slowly digging weeds out of an unkempt field in some rural wilderness!
[42] Weeds Act 1959, s.3(1).
[43] *ibid.,* s.3(2), (4).
[44] See para. 6.2.3, above.

and may easily be inferred. The question of whether the spread of weeds could constitute an actionable nuisance at common law is discussed later.[45]

Invasive Non-native Species

6.2.11   In order to protect the native flora, and the country in general, from invasive alien species, the law prohibits the release into the wild of a number of plants which aggressively take over any habitat where they become established. It is an offence to plant or otherwise cause to grow[46] in the wild any plant listed in Part II of Schedule 9 to the Wildlife and Countryside Act 1981.[47] The plants listed include giant hogweed, Japanese knotweed and several species of seaweed.[48] It is a defence that the accused took all reasonable steps and exercised all due diligence to avoid committing the offence, but where this defence involves an allegation that another person's act or default was responsible for the commission of the offence, prior notice identifying that person must be given to the prosecutor.[49] Those authorised by the Minister enjoy a power of entry to land (other than a dwelling) to ascertain whether an offence has been committed, and obstruction of such an investigation is an offence.[50]

Plant health

6.2.12   Although designed to control pests and diseases injurious to trees and bushes and to agricultural and horticultural crops,[51] the legislation on plant health is broad enough in its scope to encompass all plants growing wild, necessarily so as wild plants may harbour threats to their cultivated relatives. The Plant Health Act 1967 and the Orders made under it confer on the "competent authorities" wide powers to take action to prevent or control pests, defined as including all forms of harmful insects, bacteria, fungi, plant and animal organisms, and all other agents causative of transmissible disease.[52] The "competent

---

[45] See section 8.8, below.

[46] The precise scope of this phrase remains to be tested, *e.g.* in what circumstances, if any, would failing to prevent the spread of a plant from a garden to the wild be regarded as having "caused it grow" there?

[47] WCA 1981, s.14(2); as usual, licences may be granted to authorise such conduct (*ibid.*, s.16(4); see Appendix C).

[48] See Appendix A.

[49] WCA 1981, s.14(3), (4).

[50] *ibid.*, s.14(5), (6) in Scotland; in England and Wales superseded by the wider enforcement powers of wildlife inspectors (*ibid.*, s.19ZA, added by CRWA 2000, Sched. 12, para. 8).

[51] Plant Health Act 1967, s.1(1).

[52] *ibid.*

authorities" are ministers, and the Forestry Commission for matters relating to forest trees and timber.[53] Orders made under the Act can require local authorities (counties and metropolitan districts in England) to take the necessary steps to carry the measures into effect.[54]

The 1967 Act itself is an enabling provision, allowing for orders to be made to deal with specific problems and to comply with European Community requirements. The powers available include the removal, treatment or destruction of any crops, plant or seed found to be infected, the prohibition of the sale or keeping of any living specimens of a pest, the prohibition of the entry into this country of any pests or infected items, as well as powers of entry and inspection and powers to take direct action in default of compliance with official requirements. The detailed provisions are to be found in the orders made under the 1967 Act, of which the two most general are the much amended Plant Health (Great Britain) Order 1993[55] and Plant Health (Forestry) (Great Britain) Order 1993.[56] These specify a number of pests, and in relation to these impose import restrictions in relation to any plants, soil or other growing medium and machinery which might be infected, prohibit the keeping of living specimens of the pests and establish a regime of phytosanitary certificates to ensure the health of material being imported and exported. Further restrictions are imposed in relation to specific problems such as the Colorado beetle and progressive wilt disease of hops.

6.2.13

Only in a few cases are these provisions likely to have much effect on nature conservation, but the potential is there and has been demonstrated by the provisions made under the 1967 Act in relation to Dutch Elm Disease. In order to prevent the spread of the disease, the Dutch Elm Disease (Local Authorities) Order 1984[57] and its predecessors gave powers to local authorities in the specified areas to serve notices requiring particular elm trees to be cut down, destroyed by fire or subjected to specified treatments. The ravages of the disease itself and of such preventive action during the height of the outbreak around 1980 wrought significant changes to the landscape and local habitats in many of the affected areas. An outbreak of some other pest or disease which affects both cultivated and wild plants could similarly lead to widespread action which could have major consequences for the flora of particular areas, and consequently for the habitat as a whole.

6.2.14

---

[53] *ibid.*, s.1(2).
[54] *ibid.*, s.5 (amended for England and Wales by Local Government Act 1972, Sched. 29, Pt. II, para. 34; for Scotland by Local Government etc. (Scotland) Act 1994, Sched. 13, para. 68; for Wales by Local Government (Wales) Act 1994, Sched. 16, para. 28).
[55] S.I. 1993 No. 1320.
[56] S.I. 1993 No. 1283.
[57] S.I. 1984 No. 687.

HEDGEROWS

6.3.1   The conservation value of hedgerows has long been recognised, both as a habitats in their own right and for their role as "corridors" linking other fragmented habitats.[58] They are also valued for their contribution to the landscape.[59] The loss of hedgerows has long been identified as a significant matter,[60] but a specific legal response was introduced only in 1997. Prior to that, uncertainty over whether the mix of "tree" and "shrub" species in a hedgerow permitted the use of Tree Preservation Orders had constrained the use of that mechanism to provide some legal protection,[61] and the absence of other provisions had stimulated the investigation of innovative legal approaches. Thus in *Seymour and Yorkshire Wildlife Trust v. Flamborough Parish Council*[62] campaigners convinced the county court that an Inclosure Act of 1765 imposed a continuing obligation on the Parish Council to maintain a living hedge at a particular location. Apart from the fact that this success depended on the specific wording of the Act in question, subsequent cases have suggested that difficulties over establishing *locus standi*[63] and the interaction with more modern legislation, such as the planning system,[64] may limit the effectiveness of this approach, although in some cases reliance on Inclosure Acts may still offer a way to protect hedges that fall outwith the new statutory scheme.

6.3.2   Specific statutory protection for hedgerows is provided by the Hedgerows Regulations 1997,[65] but extends to England and Wales only.[66] Protection is provided for "important" hedgerows and much of

---

[58] Hedgerows are a prime example of the features which Member States must endeavour to have managed with a view to their wildlife importance under art.10 of the Habitats and Species Directive: "features ... which by virtue of their linear and continuous structure (such as ... traditional systems for marking field boundaries) are essential for the migration, dispersal and genetic exchange of wild species."; see para. 7.4.27, below.

[59] See generally: House of Commons Environment, Transport and Regional Affairs Committee, *Protection of Field Boundaries*, 13th Report of 1997–98 (1997–98 H.C. 969); J. Holder, "Law and Landscape: the legal construction and protection of hedgerows" (1999) 62 M.L.R. 100; C. Mynors, "Hedgerows: Biodiversity or Rupert Bear" in N. Herbert-Young (ed.), *Law, Policy and Development in the Rural Environment* (1999); J. Holder, "Hedgerows, Laws and Cultural Landscape" in J. Holder and D. McGillivray, *Locality and Identity: Environmental Issues in Law and Society* (1999).

[60] See, *e.g. Biodiversity: the U.K. Action Plan* (Cm.2428, 1994) pp. 94–98.

[61] See para.6.5.6, below.

[62] 1997; unreported but discussed in the Select Committee Report (note 5a, above) at paras 106–119 and Mynors, *op. cit.*, at pp. 153–157.

[63] *Marlton v. Turner* [1998] 3 E.G.L.R. 185.

[64] *R. v. Solihull Borough Council, ex p. Berkswell Parish Council* (1998) 77 P.&C.R. 312.

[65] S.I. 1997 No.1160, made under EA 1995, s.97.

[66] See generally *The Hedgerow Regulations 1997: A Guide to the Law and Good Practice* (DETR / Welsh Office, 1997) which both helps to explain the scheme and provides practical advice.

the Regulations is taken up with attempting to define this concept, although there is no definition of "hedgerow" itself. The Regulations apply only to hedgerows in or adjacent to common land, land used for agriculture, forestry or grazing horses or land designated as a National Nature Reserve or SSSI, and exclude those within the curtilage or marking the boundary of a dwelling-house. The hedgerow must be at least 20 metres long, with additional provisions to deal with gaps in the length and where a shorter stretch meets another hedgerow.

The basic scheme is that for such hedgerows the owners of the land, or utility operators[67] if they are to be responsible for the work, must give the local planning authority notice of their intention to remove or destroy the hedgerow. The authority then has 42 days in which to consult the local parish or community council and decide whether to permit the work to proceed. A hedgerow retention notice preventing the removal can be served only if the hedgerow meets the criteria for being "important", but the authority is under a duty to serve a retention notice for important hedgerows unless satisfied that the circumstances justify their removal, having particular regard to the reasons for removal. There are rights of entry to assist the authority in its function and a right of appeal to the Minister (in practice the Planning Inspectorate) against a hedgerow retention notice.

6.3.3

Where the Regulations apply, it is an offence intentionally or recklessly to remove[68] a hedgerow, or to cause or permit its removal, without giving notice, without acting in accordance with the terms of the notice given or without either having approval from the authority or waiting 42 days from the date of the notice before starting the work. An unchallenged hedgerow removal notice authorises work during the next two years only. Defences apply where the work is authorised by an express grant of planning permission,[69] where the removal is for reasons of national defence or to give access to land in an emergency in circumstances where any other means of access would entail disproportionate cost, where the work is required for flood defence or land drainage, where the removal is to prevent the spread of plant or tree pests, or where the work is undertaken in order to prevent obstruction or danger in relation to electricity lines or as part of the Minister's functions as highway authority. A further defence applies where the removal of the hedgerow is to provide a new access to land in substitu-

6.3.4

---

[67] Essentially electricity, gas, telecommunications, water or sewerage undertakers; Hedgerows Regulations 1997, reg. 2.
[68] "Remove" means to uproot or otherwise destroy (EA 1995, s.97(8)) so that the Regulations do nothing to protect a hedgerow from gradual deterioration (see para. 6.3.6, below); cf. the meaning of "destroy" in relation to tree preservation orders (para. 6.5.12, below).
[69] Works granted permission through the operation of the General Permitted Development Order therefore do not qualify.

6.3.5

tion for an existing one, provided that the old gap is filled within eight months by planting a hedge. Finally, no offence is committed by work which is required for the proper management of the hedgerow.

The definition of important hedgerows is crucial to the Regulations and is provided in great detail. In order to be important, the hedgerow must be at least 30 years old and satisfy at least one of the eight criteria in Schedule 1 to the Regulations. The criteria are divided into two broad groups. The first group relates to archaeology and history, including the fact that the hedgerow marks the historic boundary of a parish or township since before 1850, the boundary of an estate or manor from before 1600, is part of a field system pre-dating the Inclosure Acts or is within a scheduled ancient monument. The second group relates to wildlife and landscape and depends on the presence of rare or specially protected species of birds, plants and animals, or the presence of certain numbers and mixes of species of woody, woodland and other plants, the number and mix varying depending on the setting of the hedgerow and between the north and south of England. Further provisions specify exactly which species qualify (*e.g.* listing the 56 woody species and 57 woodland species to be looked for), how hybrids and multi-stemmed trees are to be counted and the sources and dates to be used in the process. The overall effect is overwhelming.

6.3.6

The Hedgerows Regulations 1997 thus create an astonishingly detailed scheme for protecting some hedgerows in the countryside. The scheme has been criticised for its reliance on a centrally determined and technical definition of importance, its virtual uniformity across the whole of England and Wales, its lack of emphasis on the contribution of hedgerows to landscape, and the rigidity of the permitted sources which prevent new information being taken into account. Further points include the failure to protect hedgerows against gradual deterioration (as a result of which a valuable hedgerow may decline so that it is no longer important) or to protect young or damaged hedgerows which may mature or recover to meet the criteria for importance. There is also the question of whether hedgerows in urban and suburban settings should benefit from similar specific protection, as opposed to relying on the fact that the most likely causes of removal in such settings will lead to some scrutiny as planning permission will be required. The Regulations were introduced in March 1997, and a review was announced in May 1997, before they even took effect. It has seemed likely that the scheme would be amended,[70] but the legislative oppor-

---

[70] *Review of the Hedgerows Regulations 1997* (DETR, 1998). The need for rapid reconsideration was at least partly due to the haste to get some Regulations, albeit far from perfect, in place before the General Election in 1997. See also the Government Response to the House of Commons Environment, Transport and Regional Affairs Committee Report on *The Protection of Field Boundaries* (Cm. 4200, 1999).

tunity presented by the Countryside and Rights of Way Bill was passed over.

The separate issue of high hedges causing disputes between neigh- **6.3.7**
bours has been the subject of consultation papers from the Department of the Environment, Transport and the Regions and the Scottish Execut-ive.[71] Any legislative initiatives on this issue appear likely to be in the form of establishing a complaints system with a mechanism for requir-ing remedial action to be taken, and there is no indication of special attention being paid to nature conservation issues other than as part of a general assessment of all the circumstances of the case.

Trees: Forestry

Trees are the subject of a variety of special legal and administrative **6.4.1**
provisions. Almost all of the woodland in Great Britain has been man-aged or exploited at some time in the past, and even those which do not reveal signs of recent human intervention are referred to as "ancient" or "semi-natural" woodland, rather than as being truly natural, reflecting the likelihood of past human interference. Throughout the centuries trees have been planted to provide shelter, for their wood and other products, and as a decorative feature of the landscape.

The area of woodland in Britain had been constantly reduced for **6.4.2**
centuries as timber was harvested and land was cleared for other pur-poses, but during the twentieth century the conscious policy of reducing the country's dependence on imported timber, initially for strategic but now for commercial reasons, has led to considerable new planting and a significant increase in the area supporting trees.[72] However it is only in the last couple of decades that environmental considerations have been taken into account in the preservation of ancient woodlands and the design of new plantations.

Woodlands of various sorts are important for biodiversity and are **6.4.3**
well represented in the habitats selected for protection under the meas-ures already discussed in Chapter 5, *e.g.* Caledonian forest is a priority habitat type under the Habitats and Species Directive.[73] The hedgerow provisions will also protect some trees, but there are two areas of law which deal directly with trees, and although neither is primarily directed

---

[71] *High Hedges: Possible Solutions* (DETR, 1999); *Consultation Paper on High Hedges, the Extent of Problems and Possible Solutions in Scotland* (Scottish Executive Justice Department, 2000).

[72] From a level of about 5 per cent at the start of the twentieth century, about 10 per cent of the land area of the U.K. is now covered in woodland; in Scotland the figure is 17 per cent, 2 per cent semi-natural woodland and 15 per cent planted (*Forests for Scotland: The Scottish Forestry Strategy*: Scottish Executive, 2000 (SE/2000/199)).

[73] See para. 7.4.20, below.

at nature conservation, the exercise of the relevant powers may lead to considerable benefits or harm to conservation interests. Firstly, there is forestry, where the planting, maintenance and felling of trees are regulated by some direct legal controls, but even more by the effects of the grant schemes operated by the Forestry Commission. Secondly, the town and country planning system makes a number of special provisions, recognising the value of trees to the character and amenity of particular localities.

6.4.4   The regulation of forestry lies primarily in the hand of the Forestry Commission,[74] which has in recent decades shown a much greater awareness of environmental concerns. The imposition in 1985 of a duty on the Commission to seek a balance between timber production and conservation[75] reflected a change of approach which was already becoming evident. The design of plantations nowadays takes account of the interests of landscape and nature conservation, and the grant schemes no longer limit their support to woodland grown exclusively for timber production.[76] The extent to which such policies really effect major changes in British forestry will become apparent in future years as the older plantations are felled and the recent ones grow to maturity.

6.4.5   The regulatory mechanisms have recently been transformed by amended requirements for environmental assessment, which for the first time demand express approval before planting is undertaken in some circumstances.[77] The development of forestry is also shaped by the nature of the grant schemes, which have replaced taxation measures as the main economic instrument influencing forestry in this country. The tax system still contains a number of special provisions for commercial forestry,[78] but they are not so influential as in the past. Prior to 1988, the income tax system allowed a means of gaining considerable tax relief when a taxpayer was involved in the expensive stage of establishing a new plantation, but of escaping tax on the income when the timber came to be harvested. This led to claims that for short-term financial gain large plantations unsuitable and unsympathetic to local conditions were being established, and in the 1988 Budget the tax system was changed. The current position is that commercial forestry falls outwith the income tax system, so that the expenses of establishing a plantation cannot be set off against other income, but there is no tax

---

[74] See paras 2.7.10–2.7.14, above.

[75] Forestry Act 1967, s.1(3A) (added by Wildlife and Countryside (Amendment) Act 1985, s.4); see para. 2.2.8, above.

[76] See para. 6.4.12, below.

[77] See paras 6.4.25–6.4.29, below.

[78] The growing of Christmas trees does not qualify (*Jaggers (trading as Shide Trees) v. Ellis* [1997] STC 1417), whilst growing "short-rotation coppice" (defined as involving perennial tree species harvested above the ground at intervals of less than 10 years) is treated as an agricultural activity for tax purposes (Finance Act 1995, s.154).

to pay on the income when the trees are harvested.[79] For the purposes of capital gains tax, the value of growing timber is not included in any valuations,[80] and for inheritance tax, the payment of tax can be deferred until the woodland is harvested or disposed of, with no further tax due in the event of another death during the intervening period.[81]

Planting

Until 1999, the planting of trees was not subject to any direct legal controls, and today formal approval is required only in the circumstances covered by the environmental assessment regulations discussed below. In other circumstances it remains the case that no form of official permission is required to plant trees, however large an area is affected. Furthermore, it is expressly declared that the afforestation of land is not "development" for the purposes of the town and country planning system,[82] and consequently no permission is required for changing the use of land to forestry, while most forestry operations are likewise exempted from planning control.[83] However, planning authorities are encouraged to prepare indicative forestry strategies as part of the structure plans for their areas. These are intended to indicate the preferred, potential and sensitive areas for forestry, identifying areas where the physical and other conditions are suitable for commercial projects, where the ground is suitable but there are some constraining interests and other areas where there are serious or multiple constraints on forestry development.[84]

6.4.6

In most circumstances, instead of direct legal controls, the regulation of new planting is achieved through the grant schemes operated by the Forestry Commission and discussed below. Small-scale planting and planting purely for amenity may receive financial support from other public bodies, such as the Countryside Agency, Scottish National Heritage and Countryside Council for Wales in their countryside role, and accordingly come under some form of scrutiny. However unless the environmental assessment regulations apply, if no financial support is sought, there is nothing to prevent a landowner planting as much of his land with whatever sort of trees in whatever form he chooses, regardless of environmental and amenity considerations. The replanting of

6.4.7

---

[79] Finance Act 1988, s.65 and Sched. 6.
[80] Taxation of Chargeable Gains Act 1992, s.250.
[81] Inheritance Tax Act (née Capital Transfer Tax Act) 1984, ss.125–130.
[82] TCPSA 1997, s.19(2)(e); TCPA 1990, s.55(2)(e).
[83] Town and Country Planning (General Permitted Development) (Scotland) Order 1992, (S.I. 1992 No. 223), art. 3, Sched. 1, Pt 7 (class 22); Town and Country Planning General Development Order 1995, (S.I. 1995 No. 418), art. 3, Sched. 2, Pt 7.
[84] SODD Circular 9/99, DoE Circular 29/92; for a critical view, see N. Marshall, *Forestry Plan Scan '96: A Review of Indicative Forestry Strategies* (RSPB, 1996).

areas following harvesting will usually be controlled through conditions attached to the felling licence authorising the felling.[85]

6.4.8   Apart from the provision giving basic authority to pay grants,[86] the Forestry Commission's grant schemes and the procedural arrangements for them are not in statutory form, although it has been held that the Commission's decisions may be subject to judicial review.[87] The best sources of information on the schemes are the booklets produced by the Commission itself and the information on its web-pages.[88]

Procedures

6.4.9   Once an application for a grant is made, it is examined first by the Commission to consider whether the proposals are sensible in terms of silviculture, landscaping, nature conservation and other environmental concerns, then consultations will be held with a range of public bodies. The following bodies are involved when any application falls within the scope of the consultation arrangements agreed between them and the Commission:[89] the agriculture departments, local authorities, the statutory conservation bodies, the Countryside Agency, the Deer Commission and the Civil Aviation Authority. Since 1992 the Commission has maintained a public register of grant applications (available now on the internet), allowing the public access to the full applications on request, and inviting comments, as well as recording the outcome of applications.[90]

6.4.10   If there are objections to the proposal, further discussions are held to try to resolve these, the aim being to produce a final proposal acceptable to all those concerned. If no solution is possible, the case may be referred to the relevant Regional Advisory Committee. The composition of these committees is governed partly by convention and partly by statute. The relevant provisions were amended in 1991, increasing the membership from nine to twelve to allow for a greater representation of environmental interests after criticism that there was an inherent bias in favour of forestry developments in the Committees.[91] By law, at least four of the members must be appointed after consultations with organisations representing the interests of owners of woodlands and timber merchants and with organisations concerned with the study and

---

[85] See paras 6.4.17–6.4.24, below.
[86] Forestry Act 1979, s.1.
[87] *Kincardine and Deeside District Council v. Forestry Commissioners*, 1992 S.L.T. 1180.
[88] http://www.forestry.gov.uk.
[89] See the Forestry Commission's *Woodland Grant Scheme Applicant's Pack* (1998); individual bodies are not listed in the 2000 version of the Pack.
[90] Forestry Authority leaflet, *Register of New Planting* (1993).
[91] Forestry Act 1967, s.38 (amended by Forestry Act 1991, s.1).

promotion of forestry.[92] In practice these were joined by an independent chairman and one person representing each of agricultural, planning, trade union and environmental interests. Although there is no legal prescription, the government has undertaken that the three additional members will be chosen to reflect environmental interests, one of them concerned with public access and recreation.[93] There are thus four members with environmental interests to balance the four with forestry ones.

Although the Regional Advisory Committees meet in private, the proposals which are referred to them are advertised in the press and written representations from the public are welcomed; if it is thought that it would be helpful, a person who has submitted observations may be invited to attend a meeting. Again the aim of the proceedings is one of conciliation, to resolve the problem and to find a solution acceptable to all parties. In the event of failure, a report (which is published) is prepared for the Forestry Commission to make the final decision. Although there is no formal appeal, a dissatisfied applicant can make representations to the appropriate Forestry Minister, who may ask the Commission to reconsider its decision. Only a few cases are referred to the Committees,[94] but by the very nature of the procedure, they are the most controversial ones.

6.4.11

Grant schemes

The main grant scheme at present is the Woodland Grant Scheme, introduced in 1990. The purposes of the scheme reflect the Commission's shift of emphasis away from simply maximising timber production to take account of environmental, amenity and other considerations. Whereas earlier schemes stressed that "timber production must be the primary objective,"[95] the present scheme has multiple purposes:

6.4.12

"to encourage people to create new woodlands and forests to

- increase the production of wood,
- improve the landscape,
- provide new habitats for wildlife, and
- offer opportunities for recreation and sport;

---

[92] *ibid.*, s.38(3).

[93] Statements by the Earl of Lindsay during debate in the House of Lords, June 11, 1991 House of Lords Official Report, Vol. 529, cols 1073–1078.

[94] Even at a time when forestry proposals were generating a lot of controversy, between 1984 and 1990 only 113 cases were referred to the Committees from 28,598 grant applications and 11,712 applications for felling licences (*Woodland Grant Scheme Applicant's Pack* (1991), Grants and Procedures, p.12).

[95] Forestry Commission leaflet, *Forestry Grant Scheme* (1987), p.1.

- to encourage good management of forests and wood-lands,including their well timed regeneration, particularly looking after the needs of ancient and semi-natural wood-lands;
- to provide jobs and improve the economy of rural areas and other areas with few other sources of economic activity; and
- to provide a use for land instead of agriculture."[96]

6.4.13 This range of objectives is reflected in the conditions which must be met before an application for a grant is likely to be successful. In contrast to past practice, new proposals will have to include some species diversity and show that due regard is being given to landscape and conservation considerations in the overall design of the planting, the choice of species and the detailed features of the proposal, *e.g.* protecting watercourses and leaving open ground for the benefit of wildlife. Detailed plans of the planting and management plans must be submitted, and the main grants are paid in instalments, or in arrears, to ensure that good practice is maintained.

6.4.14 Under the Woodland Grant Scheme,[97] the main grants are available for the establishment of woodlands, by planting or by promoting natural regeneration. Higher sums are paid for broadleaves than for conifers, reflecting the higher establishment costs, the longer period before any income can be made from the trees, and the greater environmental value of broadleaved woodland in terms of the diversity of other species it supports and of landscape and amenity. The higher grants are also available for establishing native Scots pines north of the Forth-Clyde valley. Supplements are available for woodlands established on better quality agricultural land,[98] and for new community woodlands close to towns and cities where public access will be permitted and where the wood will be of value for informal public recreation.

6.4.15 Management grants are available to assist with the management and improvement of existing woodlands. There are various headings under which such payments can be made, including safeguarding or enhancing the special environmental value of a wood, improving woodlands that are below current environmental standards, improving or maintaining public access and managing woodlands to improve or maintain biodiversity.

6.4.16 An additional scheme, the Farm Woodland Premium Scheme, exists. There has been a change of emphasis in its purposes, from its initial

---

[96] *A Guide to the Woodland Grant Scheme* (2000), p. 3.
[97] The details of the grant schemes are all contained in the Forestry Commission's *Woodland Grant Scheme Applicant's Pack* (2000).
[98] Arable land or improved grassland; this is part of the broader policy of combatting agricultural overproduction by encouraging farmers to turn to other uses for their land.

role in encouraging farmers to take their land out of agricultural production to making a wider contribution to sustainable land use:

> "To enhance the environment through the planting of farm woodlands, in particular to improve the landscape, provide new habitats and increase biodiversity. In doing this, land managers should be encouraged to realise the productive potential of woodland as a sustainable land use."[99]

This scheme allows farmers who are receiving establishment grants under the Woodland Grant Scheme to receive additional annual payments while the trees are growing to the stage when they can produce income, the sums varying according the quality of the land which has been planted and the agricultural classification of the area. The annual payments are available for 10 or 15 years after planting, depending on the species involved, and are to make up for the fact that the farmer who has been operating on the basis of receiving an annual income from all of his land cannot make any return on the land planted with trees until they reach a certain stage of maturity. As with all the forestry schemes, planting for Christmas trees does not qualify as that is a short-term crop.

Felling

Whereas the regulation of afforestation is largely carried out indirectly through the grant schemes, the felling of trees is controlled by a legal licensing regime. Subject to many exceptions, it is a criminal offence to fell any growing trees without first having obtained a licence from the Forestry Commission.[1] The maximum penalty is a fine of level 4 on the standard scale, or twice the value of the trees which were felled, whichever is the higher.[2] In some circumstances an environmental assessment must be carried out, as discussed below.[3] The relationship between felling licences and tree preservation orders is also considered below.[4]

6.4.17

---

[99] Farm Woodland Premium Scheme 1997 (S.I. 1997 No. 829) (made under the Farm Land and Rural Development Act 1988); quotation from p. 4 of the *Farm Woodland Premium Scheme Rules & Procedures* booklet (1998). Set-aside schemes may also offer incentives to convert arable land to forestry, see para. 8.4.11, below and Regulation (E.C.) 2080/92.

[1] Forestry Act 1967, ss.9, 17 (the provisions on tree felling do not apply in Inner London (*ibid.*, s.36)); *Forestry Commission v. Grace* [1992] E.G.L.R. 28.

[2] *ibid.*, s.17 (amended by Criminal Procedure (Scotland) Act 1975, ss.289F, 289G (added by Criminal Justice Act 1982, s.54); Criminal Justice Act 1982, s.46); *Campbell v. Webster*, 1992 S.C.C.R. 167.

[3] See para. 6.4.26, below.

[4] See paras 6.5.20-6.5.23, below.

6.4.18   Topping and lopping of trees fall outwith this provision, as do the trimming and laying of hedges, the felling of trees in a garden, orchard, churchyard or public open space, and the felling of trees no more than 8 centimetres in diameter[5] (or 15 centimetres in the case of underwood or coppice).[6] The occupier of land is allowed to fell up to 5 cubic metres in any calendar quarter without a licence, provided that no more than 2 cubic metres are sold, and to fell trees of no more than 10 centimetres in diameter as thinnings.[7] Also exempt from the licensing requirement is felling in the following circumstances: in order to prevent danger or to prevent or abate a nuisance,[8] in compliance with a statutory obligation,[9] at the request of an electricity operator where the trees are close to electric lines or plant,[10] when immediately required for development authorised under the town and country planning system.[11] Further exemptions apply to felling by statutory undertakers, felling required by water and drainage authorities, the felling of elms badly affected by Dutch Elm disease,[12] and most significantly, felling in accordance with a plan of operations agreed with the Forestry Commission as part of one of its grant or dedication schemes.[13]

6.4.19   It is the landowner, or a tenant who is entitled to fell the trees, who must apply to the Forestry Commission for a licence.[14] The trees will usually be inspected, consultations similar to those for grant applications will be held and the application will appear on the public register. Where it appears to the Commission expedient in the interests of good forestry, agriculture, the amenities of the district or the maintenance of an adequate supply of growing timber, conditions may be imposed on the grant of a licence,[15] requiring that after the felling has taken place the land (or other land agreed by the applicant and the Commission) be

[5] Measured over the bark at 1.3 metres above ground level (Forestry Act 1967, s.9(6)); all of the measurements in these provisions were rendered metric by the Forestry Act 1979, s.2 and Sched. 1.

[6] Forestry Act 1967, s.9(2).

[7] *ibid.*, s.9(3) (amended by the Forestry (Modification of Felling Restrictions) Regulations 1985, (S.I. 1985 No. 1958)).

[8] *ibid.*, s.9(4).

[9] *ibid.*

[10] *ibid.*, (amended by Electricity Act 1989, Sched. 16, para. 13).

[11] *ibid.*, (amended by Planning (Consequential Provisions) (Scotland) Act 1997, Sched. 2, para. 13; Planning (Consequential Provisions) Act 1990, Sched. 2, para. 14).

[12] Forestry (Exceptions from Restriction of Felling) Regulations 1979, S.I. 1979 No. 792, (amended by Forestry (Exceptions from Restriction of Felling) (Amendment) Regulations 1988 and 1998, (S.I.s 1988 No. 970, 1998 No.603)), reg. 4.

[13] *ibid.*

[14] Forestry Act 1967, s.10; the time-limits and other procedural aspects of the licensing scheme and related matters are largely governed by the Forestry (Felling of Trees) Regulations 1979, (S.I. 1979 No. 791) (amended by the Forestry (Felling of Trees) (Amendment) Regulations 1987, (S.I. 1987 No. 632)).

[15] *ibid.*, s.10(2).

restocked with trees.[16] Such restocking conditions are usually imposed.

If a licence is refused, the applicant is entitled to compensation.[17] **6.4.20**
The sum available is the depreciation in the value of the trees which is
attributable to the deterioration in the quality of their timber as a result
of felling being refused. However, as the Commission is unlikely to
refuse permission to fell trees which are so far past their prime that
their value is diminishing, this appears to be a redundant provision in
practice.

An applicant aggrieved by the conditions imposed on a licence may **6.4.21**
request the Minister to refer the case to a special reference committee,
and the Minister must do so unless he considers the grounds for the
request to be frivolous.[18] The reference committee will give the applicant a hearing and consider the matter before reporting to the Minister
who may confirm, overturn or modify the Commission's decision. The
committee is appointed by the Minister and comprises a chairman, and
two members drawn from panels selected after consultations with the
relevant Regional Advisory Committee and organisations representing
the interests of the owners of woodland and timber merchants, and
organisations involved in the study and promotion of forestry.[19] A similar procedure is followed where an applicant is aggrieved by the refusal
of a licence, but only if a licence for the same land has been refused
more than three years previously.[20]

If a restocking condition is not complied with, the owner of the land **6.4.22**
can be served with a notice requiring him to make good the default
within a set time.[21] If the recipient considers that the specified steps
have already been taken or that they are not required in order to fulfil
the condition, he can request the Minister to refer the matter to a special
reference committee as described above, and the notice is suspended
pending its review.[22] In the absence of a reasonable excuse, failure to
carry out the steps required is a criminal offence,[23] and the Forestry
Commission has the power to enter the land and carry out the necessary
work itself,[24] recovering expenses from the landowner.[25]

If a person has been convicted of felling trees without a licence, the **6.4.23**
Commission can serve a notice requiring that the land concerned, or

---

[16] *ibid.*, s.12.
[17] *ibid.*, s.11.
[18] *ibid.*, s.16.
[19] *ibid.*, s.27.
[20] *ibid.*, s.16(4).
[21] *ibid.*, s.24(2).
[22] *ibid.*, s.25.
[23] *ibid.*, s.24(4).
[24] *ibid.*, s.24(3).
[25] *ibid.*, s.26.

other land as agreed, be restocked with trees. Such a notice can be enforced in the same way as a restocking condition in a licence.[26]

6.4.24 The Forestry Commission also has the power to direct the felling of trees in order to prevent the deterioration in the quality of the timber in the trees or to improve the growth of other trees.[27] The recipient of a felling direction can ask for it to be reviewed in the same way as a condition in a felling licence,[28] and can require the Commission to buy the trees for immediate felling or the Minister to acquire his interest in the land where that interest does not entitle the recipient to sell the trees in this way.[29] A felling direction is enforced in the same way as a restocking condition in a licence.[30]

Environmental Impact Assessment

6.4.25 Where there is a requirement for an environmental assessment, very different procedures apply, for both felling and planting, including a requirement for express permission before trees can be planted. Initially the E.C. Directive[31] on environmental assessment was implemented simply by adding the assessment to the consideration of grant applications, but this meant that projects not seeking grant support fell outwith the procedure,[32] and however unlikely this was in practice, such an arrangement was clearly inadequate to ensure that the terms of the Directive were observed. Although the amendments to the Directive led to new Regulations in 1998,[33] these took the same flawed approach.[34] Now, though, Regulations approved in 1999 do impose a clear requirement for express approval before relevant projects can go ahead.

6.4.26 The 1999 Regulations[35] apply to initial afforestation, to deforestation

---

[26] *ibid.*, ss.17A–17C (added by Forestry Act 1986, s.1).

[27] *ibid.*, s.18; this section includes a number of exceptions and factors which must be taken into account before the power is exercised—in practice the power is not used.

[28] *ibid.*, s.20.

[29] *ibid.*, s.21.

[30] *ibid.*, s.24.

[31] See section 8.3, below for a discussion of the Directive and its requirements.

[32] Environmental Assessment (Afforestation) Regulations 1988, (S.I. 1988 No.1207). The fact that even this imperfect implementation was late led to litigation; *Kincardine and Deeside District Council v. Forestry Commissioners*, 1992 S.L.T. 1180.

[33] Environmental Assessment (Forestry) Regulations 1998, (S.I. 1998 No.1713).

[34] The adequacy of the 1988 and 1998 Regulations was challenged in *Swan v. Secretary of State for Scotland*, 1998 S.C. 479, but as the 1999 Regulations were in place before the final resolution of that case, this issue was not considered when the substantive issues were finally dealt with by the court; *Swan v. Secretary of State for Scotland (No.2)* [2000] Env. L.R. 60.

[35] Environmental Impact Assessment (Forestry) (Scotland) Regulations 1999, (S.S.I. 1999 No.43); Environmental Impact Assessment (Forestry) (England and Wales) Regulations 1999, (S.I. 1999 No.2228). The two sets of Regulations are almost identical and the following regulation numbers apply to both.

for the purpose of converting the land to another use and to forest road and quarry works, where the project is likely to have significant effects of the environment, but not where the work is already covered by the need for express planning permission or the more general environmental impact assessment provisions.[36] A project is to be taken as not likely to have such effects if its area falls below certain specified thresholds, ranging from five hectares for planting (one hectare for deforestation) in land free from environmental designations, through two hectares (half a hectare) in a National Scenic Area or Area of Outstanding Natural Beauty, to zero where an SSSI or European Site is concerned.[37] A formal opinion on the need for an assessment can be requested from the Forestry Commission, with further reference to the Minister.[38]

Where the Regulations apply, consent from the Commission must be **6.4.27** sought before any work begins, and the work must be carried out in compliance with any conditions imposed on the consent.[39] The application must be presented with an environmental statement and the standard requirements for consultation, publicity and co-operation from other bodies apply, and the Commission is specifically directed to consider the environmental factors listed in Schedule 4 to the Regulations.[40] All consents are subject to a condition that the work must be begun and completed within the periods specified by the Commission (not more than five and ten years, respectively), but the Commission is free to add further conditions.[41] There is a right of appeal to the Minister against a refusal of consent or the imposition of conditions (other than specifying the maximum periods just noted), and any person aggrieved has the right to apply to the courts on the grounds that he or she has been substantially prejudiced by a failure to take account of representations or other material considerations.[42] A public register is maintained of all applications, environmental statements and decisions.[43]

The Forestry Commission has the power to serve an enforcement **6.4.28** notice in the event of work proceeding other than in full accordance with a consent. Again there is a right of appeal to the Minister, which has the effect of suspending the notice. Failure to comply with an enforcement notice is a criminal offence, punishable with a fine of up to level 5 on the standard scale, and if any remedial work specified in the notice is not carried out, the Commission enjoys a power to enter

---

[36] *ibid.*, reg. 3.
[37] *ibid.*, reg. 3 and Sched. 2.
[38] *ibid.*, regs 5–8.
[39] *ibid.*, reg. 4.
[40] *ibid.*, regs 9–16; see section 8.3, below.
[41] *ibid.*, regs 15, 18.
[42] *ibid.*, regs 17, 19.
[43] *ibid.*, reg. 24.

the land and carry out the work itself, recovering the costs from the defaulter. There are also powers of entry to land where it is reasonably suspected that unauthorised work is being carried out.[44]

6.4.29 These provisions may seem unremarkable when compared with the town and country planning system, and indeed aspects of the system of felling licences, but they do represent a major change in the regulation of countryside activities. Agriculture and forestry have in the past operated essentially outwith the planning and many other formal regulatory systems, and changes in rural land use have generally not been subject to any such direct control. For many projects it will still be the indirect control exercised through grant schemes that matters, but the imposition of such a formal consent procedure is a significant departure from the reliance on the voluntary principle which has been so dominant in the regulation of the countryside.

TREES: PLANNING

6.5.1 The importance of trees for the appearance and amenity of an area is recognised by the town and country planning system in several ways. Most important is the scheme for tree preservation orders (TPOs), but other provisions are also worthy of note. The most general is the requirement that planning authorities ensure where appropriate that conditions in a grant of planning permission should be used to ensure the preservation or planting of trees.[45] There is also in England and Wales a general power for local authorities to plant trees on land in their area for the purposes of preserving or enhancing natural beauty.[46]

6.5.2 Special rules exist for trees within conservation areas. Although the aim of such areas is to protect and enhance areas of special architectural and historical interest,[47] natural features will often play a major part in the overall appearance of the area. It is an offence in most circumstances to cut down, top, lop, uproot, or wilfully damage or destroy a tree in a conservation area unless notice has been given in advance to the planning authority, and either the authority has given its consent or six weeks have elapsed.[48] The aim of this provision is to allow time for the authority to decide whether a TPO should be made to protect the trees in question, and for this reason the provision does not apply to

---

[44] *ibid.*, regs 20–23.
[45] TCPSA 1997, s.159; TCPA 1990, s.197.
[46] NPACA 1949, s.89(1).
[47] Planning (Listed Buildings and Conservation Areas) (Scotland) Act 1997, s.61; Planning (Listed Buildings and Conservation Areas) Act 1990, s.69; see para. 5.12.11, above.
[48] *ibid.*, s.172; TCPA 1990, s.211.

trees which are already subject to such an order.[49] The planning authority is not, however, prevented from making an order after the six weeks have elapsed.[50] If the operations have not been carried out within two years of the notice, a new notice must be served before the operations are lawful.[51] The planning authority must keep a register of the notices which it receives under these provisions.[52]

The criminal offence, which is subject to the same penalties as a **6.5.3** breach of a TPO,[53] is committed by the person who carries out the unlawful felling, etc., but the owner of the land also becomes liable to plant another tree of appropriate size and species at the same place as the one unlawfully felled, uprooted or destroyed.[54] Replanting may also be required where the removal of the tree was not unlawful, but only because it fell within certain of the exceptions discussed below. It is made clear that this obligation is owed by the owner of the land from time to time, regardless of his involvement in the offence, although the owner can apply to the planning authority to dispense with this requirement. The obligation can be enforced in the same way as the replacement provisions relating to TPOs.[55]

Where a tree is already covered by a TPO, this more general offence **6.5.4** does not apply, and several further categories of trees and operations are excluded from the provisions, in line with the exceptions which apply in relation to TPOs themselves.[56] Trees which are no bigger than 75 millimetres in diameter are exempt (100 mm. if the tree is in woodland and is uprooted or felled to improve the growth of others).[57] Felling in accordance with a plan of operations agreed with or a felling licence granted by the Forestry Commission is exempt, as are actions by a planning authority and by a range of statutory undertakers on land which they occupy. More generally no offence is committed if the uprooting, felling or lopping is in the interests of safety, or necessary for the prevention or abatement of nuisance.[58] Steps taken in compli-

---

[49] *ibid.*, s.172 (2); *ibid.*, s.211(2).
[50] *R. v. North Hertfordshire District Council, ex parte Hyde* (1990) 88 L.G.R. 426.
[51] TCPSA 1997, s.172 (3); TCPA 1990, s.211(3).
[52] *ibid.*, s.175; *ibid.*, s.214.
[53] *ibid.*, s.172(4); *ibid.*, s.211(4); see para. 6.5.13, below.
[54] *ibid.*, s.174; *ibid.*, s.213.
[55] See para. 6.5.18, below.
[56] Town and Country Planning (Tree Preservation Order and Trees in Conservation Areas) (Scotland) Regulations 1975, (S.I. 1975 No. 1204), reg. 11; Town and Country Planning (Trees) Regulations 1999, (S.I. 1999 No. 1892), reg. 10. The wording of the English legislation differs slightly from the Scottish, and the differences may be significant in some cases; this is discussed more fully at paras 6.5.14–6.5.16, below.
[57] The measurement is to be taken 1.5m above the ground as opposed to at 1.3m for felling licences; does this mean that planning officers are taller than foresters?
[58] The precise exceptions here are the same as relate to TPOs; see paras 6.5.14–6.5.16, below.

ance with an obligation imposed by an Act of Parliament are exempt, together with ministerially approved action taken to avoid danger or hindrance to air navigation.

6.5.5 Tree Preservation Orders offer the strongest protection to trees under the planning legislation, but also the most complex.[59] The issue is often a controversial one, not only because mature trees are a very conspicuous feature of the landscape, but also because the protection of even a single tree may thwart any plans for developing a particular site. In any event, the whole idea of tree "preservation" is somewhat odd, as trees are living organisms which grow old and die, and perhaps only fossilisation can truly "preserve" a tree effectively. Many of the most striking trees in the landscape are already mature, if not past their prime, and rather than trying to protect a tree in its declining years it may often be better in the long-term for efforts to be made to secure the planting and tending of young trees to ensure the regeneration and sustainability of attractive features. This is particularly the case in parks and avenues where all the trees may well have been planted together at the same time; unless thought is given to their replacement decades before the trees reach the end of their natural life, the result will be many years of barren landscape as the trees die and young replacements grow slowly.

6.5.6 The legislation offers no definition of "tree," and this basic issue can cause difficulties, particularly in relation to hedgerows, where there may well be plants of differing sizes and species, some normally viewed as trees, others as shrubs. In one case Lord Denning expressed the view that, in woodland at least, only something over seven or eight inches in diameter should count as a tree,[60] but there seems to be no basis for such a requirement[61] and his view has been rejected by later courts.[62] The test appears to be left to common sense, and in *Bullock v. Secretary of State for the Environment*[63] Phillips J. said that an order could refer to anything which one would ordinarily call a tree, as

---

[59] The legislation in Scotland is TCPSA 1997, ss.160–171, and the Town and Country Planning (Tree Preservation Order and Trees in Conservation Areas) (Scotland) Regulations 1975, (S.I. 1975 No. 1204) (significantly amended by the Town and Country Planning (Tree Preservation Order and Trees in Conservation Areas) (Scotland) Amendment Regulations 1981 and 1984, (S.I.s 1981 No. 1385, 1984 No. 329))—hereafter the 1975 Regulations; in England and Wales, TCPA 1990, ss.198–214D (significantly amended by the Planning and Compensation Act 1991 s.23) and the Town and Country Planning (Trees) Regulations 1999, (S.I. 1999 No. 1892)—hereafter the 1999 Regulations.

[60] *Kent County Council v. Batchelor* (1976) 33 P. & C.R. 185 at p. 189.

[61] *e.g.*, the express exemption for trees below certain sizes in conservation areas clearly suggests that the legislation contemplates smaller plants counting as trees.

[62] *Bullock v. Secretary of State for the Environment* (1980) 40 P. & C.R. 246 at p. 251; see also *Brown v. Michael B. Cooper Ltd*, 1990 S.C.C.R. 675 at p. 678. For a somewhat whimsical discussion of the issue see [1977] J.P.L. 5.

[63] (1980) 40 P. & C.R. 246.

opposed to bushes, shrubs and scrub; accordingly coppice fell within the meaning of "trees" and could be made the subject of a TPO. Hedgerows in England and Wales are now subject to the protective measures described above.[64]

Subject to the default powers of the Minister,[65] it is the planning authority which has the power to make a TPO, the test being that it is "expedient in the interest of amenity" to make provision for the preservation of trees or woodland.[66] The trees may be specified individually, as trees in a specified area, or as a woodland.[67] The way in which the trees are described may be significant, as there are minor differences in the legislation for each form of order. The description may also affect the extent to which the order applies to trees established on the site after the order has been made. In *Brown v. Michael B. Cooper Ltd*[68] it was held that an order referring to trees in a specified area applied only to trees in existence at the time when the order was made, so that young trees in the area, which could not be proven to have been in existence at that date, were not protected. Had the order referred to an area of woodland, it is likely that no such qualification would have applied.[69]

6.5.7

Before an order can come into effect it must be advertised, notified to those with an interest in the land, made available for inspection and in Scotland notified to the Forestry Commission[70] and to the Keeper of the Registers of Scotland.[71] Objections and representations may be made within 28 days and a local inquiry may be held. The planning authority must then decide whether or not to confirm the order (with or without modifications)[72], and if confirmed, the same parties must be notified, and the confirmed order advertised and deposited for public inspection.[73] In Scotland the order must be recorded in the Register of Sasines (or Land Register of Scotland;)[74] in England and Wales the

6.5.8

---

[64] See section 6.3, above.

[65] TCPSA 1997, s.164; TCPA 1990, s.202.

[66] *ibid.*, s.160(1); *ibid.*, s. 198(1).

[67] 1975 Regulations, First Schedule to Model Order; 1999 Regulations, Schedule 1 to Model Order.

[68] 1990 S.C.C.R. 675.

[69] It should be remembered that in any case a TPO will only protect trees, not any of the other vegetation which is vital to the ecological and amenity value of woodland.

[70] This requirement can be waived.

[71] 1975 Regulations, regs 5–10; 1999 Regulations, reg. 3.

[72] The modifications cannot change the area specified so as to include additional woodland beyond the boundaries of the original order; *Evans v. Waverley Borough Council*, [1995] 3 P.L.R. 80.

[73] If no copy is available for inspection the order is invalid; *Vale of Glamorgan Borough Council v. Palmer and Bowles* (1983) 81 L.G.R. 678.

[74] 1975 Regulations, reg. 10 (read in the light of the Land Registration (Scotland) Act 1979, s.29(2)).

order is registrable as a local land charge.[75] It is only when an order has been confirmed that it takes effect, unless the authority directs that it should take effect immediately without confirmation.[76] Such provisional orders lapse after the passage of six months unless they are confirmed. All orders may subsequently be revoked or modified.

6.5.9   The precise extent and effect of the order will depend on its terms, but essentially a TPO renders it a criminal offence for any person to cut down, uproot, fell, lop, or wilfully damage or destroy the protected trees without the consent of the planning authority. Such consent is applied for in the same way as an application for planning permission, and consent may be given subject to conditions.[77] If the applicant is aggrieved by a refusal of consent or the conditions imposed, there is a right of appeal to the Minister.[78] There is, however, no right of appeal against the making of the order itself. In relation to woodland, it is stated that consent shall be given so far as it accords with the principles of good forestry, except where in the planning authority's opinion refusal is necessary in the interest of amenity in order to maintain the special character of the woodland or the woodland character of the area.[79]

6.5.10   If consent is refused, or granted subject to conditions, there is generally a right to compensation for any loss or damage suffered in consequence of such refusal, an issue where the 1999 Regulations have significantly changed the law in England and Wales. Under the old law, and still the case in Scotland,[80] the most significant form of loss may be a diminution in the value of the land since its potential uses are restricted, as in *Bell v. Canterbury City Council*,[81] where the refusal of consent to fell trees meant that the landowner was not able to convert his land from woodland to agricultural use. The court there held that this was a form of loss for which compensation was due, and that it was properly attributable to the refusal of consent, not to the initial making of the order as the council had argued. Other forms of loss may include the unrealisable timber value of the trees, the cost of an expert's report on the possible threat being caused to nearby buildings[82] and the

---

[75] Local Land Charges Act 1975, s.1.

[76] TCPSA 1997, s.163; TCPA 1990, s.201; such directions are usual in order to avoid the trees being removed or damaged during the interval between notification and confirmation.

[77] TCPSA 1997, s.160(3) and 1975 Regulations, Model Order paras 3–7; TCPA 1990, s.198(1) and 1999 Regulations, Model Order, arts 6–7.

[78] 1975 Regulations, Third Schedule to Model Order paras 33–34; 1999 Regulations, Model Order, art. 7.

[79] 1975 Regulations, Model Order para. 5; 1999 Regulations, Sched. 2 to Model Order, adapting TCPA 1990, s.70.

[80] TCPSA 1997, ss.165–166 and 1975 Regulations, Model Order, paras 9–12.

[81] (1988) 56 P. & C.R. 211.

[82] *Fletcher v. Chelmsford Borough Council* [1992] J.P.L. 279.

additional costs of felling a tree in accordance with conditions attached to a consent.[83] However, no compensation will be paid if the planning authority has certified that the refusal of consent or a condition attached to it is in the interests of good forestry, or, in the case of trees other than those in woodlands, that the trees have an outstanding or special amenity value.[84] There is a right of appeal to the Minister against the making of such a certificate.

Under the new rules in England, the right to compensation is more limited.[85] There is no right to compensation for loss of development value or any other diminution in the value of the land, for any loss not reasonably foreseeable when consent was refused or granted subject to conditions, or for any loss that was reasonably foreseeable and can be attributed to the claimant's failure to take reasonable steps to mitigate or avert the loss. The costs of an appeal against the decision on consent are no longer recoverable,[86] nor is compensation for any loss under £500. The only time when losses under £500 can be recovered is where consent is refused for felling in the course of forestry operations in a woodland area, and in these circumstances recovery is limited to the amount by which the timber has depreciated in value as a result of the refusal. **6.5.11**

It is a criminal offence for any person in contravention of a TPO to cut down, top, lop, uproot, wilfully damage or wilfully destroy[87] a tree, or to cause or permit such action.[88] The offence is committed by the person who actually carries out the act, and is an offence of strict liability, committed regardless of whether the offender knows of the order and its terms.[89] Employers may be vicariously liable for the acts of **6.5.12**

---

[83] *Deane v. Bromley Borough Council* [1992] J.P.L. 279.

[84] 1975 Regulations, Model Order, paras 6, 9; the certificate must be issued at the time that the decision is taken on the application for permission to fell the trees; *Beyers v. Secretary of State for the Environment, Transport and the Regions* (2001) 82 P. & C.R. 5.

[85] 1999 Regulations, Model Order art. 9.

[86] Under the old rules (and presumably those that still apply in Scotland), appeal costs were recoverable; *Buckle v. Holderness Borough Council* (1996) 71 P. & C.R. 428.

[87] For a tree to be "destroyed" it is sufficient that so radical an injury is inflicted on it that any reasonably competent forester would decide that it ought to be felled, taking into account all the circumstances, *e.g.* a tree by a highway requires greater vigour and stability than one in a field; *Barnet London Borough Council v. Eastern Electricity Board* [1973] 1 W.L.R. 430 (where the severing of between a half and one third of the root systems of trees was held to have destroyed them, even though the trees might have survived for some years).

[88] TCPSA 1997, s.171 and 1975 Regulations, Model Order, para. 2; TCPA 1990, s.210, and 1999 Regulations, Model Order, art. 4.

[89] *Maidstone Borough Council v. Mortimer* [1980] 3 All E.R. 552, where it was said that the preservation of trees was "of the utmost importance" (Park J. at p. 554).

their employees,[90] but the occupier will not be liable if a contractor acts
in defiance of instructions not to damage a tree.[91] A contractor hired to
cut down trees should always check the legal position first as he will
still be liable for breaching the TPO even though he has been assured
by the occupier that the felling is lawful, although the penalty imposed
in such circumstances should reflect the lack of culpability.[92] It has
been suggested that there may be problems in ensuring that the person
truly at fault in such circumstances can be prosecuted,[93] although there
seems to be no reason why recourse should not be had to the general
rules of art and part guilt and of incitement, aiding and abetting.

6.5.13   The penalties for breaching a TPO can be substantial, with no limit
to the fines following conviction on indictment and in summary proceedings fines of up to £20,000 or twice the value of the trees.[94] In
assessing the fine the courts are expressly instructed to take into account
any financial benefit which appears likely to accrue to the offender as
a result of the offence.[95] Deliberate flouting of a TPO is likely to incur
a fairly large penalty,[96] and in *R. v. Razzell*[97] a developer who stood to
gain £50,000 if he had been able to develop land free of trees was fined
£10,000 on each of two charges of breaching a TPO, together with
£12,000 costs. The planning authority can seek to support a TPO with
an interdict or injunction,[98] although this is likely to be apt only where
there is some aggravating feature such as a deliberate and flagrant
flouting of the law.[99]

6.5.14   A number of exceptions are provided where the felling, etc., of a
tree will not be unlawful, despite the existence of a TPO. The wording
of some of the main exceptions differs in the two sets of legislation. In
Scotland an order cannot prohibit the uprooting, felling or lopping of
any tree if such action is urgently necessary in the interests of safety,
or is necessary for the prevention or abatement of a nuisance, provided

---

[90] *Bath City Council v. Pratt (t/a Crescent Investments)* (unreported, see [1988] C.L.Y.
  3422).
[91] *Groveside Homes Ltd v. Elmbridge Borough Council* (1987) 55 P. & C.R 214.
[92] *Maidstone Borough Council v. Mortimer*, above.
[93] C. Crawford and P. Schofield, "A Weak Branch in the Law of Trees?" [1981] J.P.L.
  316.
[94] TCPSA 1997, s.171(1); TCPA 1990, s.210(2) (amended by Planning and Compensation Act 1991, s.23). A lesser penalty is set for topping and lopping which is not likely
  to destroy the tree; TCPSA 1997, s.171(4), TCPA 1990, s.210(3).
[95] *ibid.*, s.171(3); *ibid.*, s.210(4).
[96] *e.g.* a £1,000 fine in *White v. Hamilton*, 1987 S.C.C.R. 12.
[97] (1990) 12 Cr. App. R. (S) 142.
[98] TCPSA 1997, s.146; TCPA 1990, s.214A (added by Planning and Compensation Act
  1991, s.23).
[99] *Newport Borough Council v. Khan (Sabz Ali)* [1990] 1 W.L.R. 1185 (although this
  was decided before express provision for the use of injunctions was made in the Planning and Compensation Act 1991).

that notice is given to the planning authority as soon as may be after the necessity has arisen.[1]

In England and Wales the equivalent provision exempts actions **6.5.15** affecting trees which are dying, dead or have become dangerous, or so far as may be necessary for the prevention or abatement of nuisance.[2] It has been held that the wording used means that once a tree has "become dangerous," any felling or lopping is exempt, even though it does nothing to remove or reduce the danger.[3] Whether a tree is dangerous is a matter of fact, the onus of proving which lies on the person claiming the exception,[4] and a tree may be dangerous as a result of its size and location (*e.g.* by damaging a building's foundations) even though it is perfectly healthy and safe in itself.[5] In one case it has been said that a developer cannot argue that a tree is a nuisance when he owns and occupies the land on which the nuisance is said to occur, nor that he can lawfully fell the tree as one which has become dangerous when it was his own actions as part of the continuing development which made it dangerous.[6]

Other exceptions apply in both jurisdictions. Felling required by any **6.5.16** Act of Parliament is exempt,[7] as is felling in accordance with a plan of operations approved by the Forestry Commission, and felling immediately required for a development which has been authorised by a grant of planning permission. Also exempt is felling which is necessary in order to carry out works on or for the safety of operational land held by a range of statutory undertakers and equivalents, or necessary for the safety of air navigation.[8] In England and Wales, further exceptions apply to fruit trees cultivated for fruit production or in an orchard or garden and in some circumstances where the trees are interfering with the functions of water and drainage authorities in relation to the maintenance, improvement or construction of water courses or drainage works. Express consent under the TPO may not be required for felling authorised by a felling licence from the Forestry Commission[9] or authorised for opencast coal works.[10]

---

[1] TCPSA 1997, s.160(6).
[2] TCPA 1990, s.198(6).
[3] *Smith v. Oliver* [1989] 2 P.L.R. 1.
[4] *R. v. Alath Construction Ltd* [1990] 1 W.L.R. 1255.
[5] *Smith v. Oliver*, above.
[6] *Bath City Council v. Pratt (t/a Crescent Investments)* (unreported, see [1988] C.L.Y. 3422).
[7] TCPSA 1997, s.160(6); TCPA 1990, s.198(6).
[8] 1975 Regulations, Second Schedule to Model Order (as amended by the Electricity Act 1989 (Consequential Modifications of Subordinate Legislation) Order 1990, (S.I. 1990 No. 526)); 1999 Regulations, Model Order art. 5.
[9] See paras 6.5.20–6.5.23, below.
[10] TCPSA 1997, s.160(7); TCPA 1990, s.198(7).

6.5.17 In addition to the penalty, steps can be taken to ensure the replacement of the trees. The replacement provisions apply if a tree is unlawfully removed, uprooted or destroyed in contravention of a TPO, or (except in relation to woodland) is removed, uprooted or destroyed or dies at a time when its removal, etc., is lawful only in the interest of safety. In such circumstances there is a duty on the owner of the land to plant another tree of appropriate size and species at the same place as soon as he reasonably can, or in the case of trees in woodland, to replace the trees by planting the same number of trees on or near the affected land, or on other land as agreed with the planning authority.[11] It is made clear that this obligation rests with the owner of the land for the time being, but the planning authority can waive the replanting requirement. The relevant TPO applies to any replacement trees as it applied to the original ones. In Scotland, a replanting or replacement condition can also be imposed when the authority gives consent for trees to be felled, and must be imposed in relation to any felling of woodland (other than silvicultural thinning) unless the consent was for development which has been granted planning permission or the Minister approves the planning authority's waiver of this requirement.[12] In England and Wales replanting directions can be made following consent for felling in woodland areas in the course of forestry operations.[13]

6.5.18 A replanting requirement (whether following a breach of an order or imposed as a condition to felling consent) can be enforced by the planning authority, in Scotland within two years of becoming aware of the failure to comply,[14] in England and Wales within four years of the date of the alleged failure.[15] A notice requiring compliance and specifying the necessary steps is served on the landowner, who has a right of appeal to the Minister on the grounds that he has complied with the requirement, that the requirement is not applicable or should be dispensed with, that the specified timescale or species for the replacement are unreasonable, that the planting is not required in the interest of amenity or would be contrary to good forestry practice, or that the place specified is unsuitable for the purpose.[16] If the notice is not complied with, the authority has the power to enter the land and carry out the required steps itself, the costs being recoverable from the landowner

---

[11] TCPSA 1997, s.167; TCPA 1990, s.206.
[12] 1975 Regulations, Model Order, paras 5, 7.
[13] 1999 Regulations, Model Order, art. 8.
[14] TCPSA 1997, s.168.
[15] TCPA 1990, s.207 (amended by Planning and Compensation Act 1991, s.23).
[16] TCPSA 1997, s.169; TCPA 1990, s.208 (amended by Planning and Compensation Act 1991, s.23).

who has in turn a right to recover from the person responsible for the removal of the original trees.[17]

In order to assist in the operation of all of the provisions relating to **6.5.19** TPOs, the planning authority enjoys a power of entry to land in order to ascertain whether its powers should be exercised, whether any order is being complied with and in order to take any necessary enforcement action. In the absence of co-operation, warrants can be obtained to ensure that the powers can be exercised, and wilful obstruction of anyone exercising the powers is a criminal offence.[18]

There is obviously an overlap between the provisions in the planning **6.5.20** and in the forestry legislation relating to the felling of trees. This point is dealt with in the legislation, but the two schemes are so different in their aims and procedures, that the outcome is not wholly satisfactory. On land where the Forestry Commission has given a grant for forestry or which is covered by a forestry dedication agreement,[19] a TPO can be made only if there is no agreed plan of operations for the land and the Forestry Commission agrees to the making of the order,[20] and the order cannot affect felling in accordance with any plan of operations approved by the Commission.[21]

Where both a felling licence[22] and consent under a TPO are necessary **6.5.21** for the felling of trees, the starting point is that the matter should be dealt with under the forestry legislation and no application for consent from the planning authority should be made.[23] If the Forestry Commission refuses a licence, that is the end of the matter. However, the Commission may decide to refer the matter to the planning authority for decision under the Planning Acts, and in any event, if it proposes to grant a licence, then the planning authority must be notified.[24] If the authority objects to the proposed grant of a felling licence and the objections cannot be resolved, the Commission must refer the case to the Minister for final determination and the matter is dealt with under the planning legislation.[25] Only if the matter has been referred in either of these ways will it be determined under the planning legislation; in

---

[17] *ibid.*, s.170; *ibid.*, s.209 (as amended by Planning and Compensation Act 1991, s.23).
[18] *ibid.*, ss.176–178; *ibid.*, ss.214B–214D (added by Planning and Compensation Act 1991, s.23).
[19] Under s.5 of the Forestry Act 1967; as far as new planting is concerned, the revised grant schemes have now in practice replaced this method of securing the long-term use of land for forestry.
[20] TCPSA 1997, s.162; TCPA 1990, s.200.
[21] *ibid.*, s.58(8); *ibid.*, s.200(3).
[22] See paras 6.4.17–6.4.24, above.
[23] Forestry Act 1967, s.15(5).
[24] *ibid.*, s.15(1).
[25] *ibid.*, s.15(2).

all other cases the grant or refusal of the felling licence decides the issue.

6.5.22 The legal basis on which permission to fell is refused may have a major practical significance in Scotland because of the differing schemes for compensation as a result of refusal. If the case is dealt with under the forestry legislation, the obligation to pay compensation rests with the Forestry Commission, but the sum is limited to the loss (if any) in the value of the trees as timber.[26] On the other hand, if the matter is dealt with by the refusal of consent under the tree preservation provisions, it is the planning authority which is responsible, and the measure of compensation is all of the loss suffered in consequence of the refusal. The new compensation provisions in the 1999 Regulations for England and Wales have largely removed this issue there.[27]

6.5.23 The general practice used to be for the Forestry Commission to refer applications for determination by the planning authority, but following *Bell v. Canterbury City Council*[28] it was realised that this might result in planning authorities being liable to pay very large sums in compensation, or being influenced to grant consent reluctantly in order to avoid such payments. It was therefore announced[29] that the Forestry Commission will itself give full consideration, taking into account amenity considerations, to all applications which do not involve a commitment to retaining the land as woodland. Only where the application for a felling licence includes a commitment to replanting will the matter be referred to the planning authority to determine under the planning legislation; in such cases any compensation will be insignificant—large sums are only likely where the refusal of consent hinders a profitable change in the use of the land. As discussed above, if the Commission proposes to grant a licence, the authority must be notified and if it objects the case will be dealt with under the planning legislation, by means of a reference to the Minister. Responsibility for the majority of decisions, and for any compensation, was thus effectively transferred from the planning authority to the Forestry Commission.

Miscellaneous

6.5.24 Trees also feature in other legislation which contains provisions to ensure that trees do not interfere with other activities. Thus trees or shrubs which cause a danger or obstruction to road-users or obstruct their view, a public lamp or a traffic sign (or additionally in Scotland increase the likelihood of a road being obstructed by drifting snow)

---

[26] See para. 6.4.20, above.
[27] See paras 6.5.10–6.5.11, above.
[28] (1988) 56 P. & C.R. 211; see para. 6.5.10, above.
[29] See [1988] J.P.L. 531.

may be removed by the roads or highways authority, initially by requiring action from the occupier, but with the possibility of direct action.[30] On the other hand, the roads legislation also grants express powers to plant trees.[31] Similarly action can be taken against trees which are overhanging a street in such a way as to obstruct telecommunications apparatus.[32]

---

[30] Roads (Scotland) Act 1984, s.91 (see also s.92); Highways Act 1980, ss.79, 154.
[31] *ibid.*, ss.50, 51; *ibid.*, ss.141–142, 282.
[32] Telecommunications Act 1984, Sched. 2, para. 19.

7. EUROPEAN AND INTERNATIONAL ASPECTS

7.1.1   Nature conservation law must obviously be tailored to meet the needs of each particular country—there is little point in a law protecting wild giraffes in Britain—but it should also take account of the fact that no ecosystem is wholly isolated. As far as natural connections are concerned, many birds, marine creatures and, in the case of continental states, land creatures are merely visitors to any particular country, living in or passing through several national jurisdictions as their annual or life cycles progress. Species in one country may depend on water or other resources flowing from the territory of another, and the viability of many populations may depend on contacts with individuals on the other side of international frontiers.

7.1.2   When human activities are also considered, the potential for international repercussions becomes even greater. Non-native species introduced, deliberately or accidentally, by man may threaten the native flora and fauna, as predators or as competitors for the same limited resources. Pests and diseases can be spread across the world and wreak havoc with populations never previously exposed to such threats. Human exploitation of animals can reach across the globe so that plants and animals in one country are destroyed in order to meet a demand in another country thousands of miles away. For all of these reasons, it is essential that nature conservation law should not only look to what is happening in the national environment, but also consider the issue on an international scale.

7.1.3   In Britain, the law addresses these issues in several ways. First, there are national laws regulating the introduction of non-native species to the natural environment. Secondly, commerce in wild plants and animals is controlled by measures at the national, European and international levels. Thirdly, the European Community has taken steps to protect natural habitats and wildlife throughout the Community. Fourthly, there is a growing series of international agreements under which states throughout the world have agreed to take steps to further the interests of nature conservation. Each of these must be considered.

Non-Native Species

7.2.1   Throughout history, as humans have travelled from one land to another, they have taken with them plants and animals to establish in their new home, in order to provide food or other resources, either as a commercial enterprise or merely for pleasure. In countries such as New Zealand the capacity of introductions to devastate the indigenous wildlife can be clearly seen as the introductions and their effects have been recorded over a comparatively short period. In a country such as Britain, with a long history of settlers from beyond these shores, it can be almost impossible to determine whether some species, which are firmly established here, are truly indigenous or are rather introductions of long standing, and many species generally regarded as part of the natural scene are in fact introductions within historical times, *e.g.* the rabbit. Other species such as the mink[1] and Japanese knotweed[2] have made an impact in much more recent times.

Some introductions into the wild have been deliberate, but in other cases plants and animals have escaped from the gardens, parks or farms where they were being tended and have been able to establish themselves away from human care. In recent years, major problems have been discovered in aquatic environments as a result of organisms travelling the globe in ballast water, taken on board (often at larval stage) off one continent and discharged off another. Many introductions have been beneficial to humans and caused little interference to the indigenous flora and fauna, but others have had serious and undesirable consequences.[3]

7.2.2

The introduction of new species is controlled directly by section 14 of the Wildlife and Countryside Act 1981, and indirectly as some of the import restrictions extend to cover the keeping and release of the affected species.[4] It is an offence to release or to allow to escape into the wild any animal which is not ordinarily resident in or is not a regular visitor to Great Britain in a wild state.[5] In order to prevent the reinforcement of alien species which have managed to establish a foothold here as a result of past releases and escapes (and may thus qualify as being "ordinarily resident in a wild state") the prohibition is extended to cover the specific species listed in Schedule 9, which are not native but may already be found in the wild somewhere in Great Britain.[6] This list ranges from well-known species which are now widespread (such as the grey squirrel) to the more exotic (such as the ringnecked parakeet and the red-necked wallaby) and unloved (such as New Zealand flatworms). The E.C. Birds Directive also requires that any introductions of non-native birds should not be prejudicial to the native

7.2.3

---

[1] In July 2001 SNH announced a project costing £1.65 million to eliminate from North and South Uist mink that have flourished since their escape or release from mink farms over the last 40 years (press release July 19, 2001). At the same time the RSPB is undertaking a project on these islands to trap hedgehogs, which were first released there in 1974. Both of these species are a significant threat to ground-nesting birds.

[2] J. Bailey and A. Connolly, "Prize-winners to Pariahs—A History of Japanese Knotweed *s.l.* (Polygonaceae) in the British Isles" *Watsonia* 23: 93 (2000).

[3] See generally, C. Shine, N. Williams and L. Gndling, *A Guide to Designing Legal and Institutional Frameworks on Alien Invasive Species* (IUCN, Environmental Law Centre: Environmental Policy and Law Paper No. 40 (2000)).

[4] See paras 7.3.1–7.3.5, below.

[5] WCA 1981, s.14(1)(a).

[6] *ibid.*, s.14(1)(b), Sched. 9, Pt I; see Appendix A.

flora and fauna.[7] As far as plants are concerned, it is an offence to plant
or otherwise cause to grow in the wild any of the species of plant listed
in Part II of Schedule 9 to the 1981 Act.[8]

7.2.4   In relation to these charges it is a defence for the accused to prove
that all reasonable steps were taken and that all due diligence was used
in order to avoid committing the offence.[9] Prior notice must be given
to the prosecution if this defence involves an allegation that the release
or escape was due to the act or omission of another person.[10] Licences
to authorise releases may be granted by the Minister,[11] and in England
and Wales general licences permit the release of wild-bred barn owls
that have recovered after being tended while disabled.[12] In Scotland,
those investigating whether an offence has been committed and
authorised by the enjoy a power of entry to land,[13] and obstruction of
those involved in the exercise of this power is itself a criminal
offence,[14] while in England and Wales wildlife inspectors can exercise
their powers in relation to these offences.[15]

7.2.5   The adequacy of these measures has been questioned as an increasing
number of species, especially aquatic ones, are found in British territory, and calls have been made for a more coherent effort to tackle the
issue and for the law to adopt a more precautionary approach.[16] The
government has agreed that "current procedures, both statutory and
non-statutory, are uncoordinated and outdated in their approach" and a
review of this area has been announced.[17]

7.2.6   The restrictions on the import of animals and plants provide a further
means of preventing damaging releases. In addition to the general
measures, the import of some animals is further restricted by measures
specifically designed to prevent the introduction of harmful pests. The
Destructive Imported Animals Act 1932[18] and the orders made under it

---

[7] Directive 79/409, art. 11; see para. 7.4.4, below. The Convention on Biological Divers-
     ity also requires states to "prevent the introduction of, control or eradicate those alien
     species which threaten ecosystems, habitats or species" (art. 8(h)); see para. 7.5.23,
     below.
[8] WCA 1981, s.14(2), Sched. 9, Pt II; see para. 6.2.11, above and Appendix A.
[9] *ibid.*, s.14(3).
[10] *ibid.*, s.14(4).
[11] *ibid.*, s.16(4), (9).
[12] Licences: WLF 100100 and WLF 004.
[13] WCA 1981, s.14(5).
[14] *ibid.*, s.14(6).
[15] *ibid.*, s.19ZA, as added by CRWA 2000, Sched. 12, para. 8; see para. 3.2.16, above.
[16] House of Commons Environment, Transport and Rural Affairs Committee, *UK Biodiv-
     ersity*, 20th Report of 1999–2000 (1999–2000 H.C. 441), paras 93–96.
[17] Government Response to the above report (Cm. 5072 (2001)), response to recom-
     mendation (cc).
[18] As amended to exclude imports from within the European Community (as part of the
     achievement of the Single Market) by the Destructive Imported Animals Act 1932
     (Amendment) Regulations 1992 (S.I. 1992 No. 3302).

impose controls on the importation and keeping of a number of species: musk rats,[19] grey squirrels,[20] non-indigenous rabbits,[21] mink[22] and coypus.[23] The legislation on zoos[24] and on keeping dangerous wild animals[25] also serves to ensure that alien species are unlikely to escape to the wild. The forthcoming ban on fur farming will remove a potential source of further escapes.[26]

TRADE

The import and export of animals and plants is heavily regulated, primarily in order to ensure that no pests or diseases are allowed to enter the country. British law in this area has been strict, in order to continue the natural advantage enjoyed by an island nation, as most publicly shown by the anti-rabies measures that have in the past prevented the landing of dogs without a long quarantine period.[27] The law has become more complex following Britain's membership of the European Community, as the need to ensure the free movement of goods and to establish the Single Market[28] has required both common standards and the

7.3.1

---

[19] Musk Rats (Prohibition of Importation and Keeping) Order 1933 (S.R. and O. 1933 No. 106).

[20] Grey Squirrels (Prohibition of Importation and Keeping) Order 1937 (S.R. and O. 1937 No. 478).

[21] Non-indigenous Rabbits (Prohibition of Importation and Keeping) Order 1954 (S.I. 1954 No. 927); strictly speaking, it is unlikely that any rabbits in this country are truly indigenous, and the order refers to rabbits "other than those of the species Oryctolagus Cuniculus [sic.] (commonly known as the European rabbit)."

[22] Mink (Keeping) (Scotland) Order 2000 (S.S.I. 2000 No. 400); Mink (Keeping) (Wales) Order 2000 (S.I. 2000 No. 3340); Mink (Keeping) (England) Order 2000 (S.I. 2000 No. 3402).

[23] Coypus (Prohibition on Keeping) Order 1987 (S.I. 1987 No. 2195); the populations that had established themselves in the wild in England have now been eradicated.

[24] Zoo Licensing Act 1981; see, *e.g.* s.5(3) which expressly authorises conditions in a licence requiring precautions against escapes. See also art. 3 of Directive 1999/22, requiring states to take measures to prevent animals escaping from zoos and presenting possible ecological threats to indigenous species.

[25] Dangerous Wild Animals Act 1976; see, *e.g.* s.1(3) which states that a licence will only be granted if the animal is held in accommodation which secures that it will not escape.

[26] Fur Farming (Prohibition) Act 2000, to come into force at a date to be specified, no earlier than January 1, 2003; Fur Farming (Prohibition) (Scotland) Act 2002.

[27] Now subject to the pet travel scheme making certain exceptions for cats and dogs; Pet Travel Scheme (Pilot Arrangements) (England) Order 1999 (S.I. 1999 No. 3443) (as amended).

[28] See, *e.g.* Animals and Animal Products (Import and Export) Regulations 1998 (S.I. 1998 No.190); Animals and Animal Products (Import and Export) (England and Wales) Regulations 2000 (S.I. 2000 No.1673) implementing Directives 90/425 and 91/496 (as amended).

establishment of schemes for mutual recognition of licences, certificates, etc. Most of the law is primarily directed at domesticated animals
and cultivated plants, and will not be discussed in detail here, although
wild species will also be covered by its terms. However, there are
important measures designed specifically to protect wild species from
over-exploitation, and these will be looked at more thoroughly.

7.3.2   As far as animals are concerned, the main provisions affecting their
import and export rest on the Animal Health Act 1981 and its predecessors. Under section 10 of the 1981 Act, the agriculture ministers may
make orders as they think fit to prevent the introduction to or spread
within Britain of disease through the import of animals, carcases, eggs,
or any other animate or inanimate thing by which disease can be transmitted.[29] For the purpose of this provision, "animal" and "disease" are
not restricted in their definition as they are for many other aspects of
the Act, so that although directed at domesticated species, any import
of wild animals is likely also to be affected.[30] Under this power, and
equivalent powers under earlier legislation, a large volume of delegated
legislation has been made, the most important (although now amended)
orders being perhaps the Importation of Animals Order 1977[31] and the
Rabies (Importation of Dogs, Cats and Other Mammals) Order 1974.[32]
The orders detail the various licences, certificates, quarantine and other
arrangements required for the lawful import of animals from abroad.

7.3.3   Exports are also subject to restrictions in order to prevent the spread
of diseases to other members of the European Community. The relevant
enabling provision is section 11 of the Animal Health Act 1981, and
again there is delegated legislation making provision for licences, certificates, etc., and compliance with E.C. rules.

7.3.4   Whilst fish and shellfish can be dealt with under the Animal Health
Act 1981,[33] more specific provision has also been made. Under the
Import of Live Fish (Scotland) Act 1978 and the Import of Live Fish
(England and Wales) Act 1980,[34] the Minister can make orders prohib-

---

[29] Animal Health Act 1981, s.10(1).

[30] *ibid.*, s.10(4); *e.g.* the Importation of Birds, Poultry and Hatching Eggs Order 1979
(S.I. 1979 No. 1702) expressly defines "poultry" as meaning live birds of every species (art. 2).

[31] S.I. 1977 No. 944; among other amendments over the years, the controls were
extended to cover elephants by the Importation of Animals (Amendment) Order 1996
(S.I. 1996 No. 1760).

[32] S.I. 1974 No. 2211 (now subject to the exceptions under the Pet Travel Scheme (Pilot
Arrangements) (England) Order 1999 (S.I. 1999 No. 3443) (as amended)).

[33] See, *e.g.* the Shellfish and Specified Fish (Third Country Imports) Order 1992 (S.I.
1992 No. 3301).

[34] A rare but most welcome example of non-Scottish legislation prior to devolution the
title of which properly indicated its limited application.

iting or requiring a licence for the import, keeping or release of live fish or live eggs of fish of species which are not native and which it is thought might compete with, displace, prey on or harm the habitat of any freshwater fish, shellfish or salmon.[35] There are the usual provisions creating offences, granting powers of search, etc., to give effect to the basic provision. The Diseases of Fish Act 1937 likewise confers powers to restrict imports.[36]

Plant health within Great Britain is similarly protected by restrictions on imports. Again the main statute is an enabling Act, the Plant Health Act 1967, under which some general and other more specific measures have been introduced, with the usual requirements for licences, etc.[37]

7.3.5

Endangered species

Of greater significance for nature conservation are the measures designed to restrict trade in endangered species. Since ancient times the ownership of wild animals, their skins, plumage or other products, has frequently been strongly desired in some quarters, primarily as a luxury item or as a component in perfumes or medicinal products. Inevitably considerable efforts have been made to meet this demand, and since at least Roman times, it has been apparent that the efforts of hunters supplying this market can devastate and ultimately destroy populations of certain animals. Tragically, the value of the animal may increase as it becomes rarer, encouraging even greater efforts on the part of hunters and collectors, and increasing the risk that such exploitation will eventually lead to extinction. The continuing battles against elephant and rhinoceros poachers in parts of Africa and the threat which they pose to the survival of the species demonstrate both the effects of such exploitation and the strength of the incentive to continue the hunting even once a species becomes rare.

7.3.6

A similar fate can befall species of plant. At present orchids, cacti and Mediterranean bulbs are probably most at risk, but in the past the fashion was for other species, particularly ferns, and great damage was done to many populations and whole species. In the case of both plants and animals the effect of the trade is exacerbated by the fact that the demand is usually in a part of the world distant from the supply (that, after all, is part of the attraction) and the difficulties of transporting live specimens mean that in order to supply a particular number of indi-

7.3.7

---

[35] Orders under either provision include the Import of Live Fish (Coho Salmon) (Prohibition) (Scotland) Order 1980 (S.I. 1980 No. 376), the Prohibition of the Keeping or the Release of Live Fish (Pikeperch) (Scotland) Order 1993 (S.I. 1993 No. 1288) and the Prohibition of Keeping of Live Fish (Crayfish) Order 1996 (S.I. 1996 No.1104).

[36] *e.g.* Importation of Live Fish of the Salmon Family Order 1986 (S.I. 1986 No. 283).

[37] See paras 6.2.12–6.2.13, above.

vidual specimens in good condition, many, many more are collected from the wild and perish en route.

7.3.8　　It should be recognised, however, that if properly regulated, trade in a species can actually be beneficial to its survival. The fact that a plant or animal has a commercial value can encourage measures to ensure its survival at a level permitting its long-term and sustainable exploitation. Thus its habitat may be preserved and those with an interest in its lawful trade may endeavour to protect it from accidental harm or destructive poaching. The strength of this argument and its validity in individual circumstances is, however, a point of heated debate among conservationists.

7.3.9　　If destructive trade is to be controlled, the law can obviously try to control the hunters and collectors in the countries where the specimens are to be found, but it has also been realised that there is a need to approach the problem from the other end, regulating the market for such goods so as to stifle the demand which fuels the trade. In Great Britain, this approach was first taken at a time when the fashion for colourful feathers in ladies' hats was threatening a number of tropical bird species. With the exceptions of ostrich feathers and eider down, the Importation of Plumage (Prohibition) Act 1921 prohibited the import of any plumage from wild birds unless a special licence had been obtained.[38] More recently, the problem has been tackled on a global scale.

7.3.10　　The basis for the current law at a British and European level is the Convention on International Trade in Endangered Species of Wild Fauna and Flora (CITES), concluded in Washington in 1973.[39] Many states around the world have become parties to this treaty which endeavours to regulate international trade by requiring licences to be granted before specimens of plants and animals, or items derived from them, can be imported or exported. In some cases commercial trade is essentially prohibited, in others controlled exploitation remains possible, and the needs of individual countries are taken into account both by the separate treatment of distinct populations of certain species and the potential for a state to use the CITES machinery to further its own conservation plans.

7.3.11　　The animals and plants covered by the Convention are divided into

---

[38] This Act contains many of the features of the modern legislation, most notably the use of a variable Schedule to list the species covered by or excepted from the main rules and the appointment of a specialist body to advise on what should be included in the Schedule.

[39] For a fuller account and references to more detailed works, see P. Birnie and A. Boyle, *International Law and the Environment* (2nd ed., 2002), pp. 625–631. See also the CITES Secretariat website at www.cites.org and the U.K. Government's CITES website at www.ukcites.gov.uk.

three categories.[40] Those listed in Appendix I, *e.g.* tigers, are those "threatened with extinction which are or may be affected by trade", and trade in these must be permitted only in exceptional circumstances. Appendix II is for species which "may become [threatened with extinction] unless trade in specimens of such species is subject to strict regulation in order to avoid utilisation incompatible with their survival", *e.g.* all species of southern fur seals. Also covered by Appendix II are species whose listing is necessary to ensure the effectiveness of the controls on the other Appendix II species—this allows for "look-alike" species to be listed, preventing the enforcement of the treaty being undermined by the difficulties of distinguishing between similar species, only some of which are listed. Appendix III is an optional one which allows individual states to invoke the provisions of CITES for particular species which they wish to protect but which have not been listed in the main Appendices; these are protected only in relation to trade with the states which added the species to the list. The listing applies to living and dead specimens and to "any readily recognizable part or derivative thereof".[41]

The contents of the Appendices can be amended at the regular Conferences of the Parties which are a feature of CITES,[42] and many changes have been made since the Convention was first agreed. This issue reached the public's attention during the 1990s with the arguments over the status of the African elephant, concerning whether its long-term conservation is best served by a ban on the trade in ivory or the continuation of limited and controlled trade. Geographically separate populations of a species can be treated independently when it comes to listing[43] so that it is possible for a plant or animal which is severely threatened in one part of its range to be fully protected there whilst allowing limited commercial trade from other parts where there is no risk of extinction. **7.3.12**

The basic structure of the CITES provisions is that for species in Appendix I, any trade requires both an export permit from the supplying state and an import permit from the destination state. Export permits should be granted only where the trade will not be detrimental to the survival of the species, where the specimen has been lawfully obtained and an import permit has been granted by the receiving state, and where there are appropriate facilities to ensure that any living specimen is protected during transit. An import permit should only be granted if the **7.3.13**

---

[40] CITES, art. 2.
[41] *ibid.*, art. 1(b); *The Times* on December 10, 1996 reported a postgraduate ecology student having to seek a licence in order to take rhinoceros dung into the U.K. for detailed analysis.
[42] CITES, art. 15.
[43] *ibid.*, art. 1(a).

import is for purposes not detrimental to the survival of the species, if there are appropriate facilities to house the specimen once it arrives, and the trade is not for primarily commercial purposes.[44] In essence therefore, there can be no lawful commercial trade in such species and only in exceptional cases can specimens be transferred from one country to another.

7.3.14   For species in Appendix II, it is merely an export permit which is required, the granting of such permits being subject to the same restrictions as for Appendix I, apart from the requirement for an import permit to have been issued. Imports do not require specific approval, but are subject to the prior presentation of an export permit.[45] For Appendix III, again, it is merely an export permit which is required, to be issued if the specimen was lawfully taken and appropriate transit requirements are made.[46]

7.3.15   These essentials of CITES are supported by a number of other provisions dealing with exemptions,[47] the confiscation and subsequent dealing with specimens unlawfully traded,[48] formalities for permits and certificates,[49] re-exports and the handling of goods in transit through a state,[50] the restriction of the ports, etc., through which such trade can be carried out,[51] and the landing of listed species taken on the high seas.[52] More significantly the treaty requires each party to identify a scientific authority and a management authority within the state which are to have responsibility for advising on and overseeing the operation of the treaty.[53] The treaty also requires that detailed records (open for public inspection) are kept of all trade authorised under CITES and that regular reports are made to the Secretariat.[54] This recording system ensures that the treaty does not become a dead-letter, although the experience has been that even where apparently full returns have been made, the records of imports and exports between countries rarely tally exactly. The reports also serve to demonstrate the scale and complexity of international trade in wild plants and animals.[55]

---

[44] *ibid.*, art. 3.
[45] *ibid.*, art. 4.
[46] *ibid.*, art. 5.
[47] *ibid.*, art. 7.
[48] *ibid.*, art. 8(1)–(4).
[49] *ibid.*, art. 6.
[50] *ibid.*, arts 3(4), 4(5) and 5(4).
[51] *ibid.*, art. 8(3).
[52] *ibid.*, arts 3(5) and 4(6).
[53] *ibid.*, art. 9.
[54] *ibid.*, art. 8(6)–(8); the Secretariat was established through the United Nations Environment Programme (*ibid.*, art. 12).
[55] In the latest E.C. Report, *Convention on International Trade in Endangered Species of Wild Fauna and Flora: E.C. Annual Report 1999* (2001) there are over 400 pages listing the import, export and re-export of specimens involving Member States.

The vitality of CITES is also maintained by the biennial Conferences **7.3.16**
of the Parties, at which amendments to the treaty, and in particular the
Appendices, are discussed.[56] These meetings are open to international
agencies and approved non-governmental bodies, which can participate
in discussions but not vote. In this way publicity is guaranteed and
states may have to contend with open criticism from conservation
bodies which are not affected by the broader considerations of international relations which can mute inter-governmental criticism.

As a result of these measures, CITES has in some ways proved to **7.3.17**
be a comparatively successful treaty, although there are conflicting
assessments of its true impact.[57] Moreover, because it allows both strict
conservation and regulated trade it has attracted a large number of parties, both suppliers and recipients of animals, plants and their products.
Its provisions apply directly only to trade between parties, but the parties must impose some similar requirements on trade with other states,
and the treaty expressly allows the parties to maintain stricter domestic
rules on any international or internal trade.[58] Nevertheless, there
remains a massive problem of illegal trade in wildlife and wildlife products, a trade that, perhaps in part because of the successes of CITES,
can be very profitable. The demand for some products in certain parts
of the world continues to pose a very real threat to the survival of some
species.

Both the United Kingdom, as a party to CITES, and the European **7.3.18**
Community, not formally a party but accepting its terms,[59] have taken
steps to implement its provisions. At the European level, the main provision is Regulation (E.C.) 338/97 which requires Member States to
comply with the provisions of the Convention. The Regulation goes
beyond the Convention's provisions by requiring both import and
export permits for species listed in Appendices I and II.[60] It also provides for a number of additional species to be treated as if contained
in Appendix I of CITES, and for import permits to be required in relation to others. The protected species are listed in the Annexes to the
Regulation which are regularly updated in accordance with amendments to the CITES Appendices. This measure is supported by a Regulation laying down standard requirements for the forms, certificates and
labels necessary for the operation of the controls.[61]

Information on the scientific and management authorities within each **7.3.19**

---

[56] CITES, art. 11; full details are on the CITES Secretariat website at www.cites.org.
[57] See Birnie and Boyle, *op. cit.*, pp. 629–631.
[58] *ibid.*, arts. 10 and 14(1).
[59] The "Gaborone Amendment" to the Convention to allow a "regional economic integration organisation" such as the E.C. to become a full party was agreed in 1983, but
has not yet been ratified by enough states to come into force.
[60] Only export permits are required for Appendix II species under CITES.
[61] Regulation (E.C.) 1808/2001.

of the Member States responsible for the operation of CITES and on the ports through which trade is permitted is collected and published at a European level,[62] and the Commission produces an annual report recording all the trade carried out by Member States under the CITES arrangements.[63]

7.3.20 In the United Kingdom,[64] the implementation of CITES has been rather complex as legislation to give effect to the European Community's adoption of CITES existed alongside the more general Endangered Species (Import and Export) Act 1976, enacted to give effect to the United Kingdom's individual accession to CITES. The position has now been simplified, removing the duplication, so that import and export controls are essentially achieved through the E.C. Regulations.[65] These are supported by the Control of Trade in Endangered Species (Enforcement) Regulations 1997[66] which provide for offences in relation to breaches of the Community Regulations implementing CITES[67] and contain provisions on powers of search and entry to assist in its enforcement. In the operation of the Act, the Department of the Environment, Food and Rural Affairs has been designated as the "Management Authority" required by CITES, with the statutory conservation bodies and the Joint Nature Conservation Committee serving as the "Scientific Authority" for animals and the Royal Botanic Gardens, Kew for plants.[68] The Control of Trade in Endangered Species (Designation of Ports of Entry) Regulations 1985[69] further assist the enforcement of CITES by designating particular groups of ports and airports as the only ones through which live animals of different categories may be imported.

7.3.21 In addition to the direct controls on imports and exports, it is an offence for anyone to purchase, sell, offer or expose for sale, possess or transport with a view to sale or to display in public for commercial

---

[62] Commission Information [1989] O.J. C327/01 and 327/02.

[63] *Convention on International Trade in Endangered Species of Wild Fauna and Flora: E.C. Annual Report 1999* (2001).

[64] For more details and practical guidance see the U.K. CITES website at www.ukcites.gov.uk.

[65] A match between the U.K. and E.C. restrictions was achieved by the Endangered Species (Import and Export) Act 1976 (Amendment) Order 1996 (S.I. 1996 No. 2677), and then the U.K. restrictions in effect removed by the Endangered Species (Import and Export) Act 1976 (Amendment) Regulations 1996 (S.I. 1996 No. 2684).

[66] S.I. 1997 No. 1372 (known as CoTES); these were made under the European Communities Act 1972, not the slightly more restricted delegated powers under the Endangered Species (Import and Export) Act 1976.

[67] Regulation (E.C.) 1808/2001; see para. 7.3.18, above.

[68] See para. 7.3.15, above; the JNCC handled over 21,000 applications for CITES licences in 2000–2001 (JNCC, *Annual Report 2000/2001*, p. 17).

[69] S.I. 1985 No. 1154.

purposes any plant or animal unlawfully imported.[70] Similar offences apply in relation to the further species of animal listed in Schedule 4 or plant in Schedule 5 of the 1976 Act, or anything made of these species, unless the import was prior to the end of October 1981.[71] The offences do not apply to imports authorised by a licence,[72] and it is a defence for the person charged to show that at the time of the offence he had no reason to believe that the item was restricted under these provisions, and that when it first came into his possession he made reasonable enquiries to ascertain whether it was restricted.[73] The requirement for reasonable enquiries will be satisfied if the item was acquired with a signed certificate from the supplier stating that enquiries have been made and that there is no reason to believe that the item was restricted at the time the supplier passed it on.[74] Further provisions in the 1976 Act allow the Minister to make orders restricting the airports and ports through which live animals can be imported to the United Kingdom.[75]

As well as the specific offences created by the relevant provisions, **7.3.22** any attempt to evade the restrictions on the import and export of wild animals and plants will constitute an offence under the general law relating to customs and excise.[76] This may allow for more severe penalties, including custodial sentences, than are prescribed in the more specific legislation.[77]

The European Community has also introduced a handful of other **7.3.23** measures specifically directed at the trade in wildlife products (in addition to the general laws on plant and animal health), although these have largely been overtaken by the implementation of CITES. The commercial importation of whale products is banned by the requirement for a licence for any import of any meat, oil or other products derived from cetaceans, or of goods treated with such products, coupled with a provision that no such licence is to be granted for commercial purposes.[78]

Concerns over cruelty, as well as potential over-exploitation, contrib- **7.3.24**

---

[70] Regulation (E.C.) 338/97, art. 8; Control of Trade in Endangered Species Regulations 1997 (S.I. 1997 No. 1372), reg. 8.
[71] Endangered Species (Import and Export) Act 1976, s.4(2); these Schedules are now restricted to some species that are not covered by the E.C.'s CITES Regulations (Endangered Species (Import and Export) Act 1976 (Amendment) Regulations 1996 (S.I. 1996 No. 2684), Scheds 1 and 2).
[72] *ibid.*, s.4(1B) (added by WCA 1981, Sched. 10, para.5(2)).
[73] *ibid.*, s.4(2).
[74] *ibid.*, s.4(3).
[75] *ibid.*, s.5; in practice the designation has been carried out by regulations made to give effect to the European Community's accession to CITES; see para. 7.3.20, above.
[76] Customs and Excise Management Act 1979, s.170.
[77] *R. v. Sperr* (1992) 13 Cr. App. Rep.(S.) 8.
[78] Regulation 348/81.

uted to further measures, and the commercial importation of the skins of whitecoat pups of harp seals and of the pups of hooded seals (blue-backs) is prohibited.[79] Plans to ban the import of pelts from animals caught in leg-hold traps[80] ran into difficulties on the basis that they represented a unilateral restriction of international trade, and have been suspended,[81] although agreements have been made with the major producers on standards for humane trapping.[82]

Trade and Environment

7.3.25 Concern for wildlife has featured prominently in the wider debates over the relationship between international trade and the environment. To what extent is a state entitled to impose environmental controls that act as a restriction on free trade? At both E.C. and global levels it is accepted that environmental concerns can be a legitimate ground for measures that do stand in the way of international trade, but how far this extends remains unclear and at times controversial. The perceived danger is that environmental concerns are used to dress up restrictions which are really adopted for other, protectionist or discriminatory, reasons, or that restrictions have a disproportionate effect when their legitimate aims could be met in a less disruptive way. What follows is a very brief indication of the fundamental issue in a very complex subject.[83]

7.3.26 Within the European Community, the Treaty provisions prohibit any quantitative restrictions on imports and exports between Member States and any measures that have an equivalent effect.[84] This is qualified, though, to permit restrictions to be imposed where they are necessary and proportionate for a number of reasons, including for "the protection of health and life of humans, animals or plants".[85] Moreover the law here must be formulated and interpreted in the light of the obligation

---

[79] Directive 83/129, implemented in the U.K. by the Import of Seal Skins Regulations 1996 (S.I. 1996 No. 2686); see also the Seal Fisheries (North Pacific) Act 1912 (Amendment) Regulations 1996 (S.I. 1996 No. 2685).

[80] Regulation 254/91.

[81] Regulation 1771/94.

[82] Agreements on International Humane Trapping Standards with Canada and the Russian Federation (Council Decision 98/142/E.C.), and with the USA (Council Decision 98/487/E.C.). See generally A. Nollkaemper, "The Legality of Moral Crusades Disguised in Trade Laws: An Analysis of the EC 'Ban' on Furs from Animals taken by Leghold Traps" (1996) 8 J.E.L. 237; S. Harrop, "The International Regulation of Animal Welfare and Conservation Issues through Standards dealing with the Trapping of Wild Mammals" (2000) 12 J.E.L. 334.

[83] A convenient recent source for a fuller account of the issue and for references to the primary materials and extensive literature is P. Birnie and A. Boyle, *International Law and the Environment* (2nd ed., 2002), Chap. 14 (by T. Schoenbaum).

[84] E.C. Treaty, arts. 28 and 29.

[85] *ibid.*, art. 30.

to integrate environmental protection requirements into the definition and implementation of Community policies.[86] The difficulty in practice comes in determining whether a particular measure is a legitimate means of environmental protection or an unjustified restriction on the free movement of goods. If there are any common or harmonised rules on the issue adopted at Community level, those will determine the issue of where the balance is to be struck, but in the absence of such a common position disputes can arise over the legitimacy of particular measures.

Two contrasting cases can illustrate this point. In *Commission v.* **7.3.27** *Germany*,[87] Germany imposed a total ban on imports of live crayfish in the attempt to stop the spread of disease affecting wild populations. In *Ditlev Bluhme*,[88] Denmark permitted only bees of the local variety to be kept on a certain island in order to ensure the survival of that strain. In both cases it was held that the measures did amount to a restriction on free trade, but also that the reasons for which they were imposed did fall within the permitted exceptions.[89] Therefore, since there were no E.C. norms dealing with the specific matters, the question in both cases was whether the national measures were necessary and proportionate in the circumstances. The Danish restrictions were upheld, but the European Court of Justice held that the German import ban could not be justified since other measures that had less effect on trade within the Community, such as health checks on all imports, could be equally effective in achieving the desired aim.

Essentially the same pattern applies at the global level. The General **7.3.28** Agreement on Tariffs and Trade (GATT) contains prohibitions on discriminatory trade measures,[90] but permits exceptions "necessary to protect human, animal or plant life or health" and "relating to the conservation of exhaustible natural resources if such measures are made effective in conjunction with restrictions on domestic production or consumption", provided that there is no unjustifiable discrimination between states and the measures are not in fact a disguised restriction on trade.[91] In the *Tuna-Dolphin* and *Shrimp-Turtle* cases[92] national prohibitions on imports of seafood caught in ways that threatened other vulnerable species were held not to be justified under the terms of

---

[86] *ibid.*, art. 6; see para. 2.9.3, above.
[87] (C-131/92), [1994] E.C.R. I-3303.
[88] (C-67/97), [1998] E.C.R. I-8033.
[89] *ibid.* at para. 33, where the contribution to biodiversity is expressly mentioned.
[90] GATT, arts. I, III, XI.
[91] *ibid.*, art. XX(b), (g).
[92] *US-Restrictions on Imports of Tuna* (1991) 30 I.L.M. 1598 (*Tuna-Dolphin I*); *US-Restrictions on Import of Tuna* (1994) 33 I.L.M. 839 (*Tuna-Dolphin II*); *US-Import Prohibition of Certain Shrimp and Shrimp Products* (1998) 37 I.L.M. 832 (*Shrimp-Turtle* case).

GATT. The issues of how environmental concerns fit into the GATT structure, when national measures are justified and the role for multilateral environmental agreements in establishing conservation measures that will be acceptable remain controversial, and the means of reconciling environmental concerns and the structures for free trade is a question that is increasingly recognised within the World Trade Organisation as one that requires urgent attention.[93]

EUROPEAN COMMUNITY WILDLIFE INITIATIVES

7.4.1   The measures to implement CITES discussed in the preceding section and other restrictions on the trade in wildlife fall naturally within the European Community's concern for creating a single market between Member States, but the Community has also adopted two measures aimed to provide more direct protection for wild plants and animals within its territory.[94] Even before there was an express power in the Treaty to take action on environmental matters, the Directive on the Conservation of Wild Birds[95] was made in 1979[96] and subsequently the Directive on the Conservation of Natural Habitats and of Wild Fauna and Flora[97] was made in 1992[98] although it has still not reached full implementation. Both of these require the Member States to introduce laws to secure that the species and sites identified are given protection.[99] Their requirements have been discussed at the relevant places in the previous chapters, but it is also worth looking at them in a less fragmented way.

7.4.2   As Directives, the main way in which their provisions take effect should be through the presence in the national law of each Member

---

[93] *e.g.* para. 6 of the Ministerial Declaration from the Fourth WTO Ministerial Conference (Doha, December 2001); further information on the World Trade Organisation and its activities are available at www.wto.org.

[94] The Birds Directive (by art. 1(1)) and the Habitats and Species Directive (by art. 2(1)) are limited to the European territory of the Member States, thereby excluding the French overseas territories, but including the Azores and Canary Islands. On their application beyond the territorial seas of Member States see *R. v. Secretary of State for Trade and Industry, ex parte Greenpeace Ltd (No.2)* [2000] 2 CMLR 94, [2000] Env. L.R. 221 and D. Owen, "The Application of the Wild Birds Directive beyond the Territorial Seas of European Community Member States" (2001) 13 JEL 39.

[95] Directive 79/409.

[96] Under the rather loose authority of what was art. 235 of the EEC Treaty; see para. 2.9.2, above.

[97] Directive 92/43.

[98] Under the much clearer authority of art. 130s (now art. 175) of the Treaty; see para. 2.9.2, above.

[99] A. Nollkaemper, "Habitat Protection in European Community Law: Evolving Conceptions of a Balance of Interests" (1997) 9 J.E.L. 271.

State of appropriate measures implementing their terms, and both Directives have been important in shaping the British legislation in this field. However, if the national law does not fully meet the requirements of the Directive, it should be remembered that under general Community law the courts (at national and Community level) should always interpret and apply any national provisions in the light of the Directive, and should give direct effect to any provision in the Directive which is clear, precise and unconditional. Where necessary, the terms of a Directive which are capable of having direct effect override any national law.[1] Disputes can be referred to the European Court of Justice and the European Commission can take proceedings before that court, ultimately leading to the imposition of fines, if a Member State does not properly meet the requirements imposed by a Directive. The terms of these two Directives must therefore be borne in mind whenever the British legislation on these matters is being considered.

The Birds Directive

The Directive on the Conservation of Wild Birds[2] begins by imposing a very general obligation on the Member States to take the requisite measures to maintain the population of all species of bird naturally occurring in their territory[3] at a level which corresponds to ecological, scientific and cultural requirements, while taking account of economic and recreational requirements, or to adapt the populations to that level.[4] Not surprisingly, it has been held that this provision is too vague to have direct effect,[5] and it already embodies what has been a key issue in relation to the Directive, the impact of economic factors which might conflict with conservation requirements. To achieve the stated objective, Member States are to take the requisite measures to preserve, maintain or re-establish a sufficient diversity and area of habitats for all the naturally occurring species, primarily by the creation of protected areas, the management of habitats in accordance with ecological needs, and the re-establishment or creation of habitats.[6] Again, this provision is too vague to have direct effect and is to some extent an exhortatory measure. The Directive applies to wild birds, not those raised in captiv-

7.4.3

---

[1] See paras 2.9.4–2.9.5, above.

[2] Directive 79/409; subsequent footnotes refer to this Directive unless and until otherwise stated. For a thorough analysis of the Directive see W. Wils, "The Birds Directive 15 Years Later: A survey of the case law and a comparison with the Habitats Directive" (1994) 6 J.E.L. 219.

[3] See note 94 on p. 304, above.

[4] Art. 2.

[5] *Kincardine and Deeside District Council v. Forestry Commission*, 1992 S.L.T. 1180; it was suggested that some other provisions, *e.g.* those requiring controls on the sale and hunting of birds, may be sufficiently precise to have direct effect.

[6] Art. 3.

ity, and Member States must take the necessary steps to protect all such birds that occur in the Community, even though they are not naturally present in that state's territory.[7] Where there are several sub-species of a bird, all of these are covered, even though only some occur within the Community.[8]

7.4.4 For all species, subject to certain exceptions, a general system of protection is to be established. In particular there is a prohibition on any deliberate killing or taking of birds, deliberate destruction of nests and eggs, deliberate disturbance of birds during the breeding season where this will be significant for the general aims of the Directive, and the taking and keeping of eggs; the keeping of birds other than those species which may be hunted should also be prohibited.[9] Even where hunting is permitted,[10] any methods used for the large-scale or non-selective capture or killing of birds is to be prohibited, especially those expressly listed in Annex IV(a), which includes limes, explosives, nets, artificial lights, mirrors, and semi-automatic and automatic weapons; also prohibited is hunting by the means described in Annex IV(b), namely from aircraft, motor vehicles and boats moving at above five kilometres per hour.[11] If any species of bird which does not naturally occur in the European territory of the Community is introduced, Member States must see to it that this does not prejudice the local flora and fauna.[12]

7.4.5 Whereas for most species there is a prohibition on the sale of birds, alive or dead, and of readily recognisable parts or derivatives, as well as on the transport and keeping for sale,[13] this ban is relaxed in some cases. For the species listed in Annex III/l the ban is lifted throughout the Community provided that the birds have been lawfully killed or captured or otherwise acquired.[14] For those listed in Annex III/2, Member States have a discretion whether to make exceptions to the general rule, again provided that the birds have been lawfully taken, but subject to restrictions and an examination to ensure that the marketing will not lead to the species being endangered; this examination is to be carried out jointly by the state and the Commission.[15]

7.4.6 The hunting of birds may be allowed by national legislation, but only for those species in Annex II and always subject to a requirement that the hunting does not jeopardise conservation efforts in the hunting

---

[7] *Ministère Public v. Didier Vergy* (C-149/94) [1996] E.C.R. I-299.
[8] *Van der Feesten v. Openbaar Ministerie* (C-202/94) [1996] E.C.R. I-355.
[9] Art. 5.
[10] See para. 7.4.6, below.
[11] Art. 8, Annex IV.
[12] Art. 11.
[13] Art. 6(1).
[14] Art. 6(2).
[15] Art. 6(3).

area.[16] The species listed in Annex II/1 may be hunted throughout the Community,[17] whereas those in Annex II/2 may be hunted only in the Member States specified.[18] The Commission must be informed of the relevant hunting laws, which should ensure the wise use and ecologically balanced control of the species and protect them during the rearing season.[19]

Member States are allowed to derogate from the specific prohibitions and restrictions on the killing, taking, hunting and sale of birds, but only on a limited number of grounds and where there is no other satisfactory solution.[20] Such derogations may be justified in the interests of public health and safety or of air safety, to prevent serious damage to crops, livestock, forests, fisheries and water, and for the protection of flora and fauna. Also permitted are action for teaching and education, action taken to allow for repopulation or reintroduction (including captive breeding) and other strictly supervised and selective keeping or other "judicious use" of small numbers of birds.[21] The derogations must be detailed and specific and must be notified to the Commission together with information on the authority which is empowered to declare that the criteria for the derogation have been met.[22] By granting in Great Britain a legislative exemption of indefinite duration to all "authorised persons" in relation to a number of pest species, the Wildlife and Countryside Act 1981 was considered to fall foul of this requirement for specific derogations, and the control of pests is now authorised under a scheme of more precise annual licences granted by government departments.[23]

7.4.7

As usual with such legislation, particular categories of birds are picked out for special treatment, in some cases by additional protection, in others less.[24] Special conservation measures are to be taken for the

7.4.8

---

[16] Art. 7(1).

[17] See note 94 on p. 304, above.

[18] Art. 7(2), (3).

[19] Art. 7(4); see *Association pour la Protection des Animaux Sauvages v. Préfet de Maine et Loire* (C-435/92) [1994] E.C.R. I-67.

[20] It must be shown that another solution is not available, as opposed to not convenient (*Ligue Royale Belge pour la Protection des Oiseaux v. Région Wallonne* (C-10/96) [1996] E.C.R. I-6775) and the Scottish courts have held that a satisfactory solution must be one that deals with the actual harm in question (*RSPB v. Secretary of State for Scotland*, 2000 S.L.T. 1272), so that a scheme to compensate farmers for the loss resulting from grazing by geese could not count as an alternative solution; see para. 3.3.11, above.

[21] Art. 9.

[22] *Associazione Italiana per il WWF v. Regione Veneto* (C-118/94) [1996] E.C.R. I-1223, *Commission v. Italy* (C-159/99) [2001] E.C.R. I-4007.

[23] Under WCA 1981, s.16; see paras. 3.3.8–3.3.12, above.

[24] The various Annexes have been replaced and amended at various times.

species (over 170 in number[25]) listed in Annex I of the Directive, the
listing taking account of species in danger of extinction, vulnerable to
specific changes in their habitat, with small populations or restricted
local distribution or requiring specific habitat.[26] For these species the
most suitable areas are to be classified as Special Protection Areas,[27]
where appropriate steps are to be taken to avoid pollution or deterioration of habitats or disturbance of the birds. In other areas states are to
strive to avoid pollution or deterioration of habitats.[28] Similar steps are
to be taken for regularly occurring migratory species not listed in
Annex I, paying particular attention to wetlands.[29] The Commission is
to be kept informed of the steps taken with a view to co-ordinating
such action to secure that the protective measures form a coherent
whole.[30] These sites now form part of the *Natura 2000* programme
with the Special Areas of Conservation under the Habitats and Species
Directive.[31]

7.4.9   It is the habitat protection provisions which have proved the most
controversial. At the core of the main arguments has been the extent to
and stage at which competing economic and social interests can be
taken into account in determining whether areas are to be designated
and how they are to be protected. The original text of the Directive was
essentially silent on this point, and in a series of major cases the European Court of Justice held that designation of sites was to be determined by ornithological criteria alone, and that only in the most exceptional circumstances could activities that damage or lessen the quality
of the site be permitted.[32] This approach was considered by some to be
giving too much priority to conservation, and the Habitats and Species
Directive amended the Birds Directive so as to apply to Special Protection Areas the same obligations as were being introduced for Special
Areas of Conservation, permitting an overriding public interest to take
priority over the protective requirements.[33] The more general obligation

---

[25] As they list the birds by their names in all of the Community's official languages, as
    well as by their scientific names, the Annexes provide a useful phrase book for any
    birdwatcher travelling in Europe.

[26] Art. 4(1).

[27] Art. 4(1); see paras. 5.2.2–5.2.5, above.

[28] Art. 4(4); this provision was not affected when the rest of art. 4(4) was replaced by
    the Habitats and Species Directive (see below).

[29] Art. 4(2).

[30] Art. 4(3).

[31] See para. 7.4.20, below.

[32] *Commission v. Germany* (C-57/89) [1991] E.C.R. I-883 (Leybucht Dykes); *Commis-
    sion v. Spain* (C-355/90) [1993] E.C.R. I-4223 (Santoña Marshes); *R. v. Secretary of
    State for the Environment, ex p. RSPB* (C-44/95) [1996] E.C.R. I-3805, [1997] Q.B.
    206 (Lappel Bank).

[33] Art. 7 of the Habitats and Species Directive applying art. 6 of that Directive in place
    of art. 4(4) of the Birds Directive, with effect from 1994; A. Nollkaemper, *op. cit.*, at
    pp. 273–278.

under the Directive to strive to avoid pollution or the deterioration of habitats outside the designated areas remains in force.[34]

It has been consistently emphasised, though, that the first stage of **7.4.10** designation is one determined by ornithological criteria alone. Member States have some discretion in applying the relevant criteria, but cannot decide that for any other reason it is not appropriate to designate a site. They can be held accountable before the Court if their designations cover a number and total area of sites manifestly less than that justified on scientific grounds,[35] and are required to take steps to prevent the deterioration not just of designated sites but also of areas that should have been designated as Special Protection Areas.[36]

As well as the specific measures to protect birds, the Directive **7.4.11** requires Member States to report to the Commission every three years on its implementation and to encourage research on the protection, management and use of birds.[37] It is expressly stated that Member States may introduce stricter measures than those provided for by the Directive.[38]

As in many other cases within the environmental field, the Member **7.4.12** States have not been perfect in their implementation of the Directive.[39] The Commission has taken enforcement action against several states which have failed to comply properly with its terms, and a comparatively large number of cases have reached the European Court of Justice.[40] Even where appropriate national laws are in place, there may be problems in enforcing the law at the local level.

---

[34] The last sentence of art. 4(4), unaffected by the amendments made by the Habitats and Species Directive.

[35] *Commission v. Netherlands* (C-3/96) [1998] E.C.R. I-3031; *Commission v. France* (C-166/97) [1999] E.C.R. I-1719. Reference has been made to the *Inventory of Important Bird Areas in the European Community (IBA 89)* prepared for the Commission by the Eurogroup for the Conservation of Birds and Habitats and the International Council of Bird Protection in 1989.

[36] *Commission v. France* (C-96/98) [1999] E.C.R. I-8531, at para. 41; although in this and the preceding cases, proceedings began before the amendments in the Habitats and Species Directive took effect, that this remains the correct approach was confirmed in *R. v. Secretary of State for the Environment, Transport and the Regions, ex p. First Corporation Shipping Ltd* (C-371-98) [2000] E.C.R. I-9253 (see para. 7.4.21 below).

[37] Art. 12.

[38] Art. 14.

[39] For information on progress towards designations of Special Protection Areas, see the *Natura 2000* Barometer at http://europa.eu.int/comm/environment/nature/barometer/barometer.htm.

[40] In addition to those already mentioned, cases include: *Commission v. Belgium* (247/85) [1987] E.C.R. 3029; *Commission v. Italy* (262/85) [1987] E.C.R. 3073; *Commission v. Germany* (412/85) [1987] E.C.R. 3503 (see further *Commission v. Germany* (C-345/92) [1993] ECR I-1115); *Commission v. Netherlands* (236/85) [1987] E.C.R. 3989; *Commission v. France* (252/85) [1988] E.C.R. 2243; *Commission v. Netherlands* (C-339/87) [1990] E.C.R. I-851; *Commission v. Germany* (C-288/88) [1990] E.C.R. I-2721; *Commission v. Italy* (C-157/89) [1991] E.C.R. I-57; *Commission v. Italy*

7.4.13   As far as Great Britain is concerned, the provisions in the Wildlife and Countryside Act 1981, introduced partly to secure such implementation, do achieve broad compliance with the Directive, and further refinements in the law, *e.g.* the changes relating to pest species, those introduced by the Conservation (Natural Habitats etc.) Regulations 1994 for all European Sites and the extension to some offshore activities,[41] bring our law closer into line with the Directive's requirements. There are still, though, some questions over the extent of protected areas,[42] the willingness to grant licences derogating from the protective provisions and the effectiveness in fulfilling the general obligation to prevent the deterioration of habitats.

Habitats and Species Directive

7.4.14   The Directive on the Conservation of Natural Habitats and of Wild Fauna and Flora[43] is more far-reaching and in some respects takes over from the Birds Directive. It is based on the Bern Convention[44] and aims to establish a network of protection for habitats which are of ecological value (in themselves or as the host to threatened species) and to protect rare or vulnerable species of plants and animals from harm. A novel feature of the Directive is the potential for the Community to propose for special protection sites which have not been suggested by the Member State concerned.

7.4.15   The overall objective is to "contribute towards ensuring bio-diversity through the conservation of natural habitats and wild flora and fauna,"[45] based on the network of protected sites known as *Natura 2000*. However, in the preamble it is stated that the aim is to "promote the maintenance of biodiversity, taking account of economic, social, cultural and regional requirements, [making] a contribution to the general objective of sustainable development", and one of the significant differences from the Birds Directive is the inclusion of express provisions to determine how competing conservation and other interests are to be

---

(C-334/89) [1991] E.C.R. I-93; *Commission v. Germany* (C-57/89) [1991] E.C.R. I-883; *Commission v. France* (C-374/98) [2000 E.C.R. I-10799; *Commission v. France* (C-38/99) [2000] E.C.R. I-10941; *Commission v. Italy* (C-159/99) [2001] E.C.R. I-4007.

[41] The Offshore Petroleum Activities (Conservation of Habitats) Regulations 2001 (S.I. 2001 No. 1754).

[42] On the *Natura 2000* Barometer (see no. 138, above, as updated to January 31, 2001), the U.K.'s designation is listed as "incomplete"; only Belgium, Denmark and the Netherlands are listed as "complete" and France is listed as "notably insufficient".

[43] Directive 92/43; subsequent footnotes refer to this Directive unless and until otherwise stated.

[44] Convention on the Conservation of European Wildlife and Natural Habitats; see paras. 7.5.15–7.5.21, below.

[45] Art. 2(1).

resolved. As with the Birds Directive, the scope of this new measure is limited to the European territory of the Member States.[46] Member States should have had the appropriate legislative and administrative machinery in place by May 1994, although separate timetables are provided for the designation of special areas.[47]

The targets of the Directive are species and habitats "of Community interest," a concept defined in Article 1. As far as species are concerned, this term covers those within the Community which are endangered, vulnerable, rare, or endemic and in need of particular attention.[48] Species which are endangered within the Community may be excluded if their presence in the Community is marginal to their natural range and they are not endangered or vulnerable in the broader western palaearctic region.[49] Vulnerable species are those believed likely to move into the endangered category in the near future "if the causal factors continue operating", presumably a reference to whatever causal factors are producing a decline in the species. Rare species are ones which are not at present endangered or vulnerable, but are at risk through being found in restricted geographical areas or being thinly scattered over a more extensive range. Species in all four of these categories can be listed for direct protection and to ensure protection for their habitat. **7.4.16**

The habitat provisions are directed both at particular habitat types and at the habitat necessary for species of Community interest. Habitat types of Community interest which can qualify for listing are those which are in danger of disappearance in their natural state, have a small natural range by reason of their intrinsically restricted area or as a result of their regression, or present outstanding examples of one or more of the five listed biogeographical regions: Alpine, Atlantic, Continental, Macaronesian (*i.e.* the Azores) and Mediterranean.[50] The other category of habitats which can be listed is that which provides the homes of the listed species of Community interest.[51] **7.4.17**

The Annexes of the Directive contain lists of the habitats and species **7.4.18**

---

[46] Art. 2(1); it extends beyond territorial waters to all seas under the Member States' jurisdiction (*R. v. Secretary of State for Trade and Industry, ex p. Greenpeace Ltd (No. 2)* [2000] 2 C.M.L.R. 94, [2000] Env. L.R. 221).

[47] Art. 23(1); see below for details. The first proceedings for failing to implement the Directive properly have already reached the European Court of Justice: *Commission v. Greece* (C-329/96) [1997] E.C.R. I-3749; *Commission v. France* (C-256/98) [2000] E.C.R. I-2487; *Commission v. Greece* (C-103/00) Jan. 30, 2002 (E.C.J.).

[48] Art. 1(g).

[49] Especially before the accession of Sweden and Finland in 1995, this qualification was potentially significant for the U.K., since for a few species their presence within the limits of the Community was limited to small numbers in Britain, suggesting that they should qualify as endangered, whereas they were in fact plentiful in other northern lands.

[50] Art. 1(c).

[51] Art. 4(1).

which meet these criteria. Annex I lists almost 200 habitat types of Community interest, varying from fairly general descriptions such as estuaries and large shallow inlets or bays, through more specific instances, *e.g.* Caledonian forest, to very detailed examples, *e.g. Tetra-clinis articulata* forests in Andalucia. Annex II lists the many species of animals and plants whose habitats are to be protected, with a separate list of plants for the Azores.[52] Annex IV lists the animals and plants which are to be given direct protection. The lists of animals and plants contain only a few species found in the United Kingdom, the emphasis being more on Mediterranean species. Generally the animal lists cover a broad range of animals, including not only mammals which have in the past tended to dominate such lists, but many reptiles, amphibians, fish, insects, molluscs and other invertebrates. All of the lists are, however, somewhat difficult to use, requiring considerable knowledge of the ecological classification of habitats,[53] and giving only the Latin names of individual species.[54] As usual, there is provision for the lists to be amended.[55]

7.4.19   For the habitat provisions, there are marked in Annexes I and II the "priority natural habitat types" and the "priority species" identified in accordance with the definitions in Article 1. In both cases the crucial points are that either the habitat or species is in danger of disappearing and that there is a particular responsibility on the Community for their conservation in view of the proportion of their natural range which falls within its territory.[56]

7.4.20   The aim of the habitat provisions is to establish a coherent network of Special Areas of Conservation under the title *Natura 2000*, enabling the conservation and restoration of the natural habitat types listed in Annex I and of the habitats necessary for the species listed in Annex II.[57] Each Member State is required to contribute to the creation of this network in proportion to the representation within its territory of the

---

[52] Within the U.K. there are reckoned to be 76 Annex I habitats (including 22 priority types) and 51 Annex II species have been recorded in the U.K. (although 10 of these are extinct or have been recorded only as vagrants); *First report by the United Kingdom under Article 17 on implementation of the Directive from June 1994 to December 2000* (DEFRA, 2001) (hereafter *"First Implementation Report"*), p. 8.

[53] The classification used is that produced through the Community's Corine programme, established under Council Decision 85/338, but was described as having "inherent weaknesses" (*First Implementation Report*, p. 8). The European Commission has produced an *Interpretation Manual of European Union Habitats* (version 2, 1999).

[54] From frustrating experience immediately after the Directive was made, it took several days of consulting a wide range of books and experts to discover what some of the listed species are, far less whether they are likely to occur in the U.K.

[55] Art. 19.

[56] Art. 1(d), (h).

[57] Art. 3(1).

habitats concerned, primarily through the recognition of Special Areas of Conservation.

The designation of such areas is a two-stage process. In the first place, each Member State has to propose to the Commission a list of sites identified by the application of the criteria set out in Annex III (Stage I);[58] these criteria cover such factors as the degree of conservation and potential for restoration of the habitat, the extent to which the habitat is representative of the habitat type, the proportion of the habitat or of the local population of the particular species present in relation to their presence in the state as a whole, and a global assessment of the value of the site for conserving the habitat type or species. The grounds for proposing each site must be fully stated, and any priority habitat types or habitats for priority species must be identified in the proposal. The European Court of Justice has confirmed that the designation process is to be based purely on the scientific criteria, without any place for arguments based on economic or social concerns.[59] The initial date for completing this stage was May 1, 1995. No country has provided what is described as a complete list, and in actions raised by the Commission the European Court of Justice has ruled that Ireland, Germany and France are in breach of E.C. law by failing to provide the required lists of sites.[60] The U.K. is one of five states whose lists are described as "notably insufficient".[61]

7.4.21

The second stage involves the Commission preparing, from the individual lists and in agreement with each Member State, a draft list of sites of Community importance.[62] This selection is to be carried out in accordance with the criteria set out in Annex III (Stage II), which require the selection of all sites containing priority habitats or species, and consideration of the relative value of the site at national level, the situation of the site on migration routes or as part of a continuous ecosystem straddling national frontiers, the total area of the site, the number of habitat types or species present and its global ecological value. However, where the sites containing one or more priority habitat type or species amount to more than five percent of the national territory of a state, that state can request the flexible application of these criteria.[63] The final list of sites selected as of Community importance

7.4.22

---

[58] Art. 4(1).
[59] *R. v. Secretary of State for the Environment, ex p. RSPB* (C-44/95) [1996] E.C.R. I-3805; *R. v. Secretary of State for the Environment, Transport and the Regions, ex p. First Corporation Shipping Ltd* (C-371/98) [2000] E.C.R. I-9253.
[60] *Commission v. Ireland* (C-67/99) [2001] E.C.R. I-5757; *Commission v. Germany* (C-71/99) [2001] E.C.R. I-5811; *Commission v. France* (C-220/99) [2001] E.C.R. I-5831.
[61] According to the *Natura 2000* Barometer (see note 39, above).
[62] Art. 4(2).
[63] For those wishing to have economic, social and cultural criteria taken into account when designation is being determined, the acceptance at this stage of departures from the strict scientific criteria may open the door for renewing the arguments that were

was due to be adopted by May 1998[64] by the Council of Ministers following consideration by a committee chaired by a member of the Commission and comprising representatives of the Member States.[65] The Committee and the Council can act on the basis of qualified majority votes. This timetable, however has slipped and progress has been patchy and slow.

7.4.23 This designation procedure obviously leaves the prime initiative in the hands of the Member State, and the interests of individual states are further protected by the potential for the rules to be relaxed if more than five percent of a state is likely to be designated.[66] However, in a novel feature of this Directive, the Commission has "in exceptional cases" the power to initiate the designation of a site containing priority habitat or species and which the Member State has failed to mention.[67] Consultations are to take place (for up to six months), but ultimately (within three further months) the Council, acting unanimously, can take the final decision on including the site. The requirement for unanimity in effect preserves the Member State's veto over the designation of sites in its territory, but the potential for an outside body to intervene in the selection of such sites is a major innovation.

7.4.24 Once a site has been fully recognised at Community level, the Member State must designate it as a Special Area of Conservation as soon as possible and within six years at most,[68] giving priority according to the importance of the site for the listed habitat and species and for the coherence of *Natura 2000* and to any threats to which the site is exposed.[69] The consequences of such designation are that the state shall establish the necessary conservation measures, including management plans and appropriate statutory, administrative or contractual measures to meet the ecological needs of the site. In particular steps are to be taken to avoid the deterioration of the habitat and the disturbance of the species for whose benefit the habitat has been designated.[70] These provisions for the protection of sites replace the provisions relating to Special Protection Areas under the Birds Directive.[71]

7.4.25 Where any plan or project other than one directly connected with the

---

unsuccessful in relation to the first, national stage in the *First Shipping Corporation* case (note 59, above).

[64] Art. 4(3).

[65] Arts 20 and 21.

[66] Art. 4(2).

[67] Art. 5.

[68] Action is likely long before then, but even without any failure to implement the Directive, it may still be several years before sites are fully designated at Community and national level.

[69] Art. 4(4).

[70] Art. 6(1), (2); see *Managing Natura 2000 Sites: The provisions of Article 6 of the 'Habitats' Directive 92/43/EEC* (European Commission, 2000).

[71] Art. 7.

management of the site is likely to have a significant effect on the site,[72] it must be subject to a full assessment of its implications for the conservation objectives of the site. As a general rule only if it will not affect the integrity of the site can approval for the project be given.[73] However, despite a negative assessment, if there are no alternative solutions, a plan or project may be carried out for imperative reasons of overriding public interest, including social and economic ones.[74] In such a case, appropriate compensatory measures are to be taken by the state to ensure that the overall coherence of *Natura 2000* is not harmed. Where a site contains a priority habitat or species, the only overriding factors which are acceptable without seeking an opinion from the Commission are those relating to human health or public safety, or to environmental benefits of primary importance.[75] In this way the Special Areas of Conservation are to be given very considerable protection from development which might damage them, and it is made clear that it is at this stage, not initial designation, that competing factors are to be taken into account.[76]

Member States are to be assisted in fulfilling their obligations to conserve the Special Areas of Conservation by the availability of Community funds.[77] Each state is to submit to the Commission estimates of the co-financing considered necessary to allow it to meet its obligations, and after full discussions, a "prioritized action framework of measures" to be taken when the sites in question are designated. Final decisions in the light of the funds available rest with the Council acting after consideration of the issues by the Committee referred to above.[78] **7.4.26**

Apart from their obligations with regard to Special Areas of Conservation, Member States are required generally to endeavour to improve the ecological coherence of *Natura 2000* by maintaining and developing features of the landscape of major importance for wild fauna and flora.[79] Where they consider it necessary, land use planning and development policies should encourage the management of features of value to wildlife, as being essential for the migration, dispersal and genetic **7.4.27**

---

[72] Note that there is no requirement for the project to be on the site or even neighbouring it; what counts is that the site will be affected.

[73] Art. 6(3); it is further stated that the authorities should give approval "if appropriate, after having obtained the opinion of the general public," an unclear provision which may be satisfied by the degree of advertisement, etc., which applies to projects undergoing a standard environmental assessment (see section 8.3, below).

[74] A. Nollkaemper, "Habitat Protection in European Community Law: Evolving Conceptions of a Balance of Interests" (1997) 9 J.E.L. 271, at pp. 279–284.

[75] Art. 6(4).

[76] See paras 5.2.20–5.2.24, above.

[77] Art. 8.

[78] See para. 7.4.22, above.

[79] Art. 3(3).

exchange of wild species.[80] The features identified are those whose linear or continuous structure offers corridors or pathways for wild species (*e.g.* rivers and their banks, traditional forms of field boundary) or which act as stepping stones (*e.g.* ponds or small woods). The obligation here is not strong and leaves ample discretion to the Member States, but has at least been reflected in the United Kingdom by inclusion in the development planning process under the town and country planning legislation.[81]

7.4.28   The Commission, in conjunction with the Committee established under the Directive, is to review periodically the contribution of *Natura 2000* towards the achievements of the general objectives of the Directives.[82] Such reviews may consider the declassification of Special Areas of Conservation where warranted by natural developments. To inform such reviews and other decision-making, *e.g.* in relation to the measures necessary for the species given direct protection as discussed below, Member States are required to undertake surveillance of the conservation status of the habitats and species covered by the Directive.[83]

7.4.29   The measures designed to protect particular species of plant follow a standard pattern. For the species listed in Annex IV(b), Member States are to take the requisite steps to prohibit their deliberate picking, collecting, cutting, uprooting or destruction in their natural range in the wild.[84] Also to be prohibited are the keeping, transport, sale, offer for sale or exchange of specimens taken in the wild, except those legally taken before the Directive is implemented.

7.4.30   The measures relating to animals are more complex. The main provision requires the protection of the species listed in Annex IV(a).[85] This requires the prohibition of all forms of deliberate capture or killing in the wild, or deliberate disturbance of these species especially during periods of breeding, rearing, hibernation or migration, and of deliberate destruction or taking of eggs in the wild,[86] as well as the banning of the keeping, transport, sale and offer for sale or exchange of specimens taken from the wild, except for those taken lawfully before the Directive is implemented.

7.4.31   These measures follow the standard pattern for such protective legislation, but there are two further requirements. First, Member States should prohibit the deterioration or destruction of breeding sites or

---

[80] Art. 10.
[81] CNHR 1994, reg. 37; see para. 8.2.16, below.
[82] Arts 9 and 21.
[83] Art. 11.
[84] Art. 13.
[85] Art. 12.
[86] Birds are not included in the Annex, remaining subject to the separate Birds Directive, but virtually all of the non-mammalian species listed are oviparous.

resting places of these species.[87] Although some derogations may be allowed,[88] this is a potentially significant provision, especially as the prohibition is not restricted to deliberate deterioration or destruction, and reflects the general awareness throughout the Directive of the importance of directing the law at the conservation of habitat if nature conservation measures are to be effective. Secondly, states are required to establish a system to monitor the incidental capture and killing of the listed species, and to undertake research or conservation measures to ensure that the incidental capture and killing does not have a significant negative impact on the species.[89]

Annex V contains a list of animals and plants which are not automatically entitled to protection. However, if a Member State deems it necessary in the light of its general surveillance of conservation matters, it is to take measures to ensure that any taking in the wild or exploitation of a species is compatible with its being maintained at a favourable conservation status.[90] The protective measures may include regulations regarding access to property, temporary or local prohibitions of the taking of specimens in the wild or of exploiting particular populations, regulation of the periods and methods permitted for taking specimens, the establishment of licensing or quota systems, regulation of the purchase, sale, offering for sale and keeping of specimens, and the application of hunting and fishing rules which take account of conservation. The measures may also include strictly controlled captive breeding and artificial propagation schemes with a view to reducing the taking of specimens in the wild, and should include an assessment of the effect of the measures adopted.

7.4.32

Member States may claim exceptions from the provisions offering direct protection to the species in Annexes IV and V. Such derogations are admissible only where they are not detrimental to the maintenance of the affected population at a favourable conservation status, where no satisfactory alternative exists, and where they are claimed on one of the specified grounds.[91] These permit derogations: in the interests of protecting wild fauna and flora and in conserving natural habitats; to prevent serious damage, in particular to crops, livestock, forests, fisheries and water; in the interests of public health and public safety; for other imperative reasons of overriding public interest, including those of a social or economic nature and the achievement of beneficial consequences of primary importance to the environment. Also covered is

7.4.33

---

[87] Art. 12(2).
[88] See below.
[89] Art. 12(4). On monitoring arrangements in Great Britain see the *First Implementation Report*, pp. 49–52.
[90] Art. 14; "favourable conservation status" is defined in art. 1(e).
[91] Art. 16(1).

action taken for research and education, and for repopulating an area or reintroducing species (including any breeding and artificial propagation which may be necessary). Apart from these specific grounds, Member States are permitted to allow under strictly supervised conditions, on a selective basis and to a limited extent, the taking of Annex IV species in the limited numbers determined by the appropriate national authorities.

7.4.34 Every two years the Member States must submit to the Commission a report on the derogations applied, giving details of the species affected, the reasons for the derogation, including where appropriate a reference to the alternatives considered and scientific data employed, the means of capturing or killing any animal which are permitted, the authority empowered to regulate and supervise the exceptions and the results of their supervision.[92] Within 12 months the Commission must give its opinion on the report and enforcement action may follow if the Commission considers that a state is in breach of its obligations under the Directive. The wide scope of some of the grounds for permitting exceptions, together with the general statement that social, economic, cultural and local factors are to be taken into account,[93] means that despite the apparently rigid rules laid down in the Directive, Member States will in fact enjoy a considerable discretion when it comes to carrying these provisions into practice.

7.4.35 In any case where the killing or capture of an animal listed in Annexes IV or V is permitted Member States are to prohibit the use of all indiscriminate means capable of causing the local disappearance of, or serious disturbance to, populations of the animals.[94] In particular Annex VI lists a number of methods to be banned, including explosives, electric devices, tape recorders, blind or maimed decoys, artificial lights and mirrors, night sights, non-selective nets and traps, poisons, gases and automatic and semi-automatic weapons, as well as any killing from aircraft or moving motor vehicles. Derogations are possible in relation to the specific methods listed, but not from the general obligation to prohibit the use of destructively indiscriminate methods.[95]

7.4.36 The Directive contains further provisions relating to information and research. Member States are required to prepare a report on the implementation of the Directive every six years, containing information on the impact of the measures and the results of their surveillance,[96] of the species and habitats affected.[97] On the basis of these reports, which are to be accessible to the public, the Commission is to prepare a composite

---

[92] Art. 16(2), (3).
[93] Art. 2(3).
[94] Art. 15.
[95] Art. 16(1).
[96] See para. 7.4.28, above and art. 11.
[97] Art. 17(1); see para. 7.4.37, below.

report for presentation to the Member States, the European Parliament, the Council and the Economic and Social Committee.[98] More generally, the Member States and Commission should encourage research and scientific work related to the objectives of the Directive, ensuring the exchange of information and coordination of work.[99] Particular attention should be paid to transboundary cooperation and scientific work relating to the conservation of Special Areas of Conservation and other features of landscape valuable to wildlife.

The United Kingdom's first report on implementation of the Direct- **7.4.37** ive covers the period from June 1994 to December 2000 listing the legal and other mechanisms used to ensure implementation. In Great Britain, the requirements of the Habitats and Species Directive required clear legislative changes, and resulted in the introduction of the Conservation (Natural Habitats, etc.) Regulations 1994.[1] These go a considerable way towards meeting the key elements of the Directive, but in August 2001 the Commission confirmed that it was taking enforcement action against the United Kingdom (and several other states) over gaps in the implementation. Alleged failings in the British legislation include inadequate provisions to ensure that sites do not deteriorate through neglect, inadequate surveillance to monitor the health of habitats and species, failure to assess the impact of land use development plans on sites and loopholes in the species protection provisions. As with the Birds Directive,[2] although the most important initial steps have been taken, there is likely to be a prolonged process of moving ever closer to a perfect match between the Directive and national law, with the government, official and non-official conservation bodies, the Commission, courts and individual complainants and litigants all having a role to play.

INTERNATIONAL OBLIGATIONS

As a party to a number of treaties, the United Kingdom has accepted **7.5.1** obligations in international law with respect to nature conservation. Unlike the provisions of European Community law, the terms of these treaties are not part of the law which can be relied on in the British courts. It is only if an Act of Parliament has been passed to incorporate such terms into domestic law, as has happened with the Antarctic

---

[98] Art. 17(2).
[99] Art. 18.
[1] Now supplemented by the Offshore Petroleum Activities (Conservation of Habitats) Regulations 2001 (S.I. 2001 No. 1754).
[2] And other instances such as in relation to environmental impact assessment; see para. 8.3.6, below.

Treaty Act 1967, that the treaties have any legal effect within the United Kingdom. Nevertheless, the fact that the government is bound by these obligations at the international level should have a significant impact in the policy and legislation which are adopted here.[3]

7.5.2   At the international level, there is no strict monitoring or enforcement mechanism to ensure that states are fully complying with their treaty obligations.[4] Moreover, many of the international provisions in the environmental field are what is described as "soft law", *i.e.* they take the form of provisions which are very general in their phrasing and exhortatory in their tone, setting out broad aims and intentions rather than creating precise rules and obligations which it is intended should be enforced.[5] Critics can therefore argue that these measures are not "law" at all and essentially worthless.

7.5.3   Although the weaknesses of the international law must be acknowledged, the treaties which exist do play an important role. They provide the framework for international co-operation[6] in the field of nature conservation, co-operation which is essential if long-term conservation measures are to be taken on a regional or global scale. This co-operation can take many forms, from providing protection to migratory species throughout their range, to ensuring practical support for developing countries to ensure that the demands of economic development do not always override conservation interests.[7] At the very least treaties serve as public declarations of intent on the part of the states concerned, setting a standard against which their conduct can be judged. Some treaties, such as CITES, themselves provide some continuing mechanism, such as a central Secretariat or regular meetings of the parties, to ensure that states cannot simply forget about their terms, and in the modern world pressure groups can be relied on to draw attention to governmental failings. All governments are sensitive to criticism that they are in breach of their international obligations.

7.5.4   Perhaps more in the political than in the legal world, treaties do play a significant role in shaping the conduct of states, and provide strong bargaining counters when one state is trying to influence or seek co-operation from others. In a similar way, although the United Kingdom's treaty obligations lack legal force within this country, they have helped to shape domestic law and the need to comply with international obligations can be a strong argument in persuading the government to act in

---

[3] See generally P. Birnie and A. Boyle, *International Law and the Environment* (2nd ed., 2002); M. Bowman and C. Regdwell (eds.), *International Law and the Conservation of Biodiversity* (1996).

[4] See generally S. Lyster, *International Wildlife Law* (1985), Chaps 1 and 14; Birnie and Boyle, *op. cit.*, Chap. 4.

[5] Birnie and Boyle, *op. cit.*, at pp. 24–27.

[6] *ibid.*, Chaps 1–5.

[7] *ibid.*, Chap. 11.

a particular way, even though there may be no realistic fear of any sanction being imposed if the obligation is broken.

The following conventions are discussed as examples of the main conservation treaties to which the United Kingdom is a party. There are many more agreements.[8] Some are of largely historical interest, *e.g.* the late nineteenth-century agreements on sealing in the Northern Pacific,[9] whereas others are very much the subject of heated current debate, *e.g.* the International Convention for the Regulation of Whaling.[10] The impact during the past decades of the resolutions of the International Whaling Commission established by that treaty illustrate the power which such international agreements and organisations can have, as well as the ultimate weakness arising from the absence of direct, formal sanctions to ensure that decisions are observed. A number of other treaties deal directly with nature conservation, *e.g.* the Bonn Convention,[11] whilst many more, *e.g.* those relating to marine fishing and pollution of the seas and climate change, will also have an effect on the conservation of wild flora and fauna.[12]

7.5.5

Ramsar

The Convention on Wetlands of International Importance Especially as Waterfowl Habitat was signed in 1971 in the town of Ramsar in northern Iran, from whence it takes its common name. The loss of wetlands through drainage, development and pollution was identified as being a major and widespread occurrence, threatening many species of plants and animals. The impact of such loss of habitat may be felt far distant from the wetlands themselves, as such habitat may provide breeding, feeding and resting grounds for animals, fish and birds which travel far from a particular site in their life cycles or annual migrations. The Convention imposes fairly general obligations, centred on the identi-

7.5.6

---

[8] See, *e.g.* J. Beer-Gabel and B. Labat, *La protection internationale de la faune et de la flore suavages* (1999); M. Austen and T. Richards, *Basic Legal Documents on International Animal Welfare and Wildlife Conservation* (2000); M. Bowman, "International Treaties and the Global Protection of Birds" (1999) 11 J.E.L. 87 and 281.

[9] See, *e.g.* the Behring Sea Award Act 1894 and the Seal Fisheries (North Pacific) Acts 1895 and 1912. This legislation is not wholly without current relevance; see the Seal Fisheries (North Pacific) Act 1912 (Amendment) Regulations 1996 (S.I. 1996 No. 2685), para. 7.3.24, above.

[10] Agreed in 1946; see Lyster, *op. cit.*, Chap. 2; Austen and Richards, *op. cit.*, p.121; Birnie and Boyle, *op. cit.*, pp. 666–669; and the International Whaling Commission's web-pages at www.iwcoffice.org.

[11] Convention on the Conservation of Migratory Species of Wild Animals; see Lyster, *op. cit.*, Chap. 13; Austen and Richards, *op. cit.*, p.30; Birnie and Boyle, *op. cit.*, pp. 622–625; Bowman, *op. cit.*, pp. 282–293. See web-pages at www.wcmc.org.uk/cms/.

[12] See Birnie and Boyle, *op. cit.*, Chaps 11–13.

fication of particular sites to be designated by the parties as Wetlands of International Importance.[13]

7.5.7   For the purposes of Ramsar, "wetlands" is given a broad definition covering areas of marsh, fen, peatland or water, natural or artificial, permanent or temporary, with water that is static or flowing. The water may be fresh, salt or brackish and the definition includes marine areas where the depth of water at low tide does not exceed six metres.[14] In relation to all wetlands in their territory, parties should formulate and implement their planning to promote as far as possible the wise use of wetlands,[15] and should promote the conservation of wetlands and waterfowl[16] by establishing nature reserves and providing for their wardening.[17] Parties must also encourage research and the exchange of data and publications relating to wetlands and their flora and fauna,[18] promote the training of personnel competent in relevant research, management and wardening,[19] and should endeavour through management to increase the waterfowl populations on appropriate wetlands.[20] International consultation and co-operation are required, especially where parties share a water system.[21]

7.5.8   Each party is also bound to designate suitable wetlands for inclusion in the List of Wetlands of International Importance, as discussed in Chapter 5.[22] The conservation of these wetlands should be promoted and their condition monitored,[23] and compensatory measures taken if a party in its "urgent national interest" deletes any wetland from the List or restricts it.[24] The List is to be maintained by a bureau operated by the IUCN,[25] and conferences of the parties can be called to discuss the implementation of and amendments to the Convention, and other related matters.[26]

---

[13] See generally, Lyster, *op. cit..*, Chap. 10; Austen and Richards, *op. cit.*, p. 9; Birnie and Boyle, *op. cit.*, pp. 616–620; Bowman, *op. cit.*, pp. 94–100; and web pages at www.ramsar.org.

[14] Ramsar Convention, art. 1(1); subsequent footnotes refer to this convention unless and until otherwise stated.

[15] Art. 3(1); D. Farrier and L. Tucker, "Wise Use of Wetlands under the Ramsar Convention: A Challenge for Meaningful Implementation of International Law" (2000) 12 J.E.L. 21.

[16] Defined as "birds ecologically dependent on wetlands"; art. 1(2).

[17] Art. 4(1).

[18] Art. 4(3).

[19] Art. 4(5).

[20] Art. 4(4).

[21] Art. 5.

[22] Art. 2; see paras. 5.13.4–5.13.7, above.

[23] Art. 3.

[24] Art. 4(2).

[25] Arts. 2(1), 8.

[26] Art. 6; it is expressly provided that the parties' representatives should include experts on wetlands and waterfowl (art. 7(1)).

The obligations imposed by Ramsar are not particularly strong, **7.5.9** requiring the promotion and encouragement of and endeavour towards the stated aims, rather than demanding more specific action. Although its terms may not provide any strict legal protection, nevertheless, by focusing attention on the plight of wetlands and establishing the List conferring international status on particular sites, the Convention should ensure that the parties cannot ignore the fate of wetlands and should pay some heed to their conservation in their policy and legislation. The extent to which this will be reflected in practice will obviously depend on the importance of nature conservation in the political battles within each state.

World Heritage Convention

The Convention Concerning the Protection of the World Cultural and **7.5.10** Natural Heritage was agreed in 1972 under the auspices of UNESCO.[27] The Convention is based on the idea that certain great treasures of the world, such as the Taj Mahal and the Grand Canyon, constitute part of the heritage not merely of one state but of mankind as a whole. Accordingly, such treasures should be given international recognition and protection, and the international community should provide positive and practical assistance to ensure their conservation. The aim is to ensure the long-term conservation of the outstanding natural and man-made features of the world.

The Convention imposes a general obligation on parties to ensure **7.5.11** the identification, protection, conservation and transmission to future generations of the cultural and natural heritage situated in their territory.[28] The natural heritage is defined as: natural features consisting of physical or biological formations of outstanding universal value from the aesthetic or scientific point of view; geological and physiographical formations and precise areas which constitute the habitat of threatened species of animals and plants of outstanding value from the point of view of science or conservation; natural sites or precise areas which are of outstanding universal value from the point of view of science, conservation or natural beauty.[29] The definition thus covers aesthetic merits as well as scientific ones.

In relation to this heritage, the parties are to ensure that effective and **7.5.12** active measures are taken for the protection, conservation and presenta-

---

[27] See Lyster, *op. cit.*, Chap. 11; Birnie and Boyle, *op. cit.*, pp. 620–622; and web-pages at www.unesco.org/whc.

[28] World Heritage Convention, art. 4; the words used require states to "do all [they] can to this end, to the utmost of [their] resources". Subsequent footnotes refer to this convention unless and until otherwise stated.

[29] Art. 2; the Operational Guidelines for identifying such sites is available at the web site noted above.

tion of the heritage in their territory.[30] As far as possible, each party should adopt a general policy integrating the protection of the heritage into its comprehensive planning programmes, establish services for the protection, etc., of the heritage, undertake research and develop operating methods to counteract dangers to the heritage, take legal, administrative, financial and scientific measures to ensure the identification, protection and rehabilitation of the heritage and foster the establishment of training for the protection, etc., of the heritage. Parties should also endeavour, particularly through education and information, to strengthen appreciation and respect by their peoples of the cultural and natural heritage and to keep the public broadly informed of the dangers threatening the heritage and the activities carried out under the Convention.[31]

7.5.13   In practice these obligations are focused on the sites which have been accepted for the World Heritage List, as discussed earlier,[32] but they do apply more generally and do require measures to identify the outstanding features within each state and to conserve them pending consideration for the List. With regard to other states, the parties are required to offer assistance when requested in the identification, protection, etc., of the heritage of other states, and to refrain from any deliberate measures which might damage that heritage directly or indirectly.[33] The obligation to offer assistance is given more tangible form through the World Heritage Fund,[34] to be used for financial or other assistance to states undertaking appropriate measures for the benefit of their heritage.[35] Parties may also take an active role in furthering the aims of the Convention by participating in the World Heritage Committee which is responsible for deciding on which sites are to be listed and on the use of the Fund and other forms of international assistance.[36]

7.5.14   Through the World Heritage Convention, the fate of the natural and man-made treasures of the world legitimately become the concern of the international community as a whole, not merely an internal matter for the state where each lies. For developing countries this concern can take the tangible form of financial and technical support to ensure the conservation of those treasures. For the developed world, the international attention should ensure that states live up to their declared intentions of ensuring proper protection for the sites identified. Any detailed conservation measures will remain a matter for the particular state, but

---

[30] Art. 5.
[31] Art. 27.
[32] See paras. 5.13.8–5.13.10, above.
[33] Art. 6.
[34] Arts 15–18.
[35] Arts 19–26.
[36] Arts 8–14.

the obligations in the Convention present a standard against which they can be judged by the public and by other states.

Bern Convention

The Convention on the Conservation of European Wildlife and Natural Habitats was agreed in Bern in 1979,[37] under the auspices of the Council of Europe.[38] It aims to conserve wild flora and fauna and their habitats, especially where this will require the co-operation of several states and particularly with regard to endangered and vulnerable species.[39] The Convention has played a major role in inspiring and providing the formulation for the European Community Directives on Wild Birds and on Habitats and Species.[40]   **7.5.15**

The Convention begins by imposing very general obligations on the parties to maintain the population of wild flora and fauna at, or to adapt it to, a level which corresponds to ecological, scientific and cultural requirements, taking account of economic and recreational requirements.[41] Steps are to be taken to promote national policies for the conservation of wild flora, wild fauna and natural habitats, while regard is to be paid to the requirements of such conservation in each party's planning and development policies and in measures to control pollution. Each party should also promote education and disseminate general information on the need to conserve species of wild flora and fauna and their habitats.[42] The parties undertake to co-ordinate their efforts under the Convention in relation to migratory species,[43] and to encourage and co-ordinate research related to the purposes of the Convention.[44] Also to be encouraged is the reintroduction of native species where this would contribute to the conservation of endangered species, while the introduction of non-native species is to be strictly controlled.[45]   **7.5.16**

As far as habitat is concerned, the parties are obliged to take appropriate and necessary legislative and administrative measures to ensure the conservation of the habitats of wild flora and fauna, especially those   **7.5.17**

---

[37] See Lyster, *op. cit.*, Chap. 8; Austen and Richards, *op. cit.*, p. 171; Bowman, *op. cit.*, pp. 106–119; and the Council of Europe's relevant web-pages at www.nature.coe.int.

[38] The Convention is open to signature by non-members of the Council and indeed by non-European states, as its provisions affect species which travel beyond Europe (Burkino Faso, Tunisia and Senegal have become parties); Bern Convention, art. 20; subsequent footnotes refer to this convention unless and until otherwise stated.

[39] Art. 1.

[40] See section 7.4, above.

[41] Art. 2; *cf*. Birds Directive, art. 2 (para. 7.4.3, above).

[42] Art. 3.

[43] Art. 10.

[44] Art. 11(1).

[45] Art. 11(2).

listed in Appendices I and II. As far as possible the deterioration of such habitat should be minimised by conservation requirements being taken into account in planning and development policies. Special attention should be paid to sites used by migratory species, and states should co-ordinate their efforts in relation to habitats in frontier areas.[46] Such provisions, whilst ensuring that regard should be had to the needs of conservation, do allow very considerable discretion to each party and avoid any identification of particular sites at an international level.

7.5.18 The particular species of plants in Appendix I and animals in Appendix II are to be given special protection by appropriate legislative and administrative measures. For the plants listed in Appendix I, the deliberate picking, collecting, cutting or uprooting is to be prohibited, as is their possession and sale.[47] For the animals in Appendix II, the measures should include the prohibition of all forms of deliberate capture, keeping and killing, deliberate damage to or destruction of breeding or resting sites, deliberate disturbance which is significant in relation to the aims of the Convention, deliberate destruction, taking or keeping of eggs, and the possession and trading in the animals, alive or dead.[48]

7.5.19 For a further category of animals, listed in Appendix III, measures are to be taken to ensure their protection.[49] The exploitation of such animals is permitted, but must be controlled by measures such as close seasons, temporary or local prohibitions on exploitation to allow populations to recover, and regulation of their sale and related activities.[50] Where capture and killing is permitted, either of Appendix III animals or those of Appendix II under special exceptions, all indiscriminate methods are to be prohibited, as are those capable of causing serious disturbance to the local population and those methods specified in Appendix IV.[51]

7.5.20 Exceptions to the protective measures discussed above are permitted where there is no other satisfactory solution, the exception will not be detrimental to the survival of the population concerned, and is required on one of the following grounds:

    (a) the protection of flora and fauna;
    (b) the prevention of serious damage to crops, livestock, forests, fisheries, water and other forms of property;

---

[46] Art. 4.
[47] Art. 5.
[48] Art. 6.
[49] As opposed to the "special protection" for Appendix II animals.
[50] Art. 7.
[51] Art. 8.

(c) in the interests of public health and safety, air safety or other
overriding public interests;

(d) research, education, repopulation and reintroduction;

(e) judicious and selective exploitation of certain species under
strictly supervised conditions.[52]

These exceptions must be notified in reports made every two years to
the Standing Committee established under the Convention.

As mentioned earlier, these provisions lie behind much that is in the   **7.5.21**
European Community's Birds and Habitats and Species Directives.
Since these Directives have legal force within the United Kingdom and
impose more detailed obligations, especially in relation to particular
sites and the scrutiny of any exceptions to the protection provided, it is
the Directives rather than the Convention, that will have a practical
impact. However, in extending beyond the 15 Member States the commitment to and co-operation on nature conservation, and in providing
a further layer of legal recognition for the needs of certain endangered
species, the Convention does still play a role in the conservation of
Europe's natural heritage.

Convention on Biological Diversity

The Convention on Biological Diversity was signed at the Earth   **7.5.22**
Summit in Rio de Janeiro in June 1992.[53] The aims of the Convention
are the conservation of biological diversity, the sustainable use of its
components ("genetic resources, organisms ... or any other biotic
component of ecosystems with actual or potential use or value for
humanity"), and the fair and equitable sharing of the benefits of such
use, including access to biological resources and the transfer of technology.[54] Much of the Convention, and most of the controversy surrounding its adoption, concerns the provisions on access to biological
resources, the exploitation of which is clearly stated to be a sovereign
right of the state where they are found.[55] Other states should have
access to a nation's resources on an agreed basis, which should include
arrangements for sharing the benefits of their use and the transfer of
the technology to exploit them.[56] In particular the developed countries

---

[52] Art. 9; *cf.* Habitats and Species Directive, art.16 (see para. 7.4.33, above).

[53] See Birnie and Boyle, *op. cit.*, pp. 568–589; *Handbook of the Convention on Biological
Diversity* (Secretariat of the Convention on Biological Diversity, 2001); and
www.biodiv.org.

[54] Convention on Biological Diversity, art. 1; subsequent footnotes refer to this convention unless and until otherwise stated.

[55] Art. 3.

[56] Arts. 15–19.

should provide technical and financial assistance to the developing countries to further the aims of the Convention.[57]

7.5.23 As far as conservation is concerned, there are broadly phrased obligations on all of the signatories, obligations qualified by phrases such as "as far as possible and appropriate". National strategies for the conservation and sustainable use of biological resources should be developed and integrated into the other policies of the state.[58] Protected areas should be established, and in the areas surrounding these environmentally sound and sustainable development should be promoted to further their protection. Degraded ecosystems should be rehabilitated, threatened species should be protected and the introduction of damaging aliens should be prohibited or controlled.[59] Away from the habitats in question, but preferably within the state of origin, steps should be taken to further such *in situ* measures,[60] and to promote research and training and public education and awareness.[61] Economically and socially sound measures that act as incentives for the conservation and sustainable use of biological resources should be adopted.[62] Environmental impact assessment should be employed where proposed projects are likely to have significant adverse effects on biological diversity, such effects should be minimised, and responses prepared to emergencies, natural or man-made, presenting grave and imminent danger to biological diversity.[63]

7.5.24 All of these measures, and the general exhortation to international co-operation,[64] are too vague to have any direct legal significance here. The Convention is primarily a political statement, but does try to ensure continuing attention and action through the Conferences of the Parties and the requirements on parties to report on their progress,[65] as well as through the operation of financial mechanisms to assist developing countries. The Conference has already led to one further agreement in 2000, adding to the Convention a Protocol on Biosafety, dealing with transit, handling and use of genetically modified organisms.[66] The immediate practical results of the Convention may be very limited, but it serves to place issues of conservation and sustainable use firmly on the international negotiating table.

---

[57] Art. 20; it is expressly stated that the extent to which the developing world will effectively implement its obligations will depend on the extent to which the developed world effectively implements its commitments in relation to finance and the transfer of technology (Art. 20(4)).

[58] Arts 6 and 10.

[59] Art. 8.

[60] Art. 9.

[61] Arts 12 and 13.

[62] Art. 11.

[63] Art. 14.

[64] Art. 5.

[65] See para. 1.2.4, above.

[66] Known as the Cartagena Protocol; see www.biodiv.org/biosafety.

Antarctic Treaties

Although unlikely to be of practical relevance to many readers of this **7.5.25**
book, the various treaties designed to protect the Antarctic environment
merit a brief mention since certain key provisions have been incorporated into domestic law. The parties to the Antarctic Treaty of 1959
have agreed further measures to protect that region, most notably the
Protocol on Environmental Protection agreed in 1991, which designates
Antarctica as a "natural reserve, devoted to peace and science" and
recognises protection of its environment as fundamental to all activities
in the area.[67] This was in part a reaction to the abortive Convention on
the Regulation of Antarctic Mineral Resource Activities (1988) and
supports or supersedes the earlier conservation measures, under the
Agreed Measures for the Conservation of Antarctic Fauna and Flora
(1964), the Convention for the Conservation of Antarctic Seals (1972),
and the Convention on the Conservation of Antarctic Marine Living
Resources (1980).[68]

The Antarctic Act 1994 has given effect to these provisions so that **7.5.26**
there are severe restrictions enforceable under British law.[69] For the
purposes of this legislation, Antarctica is defined as the whole area
south of the sixtieth parallel of south latitude,[70] and restrictions also
apply to certain areas north of that latitude designated as protected
places under the 1980 Convention.[71] Unless a permit has been obtained,
United Kingdom nationals[72] commit a crime under the 1994 Act if they
do any of the following in Antarctica: intentionally kill, capture, handle
or molest any native mammal or bird; intentionally disturb breeding or
moulting birds or concentrations of mammals or birds; use vehicles,
vessels or explosives to disturb such concentrations; significantly
damage concentrations of native plants or remove or damage plants so
that their local abundance or distribution is affected; do anything likely
to cause significant damage to habitat.[73] The introduction of any non-
native animal or plant is also an offence, unless they are kept on board
a vessel.[74]

Permits are required for any person to enter or remain in Antarctica **7.5.27**

---

[67] Protocol on Environmental Protection to the Antarctic Treaty (1991), arts 2 and 3(1).
[68] See Lyster *op. cit.*, Chap. 9; further information is available on the web-pages of the
British Antarctic Survey, at www.antarctica.ac.uk, in the "About Antarctica" section,
and on those of the Commission for the Conservation of Antarctic Marine Living
Resources (CCAMLR) at www.ccamlr.org.
[69] Also the Antarctic Regulations 1995 (S.I. 1995 No. 490) and the Antarctic
(Amendment) Regulations 1998 (SI 1998 No. 1007) and 2000 (S.I. 2000 No. 2147).
[70] Antarctic Act 1994, s.1.
[71] *ibid.*, s.11.
[72] Defined in the Antarctica Act 1994, s.31(1) and including British companies.
[73] *ibid.*, s.7.
[74] *ibid.*, s.8.

on a British expedition (*i.e.* one organised in or taking its final departure from the United Kingdom), for any person to stay at a British Antarctic station, or for any British vessel or aircraft to enter Antarctica, except in transit or for commercial fishing (which is separately regulated).[75] Without a specific permit it is an offence for any United Kingdom national to engage in any mineral-related activities (including surveying)[76] and separate permits are needed to enter designated protected areas.[77] In granting permits the Minister is to have regard to the terms and objectives of the 1980 Protocol.[78] No damage is to be done to Antarctic Historic Sites or Monuments. Defences exist in emergency situations and where the events were beyond the control of an accused who had taken all reasonable precautions.[79]

Other Treaties

7.5.28 Amongst other Treaties, a number relate to the conservation of particular species. These include:

- The Convention for the Conservation of Salmon in the North Atlantic Ocean.[80] This restricts fishing for salmon in the North Atlantic, within and beyond national fisheries jurisdiction, and establishes the North Atlantic Salmon Conservation Organisation, with regional Commissions. These act to gather information and assist co-operation in relation to the conservation, enhancement and rational management of salmon stocks, with limited powers to introduce regulatory measures.
- The Agreement on the Conservation of Bats in Europe (EUROBATS).[81] Under this agreement, states are required to prohibit, except under specific permit, the deliberate capture, keeping or killing of all species of bats within their territory. They should also identify and protect sites that are important for the conservation status of bats and endeavour to protect important feeding areas.
- The Agreement on the Conservation of Small Cetaceans of the Baltic and North Seas (ASCOBANS).[82] Building on the Bonn Convention,[83] this calls on states in the area to co-operate

---

[75] *ibid.*, ss. 3–5.
[76] *ibid.*, s.6.
[77] *ibid.*, s.10.
[78] *ibid.*, s.15.
[79] *ibid.*, s.18.
[80] 1982; Austen and Richards, *op. cit.*, p. 283; see www.nasco.org.uk.
[81] 1991; Austen and Richards, *op. cit.*, p. 296; see www.eurobats.org.
[82] 1992; Austen and Richards, *op. cit.*, p. 300; see www.ascobans.org.
[83] See para. 7.5.5, above.

closely in order to improve the conservation status of all toothed whales in the seas that are covered by the agreement, in particular introducing legislation to prevent the taking and killing of these animals, working towards the prevention of pollution, disturbance, fishing practices and other activities that threaten the species, carrying out joint research and establishing systems for reporting and retrieving by-catches and stranded specimens.

These and the other measures listed in this Chapter are just examples of a large body of international law affecting nature conservation in many direct and indirect ways.

8. MISCELLANEOUS

8.1.1 The previous chapters have covered the law which is most directly concerned with nature conservation, but many other areas of the law can also have a considerable impact on conservation and on the fate of wild plants and animals and their habitat. This chapter aims to draw attention to some of these further areas of law. As almost all human activities do or could have some effect on the environment many more areas of legal regulation could be included. Indeed one of the challenges for environmentalists today is to ensure that the political rhetoric on sustainability and environmental concern is matched by an awareness of the ways in which so many areas of policy and law have environmental consequences, albeit unintentionally and indirectly.

8.1.2 Town and country planning is an obvious candidate for a brief treatment here, followed by the linked topic of environmental assessment. As its effect on the countryside is so great, agriculture must be considered, and pollution control is important both for the general health of the environment and to protect sites from particular threats. The control of water resources is crucial to many habitats, while the development of genetic modification has added a new dimension to concerns about contamination of the natural world. Finally the extent to which wildlife can be a legal liability to a landowner is considered.

TOWN AND COUNTRY PLANNING

8.2.1 The system of town and country planning is the most important means by which land use is regulated in this country and is therefore of great importance to nature conservation. We have already seen in Chapter 5 how in many cases provisions designed to conserve habitats operate in conjunction with the planning legislation. This is not the place for a detailed account of the planning system, especially as the subject is so thoroughly covered by other books and journals.[1] Instead, after the briefest of outlines of the system, an indication will be given of the opportunities at various stages in the planning process for nature conservation to be taken into account.

---

[1] In Scotland, J. Rowan Robinson *et al.*, *Scottish Planning Law and Procedure* (2001), N. Collar, *Planning* (2nd ed., 1999), A. McAllister and R. McMaster, *Scottish Planning Law* (2nd ed., 1999), the *Scottish Planning Encyclopaedia* (looseleaf—B. Gill and M. Thomson (eds.)) and the journal *Scottish Planning and Environmental Law*. In England there is a very wide choice of books—the most recent general texts include R. Duxbury, *Planning Law and Procedure* (11th ed., 1999), V. Moore, *A Practical Approach to Planning Law* (7th ed., 2000), M. Grant, *Planning Law* (2nd ed., 2001); there are also a number of looseleaf works and the leading periodical is the *Journal of Environmental and Planning Law*.

The planning system is operated by a partnership (not always 8.2.2
harmonious) of central and local government. General policy is set by
the Minister, expressed primarily through the many policy guidance
notes and circulars that are of major importance in determining how
the system operates in practice. The Minister also decides appeals
against the individual decisions taken by local planning authorities and
can "call in" particular cases for initial determination. At local level,
planning functions are divided between the tiers of local government
where there is not a unitary system.

In Scotland and Wales, the unitary councils have responsibility for 8.2.3
all planning issues, with some functions on occasion to be exercised on
a joint basis between authorities. In the parts of England where there
are district and county councils, most matters, including development
control (*i.e.* the determination of individual applications for planning
permission) are in the hands of district councils. However, strategic
planning, in particular the preparation of structure plans, rests with the
county council. In the metropolitan areas the London and metropolitan
borough councils have sole responsibility, although in London the
Mayor is responsible for preparing a Spatial Development Strategy and
may become further involved in some planning matters.[2] Special rules
do or may apply for many specially designated areas, *e.g.* National
Parks,[3] urban development areas.

The system of town and country planning requires authorities to 8.2.4
establish broad plans for their areas, setting out general policies for
development.[4] It is provided that "unless material considerations indicate otherwise", individual planning decisions are to be made in accordance with these development plans.[5] As these plans will obviously be
of great significance for individual decisions, those with an interest in
land use issues must ensure that they take the opportunity to become
involved in the making of the plans, as by the time that a specific
application comes to be considered it may be too late to raise questions
of general policy.

In London and the metropolitan areas of England and Wales there 8.2.5
are unitary development plans, but elsewhere the development plans
are the combination of structure plans, prepared at the regional or
county level, and local plans, prepared at the district level. The structure
plan is designed to provide "a long-term vision, looking forward at
least 10 years, as part of an overview of an area's development requirements"[6] setting out major policies and proposals and providing strategic

---

[2] Greater London Authority Act 1999, Pt VIII.
[3] See section 5.11, above.
[4] TCPSA 1997, Pt II; TCPA 1990, Pt II.
[5] *ibid.*, s.25; *ibid.*, s.54A (added by Planning and Compensation Act 1991, s.26).
[6] NPPG 1: *The Planning System* (SEDD, 2000) para. 29.

development control policies, covering both development and protection of the built and natural heritage, and which will in turn guide the preparation of local plans. The public must have an opportunity to be involved in the making of these plans, and certain issues may form the subject of an "examination in public," a form of public inquiry. Before it can take effect the final plan must be approved by the Minister, who can make modifications to it.

8.2.6 Local plans are more specific, including a map of the area affected, and should provide clear guidance to potential developers and a clear statement of the planning authority's development control policies. Again public participation, including in many cases a local inquiry into objections, is required in the formulation of the plan, which must be in conformity with the structure plan for the area. Only exceptionally will the Minister's approval be required for the adoption of a local plan. A recurring problem is the difficulty of keeping plans up-to-date, especially where the holding of lengthy inquiries slows progress.

8.2.7 The most obvious aspect of the planning system is development control, the grant or refusal of planning permission for particular proposals.[7] The most important concept here is "development", as whether or not permission is required for a proposal depends on whether or not it qualifies as "development". In this context "development" is defined as "the carrying out of building, engineering, mining or other operations in, on, over or under land or the making of any material change in the use of any buildings or other land".[8] This definition has given rise to a wealth of case law, individual cases being complicated by the problems of multiple and ancillary uses and the difficulty of ascertaining the correct area of ground ("planning unit") in relation to which the activity in question should be considered. Only through a study of the case law can the full meaning of this evolving term be understood.[9]

8.2.8 The scope of "development" is qualified by a number of other provisions. Some things are expressly declared not to amount to development, *e.g.* the use of land for agriculture or forestry, while others are expressly declared to be development, *e.g.* the deposit of waste material (however authorised) to a height above that of the surrounding land.[10] Further qualifications exist through the Use Classes Orders,[11] which

---

[7] TCPSA 1997, Pt III; TCPA 1990, Pt III.

[8] *ibid.*, s.26(1); *ibid.*, s.55(1).

[9] "'Development' is a key word in the planners' vocabulary but it is one whose meaning has evolved and is still evolving. It is impossible to ascribe to it any certain dictionary meaning, and difficult to analyse it accurately from the statutory definition." Lord Wilberforce in *Coleshill and District Investment Co. v. Minister of Housing and Local Government* [1969] 1 W.L.R. 746 at 763.

[10] TCPSA 1997, s.26(2), (3); TCPA 1990, s.55(2), (3).

[11] Town and Country Planning (Use Classes) (Scotland) Order 1997, (S.I. 1997) No. 3061; Town and Country Planning (Use Classes) Order 1987, (S.I. 1987 No. 764).

provide that a change of use within a particular class, *e.g.* from one kind of shop to another, or between particular categories of industrial uses, is to be taken as not involving development. The General Permitted Development Orders[12] grant deemed permission to certain operations and uses, *e.g.* minor alterations to houses, agricultural and forestry operations, land drainage works; these do still count as development but within the prescribed limits they are automatically authorised by the deemed permission, without any need to apply for express planning permission for the individual project. There are thus several sources to be considered before it can be said with certainty whether a particular proposal does involve development and requires planning permission.

From the point of view of nature conservation, several of the activities falling outwith the meaning of development, and hence outwith the planning system, are of considerable significance, particularly in relation to agriculture and forestry. It does not amount to a material change of use, and hence is not development, if what is involved is "the use of land for the purposes of agriculture or forestry (including afforestation)[13] and the use for any of those purposes of any building occupied together with land so used."[14] This means that no permission is required for converting land to such uses, a change which can radically transform the nature of the land and the habitats provided.[15] Equally, the General Permitted Development Orders grant deemed permission, subject to some limitations, to agricultural buildings and operations (including mineral workings reasonably necessary for agricultural purposes on that unit)[16] and to forestry operations and buildings.[17] Thus there is no need to seek planning permission before carrying out such operations, even though they fundamentally alter the land affected, *e.g.* ploughing moorland, clear felling mature woodland. Also of potentially major significance are deemed permissions (again subject to various limitations) for land drainage works,[18] operations carried out

8.2.9

---

[12] Town and Country Planning (General Permitted Development) (Scotland) Order 1992, (S.I. 1992 No. 223); Town and Country Planning (General Permitted Development) Order 1995, (S.I. 1995 No. 418); these are subject to frequent minor amendments.

[13] This definition is not restricted to the land where the trees, crops, etc., are being grown, and can even include land some distance from the primary site; *Farleyer Estate v. Secretary of State for Scotland*, 1992 S.L.T. 476.

[14] TCPSA 1997, s.26(2)(e); TCPA 1990, s.55(2)(e).

[15] Although consent may be required under the Regulations for environmental assessment for forestry (see paras 6.4.25–6.4.29, above) and for the conversion of non-cultivated land (see para. 8.3.6, below).

[16] Town and Country Planning (General Permitted Development) (Scotland) Order 1992, (S.I. 1992 No. 223), Sched. 1, Pt 6; Town and Country Planning (General Permitted Development) Order 1995, (S.I. 1995 No. 418), Sched. 2, Pt 6.

[17] *ibid.*, Sched. 1, Pt 7; *ibid.*, Sched. 2, Pt 7.

[18] *ibid.*, Sched. 1, Pt 6, class 20; *ibid.*, Sched. 2, Pt 14.

by statutory undertakers,[19] operations relating to mineral exploration and ancillary to mineral workings,[20] and in Scotland the taking of peat for individual domestic requirements.[21]

8.2.10 If planning permission is required, an application must be made to the relevant planning authority. Full permission may be sought, or outline permission, which approves the general principle of a particular development but leaves detailed aspects for approval at a later stage, allowing developers to test the acceptability of a proposal without the effort (and cost) of preparing fully detailed plans and enabling the final development to be shaped in accordance with the planning authority's concerns as expressed in the grant of outline permission. Applications are available for inspection and must generally be notified to neighbours and in some cases advertised in the press. Members of the public have the opportunity to make representations to the planning authority before it decides whether or not to grant permission. In some instances an environmental impact assessment may be necessary.[22]

8.2.11 The authority may grant or refuse permission, or grant permission subject to conditions. It may also seek to enter an agreement with the developer to cover related matters which cannot be dealt with by means of conditions.[23] If a development goes ahead without planning permission or in breach of conditions, the authority can take enforcement action, leading ultimately to criminal prosecution if the developer fails to comply with the various forms of enforcement notice which can be served.

8.2.12 If permission is refused, or if the developer is unhappy with any conditions imposed, the developer can appeal to the Minister.[24] Although the Minister may become personally involved in major cases, appeals are usually decided by the reporters (inspectors in England and Wales) appointed to hear them, most commonly on the basis of written representations but sometimes after a public inquiry at which the developer, the authority and any objectors or others who have become involved in the process have the opportunity to present evidence and arguments before the reporter. If permission is granted, there is no right of appeal to objectors, although they may seek to challenge the decision by means of judicial review, a course also open to developers who

---

[19] *ibid.*, Sched. 1, Pt 13; *ibid.*, Sched. 2, Pt 17.

[20] *ibid.*, Sched. 1, Parts 15–19; *ibid.*, Sched. 2, Parts 19–23.

[21] *ibid.*, Sched. 1, Pt 6, class 21.

[22] See section 8.3, below.

[23] TCPSA 1997, s.75; TCPA 1990, ss.106–106B (as amended by s.12(1) of the Planning and Compensation Act 1991).

[24] These appeal mechanisms survived a challenge based on the argument that the Minister's involvement meant that there was not an "independent and impartial tribunal" as guaranteed under the Human Rights Act 1998; see para. 1.5.6, above.

consider that appeal proceedings in which they were unsuccessful were flawed.[25]

In addition to the general pattern of development control described above, special rules apply to regulate particular aspects of development.[26] As already noted in Chapter 5, there are special rules for National Parks, conservation areas and other areas designated for landscape or similar purposes.[27] Buildings of special architectural or historical interest can be listed by the Minister, becoming subject to special rules designed to conserve them,[28] while trees can become subject to Tree Preservation Orders.[29] Advertisements and mineral workings are also governed by special rules, as are the storage and use of hazardous substances.[30]   **8.2.13**

The basic planning procedures described above offer several opportunities for nature conservation to be taken into account, and this forms the subject of ministerial guidance.[31] As planning is undoubtedly a statutory function relating to land, planning authorities in the exercise of their powers are under a duty to have regard to conserving the natural heritage of Scotland (Scotland) or to the desirability of conserving the natural beauty and amenity of the countryside (England and Wales).[32] Where European sites or other designated areas are affected, more direct obligations will apply, as described in Chapter 5. Arguments based on nature conservation are thus very relevant to the planning process.   **8.2.14**

If attention is going to be paid to nature conservation, it is important that it should be considered at an early stage in proceedings. Conservation should not be seen as something to be added on at the last minute once all the important points of a plan or a proposal have been finalised. That is a recipe for conflict. Instead, nature conservation should be one   **8.2.15**

---

[25] Several statutory procedures are provided for referring matters to the courts, rather than the general judicial review procedures being used; TCPSA 1997, Pt XI, TCPA 1990, Pt XII.

[26] TCPSA 1997, Pt VII, Planning (Listed Buildings and Conservation Areas) (Scotland) Act 1997; TCPA 1990, Pt VIII, Planning (Listed Buildings and Conservation Areas) Act 1990.

[27] See sections 5.11 and 5.12, above.

[28] Planning (Listed Buildings and Conservation Areas) (Scotland) Act 1997; Planning (Listed Buildings and Conservation Areas) Act 1990.

[29] See section 6.5, above.

[30] Planning (Hazardous Substances) (Scotland) Act 1997; Planning (Hazardous Substances) Act 1990.

[31] NPPG 14: *Natural Heritage* (SEDD, 1999); PPG 9: *Nature Conservation* (DoE, 1994; a revised version was due in late 2001 but was delayed); TAN 5, *Nature Conservation and Planning* (Welsh Office, 1996).

[32] CSA 1967, s.66 (amended by NHSA, Sched. 10); CA 1968, s.11; the references to the natural heritage and the natural beauty of the countryside are expressly stated to include the flora and fauna and geological and physiographical features of the land— see para. 2.2.6, above.

of the fundamental factors considered right from the start, just as is the basic infrastructure provision. If conservation is thought about at this stage, it will often be possible to choose an option which satisfies all sides and achieves real benefits at essentially no cost. Nature conservation should help to shape the final decision, and not be seen as something fighting against it. The following aspects of the planning system offer particular opportunities to take nature conservation into account.[33] These issues are as significant in urban areas as in rural ones. The value of urban areas in conservation is slowly being appreciated, both as refuges from the pressures of intensive agriculture and as the place where most people first come into contact with wildlife, and in the urban areas it is the planning system that will be the dominant means of regulating land use and development.

Development Plans

8.2.16 Development plans must include policies on the conservation of natural beauty and amenity and improving the physical environment.[34] In particular the plans must include policies encouraging the management of features of the landscape which are of particular importance for wild flora and fauna. For this purpose these are specified as those features which by their linear or continuous structure (*e.g.* rivers, traditional field boundaries) or through their role as "stepping-stones" (*e.g.* ponds or small woodlands) are essential for the migration, dispersal or genetic exchange of wild species.[35] There is thus a direct statutory requirement to give assistance to nature conservation through the preservation of "green corridors", *i.e.* corridors of undeveloped land which link areas of park and countryside. Such corridors are very valuable in providing pathways for wildlife between different areas, enabling plants and animals to colonise new habitats and to recover from any local setbacks, thereby safeguarding the longer term conservation value of parks, etc. They are also likely to be of amenity value as walks, cycle tracks or simply breaks in otherwise built-up areas. Plans can also include policies to protect the most valuable sites, to discourage development likely to be harmful, preserve the variety of habitats in the relevant area, and to encourage the enhancement of biodiversity, especially when derelict land or old mineral sites are being restored. Such action should be seen as making a worthwhile contribution to the general amenity of an area, not simply as a matter of nature conservation.

---

[33] See PAN 60: *Planning for Natural Heritage* (SEDD, 2000).
[34] TCPSA 1997, ss.7, 11; TCPA 1990 ss.12, 31, 36.
[35] CNHR 1994, reg. 37, implementing art. 10 of the Habitats and Species Directive.

Planning Applications

Nature conservation is a material consideration in the determination of individual applications for planning permission. Conservation arguments may help to bolster the case for or against a particular development, and may be particularly relevant where the possibility of alternative sites is considered. If a proposal will cause serious damage to the natural environment, permission could be refused. Frequently, though, a concern for nature can be accommodated by fairly minor changes to the proposed development or by the imposition of conditions, *e.g.* ensuring that watercourses are protected, that areas of a site are left undisturbed, that appropriate restoration work is carried out after construction is completed. Indeed the planning legislation includes an express provision that where appropriate, conditions should be used to ensure the preservation or planting of trees.[36] More generally, it may be possible to take account of the needs of flora and fauna, not merely aesthetics, in considering the landscaping, etc., of the final development, *e.g.* providing for the creation of wildlife ponds and an appropriate mix of vegetation, and even the timing of particular operations to avoid breeding seasons. Again, such requirements can be seen as a positive factor for a developer and future occupiers; they offer good publicity, and should be no more onerous than the sort of landscaping more commonly carried out.

8.2.17

Planning Agreements

Planning agreements under section 75 of the Town and Country Planning (Scotland) Act 1997 and section 106 of the Town and Country Planning Act 1990[37] may be made "for the purpose of restricting or regulating the development or use of the land" affected. Clearly it is possible to use this device for the purposes of nature conservation, *e.g.* to ensure appropriate protection or enhancement of a local habitat, or to secure the long-term management of a site or co-operation and assistance in the conservation work being carried out by others. There is a further possibility in the power of a planning authority at any time to enter an agreement with a landowner to do whatever is thought necessary to preserve and enhance the natural beauty of the countryside.[38]

8.2.18

Conservation Areas[39]

Although the aim of conservation areas is to protect and enhance areas of special architectural and historic interest, not the natural herit-

8.2.19

[36] TCPSA 1997, s.159; TCPA 1990, s.197.
[37] As substituted by Planning and Compensation Act 1991, s.12.
[38] CSA 1967, s.49A(2) (added by Countryside (Scotland) Act 1981, s.9 and amended by NHSA 1991, Sched. 10); WCA 1981, s.39.
[39] See para. 5.12.11, above.

age,[40] the natural environment will often be a significant element in their special features. Large gardens, open spaces and mature trees may all contribute to the character and appearance of the areas which are to be preserved and enhanced, and all can make a contribution to nature conservation. Action taken to achieve the objectives of a conservation area can also be useful for nature conservation, and this aspect should be taken into account when considering how to deal with such areas.

Tree Preservation Orders

8.2.20   Tree preservation orders are also part of the town and country planning system and, as discussed in Chapter 6,[41] can be used for the benefit of nature conservation, to protect individual trees or, more usefully, groups of trees or small areas of woodland.

ENVIRONMENTAL IMPACT ASSESSMENT

8.3.1   The modern planning system has always offered an opportunity for the environmental impact of proposed development to be considered, but special emphasis is placed on assessing the environmental consequences of proposals as a result of a European Community initiative on this topic. Under a Directive made in 1985, and amended in 1997[42] there is a requirement that before certain types of major project are given official approval there should be carried out a thorough assessment of the impact of the project on the environment. This Directive has been implemented in Britain mainly by adding the requirement for an environmental impact assessment to existing procedures for approval. In most cases the mechanism involved is the planning system, as the projects in question already required planning permission before they could proceed, but for some projects the environmental assessment has had to be grafted on to other procedures, or new procedures established.

8.3.2   The Directive requires that before consent is given, projects likely to have a significant effect on the environment by virtue, *inter alia*, of their nature, size or location are subjected to an assessment of their effects.[43] The assessment must deal with the direct and indirect effects of the project on human beings, flora and fauna, soil, water, air, climate,

---

[40] Planning (Listed Buildings and Conservation Areas) (Scotland) Act 1997, s.61; Planning (Listed Buildings and Conservation Areas) Act 1990, s.69.
[41] See section 6.5, above.
[42] Directive 85/337 as amended by 97/11/EC.
[43] *ibid.*, art. 2(1).

the landscape, material assets and cultural heritage.[44] The proposer of the project must supply an environmental statement with information on the project and its environmental effects, with any public authorities holding relevant information making that available to him,[45] and the statement should be the subject of consultation with environmental bodies and the public.[46] All of the information gathered through this process must be taken into consideration in the development consent procedure, and the main reasons for the final decision given.[47]

This measure therefore does not attempt to guarantee that certain environmental consequences will be avoided. Rather it aims to ensure that those taking the decision on whether or not to approve a project are fully aware of its likely environmental effects so that these can be put in the balance with the other factors—economic, social, perhaps aesthetic—to be considered before the final determination is made. The requirement for public consultation is a significant feature of the process[48] and offers an opportunity for pressure groups and concerned individuals to ensure that environmental considerations are truly taken into account. In order to ensure that this consultation is meaningful, it is expressly stated that the information provided must include a non-technical summary[49] thereby preventing the developer from stifling public comment by providing a statement which may be technically excellent but is incomprehensible to all but experts in the various scientific fields involved.

8.3.3

The Directive states when an environmental impact assessment is required. It specifies the projects affected, dividing them into two categories. For projects listed in Annex I, an environmental assessment will always be necessary; for those in Annex II, it is only when a particular project in its individual circumstances is likely to have significant effects on the environment that the assessment must be carried out.[50] The requirement does not, however, apply to projects approved

8.3.4

---

[44] *ibid.*, art. 3.
[45] *ibid.*, art. 5.
[46] *ibid.*, art. 6; if significant effects are likely to be felt in another Member State, then cross-boundary consultation should also take place (art. 7).
[47] *ibid.*, art. 9.
[48] See *Berkeley v. Secretary of State for the Environment, Transport and the Regions (No.1)* [2001] 2 A.C. 603 (para. 8.3.12, below).
[49] Directive 85/337, Annex IV, para. 6.
[50] The decision whether an assessment is required for an Annex II project can be made by reference to national thresholds or criteria, provided that these do not exclude whole categories of project and that the projects excluded by the thresholds cannot collectively have significant effects on the environment; *World Wildlife Fund v. Autonome Provinz Bozen* (C-435/97) [1999] E.C.R. I-5613, *Commission v. Ireland* (C-392/96) [1999] E.C.R. I-5901.

by a specific act of national legislation,[51] and there is a power for Member States in exceptional cases to exempt specific projects.[52]

8.3.5   Annex I includes major projects with obvious environmental effects such as oil refineries, power stations, radioactive waste sites, integrated chemical works, motorways, airports, trading ports, waste disposal installations for the incineration, treatment or landfill of toxic and dangerous wastes, and some large intensive poultry or pig rearing installations. The list of projects in Annex II is longer and much more varied, and only some of the projects in each category will actually require an environmental assessment as being "likely to have significant effects on the environment by virtue *inter alia* of their nature, size or location".[53] More than 80 kinds of project are listed under 13 headings: Agriculture (*e.g.* intensive livestock or fish farming projects), Extractive Industry (*e.g.* mining and quarrying), Energy Industry (*e.g.* generating stations and overhead electricity transmission lines), Production and Processing of Metals (*e.g.* iron and steelworks, manufacture and assembly of motor vehicles), Mineral Industry (*e.g.* glass, cement or brick manufacture), Chemical Industry, Food Industry (*e.g.* packing and canning, slaughter of animals), Textile, Leather, Wood and Paper Industries, Rubber Industry, Infrastructure Projects (*e.g.* industrial estates, urban developments, transport works), Other Projects (*e.g.* waste disposal installations, waste water treatment plants, storage of scrap iron), Tourism and Leisure (*e.g.* ski-runs, marinas and holiday villages) and changes or extensions to previously authorised Annex I projects.

8.3.6   Implementing the requirements of the Directive in Great Britain has been a slow and complex process. The various regulations initially made to implement the original Directive were both late and incomplete, and there was a steady trickle of further regulations to fill gaps in the implementation[54] before the amendments to the Directive in 1997 required a further tide of regulations (again late in many cases) in the effort to ensure that the procedures here do provide full implementa-

---

[51] Directive 85/337/EEC, art. 1(5), subject to the proviso that the information equivalent to that required from the environmental statement is considered as part of the legislative process; *Luxembourg v. Linster* (C-287/98) [2000] E.C.R. I-6917.

[52] *ibid.*, art. 2(3).

[53] *ibid.*, art. 4(2); Annex III provides a list of the criteria to be used in determining whether this test is met.

[54] *e.g.* the Town and Country Planning (Environmental Assessment and Permitted Development) Regulations 1995, (S.I. 1995 No.417), closing a loophole whereby some projects that should be subject to formal environmental assessment could qualify as permitted development and thus not require an express application for planning permission triggering the environmental assessment procedure under the Town and Country Planning (Assessment of Environmental Effects) Regulations 1988, (S.I. 1998 No.1199).

tion. Further gaps are still being filled.[55] The regulations have generally been made under the authority of the European Communities Act 1972,[56] but since this power is limited to the making of legislation necessary to implement Community law, direct statutory powers have been granted to make it possible to extend the requirement for an assessment beyond the strict limits of the categories listed in the Directive.[57]

In most cases the projects listed in the Annexes of the Directive were already subject to formal approval through the planning system, so that the environmental assessment procedure has been added to the existing planning process.[58] Special provision has however been necessary for a number of projects which are subject to approval under different statutory procedures or for which there was no formal approval mechanism in place. Thus a requirement for environmental assessment has been added to the special rules for roads,[59] electricity projects,[60] land drainage works,[61] pipelines,[62] some harbour and coastal protection works,[63] and other infrastructure projects.[64] For fish farming in the sea, where

8.3.7

---

[55] *e.g.* it was only in late 2001 and early 2002 that regulations were made to meet the requirements for an environmental impact assessment before the conversion to intensive agricultural purposes of uncultivated land and semi-natural areas (Environmental Impact Assessment (Uncultivated Land and Semi-natural Areas) (England) Regulations 2001; (S.I. 2001 No. 3966)); and (Scotland) Regulations 2002 (S.S.I. 2002 No. 6).

[56] European Communities Act 1972, s.2(2).

[57] TCPA 1990, s.71A; TCPSA 1997, s.40.

[58] Environmental Impact Assessment (Scotland) Regulations 1999, (S.S.I. 1999 No.1), Pt II (this was the very first Scottish Statutory Instrument made by the Scottish Executive when devolution took effect); Town and Country Planning (Environmental Impact Assessment) (England and Wales) Regulations 1999, (S.I. 1998 No. 293) (amended by Town and Country Planning (Environmental Impact Assessment) (England and Wales) (Amendment) Regulations 2000, (S.I. 2000 No. 2867)).

[59] Roads (Scotland) Act 1984, ss.20A, 20B, 55A, 55B (added by Environmental Impact Assessment (Scotland) Regulations 1999, (S.S.I. 1999 No. 1), Pt III); Highways Act 1980, Pt VA (as substituted by Highways (Assessment of Environmental Effects) Regulations 1999, (S.I. 1999 No. 369)).

[60] Electricity Works (Environmental Impact Assessment) (Scotland) Regulations 2000, (S.S.I. 2000 No. 320); Electricity Works (Environmental Impact Assessment) (England and Wales) Regulations 2000, (S.I. 2000 No. 1927).

[61] Environmental Impact Assessment (Scotland) Regulations 1999, (S.S.I. 1999 No. 1), Pt IV; Environmental Impact Assessment (Land Drainage Improvement Works) Regulations 1999, (S.I. 1999 No.1783).

[62] Public Gas Transporter Pipe-line Works (Environmental Impact Assessment) Regulations 1999, (S.I. 1999 No. 1672); Pipe-line Works (Environmental Impact Assessment) Regulations 2000, (S.I. 2000 No. 1928); Offshore Petroleum Production and Pipe-lines (Assessment of Environmental Effects) Regulations 1999, (S.I. 1999 No. 360).

[63] Harbour Works (Environmental Impact Assessment) Regulations 1999, S.I. 1999 No. 3445.

[64] Transport and Works (Assessment of Environmental Effects) Regulations 1998, (S.I. 1998 No. 2226); Transport and Works (Applications and Objections Procedure) (England and Wales) Rules 2000, (S.I. 2000 No. 2190).

there was no existing statutory procedure, the environmental impact assessment (where necessary) has been made a prerequisite of the consent required from the Crown Estate Commissioners.[65] For forestry, where both afforestation and deforestation can fall within the terms of the Directive, a new procedure, incorporating the assessment has been introduced requiring projects to obtain formal consent from the Forestry Commission.[66]

8.3.8   The exemption in the Directive for projects specifically authorised by the legislature creates a potential gap in the system in view of the actual and potential use of private legislation procedure to approve major and controversial projects. This gap has been filled by changes to the detailed rules of procedure so that an environmental assessment can now be held as part of the legislative process,[67] and by the Transport and Works Act 1992 which established a wholly new procedure for authorising many projects in England and Wales which would previously have been the subject of private legislation. The procedural rules made under the 1992 Act make provision for environmental assessments.[68]

8.3.9   The various sets of regulations all follow the same pattern, giving effect to the main provisions of the Directive as described above. Thus the regulations state the test to be applied in deciding whether an assessment is necessary, namely, is the project is one for which an assessment is mandatory in accordance with Annex I of the Directive or if it falls within Annex II, is it likely to have significant effects on the environment? The regulations then specify in varying degrees of detail the information and issues to be contained in the environmental statement provided by the proposer, the obligations on the statutory conservation and other bodies to supply information useful in preparing the statement, the requirements for publicity and consultation and the obligation on the determining authority to take the results of the statement and consultation into account.

8.3.10 A difficulty in many instances is in deciding whether a particular project which falls within Annex II of the Directive meets the test of being "likely to have significant effects on the environment by virtue

---

[65] Environmental Impact Assessment (Fish Farming in Marine Waters) Regulations 1999, S.I. 1999 No. 367; the same applies where the consent power lies with Orkney or Shetland council.

[66] Environmental Impact Assessment (Forestry) (Scotland) Regulations 1999, (S.S.I. 1999 No. 43); Environmental Impact Assessment (Forestry) (England and Wales) Regulations 1999, (S.I. 1999 No. 2228); see paras 6.4.25–6.4.29, above.

[67] See B. Winetrobe, "Environmental Assessment and Private Legislation" (1992) 35 S.P.L.P. 7; J. Rowan-Robinson and B. Winetrobe, "Environmental Assessment and Private Legislation Procedures" (1992) 36 S.P.L.P. 51.

[68] Transport and Works (Applications and Objection Procedure) Rules 2000, (S.I. 2000 No. 2190).

inter alia of its nature, size or location". In some cases the opportunity has been taken to specify thresholds below which a project will be viewed not to have significant effects, but beyond that there remains considerable scope for argument. Large-scale projects and those on sites where there is an SSSI or other conservation or landscape designation are the most likely to meet the test. In the planning system it is possible for a developer to seek an opinion from the planning authority on whether an environmental assessment will be required for a particular application, subject to an application to the Minister for a final direction on the matter.[69]

The courts have generally shown themselves reluctant to interfere where it is argued that the particular circumstances of a development are such that the relevant authority should insist on a formal assessment,[70] and they have refused to impose a requirement on authorities to provide reasons for refusing to order an assessment.[71] On the other hand, the courts have been more willing to listen to arguments that there are gaps in the implementing regulations which would allow classes of project that should be subjected to assessment to escape such scrutiny. In such cases, direct effect can been given to the Directive pending legislative correction, *e.g.* in relation to old mineral consents.[72] A further issue which may require legislative attention is how best the environmental impact procedure can operate in relation to the two-stage process where outline planning permission is sought in advance of the full details of a project being formulated.[73] **8.3.11**

The importance of the process has recently been emphasised. In *Berkeley v. Secretary of State for the Environment (No.1)*[74] it was argued that although the formal procedural requirements had not been **8.3.12**

---

[69] Environmental Impact Assessment (Scotland) Regulations 1999, (S.S.I. 1999 No. 1), regs 4–6; Town and Country Planning (Environmental Impact Assessment) Regulations 1999, (S.I. 1999 No. 293), regs 4–6; most of the other regulations contain similar provisions.

[70] *e.g. R. v. Powys C.C., ex p. Andrews* [1997] Env. L.R. 170; *Swan v. Secretary of State for Scotland (No.2)* [2000] Env. L.R. 60, (1999) 73 S.P.E.L. 65; *cf. R. v. Cornwall County Council, ex p. Hardy* [2001] Env. L.R. 25, where planning permission was quashed because there was a gap in the information identified as relevant during the assessment process.

[71] *R. v. Secretary of State for the Environment, ex p. Marson* [1998] Env. L.R. 761, [1999] 1 C.M.L.R. 268.

[72] *R. v. North Yorkshire C.C., ex p. Brown* [2000] 1 A.C. 397; *R. v. Oldham Metropolitan Borough Council, ex p. Foster* [2000] Env. L.R. 395; *R. v. Durham C.C., ex p. Huddleston* [2000] 1 W.L.R. 1484; Town and Country Planning (Environmental Impact Assessment) (England and Wales) (Amendment) Regulations 2000, (S.I. 2000 No. 2867).

[73] *R. v. Rochdale MBC, ex p. Tew* [2000] Env. L.R. 1; A. Lea, "Environmental Impact Assessment—Should the regulations apply to reserved matters applications?" (2000) 2 Env. L. Rev. 131.

[74] [2001] 2 A.C. 603.

complied with, the outcome of a planning decision could be upheld since all of the relevant information had in fact been available in one form or another to those involved in the decision-making process. In rejecting that view and quashing the grant of planning permission, the House of Lords stressed that the "cornerstone of the regime"[75] is the provision of an environmental statement, "a single and accessible compilation, produced by the applicant at the very start of the application process",[76] and that this could not be replaced by a "paper chase"[77] through other documents provided at different stages throughout the process.

8.3.13   Environmental impact assessment is now a firmly established element in the approval of many different sorts of project. It must always be remembered, though, that it regulates the process by which decisions are reached, not the substantive outcomes. The value of the process in relation to protecting the natural heritage therefore depends both on the quality of the information and analysis that is provided in the environmental statement (and in contributions from other parties), and the willingness of the decision-makers to give environmental considerations weight as they reach their conclusions. One weakness of the whole system, is that too often there are inadequate procedures for revisiting the issues considered in the assessment, so that if the impact of a project turns out to be different from that predicted, there may be no straightforward way of revising the original permission, whether to tighten or relax the controls imposed at the time.

8.3.14   A further weakness has been that the process has been applied only in the context of individual projects, whereas often these are simply the manifestations of wider policy decisions that have been reached without the same rigour in the consideration of environmental impacts. This flaw is now being cured as a result of a further Directive on what is known as "strategic environmental impact assessment".[78] Under this Directive, due to be implemented by July 2004, certain draft plans or programmes produced by government at all levels must be accompanied by an environmental report setting out their likely effects on the environment and there must be an opportunity for public consultation. The details of implementing this provision in Great Britain remain to be worked out, but it is certain that this requirement will apply to development plans under the planning system and to a variety of other transport, energy, water and waste management, agriculture, forestry and fishery plans. In some cases, as with the earlier measures for individual projects, it may be a straightforward task to graft the Directive's

---

[75] *ibid.*, Lord Bingham at p. 608.
[76] *ibid.*, Lord Hoffmann at p. 617.
[77] *ibid.*
[78] Directive 2001/42/EC.

requirements onto existing procedures, but in others the need to establish formal procedures for the adoption of the policies will be a considerable innovation.

AGRICULTURE

As so much of Britain is actively farmed, changes in agricultural prac-   **8.4.1**
tices have a great impact on nature conservation. Agriculture in turn is
greatly affected by the range of subsidies and other aids by means of
which governments give effect to their agricultural policies, and by the
laws which regulate the rights of agricultural tenants and others
involved in the industry. Indeed, changing agricultural practices during
the second half of the twentieth century have almost certainly had a
greater effect on nature conservation than any other factor. Therefore,
any thorough examination of the law affecting nature conservation must
at least mention the law relating to agriculture.[79]

The agricultural policy adopted by the British government and by the   **8.4.2**
European Community through the Common Agricultural Policy (CAP)[80]
used to have the simple goal of stimulating production. This has led in
Britain to highly mechanised and highly specialised agricultural units
which produce high yields but require large fields for intensive crop
growing or industrial buildings for intensive livestock rearing, in all cases
calling for the substantial use of fertilisers, pesticides and herbicides.
Such developments have been encouraged by a range of grants and other
aids available to farmers wishing to "improve" their land through the
construction of new buildings, drainage, or the cultivation of rough grassland or heath. These changes have been harmful to the "traditional"
countryside and to the flora and fauna which it supports.

Now, however, it has been realised that this policy has been too   **8.4.3**
successful and the Community is faced with twin problems. The first
is the overproduction of many agricultural products, which cannot be
sold on the open market but which are still paid for in order to prevent
agricultural collapse leading to the depopulation of large areas of rural
Europe. The second has been the realisation of the unsustainable nature
of certain agriculture practices and the risk to the environment from
incentives to greater intensity and further production.[81] At the same

---

[79] See generally, W. Howarth and C.P. Rodgers (eds.), *Agriculture, Conservation and Land Use* (1992); N. Hawke and N. Kovaleva, *Agri-Environmental Law and Policy* (1998); I. Hodge, "Agri-environmental Policy: A U.K. Perspective" in D. Helm (ed.), *Environmental Policy: Objectives, Instruments and Implementation* (2000); J. Usher, *E.C. Agricultural Law* (2nd ed., 2002).

[80] See generally, J. McMahon, *Law of the Common Agricultural Policy* (2000).

[81] B. Jack, "Protecting the European environment from the Community: the case of agriculture" (2001) 3 Env. L. Rev. 44.

time, the existing structure of subsidies risks falling foul of the free
trade rules at an international level. Agricultural policies are changing,
and one aspect of this is the view that the farmers' role in protecting
the rural environment and managing the landscape should be recognised more fully and remunerated accordingly.[82]

8.4.4   This change of attitude is reflected in several specific schemes and
in broader measures, such as the obligation on the agriculture ministers
to seek a balance between the promotion of agriculture and the conservation and enjoyment of the countryside.[83] Some of the specific
schemes are mentioned below; these schemes are constantly changing
and the position is complicated by the fact that many involve commitments over several years so that land continues to be affected by
arrangements under schemes that are no longer available to new applicants. In the long term, though, of greater significance will be whether
the totality of agricultural reforms affecting policy, subsidies and markets will lead to general changes in practice as thorough as those produced in past decades by the drive for maximum production. Although
the proportion is rising, less than 5 percent of the funding provided by
means of direct payment schemes at EC and national levels is directed
through "agri-environment" programmes.[84]

8.4.5   At Community level there have been two main stages in the introduction of environmental concerns into agricultural policy, although some
measures were introduced earlier.[85] The first came with the launch of
the "agri-environment" programme in 1992 which made provision for
schemes to encourage agricultural methods compatible with the requirements for the protection of the environment and the maintenance of the
countryside.[86] This allows for support to be given to farmers to reduce
their use of fertilisers, herbicides and pesticides, to introduce organic
methods, to change to less intensive forms of farming, to use farming
practices compatible with the maintenance of the countryside, to set
aside land for at least 20 years to establish nature reserves and to
manage the land for public access and enjoyment.[87] By authorising the

---

[82] "The integration of environmental goals into the CAP and the development of the role
     farmers can and should play in terms of management of natural resources and land-
     scape conservation are another increasingly important objective for the CAP." Agenda
     2000, COM (97) 2000 vol. I at p. 27.

[83] See para. 2.2.8, above.

[84] At E.C. level, see the Court of Auditor's Special Report No. 14/2000 on *Greening the
     CAP* ([2000] OJ C 353/1). In Scotland, although the total spent on agri-environment
     schemes rose from £6.4 million in 1996 to £21.2 million in 1999, payments through
     other schemes totalled over £450 million; see *Agricultural Facts and Figures 2000*
     (SERAD, 2000).

[85] *e.g.* the provisions that led to the creation of Environmentally Sensitive Areas; see
     para. 5.9.1, above.

[86] Regulation 2078/92.

[87] *ibid.*, art. 2.

use of state funds in these ways, the agri-environment programme enabled Member States to develop their own schemes to support environmentally beneficial activities.[88] Assessments of the programme have, however, suggested that it has had limited impact in changing the nature of farming across Europe. It has provided some incentives for the maintenance of extensive (*i.e.* non-intensive) farming practices, but the environmental potential of set-aside has not been realised, overgrazing has not been tackled and incentives remain for environmentally damaging crop production; "with the 1992 reform, the Community may have succeeded in 'greening' its CAP but not necessarily agriculture".[89]

The second stage has come as part of the Agenda 2000 programme, which as well as addressing the challenges of possible enlargement of the Community has endeavoured to respond to the higher priority for environmental considerations embedded into the Treaty provisions by the Amsterdam Treaty.[90] This has led to a greater integration of environmental issues into new agricultural measures, and to a closer link between agricultural and rural development policy, recognising what has been referred to as the "multifunctionality of agriculture", *i.e.* the many roles of the farming community over and above the production of food, encompassing its wider contribution to the overall social, environmental and economic health and sustainability of rural areas. A key development has been the insistence on basic environmental standards as a mandatory condition of receiving grant aid, with penalties, including cancellation of any grants, where the basic standard is not observed, and with agri-environmental benefits being paid only in the case of commitments beyond usual good practice.[91]

8.4.6

A further development has been what is known as "modulation",[92] the capacity of Member States to divert spending from agricultural subsidies for production in order to increase funding for agri-environment and rural development initiatives. States are permitted to modulate up to 20 percent of their agricultural spending under the CAP, but must provide matching funds. The U.K. government is taking advantage of this scheme to transfer a portion of its CAP funding, initially 2.5 percent in 2001, rising to 4.5 percent in 2005, to other programmes, primarily those in the agri-environment area.[93] This is a further step in the

8.4.7

---

[88] N. Hawke and N. Kovaleva, *op. cit.* (1998), Chap. 5.

[89] Court of Auditor's Special Report No.14/2000 on *Greening the CAP* ([2000] OJ C 353/1), para. 91.

[90] E.C. Treaty, art. 6; see para. 2.9.3, above.

[91] *e.g.* Regulation (EC) 1259/1999, art. 3; Regulation (EC) 1257/1999, art. 23.

[92] "We are appalled by the term 'modulation' but unfortunately, for the purposes of this report, we are unable to find a way around using it"; House of Commons Environment, Transport and Regional Affairs Committee, *Rural White Paper*, 7th report of 1999–2000 (1999–2000 HC 32), para. 50.

[93] *ibid.*, paras 50–52; also the Committee's 20th report of 1999–2000, *U.K. Biodiversity* (1999–2000 HC 441), paras 74–75; see, *e.g.*, the Common Agricultural Policy Support Schemes (Modulation) (Scotland) Regulations 2000, (S.S.I. 2000 No. 429).

direction of a more environmentally-aware agricultural policy, but the vast majority of agricultural support will continue to be directed through schemes based on production.[94]

8.4.8　　It is not just the grand thrust of Community policy that is important, but also the precise terms. The reshaping of the details of support schemes can remove incentives to environmentally damaging practices, *e.g.* by converting the support for hill farmers from schemes based on the number of livestock to those based on the area farmed, a key incentive for overstocking and thus harmful overgrazing of the land is being removed.[95] Similarly, care must be taken that what appear to be simple administrative rules do not inadvertently stand in the way of beneficial practices, as shown by the negotiations over the rules on how areas of arable land are to be measured, which threatened to penalise significantly farmers who left wide field margins for their cultivated fields, despite the considerable benefits of this practice for wildlife of many kinds.[96]

8.4.9　　An early scheme recognising the relationship between agriculture and nature conservation is that for Environmentally Sensitive Areas.[97] Under a European Community Regulation that pre-dated the agri-environment programme,[98] Member States were permitted to develop their own schemes to assist farmers who undertake to farm environmentally important areas so as to preserve or improve the environment there. This was given effect here through the system of Environmentally Sensitive Areas introduced by section 18 of the Agriculture Act 1986. This scheme recognises the importance of traditional farming methods in preserving the habitat and landscape in many areas, and within the designated areas offers payments to farmers willing to continue such methods, in order to discourage them from changing to more intensive methods which might offer them a greater yield. The scheme has been considerably extended since the first group of designations was made, but is in part being overtaken by the more general schemes introduced subsequently.

8.4.10　　Other agricultural support schemes which give effect to the increasing role of environmental considerations are constantly changing, but in recent years there have been moves towards consolidation. There is

---

[94]　See note 84, above.

[95]　This is leading to the replacement of the Hill Livestock Compensatory Allowances with the Hill Farm Allowance Scheme.

[96]　House of Commons Environment, Transport and Regional Affairs Committee, *U.K. Biodiversity*, 20th report of 1999–2000 (1999–2000 HC 441), para. 83.

[97]　See section 5.9, above.

[98]　Regulation 797/85, art. 19.

now one main scheme in each part of Great Britain: the Rural Stewardship Scheme in Scotland, the Countryside Stewardship Scheme in England and the Land in Care Scheme (Tir Gofal) in Wales.[99] The Scottish Regulations, for example, lay down certain general environmental conditions for grant support (*e.g.* the preservation of the conservation interest of rough grazing and machair by not undertaking drainage, seeding, fertilising or other cultivation), then specifies a number of management activities (*e.g.* management of grassland for birds) and capital projects (*e.g.* creation or restoration of ponds). The scheme thus operates both by disqualifying those who undertake harmful activities and rewarding a wide range of activities which produce benefits for biodiversity, landscape and amenity rather than furthering agricultural production.

The agricultural set-aside scheme that was so prominent in the 1990s **8.4.11** also incorporates environmental concerns to some extent.[1] Although the primary aim is a reduction in the quantity of crops being produced, the details of the scheme have been shaped with some regard for conservation. Thus within the scheme there are specific management options for the land that are expressly directed at conservation targets, *e.g.* wild bird cover, whilst the general conditions insist that the land be managed in a way that preserves features of conservation value, such as hedges, trees, ponds and streams.[2] Likewise, the Farm Woodland Premium Scheme takes into account the environmental benefits of woodland, not merely its commercial potential.[3]

Particular aspects of agricultural activity which might have implica- **8.4.12** tions for nature conservation are also regulated. Some regulatory schemes allow action to be taken which might be prejudicial to the wild flora and fauna, but often limitations are imposed which should reduce the harm resulting. There are detailed legal schemes on animal and plant health which include powers to destroy diseased or suspect animals and plants, including those in the wild.[4] A range of pest control measures allows action to be taken against particular species, primarily rodents, but at the same time places restrictions on the use of indiscriminate measures.[5] The use of pesticides is controlled by Part III of the Food and Environment Protection Act 1985 and associated regulations. Under these provisions pesticides must gain ministerial approval before

---

[99] Rural Stewardship Scheme (Scotland) Regulations 2001, (S.S.I. 2001 No. 300); Countryside Stewardship Regulations 2000, (S.I. 2000 No. 3048); Land in Care Scheme (Tir Gofal) Regulations 1999, (S.I. 1999 No. 1176).

[1] N. Hawke and N. Kovaleva, Chap. 4.

[2] Arable Area Payment Regulations 1996, (S.I. 1996 No. 3142).

[3] See para. 6.4.16, above.

[4] Animal Health Act, 1981, see para. 4.5.11, above; Plant Health Act 1967, see paras 6.2.12–6.2.14, above.

[5] See section 4.5, above.

they can be advertised, sold or used, and the conditions in any approval will include a duty to take all reasonable precautions to safeguard the environment.[6]

8.4.13 Fire has long been used as an agricultural tool, but can be particularly destructive to natural habitats. Legal controls affect both muirburn and the burning of crop residues. As far as muirburn is concerned in Scotland, the basic rule is that it is an offence to make muirburn except before April 16 or after September 30 in any year, although for the proprietor of land (or tenant with the proprietor's approval) the permitted period is extended to April 30, or May 15 for land over 450 metres. A direction from the Minister can extend the generally permitted period until a specified date not later than May 1, or May 16 in the case of land over 450 metres.[7] It is an offence to make muirburn between one hour after sunset and one hour before sunrise, and in all cases the person responsible must notify neighbours and provide sufficient staff and equipment to control the burning operations so as to prevent damage to woodlands and all neighbouring land and property.[8] Making muirburn without due care so as to cause damage to adjoining lands is a criminal offence[9] as well as giving rise to civil liability.[10]

8.4.14 In England and Wales the burning of heather, bracken, grass and vaccinium is controlled by regulations made by the Minister.[11] These prohibit burning between March 31 and November 1, or between April 15 and October 1 in upland areas,[12] although a special licence from the Secretary of State can authorise burning at other times.[13] No burning is allowed between sunset and sunrise, neighbours must be notified, sufficient staff and equipment must be provided to control the fires and all reasonable precautions must be taken to prevent injury or damage to adjoining property.[14] The prohibitions do not apply to pleasure grounds, private gardens and allotments,[15] and special rules apply for railway land.

8.4.15 The burning of crop residues is now also subject to strict legal con-

---

[6] See para. 4.4.2, above.

[7] Hill Farming Act 1946, s.23 (amended by Agriculture (Adaptation of Enactments) (Scotland) Regulations 1977, (S.I. 1977 No. 2007)); WCA 1981, s.72).

[8] *ibid.*, s.25.

[9] *ibid.*, ss.25, 27.

[10] *Mackintosh v. Mackintosh* (1864) 2 M. 1357; *Lord Advocate v. Rodger*, 1978 S.L.T. (Sh.Ct) 31.

[11] Heather and Grass, Etc. (Burning) Regulations 1986, (S.I. 1986 No. 428) (amended by Heather and Grass, Etc. (Burning) (Amendment) Regulations 1987, (S.I. 1987 No. 1208)), made under the Hill Farming Act 1946, s.20 (amended by Hill Farming (Amendment) Act 1985).

[12] As defined on maps kept for this purpose; *ibid.*, reg. 2(1).

[13] *ibid.*, reg. 6; the provisions governing licences are in reg. 7.

[14] *ibid.*, reg. 5.

[15] *ibid.*, reg. 3.

trol, as much to prevent nuisance, air pollution and the dangers from smoke obstructing visibility on roads, as to avoid the dangers of fires getting out of control. The Minister has the power to make regulations to prohibit or restrict the burning of crop residues on agricultural land by persons engaged in agriculture,[16] but so far this power has only been exercised in relation to England and Wales.

Under the Crop Residues (Burning) Regulations 1993[17] it is an offence to burn on agricultural land any of the specified crop residues[18] except for the purposes of education or research, or for disease control under statutory notices.[19] Where burning of these residues is permitted, or where linseed residues are burnt, very detailed requirements must be complied with. These extend to such matters as the times and dates of burning (not at weekends or on bank holidays), the precautions to prevent fire or smoke affecting buildings, trees, hedges, nature reserves, ancient monuments, roads and railway lines, the notice to be given to various authorities, and the fire-fighting equipment and personnel to be available, as well as imposing an obligation to incorporate the ash into the soil within 24 hours.[20] Burning is permitted for the disposal of straw stack remains or broken bales. **8.4.16**

Special measures have also been taken to prevent water pollution arising from agricultural activities, particularly in an attempt to control the build-up of nitrates in lochs, rivers and groundwater. As well as its potential to harm human health, the presence of nitrates in water can radically affect the fauna and especially the flora which it supports. The eutrophication of water previously low in nutrients destroys the habitat of many species which have evolved to take advantage of poor conditions and can lead to huge "blooms" of algae, which can stifle all other life in the water and can in themselves be poisonous to animals and man. This phenomenon is largely attributable to years of intensive cultivation, as both inorganic fertilisers and natural processes working on the much increased volumes of vegetable matter have led to nitrates entering and accumulating in the water system. Any measures taken now can at most prevent the accelerated deterioration of the situation; there are decades of accumulated damage to be dealt with, and the slow leaching of nitrates currently in the soil will continue to affect the water system for years to come. **8.4.17**

Action against nitrate pollution has been led by developments within the European Community. The Directive on protecting waters against **8.4.18**

---

[16] EPA 1990, s.152.
[17] S.I. 1993 No. 1366.
[18] Cereal straw or stubble, and residues of oil-seed rape or of field beans or peas harvested dry; *ibid.*, Sched. 1.
[19] Plant Health (Great Britain) Order 1993, (S.I. 1993 No. 1320), art. 22.
[20] Crop Residues (Burning) Regulations 1993, Sched. 2.

pollution caused by nitrates from agricultural sources[21] requires Member States to identify waters which contain more than 50 mg/l of nitrates, fall foul of the limits set in Community legislation on drinking water,[22] are found to be subject to eutrophication, or may fall into any of these categories if steps are not taken. The areas draining into such waters are to be designated as vulnerable zones, and within these action programmes are to be implemented in the endeavour to reduce water pollution caused or induced by nitrates from agricultural sources and to prevent further such pollution. These programmes, and supporting voluntary codes of practice, deal with issues such as the periods during which the application of fertilisers[23] is inappropriate, the methods of application, the ground conditions in which application is inappropriate (*e.g.* saturated or frozen ground, steeply sloping ground), and the storage of livestock manure to prevent run-off. Other matters such as crop rotation, the maintenance of vegetation cover on the soil, the prevention of run-off and individual fertiliser limits for farms may also be included.

8.4.19　　British farmers challenged the validity and implementation of the Directive on the grounds that it was wrong for nitrate vulnerable zones to be declared where agriculture was not the only source of the nitrates and that the action programmes by imposing restrictions on farmers alone, even though there might be other sources of nitrates, constituted a disproportionate response to the problem and offended against the principles of polluter pays and rectifying pollution at source,[24] as well as infringing the farmers' rights to deal with their own property as they wished. This challenge was rejected by the European Court of Justice on both grounds; the Directive did not require agriculture sources to be the sole source of nitrate pollution, provided that they made a significant contribution to the pollution, whilst the Directive's provisions were sufficiently flexible to allow Member States to avoid offending against any of the general principles relied on by the farmers.[25]

8.4.20　　The implementation of this Directive in Great Britain has not been straightforward, and the United Kingdom has been held to be in breach of its duty to implement it, as a result of the initial failure to take any action in Northern Ireland and of assessing only waters from which drinking water is extracted when identifying the waters at risk of nitrate

---

[21] Directive 91/676.

[22] Established under Directive 75/440 (as amended).

[23] All forms of fertiliser containing nitrogen compounds are included, including animal manure and sewage sludge.

[24] These principles are embedded in the environmental provisions of the E.C. Treaty, now at art. 174.

[25] *R. v. Secretary of State for the Environment, ex p. Standley* (C–293/97) [1999] E.C.R. I–2603, [1999] Q.B. 1279.

pollution.[26] The position has still not been fully rectified and the European Commission has notified its intention of taking further action against the United Kingdom in relation to its continuing non-compliance.[27] Consultation papers issued in late 2001 and early 2002 propose the designation as Nitrate Vulnerable Zones of at least 80 percent of England and in Scotland virtually all of the arable land on the east coast and Nithsdale.[28]

Initially the approach in Britain was based on Nitrate Sensitive **8.4.21** Areas, where although there was the potential for stronger measures, the emphasis was on voluntary agreements under which farmers accepted obligations in respect to the management of their land designed to prevent pollution by nitrates in exchange for payments.[29] Now implementation rests on the stronger provisions for Nitrate Vulnerable Zones. In such Zones, the action programme imposes (without compensation) mandatory restrictions on agricultural activity in order to prevent the accumulation of nitrates.[30] These deal with the quantity, timing and method of applying nitrogen, chemical and organic fertilisers (including manure and slurry), and the treatment of unharvested residues of certain crops, as well as specifying the data to be kept for monitoring purposes. Failure to observe the requirements of the programme is a criminal offence, although an enforcement notice may be served as the initial step when failure to comply is detected. Some grants may still be available, *e.g.* towards facilities for storing or treating manure, slurry and silage effluent.[31]

Further measures include the Control of Pollution (Silage, Slurry and **8.4.22** Agricultural Fuel Oil) (Scotland) Regulations 2001[32] and their equiva-

---

[26] *Commission v. United Kingdom* (C-69/99) [2000] E.C.R. I-10979.

[27] Press Release IP/01/1528 of October 30, 2001.

[28] *How Should England Implement the 1991 Nitrates Directive?* (DEFRA, 2001); *Protection of Scotland's Water Environment* (SERAD, 2002). Designation is also proposed for a much smaller area of Wales; *The Protection of Waters against Agricultural Nitrate Pollution in Wales* (Welsh Ass., 2002).

[29] Control of Pollution Act 1974, ss.31B–31D (added by Water Act 1989, Sched. 23); Water Resources Act 1991, ss.94–96; Nitrate Sensitive Areas (Designation) Order 1990, (S.I. 1990 No. 1013); Nitrate Sensitive Areas Regulations 1994, (S.I. 1994 No. 1729); Hawke and Kowaleva, *op. cit.*, pp.170–174.

[30] Protection of Water against Agricultural Nitrate Pollution (England and Wales) Regulations 1996 (S.I. 1996 No.888); Action Programme for Nitrate Vulnerable Zones (England and Wales) Regulations 1998 (S.I. 1998 No. 1202); Protection of Water against Agricultural Nitrate Pollution (Scotland) Regulations 1996, (S.I. 1996 No.1564); Action Programme for Nitrate Vulnerable Zones (Scotland) Regulations 1998 (S.I. 1998 No. 2927); Designation of Nitrate Vulnerable Zones (Scotland) Regulations 2000 (S.S.I. 2000, No. 26).

[31] Farm Waste Grant (Nitrate Vulnerable Zones) (England) (No. 2) Scheme 2000 (S.I. 2000 No. 2911).

[32] S.S.I. 2001 No. 206.

lent for England and Wales.[33] These contain requirements on the construction and siting of tanks for the making of silage and the storage of silage, slurry and oil in order to prevent water pollution, including the leaching of nitrates into the soil. The requirements apply to facilities built or significantly modified after March 1991, but the environment agencies can serve a notice requiring work to be carried out on older structures where there is a significant risk of pollution. There is also provision for Codes of Practice to be issued giving practical advice and promoting good practice with a view to preventing or minimising water pollution arising from agricultural activities.[34] A breach of such codes does not give rise to any civil or criminal liability but is a factor to be taken into account when the environment agencies consider whether to exercise their other powers.

8.4.23   A final point to note in relation to agriculture is the potential significance of the law on land tenure in restricting the extent to which the occupier of agricultural land can give priority to nature conservation. Much of the countryside is held under the terms of agricultural tenancies, which impose obligations on the tenant to farm the land in an efficient manner. The rights of the landowner to trees,[35] minerals, game and other aspects of the land may also affect the ability or willingness of tenants to manage their land in particular ways. Notice to quit can be served on tenants who are failing to farm the land in accordance with the rules of good husbandry.[36] A landlord can apply to the Land Court (Scotland) or the Agricultural Land Tribunal (England and Wales) for a certificate to this effect,[37] and once this has been granted a notice to quit on that basis is not subject to further scrutiny.[38] Similarly one of the statutory conditions applied to crofts is that the crofter shall cultivate the croft.[39]

8.4.24   The rules of good husbandry require that the tenant maintains a reas-

---

[33] Control of Pollution (Silage, Slurry and Agricultural Fuel Oil) Regulations 1991 (S.I. 1991 No. 324) (as amended by the Control of Pollution (Silage, Slurry and Agricultural Fuel Oil) (Amendment) Regulations 1996 and 1997 (S.I.s 1996 No. 2044 and 1997 No. 547).

[34] Control of Pollution Act 1974, s.51 (substituted by Water Act 1989, Sched. 23, para. 5); Water Resources Act 1991, s.97. Codes have been approved by the Water (Prevention of Pollution) (Code of Practice) (Scotland) Order 1997 (S.I. 1997 No. 1584), and the Water (Prevention of Pollution) (Code of Practice) Order 1998 (S.I. 1998 No. 3084).

[35] For example, special legislation was necessary to enable crofters to use common grazings for forestry purposes; Crofter Forestry (Scotland) Act 1991 (see now Crofters (Scotland) Act 1993, s.50).

[36] See below.

[37] Agricultural Holdings (Scotland) Act 1991, s.26; Agricultural Holdings Act 1986, Sched. 3, Pt I Case C, Pt II, para. 9.

[38] *ibid.*, s.22; *ibid.*, s.26.

[39] Crofters (Scotland) Act 1993, s.5, Sched. 2, paras 3, 13.

onable standard of efficient production, and in Scotland specify such matters as the proper stocking of livestock units, regular muirburn on hill farms, and systematic control of vermin, bracken, whins, broom and injurious weeds.[40] However, practices adopted as the result of obligations arising from the designation of a Nitrate Sensitive Area may be disregarded.[41] The English rules are similar,[42] but it is stated that any practice adopted in pursuance of any term of the tenancy or other agreement between tenant and landlord which has as its objective the conservation of flora, fauna or geological or physiographical features, or the protection of buildings or sites of archaeological, architectural or historic interest, or the conservation and enhancement of the natural beauty and amenity of the countryside, should be disregarded.[43] However, such qualifications give no protection to an agricultural tenant who at his own initiative takes measures which may benefit nature conservation but which do not result in efficient agricultural production.[44] Moreover it has been held that the Land Court has no discretion to refuse a certificate of bad husbandry once it has concluded that the rules are being broken, regardless of mitigating circumstances.[45] The extent to which occupiers may dedicate their land to nature conservation may thus be restricted by their status as agricultural tenants.[46]

CONTROL OF POLLUTION

The environment is now protected by a large number of measures designed to prevent or restrict pollution. Most of these have been introduced with a view to human health and comfort, but obviously they will also serve to benefit wild flora and fauna. Such measures are found

8.5.1

---

[40] Agriculture (Scotland) Act 1948, Sched. 6 (applied by Agricultural Holdings (Scotland) Act 1991, s.85(2)).

[41] Agricultural Holdings (Scotland) Act 1991, s.26(2).

[42] Agriculture Act 1947, s.11 (applied by Agricultural Holdings Act 1986, s.96(3)).

[43] Agricultural Holdings Act 1986, Sched. 3, Pt II, para. 9(2) (amended by Water Consolidation (Consequential Provisions) Act 1991, Sched. 1, para. 43).

[44] In Scotland it is proposed that the law be changed to permit tenants to undertake conservation activities in compliance with official agri-environment or conservation schemes, but with landlords having a right to object where their interests would be materially prejudiced; *Agricultural Holdings: Proposals for Legislation* (Scottish Executive, 2000), paras 3.7–3.8.

[45] *Cambusmore Estate Trustees v. Little*, 1991 S.L.T. (Land Ct.) 33.

[46] See M. Cardwell, "Set-aside Schemes and Alternative Land Uses: Some Problems for the Tenant Farmer" [1992] Conv. 180. See also *Williams v. Schellenberg*, 1988 G.W.D. 29–1254 where one *pro indiviso* owner of land argued that her interest had been damaged by the proprietor in occupation encouraging the designation of the land as an SSSI, thereby restricting its management and reducing its value.

in European legislation, Acts of Parliament and detailed statutory regulations and operate in a number of ways, imposing emission controls, setting quality standards for air and water, and providing product standards so that only goods meeting certain anti-pollution requirements can enter the market. The volume of legislation involved is daunting.[47]

8.5.2   With a steady flow of new legislation, as well as the gradual coming into force of provisions once they have been made, any attempt here to sketch even the outline of the law on pollution would not only be hopelessly inadequate, but is likely to be either out of date or premature. The extension of more thorough pollution controls to some food-processing and intensive agricultural activities[48] demonstrates the increasing reach of the anti-pollution legislation, well beyond the stereotype of a dirty factory belching out dark fumes and foaming effluent. Increasingly, though, there is concern that as the problems caused by major "point-source" pollution come under control, the overall health of the environment is at greater risk from diffuse pollution, the cumulative effects of the many small-scale emissions which inevitably fall below the threshold for significant direct regulation.[49]

8.5.3   What is worthy of note, though, is the extent to which the broader environment, including the health of flora and fauna, is now included in the aims of the anti-pollution measures. The general duties of the Environment Agency and the Scottish Environment Protection Agency include duties to have regard to the conservation of the natural heritage[50] and to promote the conservation of flora and fauna dependent on an aquatic environment.[51] The Pollution Prevention and Control Act 1999 authorises measures designed to prevent environmental pollution that may give rise to any harm, and such terms are defined in a way which protects other species in addition to man; "harm" includes "impairment of, or interference with, the ecological systems of which any living organisms form part".[52] Similar broad definitions are used in other areas, *e.g.* the provisions on waste management define "harm" as including "harm to the health of living organisms or other interfer-

---

[47] For general surveys see: S. Bell and D. McGillivray, *Environmental Law* (5th ed.) (2000), C. Reid (ed.) *Environmental Law in Scotland* (2nd ed.) (1997); the sheer bulk of the multi-volume loose-leaf encyclopaedias on the topic demonstrate the amount of legislation and official guidance in this area: *Encyclopaedia of Environmental Law* (1993–), *Garner's Environmental Law* (1992–).

[48] Pollution Prevention and Control (England and Wales) Regulations 2000 (S.I. 2000 No.1973); Pollution Prevention and Control (Scotland) Regulations 2000 (S.S.I. 2000 No.323), both made under the Pollution Prevention and Control Act 1999 to implement Directive 96/61/EC.

[49] *e.g.*, SEPA, *Improving Scotland's Water Environment* (1999), p. 54.

[50] EPA 1990 ss.7, 32.

[51] EPA 1990 ss.6, 34.

[52] Pollution Prevention and Control Act 1999, s.1(3).

ence with the ecological systems of which they form part",[53] whilst specific powers can be exercised in the interests of wildlife, *e.g.* one of the grounds on which the Minister can direct the revocation or modification of a consent to discharge into waters is for "the protection of ... flora and fauna dependent on an aquatic environment".[54] Designated sites are also given recognition by means of additional consultation requirements when they may be affected, both as a general obligation[55] and as a specific part of particular procedures, *e.g.* in relation to waste management proposals.[56] The powers to control pollution are therefore to be exercised for the benefit of plants and animals as well as man.

WATER RESOURCES

Many communities and species of plants and animals depend directly on an aquatic environment, from otters and kingfishers to the less appreciated midges whose larval stages are aquatic. Moreover the maintenance of the underlying water table at particular levels is crucial to the existence of many kinds of habitat, including water meadows, marshes and fens. The conservation of water resources is thus of great significance. Threats to a healthy aquatic environment come from drainage, pollution and the over-use of water taken from rivers, lochs and underground strata. All of these are to some extent regulated by law.   **8.6.1**

The law in this field is complex. To a background mixture of common law and statute, balancing the rights of landowners to do as they wish on their land both with the protection of the rights of neighbours and of downstream owners and with the public interest, in preventing abuses of water resources and in ensuring that individual landowners cannot prevent or hinder schemes which offer a wider benefit,[57] there has been added a flood of domestic and E.C. legislation limiting discharges and setting quality standards for waters used for different purposes.[58] Statutory controls exist over discharges into water[59]   **8.6.2**

---

[53] EPA 1990, s.29(5).
[54] Control of Pollution Act 1974, s.37(2) (substituted by the Water Act 1989, Sched. 23); Water Resources Act 1991, Sched.10 para. 7(4).
[55] EPA 1990, ss.8, 35.
[56] EPA 1990, s.36(7).
[57] See generally, F. Lyall, "Water and Water Rights" in *The Laws of Scotland: Stair Memorial Encyclopaedia*, vol.25 (1989); W. Howarth, *Wisdom's Law of Watercourses* (5th ed.) (1992); W. Howarth, *Legal Aspects of Flooding and Land Drainage* (2002).
[58] The 1200 pages of W. Howarth and D. McGillivray, *Water Pollution and Water Quality Law* (2001) themselves testify to the volume and complexity of the law here.
[59] Control of Pollution Act 1974, Part II (much amended by Water Act 1989, Sched.23); Water Resources Act 1991, Part III.

(including dumping at sea),[60] land drainage,[61] and the abstraction of water,[62] with further powers in relation to flood control[63] and drought.[64] A range of public authorities is involved in its administration.[65] The detailed working of these arrangements can obviously have a major impact on water quality and thus on conservation.

8.6.3   In England and Wales, one feature of the structural reforms and statutory consolidation that took place during the 1980s and 1990s has been the inclusion in the relevant statutory provisions of express duties on the various authorities to have regard to and to further the interests of nature conservation. Thus the Environment Agency, is under a general duty, so far as it considers desirable, to promote the conservation of flora and fauna which are dependent on an aquatic environment,[66] in addition to the general duty on the Agency and Ministers to further the conservation of flora and fauna.[67] There is also provision for the preparation of Codes of Practice giving practical guidance and promoting good practice on such matters.[68] Similar obligations are present in the other legislation, applying to Ministers, water and sewerage undertakers and regulators.[69]

8.6.4   In Scotland, the restructuring of the water industry during the 1990s also gave the opportunity for a recasting of the environmental obligations of the various authorities. The Ministers and the water and sewerage authorities are under an obligation to further the conservation of flora, fauna and geological and physiographical features of special interest, so far as is consistent with their other functions,[70] and designated sites are subject to additional consultation requirements.[71] The law, however, remains more fragmented than in England and Wales

---

[60] Food and Environment Protection Act 1985, Part II.

[61] Land Drainage (Scotland) Acts 1930, 1941 and 1958; Land Drainage Acts 1976, 1991 and 1994.

[62] Water (Scotland) Act 1980, Natural Heritage (Scotland) Act 1991, Part II; Water Resources Act 1991, Part II, Chap. II.

[63] Flood Prevention (Scotland) Act 1961; Water Resources Act 1991, Part IV.

[64] Natural Heritage (Scotland) Act 1991, Part III; Water Resources Act 1991, Part II, Chap. III.

[65] See paras 2.7.21–2.7.23, above.

[66] EA 1995, s.6.

[67] *ibid.*, s.7.

[68] Water Industry Act 1991, s.5; EA 1995, s.9; Water and Sewerage (Conservation, Access and Recreation) (Code of Practice) Order 2000 (S.I. 2000 No. 477).

[69] *e.g.* Water Industry Act 1991, s.3; Land Drainage Act 1991, ss.61A–61C (added by the Land Drainage Act 1994, s.1); Food and Environment Protection Act 1985, s.8; see paras 2.2.10, 2.7.19, above.

[70] Water (Scotland) Act 1980, s.1 (as substituted by the Local Government etc. (Scotland) Act 1994, s.65).

[71] Local Government etc. (Scotland) Act 1994, s.73. See Addendum, above.

and in some areas lacks the explicit environmental duties imposed there in recent years.[72]

The law in this area will have to be significantly recast over the coming years in order to implement the E.C. Water Framework Directive.[73] This requires water resources (surface water, groundwater and coastal waters) to be managed on the basis of river basin districts,[74] with controls on point source and diffuse pollution, abstraction, impoundment and engineering works such as land drainage and flood and coastal protection that affect the water systems.[75] The aim of these measures is to meet the environmental objectives, or quality targets, established for each body of water under the management plan for each river basin district,[76] and significantly these objectives are based primarily on ecological criteria.[77] Nature conservation issues will inevitably play a significant part as the plans to implement these measures are refined.

8.6.5

GENETICALLY MODIFIED ORGANISMS

A new threat to the conservation of flora and fauna is posed by the creation of genetically modified organisms. For thousands of years man has been involved in genetic manipulation through the selective breeding of crops and domesticated animals, but now much more rapid and much more far-reaching changes to plants and animals are possible. The long-term effects of such modified organisms being released and coming into contact with wild plants and animals are largely unknown. Many interactions with wildlife and domesticated plants and animals are possible—as competitors, as predators or grazers, as food-plants or prey that alter nutritional intake or introduce toxins, or as breeding partners that spread new genes and create new hybrids. The experience of releases of natural but geographically alien species such as mink or Japanese knotweed has shown the damage which can be caused. Moreover, there is concern about indirect effects arising from changes in agricultural practices that might follow the introduction of genetically modified crops. In the late 1990s this issue became one of great public controversy in Britain, initially in relation to the presence of genetic-

8.7.1

---

[72] *e.g.*, there is no direct equivalent in the Scottish land drainage legislation of the obligations added south of the border by the Land Drainage Act 1994.

[73] Directive 2000/60/EC; the necessary legal and administrative measures for implementation should be in place by December 22, 2003.

[74] *ibid.*, art. 3.

[75] *ibid.*, art. 11.

[76] *ibid.*, art. 4.

[77] *ibid.*, Annex V.

ally-modified ingredients in food and then focused on the programme
of field-scale trials of genetically modified crops. Attention has therefore been drawn to the legal measures controlling the circumstances
and conditions under which genetically modified organisms can be
released into the environment. This has led to developments at
domestic, European and international levels, including the Cartagena
Protocol on Biosafety, agreed in January 2000.[78]

8.7.2   In Great Britain the issue is governed by Part VI of the Environmental Protection Act 1990 and detailed Regulations that implement
European Community measures on the topic.[79] The Act gives a broad
definition of "genetically modified organisms", allowing the term to
cover all forms of genetic manipulation other than those involving
merely assistance to naturally occurring reproductive processes, *e.g.*
selective breeding,[80] and more precise and technical definitions are provided in the Regulations. Broad definitions are also given to phrases
such as "damage to the environment" and "harm", which ensure that
effects on flora and fauna are to be fully considered, and organisms are
"released" or "escape" when they are no longer subject to physical,
chemical or biological barriers for ensuring that the organisms do not
enter the environment or do not produce descendants which are not
contained, or for ensuring that they or their descendants are harmless.[81]
Field-trials of genetically modified crops therefore count as a release to
the environment.

8.7.3   Under the Act, risk assessments are required from anyone intending
to import, acquire, release or market genetically modified organisms,
and notification to the Minister may be required.[82] If there is a risk of
damage to the environment despite the precautions which are to be
taken, the organism should not be imported, kept, etc., and at all times
the best available techniques not entailing excessive costs should be
used to prevent damage to the environment.[83] The Minister can prohibit
any dealings with organisms[84] or require that consents be obtained
before organisms are imported, kept, released, etc., the conditions of
such consents including continuing obligations on the person authorised
to keep informed of any risks involved and to inform the Minister if

---

[78] This agreement, a protocol to the Convention on Biological Diversity has been signed
   by over 100 states, including the U.K., and by the European Community, but has not
   yet been ratified by sufficient parties to enter into force; see www.biodiv.org/biosafety.
[79] Changes in the Regulations are imminent to implement new E.C. measures; see para.
   8.7.6, below.
[80] EPA 1990, s.106 (4),(5).
[81] *ibid.*, s.107.
[82] *ibid.*, s.108.
[83] *ibid.*, s.109.
[84] *ibid.*, s.110.

the risks appear more serious than at the time the consent was given.[85] As usual, there are a number of powers granted to assist the enforcement of these controls, and the Minister has the power to act immediately in the case of imminent danger to the environment in order to render any genetically modified organism harmless.[86] In all cases there are registers of notifications, applications and consents, so that the public can be informed of the nature of the organisms and where they are being released.

The detailed Regulations[87] on the deliberate release to the environ- **8.7.4** ment of genetically modified organisms follow the terms of E.C. legislation,[88] and are due to be revised to implement the new E.C. measures agreed during 2001.[89] The Regulations distinguish between consent to put products on the market and other forms of release, *e.g.* for research and development. In the latter case ("Part B consents"), applicants must provide a dossier of information in response to the long list of issues to be addressed as part of the risk assessment; the list for higher plants[90] contains 41 items, that for other organisms 90. These include details of the organism, its origins and any selective advantages or disadvantages arising from the modification, of the location where it is to be released, of other organisms at the site with which it might interact in any way and of precautions to keep the test organism separated from others. Where the organism is not a higher plant, the longer list includes measures to protect the site from intrusion by unauthorised individuals. Applications are placed on the public register, a range of statutory authorities is consulted and all applications are carefully examined by the United Kingdom Advisory Committee on Releases to the Environment (ACRE), which advises the Minister taking the decision. Consents include monitoring requirements both during and after the experimental period.

In the case of applications to market genetically modified products **8.7.5** ("Part C consents"), *e.g.* to sell modified seed, consent must be given at E.C. level, involving consultation with all Member States. Decision-making lies initially in the hands of the state that receives the application for consent, but there are provisions for referral to the Commission

---

[85] EPA 1990, s.112.

[86] *ibid.*, s.117.

[87] Genetically Modified Organisms (Deliberate Release) Regulations 1992 (S.I. 1992 No. 3280), as amended by the Genetically Modified Organisms (Deliberate Release) Regulations 1993 and 1995 (S.I.s 1993 No. 152 and 1995 No. 304), and the Genetically Modified Organisms (Deliberate Release and Risk Assessment Amendment) Regulations 1997 (S.I. 1997 No. 1900).

[88] Directive 90/220 amended by Dir. 94/15/EC and 97/35/EC and now repealed by Dir. 2001/18/EC.

[89] Directive 2001/18/EC; see para. 8.7.6, below.

[90] *Gymnospermae* and *Angiospermae*.

and ultimately the Council if some Member States object. Applications must be advertised, the statutory conservation bodies (and many other bodies) must be consulted and full information on the proposed release and its effects provided, much as for Part B consents.[91] Separate Regulations,[92] again following E.C. measures,[93] deal with the contained use of genetically modified organisms, including requirements to notify the Health and Safety Executive of the intention to use premises for this purpose and to carry out a risk assessment (submitted to the Executive) for each particular operation, while in some cases ministerial consent is required. Exposure of humans and the environment to genetically modified micro-organisms is to be reduced to the lowest level that is reasonably practicable and emergency plans for dealing with any escape may also be required.

8.7.6   The existing Regulations will have to change in response to the new Directive on genetically modified organisms that was adopted in March 2001 and is due to be implemented by October 17, 2002.[94] In addition to consolidating the changes already made since 1990, the revised Directive emphasises that action is to be taken in accordance with the precautionary principle and that "all appropriate measures are taken to avoid adverse effects on human health and the environment".[95] Public consultation becomes a mandatory feature of the E.C. regime and for higher plants the consequences of likely changes in management, including changes in agricultural practices, are added to the factors to be addressed in the risk assessment. Consents for release onto the market will be limited to 10 years' duration, and subject to monitoring and labelling requirements.

8.7.7   The legislation aims to ensure that genetically modified organisms are used only after a thorough assessment of the known risks involved, but it is the unknown risks that perhaps lie at the core of present debate. Should society permit the experiments that will enable these risks to be better understood, when those experiments themselves carry a risk of creating the very dangers which the regulatory system is designed to prevent? The precautionary principle suggests that in this area which is very much at the frontier of scientific knowledge and technology the law should ensure that there are adequate safeguards against the potential dangers arising from genetic modifications, even at the cost of hindering beneficial advances.

---

[91] Genetically Modified Organisms (Deliberate Release) Regulations 1992 and 1993 (S.I.s 1992 No. 3280, 1993 No. 152).
[92] Genetically Modified Organisms (Contained Use) Regulations 2000 (S.I. 2000 No. 2831).
[93] Directive 90/219, amended by Dir. 94/51/EC and 98/81/EC.
[94] Directive 2001/18/EC.
[95] *ibid.*, art. 4.

LIABILITY FOR WILDLIFE

The encouragement of wild plants and animals on a piece of land may cause problems if the result is an increase in what others regard as weeds and pests which then spread to neighbouring land. There are a number of statutory measures under which a landowner can be forced to take action to control "injurious weeds"[96] or pests[97] on his land, but there is also the question of whether the neighbour who claims that his property is being damaged is entitled to compensation. This issue is currently one of some difficulty as it is not wholly clear how far the law has moved from its once definite position that no compensation was available in such circumstances. In practice, anyone seeking compensation may also face difficulties in establishing that the defenders' land is indeed the source of the problem, that the problem has been worsened by their action, and that the level of damage caused by the weeds or pests is greater than could normally be expected.

8.8.1

A convenient starting point for both Scots and English law is *Giles v. Walker*,[98] where a farmer sought to sue his neighbour for the damage caused by thistles spreading from the latter's land after it had been cleared of trees and brought into cultivation. This claim was rejected by the court which asserted that there could be "no duty as between adjoining occupiers to cut the thistles, which are the natural growth of the soil."[99] This approach was followed in both jurisdictions in relation to rats in *Steam v. Prentice Bros. Ltd*,[1] pheasants in *Seligman v. Docker*,[2] and rabbits in *Marshall v. Moncrieffe*,[3] *Gordon v. Huntly Lodge Estates Co. Ltd*,[4] and *Forrest v. Irvine*.[5] In these cases though, the courts noted that the defender had not been taking any active or unusual steps to encourage the offending wildlife and left open the possibility of the position being different if such steps had been taken.[6] Unless the measures taken were specifically designed for the multi-

8.8.2

---

[96] See paras 6.2.8–6.2.10, above.
[97] See section 4.5, above.
[98] (1890) 24 Q.B.D. 656.
[99] *ibid.*, at p. 657, Lord Coleridge C.J.
[1] [1919] 1 K.B. 394.
[2] [1949] Ch. 53.
[3] (1912) 28 Sh. Ct. Rep. 343.
[4] (1940) 56 Sh. Ct. Rep. 112.
[5] (1953) 69 Sh. Ct. Rep. 203; also *McDonald v. British Railways Board* (unreported, Aberdeen Sheriff Court, November 5, 1986) and *Hall v. Dart Valley Light Railway plc* [1998] C.L.Y. 3933.
[6] In *Pole v. Peake, The Times*, July 22, 1998 it was held that the holder of sporting rights including the right to rear game was not liable to the owner of the land for damage caused by the pheasants introduced or reared in the reasonable exercise of those rights.

plication of the damaging species, it seems unlikely that nature conservation measures would fall into that category.

8.8.3   More recent developments in England and related jurisdictions have overturned this general rule that a landowner cannot be liable for the spread of naturally occurring items from his land. In an Australian case, *Goldman v. Hargrave*[7] the Privy Council imposed liability for the spread of a naturally occurring fire, while the New Zealand courts have allowed compensation for the harm caused by the spread of thistles to grazing land.[8] Finally, *Giles v. Walker* was formally overruled[9] by the English courts in *Leakey v. National Trust for Places of Historic Interest and Scenic Beauty*,[10] where it was held that a landowner was liable for the fall of earth due to natural causes from a steep bank overlooking another's house.

8.8.4   It follows that in these jurisdictions the law may allow compensation for harm caused by the spread of naturally occurring things from one piece of land to another. However, liability does not rest on the fact of harm alone. Strict liability exists under the rule in *Rylands v. Fletcher*[11] only in cases of non-natural use of the land (which appears to rule out liability arising as a result of all but the most eccentric nature conservation measures), so that in the absence of deliberate harm, one is left with a claim based directly on negligence or on the arguments in *Leakey*.[12] There, although the claim was held to be appropriately framed in nuisance,[13] liability rested on a failure of the landowner to take such steps as were reasonable to prevent or minimise the risk of harm which the landowner knew or ought to have known would be caused to his neighbour. Therefore, whether the claim is framed in nuisance or negligence, there must be shown some failure to take reasonable care on the part of the landowner from whose land the danger has spread.

8.8.5   In *Goldman v. Hargrave*[14] and *Leakey*[15] the harm was caused by a one-off occurrence against which specific preventive action might have been taken, but assessing whether reasonable steps have been taken will be much harder where the injury is in the form of more diffuse harm, such as that caused by weeds or rabbits or other pests. In *French*

---

[7] [1967] 1 A.C. 645.
[8] *French v. Auckland City Corporation* [1974] 1 N.Z.L.R. 340.
[9] The fact that *Giles v. Walker* has been overruled did not stop it being relied on in *Hall v. Dart Valley Light Railway plc* [1998] C.L.Y. 3933, but the outcome there can be supported by other authorities.
[10] [1980] Q.B. 485.
[11] (1868) L.R. 3 H.L. 330.
[12] [1980] Q.B. 485.
[13] Megaw L.J., *ibid.*, at p. 514; *cf.* McMullin J. in *French v. Auckland City Corporation* [1974] 1 N.Z.L.R. 340 at p. 350.
[14] [1967] 1 A.C. 645.
[15] [1980] Q.B. 485.

v. Auckland City Corporation,[16] where liability was imposed for damage caused by thistles growing from seed blown from neighbouring land, the court emphasised that everything depended on the surrounding circumstances, such as the extent of the spread of weeds, the damage likely to ensue, the cost and practicality of preventing the spread and the location of the properties. It was suggested in *French* and in *Goldman* that the individual circumstances of the parties may be relevant in assessing this, *i.e.* a poor defendant may not be required to do what might be expected of a rich one, and the duty may in some circumstances be satisfied simply by the defendant enabling the claimant to enter the land to take remedial steps as he thinks fit. It may therefore be difficult to predict whether liability will exist in any particular case, but it is clear that the courts will be looking for something much more than mere annoyance arising from generally acceptable land management practices employed by a neighbour.

The latest significant case, *Wandsworth London Borough Council v. Railtrack plc*[17] confirms the trend toward potential liability, but relates to rather special circumstances. The action was brought in public nuisance, based on the extent to which the droppings from pigeons roosting under a railway bridge owned by the defendant were causing a nuisance to pedestrians passing under the bridge and additional costs to the council which had responsibility for cleaning the road. Railtrack was found liable, on the basis that once it was aware of the problem it had failed to take reasonable steps to remedy the nuisance. It did not matter that the nuisance was not the result of its own actions.[18] Since the argument on public nuisance was successful, issues of private nuisance or negligence were not considered. At first instance, though, doubts were expressed whether the council would have a claim on those grounds in the absence of physical damage to its property. The thorough examination of the law by Gibbs J. at first instance shows the potential for liability, confirmed on appeal, but also shows the wide range of issues to be considered in deciding on the existence and extent of liability, including the potential for earlier mitigating action.

8.8.6

As yet, the Scottish courts have not given any indication of whether they would be prepared to follow the English movement away from the position stated in *Giles v. Walker*, a position expressly approved in the Scottish cases noted above.[19] In any event, it has been made abundantly clear in *R.H.M. Bakeries (Scotland) Ltd. v. Strathclyde Regional Coun-*

8.8.7

---

[16] [1974] 1 N.Z.L.R. 340.
[17] [2002] 2 W.L.R. 51; the decision at first instance is reported at [2001] 1 W.L.R. 368.
[18] *Attorney General v. Tod Heatley* [1897] 1 Ch. 560; see also Rowlatt J. in *Noble v. Harrison* [1976] 2 Q.B. 332 at p. 338.
[19] See W.M. Gordon, "Is Moving Land a Nuisance?" (1980) 25 J.L.S.S. 323.

cil[20] that the basis of liability in nuisance is *culpa*,[21] so that some fault on the part of the landowner would have to be established. As discussed above, this raises issues as to the extent to which the management of land in a way which causes unintentional but foreseeable harm to others can be classed as culpable when the harm arises not from any specific danger but from an allegedly greater incidence of a sort of naturally occurring harm which everyone must accept as part of the everyday risks of owning land.

8.8.9   Although it cannot be wholly ruled out, it therefore seems unlikely that a landowner taking measures on his own land to further nature conservation will be liable to a neighbour who claims to have suffered damage as a result of wild plants or animals being encouraged.

---

[20] 1985 S.L.T. 214.
[21] See generally G. Cameron, "Nuisance in the Common Law of Scotland" (1999) 3 S.L.P.Q. 1.

APPENDIX A

Schedules to the Wildlife and Countryside Act 1981

Each Schedule is accompanied by a note in the following terms:

"The common name or names given in the first column of this Schedule are included by way of guidance only; in the event of any dispute or proceedings, the common name or names shall not be taken into account."

Schedule 1

Birds which are protected by special penalties

Part I: At all times

Common name	Scientific name
Avocet	Recurvirostra avosetta
Bee-eater	Merops apiaster
Bittern	Botaurus stellaris
Bittern, Little	Ixobrychus minutus
Bluethroat	Luscinia svecica
Brambling	Fringilla montifringilla
Bunting, Cirl	Emberiza cirlus
Bunting, Lapland	Calcarius lapponicus
Bunting, Snow	Plectrophenax nivalis
Buzzard, Honey	Pernis apivorus
Capercaillie (Scotland only)	Tetrao urogallus
Chough	Pyrrhocorax pyrrhocorax
Corncrake	Crex crex
Crake, Spotted	Porzana porzana
Crossbills (all species)	Loxia
Curlew, Stone	Burhinus oedicnemus
Divers (all species)	Gavia
Dotterel	Charadrius morinellus
Duck, Long-tailed	Clangula hyemalis
Eagle, Golden	Aquila chrysaetos
Eagle, White-tailed	Haliaetus albicilla
Falcon, Gyr	Falco rusticolus
Fieldfare	Turdus pilaris
Firecrest	Regulus ignicapillus
Garganey	Anas querquedula
Godwit, Black-tailed	Limosa limosa
Goshawk	Accipiter gentilis
Grebe, Black-necked	Podiceps nigricollis
Grebe, Slavonian	Podiceps auritus

Common name	*Scientific name*
Greenshank	Tringa nebularia
Gull, Little	Larus minutus
Gull, Mediterranean	Larus melanocephalus
Harriers (all species)	Circus
Heron, Purple	Ardea purpurea
Hobby	Falco subbuteo
Hoopoe	Upupa epops
Kingfisher	Alcedo atthis
Kite, Red	Milvus milvus
Merlin	Falco columbarius
Oriole, Golden	Oriolus oriolus
Osprey	Pandion haliaetus
Owl, Barn	Tyto alba
Owl, Snowy	Nyctea scandiaca
Peregrine	Falco peregrinus
Petrel, Leach's	Oceanodroma leucorhoa
Phalarope, Red-necked	Phalaropus lobatus
Plover, Kentish	Charadrius alexandrinus
Plover, Little Ringed	Charadrius dubius
Quail, Common	Coturnix coturnix
Redstart, Black	Phoenicurus ochruros
Redwing	Turdus iliacus
Rosefinch, Scarlet	Carpodacus erythrinus
Ruff	Philomachus pugnax
Sandpiper, Green	Tringa ochropus
Sandpiper, Purple	Calidris maritima
Sandpiper, Wood	Tringa glareola
Scaup	Aythya marila
Scoter, Common	Melanitta nigra
Scoter, Velvet	Melanitta fusca
Serin	Serinus serinus
Shorelark	Eremophila alpestris
Shrike, Red-backed	Lanius collurio
Spoonbill	Platalea leucorodia
Stilt, Black-winged	Himantopus himantopus
Stint, Temminck's	Calidris temminckii
Swan, Bewick's	Cygnus bewickii
Swan, Whooper	Cygnus cygnus
Tern, Black	Chlidonias niger
Tern, Little	Sterna albifrons
Tern, Roseate	Sterna dougallii
Tit, Bearded	Panurus biarmicus
Tit, Crested	Parus cristatus
Treecreeper, Short-toed	Certhia brachydactyla
Warbler, Cetti's	Cettia cetti
Warbler, Dartford	Sylvia undata
Warbler, Marsh	Acrocephalus palustris
Warbler, Savi's	Locustella luscinioides

Common name	Scientific name
Whimbrel	Numenius phaeopus
Woodlark	Lullula arborea
Wryneck	Jynx torquilla

[As amended by the Wildlife and Countryside Act 1981 (Amendment) (Scotland) Regulations 2001, S.S.I. 2001 No. 337]

Part II: During the close season

Common name	Scientific name
Goldeneye	Bucephala clangula
Goose, Greylag (in Outer Hebrides, Caithness, Sutherland and Wester Ross only)	Anser anser
Pintail	Anas acuta

Schedule 2

Birds which may be killed or taken

Part I: Outside the close season

Common name	Scientific name
Capercaillie (in England and Wales only)	Tetrao urogallus
Coot	Fulica atra
Duck, Tufted	Aythya fuligula
Gadwall	Anas strepera
Goldeneye	Bucephala clangula
Goose, Canada	Branta canadensis
Goose, Greylag	Anser anser
Goose, Pink-footed	Anser brachyrhynchus
Goose, White-fronted (in England and Wales only)	Anser albifrons
Mallard	Anas platyrhynchos
Moorhen	Gallinula chloropus
Pintail	Anas acuta
Plover, Golden	Pluvialis apricaria
Pochard	Aythya ferina
Shoveler	Anas clypeata
Snipe, Common	Gallinago gallinago
Teal	Anas crecca
Wigeon	Anas penelope
Woodcock	Scolopax rusticola

[As amended by Wildlife and Countryside Act 1981 (Amendment) (Scotland) Regulations 2001, S.S.I. 2001 No. 337]

Part II: by Authorised persons at all times

[All the birds previously listed in this Part of the Schedule were removed by the Wildlife and Countryside Act 1981 (Variation of Schedules 2 and 3) Order 1992, S.I. 1992 No. 3010]

Schedule 3

Birds which may be sold

Part I: Alive at all times if ringed and bred in captivity

Common name	Scientific name
Blackbird	Turdus merula
Brambling	Fringilla montifringilla
Bullfinch	Pyrrhula pyrrhula
Bunting, Reed	Emberiza schoeniclus
Chaffinch	Fringilla coelebs
Dunnock	Prunella modularis
Goldfinch	Carduelis carduelis
Greenfinch	Carduelis chloris
Jackdaw	Corvus monedula
Jay	Garrulus glandarius
Linnet	Carduelis cannabina
Magpie	Pica pica
Owl, Barn	Tyto alba
Redpoll	Carduelis flammea
Siskin	Carduelis spinus
Starling	Sturnus vulgaris
Thrush, Song	Turdus philomelos
Twite	Carduelis flavirostris
Yellowhammer	Emberiza citrinella

Part II: Dead at all times

Common name	Scientific name
Woodpigeon	Columba palumbus

[As amended by the Wildlife and Countryside Act 1981 (Variation of Schedules 2 and 3) Order 1992, S.I. 1992 No. 3010]

Part III: Dead from 1 September–28 February

Common name	Scientific name
Capercaillie (in England and Wales only)	Tetrao urogallus
Coot	Fulica atra
Duck, Tufted	Aythya fuligula
Mallard	Anas platyrhynchos
Pintail	Anas acuta
Plover, Golden	Pluvialis apricaria

Common name	Scientific name
Pochard	Aythya ferina
Shoveler	Anas clypeata
Snipe, Common	Gallinago gallinago
Teal	Anas crecca
Wigeon	Anas penelope
Woodcock	Scolopax rusticola

[As amended by Wildlife and Countryside Act 1981 (Amendment) (Scotland) Regulations 2001, S.S.I. 2001 No. 337]

Schedule 4

Birds which must be registered and ringed if kept in captivity

Common name	Scientific name
Bunting, Cirl	Emberiza cirlus
Bunting, Lapland	Calcarius lapponicus
Bunting, Snow	Plectrophenax nivalis
Buzzard, Honey	Pernis apivorus
Chough	Pyrrhocorax pyrrhocorax
Crossbills (all species)	Loxia
Eagle, Adalbert's	Aquila adalberti
Eagle, Golden	Aquila chrysaetos
Eagle, Great Philippine	Pithecophaga jefferyi
Eagle, Imperial	Aquila heliaca
Eagle, New Guinea	Harpyopsis novaeguineae
Eagle, White-tailed	Haliaeetus albicilla
Falcon, Barbary	Falco pelegrinoides
Falcon, Gyr	Falco rusticolus
Falcon, Peregrine	Falco peregrinus
Fieldfare	Turdus pilaris
Firecrest	Regulus ignicapillus
Fish-Eagle, Madagascar	Haliaeetus vociferoides
Forest-Falcon, Plumbeous	Micrastur plumbeus
Goshawk	Accipiter gentilis
Harrier, Hen	Circus cyaneus
Harrier, Marsh	Circus aeruginosus
Harrier, Montagu's	Circus pygargus
Hawk, Galapagos	Buteo galapagoensis
Hawk, Grey-backed	Leucopternis occidentalis
Hawk, Hawaiian	Buteo solitarius
Hawk, Ridgway's	Buteo ridgwayi
Hawk, White-necked	Leucopternis lacernulata
Hawk-Eagle, Wallace's	Spizaetus nanus
Hobby	Falco subbuteo
Honey-Buzzard, Black	Henicopernis infuscatus
Kestrel, Lesser	Falco naumanni

Common name	Scientific name
Kestrel, Mauritius	Falco punctatus
Kite, Red	Milvus milvus
Merlin	Falco columbarius
Oriole, Golden	Oriolus oriolus
Osprey	Pandion haliaetus
Redstart, Black	Phoenicurus ochruros
Redwing	Turdus iliacus
Sea-Eagle, Pallas'	Haliaeetus leucoryphus
Sea-Eagle, Steller's	Haliaeetus pelagicus
Serin	Serinus serinus
Serpent-Eagle, Andaman	Spilornis elgini
Serpent-Eagle, Madagascar	Eutriorchis astur
Serpent-Eagle, Mountain	Spilornis kinabaluensis
Shorelark	Eremophila alpestris
Shrike, Red-backed	Lanius collurio
Sparrowhawk, New Britain	Accipiter brachyurus
Sparrowhawk, Gundlach's	Accipiter gundlachi
Sparrowhawk, Imitator	Accipiter imitator
Sparrowhawk, Small	Accipiter nanus
Tit, Bearded	Panurus biarmicus
Tit, Crested	Parus cristatus
Warbler, Cetti's	Cettia cetti
Warbler, Dartford	Sylvia undata
Warbler, Marsh	Acrocephalus palustris
Warbler, Savi's	Locustella liuscinioides
Woodlark	Lullula arborea
Wryneck	Jynx torquilla

Any bird one of whose parents or other lineal ancestor was a bird of a kind specified in the foregoing provisions of this Schedule.

[As amended by the Wildlife and Countryside Act 1981 (Variation of Schedule 4) Order 1994, S.I. 1994 No. 1151]

Schedule 5

Animals which are protected

Those that are marked with an asterisk are also European Protected Species under the Conservation (Natural Habitats, etc.) Regulations 1994, Schedule 2

Common name	Scientific name
Adder (in respect of s.9(1) so far as it relates to killing and injuring and s.9(5) only)	Vipera berus

Common name	Scientific name
Allis Shad (in respect of s.9(1) and 9(4)(a) only)	Alosa alosa
Anemone, Ivell's Sea	Edwardsia ivelli
Anemone, Startlet Sea	Nematosella vectensis
Apus	Triops cancriformis
Atlantic Stream Crayfish (in relation to s. 9(1) so far as it relates to taking and s.9(5) only)	Austropotamobius pallipes
*Bats, Horseshoe (all species)	Rhinolophidae
*Bats, Typical (all species)	Vespertilionidae
Beetle	Graphoderus zonatus
Beetle	Hypebaeus flavipes
Beetle	Paracymus aeneus
Beetle, Lesser Silver Water	Hydrochara caraboides
Beetle, Mire Pill (in respect of s.9(4)(a) only)	Curimopsis nigrita
Beetle, Rainbow Leaf	Chrysolina cerealis
Beetle, Stag (in respect of s.9(5) only)	Lucanus cervus
Beetle, Violet Click	Limoniscus violaceus
Burbot	Lota lota
Butterfly, Heath Fritillary	Mellicta athalia (otherwise known as Melitaea athalia)
*Butterfly, Large Blue	Maculinea arion
Butterfly, Swallowtail	Papilio machaon
Butterfly, Northern Brown Argus (in respect of s.9(5) only)	Aricia artaxerxes
Butterfly, Adonis Blue (in respect of s.9(5) only)	Lysandra bellargus
Butterfly, Chalkhill Blue (in respect of s.9(5) only)	Lysandra coridon
Butterfly, Silver-studded Blue (in respect of s.9(5) only)	Plebejus argus
Butterfly, Small Blue (in respect of s.9(5) only)	Cupido minimus
Butterfly, Large Copper	Lycaena dispar
Butterfly, Purple Emperor (in respect of s.9(5) only)	Apatura iris
Butterfly, Duke of Burgundy Fritillary (in respect of section 9(5) only)	Hamearis lucina
Butterfly, Glanville Fritillary (in respect of s.9(5) only)	Melitaea cinxia
Butterfly, High Brown Fritillary (in respect of s.9(5) only)	Argynnis adippe
Butterfly, Marsh Fritillary	Eurodryas aurinia
Butterfly, Pearl-bordered Fritillary (in respect of s.9(5) only)	Boloria euphrosyne

Common name	Scientific name
Butterfly, Black Hairstreak (in respect of s.9(5) only)	Strymonidia pruni
Butterfly, Brown Hairstreak (in respect of s.9(5) only)	Thecla betulae
Butterfly, White Letter Hairstreak (in respect of s.9(5) only)	Stymonida w-album
Butterfly, Large Heath (in respect of s.9(5) only)	Coenonympha tullia
Butterfly, Mountain Ringlet (in respect of s.9(5) only)	Erebia epiphron
Butterfly, Chequered Skipper (in respect of s.9(5) only)	Carterocephalus palaemon
Butterfly, Lulworth Skipper (in respect of s.9(5) only)	Thymelicus acteon
Butterfly, Silver Spotted Skipper (in respect of s.9(5) only)	Hesperia comma
Butterfly, Large Tortoiseshell (in respect of s.9(5) only)	Nymphalis polychloros
Butterfly, Wood White (in respect of s.9(5) only)	Leptidea sinapis
*Cat, Wild	Felis silvestris
Cicada, New Forest	Cicadetta montana
Cricket, Field	Gryllus campestris
Cricket, Mole	Gryllotalpa gryllotalpa
Damselfly, Southern	Coenagrion mercuriale
*Dolphins (all species)	Cetacea
*Dormouse	Muscardinus avellanarius
Dragonfly, Norfolk Aeshna	Aeshna isosceles
Frog, Common (in respect of s.9(5) only)	Rana temporaria
Goby, Couch's	Gobius couchii
Goby, Giant	Gobius cobitis
Grasshopper, Wart-biter	Decticus verrucivorus
Hatchet Shell, Northern	Thyasira gouldi
Hydroid, Marine	Clavopsella navis
Lagoon Snail	Paludinella littorina
Lagoon Snail, De Folin's	Caecum armoricum
Lagoon Worm, Tentacled	Alkmaria romijni
Leech, Medicinal	Hirudo medicinalis
*Lizard, Sand	Lacerta agilis
Lizard, Viviparous (in respect of s.9(1) so far as it relates to killing and injuring and s.9(5) only)	Lacerta vivipara
Marten, Pine	Martes martes
Mat, Trembling Sea	Victorella pavida
Moth, Barberry Carpet	Pareulype berberata
Moth, Black-veined	Siona lineata (otherwise known as Idaea lineata)

Common name	Scientific name
Moth, Essex Emerald	Thetidia smaragdaria
Moth, Fiery Clearwing	Bembecia chrysidiformis
Moth, Fisher's Estuarine	Gortyna borelii
Moth, New Forest Burnet	Zygaena viciae
Moth, Reddish Buff	Acosmetia caliginosa
Moth, Sussex Emerald	Thalera fimbrialis
Mussel, Fan (in respect of s.9(1), 9(2) and 9(5) only)	Atrina fragilis
Mussel, Freshwater Pearl	Margaritifera margaritifera
*Newt, Great Crested (otherwise known as Warty newt)	Triturus cristatus
Newt, Palmate (in respect of s.9(5) only)	Triturus helveticus
Newt, Smooth (in respect of s.9(5) only)	Triturus vulgaris
*Otter, Common	Lutra lutra
*Porpoises (all species)	Cetacea
Sandworm, Lagoon	Armandia cirrhosa
Sea Fan, Pink (in respect of s.9(1), 9(2) and 9(5) only)	Eunicella verrucosa
Sea Slug, Lagoon	Tenellia adspersa
Shad, Twaite (in respect of s.9(4)(a) only)	Alosa fallax
Shark, Basking	Cetorhinus maximus
Shrimp, Fairy	Chirocephalus diaphanus
Shrimp, Lagoon Sand	Gammarus insensibilis
Slow-worm (in respect of s.9(1) so far as it relates to killing and injuring and s.9(5) only)	Anguis fragilis
Snail, Glutinous	Myxas glutinosa
Snail, Sandbowl	Catinella arenaria
Snake, Grass (in respect of s. 9(1) so far as it relates to killing and injuring and s.9(5) only)	Natrix helvetica
*Snake, Smooth	Coronella austriaca
Spider, Fen Raft	Dolomedes plantarius
Spider, Ladybird	Eresus niger
Squirrel, Red	Sciurus vulgaris
*Sturgeon	Acipenser sturio
Toad, Common (in respect of s.9(5) only)	Bufo bufo
*Toad, Natterjack	Bufo calamita
*Turtles, Marine (all species)[a]	Dermochelyidae and Cheloniidae
Vendace	Coregonus albula
Vole, Water (in respect of s.9(4) only)	Arvicola terrestris

Common name	**Scientific name**
Walrus	Odobenus rosmarus
*Whale (all species)	Cetacea
Whitefish	Coregonus lavaretus

[a]In the Conservation (Natural Habitats, etc.) Regulations 1994, Sched.2 the entry is:

Turtles, Marine	Caretta caretta
	Chelonia mydas
	Lepidochelys kempii
	Eretmochelys imbricata
	Dermochelys coriacea

[As amended by the Wildlife and Countryside Act 1981 (Variation of Schedules) Orders 1988, 1989 and 1991 and by the Wildlife and Countryside Act 1981 (Variation of Schedules 5 and 8) Orders 1992 and 1998, S.I.s 1988 No. 288, 1989 No. 906, 1991 No. 367, 1992 No. 2350 and 1998 No. 878]

Schedule 6

Animals which may not be killed or taken by certain methods

Common name	**Scientific name**
Badger	Meles meles
Bats, Horseshoe (all species)	Rhinolophidae
Bats, Typical (all species)	Vespertilionidae
Cat, Wild	Felis silvestris
Dolphin, Bottle-nosed	Tursiops truncatus (otherwise known as Tursiops tursio)
Dolphin, Common	Delphinis delphis
Dormice (all species)	Gliridae
Hedgehog	Erinaceus europaeus
Marten, Pine	Martes martes
Otter, Common	Lutra lutra
Polecat	Mustela putorius
Porpoise, Harbour (otherwise known as Common porpoise)	Phocaena phocaena
Shrews (all species)	Soricidae
Squirrel, Red	Sciurus vulgaris

[See the end of this Appendix for the list of species similarly protected under the provisions of the Conservation (Natural Habitats, etc.) Regulations 1994, S.I. 1994 No. 2716.]

Schedule 8

Plants which are protected

Those that are marked with an asterisk are also European Protected Species under the Conservation (Natural Habitats, etc.) Regulations 1994, Schedule 4

Common name	*Scientific name*
Adder's-tongue, Least	Ophioglossum lusitanicum
Alison, Small	Alyssum alyssoides
Anomodon, Long-leaved	Anomodon longifolius
Beech-lichen, New Forest	Enterographa elaborata
Blackwort,	Southbya nigrella
Bluebell (in respect of s.13(2) only)	Hyacinthoides non-scripta
Bolete, Royal	Boletus regius
Broomrape, Bedstraw	Orobanche caryophyllacea
Broomrape, Oxtongue	Orobanche loricata
Broomrape, Thistle	Orobanche reticulata
Cabbage, Lundy	Rhynchosinapis wrightii
Calamint, Wood	Calamintha sylvatica
Caloplaca, Snow	Caloplaca nivalis
Catapyrenium, Tree	Catapyrenium psoromoides
Catchfly, Alpine	Lychnis alpina
Catillaria, Laurer's	Catellaria laureri
Centaury, Slender	Centaurium tenuiflorum
Cinquefoil, Rock	Potentilla rupestris
Cladonia, Convoluted	Cladonia convoluta
Cladonia, Upright Mountain	Cladonia stricta
Clary, Meadow	Salvia pratensis
Club-rush, Triangular	Scirpus triquetrus
Colt's-foot, Purple	Homogyne alpina
Cotoneaster, Wild	Cotoneaster integerrimus
Cottongrass, Slender	Eriophorum gracile
Cow-wheat, Field	Melampyrum arvense
Crocus, Sand	Romulea columnae
Crystalwort, Lizard	Riccia bifurca
Cudweed, Broad-leaved	Filago pyramidata
Cudweed, Jersey	Gnaphalium luteoalbum
Cudweed, Red-tipped	Filago lutescens
Cut-grass	Leersia oryzoides
Deptford Pink (in England and Wales only)	Dianthus armeria
Diapensia	Diapensia lapponica
*Dock, Shore	Rumex rupestris
Earwort, Marsh	Jamesoniella undulifolia
Eryngo, Field	Eryngium campestre
Feather-moss, Polar	Hygrohypnum polare

Common name	Scientific name
Fern, Dickie's Bladder	Cystopteris dickieana
*Fern, Killarney	Trichomanes speciosum
Flapwort, Norfolk	Leiocolea rutheana
Fleabane, Alpine	Erigeron borealis
Fleabane, Small	Pulicaria vulgaris
Frostwort, Pointed	Gymnomitrion apiculatum
Fungus, Hedgehog	Hericium erinaceum
Galingale, Brown	Cyperus fuscus
Gentian, Alpine	Gentiana nivalis
Gentian, Dune	Gentianella uliginosa
*Gentian, Early	Gentianella anglica
Gentian, Fringed	Gentianella ciliata
Gentian, Spring	Gentiana verna
Germander, Cut-leaved	Teucrium botrys
Germander, Water	Teucrium scordium
Gladiolus, Wild	Gladiolus illyricus
Goblin Lights	Catolechia wahlenbergii
Goosefoot, Stinking	Chenopodium vulvaria
Grass-poly	Lythrum hyssopifolia
Grimmia, Blunt-leaved	Grimmia unicolor
Gyalecta, Elm	Gyalecta ulmi
Hare's-ear, Sickle-leaved	Bupleurum falcatum
Hare's-ear, Small	Bupleurum baldense
Hawk's-beard, Stinking	Crepis foetida
Hawkweed, Northroe	Hieracium northroense
Hawkweed, Shetland	Hieracium zetlandicum
Hawkweed, Weak-leaved	Hieracium attenuatifolium
Heath, Blue	Phyllodoce caerulea
Helleborine, Red	Cephalanthera rubra
Helleborine, Young's	Epipactis youngiana
Horsetail, Branched	Equisetum ramosissimum
Hound's-tongue, Green	Cynoglossum germanicum
Knawel, Perennial	Scleranthus perennis
Knotgrass, Sea	Polygonum maritimum
*Lady's-slipper	Cypripedium calceolus
Lecanactis, Churchyard	Lecanactis hemisphaerica
Lecanora, Tarn	Lecanora archariana
Lecidea, Copper	Lecidea inops
Leek, Round-headed	Allium sphaerocephalon
Lettuce, Least	Lactuca saligna
Lichen, Arctic Kidney	Nephroma arcticum
Lichen, Ciliate Strap	Heterodermia leucomelos
Lichen, Coralloid Rosette	Heterodermia propagulifera
Lichen, Ear-lobed Dog	Peltigera lepidophora
Lichen, Forked Hair	Bryoria furcellata
Lichen, Golden Hair	Teloschistes flavicans
Lichen, Orange Fruited Elm	Caloplaca luteoalba
Lichen, River Jelly	Collema dichotomum

Common name	Scientific name
Lichen, Scaly Breck	Squamarina lentigera
Lichen, Stary (*sic.*) Breck	Buellia asterella
Lettuce, Least	Lactuca saligna
Lily, Snowdon	Lloydia serotina
Liverwort	Petallophyllum ralfsi
Liverwort, Lindenberg's Leafy	Adelanthus lindenbergianus
Marsh-mallow, Rough,	Althaea hirsuta
*Marshwort, Creeping	Apium repens
Milk-parsley, Cambridge	Selinum carvifolia
Moss	Drepanocladius vernicosus
Moss, Alpine Copper	Mielichoferia mielichoferi
Moss, Baltic Bog	Sphagnum balticum
Moss, Blue Dew	Saelania glaucescens
Moss, Blunt-leaved Bristle	Orthotrichum obtusifolium
Moss, Bright Green Cave	Cyclodictyon laetevirens
Moss, Cordate Beard	Barbula cordata
Moss, Cornish Path	Ditrichum cornubicum
Moss, Derbyshire Feather	Thamnobryum angustifolium
Moss, Dune Thread	Bryum mamillatum
Moss, Flamingo	Desmatodon cernuus
Moss, Glaucous Beard	Barbula glauca
Moss, Green Shield	Buxbaumia viridis
Moss, Hair Silk	Plagiothecium piliferum
Moss, Knothole	Zygodon forsteri
Moss, Large Yellow Feather	Scorpidium turgescens
Moss, Millimetre	Micromitrium tenerum
Moss, Multifruited River	Cryphaea lamyana
Moss, Nowell's Limestone	Zygodon gracilis
Moss, Rigid Apple	Bartramia stricta
Moss, Round-leaved Feather	Rhyncostegium rotundifolium
Moss, Schleicher's Thread	Bryum schleicheri
Moss, Triangular Pygmy	Acaulon triquetrum
Moss, Vaucher's Feather	Hypnum vaucheri
Mudwort, Welsh	Limosella australis
Naiad, Holly-leaved	Najas marina
*Naiad, Slender	Najas flexilis
Orache, Stalked	Halimione pedunculata
Orchid, Early Spider	Ophrys sphegodes
*Orchid, Fen	Liparis loeselii
Orchid, Ghost	Epipogium aphyllum
Orchid, Lapland Marsh	Dactylorhiza lapponica
Orchid, Late Spider	Ophrys fuciflora
Orchid, Lizard	Himantoglossum hircinum
Orchid, Military	Orchis militaris
Orchid, Monkey	Orchis simia
Pannaria, Caledonia	Pannaria ignobilis
Parmelia, New Forest	Parmelia minarum
Parmentaria, Oil Stain	Parmentaria chilensis

Common name	Scientific name
Pear, Plymouth	Pyrus cordata
Penny-cress, Perfoliate	Thlaspi perfoliatum
Pennyroyal	Mentha pulegium
Pertusaria, Alpine Moss	Pertusaria bryontha
Physcia, Southern Grey	Physcia tribacioides
Pigmyweed	Crassula aquatica
Pine, Ground	Ajuga chamaepitys
Pink, Cheddar	Dianthus gratianopolitanus
Pink, Childling	Petroraghia nanteuilii
*Plantain, Floating[-leaved] Water	Luronium natans
Polypore, Oak	Buglossoporus pulvinus
Pseudocyphellaria, Ragged	Pseudocyphellaria lacerata
Psora, Rusty Alpine	Psora rubiformis
Puffball, Sandy Stilt	Battarraea phalloides
Ragwort, Fen	Senecio paludosus
Ramping-fumitory, Martin's	Fumaria martinii
Rampion, Spiked	Phyteuma spicatum
Restharrow, Small	Ononis reclinata
Rock-cress, Alpine	Arabis alpina
Rock-cress, Bristol	Arabis stricta
Rustworth, Western	Marsupella profunda
Sandwort, Norwegian	Arenaria norvegica
Sandwort, Teesdale	Minuartia stricta
Saxifrage, Drooping	Saxifraga cernua
*Saxifrage, [Yellow] Marsh	Saxifraga hirculus
Saxifrage, Tufted	Saxifraga cespitosa
Solomon's-seal, Whorled	Polygonatum verticillatum
Solenopsora, Serpentine	Solenopsora liparina
Sow-thistle, Alpine	Cicerbita alpina
Spearwort, Adder's-tongue	Ranunculus ophioglossifolius
Speedwell, Fingered	Veronica triphyllos
Speedwell, Spiked	Veronica spicata
Spike-rush, Dwarf	Eleocharis parvula
Stack Fleawort, South	Tephroseris integrifolia (ssp. maritima)
Star-of-Bethlehem, Early	Gagea bohemica
Starfruit	Damasonium alisma
Stonewort, Bearded	Chara canescens
Stonewort, Foxtail	Lamprothamnium papulosum
Strapwort	Corrigiola litoralis
Sulphur-tresses, Alpine	Alectoria ochroleuca
Threadmoss, Long-leaved	Bryum neodamense
Turpswort	Geocalyx graveolens
Viper's-grass	Scorzonera humilis
Violet, Fen	Viola persicifolia
Water-plantain, Ribbon-leaved	Alisma gramineum
Wood-sedge, Starved	Carex depauperata
Woodsia, Alpine	Woodsia alpina

Common name	Scientific name
Woodsia, Oblong	Woodsia ilvensis
Wormwood, Field	Artemisia campestris
Woundwort, Downy	Stachys germanica
Woundwort, Limestone	Stachys alpina
Yellow-rattle, Greater	Rhinanthus serotinus

[As amended by the Wildlife and Countryside Act 1981 (Variation of Schedules Order 1988 and the Wildlife and Countryside Act 1981 (Variation of Schedules 5 and 8) Orders 1992 and 1998, S.I.s Nos. 1988 No. 288, 1992 No. 2350 and 1998 No. 878]

Schedule 9

Animals and Plants to which section 14 applies
[Non-native species not to be released to the wild]

Part I: Animals which are established in the wild

Common name	Scientific name
Bass, Large-mouthed Black	Micropterus salmoides
Bass, Rock	Ambloplites rupestris
Bitterling	Rhodeus sericeus
Budgerigar	Melopsittacus undulatus
Capercaillie	Tetrao urogallus
Coypu	Myocastor coypus
Crayfish, Noble	Astacus astacus
Crayfish, Signal	Pacifastacus leniusculus
Crayfish, Turkish	Astacus leptodactylus
Deer, any hybrid one of whose parents or other lineal ancestor was a Sika deer	Any hybrid of Cervus nippon
With respect to the Outer Hebrides and the islands of Arran, Islay, Jura and Rum—	
(a) Deer, Cervus (all species)	Cervus
(b) Deer, any hybrid one of whose parents or other lineal ancestor was a Sika deer	Any hybrid of the genus Cervus
Deer, Muntjac	Muntiacus reevesi
Deer, Sika	Cervus nippon
Dormouse, Fat	Glis glis
Duck, Carolina Wood	Aix sponsa
Duck, Mandarin	Aix galericulata
Duck, Ruddy	Oxyura jamaicensis
Eagle, White-tailed	Haliaetus albicilla
Flat-worm, New Zealand	Artiposthia triangulata
Frog, Edible	Rana esculenta

Common name	Scientific name
Frog, European Tree (otherwise known as Common tree frog)	Hyla arborea
Frog, Marsh	Rana ridibunda
Gerbil, Mongolian	Meriones unguiculatus
Goose, Canada	Branta canadensis
Goose, Egyptian	Alopochen aegyptiacus
Heron, Night	Nycticorax nycticorax
Lizard, Common Wall	Podarcis muralis
Marmot, Prairie (otherwise known as Prairie dog)	Cynomys
Mink, American	Mustela vison
Newt, Alpine	Triturus alpestris
Newt, Italian Crested	Triturus carnifex
Owl, Barn	Tyto alba
Parakeet, Ring-necked	Psittacula krameri
Partridge, Chukar	Alectoris chukar
Partridge, Rock	Alectoris graeca
Pheasant, Golden	Chrysolophus pictus
Pheasant, Lady Amherst's	Chrysolophus amherstiae
Pheasant, Reeves'	Syrmaticus reevesii
Pheasant, Silver	Lophura nycthemera
Porcupine, Crested	Hystrix cristata
Porcupine, Himalayan	Hystrix hodgsonii
Pumpkinseed (otherwise known as Sun-fish or Pond-perch)	Lepomis gibbosus
Quail, Bobwhite	Colinus virginianus
Rat, Black	Rattus rattus
Snake, Aesculapian	Elaphe longissima
Squirrel, Grey	Sciurus carolinensis
Terrapin, European Pond	Emys orbicularis
Toad, African Clawed	Xenopus laevis
Toad, Midwife	Alytes obstetricans
Toad, Yellow-bellied	Bombina variegata
Wallaby, Red-necked,	Macropus rufogriseus
Wels (otherwise known as European catfish)	Silurus glanis
Zander	Stizostedion lucioperca

Part II: Plants

Common name	Scientific name
Hogweed, Giant	Heracleum mantegazzianum
Kelp, Giant	Macrocystis pyrifera
Kelp, Giant	Macrocystis angustifolia
Kelp, Giant	Macrocystis integrifolia
Kelp, Giant	Macrocystis laevis
Kelp, Japanese	Laminaria japonica
Knotweed, Japanese	Polygonum cuspidatum

Common name	*Scientific name*
Seafingers, Green	Codium fragile tomentosoides
Seaweed, Californian Red	Pikea californica
Seaweed, Hooked Asparagus	Asparagopis armata
Seaweed, Japanese	Sargassum muticum
Seaweeds, Laver (except native species)	Porphyra spp except—
	—p. amethystea
	—p. leucosticta
	—p. linearis
	—p. miniata
	—p. purpurea
	—p.umbilicalis
Wakame	Undaria pinnatifida

[As amended by the Wildlife and Countryside Act 1981 (Variation of Schedule) Order 1992, the Wildlife and Countryside Act 1981 (Variation of Schedule) (No. 2) Order 1992 and the Wildlife and Countryside Act 1981 (Variation of Schedule 9) Orders 1997 and 1999, S.I.s 1992 Nos. 320, 2674, 1997 No. 226, 1999 No. 1002]

Schedules to the Conservation (Natural Habitats, etc.) Regulations 1994

Each Schedule is accompanied by a note in the following terms:

"The common name or names given in the first column of this Schedule are included by way of guidance only; in the event of any dispute or proceedings, the common name or names shall not be taken into account."

Schedule 2

European Protected Species of Animal
These are marked by an asterisk in Schedule 5 to the Wildlife and Countryside Act 1981 (above).

Schedule 3

Animals which may not be taken or killed in certain ways

Common name	*Scientific name*
Barbel	Barbus barbus
Grayling	Thymallus thymallus
Hare, Mountain	Lepus timidus

Common name	Scientific name
Lamprey, River	Lampetra fluviatilis
Marten, Pine	Martes martes
Polecat	Mustela putorius (otherwise known as Putorius putorius)
Salmon, Atlantic	Salmo salar (only in fresh water)
Seal, Bearded	Erignathus barbatus
Seal, Common	Phoca vitulina
Seal, Grey	Halichoerus grypus
Seal, Harp	Phoca groenlandica (otherwise known as Pagophilus groenlandicus)
Seal, Hooded	Cystophora cristata
Seal, Ringed	Phoca hispida (otherwise known as Pusa hispida)
Shad, Allis	Alosa alosa
Shad, Twaite	Alosa fallax
Vendace	Coregonus albula
Whitefish	Coregonus lavaretus

Schedule 4

European Protected Species of Plants
These are marked by an asterisk in Schedule 8 to the Wildlife and Countryside
Act 1981 (above)

APPENDIX B

Open Seasons

Birds

	Scotland	England & Wales	Authority
Red grouse	Aug. 12–Dec.10	Aug. 12–Dec.10	1772/1831[1]
Ptarmigan	Aug. 12–Dec. 10	–	1772/1831
Black grouse	Aug. 20–Dec. 10	Aug. 20–Dec. 10	1772/1831
Pheasant	Oct. 1–Feb. 1	Oct. 1–Feb. 1	1772/1831
Partridge	Sep. 1–Feb. 1	Sep. 1–Feb. 1	1772/1831
Common snipe	Aug. 12–Jan. 31	Aug. 12–Jan. 31	WCA[2]
Woodcock	Sep. 1– Jan. 31	Oct. 1–Jan. 31	WCA
Wild duck and geese (below high-water mark)	Sep. 1–Feb. 20	Sep. 1–Feb. 20	WCA
All other cases	Sep. 1–Jan. 31	Sep. 1–Jan. 31	WCA

Notes
1. Game (Scotland) Act 1772, s.1; Game Act 1831, s.3.
2. Wildlife and Countryside Act 1981, s.2(4).

Deer

		Scotland[1]	England & Wales[2]
Red Deer[3]	stags	July 1–Oct.20	Aug. 1–April 30
	hinds	Oct. 21–Feb. 15	Nov. 1–Feb. 28/29
Sika Deer[3]	stags	July 1–Oct. 20	Aug. 1–April 30
	hinds	Oct. 21–Feb. 15	Nov. 1–Feb. 28/29
Fallow Deer	bucks	Aug. 1–April 30	Aug. 1–April 30
	does	Oct. 21–Feb. 15	Nov. 1–Feb. 28/29
Roe Deer	bucks	April 1–Oct. 20	April 1–Oct. 31
	does	Oct. 21–March 31	Nov. 1–Feb. 28/29

Notes
1. Deer (Scotland) Act 1996, s.5; Deer (Close Seasons) (Scotland) Order 1984, S.I. 1984 No. 76.
2. Deer Act 1991, Sched. 1.
3. In Scotland, expressly including hybrids.

Permitted Firearms
Scotland[1]

All deer	Rifle	Bullet of expanding type not less than 100 grains; muzzle velocity not less than 2450 feet per second; muzzle energy not less than 1750 foot pounds.

	Shotgun[2]	Not less than 12 bore; rifled slug not less than 380 grains or cartridge of not less than 450 grains of shot not smaller than 0.268 inches in diameter (size SSG).
Roe Deer	Rifle	Bullet of expanding type of not less than 50 grains; muzzle velocity not less than 2450 feet per second; muzzle energy not less than 1000 foot pounds.
	Shotgun[2]	Not less than 12 bore; cartridge of not less than 450 grains of shot not smaller than 0.203 inches in diameter (size AAA).

England and Wales[3]

All deer	Rifle	Calibre not less than 0.240 inches or muzzle energy of 1700 foot pounds; bullet soft or hollow-nosed.
All deer	Shotgun[2]	Not less than 12 bore; slug not less than 350 grains or cartridge of shot not smaller than 0.203 inches in diameter (size AAA).

Notes
1. Deer (Firearms) (Scotland) Order 1985, S.I. 1985 No. 1168.
2. The use of shotguns is permitted only in preventing serious damage on cultivated or enclosed land.
3. Deer Act 1991, s.7(2), Sched. 2.

APPENDIX C

Licences

Under s.16 of the Wildlife and Countryside Act 1981, licences authorising conduct otherwise unlawful under the provisions of Part I of the Act may be granted for the following purposes by the authorities shown.

In Relation to Birds

Purpose(s)	*Authority*
Scientific or educational	Minister or statutory conservation
Ringing, marking or examining any	body
ring or mark on wild birds	
Conserving wild birds	
Protecting any collection of wild	Minister
birds	
Falconry or aviculture	
Public exhibition or competition	
Taxidermy	
Human consumption[1]	
Sale or advertising for sale	
Photography	Statutory conservation body
Preserving public health or public or	Agriculture Minister
air safety	
Preventing the spread of disease	
Preventing serious damage to	
livestock, foodstuffs for livestock,	
crops, vegetables, fruit, growing	
timber or fisheries	

Notes
1. Gannets on Sula Sgeir, gulls' eggs and lapwings' eggs (before April 15 only).

In Relation to Animals and Plants

Purpose(s)	*Authority*
Scientific or educational	Statutory conservation body
Ringing, marking or examining any	
ring or mark on wild animals	
Conserving wild animals or wild	
plants or introducing them to	
particular areas	

Protecting any zoological or
   botanical collection
Photography

Preserving public health or safety   Agriculture Minister
Preventing the spread of disease
Preventing serious damage to
   livestock, foodstuffs for livestock,
   crops, vegetables, fruit, growing
   timber or to any other form of
   property or to fisheries

Sale or advertising for sale   Minister
Introduction of foreign species   (Agriculture Minister)
   (Fish or shellfish)

Note

In Wales ministerial powers under s.16 of the 1981 Act are exercisable by
   National Assembly for Wales concurrently with UK ministers: National
   Assembly for Wales (Transfer of Functions) Order 1999, S.I. 1999 No.
   672, Sched. 1.

INDEX